# The Big
# AUSTRALIAN
# RECIPE
# BOOK

# The Big
# AUSTRALIAN RECIPE BOOK

## Over 1200 Recipes

First published in this edition 1981
by Lloyd O'Neil Pty Ltd
for J. W. Books Pty Ltd
16 Cross St, Brookvale 2100
New South Wales, Australia

Designed by Zoë Murphy
Illustrations by
Peter Hirst
and Zoë Murphy

Printed in Australia at The Dominion Press, Blackburn, Victoria
ISBN 0 85550 728 4

# Meat & Chicken

# Casserole & Stew

# Family Favourites

# Low Calorie & Health

# Chinese & Asian

# MEAT & CHICKEN

# Contents

# Introduction

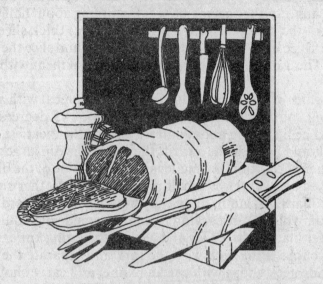

## CARVING MEAT

Next to the meat, the most important factor in good carving is good equipment. The very least you can get away with are a good knife, carving fork and sharpening steel; at the most you can use a variety of knives, saws, sharpening utensils and boards.

A French cook's knife has a triangular blade about 23 centimetres (9 in) long. It is widely used in preparing meat (trimming, cubing, etc.) and is useful for carving poultry or slicing small meat surfaces, such as canned meat. A slicing (or carving) knife is about 30 centimetres (12 in) long, straight-edged and narrow-bladed. It is used for carving all large roasts, and meats such as corned beef. A boning knife has a narrow blade which curves upward at the point. It should be about 20 centimetres (8 in) long, and is used to remove meat from the bone (both before and after cooking) and for trimming in preparing meat.

A carving fork is a great help as it keeps the meat steady while you slice. The best type of carving fork has two long prongs, is short-shafted, and has a permanent guard separating the shaft from the handle. A sharpening steel is essential. It should be as long as the blade of your largest carving knife, should have a fixed safety guard, and should have grooves running from the hilt to the point.

A meat saw is a very useful utensil in the kitchen and can be used for cutting bones too large for a knife. A cutting board should have grooves around the edges to catch the juice, and should be large enough to hold a large roast.

## Lamb

The most common lamb roasts are the leg, shoulder and forequarter. To carve a leg of lamb, wrap the bone in a clean cloth, grasp firmly and hold the leg at a 45 degree angle to the carving board. Beginning about half way along the meatiest side of the bone, make 1 centimetre (½ in) thick slices towards the carver's hand. Slice until the bone is reached, turn and slice the other side in the same way. This results in large, attractive slices of meat with very little left on the bone.

To carve a shoulder of lamb with bone in, secure the meat with a fork near the bone at the leg end. Hold the joint at an angle of 45 degrees from the carving board and begin slicing about half way along the meatiest side of the joint. The knife should be worked towards the fork. Carve in large slices until you meet bone, then slice from the smaller side of the spine of the blade bone. Turn shoulder over and carve the small pieces from the other side.

To carve a forequarter of lamb, place the joint on carving board with neck pointing away from you. Insert carving fork on near side of shoulder blade. Cut below shoulder blade between leg and neck with boning knife to separate shoulder and rib chops. Pull back with the fork and separate the joint into two sections. Divide neck chops with carving knife, and carve shoulder at an angle across the top towards the fork. When you meet the bone, rotate joint and carve the other side. Finally, carve the underside of the blade bone.

## Beef

The most common cuts of beef for roasting are rib, rolled rib and sirloin roasts, and rump and fillet roasts. The same basic rules apply to carving all beef: use a slicing (not a sawing) motion, apply only enough pressure to cut the meat fibres; and always carve across the grain of the meat if possible. A rib roast should be held securely with a carving fork, fat side up. Insert the point of the knife into the end of the joint just above the bone. Work along the bone towards the carver. This will separate the meat from the bone enough to commence slicing. Remove the tail of the joint in one piece and slice. Then slice the main joint down firmly towards the bone.

Rolled roasts should be held securely on their side with a fork. Carve downwards towards the carving board.

Slice a rump of beef by securing with a fork and carving slices across the grain.

Slice a fillet by removing string, holding securely with a fork, and slicing downwards across the grain of the meat with a long-bladed knife.

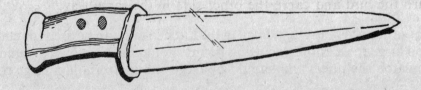

# Chicken

Chicken is one of the most versatile foods available, lending itself beautifully to many different sauces and flavourings. Though once considered a luxury in Australia, this is no longer the case—supermarket freezers are piled with frozen chickens (some of which will even baste themselves!) and fresh chickens and chicken pieces are readily available.

When buying a fresh chicken, look for creamy white or yellowish skin. The skin of fresh poultry should feel slightly waxy. Chicken pieces are more expensive than a whole chicken, but can be very convenient when only certain portions (such as breasts) are wanted for a particular dish. Wings and backs are very inexpensive and are excellent for making stock.

The main advantage of frozen chickens is convenience—they are a good stand-by if you have a freezer. To thaw a frozen chicken, leave at room temperature for 4-6 hours, depending on size. **Do not refreeze** a chicken once it has been thawed, and be sure to get a frozen chicken into the freezer as soon as possible after buying it. Remember to remove the bag of giblets from bird when it is thawed.

To roast a chicken (or other fowl), rinse with cold water and dry. Rub the inside of the bird with salt, then add stuffing if desired. Stuffing expands while the bird is cooking, so do not pack it in too tightly. Truss the bird by putting it on its back and lifting the legs until they are at right angles to the body. Tie leg ends together with strong string, and wrap the string around the tail. Then fold the wings with the tips under the back and secure tips with skewers to the neck skin. Tie wings in position with string.

Grease the skin with melted butter and place in a shallow pan on a rack with the breast down. Cover the bird with buttered cloth or grease-proof paper and bake in a moderate oven. Turn the bird over half way through cooking and allow breast to brown. The bird is done when the legs move easily when moved up and down—the leg joint may even break.

While the bird is roasting, cook the giblets in water with salt, peppercorns and celery leaves or parsley. Use the stock to make gravy from the pan drippings. Giblets may be diced and added to gravy if desired.

To carve a roast chicken or turkey, place bird on heated platter on its back. Remove legs by cutting through the skin and holding leg away from the body until the joint is revealed. Cut through gristle with knife. Separate drumstick from thigh and slice meat from drumstick if desired. Remove wings by placing knife at right angles to breast 2.5-5 centimetres (1-2 inches) above wing joint, then cut straight down through joint. Hold the bird steady with fork through one side of the breast or across top breast bone, and slice breast meat with a sawing motion. Continue until all meat is removed from one side, then turn the bird and carve the other side in the same way.

# Lamb

## LAMB CHOPS WITH MUSHROOMS

*40 minutes cooking time*

*Ingredients for 4-5 servings*

5 lamb chops
1-2 tablespoons butter
315 g (10 oz) mushrooms
¼ teaspoon white pepper

30 g (1 oz) plain flour
1¼ cups beef stock
½ teaspoon salt

1   Fry the chops and mushrooms in butter.
2   Remove when cooked.
3   Stir in flour and cook for 5 minutes.
4   Add stock and season with salt and pepper.
5   Return chops and mushrooms to pan and reheat for 15 minutes.
6   Serve immediately.

# LAMB SHANKS AND BARBECUE SAUCE

*2 hours cooking time*

*Ingredients for 4-5 servings*

4 tablespoons butter
2 onions, sliced
4 rashers bacon
6 lamb shanks
seasoned flour
440 ml (8 oz) can tomato soup
2 cups water

2 tablespoons brown sugar
2 teaspoons mustard
2 tablespoons Worcestershire sauce
½ cup vinegar
4 cups cooked rice
3 tablespoons shredded green pepper
1 teaspoon salt

1  Melt butter and sauté onion and bacon.
2  Remove.
3  Roll shanks in seasoned flour and place in pan.
4  Sauté.
5  Drain off excess fat.
6  Mix tomato soup, water, salt, sugar, mustard, Worcestershire sauce, vinegar, onion and bacon.
7  Pour over shanks and simmer for 2 hours over direct heat.
8  Serve with rice and green peppers.

# LAMBURGERS

*10 minutes cooking time*

*Ingredients for 4-5 servings*

1 kg (2 lb) shoulder of lamb, minced
3-4 tablespoons butter
juice of 2 lemons
2 onions, chopped

1 tablespoon chopped chives
1 teaspoon dill
1 clove garlic, crushed
2 teaspoons paprika

1  Combine all ingredients together.
2  Shape into 6 patties.
3  Place under griller and grill for 5-10 minutes.
4  Serve immediately.

# NECK OF LAMB

*Ingredients for 5-6 servings*

*1½ hours cooking time*

| | |
|---|---|
| **1 kg (2 lb) neck of lamb** | **1 beef stock cube** |
| **3-4 tablespoons butter** | **1 teaspoon dry mustard** |
| **2 sticks celery** | **1 teaspoon salt** |
| **2 tomatoes** | **¼ teaspoon white pepper** |
| **½ cup water** | **½ cup vinegar** |

1  Cube meat and melt butter.
2  Sauté meat quickly and add peeled and chopped vegetables.
3  Sauté about 5 minutes.
4  Add beef cube and water, mustard, salt and pepper.
5  Cook for 2 minutes then add vinegar.
6  Simmer for 1½ hours.
7  Serve immediately.

# LAMB WITH SOUR CREAM

*2 hours cooking time*

*Ingredients for 5-6 servings*

| | |
|---|---|
| **3-4 tablespoons butter** | **2 teaspoons paprika** |
| **1 kg (2 lb) shoulder of lamb** | **2 cups tomato purée** |
| **3 onions, sliced** | **chopped parsley** |
| **1 teaspoon salt** | **1 cup sour cream** |

1  Cube meat and sauté in butter.
2  Add onions and sprinkle with paprika.
3  Stir in tomato purée and parsley.
4  Cover and simmer for 1½ hours.
5  Just before serving add sour cream and reheat for 15 minutes.

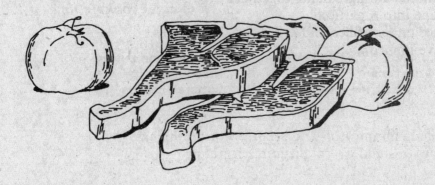

# CHOPS TOPPED WITH CHEESE

*15 minutes cooking time*

*Ingredients for 3-4 servings*

8 short loin chops
1 cup grated cheddar cheese
¼ teaspoon cayenne pepper

1 egg, beaten
½ teaspoon salt
chopped parsley

1   Prepare chops and place under griller.
2   Combine the grated cheese, egg, salt and cayenne pepper.
3   Spread on top of chops and place under griller.
4   Garnish with parsley and serve.

# LAMB IN JELLY

*30 minutes cooking time*

*Ingredients for 4-5 servings*

2 carrots
2 onions
fresh mint
1 teaspoon salt

2 tablespoons warm water
250 g (8 oz) diced lamb
new potatoes
3 teaspoons gelatine

1   Simmer carrots, onions and mint together for 30 minutes.
2   Strain and add salt.
3   To dissolved gelatine add stock and allow to cool.
4   When jelly begins to thicken add meat and pour into cake tin.
5   Allow to set.
6   Serve with new potatoes, carrots and peas.

# NOISETTES OF LAMB

*15 minutes cooking time*

*Ingredients for 4-5 servings*

small loin lamb, boned and skinned
125 g (4 oz) bacon
315 g (10 oz) button mushrooms
peas

1 tablespoon butter
fried bread
buttered carrots

1   Make lamb into roll and secure with toothpicks.
2   Allow to stand overnight in refrigerator.

3  Cut into slices and wrap bacon around each piece.
4  Peel mushrooms and sauté in butter.
5  Place lamb under griller and top with mushrooms.
6  Serve with fried bread, carrots and peas.

# LAMB CUTLETS IN WHITE SAUCE

*30 minutes cooking time*

*Ingredients for 3-4 servings*

8 lamb cutlets
seasoned plain flour
1 egg, beaten
3 tablespoons milk
3-4 spring onions

1 cup breadcrumbs
60 g (¼ cup) butter
¼ teaspoon white pepper
½ teaspoon salt
chopped ham

1  Prepare white sauce and add spring onions and chopped ham. Simmer, but do not boil.
2  Dip cutlets into seasoned flour, then egg, then breadcrumbs.
3  Place in egg mixture then breadcrumbs once again.
4  Melt butter and fry cutlets for 10 minutes.
5  Serve with white sauce and garnish with parsley.

# SPICED LAMB

*2½ hours cooking time*

*Ingredients for 4-5 servings*

1 kg (2 lb) lamb shoulder
1 cup white wine
2 onions, sliced
pinch thyme
¼ cup raisins

2 cups water
1 cup cooked rice
1 teaspoon salt
pinch marjoram

1  Cube meat and marinate for 1 hour in white wine.
2  Add sliced onion, salt, pepper, thyme and marjoram.
3  Place in a greased frying pan and add water.
4  Simmer for 1½ hours and add rice, raisins and cook for 1 hour.
5  Serve with boiled new potatoes and sour cream with chives.

# FRICASSÉE OF LAMB

*2½ hours cooking time*

*Ingredients for 3-4 servings*

| | |
|---|---|
| 1 kg (2 lb) chump chops | 2½ cups stock |
| 2 onions | 60 g (¼ cup) butter |
| 1 turnip | 30g (1 oz) flour |
| 2 sticks celery | 1¼ cups milk |
| ½ teaspoon salt | ¼ teaspoon cayenne pepper |
| 6 peppercorns | chopped parsley |

1   Cube meat into 5 centimetre (2 in) squares.
2   Prepare vegetables and place in saucepan with salt and peppercorns.
3   Cover with stock and simmer until tender.
4   Strain.
5   Reserve 1 cup of stock.
6   Melt butter and add seasoned flour.
7   Add reserved liquid and boil for 2 minutes.
8   Add milk and meat, season with salt and cayenne pepper.
9   Garnish with parsley.

# LAMB CURRY

*2 hours cooking time*

*Ingredients for 3-4 servings*

| | |
|---|---|
| 750 g (1½ lb) lamb chops | 2 teaspoons curry powder |
| 8 dried apricots | 8 dates |
| 60 g (2 oz) lima beans | ½ teaspoon salt |
| ¼ teaspoon white pepper | juice of 1 lemon |
| 2 cups water | 2 tablespoons butter |

1   Lima beans and apricots should be soaked overnight in water.
2   Melt butter and sauté the chops.
3   Add curry powder and cook for 2 minutes.
4   Add dates and soaked fruit and beans.
5   Add water.
6   Bring to the boil, season with salt and pepper.
7   Add lemon juice and simmer for 2 hours.

# LAMB CUTLETS WITH TOMATOES

*20 minutes cooking time*

*Ingredients for 4-5 servings*

**10 lamb cutlets**
**2 teaspoons butter**
**½ teaspoon salt**

**2 tomatoes**
**¼ teaspoon white pepper**

1 Preheat frypan and grease.
2 Trim meat and place cutlets in frypan.
3 Cook for 5 minutes on each side.
4 Remove to oven and keep warm.
5 Garnish with tomato slices.

# FRUITED LAMB

*2½ hours cooking time*

*Ingredients for 4-5 servings*

**¼ teaspoon white pepper**
**5 lamb shanks**
**1 cup currants**
**1 cup cooked apricots**
**2 tablespoons lemon juice**
**½ cup sugar**
**¼ teaspoon ground cloves**

**½ teaspoon salt**
**2 teaspoons plain flour**
**1 cup cooked prunes**
**2 tablespoons vinegar**
**2 tablespoons honey**
**2 cups water**

1 Season meat with salt and pepper.
2 Roll in flour and place in greased frying pan.
3 Simmer for 1-2 hours.
4 Mix prunes, currants, apricots, vinegar, lemon juice, honey, sugar, cloves and a little salt.
5 Place in saucepan with water and boil for 5 minutes. Drain and reserve a little juice.
6 Drain fat from meat and pour fruit over.
7 Place all ingredients into another greased frying pan and simmer for 1 hour.
8 Serve immediately.

# LAMB AND OLIVES

*15 minutes cooking time*

*Ingredients for 4-5 servings*

12 short loin chops
½ teaspoon salt
2 teaspoons dry mustard
½ cup sour cream

¼ teaspoon white pepper
½ teaspoon tarragon
3 tablespoons dry sherry
3 tablespoons stuffed green olives

1 Grill meat and season with salt and pepper.
2 Remove to serving dish and keep hot.
3 To pan add tarragon, mustard and sherry.
4 Simmer for 2 minutes and stir in sour cream.
5 Add sliced olives and reheat.
6 Pour over chops.
7 Serve immediately.

# MINCED LAMB

*15 minutes cooking time*

*Ingredients for 4-5 servings*

2 cups cold cooked lamb
2 tablespoons chopped parsley
⅛ teaspoon white pepper

1 cup white sauce
toast triangles
1 teaspoon salt

1 Dice meat and add to parsley.
2 Combine thoroughly.
3 Mix with prepared white sauce and heat.
4 Serve on toast.

# BREADED LAMB CHOPS

*20 minutes cooking time*

*Ingredients for 4 servings*

8 short loin chops
1½ cups plain flour
3 eggs, beaten
3 tablespoons butter

2 cups breadcrumbs
1 teaspoon salt
¼ teaspoon white pepper

1 Roll chops in flour and dip into eggs.
2 Roll in breadcrumbs and season with salt and pepper.
3 Sauté chops in butter and serve with white sauce and parsley.

## MUTTON WITH BEANS

*Ingredients for 4-5 servings*

*30 minutes cooking time*

**200 g (6 oz) beans**
**1 kg (2 lb) neck of mutton**
**2 onions**
**4 carrots**
**2 turnips**

**boiling water**
**1 teaspoon salt**
**½ teaspoon white pepper**
**2 tablespoons Worcestershire sauce**
**1 tablespoon olive oil**

1 Soak beans in water overnight.
2 Cut meat into serving pieces and trim off fat.
3 Peel and slice vegetables.
4 Brown meat in oil and add vegetables.
5 Fry for 5 minutes.
6 Add boiling water and cover.
7 Beans should be added 10 minutes before serving.

## CHINESE CHOPS

*Ingredients for 4-5 servings*

*1 hour cooking time*

**8 short loin lamb chops**
**½ teaspoon ginger**
**2 tablespoons olive oil**
**½ cup soy sauce**
**¼ cup water**

**2 tablespoons plain flour**
**½ teaspoon chives**
**4 canned pineapple slices**
**2 teaspoons cornflour**
**¼ cup sugar**

1 Place chops in mixed ginger, flour and chives.
2 Brown in oil on both sides and place pineapple on top of chops.
3 Blend remaining ingredients and pour over chops.
4 Serve immediately.

# LAMB SAUTÉ

*30 minutes cooking time*

*Ingredients for 3-4 servings*

1 kg (2 lb) thick chump lamb chops
1 onion, chopped
½ teaspoon salt
1 red pepper, chopped
60 g (¼ cup) butter
4 teaspoons curry powder
2 bay leaves

2 cloves garlic, crushed
1 green pepper, chopped
6 small onions
3 tablespoons olive oil
cooked rice
1½ cups water
2 tablespoons plain flour

1   Cube meat and leave for 5 minutes.
2   Sauté onion, green and red peppers in butter.
3   Stir in half of curry powder. Cook for 5 minutes.
4   Add flour and mix well for 2 minutes, then add water.
5   Add garlic and salt, bring to the boil and stir.
6   Sprinkle remaining powder on lamb cubes and sauté with onions.
7   Thread on skewers and lay in simmering sauce for 15 minutes.
8   Serve with hot rice and pour sauce over.

# LAMB OREGANO

*30 minutes cooking time*

*Ingredients for 3-4 servings*

1 kg (2 lb) boned lamb
2 onions, chopped
½ teaspoon salt
125 g (½ cup) butter
3 cups beef stock

3 teaspoons oregano
¼ teaspoon white pepper
1 teaspoon tomato purée
1 cup rice

1   Sauté lamb cubes in butter and add onions.
2   Add rice and cook, stirring constantly.
3   Add stock, oregano and seasonings.
4   Cover and cook for 30 minutes.
5   Add tomato purée 10 minutes before serving with a little butter.

# LAMB MARINADE

*25 minutes cooking time*

*Ingredients for 3-4 servings*

1 kg (2 lb) lean lamb
½ teaspoon salt
4 tablespoons oil
3 tablespoons soy sauce

¼ teaspoon white pepper
2 onions, grated
3 tablespoons lemon juice

1 Mix all ingredients together to make a marinade.
2 Cut lamb into cubes and leave in marinade.
3 Thread on skewers and grill until cooked.

# LAMB CUTLETS AND TOMATOES

*1 hour cooking time*

*Ingredients for 5-6 servings*

8 lamb cutlets
1 cup breadcrumbs
¼ teaspoon white pepper

3 onions, chopped
4 tomatoes, sliced
½ teaspoon salt

1 Rub cutlets in seasoned flour and place in greased frying pan.
2 Cover with onion, tomatoes and breadcrumbs.
3 Add 2 cups water and dot with butter.
4 Cook for 1 hour and serve with chopped parsley.

# LAMB COOKED IN MINT

*15 minutes cooking time*

*Ingredients for 4-5 servings*

½ cup red wine
2 cloves garlic, crushed
½ teaspoon salt

6 sprigs fresh mint, chopped
6 chump chops

1 Mix wine, chopped mint and garlic and marinate chops in this mixture for 3 hours.
2 Remove chops and grill.
3 Sprinkle with salt.

# *Beef*

## GRILLED FILLET

*10 minutes cooking time*

*Ingredients for 2 servings*

2 fillet steaks
¼ teaspoon white pepper

½ teaspoon salt
2 teaspoons butter

1   Turn griller on and leave until red hot.
2   Trim and prepare meat.
3   Place on tray and sear quickly.
4   Reduce heat and turn.
5   Cook for 10 minutes.
6   Serve with a little butter.

# SIRLOIN AND ONIONS

*1 hour cooking time*

*Ingredients for 4-5 servings*

1 kg (2 lb) sirloin steak
4 tablespoons plain flour
3 eggs, beaten
¼ teaspoon white pepper
2 tablespoons milk

4 tablespoons butter
4 onions, sliced
½ teaspoon salt
½ cup beef stock
2 cups breadcrumbs

1  Cut meat into serving pieces.
2  Prepare flour, eggs, milk and breadcrumbs.
3  Dip meat into the above ingredients.
4  Sauté meat in butter.
5  Remove from pan.
6  Add onions and sauté.
7  Place steak on top of onions, season with salt and pepper.
8  Add stock.
9  Cover and simmer for 50 minutes.
10 Serve immediately.

# FILET MIGNON

*15 minutes cooking time*

*Ingredients for 3 servings*

3 pieces eye fillet, thickly cut
150 g (5 oz) butter
peas
potatoes

4 croutes fried bread
150 g (5 oz) mushrooms
tomatoes

1  Cook meat under griller.
2  Peel mushrooms and leave in one piece.
3  Sauté mushrooms in butter.
4  Dot steak with butter, sprinkle with mushrooms.
5  Place on bread and serve.
6  Serve with tomatoes, peas, potatoes.

# BEEF WITH YORKSHIRE PUDDING

*3½ hours cooking time*

*Ingredients for 4-5 servings*

| | |
|---|---|
| **2 kg (4-5 lb) sirloin roast** | **1 tablespoon fat** |
| **½ teaspoon salt** | **¼ teaspoon white pepper** |

1  Preheat oven to 230°C (450°F).
2  Rub meat with salt and pepper.
3  Place meat in baking dish with fat and put in top of oven.
4  Bake 15 minutes then reduce temperatures to 190°C (375°F).
5  Bake for 3 hours.
6  Place on serving dish and serve with vegetables and gravy.
7  Add Yorkshire pudding to plate.
8  Serve immediately.

# PAN-FRIED STEAK

*10 minutes cooking time*

*Ingredients for 2 servings*

| | |
|---|---|
| **2 pieces fillet** | **½ teaspoon salt** |
| **fat** | |

1  Heat fat in a heavy pan.
2  Place meat in and sear quickly on both sides.
3  Reduce heat.
4  Keep turning until cooked.
5  Pour off fat from meat.
6  Serve with green vegetables and onions.

# BEEF WITH CARROTS

*30 minutes cooking time*

*Ingredients for 4-5 servings*

| | |
|---|---|
| **750 g (1½ lb) fillet of beef** | **olive oil** |
| **2 tablespoons soy sauce** | **2 carrots, finely chopped** |
| **3 tablespoons dry sherry** | **2 green peppers, chopped** |
| **2 teaspoons crushed garlic** | **2 teaspoons grated ginger** |

1   Shred beef and marinate in mixture of soy sauce, sherry, garlic and ginger for 1 hour.
2   Sauté in oil, and add carrots and peppers.
3   Cook until all ingredients are tender and serve immediately.

# STEAK DIANNE

*10 minutes cooking time*

*Ingredients for 3-4 servings*

**4 fillets**
**½ teaspoon salt**
**90 g (3 oz) butter**
**2 tablespoons chopped parsley**

**2 cloves garlic**
**¼ teaspoon white pepper**
**1 tablespoon Worcestershire sauce**

1   Prepare meat and flatten.
2   Season with salt and pepper.
3   Melt butter and sauté meat.
4   Sprinkle with parsley and garlic.
5   Add Worcestershire sauce and leave for 5 minutes or until cooked.
6   Place meat on serving dish and add sauce.

# BEEF AND ONIONS

*20 minutes cooking time*

*Ingredients for 3-4 servings*

**750 g (1½ lb) fillet**
**1 teaspoon salt**
**1 egg white**
**5 tablespoons olive oil**
**1 tablespoon cornflour**

**1 tablespoon dry sherry**
**1 tablespoon sugar**
**1 tablespoon soy sauce**
**4 onions, sliced**

1   Pound beef and slice thinly into strips.
2   Mix meat with salt, pepper, white of egg and cornflour.
3   Heat oil and sauté onions, remove to warmed plate.
4   Fry meat for 2 minutes, adding oil as necessary.
5   Replace onions, then add wine, sugar, soy sauce.
6   Stir constantly.
7   Bring to the boil and serve immediately.

# KEBABS

*20 minutes cooking time*

*Ingredients for 5-6 servings*

1 kg (2 lb) sirloin steak
1 cucumber

500 g (1 lb) small mushrooms
250 g (8 oz) tomatoes

## MARINADE

½ cup olive oil
¼ cup vinegar
¼ cup chopped onion

½ teaspoon salt
¼ teaspoon white pepper
2 teaspoons Worcestershire sauce

1  Mix marinade mixture and pour over beef.
2  Stand for 2 hours.
3  Drain.
4  On skewer place beef, mushrooms, cucumber and tomatoes alternately.
5  Place under griller for 20 minutes.
6  Baste with marinade mixture.
7  Serve with rice or buttered noodles.

# BRAISED RUMP

*2 hours cooking time*

*Ingredients for 4-5 servings*

2 kg (4 lb) rump steak
¼ teaspoon white pepper
2 tablespoons olive oil
1 tablespoon honey
2 tablespoons soy sauce

2 teaspoons celery salt
2 cloves garlic, crushed
1 cup water
1 tablespoon vinegar
1 teaspoon ginger, ground

1  Rub serving pieces of meat with celery salt and pepper.
2  Sauté garlic in oil and remove when cooked.
3  Brown meat in oil and combine honey, water, vinegar, soy sauce and ginger.
4  Pour over meat.
5  Cover and simmer for 2 hours.
6  Transfer meat to serving dish and pour gravy over.
7  Serve immediately.

# FILLET ROSSINI

*Ingredients for 4 servings*

*15 minutes cooking time*

**4 small trimmed fillets of beef**
**90 g (3 oz) butter**

**4 thick slices paté**
**4 croutons fried in butter**

1  Heat butter and sauté fillets in pan.
2  Remove and keep hot.
3  Place each piece of steak on fried crouton.
4  Place paté slices on meat.
5  Pour pan juices over meat and serve immediately.


# BEEF OLIVES

*Ingredients for 4-5 servings*

*2 hours cooking time*

**1 kg (2 lb) topside steak**
**chopped parsley**
**¼ teaspoon white pepper**
**2 teaspoons butter**
**2 cups water**

**½ cup breadcrumbs**
**1 teaspoon salt**
**mixed herbs**
**juice of 1 lemon**
**2 tablespoons plain flour**

1   Cut meat into 10 centimetre (4 in) slices.
2   Combine breadcrumbs, chopped parsley, salt, pepper, herbs and lemon juice together.
3   Spread on steak.
4   Roll up and tie securely.
5   Brown meat in melted butter until cooked.
6   Remove.
7   Add flour to pan and stir in water.
8   Allow to thicken then add meat, salt and pepper.
9   Allow to simmer for 1½ hours.
10  Place on serving dish.
11  Pour over gravy.

# SIRLOIN NICOISE

*30 minutes cooking time*

*Ingredients for 4-5 servings*

4 tomatoes
2 cloves garlic, crushed
8 pieces sirloin
½ teaspoon salt
string beans, cooked in butter
chopped parsley

4 tablespoons butter
1 teaspoon tarragon
extra butter
¼ teaspoon white pepper
small potatoes

1  Prepare tomatoes then simmer in butter with crushed garlic.
2  Add the tarragon at very low heat.
3  Cook for 5 minutes.
4  Sauté steaks in butter and season with salt and pepper.
5  Remove when cooked and place in oven to keep warm.
6  Place tomatoes on top of steak and surround with beans and potatoes.
7  Garnish with chopped parsley.

# TOPSIDE WITH DRIED APRICOTS

*2 hours cooking time*

*Ingredients for 5-6 servings*

½ cup dried apricots
¼ teaspoon white pepper
1.75 kg (3½ lb) topside steak
3 tablespoons butter
½ cup stock

½ teaspoon salt
2 onions, chopped
2 tablespoons water
lemon rind

1  Cover dried apricots with water and soak overnight.
2  Brown meat in butter.
3  Season with salt and pepper.
4  Add onion, water, lemon rind.
5  Cover and simmer for 2 hours.
6  Add apricots and stock in last 30 minutes of cooking.
7  Place apricots and meat on serving dish.
8  Thicken gravy and pour over meat.

# SEASONED TOPSIDE

*2 hours cooking time*

*Ingredients for 5-6 servings*

2 cups breadcrumbs
1 tablespoon butter
¼ teaspoon white pepper
2 onions chopped

2 teaspoons grated lemon rind
½ teaspoon salt
½ teaspoon mixed herbs
1 egg, beaten

1  Preheat oven to 200°C (400°F).
2  Rub butter into breadcrumbs.
3  Add remainder of ingredients and blend well.
4  Bind with egg.
5  Cut pocket into steak and pack stuffing.
6  Sew securely.
7  Melt fat and brown meat.
8  Add water and cover pan.
9  Place in oven and bake for 10 minutes.
10  Reduce heat to 190°C (375°F) and bake a further 1¾ hours.
11  Serve with baked potatoes, peas, carrots and turnips.

# STEAK AND MUSHROOM KEBABS

*25 minutes cooking time*

*Ingredients for 4-5 servings*

1 kg (2 lb) grilling steak
12 mushrooms
½ cup claret
¼ teaspoon white pepper
1 teaspoon Worcestershire sauce
2 cloves garlic, crushed

2 tablespoons tomato sauce
1 teaspoon sugar
½ teaspoon salt
½ cup oil
1 tablespoon vinegar
rosemary

1  Cube steak and peel mushrooms.
2  Mix other ingredients and pour over meat.
3  Leave to marinate for 4 hours.
4  Thread onto skewers, alternating mushrooms and steak.
5  Grill until cooked.
6  Serve immediately.

# APRICOT ROLL UPS

*2 hours cooking time*

*Ingredients for 5-6 servings*

1 kg (2 lb) round steak
1 cup dried apricots
1 stick celery
¼ teaspoon white pepper
2 slices bread
2 onions, sliced

½ teaspoon sugar
2 tablespoons butter
½ teaspoon salt
2 cups water
2 teaspoons soy sauce

1   Soak apricots overnight in water.
2   Pound steak and cut into pieces 10 by 12 centimetres (4 by 5 in).
3   Chop apricots and celery.
4   Crumble bread and mix with sugar.
5   Spread mixture on meat and roll up.
6   Secure with toothpicks.
7   Melt butter and brown meat.
8   Season with salt and pepper.
9   Add water, soy sauce and onions.
10  Cover and simmer for 2 hours.

# ECONOMY ROUND STEAK

*3 hours cooking time*

*Ingredients for 5-6 servings*

1 kg (2 lb) round steak
2 onions, chopped
2 carrots, chopped
2 stalks celery, chopped

1 parsnip, diced
1 teaspoon salt
¼ teaspoon white pepper
1 tablespoon plain flour

1   Cube meat and cover with boiling water.
2   Simmer for 2-3 hours.
3   Add onion, carrot, parsnip, salt, pepper and celery.
4   Simmer for another hour and thicken with flour.
5   Serve immediately.

# BRAISED ROUND STEAK

*2½ hours cooking time*

*Ingredients for 5-6 servings*

1.25 kg (2½ lb) round steak
3 tablespoons butter
4 tablespoons plain flour
4 tablespoons chopped onion

2 teaspoons lemon juice
3 cloves
1½ teaspoons salt
¼ teaspoon white pepper

1  Cut meat into squares and sauté in butter.
2  Remove meat.
3  Add flour and stir well.
4  Add other ingredients and simmer for 5 minutes.
5  Add meat and simmer for 2-2½ hours.
6  Serve immediately.

# STEAK AND BEANS

*20 minutes cooking time*

*Ingredients for 5-6 servings*

1 kg (2 lb) skirt steak
500 g (1 lb) french beans
6 spring onions
1 teaspoon salt

2 cloves garlic
½ cup stock
60 g (¼ cup) butter
2 teaspoons cornflour

1  Cut meat into 4 centimetre (1½ in) squares.
2  Chop beans into 8 centimetre (3 in) lengths and onions into 5 centimetre (2 in) lengths.
3  Chop garlic and fry in butter.
4  Add salt and steak and sauté with garlic.
5  Remove from heat and place on hot plate.
6  Add beans and fry for 2 minutes.
7  Stir constantly.
8  Add stock and simmer for 10 minutes.
9  Add meat, onion and salt. Stir and cook for 5 minutes.
10  Thicken with cornflour and serve.

# SPARERIBS AND CABBAGE

*1 hour cooking time*

*Ingredients for 4-5 servings*

1.5 kg (3 lb) spareribs
1 teaspoon salt

6 cups cabbage
1 tablespoon butter

1 Boil cabbage and when cooked and drained let stand in saucepan with butter on top.
2 Divide spareribs and sprinkle with salt.
3 Place in frying pan and cover with water.
4 Bring to boil and reduce heat. Simmer for 30 minutes.
5 Add cabbage and simmer for further 15 minutes.
6 Serve immediately.

# BEEF WITH NOODLES

*25 minutes cooking time*

*Ingredients for 2-3 servings*

250 g (8 oz) minced beef
2 teaspoons cornflour
90 g (3 oz) dry noodles
1 onion, chopped
½ green pepper, chopped
2 tablespoons olive oil

1¼ cups beef stock
2 teaspoons soy sauce
oil for frying
2 cloves garlic, crushed
4 tomatoes

1 Sauté minced beef in oil.
2 Add pepper and tomatoes to meat.
3 Stir in stock and simmer for 10 minutes.
4 Add garlic and soy sauce.
5 Blend cornflour and simmer with a little more water.
6 Serve with fried or boiled noodles.

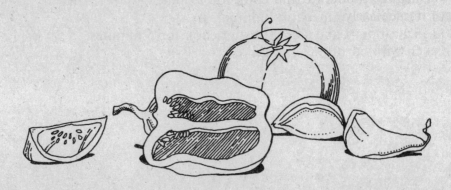

# TOMATO MINCE

*Ingredients for 5-6 servings*

*35 minutes cooking time*

**500 g (1 lb) minced steak**
**2 cloves garlic**
**1 green pepper, chopped**
**½ teaspoon salt**
**2 tablespoons butter**

**1 tin tomato paste**
**1 red pepper, chopped**
**¼ teaspoon white pepper**
**2 onions, chopped**
**noodles**

1  Sauté onion, garlic, red and green peppers in butter.
2  Put tomato paste and mince in saucepan and simmer for 20 minutes.
3  Add fried ingredients and simmer for further 10-15 minutes.
4  Boil noodles and when cooked run boiling water over them.
5  Dot with butter and combine with other ingredients.
6  Serve with chopped parsley.

# GLAZED SPARERIBS

*Ingredients for 3-4 servings*

*1 hour 40 minutes cooking time*

**1.25 kg (2½ lb) spareribs**
**½ teaspoon salt**
**½ cup sherry**
**3 tablespoons vinegar**
**2 cloves garlic, crushed**

**¼ teaspoon white pepper**
**½ can tomato purée**
**½ cup honey**
**3 tablespoons onion, chopped**
**½ teaspoon Worcestershire sauce**

1  Sprinkle spareribs with salt and pepper.
2  Place in frying pan and cook for 40 minutes.
3  Drain off fat that has collected.
4  Mix tomato purée, sherry, honey, vinegar, onion, garlic and Worcester-shire sauce. Pour over spareribs.
5  Lower heat to moderate and cook for 1 hour.
6  Serve immediately.

# BEEF AND WORCESTERSHIRE SAUCE

*20 minutes cooking time*

*Ingredients for 4-5 servings*

2 cups grated cheddar cheese
2 cups corned beef, chopped
3 cups strained tomatoes
3 eggs, beaten

2 teaspoons Worcestershire sauce
3 teaspoons butter
⅛ teaspoon white pepper

1   Place cheese, beef and tomatoes in frying pan.
2   Simmer until cheese melts.
3   Stir constantly.
4   Add butter, pepper and a little salt.
5   Add eggs and Worcestershire sauce, making sure to stir constantly.
6   Heat and serve immediately on toast.

# CHEESE LOAF

*1 hour cooking time*

*Ingredients for 3-4 servings*

500 g (1 lb) minced steak
1 egg, beaten
½ cup milk
½ cup grated cheese
1 teaspoon Vegemite

½ teaspoon salt
¼ teaspoon white pepper
½ cup chopped onion
1 cup crushed corn flakes

1   Oven should be pre-heated to 180°C (350°F).
2   Combine all ingredients and form a loaf.
3   Place on a sheet of foil.
4   Fold and place in baking tray.
5   Bake for 40 minutes.
6   For last 5 minutes of baking, open foil to brown top of loaf.
7   Serve immediately.

# MEAT SOUFFLÉ

*Ingredients for 2-3 servings*

*45 minutes cooking time*

2 cups milk
1 tablespoon flour
2 tablespoons butter
¼ teaspoon white pepper
1 cup breadcrumbs

1 egg yolk
1 tablespoon chopped parsley
3 tablespoons chopped onion
1 stalk celery, chopped
2 cups chopped cooked meat

1   Melt butter and stir in flour.
2   Add milk, salt, pepper and cook for 10 minutes.
3   Add crumbs, parsley, onion and celery.
4   Cook for further 5 minutes.
5   Add meat and beaten egg yolk, mix well.
6   Pour into greased frying pan and simmer for 30 minutes.
7   Serve immediately.

# MINCE ON TOAST

*Ingredients for 4 servings*

*20 minutes cooking time*

1 tablespoon chopped onion
3 tablespoons butter
375 g (12 oz) minced beef
½ teaspoon salt
¼ teaspoon white pepper

1 oup water
1 tablespoon plain flour
4 toast slices
4 slices tomato

1   Sauté onion in butter and add minced beef.
2   Add salt.
3   When mince is brown pour in water and bring to the boil.
4   Simmer for 10 minutes.
5   Blend flour with a little cold water and stir into meat.
6   Cook for 5 minutes, reducing heat and allowing to thicken.
7   Serve on buttered toast, garnished with tomato.

# STUFFED STEAK

*1½ hours cooking time*

*Ingredients for 4-5 servings*

**750 g (1½ lb) flank steak**
**½ teaspoon white pepper**
**1½ cups stuffing**

**1 tablespoon plain flour**
**½ teaspoon salt**

1 Cut steak into long strips and season with salt and pepper.
2 Coat in flour.
3 Spread stuffing on meat, roll up and fasten with skewers.
4 Place in frying pan with a little fat or butter and sauté for 5 minutes.
5 Remove.
6 Place under grill until cooked.

# SAUSAGES AND CABBAGE

*10 minutes cooking time*

*Ingredients for 4-5 servings*

**1 kg (2 lb) beef sausages**
**4 cups chopped cabbage**
**chopped parsley**

**1 teaspoon salt**
**¼ teaspoon white pepper**

1 Fry sausages in frying pan for 5-10 minutes.
2 Drain.
3 Make sure there are only 3-4 tablespoons fat in pan then place cabbage in.
4 Sprinkle with salt, pepper and parsley.
5 Serve immediately.

# CORNED BEEF

*Ingredients for 5-6 servings*

**2.5 kg (5 lb) beef**
**60 g (2 oz) black pepper**
**60 g (2 oz) oregano**

**6 cloves garlic**
**½ teaspoon salt**
**4 bay leaves**

1 Let meat stand in cold water for 24 hours.
2 Add fresh water and spices.
3 Stand for 2 weeks in cool place.
4 Add more salt.

# CHILLI MINCE

*2 hours cooking time*

*Ingredients for 5-6 servings*

3 tablespoons butter
2 onions, sliced
500 g (1 lb) minced steak
1 green pepper, chopped
½ cup water

3 cloves
1 bay leaf
3 tablespoons chilli powder
1 large can tomatoes
1½ teaspoons salt

1  Brown onion in melted butter.
2  Add meat and green pepper.
3  Brown and stir.
4  Add tomatoes, salt, cloves, bay leaves, and chilli powder.
5  Cover and simmer for 2 hours.
6  Serve immediately.

# CHEESEBURGERS

*20 minutes cooking time*

*Ingredients for 5-6 servings*

500 g (1 lb) minced steak
1 teaspoon salt
½ teaspoon white pepper
2 onions, chopped

½ cup breadcrumbs
1 cup grated cheddar cheese
tomato slices
buns

1  Mould meat, salt, pepper, onion and breadcrumbs together.
2  Mould into 6 burgers.
3  Let stand for 1 hour.
4  Place in a lightly greased frying pan and cook for 5 minutes.
5  Turn.
6  When cooked place cheddar slices on meat and then remove and place under griller until cheese is browned.
7  Serve on toasted buns with tomato slices.

# BEEF CUTLETS

*10 minutes cooking time*

*Ingredients for 4-5 servings*

2 cups beef mince
1 teaspoon onion juice
white sauce
2 tablespoons water

2 tablespoons chopped parsley
1 egg
1 cup breadcrumbs

1 Add onion to white sauce and leave.
2 Add parsley to meat and mix well.
3 Mould into cutlets.
4 Dip in beaten egg and roll in breadcrumbs.
5 Fry in fat for 5-10 minutes and drain.
6 Serve immediately with white sauce.

# CREAMED MEAT

*30 minutes cooking time*

*Ingredients for 4-5 servings*

2 cups cooked chopped cold meat
white sauce

½ cup boiled peas
½ cup sliced boiled mushrooms

1 Add other ingredients to prepared white sauce and simmer for 15 minutes.
2 Serve immediately with grated cheese on top.

# BEEF SAUSAGE MEAT

*1 hour cooking time*

*Ingredients for 4-5 servings*

1 kg (2 lb) chopped beef
2 teaspoons salt
1 teaspoon powdered sage
½ teaspoon black pepper

3 tablespoons chopped parsley
3 cups stale breadcrumbs
1 egg beaten
¼ teaspoon paprika

1 Mix all ingredients thoroughly.
2 Tie in cloth.
3 Drop in boiling water and boil for 1 hour.
4 Remove cloth and serve in thin pieces.

# FRIED CORNED BEEF

*20 minutes cooking time*

*Ingredients for 4-5 servings*

3 tablespoons butter
6 thick slices corned beef
½ teaspoon salt

5 cups boiled cabbage
¼ teaspoon white pepper

1 Sauté the meat in butter and remove to hot plate.
2 Add cabbage to pan and sauté.
3 Sprinkle with salt and pepper.
4 Dot with butter and serve immediately.


# MINCE ROLLS

*1 hour cooking time*

*Ingredients for 3-4 servings*

8 cabbage leaves
½ teaspoon salt
500 g (1 lb) minced steak
2 onions, chopped
½ teaspoon salt

1 cup cooked rice
1 egg
440 ml (16 oz) can tomato purée
1 tablespoon butter
¼ teaspoon white pepper

1 Preheat oven to 180°C (350°F).
2 Par-boil cabbage leaves in boiling salted water.
3 Strain.
4 Combine steak, onion, salt, pepper, rice and egg.
5 Mix well.
6 Shape and place on cabbage leaves.
7 Wrap cabbage and tie securely.
8 Place in greased casserole dish and pour tomato purée over.
9 Bake for 1 hour.
10 Serve immediately.

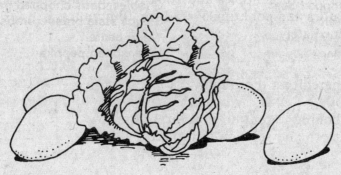

# BEEF CURRY

*2½ hours cooking time*

*Ingredients for 3-4 servings*

750 g (1½ lb) bladebone steak, cut
   cut into 1 centimetre (½ in) pieces
3 tablespoons butter
2 tablespoons flour
2 onions, chopped
¼ teaspoon white pepper
1 banana, sliced

1 tablespoon sultanas
1 tablespoon curry powder
1 tablespoon chutney
1¼ cups water
½ teaspoon salt
1 apple, chopped
juice of 2 lemons

1  Fry onions, apples, and banana in butter.
2  Add meat and curry powder.
3  Cook for 5 minutes.
4  Add flour and brown.
5  Pour in liquid and add chutney, sultanas, salt, pepper and lemon juice.
6  Bring to the boil and simmer for 2 hours.
7  Serve immediately with boiled rice.

# SPANISH STEAK

*1 hour cooking time*

*Ingredients for 3-4 servings*

2 tablespons butter
750 g (1½ lb) bladebone steak
½ teaspoon salt
¼ teaspoon white pepper
½ cup water

2 onions, sliced
1 potato, sliced
2 apples, peeled and sliced
1 tomato, skinned and sliced

1  Sauté cubed meat in butter and season with salt and pepper.
2  Add water, cover and cook for 20 minutes.
3  Add onions and cook for 20 minutes.
4  Add sliced potatoes, apples and cook for 5 minutes.
5  Add tomatoes and cook uncovered for 10 minutes.
6  Serve immediately.

# BEEF TERIYAKI

*20 minutes cooking time*

*Ingredients for 4-5 servings*

**1.25 kg (2½ lb) chuck steak**
**½ cup sugar**
**½ teaspoon monosodium**
  **glutamate (optional)**

**1 clove garlic, crushed**
**2 cups soy sauce**
**1 teaspoon grated ginger**

1  Cut meat into serving pieces and place in bowl.
2  Combine soy sauce, ginger and monosodium glutamate and sugar.
3  Heat until sugar dissolves.
4  Pour over meat and marinate for 3 hours.
5  Remove from marinade and grill till cooked.

# COLD MEAT AND RICE

*10 minutes cooking time*

*Ingredients for 4-5 servings*

**2 tablespoons butter**
**2 onions**
**125 g (4 oz) mushrooms, sliced**
**250 g (8 oz) cold cooked meat**
**½ teaspoon salt**
**green peas**

**2 cups stock**
**125 g (4 oz) uncooked rice**
**chopped parsley**
**¼ teaspoon white pepper**
**tomatoes**

1  Sauté the onions and mushrooms in butter.
2  Add meat, salt, pepper and rice.
3  Simmer for 5 minutes.
4  Add tomatoes and stock.
5  Simmer until rice is cooked and garnish with mushrooms, tomatoes and peas.

# STACKUPS

*Ingredients for 3-4 servings*

*30 minutes cooking time*

750 g (1½ lb) minced steak
2 onions, chopped
1 egg, beaten
1 cup breadcrumbs
1 tablespoon tomato purée

2 teaspoons mustard
½ teaspoon salt
¼ teaspoon white pepper
8 slices cheddar cheese

1 Place steak, onion, egg, breadcrumbs, tomato purée and mustard in a bowl.
2 Blend thoroughly and divide into 8 pieces.
3 Form into hamburgers and sauté in butter.
4 Place cheese on top of each burger and place under griller.

# Pork
# Bacon
# Ham

## PORK AND SOY SAUCE

*35 minutes cooking time*

*Ingredients for 4-5 servings*

| | |
|---|---|
| 1 kg (2 lb) pork fillet, cubed | 1 teaspoon brown sugar |
| ¼ teaspoon white pepper | ½ teaspoon salt |
| 3 tablespoons soy sauce | 1 teaspoon ground coriander |
| dash ginger | 1 cup thinly sliced onion |
| 1 cup lemon juice | |

1  In small bowl combine all ingredients except pork to make a marinade.
2  Pour marinade over pork cubes and leave for 3 hours.
3  Arrange pork on skewers and drain marinade.
4  Brush marinade on to cubes and place under griller for 5 minutes.
5  Turn.
6  Baste and grill for further 5 minutes.
7  Continue doing this until cooked.
8  Serve with saffron rice and salad.

# PORK IN SOUR CREAM

*2-3 hours cooking time*

*Ingredients for 4-5 servings*

4 thick slices pork
2 spring onions, chopped
2 cloves garlic, crushed
½ teaspoon salt
1 cup sour cream
3 tablespoons plain flour
2 tablespoons lemon juice

2 onions, sliced
2 carrots, diced
1 kg (2 lb) round steak
¼ teaspoon white pepper
1 cup red wine
3 tablespoons water

1  Add slices of pork to frying pan with onion, carrots and garlic.
2  Sauté lightly.
3  Remove vegetables and rub round steak with salt and pepper.
4  Place in pan and brown.
5  Reduce heat.
6  Stir in wine and sour cream.
7  Add vegetables again and cover. Simmer for 2-3 hours.
8  Place meat and vegetables on serving dish in oven.
9  Blend flour and water into juices and simmer.
10  Add lemon juice and pour over meat.
11  Serve immediately.

# PORK WITH DRESSING

*1 hour cooking time*

*Ingredients for 3-4 servings*

6 pork chops
2 onions, chopped
2 cups breadcrumbs
2 eggs

¼ teaspoon white pepper
1 teaspoon salt
2 tablespoons pork fat, chopped

1  Mix onion, breadcrumbs, fat, salt, pepper and beaten eggs.
2  Add ½ cup water and spread on chops.
3  Place chops in frying pan and cover bottom of pan with water.
4  Simmer for 1 hour.
5  Serve immediately.

# PORK AND BAMBOO SHOOTS

*25 minutes cooking time*

*Ingredients for 3-4 servings*

250 g (8 oz) pork
small can bamboo shoots
3 tablespoons olive oil
1 cup beef stock

1 teaspoon ginger
2 tablespoons sherry
½ teaspoon salt
1 tablespoon cornflour

1 Cut pork and bamboo shoots into small pieces.
2 Heat 2 tablespoons olive oil and fry shoots for 3 minutes.
3 Drain.
4 Blend ginger, sherry, cornflour and salt.
5 Coat pork in this mixture.
6 Add remaining oil and sauté pork for 15 minutes.
7 Replace shoots in pan with stock and cook for further 5 minutes.

# PORK CURRY

*1 hour cooking time*

*Ingredients for 4-5 servings*

2 tablespoons butter
750 g (1½ lb) fillet of pork
1 onion, chopped
1 carrot, chopped
¼ teaspoon white pepper
1 tomato, sliced
1 tablespoon curry powder

1 cup water
2 teaspoons tomato purée
2 teaspoons chutney
½ teaspoon salt
10 dried apricots
10 dried prunes

1 Sauté meat in butter until brown and remove.
2 Add to pan onion, carrot and tomato and sauté.
3 Add curry powder and cook for 5 minutes.
4 Add water and bring to the boil.
5 Add all remaining ingredients and simmer for 45 minutes.
6 Add a little more water if necessary.
7 Serve immediately.

# PICKLED PORK

*1½ hours cooking time*

*Ingredients for 4-5 servings*

1 kg (2 lb) pickled pork
2 onions, peeled
parsley, chopped
7 peppercorns

1 bay leaf
carrots, turnips, parsnips
8 cloves

1  Soak pork in cold water for 1 hour.
2  Remove.
3  Place in a saucepan with fresh water and bring to the boil slowly.
4  Add onions, cloves, peppercorns and bay leaf.
5  Cover and simmer for 1-2 hours.
6  When cooked place on serving dish and surround with vegetables.
7  Garnish with parsley.

# CHINESE PORK

*20 minutes cooking time*

*Ingredients for 4-5 servings*

500 g (1 lb) lean pork
2 tablespoons butter
2 onions, sliced
500 g (1 lb) green beans, cooked

1 tablespoon soy sauce
¼ teaspoon white pepper
boiled rice

1  Cut pork into thin strips and melt butter.
2  Sauté pork and onions and season with salt and pepper.
3  Add beans and cook for 5 minutes.
4  Stir in soy sauce and serve with rice.

# GRILLED PORK CHOPS

*30 minutes cooking time*

*Ingredients for 4-5 servings*

8 pork chops
1 teaspoon salt

¼ teaspoon white pepper
2 tablespoons butter

1  Grill chops at very high heat.
2  Reduce heat and grill for 20 minutes.

3  Sprinkle with salt and pepper.
4  Dot with butter.
5  Serve immediately.

# CANDIED PORK CHOPS

*1 hour cooking time*

*Ingredients for 4-5 servings*

| | |
|---|---|
| **8 pork chops** | **1 teaspoon salt** |
| **8 boiled sweet potatoes** | **¼ teaspoon white pepper** |
| **¼ cup brown sugar** | **2 tablespoons plain flour** |

1  Fry chops in butter and season with salt and pepper.
2  Add sliced potatoes and sprinkle with sugar and salt.
3  Simmer for 45 minutes.
4  Remove meat and potatoes and thicken gravy.
5  Serve immediately.

# SMOTHERED CHOPS

*1½ hours cooking time*

*Ingredients for 6-8 servings*

| | |
|---|---|
| **1.5 kg (3 lb) pork chops, cut thickly** | **2 cups tomato purée** |
| **2 lemons, sliced** | **2 green peppers, cut in rings** |
| **1 large onion, chopped** | **1 teaspoon salt** |
| **2 tablespoons butter** | |

1  Place chops in frying pan and cover with lemon, onion and pepper.
2  Sprinkle with salt and pour tomato purée over.
3  Dot with butter and cook for 1-1½ hours.
4  Lift on to serving dish and place pepper rings on top.
5  Serve immediately.

# PORK AND TOMATO COMBINATION

*1 hour cooking time*

*Ingredients for 5-6 servings*

2 tablespoons butter
2 cloves garlic
6 pork chops
¼ teaspoon white pepper
2 tablespoons tomato purée

2 cups water
2 green peppers
250 g (½ lb) mushrooms, sliced
½ teaspoon salt

1  Melt butter and sauté garlic and chops.
2  Season with salt and pepper.
3  Remove from pan.
4  Dilute purée with water and add peppers and mushrooms to pan.
5  Simmer for 10 minutes and replace meat in the pan with mushrooms and peppers.
6  Simmer until cooked and serve.

# PORK UNIVERSAL

*20 minutes cooking time*

*Ingredients for 2 servings*

1 tablespoon butter
500 g (1 lb) pork, cut in strips
1 cup stock
100 g (¼ lb) beans
2 onions, sliced

½ cabbage, shredded
½ teaspoon salt
2 sticks celery
2 teaspoons cornflour
2 tablespoons water

1  Melt butter and add meat.
2  Cook and stir constantly.
3  Remove meat.
4  Add celery which has been cut into 2 centimetre (1 in) pieces.
5  Add beans and onions, fry for 10 minutes.
6  Add cabbage, salt, stock and a little pepper.
7  Return meat to pan and cook for 10-15 minutes.
8  Thicken with cornflour and serve immediately.

# BACON ROLLS

*30 minutes cooking time*

*Ingredients for 4-5 servings*

12 slices bacon
2 cups breadcrumbs
1 cup celery, chopped
2 tablespoons chopped green pepper
1 egg

½ cup milk
1 onion, chopped
1 teaspoon salt
¼ teaspoon white pepper

1  Combine breadcrumbs, celery, pepper and onion.
2  Season with salt and pepper.
3  Add egg-milk mixture and place a tablespoon of this dressing on each piece of bacon.
4  Roll and secure with a toothpick.
5  Place under griller until cooked and serve immediately.

# BACON AND APPLES

*10 minutes cooking time*

*Ingredients for 4-5 servings*

12 slices bacon
4 green apples

3 tablespoons sugar
chopped parsley

1  Fry bacon and remove to warmed plate.
2  Quarter apples and place them in bacon fat.
3  Cover and simmer until soft.
4  Sprinkle with sugar and continue to cook.
5  Serve hot with bacon.

# FRIED HAM AND RICE

*20 minutes cooking time*

*Ingredients for 4-5 servings*

2 tablespoons butter
2 tablespoons chopped onion
1 tablespoon chopped parsley
2 cups chopped, cooked ham

2 cups boiled rice
1 teaspoon salt
1 egg
¼ teaspoon white pepper

1 Melt butter and sauté onion, parsley and ham.
2 Add rice.
3 Season with salt and pepper.
4 Mix well and add beaten egg and salt.
5 Serve immediately.

# HAMLETS

*15 minutes cooking time*

*Ingredients for 4-5 servings*

2 cups minced ham
2 tablespoons milk
5 slices bread
1 cup grated cheddar cheese

¾ teaspoon Worcestershire sauce
2 eggs
5 slices bacon

1 Wet ham with milk and spread on bread.
2 Cream cheese and Worcestershire sauce.
3 Beat egg and blend with these ingredients.
4 Spread on ham.
5 Place bacon slice on top and grill for 10-15 minutes.
6 Serve immediately.

# CREAMED HAM

*Ingredients for 4-5 servings*

3½-4 cups whipped cream
½ teaspoon salt
chopped parsley

2 tablespoons dry mustard
¼ teaspoon white pepper
8 pieces thick ham

1 Whip cream and beat in mustard with salt and pepper.
2 Place on ham and sprinkle with parsley.

# HAM IN WHITE WINE SAUCE

*20 minutes cooking time*

*Ingredients for 5-6 servings*

90 g (3 oz) butter
8-10 slices ham
2 tablespoons plain flour
¼ teaspoon white pepper

¼ cup red currant jelly
1 teaspoon mustard
½ teaspoon salt
1¼ cups dry white wine

1  Sauté meat in butter for 5 minutes.
2  Remove.
3  Stir in flour and add white wine, jelly and mustard.
4  Season with salt and pepper.
5  Pour over ham.
6  Serve immediately.

# COUNTY HAM

*2 hours cooking time*

*Ingredients for 4-5 servings*

2 teaspoons butter
4 slices ham, thickly cut
2 onions, chopped
4 carrots, sliced

4 tablespoons raisins
2 tablespoons plain flour
2 oranges

1  Sauté ham in butter and add onions.
2  Simmer for 2 minutes.
3  Add carrots, raisins and water.
4  Simmer for 1 hour.
5  Mix flour and orange juice.
6  Combine with mixture in pan and bring to the boil.
7  Serve immediately.

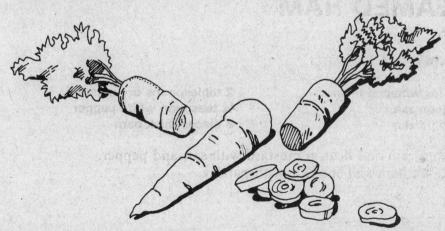

# FRIED HAM AND POTATOES

*1 hour cooking time*

*Ingredients for 4-5 servings*

| | |
|---|---|
| 1 kg (2 lb) ham | 24 cloves |
| 1 cup brown sugar | 10 new potatoes |
| 1 tablespoon breadcrumbs | 1 cup pineapple |

1  Rub ham with brown sugar and breadcrumbs.
2  Dot with cloves.
3  Cut potatoes in halves.
4  Arrange around ham in frying pan and pour over pineapple.
5  Simmer for 1 hour and serve immediately.

# HAM AND GINGER

*30 minutes cooking time*

*Ingredients for 4-5 servings*

| | |
|---|---|
| 1 kg (2 lb) ham, sliced thickly | 3 teaspoons ginger |
| ¼ cup soy sauce | ¼ cup sherry |
| ½ cup spring onions, chopped | ¼ cup water |
| 2 tablespoons olive oil | |

1  Combine soy sauce, sherry, spring onions, ginger and water.
2  Place ham in this mixture and stand for 2 hours.
3  Remove ham and dry. Reserve marinade.
4  Sauté ham in oil and pour over marinade.
5  Simmer for 30 minutes.

# *Chicken*

## WHOLE FRIED CHICKEN

*1½ hours cooking time*

*Ingredients for 2-4 servings*

1 1-kg (2-lb) chicken
juice of 1 lemon
1 teaspoon salt
2 lemons, quartered

2 tablespoons cornflour
4 cups vegetable oil
1 tablespoon honey

1  Rub chicken with lemon juice and salt.
2  Brush chicken with honey mixed with 2 tablespoons hot water.
3  Dust with cornflour.
4  Tie string to neck or feet and hang where the coating can dry out.
5  Heat oil in a deep saucepan or wok, spoon hot oil inside the chicken first, then over the outside of the chicken until golden.
6  Finish cooking by putting the chicken into oil; continue basting.
7  Drain thoroughly.
8  Cut into pieces with cleaver through the bone.
9  Serve with lemon, cut into quarters.

# CHEDDAR CHICKEN

*1¼ hours cooking time*

*Ingredients for 6 servings*

6 whole chicken breasts, split
2 cups water
3 spring onions
3 celery tops
½ cup cashew nuts

125 g (4 oz) shredded Cheddar cheese
2 cans cream of chicken soup
¾ cup crushed Jatz biscuits
1 cup macaroni

1   Simmer chicken breasts in water with onions (cut into 4 pieces) and celery tops for about 25 minutes.
2   Strain broth and reserve.
3   Let chicken cool, then skin and remove meat from bones in chunks.
4   Cook macaroni in boiling salted water until almost tender.
5   Drain and put in a greased casserole.
6   Sprinkle shredded cheese over macaroni, cover with chicken.
7   Sprinkle with nuts; pour over the soup, mixed with ¾ cup of chicken stock.
8   Top with biscuit crumbs and bake, uncovered, in a moderate oven 180°C (350°F) for 30 minutes.

# CHICKEN WITH FRUIT

*1 hour cooking time*

*Ingredients for 6-8 servings*

6-8 chicken breasts
½ cup flour
1½ teaspoons salt
½ teaspoon paprika
1 teaspoon curry powder
4 tablespoons salad oil

1 orange, segmented
1 cup pitted cherries
6-8 pineapple rings
1 avocado, cut in crescents
4 pieces fresh mint
1 cup dry white wine

1   Coat chicken pieces with mixture of flour, salt, paprika, and curry.
2   Brown gently on all sides in oil, then put in large ovenproof dish.
3   Add the wine, cover, and bake in a moderately hot oven 190°C (375°F) for 20 minutes.
4   Remove from oven and arrange orange segments, cherries and pineapple spears over the chicken and add half cup more wine if liquid has cooked away.
5   Return to oven and bake, uncovered, for 20 to 25 minutes until chicken is tender.
6   Garnish servings with crescents of avocado and sprigs of fresh mint.

# SESAME CHICKEN

*1¾ hours cooking time*

*Ingredients for 4-5 servings*

1 1.5-kg (3-lb) chicken
8 tablespoons flour
8 tablespoons sesame seed
½ teaspoon salt

¼ teaspoon pepper
⅛ cup salad oil
¼ cup white wine
¼ cup chicken stock

## SAUCE

125 g (4 oz) mushrooms, cut in pieces
2 stalks celery, chopped
1 medium carrot, chopped
chicken drippings

½ onion, chopped
½ teaspoon tarragon
¾ cup white sauce
½ cup sour cream

1  Cut chicken into pieces and coat with mixture of flour, sesame seed, salt and pepper.
2  Brown chicken in salad oil and transfer pieces to a large casserole.
3  Pour wine and chicken stock over chicken, cover and bake in a moderate oven 180°C (350°F) for 45 minutes.
4  Prepare sauce by simmering vegetables for 10 minutes in chicken drippings in frying pan.
5  Add mushroom pieces, tarragon, white sauce and sour cream.
6  Pour sauce over chicken and bake, uncovered, for an additional 20 minutes.

# BARBECUED CHICKEN LIVERS

*10 minutes cooking time*

*Ingredients for 6 servings*

500 g (1 lb) chicken livers
½ cup oil
½ cup soy sauce

½ cup sherry
1 clove garlic, crushed
1 tablespoon honey

1  Mix oil, soy sauce, sherry, garlic and honey in large bowl, add chicken livers and marinate for 2 hours.
2  Place 6-8 livers on each skewer.
3  Grill over medium coals or under grill for 4 minutes on one side, then 3 minutes on the other.

# MEXICAN CHICKEN

*1½ hours cooking time*

*Ingredients for 4 servings*

1 1.25-kg (2½-lb) chicken
2 tablespoons seasoned flour
4 tablespoons cooking oil
1 medium-sized onion, peeled and
  finely chopped
2 cups peeled tomatoes
185 g (6 oz) peas

185 g (6 oz) pimentos, diced
2 chicken stock cubes
8 stuffed olives
185 g (6 oz) rice
250 g (8 oz) sausages
salt and pepper

1  Cut the chicken into pieces and then toss in seasoned flour.
2  Heat the oil and brown the chicken, keep warm.
3  Add the onion to the pan and brown.
4  Drain the tomatoes, add water to the juice until liquid totals 2½ cups.
5  Add the tomatoes, liquid, pimentos, crumbled stock tablets, olives, rice
   and sliced sausages.
6  Stir well and season.
7  Arrange the chicken on top, and cover.
8  Simmer for 40 minutes, stirring occasionally.
9  Add peas and simmer for 15 minutes more.

# CHICKEN WITH GRAPES

*1½ hours cooking time*

*Ingredients for 6-8 servings*

6 whole chicken breasts, split
1 teaspoon salt
½ teaspoon pepper
¼ cup flour
8 tablespoons butter

¼ cup chicken stock
¾ cup dry white wine
250 g (8 oz) mushrooms, sliced
2 cups seedless grapes
2 large onions, finely chopped

1  Sprinkle chicken with salt and pepper and coat lightly with flour.
2  Heat 5 tablespoons of butter and brown chicken on all sides.
3  Arrange pieces closely together in a single layer in a large shallow pan.
4  Add onion to butter, cook until soft, and add chicken broth and wine;
   bring to boil, then pour over chicken.
5  Bake, covered, in a moderately hot oven 190°C (375°F) for 40 minutes.
6  Fry mushrooms gently in 3 tablespoons of butter.
7  When chicken has cooked for 40 minutes, add mushrooms and grapes;
   continue baking, covered, until grapes are just heated (about 10 minutes).

# CHICKEN AND YOGHURT

*2½ hours cooking time*

*Ingredients for 6 servings*

| | |
|---|---|
| 1 1.5-kg (3-lb) chicken | ¾ cup tinned tomato soup |
| 1 tablespoon flour | 2 teaspoons paprika |
| ½ teaspoon salt | ¾ cup water |
| ¼ teaspoon pepper | ½ cup yoghurt |
| 4 tablespoons oil | 1 tablespoon chopped parsley |
| 2 onions, sliced | 1 clove garlic, minced |

1  Cut chicken into serving pieces and dust with seasoned flour.
2  Fry chicken joints until brown.
3  Transfer to an ovenproof dish.
4  Fry onions and garlic in remaining oil.
5  Stir in tomato soup, paprika and water.
6  Boil and pour sauce into dish.
7  Cook, tightly covered, in a moderate oven 180°C (350°F) for 2 hours.
8  Remove from oven, check seasoning and mix in yoghurt.
9  Sprinkle with chopped parsley.

# CHICKEN AND APPLE CASSEROLE

*2 hours cooking time*

*Ingredients for 6 servings*

| | |
|---|---|
| 1 1.5-kg (3-lb) chicken | ½ teaspoon salt |
| 1 tablespoon flour | ¼ teaspoon pepper |
| 2 tablespoons butter | ½ cup apple cider |
| 1 onion, sliced | ½ cup chicken stock |
| 60 g (2 oz) bacon, chopped | 1 bay leaf |
| 2 apples, cored, peeled and quartered | ¼ teaspoon thyme |

1  Cut chicken into pieces, remove skin and coat with flour.
2  Fry chicken in butter until brown and put into a casserole.
3  Add onion and bacon to pan and cook 3-4 minutes, then add to casserole.
4  Add apples, salt, pepper, cider, bay leaf, thyme and stock.
5  Cover and cook in a moderate oven 180°C (350°F) about 1½ hours.

# SAFFRON CHICKEN

*2 hours cooking time*

*Ingredients for 6 servings*

1 1-kg (2-lb) chicken
1 teaspoon salt
¼ teaspoon pepper
½ teaspoon paprika
2 tablespoons butter
250 g (8 oz) onions, sliced

1 cup chicken stock
pinch coriander
¼ cup rice
2 teaspoons lemon juice
2 tablespoons chopped parsley
¼ teaspoon saffron powder

1 Cut chicken into pieces, remove skin, sprinkle with salt, pepper and paprika.
2 Fry chicken in butter until brown, then put into a casserole.
3 Fry onions in butter and add to casserole.
4 Sprinkle with saffron and coriander; pour on stock.
5 Cook covered in a moderate oven 180°C (350°F) about 1½ hours.
6 Put half the boiled rice into dish, put chicken piecs on top and pour on some of the juice from casserole.
7 Cover with remaining buttered rice, sprinkle with lemon juice and top with parsley.

# CHICKEN-VEGETABLE CASSEROLE

*40 minutes cooking time*

*Ingredients for 4 servings*

375 g (12 oz) chicken, cooked and
   sliced
½ cup cooked peas
½ cup cooked carrots
2 tablespoons cornflour
1 packet chicken vegetable soup
1 can creamed corn

2 cups water
1 teaspoon Worcestershire sauce
1 teaspoon salt
½ teaspoon pepper
60 g (2 oz) grated cheese
½ cup fresh breadcrumbs

1 Layer cooked chicken, peas and carrots in a casserole.
2 Combine cornflour, chicken vegetable soup and corn.
3 Stir well before adding water and Worcestershire sauce.
4 Continue to stir until mixture boils.
5 Add salt and pepper and pour into casserole.
6 Sprinkle mixed cheese and breadcrumbs over top and cook for half an hour in a moderately hot oven 200°C (400°F).
7 Put under hot grill to brown.

# CHICKEN WITH CRANBERRY DIP

*1 hour cooking time*

*Ingredients for 6 servings*

6 chicken legs
2 eggs
½ teaspoon salt
pinch black pepper

1 tin cranberry jelly
½ teaspoon prepared mustard
1 tablespoon vinegar
125 g (4 oz) dry breadcrumbs

1  Dip the chicken legs in beaten and seasoned egg and coat with breadcrumbs.
2  Place on a greased baking tray and bake in the centre of a moderate oven for 1 hour.
3  Crush the cranberry jelly with a fork and mix in the mustard and vinegar; chill and serve with the chicken.

# CHICKEN DIVAN

*1 hour cooking time*

*Ingredients for 6-8 servings*

6 chicken breasts
2 cups water
3 teaspoons salt
oolcry leaves
1 onion
1 kg (2 lb) fresh broccoli
2 cups medium white sauce

¾ teaspoon salt
4 tablespoons sherry
1 teaspoon Worcestershire sauce
1 cup grated Parmesan cheese
½ cup whipping cream
½ cup Hollandaise sauce (canned or
    your own recipe)

1  Simmer chicken in water with 3 teaspoons salt, celery leaves and onion (cut into quarters) until tender, about 25 minutes.
2  Cool, remove skin and bones and slice the chicken meat.
3  Separate broccoli into flowerets, cook in boiling salted water until tender, about 15 minutes.
4  Combine white sauce (made with half milk and half chicken stock), Hollandaise sauce, ¾ teaspoon salt, sherry and Worcestershire sauce.
5  Arrange broccoli around edge of large shallow baking dish.
6  Sprinkle with half the grated cheese, and arrange sliced chicken on top.
7  Whip cream, fold into combined sauces and spoon over chicken.
8  Sprinkle with remaining cheese.
9  Bake, uncovered, in a hot oven 200°C (400°F) for 20 minutes only.
10  Then place about 12 centimetres (5 in) under griller and grill until lightly browned.

# MACARONI AND CHICKEN

*1¼ hours cooking time*

*Ingredients for 4 servings*

185 g (6 oz) macaroni
1 small onion, peeled and grated
4 carrots, cooked and diced
salt and pepper
4 eggs

1 teaspoon paprika
630 g (1¼ lb) cooked chicken, diced
1 green pepper, chopped
2½ cups milk

1  Cook macaroni in boiling salted water until tender, then drain well.
2  Add onion, carrot, paprika, green pepper and chicken to cooked macaroni.
3  Mix well and put in buttered casserole.
4  Pour beaten eggs and milk in casserole.
5  Stand covered casserole in hot water and cook for 1 hour in moderate oven 180°C (350°F).

# SPAGHETTI AND CHICKEN

*2½ hours cooking time*

*Ingredients for 6 servings*

1 1.5-kg (3-lb) chicken
3 tablespoons olive oil
1 onion
1 green pepper
1 25-cm (10-in) stick celery, chopped
¾ teaspoon chilli powder

125 g (4 oz) mushrooms
1 tin tomatoes
1 teaspoon salt
½ teaspoon pepper
125 g (4 oz) spaghetti
grated Parmesan cheese

1  Cut chicken into small pieces and brown in oil.
2  Remove chicken and add onion, green pepper, celery, chilli powder, mushrooms and tomatoes to pan and fry for 10 minutes.
3  Add salt and pepper.
4  Break spaghetti into 10 centimetre (4 in) lengths and boil in salted water until tender.
5  Arrange chicken, spaghetti and sauce in a casserole.
6  Add a little stock if sauce is too thick.
7  Cover and cook in a slow oven 160°C (325°F) about 1¾ hours.
8  Sprinkle with cheese and brown 20 minutes.

# CHICKEN WITH LEMON AND MINT

*1 hour cooking time*

*Ingredients for 3-4 servings*

2 chicken breasts, halved
4 chicken thighs
2 lemons
¼ cup flour
1 teaspoon salt

4 tablespoons oil
2 tablespoons brown sugar
1 cup chicken stock
4 sprigs fresh mint
½ teaspoon paprika

1 Grate peel from lemon and save.
2 Squeeze lemon juice over pieces of chicken, rubbing each piece with juice.
3 Coat chicken with flour, salt and paprika and brown slowly in oil.
4 Arrange in casserole or baking dish.
5 Sprinkle grated lemon peel over chicken, add brown sugar and cover with one thinly sliced lemon.
6 Pour in stock and place mint over top.
7 Cover and bake in moderately hot oven 190°C (375°F) 40 to 45 minutes or until chicken is tender.
8 Remove mint before serving.

# GINGER CHICKEN

*1¼ hours cooking time*

*Ingredients for 6 servings*

3 whole chicken breasts, split
6 chicken thighs
2 tablespoons butter
250 g (8 oz) mushrooms, sliced
½ cup flour
2 teaspoons salt

1 teaspoon sage
½ teaspoon pepper
1 lemon
1½ teaspoons shredded fresh ginger
2 packages frozen green beans, thawed
1 teaspoon thyme

1 Fry mushrooms gently in 2 tablespoons butter for about 5 minutes and remove from pan.
2 Mix flour, salt, thyme, sage and pepper.
3 Rub chicken with lemon and dust lightly with flour mixture.
4 Melt remaining 4 tablespoons butter and brown chicken well.
5 Put chicken in casserole and sprinkle with ginger.
6 Dust green beans with seasoned flour; brown lightly in same pan, adding more butter if needed.
7 Mix beans and mushrooms and spread over chicken.
8 Bake, covered, in a hot oven 200°C (400°F) about 40 minutes.

# POTATO-CHICKEN CASSEROLE

*1 hour cooking time*

*Ingredients for 4 servings*

750 g (1½ lb) potatoes
500 g (1 lb) leeks, sliced
1 onion
2 tablespoons barley
4 rashers bacon
1 1-kg (2-lb) chicken

1 teaspoon salt
¼ teaspoon pepper
2½ cups chicken stock
1 bay leaf
¼ teaspoon thyme
2 tablespoons chopped parsley

1 Peel potatoes, slice 5 millimetres (¼ in) thick.
2 Wash leeks carefully and slice 5 millimetres (¼ in) thick.
3 Combine half onion, leek and potato mixture in casserole, with barley sprinkled on top.
4 Chop bacon and add.
5 Add skinned chicken pieces, bay leaf, thyme and cover with remaining vegetables.
6 Pour chicken stock over casserole and cover tightly.
7 Cook in a moderate oven 180°C (350°F) for 1 hour.
8 Sprinkle with parsley before serving.

# CHICKEN AND DUMPLINGS

*1½ hours cooking time*

*Ingredients for 4 servings*

1 stewing chicken, cut in quarters
2 teaspoons salt
1 teaspoon pepper
3 tablespoons butter
2 whole cloves
10 fresh mushrooms
10 small white onions, peeled
3 carrots
1 clove garlic, minced

¼ teaspoon marjoram
¼ teaspoon thyme
2 sprigs parsley
1 bay leaf
⅔ cup white wine
1 cup sour cream
1 cup packaged scone mix
6 tablespoons milk

1 Season chicken with salt and pepper and brown in butter in heavy roasting pan with a tight-fitting cover.
2 Stick cloves in one onion.
3 Add mushrooms, carrots, onions, garlic and seasonings to chicken.
4 Pour in wine.
5 Cover and bake in moderately hot oven 190°C (375°F) until chicken is tender, about 1 hour.

6  Make dumplings by stirring milk into scone mix with fork until well moistened.
7  Heat sour cream and add to chicken.
8  Place over medium heat on top of the range, and when mixture is bubbling, drop dumplings from teaspoon around edge of pan.
9  Simmer for 10 minutes uncovered, then 10 minutes covered.

# CHINESE CHICKEN CASSEROLE

*2 hours cooking time*

*Ingredients for 4-6 servings*

1 1.25-kg (2½-lb) chicken
2 tablespoons salad oil
60 g (2 oz) mushrooms, sliced
¼ cup water chestnuts, sliced
1 small can bean sprouts
1 small chilli pepper, chopped

1 clove garlic, minced
2 chicken stock cubes
1 tablespoon soy sauce
⅛ cup red wine
1 tablespoon cornflour
2 cups water

1  Cut chicken into pieces and remove skin, then fry until golden brown.
2  Put chicken into ovenproof dish with mushrooms, water chestnuts, bean sprouts, chilli pepper and garlic.
3  Put crumbled stock cube and cornflour into the pan in which chicken was browned and stir thoroughly, then add water.
4  Continue stirring until mixture boils before adding soy sauce and red wine.
5  Pour sauce over chicken and cook covered in a slow oven 160°C (325°F) for 1½ hours, until chicken is tender.

# OLIVE CHICKEN

*1½ hours cooking time*

*Ingredients for 4 servings*

1 1.75-kg (3½-lb) chicken, cut into serving pieces
4 tablespoons butter
12 large stuffed olives, sliced

1 clove garlic
½ cup tomato sauce
1 bay leaf
salt and pepper

1  Brown chicken pieces in butter.
2  Add minced garlic and olives and brown lightly.
3  Stir in tomato sauce, with salt and pepper to taste.
4  Cover and simmer until tender, adding more tomato sauce, broth or water if it becomes too dry.

# CHICKEN AND MUSHROOMS IN CREAM

*1½ hours cooking time*

*Ingredients for 4 servings*

1 1.5-kg (3-lb) chicken
½ cup plain flour
1 teaspoon salt
1¼ cups thin cream

500 g (1 lb) mushrooms, sliced
2 tablespoons chopped parsley
¼ teaspoon pepper

1  Cut chicken into pieces and cover with seasoned flour.
2  Put in shallow baking dish, cover with cream, and bake in moderate oven 180°C (350°F) for 1 hour.
3  Turn and add mushrooms.
4  Cook for another 30 minutes.
5  If gravy is too thick, add more cream.
6  Sprinkle with parsley.

# CHICKEN RAREBIT

*1 hour cooking time*

*Ingredients for 4 servings*

4 chicken breasts
125 g (4 oz) butter
2 tablespoons chopped onion
¼ teaspoon dried thyme
½ cup stock
3 tablespoons cornflour

½ cup dry cider
2-3 tablespoons single cream
125 g (4 oz) strong Cheddar cheese, grated
salt and pepper
2 teaspoons mild mustard

1  Fry the chicken breasts in hot butter, turning frequently — about 20 minutes.
2  Remove them to an ovenproof dish and keep hot.
3  Simmer the onion with a good pinch of thyme in the stock for 10 minutes.
4  Strain the stock and return it to the pan.
5  Blend the cornflour with a little cold water; add a little of the hot stock and mix; then return the mixture to the pan.
6  Boil, stirring constantly, and stir in the cider.
7  Remove from the heat and stir in the cream, half the cheese and the seasonings.
8  Pour the sauce over the chicken, sprinkle with the remaining cheese and place under a very hot griller until golden brown.

# CHICKEN WITH BLACK OLIVES

*3 hours cooking time*

*Ingredients for 6 servings*

1 1.25-kg (2½-lb) chicken
¼ cup bacon, chopped
1 tablespoon flour
1 onion, chopped
125 g (4 oz) mushrooms, chopped
1 green pepper, chopped

½ cup tomato paste
10 black olives, pitted and chopped
1 cup chicken stock
1 teaspoon salt
¼ teaspoon pepper
1 clove garlic, minced

1  Cut chicken into pieces and coat with flour.
2  Fry bacon until it is brown, then add chicken and brown.
3  Remove chicken and bacon to a casserole, then fry onion, mushrooms garlic and green pepper for 5 minutes.
4  Add tomato paste, olives and stock.
5  Stir until mixture boils then pour into casserole.
6  Add seasonings and cover.
7  Cook in a slow oven 160°C (325°F) for 2 hours.

# SPANISH CHICKEN AND PORK

*3½ hours cooking time*

*Ingredients for 4-6 servings*

1 1.75-kg (3½-lb) chicken
250 g (8 oz) lean pork
½ cup olive oil
2 large onions, chopped
2 cloves garlic, minced
¼ cup sherry

375 g (12 oz) long-grain rice
3 tomatoes
2 red peppers
4 cups stock
pinch saffron

1  Cut the chicken and the pork into small pieces.
2  Heat the olive oil in a shallow frying pan and fry the chicken and pork until they are golden brown; then put them in a casserole.
3  Fry the onion and garlic in the olive oil until they are lightly brown.
4  Add the rice and cook for 2 minutes.
5  Add sliced tomatoes and red peppers and cook for another 2 minutes.
6  Pour this mixture over the chicken in the casserole.
7  Add the boiling stock, saffron and sherry and cook in the centre of moderate oven 180°C (350°F) for about 1 hour.

# THICK CHICKEN AND OYSTER STEW

*1¾ hours cooking time*

*Ingredients for 8 servings*

1 1.5-kg (3-lb) chicken
1 teaspoon salt
½ teaspoon pepper
125 g (4 oz) butter
½ cup milk

¼ teaspoon powdered dried sage
250 g (8 oz) oysters
½ cup thick cream
¼ teaspoon powdered dried basil

1　Cut chicken into serving pieces and sprinkle with half the salt and pepper.
2　Heat the butter in a large pan and sauté the chicken pieces (uncovered) for 10 minutes, turning them once.
3　Put into a large baking dish, pour the milk over the top and sprinkle with the rest of the salt and pepper and the sage.
4　Cover with foil and bake in the centre of a hot oven 190°C (375°F) for 1¼ hours.
5　Uncover the dish, add the drained oysters, cream and basil, cover and bake for another 20 minutes.
6　Serve in soup plates, with a fork and spoon.

# CHICKEN AND SOUR CREAM

*1 hour cooking time*

*Ingredients for 4 servings*

6 tablespoons butter
4 chicken breasts
¾ cup white wine

1 cup commercial sour cream
salt and white pepper to taste
1 small onion, chopped

1　Melt 4 tablespoons butter in frying pan; add the chicken breasts with skin removed, and cook until brown , turning occasionally.
2　Sprinkle half cup wine over the chicken, cover, and steam 20 to 25 minutes until tender.
3　Melt 2 tablespoons butter in another pan; cook onion in it until transparent.
4　Stir in remaining wine and sour cream; remove from heat.
5　Pour sour cream sauce over cooked chicken, add salt and white pepper to taste, and heat 5 minutes.

# CHICKEN FLAMBÉ

*45 minutes cooking time*

*Ingredients for 4-6 servings*

| | |
|---|---|
| 4-6 chicken breasts | 4 tablespoons salad oil |
| ½ cup flour | ¾ cup white wine |
| ½ teaspoon paprika | 1½ cups pitted cherries |
| ¼ teaspoon garlic salt | ½ cup brandy |
| 1½ teaspoons salt | |

1 Coat chicken breasts with mixture of flour, garlic salt, salt and paprika.
2 Fry slowly in salad oil to golden brown.
3 Arrange in baking pan and add wine.
4 Cover and bake in a moderately hot oven 190°C (375°F) for 20 minutes.
5 Remove cover and add cherries.
6 Return to oven uncovered for 15 to 20 minutes longer, or until chicken is tender.
7 Place on top of range, pour over brandy and heat until brandy is warm but not boiling, then set aflame.
8 When brandy stops burning, serve chicken with the cherries and sauce.

# VIENNA CHICKEN

*1 hour cooking time*

*Ingredients for 2-4 servings*

| | |
|---|---|
| 4 chicken breasts, halved | 1 egg and 1 egg yolk |
| ¼ cup lemon juice | ½ cup breadcrumbs |
| ⅓ cup olive oil | ½ cup milk |
| ¼ teaspoon thyme | 125 g (4 oz) mushrooms |
| 1 tablespoon chopped parsley | 1 teaspoon salt |
| 1 bay leaf | ¼ teaspoon pepper |

1 Soak chicken breasts for 3 hours in half the lemon juice and some olive oil, with the parsley, bay leaf and thyme.
2 Dip the chicken in beaten egg, coat with breadcrumbs and fry in hot fat until golden and tender.
3 Meanwhile mix the egg yolk with the milk, mushrooms, salt and pepper and cook until thick.
4 Pour in the remaining lemon juice and pour the sauce around the fried chicken.

# CHICKEN AND HAM WITH CUCUMBER

*1½ hours cooking time*

*Ingredients for 4 servings*

4 chicken breasts
1 tablespoon oil
2 tablespoons butter
1 onion, sliced
2 cloves garlic, skinned
1 tablespoon flour
½ cup stock

bouquet garni
1 small cucumber, peeled and sliced
60 g (2 oz) ham, chopped
salt and pepper
2 egg yolks
3 tablespoons thin cream
½ cup medium white wine

1  Fry the chicken in the oil and 1 tablespoon of the butter until golden brown, then remove from the pan.
2  Add the onion and garlic to the fat and brown.
3  Sprinkle on the flour and stir until brown.
4  Gradually add the stock and wine, bring to the boil and cook until thickened.
5  Replace the chicken, add the bouquet garni and simmer on top of the stove for 30 minutes.
6  Cook the cucumber in the remaining butter.
7  Add the ham and seasoning and simmer for a further 4-5 minutes.
8  When the chicken joints are tender, strain off the liquor.
9  Mix the egg yolks and cream and add a little of the chicken liquor.
10  Add this mixture and the remaining chicken liquor to the pan containing the cucumber and ham and heat very gently until the sauce thickens.
11  Pour the sauce over the chicken to serve.

# CHICKEN AND WALNUTS

*2½ hours cooking time*

*Ingredients for 7-8 servings*

1 2-kg (4-lb) chicken
3 tablespoons sherry
2 teaspoons castor sugar
4 tablespoons oil
750 g (1½ lb) button mushrooms, washed and sliced

185 g (6 oz) water chestnuts, drained and diced
2½ cups chicken stock
2 tablespoons cornflour
125 g (4 oz) halved walnuts
1 tablespoon butter

1 Place the chicken in a dish, pour the sherry and castor sugar over it and leave for 1-2 hours.
2 Heat the oil in a frying pan and brown the drained chicken pieces.
3 Place the mushrooms and the chestnuts in a large casserole, with chicken pieces on top.
4 Pour the chicken juices and stock into the casserole, cover and bake in the centre of a moderate oven 180°C (350°F) for 2 hours.
5 Drain off the juice, keep the chicken hot and thicken the juice with the cornflour.
6 Brown the walnuts in melted butter for 4-5 minutes and drain.
7 Dish up the chicken and vegetables, pour some of the gravy over them and garnish with the browned walnuts.
8 Serve remaining gravy separately.

# TROPICAL FRIED CHICKEN

*1½ hours cooking time*

*Ingredients for 6 servings*

1 1.25-kg (2½-lb) chicken
½ cup olive oil
1 teaspoon salt
½ teaspoon pepper
1 red pepper, chopped
1 green pepper, chopped
2 pineapple rings, diced

125 g (4 oz) bacon, cut into small pieces
315 g (10 oz) long-grain rice
2 cups chicken stock
1 tablespoon chopped parsley
2 onions, chopped

1 Cut the chicken into joints and soak in the seasoned olive oil for about 30 minutes.
2 Boil the back, neck and giblets to make stock.
3 Heat 2 tablespoons oil in pan and fry the bacon, onions and peppers.
4 Add the rice and fry until it is opaque.
5 Add enough chicken stock to cover.
6 Season well, and simmer until all the liquid is absorbed and the rice is tender; add the diced pineapple 5 minutes before the rice finishes cooking.
7 In another pan fry the chicken in hot oil until tender and golden.
8 Arrange chicken on the rice and serve sprinkled with chopped parsley.

# HOT BARBECUED CHICKEN

*1½ hours cooking time*

*Ingredients for 6 servings*

| | |
|---|---|
| 125 g (4 oz) butter | 3 cloves garlic, minced |
| ½ teaspoon cayenne pepper | 1 onion, minced |
| ½ teaspoon prepared mustard | 2 tablespoons lemon juice |
| ¾ cup salad oil | ½ teaspoon Tabasco sauce |
| 1 cup tomato sauce | 3 1-kg (2-lb) chickens |
| 4 tablespoons Worcestershire sauce | salt and pepper |

1  Make the barbecue sauce by melting butter in saucepan, then add the rest of the ingredients except salt or pepper.
2  Simmer, stirring occasionally, for 15 minutes.
3  When barbecue coals are glowing, rub the chicken halves with salt and pepper; then put the chicken on the grill and cook for about 1 hour, or until tender.
4  Baste frequently with the sauce and turn them every 10 minutes.

# CHICKEN KIEV

*10 minutes cooking time*

*Ingredients for 2-4 servings*

| | |
|---|---|
| 4 chicken breasts, boned | 1 egg, beaten |
| 125 g (4 oz) soft butter | 125 g (4 oz) fresh breadcrumbs |
| 2 tablespoons chopped parsley | ⅔ cup salad oil |

1  Beat butter and parsley together, form into a roll and chill.
2  Beat the boned chicken until very thin.
3  Divide the butter into 4 pieces, place a piece on each of the chicken breasts, wrap the chicken around the butter like a parcel and tie with string.
4  Dip each parcel in beaten egg and coat with breadcrumbs.
5  Heat oil, then fry the chicken for 5 minutes.
6  Remove from the fat, drain on kitchen paper and remove the string before serving.

# CHICKEN IN CHEESE SAUCE

*2½ hours cooking time*

*Ingredients for 6 servings*

1 2-kg (4-lb) chicken
1 bunch spinach or broccoli
1 teaspoon salt

¼ teaspoon pepper
2 cups medium thick white sauce
½-1 cup grated Parmesan cheese

1  Boil the chicken until it is tender and remove the meat from the bones.
2  Wash and trim the spinach or broccoli and cook until barely tender.
3  Chop spinach or slice broccoli and place in the bottom of a greased casserole dish.
4  Season with salt and pepper.
5  Prepare the sauce (with half milk and half chicken broth).
6  Add half the grated cheese to white sauce.
7  Cover the spinach or broccoli with the chicken; cover with the sauce.
8  Sprinkle the remainder of the cheese over the top and bake in a moderate oven until the cheese browns.

# CHICKEN PILAU

*2½ hours cooking time*

*Ingredients for 6 servings*

1 1.5-kg (3-lb) chicken
2 cups long-grain rice
2 teaspoons salt
½ teaspoon pepper

1 chopped onion
½ cup chopped celery
3 sliced tomatoes
3 tablespoons butter

1  Boil 10 cups water in saucepan, add rice and chicken.
2  Cover and simmer until chicken is tender, about 1½ hours adding salt and pepper for last 30 minutes of cooking.
3  Melt butter in frying pan and brown vegetables.
4  Add to chicken.
5  Cover and simmer 30 minutes longer.

# STOVE BARBECUED CHICKEN

*1 hour cooking time*

*Ingredients for 4 servings*

1 1.5-kg (3-lb) chicken
6 tablespoons salad oil
½ onion, chopped
1 clove garlic, minced
1 tablespoon brown sugar
⅓ cup tomato sauce
1½ teaspoons Worcestershire sauce

2 tablespoons vinegar
1 teaspoon salt
½ teaspoon pepper
½ teaspoon celery seed
½ teaspoon parsley flakes
¼ cup water

1   Cut chicken into pieces, simmer giblets in pan with 1½ cups water.
2   Wash the chicken pieces and drain well.
3   In large heavy frying pan, heat salad oil and fry onion and garlic lightly, then combine with brown sugar, tomato sauce, Worcestershire sauce, vinegar, salt, pepper, celery seed, parsley flakes, and water.
4   Add chicken pieces, cook uncovered over medium heat.
5   Cook until brown on all sides and tender, about 40 minutes.
6   Remove chicken.
7   Skim oil from sauce in pan.
8   Add 1 cup stock from cooking giblets and stir to loosen all the browned particles in pan.
9   Add chopped giblets.
10   Pour sauce over chicken to serve.

# SOUTH AFRICAN PIE

*2 hours cooking time*

*Ingredients for 6 servings*

1 1.5-kg (3-lb) chicken
6 cups water
2 onions, quartered
2 sticks celery, sliced
2 tablespoons chopped parsley
60 g (2 oz) ham, cut into 5 cm (2 in) squares
1 tablespoon salt
1 teaspoon whole allspice
1 teaspoon whole peppercorns
2 bay leaves

3 carrots, sliced
2 hardboiled eggs, sliced
1 tablespoon butter
1 tablespoon flour
1 tablespoon lemon juice
1 teaspoon sugar
3 tablespoons sherry
¼ teaspoon ground mace
¼ teaspoon pepper
1 egg yolk
250 g (8 oz) shortcrust pastry

1 Put cut up chicken in a large pan with the water, vegetables, salt, allspice, peppercorns, bay leaves and parsley.
2 Cover and simmer for 30 minutes.
3 Strain the stock.
4 Cut the meat from the chicken bones and put layers of chicken and vegetables, ham and hardboiled egg into a pie dish.
5 Melt the butter and gradually stir in the flour, 1¼ cups of the chicken stock, sugar, sherry, lemon juice, mace and pepper.
6 Cook until the sauce is thick and smooth.
7 Stir beaten egg yolk into the sauce slowly and heat gently, while stirring, until thick.
8 Pour sauce over the chicken and vegetables, cover the pie with pastry.
9 Cut a circle in centre of pastry, and brush with beaten egg to glaze.
10 Bake in hot oven 220°C (425°F) for 20 minutes.

# BUBBLY CHEESE FLAN

*40 minutes cooking time*

*Ingredients for 4 servings*

**125 g (4 oz) shortcrust pastry**
**1 onion, sliced**
**125 g (4 oz) butter**
**2 pieces of celery, chopped**
**1 tablespoon flour**

**1¼ cups milk**
**salt and pepper**
**125 g (4 oz) cooked chicken, chopped**
**90 g (3 oz) grated cheese**

1 Line a flan ring with the pastry.
2 Bake in a hot oven 220°C (425°F) for 15 minutes, or until pastry has set.
3 Fry the onion and celery in half the butter until golden brown.
4 Make a white sauce with the remaining butter, flour and milk; bring to the boil and pour on to the vegetables, season and add the chicken and half the cheese.
5 Fill the flan case with this mixture, cover with the remaining cheese and brown under a hot grill.

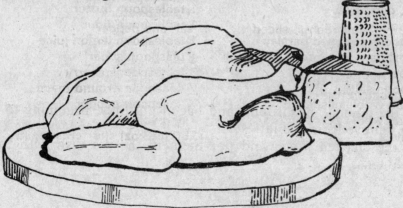

# CHICKEN PIE

*3 hours cooking time*

*Ingredients for 6 servings*

1 2-kg (4-lb) chicken
1 sliced carrot
1 stalk celery, chopped
1 sprig parsley
1 sliced onion

⅛ teaspoon pepper
plain pie pastry
4 tablespoons flour
250 g (8 oz) sliced sautéed mushrooms
1 teaspoon salt

1 Put chicken in saucepan and cover with water.
2 Add carrot, celery, parsley, onion, salt and pepper.
3 Bring to boiling point.
4 Reduce heat, cover, and let simmer 2 hours until chicken is tender.
5 Season with salt and pepper when half done.
6 Remove chicken from pan and remove skin and bones, keeping meat in large pieces.
7 Line the sides of a baking dish with plain pie pastry.
8 Put in chicken.
9 Reduce chicken stock to 3 cups by boiling and skim off fat and strain.
10 Mix flour to a smooth paste in cold water and add to stock.
11 Bring stock to boiling point, stirring constantly.
12 Add stock and mushrooms to chicken.
13 Cover with pie pastry.
14 Bake at 230°C (450°F) for 15 minutes or until well browned.

# CHICKEN AND MUSHROOM PIE

*1½ hours cooking time*

*Ingredients for 6 servings*

250 g (8 oz) flaky pastry
1 1-kg (2-lb) chicken
2 tablespoons flour
250 g (8 oz) mushrooms, sliced
2 onions, chopped

125 g (4 oz) bacon, chopped
3 tablespoons oil
1¼ cups stock
salt and pepper

1 Make the pastry.
2 Flour chicken pieces.
3 Fry the onions, mushrooms and bacon until just beginning to colour, then remove from the fat.
4 Fry the chicken joints and put them in the pie dish with the fried ingredients

5  Add flour to the fat, add the stock slowly and bring to the boil; season well and pour into pie dish.

6  Cover with the pastry, brush with egg and cook in the centre of hot oven 220°C (425°F) for 20 minutes longer.

7  Reduce the temperature to moderate 180°C (350°F) and cook 25-30 minutes.

8  Serve hot.

# CASHEW CHICKEN

*1 hour cooking time*

*Ingredients for 6 servings*

**3 whole chicken breasts**
**250 g (8 oz) fresh green peas, shelled**
**250 g (8 oz) mushrooms**
**1 can bamboo shoots, drained**
**1 cup chicken stock (can use stock cubes)**

**¼ cup soy sauce**
**2 tablespoons cornflour**
**½ teaspoon sugar**
**¼ cup salad oil**
**125 g (4 oz) cashew nuts**

1  Bone chicken breasts and remove skin.

2  Slice horizontally in 2 millimetre (⅛ in) slices, then cut in 2.5 centimetre (1 in) squares.

3  Wash and slice mushrooms.

4  Cut the green part of the onions into 2.5 centimetre (1 in) lengths and then slash both ends several times making small fans; slice the white part 4 millimetres (¼ in) thick.

5  Slice bamboo shoots.

6  Mix together soy sauce, cornflour, sugar, and salt.

7  Heat 1 tablespoon of the oil over moderate heat, add nuts and cook for 1 minute, shaking pan, until lightly toasted; remove from pan and set aside.

8  Add remaining oil to pan, add chicken, and cook quickly, turning, until it turns opaque.

9  Add peas and mushrooms; pour in stock, cover, and simmer 2 minutes.

10  Add bamboo shoots.

11  Stir the soy sauce mixture into the pan juices, and cook until sauce is thickened, stirring constantly; then simmer 1 minute uncovered.

12  Mix in the spring onions and sprinkle with nuts.

# ALMOND-ORANGE CHICKEN

*1 hour cooking time*

*Ingredients for 3-4 servings*

1 1.75-kg (3½-lb) chicken
1 teaspoon salt
¼ teaspoon pepper
1 teaspoon paprika
1 cup orange juice

1 teaspoon cornflour
⅔ cup slivered almonds or chopped filberts, toasted
⅓ cup butter

1  Cut chicken into pieces and coat with salt, pepper and paprika.
2  Melt butter in a large pan with a lid.
3  Sauté the chicken pieces until brown.
4  Cover the pan, reduce heat and cook for 30 minutes, or until chicken is tender.
5  Remove chicken and keep hot in oven.
6  Pour the orange juice into the pan, stir to loosen all the browned particles.
7  Combine cornflour with 1 teaspoon water, stir into orange juice, then cook over high heat until it is reduced by half.
8  Pour sauce over the chicken and sprinkle with toasted almond slivers.

# CHINESE FRIED CHICKEN

*40 minutes cooking time*

*Ingredients for 2-4 servings*

250 g (8 oz) raw white chicken meat
⅛ cup oil
1 onion
1 green pepper
125 g (4 oz) mushrooms

2 cloves garlic
salt and pepper
3 tablespoons cooking sherry
sugar

1  Slice the chicken thinly and coat the pieces with oil.
2  Cut pepper into 2.5 centimetre (1 in) pieces.
3  Slice mushrooms and onion.
4  Rub the inside of the frying pan with the garlic and heat the oil.
5  Fry the onion and pepper until just cooked, season to taste; remove and keep hot.
6  Fry the chicken slices in shallow oil over a brisk heat until almost tender.
7  Add the vegetables, sherry and a little sugar and stir well before serving.

# CHICKEN MAYONNAISE

*1¼ hours cooking time*

*Ingredients for 4 servings*

| | |
|---|---|
| **1 kg (2 lb) chicken breasts and legs** | **1 cup breadcrumbs** |
| **¼ teaspoon onion salt** | **½ teaspoon pepper** |
| **1 teaspoon garlic salt** | **½ teaspoon curry powder** |
| **1 cup mayonnaise** | |

1   Coat chicken pieces with mixture of the breadcrumbs, garlic salt, onion salt and curry powder.
2   Arrange crumb-coated chicken in a greased baking dish, skin side up and with no overlapping.
3   Place in a hot oven 200°C (400°F) for 15 minutes to set the crumbs so they will stick to the chicken.
4   Remove from oven; coat chicken generously with mayonnaise.
5   Reduce heat to low 150°C (300°F) and bake for 1 hour, or until chicken is done but not dry.
6   Serve hot or cold.

# CHICKEN AND MUSHROOM OMELETTES

*30 minutes cooking time*

*Ingredients for 4 servings*

| | |
|---|---|
| **185 g (6 oz) mushrooms** | **6 eggs** |
| **60 g (2 oz) butter** | **1 teaspoon salt** |
| **185 g (6 oz) cooked chicken, diced** | **¼ teaspoon pepper** |
| **2½ cups seasoned white sauce** | **2 tablespoons grated Parmesan cheese** |

1   Cook the mushrooms in butter for 5 minutes, add the chicken and half the sauce, mix well and cook, stirring, for 2-3 minutes longer.
2   Make as many small omelettes as possible, using 2 tablespoons of mixture to each omelette.
3   Cook as little as you can.
4   Spread some of the filling on each omelette and roll before placing in a shallow buttered casserole.
5   Cover with remaining sauce and sprinkle with cheese.
6   Bake in hot oven 220°C (425°F) for 10-15 minutes.

# CHICKEN-FILLED EGGPLANT

*Ingredients for 2 servings*

*45 minutes cooking time*

2 small aubergines
250 g (8 oz) cooked chicken, chopped
2 onions, chopped
1 can tomatoes, chopped

2 tablespoons olive oil
1 teaspoon salt
½ teaspoon pepper
1 tablespoon chopped parsley

1  Cover eggplants with boiling water, leave for 10 minutes, then dry them well.
2  Cut each in half and take out the flesh, do not break the skin.
3  Cook the chicken, tomatoes and onion together in olive oil, season with salt and pepper, add the chopped parsley, then add the flesh of the eggplants and mix well.
4  Fill the skins with this mixture, put them in a greased ovenproof dish and bake in reasonably hot oven 200°C (400°F) until the top is browned.

# CHICKEN BREASTS IN WINE
# WITH AVOCADO

*Ingredients for 6 servings*

*1 hour cooking time*

6 large chicken breasts
1 teaspoon salt
1 teaspoon paprika
4 tablespoons butter
¼ cup finely chopped onion

¼ cup tomato sauce
3 tablespoons wine vinegar
1½ teaspoons Worcestershire sauce
1 cup white wine
1 large avocado, sliced

1  Remove skin from chicken breasts and cover with a mixture of salt, paprika and flour.
2  Brown chicken in melted butter.
3  Combine onion, tomato sauce, vinegar, Worcestershire sauce and wine and pour over chicken.
4  Cover, and simmer about 45 minutes until chicken is tender.
5  Heap hot buttered rice on plate and arrange chicken and avocado slices around it.

# CHICKEN SOUFFLÉ

*1 hour cooking time*

*Ingredients for 4 servings*

2 tablespoons butter
1 tablespoon flour
1¼ cups milk
4 large eggs, separated

250 g (8 oz) cooked chicken, chopped
juice of ½ lemon
salt and pepper

1  Grease a 5-cup soufflé dish.
2  Melt the butter, stir in the flour and cook for 3 minutes.
3  Gradually stir in the milk and cook for 4 minutes.
4  Beat in egg yolks, then stir in the chicken, lemon juice and salt and pepper.
5  Fold in the stiffly whisked egg whites thoroughly.
6  Turn the mixture into the dish and bake in the centre of a moderate oven 180°C (350°F) for about 45 minutes, until well risen and golden brown.

# CHICKEN VEGETABLE CUPS

*Ingredients for 4-5 servings*

3 cups cooked chicken, diced
¼ cup chopped celery
2 tablespoons lemon salad dressing
1½ tablespoons finely chopped lemon
1 chicken cube
1 cup cooked mixed vegetables, diced
3 drops chilli sauce

2 hardboiled eggs, chopped
¼ teaspoon white pepper
½ teaspoon salt
3 teaspoons gelatine
1 cup water
½ cup dry white wine

1  Combine chicken, vegetables, eggs, dressing, lemon and seasonings.
2  Place wine, chicken cube and gelatine in water and stir over heat until gelatine dissolves.
3  Add to the other ingredients and add chilli sauce.
4  Pour into small moulds and allow to set.
5  Serve with crisp salad greens, tossed with extra salad dressing.

# CHICKEN AND SAUSAGES

*3 hours cooking time*

*Ingredients for 4 servings*

1 1.5-kg (3-lb) chicken
1 tablespoon butter
1 small onion, chopped
2 rashers bacon
1 tablespoon flour
1¼ cups stock or water

1 carrot, chopped
2 stalks celery, chopped
1 tablespoon tomato paste
½ small cabbage, shredded
185 g (6 oz) pork sausages
salt, pepper and nutmeg

1  Cut chicken into pieces.
2  Heat the butter in a saucepan, then cook the chopped onion until it is golden brown; add the pieces of chicken and streaky bacon and allow to brown on all sides.
3  Stir in the flour and allow to cook a moment or two before gradually adding the stock, while stirring.
4  Add salt, pepper, nutmeg, carrot, celery and tomato paste.
5  Cover and cook slowly for 2 hours (until the chicken is tender).
6  15 minutes before serving, add the cabbage and the sausages, cut into small pieces.

# PEPPER CHICKEN

*2½ hours cooking time*

*Ingredients for 6 servings*

1 1.5-kg (3-lb) chicken
2 tablespoons oil
2 onions, chopped
1 clove garlic, minced
½ carrot, chopped
2 teaspoons paprika
1 large tomato, peeled

1 green pepper
1 cup chicken stock
2 tablespoons plain flour
1¼ cups sour cream
½ parsnip, chopped
½ teaspoon salt

1  Cut the chicken into pieces.
2  Heat the oil and fry chopped onion and minced garlic until lightly browned.
3  Add carrot, parsnip and paprika, and cook for 5 minutes.
4  Add the chicken pieces and cook until they are brown on all sides.
5  Add salt, then sliced tomato, diced green pepper and stock.
6  Stir until it boils, then cover and simmer about 1 hour until the chicken pieces are tender.

7 Blend the flour with a little water, add to the mixture and stir until the sauce boils and thickens.
8 Stir in cream and heat through but do not boil.
9 Serve with either boiled rice, noodles, spaghetti or potatoes.

## CHICKEN FRICASSÉE

*2¼ hours cooking time*

*Ingredients for 6 servings*

**1 chicken**
**2 cups white sauce**
**¼ cup cream**

**2 egg yolks**
**4 tablespoons lemon juice**
**salt and pepper**

1 Boil chicken until tender, cut into neat joints.
2 Make white sauce, put in pieces of chicken, and cook gently for 15 minutes.
3 Mix egg yolks and cream, add to sauce and stir over low heat until it thickens. Do not boil.
4 Season and add lemon juice.
5 Arrange chicken on hot plate, pour sauce over.

## ITALIAN CHICKEN STEW

*2½ hours cooking time*

*Ingredients for 4 servings*

**1 1.5-kg (3-lb) chicken, jointed**
**1 stalk celery, diced**
**1 teaspoon chopped parsley**
**1 tablespoon tomato paste**
**125 g (4 oz) sliced mushrooms**

**1 small onion, chopped**
**1 carrot, chopped**
**1 tablespoon butter**
**1¼ cups stock or water**
**pepper and salt**

1 Heat the butter in a saucepan and cook the chopped vegetables for 5 minutes, then add the chicken and brown on all sides.
2 Add stock, mushrooms and tomato paste diluted with a little stock or water.
3 Cover the pan and simmer gently for 2 hours or until the chicken is tender, adding a little more stock if necessary during the cooking time.

# CHICKEN AND SWEETBREADS

*1½ hours cooking time*

*Ingredients for 6 servings*

125 g (4 oz) sliced mushrooms
2 tablespoons chopped onions
3 tablespoons butter
¼ cup flour
1 cup chicken stock
½ cup milk
½ cup light cream

1 cup diced cooked chicken
½ cup chopped cooked sweetbreads
¼ cup blanched almonds
1 teaspoon salt
¼ teaspoon pepper
¼ cup buttered breadcrumbs

1 Sauté mushrooms and onion in butter until lightly browned; stir in flour, add stock and milk gradually and cook, stirring, until thickened.
2 Add cream, chicken, sweetbreads, almonds, salt and pepper, and bring to boiling point.
3 Turn into greased individual casseroles and cover with crumbs.
4 Bake in moderate oven 180°C (350°F) until well browned.

# SKEWERED CHICKEN AND PINEAPPLE

*3 hours cooking time*

*Ingredients for 5-6 servings*

1 1.25-kg (2½-lb) chicken
½ cup dry sherry
1 tablespoon soy sauce
2 green peppers
2 tablespoons pineapple juice

2 tablespoons salad oil
1 clove garlic, crushed
1 onion
10 cm (4 in) fresh ginger

1 Bone raw chicken and cut into 5 centimetre (2 in) pieces.
2 Mix sherry, soy sauce, pineapple juice, oil and garlic and pour over chicken.
3 Leave about 3 hours, stirring occasionally.
4 Place chicken on skewers, alternating with thinly sliced ginger, pineapple chunked and 5 centimetre (2 in) squares of pepper and onion.
5 Grill about 5 minutes on each side, until chicken is tender, basting with sauce.

# CHICKEN TERIYAKI

*1 hour cooking time*

*Ingredients for 4 servings*

1 1.5-kg (3-lb) chicken
¾ cup soy sauce
¼ cup sugar

2 teaspoons grated fresh ginger
1 small clove garlic, crushed
¼ cup dry sherry

1   Using a meat cleaver, cut thighs and legs into 2 pieces each.
2   Cut halved breasts into 3 pieces each.
3   Discard wing tips, and cut remainder of each wing in two.
4   Cut back into 4 or 5 pieces.
5   Place cut chicken in a shallow bowl and cover with Teriyaki sauce made by blending all the remaining ingredients.
6   Cover and refrigerate for 2 to 3 hours, turning occasionally.
7   Drain chicken, reserving marinade.
8   Place pieces, skin side down, in a single layer in a greased baking pan.
9   Bake in a hot oven 230°C (450°F) for 10 minutes.
10  Turn chicken; bake for 10 minutes more.
11  Reduce oven temperature to 180°C (350°F), pour off and discard pan liquid.
12  Continue baking for 30 minutes longer, or until tender, brushing 2 or 3 times with some of the reserved marinade.
13  Grill about 15 centimetres (6 in) from heat for 3 minutes, or until chicken is well browned.
14  Serve with some pan drippings poured over it you like.

# BAKED CHICKEN PAPRIKA

*50 minutes cooking time*

*Ingredients for 4 servings*

1 1.5-kg (3-lb) chicken, cut in pieces
   (omit back)
1 teaspoon paprika

¾ teaspoon salt
½ teaspoon sugar
⅛ teaspoon pepper

1   Wash and drain chicken pieces; arrange skin side up in a single layer in a buttered baking pan.
2   Sprinkle with a mixture of paprika, salt, sugar and pepper.
3   Bake in a hot oven 200°C (400°F) for 35 minutes; turn pieces and cook 10 to 15 minutes longer.

# HAM AND CHICKEN IN CREAM

*25 minutes cooking time*

*Ingredients for 6 servings*

| | |
|---|---|
| 2 tablespoons butter | ¼ cup cooked green peas |
| 2 tablespoons plain flour | 2 teaspoons chopped parsley |
| 1 cup chicken stock | 1 egg |
| ⅜ cup cream | ¾ teaspoon salt |
| ½ cup chopped cooked chicken | ¼ teaspoon pepper |
| ¾ cup chopped cooked ham | |

1   Mix flour in melted butter, and cook 1 minute before adding the chicken stock.
2   Stir until sauce boils and thickens and add the cream.
3   Stir in ham, chicken, peas and parsley.
4   Pour 4 tablespoons into beaten egg, mix well, then stir back into the chicken mixture.
5   Simmer for 3 to 5 minutes.
6   Season with salt and pepper.
7   Serve over toast.

# JAPANESE CHICKEN CUSTARD

*30 minutes cooking time*

*Ingredients for 6 servings*

| | |
|---|---|
| 155 g (5 oz) chopped cooked chicken | 5 large mushrooms, cut in half |
| 12 cooked prawns, peeled and de-veined | 2 tablespoons soy sauce |
| | 3½ cups chicken stock |
| 1½ cups spinach, torn in 2.5 cm (1 in) pieces | 8 well-beaten eggs |
| | ¼ teaspoon salt |

1   Mix chicken with soy sauce.
2   In large custard cups or individual casseroles place an equal amount of chicken, prawns, spinach, mushrooms and lemon.
3   Fill with stock beaten with eggs and salt.
4   Set cups in a large shallow pan of hot water over direct heat (water should be deep enough to come halfway up sides of cups), and lay a baking sheet over cups to cover if they have no lids.
5   Poach in hot — not boiling — water until custard is firm in the centre when dish is shaken — 25 to 30 minutes.
6   Serve hot.

# CASSEROLE OF SAUSAGE AND CHICKEN

*2 hours cooking time*

*Ingredients for 6 servings*

**1 1.5-kg (3-lb) chicken**
**250 g (8 oz) pork sausage meat**
**1 teaspoon salt**
**½ teaspoon pepper**
**1 tablespoon flour**
**1 chopped onion**

**½ cup sliced mushrooms**
**1 tablespoon butter**
**½ cup cider**
**12 small whole onions**
**12 small whole mushrooms**

1  Stuff chicken with sausage and coat with flour, salt and pepper.
2  Cook mushrooms and onion in butter over low heat for 4-5 minutes.
3  Raise heat and brown chicken.
4  Put chicken and vegetables in casserole; add cider.
5  Cook, covered tightly, for 1½ hours in a moderate oven 190°C (275°F).
6  Add whole onions and mushrooms 30 minutes before serving.

# HOT CHICKEN WITH SESAME SEEDS

*1¾ hours cooking time*

*Ingredients for 4 servings*

**1 1.5 kg (3-lb) chicken, quartered**
**½ cup toasted sesame seeds**
**¼ cup oil**
**1 finely chopped onion**
**1 teaspoon salt**
**½ teaspoon ground cardamom**

**2 cloves garlic, crushed**
**2.5 cm (1 in) grated fresh ginger**
**¼ teaspoon cloves**
**½ teaspoon chilli powder**
**2 tablespoons plain flour**
**1 cup chicken stock**

1  Cut chicken into pieces, place in shallow baking dish, skin side down.
2  Mix all ingredients, except flour and chicken stock, and pour half over chicken.
3  Bake in moderate oven 180°C (350°F) for 40 minutes, basting every 10 minutes with sesame mixture.
4  Turn chicken, bake 30 minutes longer, then put under griller for 10 minutes.
5  Remove chicken to hot platter.
6  Add flour to baking dish and cook until golden, stir in chicken stock, and continue stirring until smooth and thickened.
7  Serve gravy with chicken and buttered rice.

# CAMEMBERT CHEESE CHICKEN

*1 hour cooking time*

*Ingredients for 4-6 servings*

1 1.5-kg (3-lb) chicken
250 g (8 oz) butter
1 ripe soft Camembert cheese

¾ cup fresh breadcrumbs
salt and pepper

1 Brush inside of chicken with melted butter and season with salt and pepper.
2 Cut cheese into 6 pieces and place inside chicken.
3 Cover skin with melted butter, salt, pepper and a thick layer of breadcrumbs.
4 Place in a greased baking dish.
5 Roast in hot oven 200°C (400°F) for 30 minutes.
6 Pour the rest of the melted butter over the chicken and return to oven.
7 Baste every 10 minutes with pan juices and melted cheese from inside the chicken until chicken is cooked.

# CHICKEN CACCIATORE

*1½ hours cooking time*

*Ingredients for 4-6 servings*

1 1.75-kg(3½-lb) chicken
salt and pepper
flour
¼ cup olive oil
1 large clove garlic, finely chopped
12 whole small white onions, peeled
2 green peppers, chopped
1 bay leaf

2 cups tinned tomatoes, strained
1 pimento, chopped
1 cup red wine
½ teaspoon oregano
1 cup sliced mushrooms
¼ teaspoon pepper
¼ teaspoon thyme

1 Cut chicken into pieces and dust with seasoned flour.
2 Brown chicken quickly on all sides in oil.
3 Add garlic, onions and green pepper and brown.
4 Add tomatoes, pimento, wine, oregano, pepper, bay leaf and thyme.
5 Transfer to a covered casserole and cook in moderate oven until tender, 45 minutes.
6 Add sliced mushrooms and simmer 25 minutes.

# DEVIL'S CHICKEN

*1½ hours cooking time*

*Ingredients for 4 servings*

1 chicken, cut in serving pieces
4 tablespoons butter
2 tablespoons olive oil
6 spring onions, sliced 1 cm (½ in) thick
1 clove garlic, minced

½ teaspoon salt
⅔ cup red wine
2 small red chilli peppers, finely crushed, or 1 teaspoon hot chilli powder
½ cup tomato paste

1  Brown chicken pieces on all sides in butter and oil.
2  Add onion, garlic and salt and cook until browned.
3  Add wine and chilli peppers and stir well, then add tomato sauce.
4  Cover and simmer 1 hour.

# CHICKEN CREOLE

*2½ hours cooking time*

*Ingredients for 6 servings*

1 1.5-kg (3-lb) chicken
salt and pepper
⅔ cup butter
4 large sliced onions
2 cloves garlic, minced
2 thinly sliced green peppers
1 cup sliced fresh mushrooms

1 large can peeled tomatoes
12 stoned and sliced green olives
1 bay leaf
4 sprigs parsley
1 sprig thyme
2 whole cloves
1 cup dry white wine

1  Melt ⅓ cup of butter and fry the onion, garlic and green pepper gently for 10 minutes.
2  Then add the mushrooms, tomatoes, olives and the bouquet garni and cloves.
3  Cover and simmer for about 30 minutes, stirring occasionally.
4  Discard the bouquet garni and cloves.
5  Add the wine and simmer.
6  Cut chicken into pieces.
7  Sprinkle each piece with salt and pepper and fry in ⅓ cup of butter until brown.
8  Drain, place in a casserole dish, cover with sauce, cover, and bake in a moderate oven for 1 hour or until the chicken is tender.
9  Arrange the chicken pieces on a hot platter.
10  Reduce the sauce by half by simmering uncovered for about 10 minutes.
11  Serve with freshly boiled rice.

# CHICKEN TARRAGON

*1¼ hours cooking time*

*Ingredients for 4 servings*

1 1.25-kg (2½-lb) chicken, cut up
¼ cup flour
1 teaspoon salt
¼ teaspoon pepper
1 clove garlic, minced
3½ tablespoons butter
1 tablespoon bacon drippings

1 tablespoon chopped parsley
1½ cups dry white wine
2 tablespoons finely chopped fresh
   tarragon, or 1 teaspoon dry tarragon
salt and pepper to taste
1 cup sour cream
2 tablespoons chopped spring onion

1   Dust chicken with flour, salt and pepper.
2   Brown chicken and garlic in 2 tablespoons butter and bacon drippings.
3   Pour off excess fat.
4   In a small saucepan fry onion and parsley in 1½ tablespoons butter for about 2 minutes.
5   Add 1½ tablespoons flour and stir until brown.
6   Add wine, tarragon and salt and pepper.
7   Pour sauce over chicken, cover, and cook over low heat for 45 minutes or until chicken is tender, stirring occasionally.
8   Serve with sauce and a sour cream topping.

# SPICY CHICKEN

*45 minutes cooking time*

*Ingredients for 4 servings*

1 1.5-kg (3-lb) chicken, cut up
2 cups orange juice
1¼ teaspoons salt
½ teaspoon nutmeg
1 teaspoon sweet basil

1 clove garlic, halved
1½ cups sliced fresh peaches
2 tablespoons flour
dash pepper

1   Put the chicken, orange juice, 1 teaspoon salt, nutmeg, sweet basil and garlic into pan; simmer about 40 minutes or until chicken is tender.
2   Remove chicken to a warm dish, and arrange the sliced peaches on top; keep warm in oven.
3   Strain 1½ cups of stock, and gradually stir this into flour, keeping the mixture smooth.
4   Add quarter teaspoon salt and pepper.
5   Cook over medium heat, stirring until thickened.
6   Pour over the chicken and peaches.

# CHICKEN AND OYSTER PIE

*1¼ hours cooking time*

*Ingredients for 6 servings*

| | |
|---|---|
| **2 cups diced cooked chicken** | **1 teaspoon salt** |
| **1 cup milk** | **¼ teaspoon pepper** |
| **1 cup small oysters** | **1 tablespoon chopped parsley** |
| **1 tablespoon flour** | **1 tablespoon chopped celery** |
| **1 tablespoon butter** | **plain pie pastry** |

1  Put chicken in saucepan, add milk and oysters and simmer for 30 minutes.
2  Melt butter and mix to a smooth paste with flour, stir into mixture in pan.
3  Bring to boil.
4  Add salt, pepper, parsley, celery.
5  Line a greased baking dish with plain pie pastry.
6  Pour in mixture.
7  Cover with pie pastry.
8  Bake in moderate oven 180°C (350°F) until well browned, about 20 to 25 minutes.
9  Serve hot.

# ROYAL BAKED CHICKEN

*1 hour cooking time*

*Ingredients for 4 servings*

| | |
|---|---|
| **1 1.25-kg (2½-lb) chicken** | **¼ cup chopped parsley** |
| **⅓ cup grated Parmesan cheese** | **1½ teaspoons salt** |
| **1 clove garlic** | **¼ teaspoon pepper** |
| **2 cups fresh breadcrumbs** | **1 cup melted butter** |

1  Combine cheese, breadcrumbs, crushed garlic, parsley, salt and pepper.
2  Dip each piece of chicken in melted butter, then coat with the crumb mixture.
3  Place in a large shallow baking dish.
4  Pour the remaining butter over the chicken and bake in a moderate oven for about 1 hour.
5  Baste the chicken pieces during cooking but do not turn.

# CHICKEN MORNAY

*20 minutes cooking time*

*Ingredients for 4 servings*

2 teaspoons lemon juice
2 teaspoons salt
½ teaspoon cayenne pepper
250 g (8 oz) cooked chicken, chopped

2½ cups white sauce
2 tablespoons grated cheese
2 tablespoons fried breadcrumbs

1  Add lemon juice, salt, cayenne and chicken to white sauce.
2  Grease ovenproof dish and spread mixture in it.
3  Sprinkle cheese and breadcrumbs on top, and brown lightly in oven or
   under griller.

# ORIENTAL BRAISED CHICKEN

*1 hour cooking time*

*Ingredients for 4 servings*

125 g (4 oz) dried mushrooms
3 tablespoons soy sauce
3 tablespoons salad oil
2 cloves garlic, mashed or minced
½ teaspoon pepper
1 1.5-kg (3-lb) chicken, cut in small
   pieces if possible

1 large onion, cut into 8 wedges
2 stalks celery, cut diagonally
   in 2.5 cm (1 in) pieces
½ cup toasted slivered almonds
4 spring onions and tops, cut in
   2.5 cm (1 in) lengths

1  Wash mushrooms well, cover with 1 cup cold water and let stand
   overnight.
2  Combine soy sauce, 1 tablespoon salad oil, garlic, and pepper and pour
   over chicken; marinate 30 minutes.
3  Heat remaining 2 tablespoons salad oil in a frying pan; remove chicken
   from marinade, drain well, and brown slowly.
4  Remove stems from mushrooms and slice tops in strips 5 millimetres
   (¼ in) wide.
5  Add mushrooms to the browned chicken along with ½ cup of the
   mushroom liquid, onion, celery, and the remaining marinade.
6  Cover and simmer until chicken is tender (about 40 minutes).
7  Garnish with almonds and spring onions.

# SIMPLE CHICKEN CASSEROLE

*1¼ hours cooking time*

*Ingredients for 4-6 servings*

| | |
|---|---|
| 1 chicken | 1 bay leaf |
| 60 g (2 oz) bacon | 1¼ cups stock |
| 1 onion | strip lemon rind |
| 2 tablespoons chopped parsley | |

1  Dice bacon and fry with the onion, put into a casserole.
2  Cut chicken into neat joints, dust well with flour, fry in the same pan gently for about 10 minutes.
3  Add stock, chicken and seasonings to casserole.
4  Cook in oven at 180°C (350°F) for 2 hours.
5  Remove fat, bay leaf and lemon rind before serving.

# CHICKEN BREASTS IN ORANGE SAUCE

*1¼ hours cooking time*

*Ingredients for 6 servings*

| | |
|---|---|
| ½ cup plain flour | ½ cup chicken stock |
| ½ teaspoon salt | ½ cup orange juice |
| ½ teaspoon paprika | ½ cup dry white wine |
| dash pepper | ¼ teaspoon nutmeg |
| 1 clove garlic | 2 teaspoons brown sugar |
| 6 halved chicken breasts | 2 cups thickly sliced carrots |
| 6 tablespoons olive oil | 1 can condensed cream of mushroom |
| 1 small can whole mushrooms | soup |

1  Mix flour, salt, paprika and pepper.
2  Coat chicken with the flour mixture.
3  Heat oil in frying pan; brown minced garlic and chicken breasts well on both sides in the hot oil.
4  Drain the mushrooms, reserving juice; scatter mushrooms over chicken.
5  Blend soup, reserved mushroom juice, chicken stock, orange juice, wine, nutmeg and brown sugar until smooth; pour soup mixture over chicken.
6  Cover and simmer about 30 minutes or until chicken is tender.
7  About 15 minutes before chicken is done, stir in carrots; continue cooking until tender.

# APRICOT CHICKEN

*30 minutes cooking time*

*Ingredients for 6 servings*

1 green pepper, chopped
4 tomatoes, peeled and sliced
3 small onions, sliced
2 tablespoons butter
2 tablespoons plain flour
1 tablespoon chopped parsley

1 large tin apricot nectar
½ teaspoon salt
¼ teaspoon pepper
1 steamed 1.25-kg (2½-lb) chicken
2 tablespoons dried breadcrumbs

1   Melt butter, add flour and cook, stirring for 1 minute.
2   Add apricot nectar and stir until thickened.
3   Add onions, green pepper, salt and pepper, and simmer 15 minutes.
4   Cut chicken into small pieces, place in casserole dish and cover with sliced
    tomatoes, cover with sauce, and sprinkle with breadcrumbs and parsley.
5   Place in medium oven until hot.

# NORTH ITALIAN CHICKEN

*1¼ hours cooking time*

*Ingredients for 4 servings*

3 chicken breasts, cut in half
1 tablespoon butter
1 onion, chopped
1 teaspoon chopped parsley
4 tablespoons flour
1 tablespoon chopped fennel

2 chicken livers
500 g (1 lb) shelled green peas
1¼ cups chicken stock
2 tablespoons lemon juice
2 egg yolks
salt and pepper

1   Heat the butter and brown the chopped onion and parsley; add chicken
    dusted with flour and brown.
2   Add the chopped fennel and the hot stock; cover and cook for 30 minutes.
3   In the meantime cook the peas in boiling salted water until barely tender,
    drain and add to the saucepan together with the chicken livers and
    seasoning; cook for 10 more minutes.
4   Remove from the stove and stir in the beaten egg yolks mixed with the
    lemon juice.

# CHICKEN SUPREME

*2 hours cooking time*

*Ingredients for 4 servings*

1 1.75-kg (3½-lb) chicken
375 g (12 oz) ham, sliced 6 mm
  (¼ in) thick
1 sliced onion
6 tablespoons butter
salt and pepper

1 cup celery, diced
8 pineapple rings
8 canned artichoke hearts
6 ground cooked chicken livers
1 cup grated coconut

1  Dust chicken with ½ cup flour, salt and pepper.
2  Cut chicken into pieces and brown in 4 tablespoons butter.
3  Place in large saucepan, cover with water, add a slice of onion, salt and pepper and a cup of diced celery, and boil until chicken is tender.
4  Remove from pan and strain broth.
5  Discard onion but reserve celery for casserole.
6  Place slices of grilled ham in the bottom of a large casserole, adding 2 drained pineapple rings and 2 artichoke hearts for each serving, the celery, and chicken (which has been removed from the bone).
7  Skim fat from broth and use broth in making sauce.
8  Melt 2 tablespoons of butter, stir in 2 tablespoons of flour and cook for 1 minute.
9  Add broth and stir until it boils and thickens.
10  Pour over chicken in casserole and add chicken livers.
11  Prepare dumplings.
12  Drop on top of casserole mixture.
13  Cover and place in a moderately hot oven 200°C (400°F) for 15 minutes or until dumplings are done.
14  Before serving sprinkle with freshly grated coconut which has been toasted.
15  Serve with boiled rice.

## DUMPLINGS

1 cup flour
1 teaspoon baking powder

⅓ teaspoon salt
⅓ cup chopped suet

1  Mix and sift flour, baking powder and salt.
2  Add suet and enough cold water to just bind.
3  Mix well.
4  Drop a tablespoon at a time into chicken stew 20 minutes before serving time.

# CHICKEN AND PINEAPPLE

*2 hours cooking time*

*Ingredients for 4-6 servings*

1 1.5-kg (3-lb) chicken
1 large can pineapple pieces
1 cup uncooked long-grain rice
2 tablespoons finely chopped green
  pepper

1 teaspoon butter
2 tablespoons minced onion
1 teaspoon salt
¼ teaspoon pepper
1 tablespoon fresh grated ginger

1  Add ½ cup water to ½ cup pineapple syrup and combine in a pan with the rice, green pepper, butter, onion, salt, pepper and half the ginger.
2  Boil, lower the heat and simmer gently until the rice is barely tender.
3  Add the pineapple pieces and stuff the chicken with rice combination.
4  Bake covered with foil in a moderate oven for 1 hour.
5  Remove the foil and bake for another 30 minutes or until the chicken is tender, basting with remaining pineapple juice and 2 teaspoons of ginger.

# CHICKEN LIVER PATÉ

*Ingredients for 6 servings*

375 g (12 oz) chicken livers, chopped
½ cup white wine
1½ tablespoons brandy
185 g (6 oz) butter
1 clove garlic, crushed

1 tablespoon minced onion
1 teaspoon finely chopped thyme,
  marjoram and parsley
¾ teaspoon salt
¼ teaspoon pepper

1  Soak chicken livers in white wine and brandy for 3 hours.
2  Drain livers and save liquid.
3  Chop livers coarsely and sauté in 2 tablespoons melted butter with garlic and onion for 5 minutes, turning constantly.
4  Add thyme, marjoram and parsley, and stir well.
5  Pour wine and brandy into the juices left in the pan and boil vigorously.
6  Remove from heat and stir in 1 tablespoon butter.
7  Add mixture to puréed livers and pour into a small mould.
8  Seal mould with remaining butter.

# CHICKEN BAKED WITH SESAME

*1 hour cooking time*

*Ingredients for 4-6 servings*

1 tablespoon soy sauce
1/3 cup lemon juice
1/4 cup salad oil
1/2 teaspoon salt
1/2 teaspoon pepper
1 teaspoon grated lemon rind
1 clove garlic, crushed
1 1.5-kg (3-lb) chicken

1/4 cup flour
1 teaspoon salt
1/4 teaspoon pepper
1 egg
3 tablespoons milk
1/4 cup toasted sesame seeds
1/2 cup cracker biscuit crumbs
1/4 cup melted butter

1   Combine soy sauce, lemon juice, salad oil, salt, pepper, lemon rind and garlic to make a sauce and refrigerate.
2   To toast, place sesame seeds on a tray and bake in a moderate oven for about 5 minutes.
3   Cut the chicken into pieces, coat with seasoned flour, dip in the egg and milk mixture and cover with the combined sesame seeds and cracker crumbs.
4   Place chicken pieces in a shallow dish, skin side down.
5   Brush them with the melted butter and bake uncovered at 200°C (400°F) for about 30 minutes.
6   Turn chicken and cover with the sauce.
7   Bake for 30 minutes more, or until the chicken is tender.

# CHICKEN A LA RENO

*20 minutes cooking time*

*Ingredients for 2-3 servings*

1 roast chicken
250 g (8 oz) black olives

6 tomatoes, sliced
250 g (8 oz) mushrooms

1   Stone olives.
2   Wash mushrooms and carefully peel skin off.
3   Now place chicken in oven with mushrooms, olives and tomatoes and bake for 15 minutes.
4   Garnish with parsley.

# FRENCH CHICKEN WITH HERBS

*2½ hours cooking time*

*Ingredients for 6 servings*

1 1.5-kg( 3-lb) chicken
¼ cup plain flour
1 teaspoon salt
½ teaspoon pepper
2 tablespoons butter
4 small onions
1 clove garlic
¼ teaspoon dried thyme

2 or 3 sprigs celery leaves
3 tablespoons chopped parsley
¾ cup sliced mushrooms
1 bay leaf
¾ cup chicken stock
¾ cup red wine
2 sliced carrots

1   Cut the chicken into pieces.
2   Mix the flour, salt and pepper and dust the chicken pieces.
3   Slowly fry the chicken in butter until brown on all sides and remove from pan.
4   Add peeled onions, crushed garlic and carrots.
5   Cover and cook for 5 minutes.
6   Arrange the chicken, cooked vegetables, thyme, celery leaves, parsley, bay leaf and mushrooms in a casserole.
7   Place the chicken stock and wine in the pan in which the chicken was fried and stir until boiling, scraping all the browning from the bottom.
8   Pour over the ingredients in the casserole, cover and bake in a moderate oven for 2 hours or until the chicken is tender.
9   Remove bay leaf and celery leaves.

# CHICKEN MOULDS

*40 minutes cooking time*

*Ingredients for 4-5 servings*

2 cups wholewheat breadcrumbs
2 chopped shallots
½ cup grated cheddar cheese
¼ teaspoon white pepper

4 cups cooked chicken
½ cup chopped parsley
½ teaspoon salt
2 beaten eggs

1   Combine breadcrumbs, chicken, shallots and salt.
2   Blend and mix thoroughly.
3   Add beaten eggs, parsley, cheese and pepper.
4   Combine with other ingredients and mix thoroughly.
5   Place in buttered tin and bake for 40 minutes in a moderate oven.

# CHICKEN PAPRIKA

*25 minutes cooking time*

*Ingredients for 2-3 servings*

1 roasted chicken
1 clove garlic
1 bay leaf
½ cup sour cream
500 g (1 lb) tomatoes, peeled and
  halved
½ cup chicken stock

1 onion, chopped
1 tablespoon butter
3 teaspoons paprika
1 tablespoon plain flour
½ teaspoon salt
¼ teaspoon pepper

1  Saute onion in butter and add paprika.
2  Remove from heat and add flour, stock and tomatoes.
3  Bring to the boil.
4  Add salt and pepper.
5  Add garlic and bay leaf.
6  Simmer until liquid is reduced.
7  Strain the sauce.
8  Cut chicken into pieces and place in casserole dish.
9  Cover chicken with sauce and simmer for 15 minutes.
10  Five minutes before serving, add sour cream.

# BRAISED CHICKEN

*2 hours cooking time*

*Ingredients for 4-5 servings*

1 2-kg (4-lb) frying chicken
2 chopped shallots
1 can tomatoes
2 cups water

½ teaspoon salt
wholewheat flour
1 tablespoon sugar
4 tablespoons butter

1  Dust chicken with flour and salt.
2  Brown the chicken in butter and remove.
3  Place in a casserole dish with shallots, tomatoes and sugar.
4  Pour over water.
5  Cover and bake for 2 hours.
6  Thicken mixture with 2 teaspoons flour 10 minutes before serving.

# GRILLED CHICKEN

*1 hour cooking time*

*Ingredients for 4-5 servings*

| | |
|---|---|
| 1 2-kg (4-lb) chicken | 3 tablespoons butter |
| 1 teaspoon salt | ½ teaspoon cayenne pepper |

1 Melt the butter and stand.
2 Cut chicken into pieces.
3 Rub chicken with butter thoroughly.
4 Season with salt and cayenne pepper.
5 Place on oiled rack.
6 Grill for 30 minutes.
7 Remove and bake for 30 minutes.

# CHICKEN WITH MUSHROOMS AND ALMONDS

*20 minutes cooking time*

*Ingredients for 4-5 servings*

| | |
|---|---|
| 3 tablespoons butter | 250 g (8 oz) mushrooms, sliced |
| 2 onions, sliced | ½ teaspoon salt |
| ¼ teaspoon pepper | 3 tablespoons flour |
| 2½ cups chicken stock | 3 cups diced cooked chicken |
| 1 large can evaporated milk | ½ cup white wine |
| 2 cups fluffy rice | ½ cup toasted almonds |

1 Melt the butter over a low heat.
2 Sauté the mushrooms and onions, then sprinkle with salt, pepper and flour.
3 Stir through the stock and the milk.
4 Bring to the boil and then simmer for 10 minutes.
5 Add to diced chicken and white wine.
6 Serve with fluffy boiled rice and sprinkle over the almonds.

# CHICKEN CATALINA

*30 minutes cooking time*

*Ingredients for 4-5 servings*

2 tablespoons butter
2 tablespoons flour
2 cups sliced mushrooms
¼ teaspoon pepper
¼ teaspoon celery salt
½ cup white wine
½ cup evaporated milk
¼ cup Parmesan cheese

2 tablespoons finely chopped onion
1 teaspoon salt
½ cup chicken stock
2 cups chopped cooked chicken
125 g (4 oz) fine vermicelli, cooked for 10 minutes in boiling salted water

1  Melt the butter in a saucepan and add onion and cook over low heat.
2  Add the flour, mushrooms and seasonings.
3  Stir in the stock and evaporated milk.
4  Cook over a low heat until mixture thickens.
5  Stir constantly.
6  Add the chicken and wine. Place the cooked vermicelli in a greased ovenproof dish and press to the sides of the casserole.
7  Pour chicken mixture into centre, and sprinkled with grated cheese.
8  Bake in moderate oven 180°C (350°F) until heated through and browned on top.

# BARBECUED CHICKEN TARRAGON

*25 minutes cooking time*

*Ingredients for 6 servings*

6 large chicken breasts
3 tablespoons butter
1 teaspoon tarragon
2½ tablespoons chives

3 tablespoons chopped parsley
1 teaspoon salt
½ teaspoon paprika

1  Mix tarragon, chives, parsley, salt and paprika with the butter and spread over chicken pieces underneath skin.
2  Place chicken on foil-covered grill and cook 25 minutes until golden brown, basting with butter mixture occasionally.

# PINEAPPLE CHICKEN BARBECUE

*20 minutes cooking time*

*Ingredients for 4-5 servings*

1.5 kg (3 lb) chicken pieces
1 can crushed pineapple
1½ tablespoons mustard
¾ cup brown sugar
1 teaspoon ground black pepper

1½ teaspoons vinegar
juice of 1 lemon
3 tablespoons butter
1 teaspoon salt

1  Sprinkle chicken pieces with salt and pepper, dot with knobs of butter and grill 20 minutes, brushing with butter.
2  Mix thoroughly pineapple, mustard, brown sugar, vinegar and lemon juice and spoon over chicken 10 minutes before it is cooked.
3  Baste with pineapple sauce until cooked.

# CHICKEN GUMBO

*2 hours cooking time*

*Ingredients for 4-5 servings*

125 g (4 oz) bacon rashers
seasoned flour
1 medium can sliced mushrooms
2 teaspoons salt
1 bay leaf
½ teaspoon thyme
½ teaspoon brown sugar
1 cup long-grain rice

1 kg (2 lb) chicken wings
1 onion, chopped
2 tablespoons chopped parsley
2 large cans tomatoes
4 cups hot water
1 clove garlic, crushed
¼ teaspoon cayenne pepper
½ cup white wine

1  Dice the bacon and fry in a deep pan until fat is transparent. Remove.
2  Cut the chicken wings in halves and dredge in seasoned flour, then brown in bacon fat.
3  Add the remaining ingredients except the wine, rice and parsley.
4  Simmer for 1-2 hours and add extra water when needed.
5  30 minutes before serving add wine, rice and parsley.
6  Stir and remove the bay leaf before serving.
7  Sprinkle with chopped parsley.

# FRUITY CHICKEN BARBECUE

*35 minutes cooking time*

*Ingredients for 4 servings*

1 1.75-kg (3½-ib) chicken
3 tablespoons butter
¼ cup brandy
¼ cup brown sugar
6 fresh apricots

1 cup sweet cherries
1 teaspoon salt
½ teaspoon pepper
juice of 1 lemon

1  Melt the butter and mix with brandy, sugar and lemon juice.
2  Sprinkle chicken with salt and pepper.
3  Place on grill, cover and cook about 35 minutes, basting occasionally with brandy mixture.
4  Cut apricots in half and brush cherries and apricot halves with baste.
5  Place fruit in separate containers made of aluminium foil, cook and smoke about 10 minutes.
6  Serve chicken with fruit.

# CHICKEN WITH HONEY BASTE

*1¼ hours cooking time*

*Ingredients for 6-8 servings*

2 1.5-kg (3-ib) chickens
4 tablespoons butter
2 tablespoons honey
1 onion, chopped
2 tablespoons soy sauce

2 teaspoons finely chopped ginger
1 teaspoon salt
1 cup sherry
½ teaspoon pepper

1  Secure chickens tightly, spit and cook 45 minutes, brushing with melted butter frequently.
2  Mix thoroughly honey, chopped onion, soy sauce, ginger, sherry, salt and pepper and pour over chicken.
3  Cook another 30 minutes until golden brown, using honey sauce as baste while cooking.

# MARINATED CHICKEN

*40 minutes cooking time*

*Ingredients for 4-5 servings*

| | |
|---|---|
| 1 1.5-kg (3-lb) chicken | ½ cup soy sauce |
| 1 cup hock | 1 teaspoon prepared mustard |
| 2 tablespoons salad oil | |

1 Combine salad oil, mustard, soy sauce and hock in frying pan.
2 Mix thoroughly.
3 Place chicken in this mixture and stand for 1 hour.
4 Remove chicken and grill for 15 minutes.
5 Remove.
6 Bake for 20-30 minutes, brushing with marinade.
7 Serve with rice.

# BARBECUED CHICKEN SUZETTE

*1½ hours cooking time*

*Ingredients for 4-6 servings*

| | |
|---|---|
| 1 2-kg (4-lb) chicken | ½ teaspoon salt |
| 1 small stalk celery, finely chopped | ¼ teaspoon pepper |
| 2 tablespoons chopped parsley | ⅔ cup redcurrant jelly |
| ½ teaspoon mixed herbs | juice of 1 lemon |
| ½ cup breadcrumbs | juice of 1 orange |
| ¼ cup milk | 1 teaspoon mustard |
| 1 onion, chopped | 1 teaspoon ginger |
| ½ teaspoon cayenne pepper | |

1 Wash and dry chicken and salt the cavity.
2 Soften breadcrumbs with milk and mix with celery, onion, parsley, herbs, salt and pepper.
3 Stuff chicken, fasten openings, and tie securely, crossing legs and securing wings.
4 Thread onto spit and roast over medium heat about 1½ hours.
5 Mix together redcurrant jelly, lemon and orange juice, mustard, ginger, cayenne.
6 Heat gently until smooth and baste chicken occasionally.

# CHICKEN AND TOMATOES

*20 minutes cooking time*

*Ingredients for 4-5 servings*

4 cups cooked chicken, diced
1 can tomatoes, drained
½ teaspoon salt
½ cup chopped parsley

1 cup chicken stock
2 cups cream
¼ teaspoon white pepper
2 tablespoons butter

1. Brown chicken in butter and add tomatoes.
2. Simmer for 5 minutes.
3. Season with salt and pepper.
4. Add cream and stock.
5. Simmer for further 5 minutes.
6. Dot with chopped parsley and simmer for 20 minutes.
7. Serve immediately.

# DUCKLING A L'ORANGE

*2 hours cooking time*

*Ingredients for 4 servings*

2 kg (4 lb) duckling
½ cup soy sauce
½ cup sake

3 oranges
1 cup honey (melted)
1 tablespoon cornflour

1. Soak duckling in soy sauce and honey for 4 hours, basting occasionally.
2. Peel 2 oranges. Remove pith. Cook in sake for 10 minutes at low heat.
3. Remove duckling from marinade and roast at 200°C (400°F) for 20 minutes.
4. Continue cooking for further 1½ hours at 150°C (300°F).
5. Blend cornflour with a little water. Add slowly to orange sauce, stirring continually until thickened (approximately 5 minutes).
6. Serve duckling garnished with orange slices and accompanied by sauce in a jug.

# CHICKEN SALAD

*Ingredients for 4-5 servings*

2 lettuces, broken
½ cup grated Parmesan cheese
vinegar

6 cups cooked chicken, cubed
1 cup salad oil
2 teaspoons prepared mustard

1  Combine all ingredients and season with salt and pepper.
2  If you prefer, add more oil and stand for 10 minutes before serving.

# MOULDED ORANGE-CHICKEN SALAD

*Ingredients for 6 servings*

2 packets orange jelly
3½ cups orange juice
½ cup lemon juice
2 cups cooked chicken, finely diced
½ cup mayonnaise

¼ teaspoon dry mustard
½ teaspoon salt
¼ teaspoon pepper
1 tablespoon chopped parsley
¼ cup blanched toasted almonds

1  Mix jellies with fruit juices, heat gently until dissolved.
2  Cool, and when it begins to set, place weighted cup into jelly to make a
   well.
3  Chill until firm.
4  Combine parsley, seasoned mayonnaise, chicken and almonds, and fill
   well in jelly with chicken mixture.

# TROPICAL CHICKEN SALAD

*Ingredients for 6 servings*

3 cups diced cooked chicken
2 spring onions, chopped
¾ cup celery, chopped
1 tablespoon lemon juice
½ teaspoon salt
1 tablespoon capers

1 large can mandarin pieces
1 large can pineapple pieces
½ cup chopped almonds
1½ teaspoons lemon rind, grated
½ cup mayonnaise
1 tablespoon chopped parsley

1 Combine chicken, onions, celery, salt, capers and lemon juice.
2 Put in refrigerator for 1 hour.
3 Mix mayonnaise and lemon rind and chill.
4 To serve, add the mandarin pieces and pineapple to the chicken and stir in the mayonnaise mixture.
5 Sprinkle almonds on top.

# APRICOT CHICKEN SALAD

*Ingredients for 6 servings*

2 cups fresh apricots, peeled and chopped
2 cups cooked chicken, chopped
1½ cups celery, chopped
½ teaspoon salt

2 spring onions, chopped
½ cup mayonnaise
½ cup sour cream
1½ tablespoons lemon juice

1 Make a sauce of mayonnaise, sour cream, lemon juice and salt.
2 Pour over other ingredients, mix gently and refrigerate for 30 minutes.

# CRUNCHY CHICKEN SALAD

*Ingredients for 8 servings*

4 cups diced cooked chicken
1 tin pineapple pieces
3 tablespoons spring onions, sliced
1 cup water chestnuts
⅓ cup slivered almonds

1 cup commercial sour cream
2 teaspoons fresh grated ginger
¾ teaspoon salt
¼ teaspoon pepper

1 Combine chicken, chopped onions, pineapple and water chestnuts.
2 Mix sour cream, ginger, salt and pepper and stir into chicken mixture.
3 Sprinkle with toasted almonds.

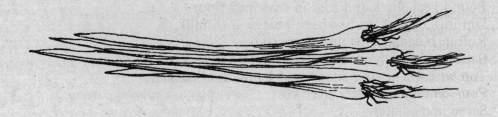

# Veal

## WIENER SCHNITZEL

*20 minutes cooking time*

*Ingredients for 6-7 servings*

| | |
|---|---|
| 8 thin slices veal steak | 8 slices lemon |
| plain flour | 8 slices hardboiled egg |
| 1 egg, beaten | 8 anchovies |
| 2 tablespoons milk | juice of 2 lemons |
| breadcrumbs | 125 g (4 oz) butter |
| ¼ teaspoon white pepper | ½ teaspoon salt |
| parsley, chopped | |

1  Pound veal slices and toss in seasoned flour.
2  Dip into egg which has been beaten with milk.
3  Roll in breadcrumbs and press flat.
4  Sauté veal slowly in butter, turning once.
5  Top with anchovies, squeeze of lemon and parsley.
6  Pour remaining butter over veal.
7  Serve immediately.

# VEAL AND CASHEWS

*1½-2 hours cooking time*

*Ingredients for 6-7 servings*

2 cups cashews
1.5 kg (3 lb) veal, sliced
½ teaspoon salt
2 onions, chopped
1 teaspoon prepared mustard
1 teaspoon Worcestershire sauce

5 tablespoons butter
¼ teaspoon white pepper
2 teaspoons plain flour
4 cloves garlic, crushed
2 cups water

1 Sauté cashews in butter and remove after 5 minutes.
2 Season sliced veal and dust with flour.
3 Sauté in butter and add onions, garlic, mustard and salt.
4 Add boiling water, Worcestershire sauce.
5 Cover and cook for 1½-2 hours.
6 About 10 minutes before serving, add cashews.

# ESCALOPES IN CREAM

*30 minutes cooking time*

*Ingredients for 4-5 servings.*

3 Granny Smith apples
½ teaspoon salt
6 pieces fillet veal
2 teaspoons plain flour

¼ teaspoon white pepper
3 tablespoons butter
2 tablespoons rum
300 ml (1¼ cups) thickened cream

1 Peel and core the apples and cut into slices.
2 Dust veal with seasoned flour.
3 Melt butter and fry veal for 2 minutes on each side.
4 Remove and place on dish in warm oven.
5 Add more butter to pan and fry apples gently until soft.
6 Pour brandy on top and set alight.
7 When flame dies down, remove apples, add the cream and bring to the boil.
8 Pour sauce over veal and serve with green beans.

# VEAL PARMESAN

*20 minutes cooking time*

*Ingredients for 4-5 servings*

6 veal cutlets
2 tablespoons plain flour
1 egg, beaten
2 tablespoons milk

125 g (4 oz) grated parmesan cheese
125 g (4 oz) butter
450 g (16 oz) can pears, drained
155 g (5 oz) breadcrumbs

1   Pound veal and toss in seasoned flour.
2   Dip in egg and milk mixture.
3   Mix parmesan cheese with breadcrumbs.
4   Coat veal in this mixture.
5   Sauté veal in butter and serve with sliced pears.

# VEAL BROCHETTE

*40 minutes cooking time*

*Ingredients for 4-5 servings*

1 kg (2 lb) veal steak
500 g (1 lb) fresh pork
⅛ teaspoon white pepper

½ cup plain flour
1 teaspoon salt
4 tablespoons butter

1   Cut veal into squares and pork into thin squares.
2   Roll in flour, salt and pepper.
3   Place alternate slices of meat on skewers and melt butter in pan.
4   Brown meat on skewers and cook slowly for 35-40 minutes.
5   Serve with gravy and green beans.

# WESTERN VEAL CHOPS

*30 minutes cooking time*

*Ingredients for 4-5 servings*

8 veal chops
1 onion, chopped
1 450 g (16 oz) can peeled tomatoes

1 310 g (10 oz) can sweet corn
1 teaspoon plain flour
½ teaspoon sage

1   Brown chops in frying pan and keep warm.
2   Add onion and cook for 4 minutes.
3   Add strained tomatoes and sweet corn.

4 Blend tomato juice with flour and sage.
5 Pour over ingredients in pan, season with salt and pepper and cook until tender.
6 Serve with new potatoes and beans.

# VEAL AND CHEDDAR CHEESE

*15 minutes cooking time*

*Ingredients for 5-6 servings*

| | |
|---|---|
| **6 veal steaks** | **3 tablespoons oil** |
| **¼ teaspoon white pepper** | **½ teaspoon salt** |
| **1 cup grated cheddar cheese** | **300 ml (1¼ cups) sour cream** |

1 Sauté veal in oil and cook until tender.
2 Season with salt and pepper.
3 Remove to warmed serving dish.
4 Stir cheese into sour cream and heat slowly.
5 Return meat to sauce and serve immediately.

# VEAL SUPREME

*30 minutes cooking time*

*Ingredients for 4-5 servings*

| | |
|---|---|
| **3 tablespoons butter** | **6 veal fillets** |
| **4 tablespoons finely chopped onion** | **2 tablespoons butter** |
| **150 g (5 oz) mushrooms, chopped** | **½ cup white wine** |
| **60 g (2 oz) ham, chopped** | **2 carrots, chopped** |
| **2 teaspoons chopped parsley** | **1 bay leaf** |
| **¼ teaspoon white pepper** | **½ teaspoon salt** |

1 Melt half of the butter and sauté onions, mushrooms, chopped ham, and parsley.
2 Divide and spread on each piece of veal.
3 Roll up and tie securely.
4 Melt remaining butter in separate saucepan and add veal.
5 Pour over wine, add carrots and bay leaf.
6 Season with white pepper and salt.
7 Simmer for 25 minutes.
8 Remove strings and serve immediately.

# VEAL MARYLAND

*20 minutes cooking time*

*Ingredients for 4-5 servings*

| | |
|---|---|
| 1 kg (2 lb) veal slices | 1 teaspoon salt |
| 1 cup plain flour | ¼ teaspoon white pepper |
| 1 cup breadcrumbs | 3 tablespoons butter |
| chopped parsley | new potatoes |
| 1 beaten egg | |

1  Wipe meat and coat in flour.
2  Dip in egg and then roll in breadcrumbs.
3  Season with salt and pepper.
4  Place in greased frying pan and dot with butter.
5  Fry until cooked through, turning once.
6  Serve with white sauce, parsley and new potatoes.

# VEAL AND BRANDY

*40 minutes cooking time*

*Ingredients for 4-5 servings*

| | |
|---|---|
| 125 g (½ cup) butter | 1 cup stock |
| 8 thin slices veal | 1 tablespoon finely chopped fresh |
| 8 spring onions | ginger |
| 1 tablespoon brandy | 450 g (16 oz) can pears |
| 2 teaspoons chopped parsley | ¼ teaspoon white pepper |
| ½ teaspoon salt | 2 tablespoons cream |

1  Sauté veal with chopped spring onions, brandy, and chopped parsley in butter.
2  Add cream and stock.
3  Simmer for 2 minutes.
4  Add sliced pears, ginger, salt, pepper and a little more parsley.
5  Simmer for 30 minutes.

# VEAL WITH TOMATOES AND SPAGHETTI

*30 minutes cooking time*

*Ingredients for 4-5 servings*

5 veal steaks
1 egg
2 tablespoons butter
1 onion, chopped
125 g (4 oz) mushrooms

1 small green pepper
1 cup breadcrumbs
4 tomatoes
extra butter
155 g (5 oz) spaghetti

1  Coat meat in beaten egg and then in seasoned breadcrumbs.
2  Melt half of the butter and fry onion and pepper.
3  Add mushrooms and cook for 5 minutes.
4  Add tomatoes and cook 2 minutes longer.
5  Fry veal steaks in another frying pan in butter.
6  Cook spaghetti in salted water and drain.
7  Dot with butter.
8  Serve combined ingredients on serving platter.

# VEAL LEMON STEAK

*30 minutes cooking time*

*Ingredients for 4 5 servings*

1 kg (2 lb) veal steak
4 tablespoons butter
¼ teaspoon salt
2 onions, sliced
½ cup stock

2 cloves garlic, halved
2 lemons, sliced
½ teaspoon paprika
2 tomatoes, chopped
chopped parsley

1  Rub meat with garlic and cut into slices.
2  Sauté meat in butter.
3  Squeeze lemon juice over meat and season with salt and paprika.
4  Arrange tomato and onion over meat.
5  Pour stock over and simmer for 15 minutes.
6  Add remaining lemon and cook for 15 minutes more.
7  Place on serving dish and dot with parsley.
8  Serve immediately.

# VEAL AND ASPARAGUS

*40 minutes cooking time*

*Ingredients for 4-5 servings*

750 g (1½ lb) veal fillets
¼ teaspoon white pepper
½ teaspoon salt
2 tablespoons butter
1 teaspoon sugar

310 g (10 oz) can asparagus tips
½ teaspoon white pepper
3 tablespoons butter
1¼ cups stock

1  Cut veal into pieces and coat in flour.
2  Season with salt and pepper.
3  Sauté in butter and pour off excess butter.
4  Add stock and cover.
5  Simmer for 25 minutes.
6  Strain liquid and heat asparagus in butter.
7  Add sugar and salt.
8  When serving place asparagus tips on top of veal.
9  Serve immediately.

# FRENCH VEAL

*2 hours cooking time*

*Ingredients for 5-6 servings*

1 kg (2 lb) fillet veal
2 onions
½ teaspoon salt
1¼ cups stock
2 tablespoons butter
4 shallots

yolks of 4 eggs
¼ teaspoon cayenne pepper
chopped parsley
100 ml (3 oz) cream
mashed potatoes and buttered peas

1   Cut veal into serving pieces.
2   Chop vegetables and place in saucepan with stock.
3   Simmer for 1½ hours.
4   Lift out meat and drain.
5   Heat butter and sauté shallots.
6   Add stock and yolks.
7   Stir but do not boil.
8   Add salt, cayenne, parsley and cream.
9   Return meat to saucepan and reheat.
10  Serve with mashed potatoes and buttered peas.

# STUFFED VEAL

*Ingredients for 4 servings*

*1 hour cooking time*

500 g (1 lb) veal steak
3 tablespoons sultanas
2 teaspoons chopped parsley
½ teaspoon salt
2 tablespoons grated cheddar cheese
1¼ cups tomato purée

2 tablespoons butter
155 g (5 oz) bacon, chopped
2 teaspoons mustard
¼ teaspoon white pepper
1 onion, chopped

1  Cut veal into slices 7 by 12 centimetres (3 by 5 in).
2  Combine sultanas, parsley, onion, cheese, bacon, mustard, salt and pepper in bowl.
3  Spread on veal and tie securely.
4  Sauté veal rolls in butter and add tomato purée.
5  Cover and simmer for 1 hour.
6  Remove cotton and serve.

# VEAL HAWAIIAN

*Ingredients for 3-4 servings*

*1½ hours cooking time*

3 tablespoons butter
4 veal loin chops
¼ teaspoon white pepper
4 pineapple rings

4 dried prunes
1 cup diced carrots
½ teaspoon salt
½ cup warm water

1  Sauté veal chops in butter.
2  Season with salt and pepper.
3  Place pineapple on top of each chop.
4  Place prune in the centre of the pineapple.
5  Add carrots, water and salt.
6  Simmer for 1½ hours.

# VEAL MARSALA

*30 minutes cooking time*

*Ingredients for 4-5 servings*

1 kg (2 lb) veal, sliced thinly
¼ teaspoon white pepper
1 tablespoon flour
2 tablespoons butter

1 cup Marsala
½ teaspoon salt
2 tablespoons stock
boiled rice

1   Pound fillets of veal and cut into pieces.
2   Sprinkle with salt and pepper.
3   Flour.
4   Sauté in butter, add Marsala and stock.
5   Cook for 10-15 minutes longer.
6   Serve on buttered rice.

# VEAL AND TOMATOES

*20 minutes cooking time*

*Ingredients for 2-3 servings*

500 g (1 lb) veal steak
1 tablespoon butter
½ teaspoon salt
1 cup tomato purée

2 eggs, lightly beaten
¼ teaspoon white pepper
buttered toast
chopped parsley

1   Chop veal finely.
2   Melt butter in saucepan and add tomato purée.
3   Combine eggs, veal and pepper.
4   Mix with butter and tomato purée.
5   Cook until thickened and serve on pieces of buttered toast, sprinkled with parsley.

# VEAL AND PINEAPPLE

*20 minutes cooking time*

*Ingredients for 4-5 servings*

1 kg (2 lb) veal, sliced thinly
¼ teaspoon white pepper
2 tablespoons butter
150 ml (5 oz) cream

4 slices pineapple, halved
½ teaspoon salt
250 g (8 oz) button mushrooms

1   Pound veal and season with salt and pepper.
2   Sauté in butter and when cooked remove.
3   Place in very hot oven on serving dish.
4   Cook pineapple in butter and place in oven with veal steaks.
5   Sauté the mushrooms in butter.
6   Stir cream into remaining butter and pour over veal, pineapple and mushrooms.
7   Serve immediately.

# BARBECUED VEAL

*10-20 minutes cooking time*

*Ingredients for 4-5 servings*

**3 tablespoons butter**
**1 kg (2 lb) breast veal**
**¼ teaspoon white pepper**
**1 cup tomato purée**
**2 cups water**
**1 tablespoon brown sugar**

**2 tablespoons Worcestershire sauce**
**1 teaspoon prepared mustard**
**½ teaspoon salt**
**1 onion, sliced**
**1 cup chopped celery**

1   Sauté meat in butter and season with salt and pepper.
2   Combine all other ingredients and pour over veal.
3   Cover and simmer for 30 minutes.
4   Serve with rice or buttered noodles.

# VEAL ROLL UPS

*20 minutes cooking time*

*Ingredients for 4-5 servings*

**6 pieces veal, thinly sliced**
**¼ teaspoon white pepper**
**3 slices ham, cut in half**
**125 g (4 oz) grated cheddar cheese**

**½ cup chopped cucumber**
**½ teaspoon salt**
**4 tablespoons butter**
**1 cup white wine**

1   Pound veal and season with salt and pepper.
2   Place slice of ham on veal and spread cheese and cucumber mixture on top.
3   Roll up and tie securely.
4   Sauté meat quickly in butter.
5   Add wine and cook for 10 minutes.
6   Serve immediately.

# VEAL PAPRIKA

*2 hours cooking time*

*Ingredients for 4-5 servings*

1 kg (2 lb) veal shank
125 g (4 oz) butter
2 onions, chopped
½ teaspoon salt
2 tablespoons paprika
1 tablespoon plain flour

2½ cups water
3 tablespoons tomato paste
¼ teaspoon white pepper
2 cloves garlic
150 ml (5 oz) sour cream
noodles

1  Cube meat and sauté in butter.
2  Remove and add onions and crushed garlic.
3  Add paprika and flour.
4  Blend thoroughly, constantly stirring.
5  Return the meat and stock and add tomato paste, salt and pepper.
6  Simmer for 2 hours.
7  30 minutes before serving add sour cream.
8  Serve with buttered noodles.

# Variety Meats

## GRILLED LIVER

*20 minutes cooking time*

*Ingredients for 4-5 servings*

1 kg (2 lb) liver
3 tablespoons butter
1 teaspoon salt

¼ teaspoon white pepper
2 lemons

1  Soak liver in boiling water for 5 minutes.
2  Brush with butter.
3  Grill.
4  Turn all the time and brush again with butter.
5  Season with salt and pepper.
6  Squeeze lemon juice over and serve.
7  Garnish with lemon wedges.

# FRENCH LIVER

*15 minutes cooking time*

*Ingredients for 4-5 servings*

500 g (1 lb) liver
2 tablespoons French dressing
1 teaspoon salt

2 cups water
8 slices bacon

1  Soak liver in salted water for 1 hour and scald in boiling water.
2  Clean and sprinkle with French dressing.
3  Stand for 1 hour.
4  Drain and slice into strips.
5  Sauté in hot fat and drain on brown paper.
6  Fry bacon and garnish.
7  Serve immediately.

# ROASTED LIVER

*1 hour cooking time*

*Ingredients for 6-8 servings*

4 tablespoons plain flour
¼ teaspoon white pepper
4 tablespoons oil
2 cups dry white wine
2 tablespoons vinegar
1 lemon, sliced

2 teaspoons salt
2 kg (4 lb) liver
2 onions, sliced
½ cup stock
¼ teaspoon ground pepper

1  Mix salt, pepper and flour.
2  Coat liver with this.
3  Heat oil and sauté liver until cooked.
4  Add onion and wine.
5  Cook for 1 minute, then add stock.
6  Season with vinegar and ground pepper and simmer for 45 minutes.
7  Remove liver to serving dish and thicken gravy.
8  Serve immediately.

# PILAU OF LIVERS

*20 minutes cooking time*

*Ingredients for 4-5 servings*

2-3 liver pieces
2 tablespoons butter
1¼ cups water or stock
½ teaspoon salt
1 onion, chopped

185 g (6 oz) rice
½ teaspoon curry powder
¼ teaspoon white pepper
pinch of saffron
1 teaspoon paprika

1  Wash the livers and cut into small pieces.
2  Sauté in a little butter.
3  Cover with stock or water and season well.
4  Simmer until tender.
5  Place remaining ingredients except liver in saucepan and simmer for 10 minutes.
6  Boil rice until tender.
7  Combine all ingredients and strain, leaving very little liquid.

# LIVER AND MUSHROOMS

*20 minutes cooking time*

*Ingredients for 4-5 servings*

4 tablespoons butter
4 sprigs parsley, chopped
juice of 2 lemons
½ cup dry white wine
½ teaspoon salt

1 kg (2 lb) liver, sliced thinly
250 g (8 oz) fresh mushrooms, washed
  and sliced
¼ teaspoon white pepper

1  Sauté mushrooms in butter and remove.
2  Add liver to butter and sauté. Sprinkle parsley on top and lower heat.
3  Add lemon juice and wine.
4  Cover and cook for 15 minutes.
5  Add salt and pepper.
6  Return mushrooms to pan and serve immediately.
7  If preferred serve with pan juices.

# LIVERS WITH CHESTNUTS

*20 minutes cooking time*

*Ingredients for 4-5 servings*

1 kg (2 lb) liver
2 tablespoons chopped spring onions
½ cup canned chestnuts
¼ cup cream

4 slices bacon
¼ cup plain flour
½ teaspoon salt
¼ cup milk

1 Cut livers in half and place bacon pieces in pan and sauté.
2 Add onion and cook for 1 minute.
3 Combine flour and salt. Coat liver in flour.
4 Add to pan and sauté.
5 Add chestnuts and milk-cream mixture.
6 Bring to the boil and serve on toast.

# LAMB'S FRY WITH BACON

*15 minutes cooking time*

*Ingredients for 3-4 servings*

8 rashers bacon
½ teaspoon salt
3 tablespoons butter
1 lamb's fry, thinly sliced
2 teaspoons cornflour

¼ teaspoon white pepper
1 cup stock
½ cup white wine
½ teaspoon mixed herbs

1 Fry bacon and remove.
2 Keep warm.
3 Sauté in butter slices of lamb's fry dipped in seasoned flour.
4 Allow to cook for 5 minutes and add stock, wine, bacon and herbs.
5 Arrange on serving dish and serve with gravy poured over.

# LIVER CROUTES

*20 minutes cooking time*

*Ingredients for 4-5 servings*

500 g (1 lb) liver
2 tablespoons melted butter
lemon juice
¼ teaspoon cayenne pepper

croutes of fried bread
3 hardboiled eggs
chopped parsley
½ teaspoon salt

1  Fry liver in half of the butter for 10 minutes.
2  Pound and add remaining butter.
3  Add lemon juice and season with salt and cayenne pepper.
4  Spread on croutes and top with egg slices.
5  Sprinkle with parsley and salt.

# LIVER AND BACON WITH ONIONS

*10 minutes cooking time*

*Ingredients for 4 servings*

1 sheep's liver
315 g (10 oz) bacon rashers
dripping
3 onions, sliced

1 tablespoon plain flour
½ teaspoon white pepper
chopped parsley

1  Thoroughly clean and wash liver.
2  Cut each rasher of bacon into 2-3 pieces and dry fry in frying pan.
3  Place on absorbent paper in oven to keep hot.
4  Add a little dripping to pan and sauté onions.
5  Remove from pan.
6  Fry liver and keep hot with bacon and onions.
7  Make a little gravy and pour over ingredients in oven on serving dish.
8  Garnish with chopped parsley.

# CREAMED SWEETBREADS

*20 minutes cooking time*

*Ingredients for 4-5 servings*

500 g (1 lb) sweetbreads
2 tablespoons butter
4 tablespoons plain flour
½ teaspoon salt

2 cups milk
2 tablespoons sherry
¼ teaspoon white pepper

1  Soak sweetbreads in water for 1 hour.
2  Place in saucepan and cover with water.
3  Simmer for 15 minutes.
4  Remove fat and skin.
5  Melt butter in separate saucepan and stir in flour.
6  Add milk and bring to the boil, stirring.
7  Simmer for 3 minutes, add chopped sweetbreads and sherry and season with salt and pepper.

# LIVER IN CREAM

*30 minutes cooking time*

*Ingredients for 4-5 servings*

500 g (1 lb) liver, cut in half
1 tablespoon shallots, minced
½ teaspoon salt
1 cup whipped cream

60 g (¼ cup) butter
¼ teaspoon white pepper
1 jigger cognac
chopped parsley

1　Sauté livers in butter along with shallots.
2　Season with salt and pepper.
3　Pour over cognac.
4　Light and allow the flames to die.
5　Add cream and cook. Sprinkle with chopped parsley.
6　Serve immediately.

# LIVER IN MADEIRA

*20 minutes cooking time*

*Ingredients for 4-5 servings*

60 g (¼ cup) butter
¼ teaspoon white pepper
2 tablespoons plain flour
½ cup Madeira wine

500 g (1 lb) liver
½ teaspoon salt
½ cup beef stock
½ cup sour cream

1　Melt butter and sauté liver pieces.
2　Cook gently.
3　Season with salt and pepper.
4　Remove and place on serving dish.
5　Add flour to the pan and stir.
6　Gradually add stock and wine.
7　Add sour cream and stir until smooth.
8　Pour sauce over meat and serve immediately.

# CHICKEN LIVERS AND RICE

*10 minutes cooking time*

*Ingredients for 4-5 servings*

500 g (1 lb) chicken livers
3 onions, chopped
2 teaspoons butter

chicken fat
1 cup cooked rice

1 Trim livers.
2 Melt chicken fat and sauté onion.
3 Fry chicken livers for 10 minutes.
4 Add to prepared rice with onions and serve.
5 Garnish with lemon wedges if desired.

# LIVER SAVOURIES

*10 minutes cooking time*

*Ingredients for 4 servings*

**500 g (1 lb) liver**
**4 mushrooms**

**4 rashers bacon**
**½ teaspoon salt**

1 Prepare liver and divide into 4 pieces.
2 Roll up each piece in bacon rasher and skewer together.
3 Place under griller and place mushroom on top of each skewer.
4 Serve on buttered toast and garnish with parsley.

# CRUMBED SWEETBREADS

*40 minutes cooking time*

*Ingredients for 4-5 servings*

**3 pairs sweetbreads**
**chopped parsley**
**1 stalk celery, chopped**
**½ teaspoon salt**

**1 cup breadcrumbs**
**2 eggs**
**3 tablespoons butter**
**¼ teaspoon white pepper**

1 Soak sweetbreads in water for 1 hour.
2 Drain.
3 Place in saucepan with parsley, celery, salt and water.
4 Bring to the boil and reduce heat.
5 Simmer for 30 minutes.
6 Cool.
7 Take sweetbreads out and cut into serving pieces.
8 Dip into breadcrumbs, then into beaten eggs.
9 Fry in butter and serve immediately.

# DEEP-FRIED SWEETBREADS WITH MUSHROOMS

*20 minutes cooking time*

*Ingredients for 4-5 servings*

| | |
|---|---|
| 3 cups cooked chopped sweetbreads | 2 tablespoons lemon juice |
| 5 tablespoons chopped mushrooms | 2 tablespoons chopped parsley |
| ¼ teaspoon white pepper | 1 cup hot white sauce |
| 1 teaspoon salt | 2 eggs |
| ½ cup plain flour | 1 cup breadcrumbs |

1  Combine sweetbreads, mushrooms, salt, pepper, parsley and lemon juice with eggs and white sauce.
2  Set aside to cool.
3  Form into patties and roll in flour.
4  Dip into breadcrumbs, then egg.
5  Deep fry in fat and serve with white sauce.

# TRIPE IN ONION JUICE

*3½ hours cooking time*

*Ingredients for 4-5 servings*

| | |
|---|---|
| 1.5 kg (3 lb) tripe | 1 teaspoon salt |
| 2 tablespoons butter | ¼ teaspoon white pepper |
| 2 tablespoons plain flour | ½ cup onion juice |
| 2 cups milk | |

1  Soak tripe in water overnight.
2  Place in saucepan with cold salted water.
3  Bring to the boil.
4  Cover and reduce heat.
5  Simmer for 3 hours.
6  Drain and keep.
7  In another saucepan melt butter and slowly add flour.
8  Blend well and add milk. Bring to the boil, stirring.
9  Add salt, pepper, and onion juice. Stir constantly.
10  Pour over tripe and serve immediately.

# FRIED TRIPE

*3 hours cooking time*

*Ingredients for 4-5 servings*

| | |
|---|---|
| 1 kg (2 lb) tripe | 2 beaten eggs |
| ¼ cup plain flour | 1 cup breadcrumbs |
| ¼ teaspoon white pepper | ½ teaspoon salt |

1  Soak tripe overnight and clean.
2  Simmer for 3 hours in salted water.
3  When cooked, remove and cut into cubes.
4  Roll in flour and dip into eggs.
5  Roll in breadcrumbs and deep fry.
6  Serve immediately.

# TRIPE WITH BREADCRUMBS

*3 hours cooking time*

*Ingredients for 4-5 servings*

| | |
|---|---|
| 1 kg (2 lb) tripe, cut into 2 cm (1 in) pieces | milk |
| 3 onions, sliced | 3 tablespoons plain flour |
| ¼ teaspoon white pepper | ½ cup water |
| ½ teaspoon salt | 2 tablespoons chopped parsley |
| 500 g (1 lb) tomatoes | ½ cup breadcrumbs |

1  Wash tripe and place in saucepan with sliced onions.
2  Add salt to saucepan and cover.
3  Simmer for 2½ hours.
4  Add chopped tomatoes and simmer.
5  Strain liquid and make up to 3 cups with milk.
6  Mix flour and water, stand for 5 minutes, add to pan and blend thoroughly.
7  Return liquid to saucepan and place chopped parsley on top.
8  Bring to boil and season with salt and pepper.
9  Serve immediately with breadcrumbs sprinkled on top.

# TRIPE IN BATTER

*3½ hours cooking time*

*Ingredients for 4-5 servings*

| | |
|---|---|
| 1 kg (2 lb) tripe | 1 egg |
| 1½ cups plain flour | 1 teaspoon vinegar |
| ½ teaspoon salt | 3 tablespoons butter |
| ¼ teaspoon white pepper | ¼ cup water |

1  Soak tripe overnight and clean.
2  Simmer for 3 hours in salted water.
3  Cut tripe into 8 pieces and leave.
4  Combine flour, salt, pepper and water.
5  Add egg, vinegar, half butter and mix well.
6  Dip tripe into this mixture and sauté in remaining butter.

# TRIPE AND ONIONS

*3½ hours cooking time*

*Ingredients for 4-5 servings*

| | |
|---|---|
| 1 kg (2 lb) tripe | 1 teaspoon salt |
| 3 tablespoons butter | ¼ teaspoon white pepper |
| 4 tablespoons chopped onion | 1 teaspoon vinegar |

1  Soak tripe overnight and clean.
2  Simmer for 3 hours in salted water.
3  Cut tripe into pieces.
4  Sauté onion in butter and add tripe.
5  Sprinkle with salt, pepper and vinegar.
6  Serve immediately with buttered noodles.

# SAUTÉED KIDNEYS

*30 minutes cooking time*

*Ingredients for 5-6 servings*

| | |
|---|---|
| 9 lamb kidneys | 1 tablespoon butter |
| 1 teaspoon salt | 12 slices crisp bacon |
| ¼ teaspoon white pepper | 2 tablespoons plain flour |

1  Soak kidneys for 1 hour in water.
2  Drain.

3 Pour boiling water over them and drain.
4 Remove veins and slice.
5 Sprinkle with salt and pepper.
6 Coat in flour and fry in butter.
7 Turn constantly.
8 Serve immediately on toast with bacon.

# KIDNEYS IN MUSTARD SAUCE

*10 minutes cooking time*

*Ingredients for 4 servings*

| | |
|---|---|
| 2 kidneys | ½ cup dry white wine |
| plain flour | 2 teaspoons lemon juice |
| 155 g (5 oz) butter | ½ cup chopped parsley |
| 2 tablespoons chopped shallots | 4 teaspoons French mustard |

1 Prepare kidneys and slice thinly.
2 Roll in seasoned flour and sauté in butter.
3 Remove and place in warmed dish.
4 Add shallots to pan with mustard and cook for 2 minutes.
5 Add white wine and lemon juice.
6 Place kidneys back in pan with other ingredients and reduce heat.
7 Add parsley and cook for 1 minute.
8 Serve immediately with buttered noodles.

# KIDNEY SPONGE

*30 minutes cooking time*

*Ingredients for 4-5 servings*

| | |
|---|---|
| 1 kg (2 lb) round steak | 1 cup self-raising flour |
| 4 kidneys, chopped and cleaned | 2 eggs, separated |
| ½ teaspoon salt | 60 g (2 oz) butter |
| 1 cup milk | |

1 Cook steak and kidney as you normally would and keep hot.
2 Sift flour and salt into basin.
3 Beat egg yolks and stir in milk.
4 Pour into flour mixture and add butter.
5 Stir.
6 Beat egg whites and fold into mixture.
7 Pour over meat in saucepan and cover.
8 Boil for 20 minutes and serve immediately.

# KIDNEY AND BACON KEBAB

*10 minutes cooking time*

*Ingredients for 4-5 servings*

**14 lamb kidneys**
**1 cup claret**
**2 tablespoons olive oil**
**½ teaspoon salt**

**7 slices bacon, cut in half**
**5 tomatoes, sliced**
**¼ teaspoon white pepper**

1  Wipe kidneys and cut in half.
2  Combine claret and oil.
3  Thread kidneys, folded bacon and tomatoes on skewers.
4  Brush with wine and oil.
5  Place on griller and baste while cooking.

# BRAINS IN WHITE SAUCE

*20 minutes cooking time*

*Ingredients for 3-4 servings*

**6 sets brains**
**1 tablespoon vinegar**
**1 tablespoon salt**
**4 peppercorns**

**4 cloves**
**2 cloves garlic**
**2½ cups water**

1  Soak brains overnight and clean carefully.
2  Combine vinegar, salt, peppercorns, cloves, garlic and water.
3  Add brains and simmer for 2 minutes.
4  Bring to boil, then reduce heat, cook for 15 minutes.
5  Serve on warmed plate and pour white sauce over.

# PRESSED TONGUE

*3 hours cooking time*

*Ingredients for 4-5 servings*

**4-5 salted tongues**

1  Rinse tongue with fresh water and cook in boiling water for 2-3 hours.
2  Remove and put tongue into a round can or cake tin.
3  Pour over a little stock and put a plate on top.
4  Chill overnight.
5  Serve.

# OX TONGUE

*3 hours cooking time*

*Ingredients for 4-5 servings*

1 tongue
5 cups water
1 tablespoon salt
1 stalk celery
6 cloves

bouquet garni
1 carrot, diced
1 bay leaf
6 peppercorns
1 onion, sliced

1   Curl tongue and place in a saucepan.
2   Add water, salt, cloves, onion, carrot, bay leaf, celery and peppercorns.
3   Bring to the boil and cover.
4   Simmer for 3 hours.
5   Allow to cool and serve sliced.

# STUFFED BRISKET

*3 hours cooking time*

*Ingredients for 5-6 servings*

stuffing
1.5 kg (3 lb) piece of brisket
2 tablespoons butter
3 onions, chopped
¼ teaspoon white pepper

250 g (8 oz) tomatoes, skinned
   and peeled
150 ml (¼ pt) stock
½ teaspoon salt

1   Lay piece of meat out and spread with stuffing.
2   Roll up and secure.
3   Melt butter and sauté onions.
4   Add meat and tomatoes.
5   Pour stock over and season with salt and pepper.
6   Cover and simmer for 3 hours.
7   Serve with gravy.

# SOUR HEARTS

*2 hours cooking time*

*Ingredients for 4-6 servings*

2 calves' hearts
3 tablespoons butter
2 onions, chopped
3 tablespoons plain flour
2 cups water

1 teaspoon salt
4 tablespoons vinegar
1 tablespoon sugar
¼ teaspoon white pepper

1 Clean hearts and cut into half lengths.
2 Sauté in melted butter and add onions.
3 Add flour and brown.
4 Add remaining ingredients and bring to the boil.
5 Cover and simmer for 2 hours.
6 Serve with noodles.

# STEWED HEARTS

*2½ hours cooking time*

*Ingredients for 4-5 servings*

2 calves' hearts
1 onion, chopped
1 stalk celery, diced
1 teaspoon salt

¼ teaspoon white pepper
2 tablespoons butter
2 tablespoons plain flour

1 Clean and wash hearts.
2 Cube and place in saucepan with cold water.
3 Bring to the boil and reduce heat.
4 Simmer for 2 hours and add onion, celery, salt and pepper.
5 Cool.
6 Cook for further half hour and add butter and flour.
7 Bring to the boil, constantly stirring.
8 Serve immediately on buttered toast.

# BAKED HEARTS

*Ingredients for 4-5 servings*

*2½ hours cooking time*

2 calves' hearts
¼ teaspoon white pepper
4 tablespoons butter

2 large rashers of bacon
½ teaspoon salt
1 cup water

1  Preheat oven to 190°C (375°F).
2  Wash hearts and clean.
3  Wrap hearts in bacon and secure with toothpick.
4  Sauté in butter quickly.
5  Place in small baking dish and add water.
6  Bake for 2-2½ hours.

# BRAISED OXTAILS

*Ingredients for 4-5 servings*

*3 hours cooking time*

4 tablespoons butter
2 sliced carrots
1 onion, chopped
1 parsnip, chopped
1 stalk celery, chopped

2 tablespoons flour
3 oxtails
1 teaspoon salt
¼ teaspoon white pepper
2 cloves

1  Melt butter and sauté onion, carrot, and parsnip.
2  Add celery and cook for 2 minutes.
3  Stir in flour.
4  Cube oxtails and add them to pan.
5  Add salt, pepper, cloves and 2 cups of water.
6  Bring to the boil.
7  Reduce heat and simmer for 3 hours.
8  Serve immediately.

# KITCHEN GUIDE

A simple conversion chart for oven temperatures is given below. Remember that the simple rule of 20 minutes cooking time per pound of meat now converts to 45 minutes cooking time per kilogram.

## Oven Temperature Guide

| | Gas | | Electric | |
|---|---|---|---|---|
| | °C | °F | °C | °F |
| Low or cool | 95 | 200 | 95 | 200 |
| Very slow | 120 | 250 | 120 | 250 |
| Slow or warm | 150 | 300 | 150-160 | 300-325 |
| Moderately slow | 160 | 325 | 160-175 | 325-350 |
| Moderate | 175 | 350 | 175-190 | 350-375 |
| Moderately hot | 190 | 375 | 190-205 | 375-400 |
| Hot | 205 | 400 | 205-230 | 400-450 |
| Very hot | 230 | 450 | 230-260 | 450-500 |

Different makes of stoves, and sometimes even individual stoves of the same make may give varying results of a stated temperature, so if in doubt it is wise to consult the manufacturer's chart for oven settings. The guide given here is approximate, and only good for general use.

## Weights and Measures

### Imperial and American Systems

All solid and fluid measurements given in this book are metric with the old Australian Standard equivalent measurement in brackets. The American and Canadian measurements of *weight* are the same as the old Imperial measurements used in Britain and Australia, but measurements of volume differ. Approximate equivalents for the most commonly used measures are included in the following tables.

### Notes:

1. All spoon measurements used in the recipes in this book are *level*, unless otherwise stated.
2. *Never* mix metric and Imperial quantities within one recipe. Use *either* metric *or* Imperial.

## Liquid Measures

| | Australian Standard | | North American | |
|---|---|---|---|---|
| | Metric | Approx. Imperial Equiv. | Metric | Approx. Imperial Equiv. |
| 1 cup | 250 ml. | 8 fl. oz. | 170 ml. | 6 fl. oz. |
| 1 tablespoon | 30 ml | 1 fl. oz. | 15 ml. | ½ fl. oz. |
| 1 dessertspoon | 20 ml. | just below 1 fl. oz. | | |
| 1 teaspoon | 5 ml. | | 5 ml. | |
| 1 pint | 600 ml. | 20 fl. oz. | 45 ml. | 16 fl. oz. |
| ½ pint (1 gill) | 150 ml. | 5 fl. oz. | 120 ml. | 4 fl. oz. |

The American and Canadian pint equals four-fifths (i.e. 16 fluid ounces) of the old British Imperial pint (20 fluid ounces).

## Solid Measures

| Metric | Australian Standard and North American Equivalents | |
|---|---|---|
| 15 grams | ½ oz. | 1 tablespoon |
| 60 grams | 2 oz. | ½ cup |
| 90 grams | 3 oz. | |
| 125 grams | 4 oz. | 1 cup |
| 185 grams | 6 oz. | |
| 375 grams | 12 oz. | |
| 500 grams | 16 oz. (1 lb.) | 4 cups |
| 1 kilo | 2 lbs. | |

# CALORIE/KILOJOULE CHART

## Bread, Biscuits and Cakes

|  | Cal | Kj |
|---|---|---|
| 1 slice packaged bread | 80 | 320 |
| 1 small bread roll | 100 | 400 |
| 1 yeast bun | 140 | 560 |
| 1 wheatmeal biscuit | 42 | 168 |
| 1 plain dry biscuit | 25-40 | 100-160 |
| 1 plain sweet biscuit | 50 | 200 |
| Plain cake, 1 small slice | 180 | 720 |
| iced or filled | 300 | 1200 |
| Sponge cake, plain, 1 slice | 90 | 360 |
| iced and filled | 300 | 1200 |
| Fruit cake, 1 small slice | 165 | 660 |

## Cereals

(not including milk and sugar)

|  | Cal | Kj |
|---|---|---|
| Plain breakfast cereal, 30 g | 105 | 420 |
| Porridge, cooked, 1 cup | 200 | 800 |

## Dairy Products

|  | Cal | Kj |
|---|---|---|
| Butter, 30 g | 210 | 840 |
| Cheese, hard, 30 g | 120 | 480 |
| Cottage cheese, 30 g | 32 | 128 |
| Cream, 15 g | 50 | 200 |
| Milk, 1 cup | 150 | 600 |
| Skim milk, 1 cup | 75 | 300 |
| Yoghurt, 30 g | 25 | 100 |

## Desserts

|  | Cal | Kj |
|---|---|---|
| Apple pie, 1 slice | 330 | 1320 |
| Lemon meringue pie, 1 slice | 300 | 1200 |
| Custard (boiled), 5 tablespoons | 80 | 320 |
| Custard (baked), 1 serve | 150 | 600 |
| Fruit salad, ½ cup sweetened | 110 | 440 |
| Ice-cream, 1 portion | 80 | 320 |
| Jelly, 1 portion | 75 | 300 |

## Drinks

|  | Cal | Kj |
|---|---|---|
| Apple cider, 1 cup | 100 | 400 |
| Cocoa, 1 cup | 165 | 660 |
| Coffee (black) | 0 | 0 |
| Soda water | 0 | 0 |
| Tea (black) | 0 | 0 |
| Tonic water, 1 cup | 80 | 320 |

## Eggs

|  | Cal | Kj |
|---|---|---|
| Boiled (1) | 80 | 320 |
| Fried (1) | 120 | 480 |
| Omelette (1) | 125 | 500 |
| Poached (1) | 80 | 320 |
| Scrambled (1), with milk and butter | 125 | 500 |

## Fish

|  | Cal | Kj |
|---|---|---|
| Crab, crayfish, lobster 120 g | 120 | 480 |
| Fish, white, 120 g, grilled or steamed | 120 | 480 |
| fried in batter | 350 | 1400 |
| Fish, oily, 120 g grilled or steamed | 200 | 800 |
| fried in batter | 400 | 1600 |
| Oysters, 6 | 40 | 160 |
| Prawns, shelled, 30 g | 25 | 100 |
| Salmon, canned, 30 g | 40 | 160 |
| Tuna, canned in brine, 30 g | 30 | 120 |

## Fruit and Vegetable Juices (unsweetened)

| | Cal | Kj |
|---|---|---|
| Apple, ½ cup | 100 | 400 |
| Apricot, ½ cup | 75 | 300 |
| Carrot, ½ cup | 25 | 100 |
| Grape, ½ cup | 60 | 240 |
| Grapefruit, ½ cup | 45 | 180 |
| Orange, ½ cup | 55 | 220 |
| Pineapple, ½ cup | 60 | 240 |
| Tomato, ½ cup | 25 | 100 |

(Diabetic fruit juices have no extra sugar added and are equal to fresh fruit juices.)

## Fresh Fruit

| | Cal | Kj |
|---|---|---|
| Apple, medium | 80 | 320 |
| Apricot, medium | 20 | 80 |
| Avocado, ½ medium | 160 | 640 |
| Banana, medium | 100 | 400 |
| Blackberries, 1 cup | 80 | 320 |
| Cantaloupe, ½ medium | 30 | 120 |
| Cherries, 1 cup | 60 | 240 |
| Figs, 3 medium | 60 | 240 |
| Gooseberries, 1 cup | 60 | 240 |
| Grapefruit, ½ medium | 70 | 280 |
| Grapes, 1 cup | 100 | 400 |
| Honeydew melon, ½ medium | 45 | 180 |
| Lemon, medium | 25 | 100 |
| Mandarin, medium | 40 | 100 |
| Orange, medium | 70 | 280 |
| Passionfruit, 1 | 20 | 80 |
| Peach, medium | 50 | 200 |
| Pear, medium | 85 | 340 |
| Pineapple, 1 slice | 40 | 160 |
| Plum, medium | 30 | 120 |
| Raspberries, 1 cup | 80 | 320 |
| Rockmelon, ½ medium | 30 | 120 |
| Strawberries, 1 cup | 60 | 240 |
| Watermelon, 1 slice | 50 | 200 |

## Meat and Poultry

| | Cal | Kj |
|---|---|---|
| Bacon, grilled, 2 rashers | 125 | 500 |
| Beef, roast, av. portion | 140 | 560 |
| Chicken, 30 g | 55 | 220 |
| Corned beef, 60 g | 135 | 540 |
| Duck, 30 g | 70 | 280 |
| Frankfurt, 1 | 145 | 580 |
| Ham, 60 g | 230 | 920 |
| Hamburger or rissole, 30 g | 90 | 360 |
| Kidneys, 60 g | 110 | 440 |

| | Cal | Kj |
|---|---|---|
| Lamb chop, 1 grilled | 130 | 520 |
| Lamb cutlet, 1 small grilled | 65 | 260 |
| Lamb, roast, 100 g | 300 | 1200 |
| Mince steak, 100 g | 300 | 1200 |
| Pork chop, 1, 100 g | 285 | 1140 |
| Pork, roast, 100 g | 285 | 1140 |
| Sausage roll, small | 100 | 400 |
| Steak, grilled, 100 g | 255 | 1020 |
| Tripe, 120 g | 60 | 240 |
| Turkey, 30 g | 70 | 280 |
| Veal, roast, 100 g | 160 | 640 |

## Vegetables

| | Cal | Kj |
|---|---|---|
| Asparagus, ½ cup | 20 | 80 |
| Aubergine (eggplant), ½ cup | 30 | 120 |
| Beetroot, ½ cup | 60 | 240 |
| Broad beans, ½ cup | 80 | 320 |
| Broccoli, ½ cup | 30 | 120 |
| Brussels sprouts, ½ cup | 30 | 120 |
| Cabbage, ½ cup | 20 | 80 |
| Carrots, ½ cup | 30 | 120 |
| Cauliflower, ½ cup | 20 | 80 |
| Celery, 1 stalk | 3 | 12 |
| Corn on the cob | 145 | 580 |
| Cucumber, medium | 10 | 40 |
| Lettuce, 1 portion | 5 | 20 |
| Marrow, ½ cup | 5 | 20 |
| Mushrooms, ½ cup | 30 | 120 |
| Onion, ½ cup | 30 | 120 |
| Peas, ½ cup | 50 | 200 |
| Peppers, green | 10 | 40 |
| Potato, boiled, 1 medium | 100 | 400 |
| Potato chips, fried, 8 chips | 220 | 880 |
| Pumpkin, ½ cup | 50 | 200 |
| Radishes, 6 | 10 | 40 |
| Spinach, ½ cup | 30 | 80 |
| Tomato, medium | 30 | 120 |

## Miscellaneous

| | Cal | Kj |
|---|---|---|
| Chocolate, 60 g | 300 | 1200 |
| Gravy (thick), 4 table-spoons | 80 | 320 |
| Honey, 1 level dessert-spoon | 60 | 240 |
| Jam, 1 level dessertspoon | 55 | 220 |
| Peanut butter, 1 level dessertspoon | 100 | 400 |
| Sugar, 1 teaspoon | 25 | 100 |

# Index

# CASSEROLE & STEW

# Contents

# Introduction

## CASSEROLES

Casserole meals are popular for three main reasons: they can be prepared ahead of time; they cook without constant attention; and they are quick and easy to serve.

Casseroles are based on a blending of the flavours of the ingredients, and most casseroles improve by being prepared in advance. Many can be fixed long before needed and frozen until used. Others lend themselves to being cooked a day in advance and refrigerated until reheated to serve. Casseroles are also excellent for last-minute meals: many can be prepared from ingredients generally in the cupboard, and can be extended to feed almost any number.

The slow cooking required for many casseroles means that they are an excellent way to utilize less expensive (and less tender) cuts of meat, which will become as tender and tasty as the most expensive steak when cooked slowly for a long time. Casseroles are an ideal way of using leftovers; combined with other ingredients they can present a 'new' meal.

Many casseroles contain all the necessary ingredients for a balanced meal —meat, vegetables and sauce—and can be served with a simple salad or crusty bread, thus relieving the cook of last-minute attention to vegetables, etc. Other casseroles (such as vegetable combinations) are designed to provide the accompaniment for simple meat dishes such as roasts or grills.

Casseroles should be served in the containers in which they are cooked; with the large number of attractive ovenproof dishes now available, it should be easy to find one with the right colour, shape and size for your personal preference.

The best part of a casserole, of course, is that it cooks itself once all the ingredients are combined (which may be well in advance of cooking), all you have to do is relax and let it cook in the oven or on the stove while you enjoy your guests or family.

# Poultry

## CHICKEN POT PIE

*20 minutes cooking time*

*Ingredients for 4 servings*

315 g (10 oz) cooked chicken,
 chopped
½ teaspoon pepper
2 cups chicken stock
1 egg, beaten
1 stick celery, chopped
2 tablespoons sherry
60 g (2 oz) butter

1 teaspoon salt
250 g (8 oz) puff pastry
60 g (2 oz) flour
¾ cup milk
185 g (6 oz) mushrooms, sliced
30 g (1 oz) blanched almonds
¼ teaspoon nutmeg

1   Roll out pastry to fit 5-cup casserole.
2   Place on baking tray and cut into 4 triangles. Brush with beaten egg and
    leave to cool.
3   Melt butter and add flour. Stir over low heat and gradually add chicken
    stock and milk. Cook until sauce boils and thickens.
4   Add chicken, almonds, mushrooms, celery, sherry, salt, pepper and
    nutmeg.
5   Cover and cook in pan for 5 minutes. Turn into casserole dish and
    arrange pastry triangles on top. Cook for 10 minutes in hot oven 230°C
    (450°F).

# STEAMED CHICKEN MOULD

*40 minutes cooking time*

*Ingredients for 4-5 servings*

| | |
|---|---|
| 1 cup cooked buttered rice | 2 cups chopped chicken |
| 1 tablespoon butter | ½ cup breadcrumbs |
| 1 beaten egg | ½ cup chicken stock |
| 1 teaspoon salt | ½ teaspoon pepper |
| 2 tablespoons chopped parsley | 1 onion, minced |

1  Butter a pudding mould and line it with rice.
2  Combine chopped chicken and butter.
3  Add breadcrumbs, beaten egg and chicken stock.
4  Season with salt and pepper. Add chopped parsley and minced onion.
5  Mix well and put into mould.
6  Top with a layer of rice and cover with greaseproof paper. Steam for 40 minutes and turn onto serving dish.

# STUFFED POT-COOKED CHICKEN

*2¼ hours cooking time*

*Ingredients for 6 servings*

| | |
|---|---|
| 2 kg (5 lb) chicken | 1 teaspoon salt |
| ½ teaspoon pepper | 1 veal knuckle |
| 2 eggs | 2 chopped carrots |
| ½ teaspoon tarragon | 2 peeled potatoes |
| 2 chopped turnips | 1 onion with 2 cloves inserted |
| 4 cabbage leaves | 125 g (4 oz) breadcrumbs |
| bouquet garni | 125 g (4 oz) pork |
| 125 g (4 oz) bacon | ¼ cup milk |
| 3 cloves garlic | 4 tablespoons chopped parsley |

1  Place wings, gizzard, heart, neck and feet of chicken with veal knuckles, vegetables, salt, pepper, bouquet garni and 15 cups of water in saucepan and bring to boil. Simmer for 1 hour, covered.
2  Mince chicken liver, bacon, pork, and garlic. Moisten breadcrumbs with milk and combine with meat. Add spices, parsley, eggs, salt and pepper.
3  Mix well and use this to stuff chicken. Poach, covered in stock, until tender.

# NORTH WALES CHICKEN PIE

*2 hours cooking time*

*Ingredients for 4 servings*

| | |
|---|---|
| **1.5 kg (3 lb) chicken** | **8 small leeks** |
| **4 sliced boiled tongues** | **4 tablespoons cream** |
| **2 tablespoons chopped parsley** | **1½ teaspoons salt** |
| **½ teaspoon mixed herbs** | **2 sticks celery, chopped** |
| **1 onion, quartered** | **1 bay leaf** |

## PASTRY

| | |
|---|---|
| **185 g (6 oz) flour** | **3 tablespoons dripping** |
| **150 ml (¼ pt) boiling water** | |

1  Place chicken in a saucepan, cover with water and bring to boil. Skim and add onion, celery, bay leaf, mixed herbs and salt.
2  Simmer for 1½ hours and remove; strain stock into a basin and cool.
3  Remove the green part of the leeks and scald the white part in boiling water.
4  Split leeks into 2.5 centimetre (1 in) lengths. Joint chicken and lay pieces in pie dish and top with slices of cold tongue.
5  Add leeks, parsley and moisten with chicken stock.
6  Sieve the flour into a basin and make a well in the centre. Add dripping which has been mixed with boiling water. Knead to correct consistency and roll out on a floured board.
7  Cover pie, leaving a small hole in the centre.
8  Bake in hot oven 220°C (425°F) until brown; remove and pour warmed cream through the opening in pie.

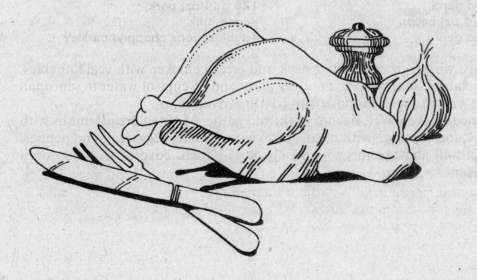

# BRISTOL CHICKEN

*1 hour 20 minutes cooking time*

*Ingredients for 4 servings*

| | |
|---|---|
| 1 kg (2 lb) chicken | 2½ cups chicken stock |
| ¼ teaspoon pepper | ½ teaspoon salt |
| 1 onion, sliced | 150 ml (½ cup) sour cream |
| 4 peppercorns | ½ teaspoon thyme |
| rind of 1 lemon | 45 g (1½ oz) flour |
| 1 tablespoon chopped parsley | 2½ cups water |
| 45 g (1½ oz) butter | ½ tablespoon curry powder |

1  Thinly slice lemon rind.
2  Place water, salt, lemon rind, parsley, thyme, peppercorns, onion, and chicken in saucepan.
3  Cover and cook for 10 minutes.
4  Remove to casserole dish and cover. Bake for 1 hour.
5  Remove chicken and strain stock. Remove meat from chicken and cut into strips.
6  Melt butter and stir in flour and curry powder, cook for 2 minutes.
7  Add chicken stock and return to heat, stir in sour cream.
8  Pour over chicken and serve.

# CHINESE CHICKEN

*30 minutes cooking time*

*Ingredients for 8 servings*

| | |
|---|---|
| 2 1.5-kg (3-lb) chickens | 8 tablespoons chicken stock |
| ½ teaspoon pepper | 1 teaspoon salt |
| 2 tablespoons sugar | 6 tablespoons soy sauce |
| 7.5 cm (3 in) fresh ginger, shredded | 5 tablespoons sherry |
| 20 dried mushrooms | 7 teaspoons sesame oil |
| 3 tablespoons oil | ½ cup chopped spring onions |

1  Chop chickens into pieces without removing bones.
2  Season with salt, soy sauce, pepper, sugar, ginger and sherry.
3  Marinate for 1 hour.
4  Soak mushrooms in hot water for 20 minutes.
5  In deep bowl, combine chicken and marinating liquid, and mushrooms.
6  Pour over peanut oil, sesame oil and stock.
7  Steam for 30 minutes and sprinkle with spring onions.

# FRUITY CHICKEN

*Ingredients for 6 servings*

*1 hour 20 minutes cooking time*

1 chicken, cut into pieces
1 slice lemon rind
1¼ cups white wine
½ teaspoon pepper
1 red pepper
4 pears, peeled, cored and sliced

3 tablespoons oil
1¼ cups chicken stock
1 teaspoon salt
1 tin prunes
3 tablespoons flour

1   Strain prunes and reserve syrup.
2   Brown chicken in oil and place in ovenproof dish. Sauté red pepper and add to dish.
3   Add pear slices and prunes. Thicken juices with flour and add stock, wine and water, some of the prune syrup and lemon rind.
4   Season and pour into casserole; cover and cook for 1 hour in moderate oven 190°C (375°F).

# CREAMY CHICKEN

*Ingredients for 4 servings*

*1½ hours cooking time*

1 1.25-kg (2½-lb) chicken
1 onion
4 peppercorns
2 tablespoons chopped parsley
rind of 1 lemon, thinly peeled
1 teaspoon salt
¼ teaspoon pepper
¼ teaspoon thyme

1½ tablespoons butter
1½ tablespoons flour
¾ tablespoon curry powder
½ teaspoon salt
2 cups chicken stock
½ cup sour cream
1½ tablespoons redcurrant jelly
2½ cups water

1   Place onion, chicken, parsley, peppercorns, thyme, pepper, lemon rind, salt and water in saucepan.
2   Cover and bring to boil, simmer for 1 hour and remove chicken. Strain and cut into cubes.
3   To make sauce, melt butter and add flour, curry powder and a little salt, cook for 2 minutes and draw to one side, slowly add chicken stock beating well.
4   Return to heat and bring to boil; when it has thickened, stir in sour cream and redcurrant jelly.
5   Put chicken in casserole, pour sauce over and bake in moderate oven for 20 minutes.

# ANGOLAN CHICKEN

*1 hour 45 minutes cooking time*

*Ingredients for 8 servings*

8 chicken breasts
3 chopped onions
4 tablespoons chopped parsley
½ teaspoon pepper
1½ cups washed rice

4 tablespoons butter
3 chopped carrots
1½ teaspoons salt
½ cup sliced paprika sausage

1 Place onions and carrots with parsley in a casserole dish.
  Season with salt and pepper.
2 Melt butter and sauté chicken pieces until brown.
3 Put chicken in casserole; add 3 cups water to pan drippings and pour over chicken.
4 Add rice and bake for 1 hour in moderate oven 190°C (375°F), covered.
5 Top with sausage and brown for 20 minutes.
6 Garnish with chopped parsley.

# BASIC CHICKEN CASSEROLE

*1½ hours cooking time*

*Ingredients for 6 servings*

1.5 kg (3 lb) chicken
24 button onions
¼ teaspoon pepper
2 cups giblet stock

60 g (2 oz) butter
250 g (8 oz) carrots, quartered
½ teaspoon salt
315 g (10 oz) frozen peas

1 Remove giblets from chicken and simmer in a little water to make the stock.
2 Heat butter in pan and fry chicken until brown.
3 Remove and place in casserole. Arrange onions and carrots around chicken. Season with salt and pepper.
4 Pour over stock and cover.
5 Bake for 1 hour at 190°C (375°F), add peas and mushrooms and cook for 20 minutes longer.

# WALLOON CHICKEN

*Ingredients for 4-5 servings*

*1½ hours cooking time*

1.5 kg (3 lb) chicken
1 calf's sweetbread
1 onion
2 cloves
½ teaspoon mixed herbs
1½ teaspoons salt

1 kg (2 lb) knuckle of veal
5 carrots
4 sticks celery
1 bay leaf
½ teaspoon pepper

## SAUCE

5 tablespoons butter
½ cup mushroom stock
½ teaspoon pepper
2 tablespoons Madeira
1 cup cream

1 cup chicken stock
½ teaspoon salt
5 egg yolks
3 tablespoons flour

1  Place knuckle of veal in a large casserole dish and cover with cold water.
2  Bring to boil and add sliced carrots, onion and celery. Stir and add herbs and seasonings.
3  Simmer for 45 minutes and add chicken and sweetbread.
4  Remove sweetbread as soon as tender and cut into cubes. Keep warm.
5  Combine half the butter with the flour and add hot chicken stock. Stir and simmer over a low heat for 30 minutes.
6  Mix yolks in basin with cream, remaining butter, Madeira and a little mushroom liquid.
7  Season with salt and pepper and beat thoroughly.
8  Add to sauce and keep on beating until sauce comes to boil.
9  Strain and place in a clean saucepan. Add sweetbreads and place chicken on hot serving dish. Pour sauce over.

# PYRENEES CHICKEN

*1¼ hours cooking time*

*Ingredients for 4 servings*

1.5 kg (3 lb) chicken
½ cup olive oil
2 red peppers
¼ teaspoon saffron
500 g (1 lb) long-grain rice
3 large onions
½ teaspoon pepper

250 g (8 oz) lean pork
4 tomatoes
4 cups stock
½ cup sherry
3 cloves garlic
1 teaspoon salt

1  Cut chicken into pieces and pork into small cubes.
2  Heat oil in shallow frying pan and brown chicken and pork.
3  Remove and place in casserole dish.
4  Chop onions and garlic, fry in oil.
5  Add rice and bay leaf and cook for 2 minutes. Add sliced tomatoes and peppers. Cook for a further 2-3 minutes and pour mixture over chicken.
6  Add boiling stock, sherry and saffron; cook in moderate oven for approximately 1 hour.

# HERBED CHICKEN

*1 hour 15 minutes cooking time*

*Ingredients for 6 servings*

6 chicken breasts
3 tablespoons olive oil
2 chopped onions
1 tablespoon flour
2 cups chicken stock

3 tablespoons tomato sauce
1 teaspoon salt
½ teaspoon pepper
2 teaspoons dried mixed herbs
250 g (8 oz) long-grain rice

1  Heat oil and fry chicken breasts until brown.
2  Place in casserole and fry chopped onions for 5 minutes, stir in flour and cook for 1 minute.
3  Gradually add stock, tomato sauce and herbs and bring to boil, stirring continuously.
4  Season and pour over chicken.
5  Cover and cook for 50 minutes in moderate oven.
6  Cook rice in boiling salted water until tender and serve under chicken.

# CHICKEN WITH MUSHROOMS

*1 hour 10 minutes cooking time*

*Ingredients for 4 servings*

1.5 kg (3 lb) chicken
6 tablespoons butter
1 teaspoon paprika
½ teaspoon pepper
¼ cup flour

½ cup dry white wine
1½ teaspoons salt
¼ teaspoon thyme
2 cups sliced mushrooms

1  Melt butter in baking dish and stir in thyme, paprika, salt and pepper.
2  Dredge pieces of chicken in flour and swish in butter.
3  Arrange in baking dish and bake in hot oven 220°C (425°F) for 30 minutes.
4  Reduce heat to 180°C (350°F) and turn over chicken. Add wine.
5  Spread mushrooms over top and cover dish with foil. Bake for a further 30 minutes and serve.


# APPLE CHICKEN

*1 hour cooking time*

*Ingredients for 4 servings*

1 kg (2 lb) chicken pieces
45 g (1½ oz) butter
1 onion, chopped
1 green pepper, deseeded and chopped
2 tablespoons chopped parsley
2 apples, peeled and chopped
¼ teaspoon pepper

125 g (4 oz) seasoned flour
¾ can condensed cream of chicken soup
125 g (4 oz) long-grain rice
1 teaspoon salt
pinch of thyme
1¼ cups water
¼ teaspoon paprika

1  Coat chicken in seasoned flour and fry in butter for 15 minutes.
2  In saucepan, combine chicken soup, parsley, onion, salt, thyme, pepper, paprika, apples and a little saffron.
3  Cook for 2 minutes and add water and rice to mixture, transfer to casserole with chicken.
4  Cook 40 minutes in moderate oven 180°C (350°F).

# WALNUT CHICKEN

*2½ hours cooking time*

*Ingredients for 5 servings*

2 kg (4 lb) chicken
1 teaspoon salt
2 cups shelled walnuts
2 tablespoons chopped parsley
15 cups water

½ teaspoon pepper
1 tablespoon paprika
3 slices white bread
1 carrot
2 onions

1   Place chicken in pot with water and onion.
2   Add carrot, parsley and salt. Cover and cook for 2 hours. When tender, remove and cool.
3   Remove skin and bones, cool and cut flesh into small pieces.
    Place walnuts through mincer twice and then add paprika.
4   Press nuts and paprika between double layers of cheesecloth to get about 2 tablespoons red oil for garnishing.
5   Soak bread in chicken stock and squeeze dry. Add walnuts and paprika. Mix well.
6   Place this mixture through mincer and add 1 cup of chicken stock. Work into a paste.
7   Divide paste in half and mix one half with minced chicken. Spread other half over chicken mixture and decorate with red walnut oil.
8   Serve cold.

# KOOLIGA CASSEROLE

*2 hours cooking time*

*Ingredients for 8 servings*

500 g (1 lb) carrots
1 teaspoon salt
2½ cups chicken stock
500 g (1 lb) tomatoes
90 g (3 oz) dripping

4 onions
2 kg (4 lb) chicken
½ teaspoon pepper
90 g (3 oz) flour

1   Peel and slice carrots and onions.
2   Sauté in dripping for 5 minutes and add tomatoes.
3   Blend flour with stock and add to pan.
4   Bring to boil and stir for 10 minutes, and season.
5   Cut chicken into joints, place in ovenproof dish with vegetable mixture and cook for 1¾ hours in moderate oven.

# SCONE-TOPPED CHICKEN

*20-25 minutes cooking time*

*Ingredients for 6 servings*

2 tablespoons butter
2½ cups chicken stock
3 tablespoons cream
60 g (2 oz) Parmesan cheese

2 tablespoons plain flour
500 g (1 lb) cooked chicken, cut into
  pieces
2 tablespoons sherry

## SCONES

1½ teaspoons salt
315 g (10 oz) self-raising flour
1 teaspoon dry mustard
2 eggs, beaten

90 g (3 oz) butter
3 tablespoons cream
¼ teaspoon pepper

1  Melt butter and add flour, cook for 1 minute, stirring, and remove from heat.
2  Stir in chicken stock and cook for 2-3 minutes or until sauce thickens.
3  Add chicken and seasonings, sherry and cream and turn into casserole dish, top with cheese.
4  Sift flour, salt, mustard, and pepper and rub in butter.
5  Mix with egg and milk. Turn onto floured board and knead. Roll out to 5 millimetre (¼ in) thickness and cut into rounds.
6  Arrange on top of chicken mixture and brush with beaten egg. Bake in hot oven 230°C (450°F) for 15-20 minutes.

# TARRAGON CHICKEN

*50-60 minutes cooking time*

*Ingredients for 4-5 servings*

1.5 kg (3 lb) chicken
2 teaspoons tarragon
1½ teaspoons salt
300 g (10 oz) cream of chicken soup

2 chopped onions
¼ teaspoon pepper
¼ cup milk
½ cup almonds, sliced

1  Arrange chicken in baking dish, skin side up.
2  Scatter onions over chicken and add tarragon, salt and pepper.
3  Mix soup with milk and spoon over chicken.
4  Bake uncovered in a moderate oven for 40 minutes and sprinkle with almonds.
5  Cook for further 10-20 minutes.

# CARIBBEAN CHICKEN

*1½ hours cooking time*

*Ingredients for 4 servings*

| | |
|---|---|
| **1.5 kg (3 lb) chicken** | **3 tablespoons butter** |
| **4 chopped spring onions** | **¼ cup chopped ham** |
| **3 green bananas** | **½ teaspoon pepper** |
| **2 tablespoons chopped parsley** | **1 teaspoon salt** |

1  Brown jointed chicken in butter.
2  Add chopped spring onions and ham.
3  Transfer to greased casserole, cover and bake in moderate oven 180°C (350°F) for 1 hour.
4  Peel bananas, halve lengthwise, then crosswise and simmer in boiling water until tender.
5  Drain and add to chicken, uncover and bake 15 minutes longer.
6  Garnish with chopped parsley and serve.


# ORANGE CHICKEN

*1 hour cooking time*

*Ingredients for 6 servings*

| | |
|---|---|
| **1½ tablespoons cornflour** | **90 g (3 oz) peanuts, chopped** |
| **6 chicken breasts** | **1 teaspoon tarragon** |
| **1½ tablespoons curacao** | **1 teaspoon salt** |
| **½ teaspoon pepper** | **3 tablespoons corn oil** |
| **2 cups white sauce** | **1¾ cups milk** |
| **315 g (10 oz) mandarin sections** | **½ cup mandarin juice** |

1  Coat chicken with seasoned cornflour.
2  Heat oil and brown chicken and remove to casserole.
3  Combine white sauce and mandarin juice with tarragon and curacao.
4  Pour over chicken and bake for 50 minutes in moderate oven 180°C (350°F).
5  Add mandarins and sprinkle with peanuts. Cook for further 10 minutes and serve.

# BUCHAREST CHICKEN

*2 hours cooking time*

*Ingredients for 6 servings*

6 chicken breasts
315 g (10 oz) onions, chopped
1½ tablespoons paprika
1 teaspoon sugar
1 bay leaf

4 tablespoons seasoned flour
2½ tablespoons butter
1¼ cups tomato juice
1 teaspoon salt
185 g (6 oz) sour cream

## DUMPLINGS

250 g (8 oz) self-raising flour
½ teaspoon garlic salt
2 tablespoons chopped parsley
1 egg, beaten

3 tablespoons cold water
1 teaspoon salt
2 tablespoons corn oil

1 Skin and coat chicken joints in seasoned flour.
2 Fry onions in butter and move to one side of pan.
3 Add chicken and fry. Combine paprika, salt, tomato juice, sugar and pour over chicken. Add bay leaf, and transfer to casserole dish.
4 Bake in moderate oven 190°C (375°F) for 2 hours.
5 Stir sour cream into sauce and reheat.
6 Sift flour and garlic salt together and add parsley.
7 Mix with oil, water and egg. Roll onto floured board and roll to 1 centimetre (½ in) thickness. Cut dough into wide strips and chop each strip into fine pieces.
8 Drop into boiling water and cook for 6-8 minutes. Drain and serve with chicken.

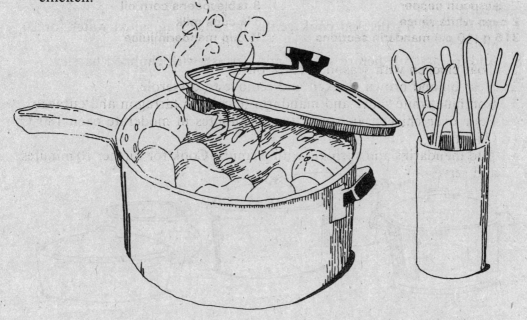

# MILANESE CHICKEN AND DUMPLINGS

*2 hours cooking time*

*Ingredients for 6 servings*

**6 chicken breasts**
**2 tablespoons chopped parsley**
**1½ tablespoons butter**
**3 sticks celery, chopped**
**½ lemon, sliced**
**185 g (6 oz) peas**
**½ teaspoon pepper**

**185 g (6 oz) carrots**
**90 g (3 oz) flour**
**3 onions, chopped**
**4 cups water**
**1 bay leaf**
**1½ teaspoons salt**
**1 cup sour cream**

## DUMPLINGS

**125 g (4 oz) self-raising flour**
**½ teaspoon salt**
**½ teaspoon oregano**

**1 tablespoon chopped parsley**
**45 g (1½ oz) shredded suet**
**1 tablespoon tomato purée**

1  Coat chicken in seasoned flour and fry in butter with onions and celery.
2  Stir in remaining flour and remove from heat, add water, stir and bring to boil.
3  Place in casserole and add lemon slices and bay leaf.
4  Cook for 1½ hours in moderate oven 180°C (350°F). Remove lemon slices and bay leaf and add carrots and peas.
5  Pour in sour cream mixed with a little water.
6  Sift flour, salt and oregano together, add suet and blend tomato purée with 3 tablespoons cold water and stir. Mix well and turn on to floured board.
7  Divide into 6 balls and cook gently in simmering salted water for 20 minutes.
8  Add to casserole before serving and garnish with chopped parsley.

# ASPARAGUS TURKEY

*30 minutes cooking time*

*Ingredients for 5-6 servings*

| | |
|---|---|
| 2½ cups diced turkey | 2 tins asparagus |
| 2 cups hot white sauce | ½ cup mayonnaise |
| 3 cups hot cooked rice | |

1 Cut asparagus into 2.5 centimetre (1 in) lengths.
2 Grease a shallow casserole dish and arrange half the turkey in a layer.
3 Cover with asparagus and top with remaining turkey.
4 Stir mayonnaise into white sauce and cool.
5 Spoon sauce over turkey.
6 Bake uncovered in a hot oven for 20-30 minutes. Serve with rice.

# TURKEY AND NOODLES

*40 minutes cooking time*

*Ingredients for 4 servings*

| | |
|---|---|
| 185 g (6 oz) wide noodles | 1 cup sour cream |
| 3 tablespoons butter | 4 tablespoons flour |
| 1 cup chicken stock | 2 cups diced turkey |
| ½ cup chopped pimentos | 1 teaspoon salt |
| 125 g (4 oz) sliced mushrooms | 2½ cups oysters, drained |
| ½ teaspoon pepper | |

1 Cook noodles as directed and drain, mix with ½ cup of sour cream.
2 Melt butter in pan and blend in flour.
3 Gradually stir in stock and cook until thickened. Stir constantly.
4 Blend in remaining sour cream and stir into noodles with the turkey.
5 Add pimentos, mushrooms, salt and pepper.
6 Turn half of the mixture into a casserole dish and arrange oysters on top.
7 Cover with remaining noodle mixture and bake uncovered for 30 minutes.

# ANTWERP GOOSE

*2 hours cooking time*

*Ingredients for 4-5 servings*

| | |
|---|---|
| 1 goose | 3 onions |
| 1¼ cups cream | 1½ teaspoons salt |
| 3 cloves | 4 peppercorns |
| ½ teaspoon pepper | 4 cups milk |
| 12 cloves garlic | 3 carrots |
| 4 rusks | 6 egg yolks |

1   Place goose in a saucepan with giblets and cover with salted warm water.
2   Bring to boil and skim.
3   Add sliced vegetables and herbs. Şimmer until tender and remove from saucepan.
4   Carve into pieces and place a little goose fat in frying pan. Brown pieces.
5   Place milk in a saucepan with skinned garlic cloves and simmer until garlic is tender.
6   Remove garlic from milk and add rusks to sauce.
7   Stir and dissolve rusks in milk.
8   Strain the sauce and beat egg yolks with cream and a little hot milk.
9   Add this mixture to milk and stir for 2-3 mintues over low heat.
10  Pour over goose and garnish with garlic cloves.

# Seafood

## FISH MOUSSE

*1 hour 10 minutes cooking time*

*Ingredients for 4 servings*

1 kg (2 lb) cod, minced
¼ cup dried breadcrumbs
250 g (8 oz) butter
1 teaspoon salt
½ teaspoon pepper

½ cup flour
1 tablespoon potato flour
4 eggs
½ teaspoon allspice
2 cups milk

1  Melt butter.
2  Grease tube tin and coat generously with breadcrumbs. Sieve flour and potato flour.
3  Mix minced fish with melted butter and beat.
4  Beat in egg yolks and sprinkle with sifted flour, salt, pepper, spice and stir in.
5  Gradually add milk and stiffly beaten egg whites.
6  Turn the mixture into prepared tin and place in large pan of boiling water. Place in moderate oven for 1 hour and cook.
7  Remove from pan and stand for 5 minutes. Carefully loosen edges with spatula and serve.

# CIDER FISH

*45 minutes cooking time*

*Ingredients for 6 servings*

3 fillets white fish
3 fillets smoked haddock
1¼ cups cider vinegar
¼ teaspoon chopped celery
2 chopped tomatoes

185 g (6 oz) champignons
1 chopped onion
1 teaspoon salt
½ teaspoon pepper

1 Cut fish into pieces and place in casserole.
2 Add remaining ingredients and pour over cider.
3 Cover and bake for 45 minutes in moderate oven.

# BERNESE FISH

*35 minutes cooking time*

*Ingredients for 6 servings*

1 kg (2 lb) flounder fillets
315 g (10 oz) mushrooms
2 tablespoons chopped parsley
4 tablespoons cream
1 teaspoon salt
125 g (4 oz) spring onions

1 tablespoon butter
5 tomatoes
1¼ cups white wine
juice of 1 lemon
⅛ teaspoon white pepper

1 Butter casserole and dot with chopped spring onions.
2 Place a layer of fillets seasoned with salt, pepper and lemon juice. Cover with chopped mushrooms and tomatoes. Dot with chopped parsley.
3 Put on another layer of fillets and moisten with white wine.
4 Cook in moderate oven until fillets are done.
5 Pour half the liquid into a saucepan and add cream, simmer until reduced and add a little chopped parsley. Pour over fish and serve.

# SMOKED FISH PIE

*40 minutes cooking time*

*Ingredients for 6 servings*

1 kg (2 lb) smoked haddock
185 g (6 oz) onion
½ teaspoon salt
125 g (4 oz) grated Cheddar cheese
3 teaspoons dry mustard
1½ tablespoons lemon juice

185 g (6 oz) butter
½ teaspoon pepper
315 g (10 oz) plain flour
2½ cups milk
4 eggs
6 anchovy fillets

1　Peel and chop onions.
2　Hardboil eggs and chop coarsely.
3　Cook and skin fish, and flake.
4　Fry onions in half the butter and stir in half the flour, the mustard and cook for 2 minutes.
5　Remove from heat, add milk gradually, and cook until sauce boils and thickens.
6　Stir in lemon juice, eggs and flaked fish.
7　Season to taste and place in casserole dish.
8　To make topping, sift remaining flour and seasonings. Rub in remaining butter and the cheese. Toss lightly. Sprinkle topping over fish and press down.
9　Bake for 40 minutes in moderate oven 180°C (350°F) and garnish with anchovy fillets.

# OREGON CRAB

*20 minutes cooking time*

*Ingredients for 4 servings*

1 crab
90 g (3 oz) roast pork
2 spring onions, chopped
lemon slices

90 g (3 oz) mushrooms
1½ cups fine breadcrumbs
1 egg

1　Remove top shell of crab and clean. Remove crab meat.
2　Drop mushrooms into very hot water and cook for 2 minutes. Mince crab meat, mushrooms and pork.
3　Combine with breadcrumbs, spring onions and beaten egg and pack into shell of crab.
4　Grill 10-15 minutes and garnish with lemon slices.

# FISH SOUFFLÉ

*35 minutes cooking time*

*Ingredients for 4 servings*

1 cup cooked fish
90 g (3 oz) flour
1 teaspoon salt
½ teaspoon grated nutmeg
2 tablespoons chopped parsley

125 g (4 oz) butter
1¾ cups milk
½ teaspoon pepper
5 eggs
¼ cup breadcrumbs

1 Make a white sauce with flour, butter and milk. Season with salt and pepper.
2 Flake fish and add to sauce together with nutmeg.
3 Stir in egg yolks and stiffly-whipped egg whites.
4 Pour into greased soufflé dish and cover with breadcrumbs.
5 Dot with melted butter and bake in moderate oven for 30 minutes. Dot with chopped parsley before serving.

# CARIBBEAN PRAWN CURRY

*45 minutes cooking time*

*Ingredients for 4 servings*

2½ cups prawns, shelled
60 g (2 oz) coconut
2 tablespoons butter
1 onion, peeled and chopped
juice of ½ lemon
1 teaspoon salt
1 tablespoon curry powder

1½ cups boiling water
4 eggs, hardboiled, shelled and halved
1 apple, peeled and cored
2 tablespoons flour
2 tablespoons tomato purée
1½ tablespoons black treacle

1 Dice apples.
2 Pour boiling water over coconut and leave until cold. Strain and reserve liquid.
3 Sauté onion and apple in butter, add flour and curry powder.
4 Cook gently for 1-2 minutes, remove from heat and gradually add liquid.
5 Cook and stir until sauce comes to boil and thickens.
6 Add tomato purée, lemon juice, treacle and seasonings.
7 Cover pan and simmer for 15 minutes.
8 Pour over prawns and eggs in casserole and heat for 15 minutes more.
9 Serve with boiled rice.

# BREAM WITH PORT

*30 minutes cooking time*

*Ingredients for 4-5 servings*

1 kg (2 lb) bream
1 teaspoon salt
1 tablespoon cream
½ cup port wine

1 tablespoon butter
½ teaspoon paprika
2 egg yolks

1  Season fish with salt and paprika.
2  Bake in butter in a covered ovenproof dish for 5 minutes and add port wine.
3  Cook until fish is tender and strain off liquid. Cook liquid quickly in saucepan, to reduce it.
4  Cook and beat in the egg yolks, add cream and reheat gently. Pour the sauce over fish and serve with rice.

# PRAWN-STUFFED FISH

*20 minutes cooking time*

*Ingredients for 8 servings*

1 1-kg (2-lb) fish
2 spring onions, chopped
¼ teaspoon white pepper
5 prawns, cleaned and chopped
2 slices fresh ginger

1 teaspoon salt
¼ teaspoon monosodium glutamate
  (optional)
1½ teaspoons sherry
1½ teaspoons cornflour

1  Scale, gut and wash fish.
2  Break spine at head and tail ends. Remove meat, leaving head, tail and skin intact.
3  Remove any small bones and chop meat.
4  Add chopped ginger, onion, sherry and seasonings to meat. Mix well and add prawns.
5  Mix to a smooth paste and spread inside the fish which has been dotted with cornflour.
6  Shape the fish into its original form.
7  Place fish on oiled plate and steam for 20 minutes.

# COLOURFUL FISH

*Ingredients for 6 servings*

*50 minutes cooking time*

| | |
|---|---|
| **1 kg (2 lb) cod fillet** | **¼ cup peas** |
| **125 g (4 oz) grated Parmesan cheese** | **2 tablespoons tomato sauce** |
| **½ teaspoon nutmeg** | **1 teaspoon salt** |
| **½ teaspoon pepper** | **3 onions** |
| **1 green pepper** | **3 tomatoes** |
| **125 g (4 oz) mushrooms** | **90 g (3 oz) butter** |
| **90 g (3 oz) flour** | **2½ cups milk** |
| **2 tablespoons chopped parsley** | **2 bay leaves** |
| **2½ cups water** | |

1  Skin fish and cut into large pieces, season with salt and pepper.
2  Peel and slice onions. Remove top and seeds of pepper and slice into thin strips.
3  Slice tomatoes fairly thickly and slice mushrooms. Place pieces of fish in casserole with prepared vegetables.
4  Melt butter in pan and stir in flour. Add milk and water gradually and bring to boil.
5  Cook for 2 minutes and add herbs, nutmeg and tomato sauce. Season with salt and pepper.
6  Pour sauce in casserole and cover. Bake for 30 minutes in moderate oven.
7  Add peas, cook 15 minutes more and serve with Parmesan cheese.

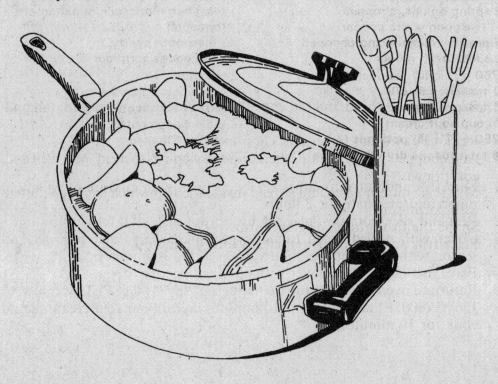

# LEATHERJACKET WITH FRUIT

*20 minutes cooking time*

*Ingredients for 6 servings*

**12 leatherjacket fillets**
**½ teaspoon pepper**
**1½ tablespoons butter**
**1½ tablespoons flour**
**4 small tomatoes**
**3 spring onions, chopped**

**1 teaspoon salt**
**1 cup white wine**
**½ cup cream**
**2 cups grapes**
**3 cloves garlic**
**2 onions, chopped**

1  Skin and slice tomatoes, season with salt and pepper.
2  Melt ½ tablespoon butter in ovenproof dish and add onion, spring onions, garlic cloves and place fish on top.
3  Spread tomato slices over and around fish. Pour wine over and cook for 10 minutes.
4  When cooked, remove fish and place on serving dish. Remove garlic and pour over cream.
5  Combine remaining butter and flour together and add to sauce, pour over fish.
6  Garnish with grapes.

# HADDOCK DUBROVNIK

*1 hour 10 minutes cooking time*

*Ingredients for 4 servings*

**750 g (1½ lb) haddock fillets**
**1 teaspoon flour**
**1 teaspoon salt**
**¾ cup sour cream**
**750 g (1½ lb) potatoes**
**4 tablespoons dry white wine**

**2 tomatoes**
**1½ teaspoons paprika**
**125 g (4 oz) bacon**
**2 tablespoons butter**
**1 onion, chopped**

1  Skin fish and cut into cubes. Place in bowl with mixture of wine and onion and marinate for 2 hours.
2  Peel and slice potatoes, place in ovenproof dish and dot with butter.
3  Cover with peeled sliced tomatoes. Sprinkle with flour, paprika and season with salt. Cook in moderate oven for 30 minutes.
4  Place fish on top and cover with chopped bacon.
5  Return to oven and bake for 15 minutes at 200°C (400°F). Lower heat to 150°C (300°F) and cook for 10 minutes more. Pour sour cream in and cook for 10 minutes.

# FISH WITH MUSTARD SAUCE

*45 minutes cooking time*

*Ingredients for 4 servings*

750 g (1½ lb) boiled fish
3 sliced onions
lemon juice

1 tablespoon butter
2 cups mashed potatoes

## SAUCE

2½ cups fish stock
1 tablespoon butter

1½ tablespoons flour
2 teaspoons prepared mustard

1 Bring the stock to the boil and blend in flour mixed with a little water, stir until it thickens. Add butter and mustard.
2 Divide fish into pieces and fry onions in butter until brown.
3 Place some of the fish at the bottom of casserole dish and add alternate layers of potatoes, onion, fish and sauce with a squeeze of lemon juice. Finish with a layer of potato and cook in oven for 30 minutes.

# CREAMY COD

*25 minutes cooking time*

*Ingredients for 6 servings*

1 kg (2 lb) cod fillet
½ teaspoon pepper
2 tablespoons chopped parsley
1 tablespoon lemon juice
2 tablespoons butter

1 teaspoon salt
6 tomatoes, baked
½ teaspoon nutmeg
2 tablespoons plain flour
2 cups milk

1 Skin fish and cut into six pieces, place in buttered casserole dish, season and sprinkle with lemon juice.
2 Pour milk round fish and cover with lid. Bake for 20 minutes.
3 Melt butter in pan and stir in flour.
4 Cook for 1 minute and drain off liquid from fish, make up to 2 cups with milk and water.
5 Bring to boil and cook for 1 minute. Season with nutmeg and place fish on serving dish.
6 Cover with sauce and sprinkle with chopped parsley. Serve with baked tomatoes.

# BANANA FISH

*30 minutes cooking time*

*Ingredients for 4 servings*

1.5 kg (3 lb) white fish
2 teaspoons sugar
3 bananas
1 teaspoon salt
4 tablespoons olive oil

3 tablespoons tomato purée
2 tablespoons water
½ teaspoon dried mixed herbs
½ teaspoon pepper

1   Split fish and place in a greased baking dish.
2   Brush with oil and sprinkle with seasonings and herbs.
3   Mix tomato purée with 2 tablespoons oil and a little sugar. Mix and add remaining sugar.
4   Add water and pour around fish. Let a little go into the centre of the fish.
5   Peel and split bananas and place round fish.
6   Bake slowly for 30 minutes, basting occasionally.

# STUFFED BREAM

*35 minutes cooking time*

*Ingredients for 4 servings*

1 kg (2 lb) bream
90 g (3 oz) prunes
1 teaspoon salt
½ teaspoon grated nutmeg

2 eggs, hardboiled
⅓ cup cooked rice
½ teaspoon pepper
2 teaspoons oil

1   Scale and clean bream, leave head on.
2   Cook and stone prunes.
3   Chop eggs and prunes and combine with rice. Season with salt, pepper and nutmeg.
4   Stuff fish with this mixture and brush with oil.
5   Place in baking dish and bake for 35 minutes in moderate oven 180°C (350°F) and serve.

# YAMBA WHITING

*45 minutes cooking time*

*Ingredients for 8 servings*

1.5 kg (3 lb) whiting fillets
1½ teaspoons salt
1½ tablespoons lemon juice

¼ teaspoon pepper
1 kg (2 lb) potatoes, diced and cooked

## SAUCE

10 rashers bacon
3 cups milk
3 tablespoons butter
½ teaspoon cayenne pepper

½ teaspoon salt
3 tablespoons flour
½ teaspoon dry mustard
185 g (6 oz) tasty cheese, grated

1  Cook and crumble bacon rashers.
2  Wash and dry fillets, remove skin and place in large casserole dish with lemon juice.
3  Season with salt and pepper.
4  Melt butter in saucepan and add flour. Cook and add milk. Stir until smooth and thick.
5  Season with salt, cayenne and mustard. Stir in potatoes and half of the cheese. Spoon over fish and bake in moderate oven for 30 minutes.
6  Remove and sprinkle with bacon and remaining cheese.
7  Return to oven and brown cheese.

# FLOUNDER BAKE

*20-25 minutes cooking time*

*Ingredients for 6 servings*

750 g (1½ lb) flounder fillet
½ teaspoon pepper
8 tablespoons breadcrumbs
2 tablespoons chopped parsley
185 g (6 oz) mushrooms, chopped

1 teaspoon salt
3 tomatoes, halved
4 tablespoons milk
2 tablespoons chopped onion
2 tablespoons butter

1  Cut fillet into serving pieces and arrange in buttered casserole dish.
2  Season with salt and pepper.
3  Sauté onion and mushrooms in butter and add parsley, milk and breadcrumbs. Mix and spread over fish.
4  Arrange tomatoes in between portions and bake for 20 minutes in moderate oven 180°C (350°F).

# FISH WITH TRUFFLES

*1½ hours cooking time*

*Ingredients for 4 servings*

| | |
|---|---|
| 1.5 kg (3 lb) white fish | 125 g (4 oz) butter |
| 4 fresh mushrooms | 6 eggs |
| 2 truffles | 2½ cups mushroom soup |
| 3 slices bread | 1 teaspoon salt |
| 1¼ cups milk | ½ teaspoon pepper |

1  Wash fish, remove skin and bones, cut flesh into small pieces and pound.
2  Remove crusts from bread and soak in milk. Mix soaked bread with fish and season with salt and pepper.
3  Sieve the mixture and melt butter in pan.
4  Add chopped mushrooms and half the soup and cook slowly for a few minutes, stirring occasionally.
5  Add mixture to fish and beat in egg yolks.
6  Beat egg whites until stiff and fold in. Pour mixture into a buttered mould which has been decorated with truffles.
7  Steam for 1 hour. Pour over remaining half of the mushroom soup and serve.

# HERMAN'S FISH

*45 minutes cooking time*

*Ingredients for 4 servings*

| | |
|---|---|
| 1 kg (2 lb) cod | 2 tablespoons olive oil |
| 1 onion | 3 cups water |
| 1 teaspoon salt | 1 teaspoon allspice |
| 3 cups cooked rice | |

1  Flake fish and fry in oil. Drain.
2  Fry onion until brown.
3  Wash rice and cover with boiling salted water.
4  Simmer for about 15 minutes and stir in allspice. Drain.
5  Place alternate layers of fish and rice in a greased casserole dish. Bake in moderate oven for 20 minutes.

# SOLE ROLL-UPS

*1 hour cooking time*

*Ingredients for 6 servings*

250 g (8 oz) small mushrooms
2 tablespoons chopped parsley
2 tablespoons butter
1 teaspoon salt
12 125-g (4-oz) sole fillets
60 g (2 oz) fresh breadcrumbs

1 tablespoon butter
125 g (4 oz) peeled prawns
2 tablespoons lemon juice
½ teaspoon pepper
⅛ cup milk

1 Chop mushroom stalks and sauté in butter for 5 minutes. Remove from heat and stir in breadcrumbs. Add parsley, seasonings and milk to bind.
2 Skin fish and divide stuffing between them. Roll up each fillet and place in casserole dish.
3 Melt butter and stir in lemon juice, pour over fish and add mushroom caps to casserole.
4 Cover and bake for 40 minutes in 190°C (375°F) oven. 5-10 minutes before serving add prawns and garnish with chopped parsley.

# Beef

## BEEF STROGANOFF

*Ingredients for 4-6 servings*

*1½-2 hours cooking time*

**750 g (1½ lb) topside steak**
**45 g (1½ oz) copha**
**250 g (8 oz) tomatoes**
**1¼ cups water**
**1 onion, chopped**

**½ cup unsweetened evaporated milk**
**1 tablespoon flour**
**1 clove garlic**
**1 packet mushroom soup**
**2 teaspoons vinegar**

1   Cut meat into small cubes.
2   Roll in the flour.
3   Melt fat and fry steak until brown.
4   Add onion and garlic, cubed tomatoes, mushroom soup.
5   Blend in with water.
6   Place in oven, using the lower rack.
7   Simmer for 1½ hours.
8   Add vinegar and milk before serving.
9   Serve with noodles and parsley.

# PAPRIKA GOULASH

*2 hours cooking time*

*Ingredients for 5-6 servings*

750 g (1½ lb) chuck or bladebone
  steak
1 tablespoon paprika
2 teaspoons tomato purée
1 bouquet garni
¼ teaspoon salt
1 green pepper
4 tablespoons sour cream

2 tablespoons dripping
250 g (8 oz) onions
1 tablespoon flour
2½ cups stock
1 clove garlic, crushed
⅛ teaspoon white pepper
2 large tomatoes

1  Cut meat into large squares.
2  Brown quickly in pan of hot dripping.
3  Take out when completely browned.
4  Lower heat and put in sliced onions.
5  After 3-4 minutes add paprika.
6  Cook slowly for 1 minute, then add flour, tomato purée, and stock.
7  Stir until boiling.
8  Replace meat, add bouquet garni, garlic and seasoning.
9  Cover and simmer gently for 2 hours in moderate oven 160°C (325°F).
10  Blanch, peel and shred the pepper.
11  Scald and peel the tomatoes, remove hard core and seeds, then slice flesh.
12  Add tomatoes and pepper to goulash.
13  Bring slowly to the boil.
14  Serve over noodles and add a spoon of sour cream.

# BEEF AND EGGPLANT CASSEROLE

*1 hour cooking time*

*Ingredients for 4-6 servings*

1 kg (2 lb) round steak
1 eggplant
4 onions
2 green peppers
3 tablespoons butter
¼ teaspoon white pepper

4 tomatoes
2 tablespoons plain flour
1 cup water
1 beef stock cube
½ teaspoon salt

1   Cube meat and peel and slice eggplant, onions and tomatoes.
2   Melt butter and brown meat on all sides.
3   Place eggplant and onion over half the meat in ovenproof dish.
4   Top with browned meat.
5   Add peppers and tomatoes.
6   Blend flour and remaining butter, cook for 2 minutes.
7   Remove from heat, gradually add water in which stock cube has been dissolved, return to heat.
8   Season with salt and pepper.
9   Pour over tomatoes, cover and bake in a moderate oven 180°C (350°F) for 1 hour.

# QUICK BEEF CURRY

*15 minutes cooking time*

*Ingredients for 3-4 servings*

450 g (15 oz) can braised steak and onions
1 cup chopped red pepper
1 cup chopped celery

½ cup finely chopped red apples
2 teaspoons curry powder
1 teaspoon salt
1 cup water

1   Combine all ingredients in saucepan.
2   Heat, stirring constantly.
3   Bring to boil.
4   Reduce heat and add salt to taste.
5   Serve with hot fluffy rice.
6   Serve immediately.

# CHABLIS SPAGHETTI BEEF

*2½ hours cooking time*

*Ingredients for 6-8 servings*

6 slices bacon
1 green pepper, chopped
1 teaspoon salt
500 g (1 lb) minced beef
1 cup grated cheese

1 onion, chopped
2 cloves garlic
500 g (1 lb) tomatoes
2 cups broken spaghetti
1½ cups Chablis

1   After frying bacon, remove.
2   Add chopped onion, green pepper and garlic with salt.
3   Cook slowly.
4   Add minced beef and cook.
5   Crumble bacon and add to this mixture.
6   Add tomatoes and wine, cover and cook for 1 hour.
7   Cook spaghetti, drain and rinse, mix with the sauce and cheese.
8   Pour into casserole dish, cover and bake slowly for 1 hour. Brown slightly, 20 minutes before serving.

# POT ROAST WITH ROSEMARY AND TOMATO

*2 hours cooking time*

*Ingredients for 4-6 servings*

1.5 kg (3 lb) round steak
2 cloves garlic
little butter or oil
½ teaspoon dried rosemary
2 medium onions

½ teaspoon salt
¾ teaspoon white pepper
2 teaspoons prepared mustard
3 large tomatoes
½ cup beef stock

1   Prepare the vegetables, peel and slice tomatoes, slice onions.
2   Trim excess fat from meat, and heat oil in heavy saucepan.
3   Brown the meat on all sides, then season with salt and pepper.
4   Add rosemary and spread meat with mustard.
5   Add tomatoes, onions and stock to pan.
6   Cover tightly and simmer until meat is tender.
7   Check liquid during cooking time, if more liquid is necessary, add a little tomato juice.

# SAUERBRATEN VON MUNCHEN

*2½ hours cooking time*

*Ingredients for 5-6 servings*

1.5 kg (3 lb) piece silverside
  (not corned)
1 cup water
1 cup vinegar
2 tablespoons brown sugar
1 teaspoon salt
¼ teaspoon white pepper
6 peppercorns
2 cloves

1 bay leaf
1 clove garlic
1 onion, chopped
1 carrot, diced
1 tablespoon dripping
1 tablespoon chopped parsley
1 tablespoon plain flour
1 tablespoon sour cream

1   Place meat in an earthenware or glass dish with a close-fitting lid.
2   Combine water, vinegar, sugar, salt, pepper, peppercorns, cloves, bay leaf and garlic.
3   Mix well, then pour over meat in dish.
4   Cover and allow to stand 4-5 days in refrigerator.
5   Turn meat every day.
6   After the meat is well marinated, lift it out of the marinade, drain well and pat dry with a clean, dry cloth. Reserve the liquid. Rub plain flour over the surface of the meat.
7   Melt the dripping in a saucepan large enough to take the meat.
8   Brown the meat well on all sides in hot dripping.
9   Add about a third of marinade liquid together with carrot and parsley.
10  Place lid on saucepan and bring to the boil.
11  Reduce heat and cook gently for 2½ hours, adding extra liquid if necessary.
12  When tender, remove meat only and place on a hot serving dish.
13  Blend flour with a little water; add to the liquid in saucepan and stir well. Add cream to make a rich, smooth gravy.

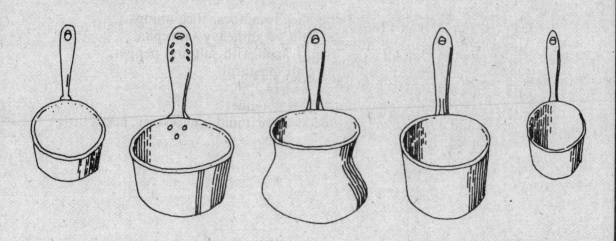

# INDIAN BEEF CURRY

*65 minutes cooking time*

*Ingredients for 5-6 servings*

1 kg (2 lb) round steak
2 onions
1 clove garlic
2 tablespoons butter
juice of 1 lemon

2 tablespoons curry powder
250 g (8 oz) can tomato purée
1 tablespoon water
1 teaspoon salt
½ teaspoon pepper

1   Cube meat, chop onion and crush garlic.
2   Melt butter in saucepan and add onion.
3   Sauté.
4   Add meat and brown well.
5   Add garlic, curry powder and pepper.
6   Add tomato paste and water.
7   Cover and simmer for 1 hour.
8   Season to taste with salt and pepper.
9   Serve with boiled rice.

# OXTAIL CIVET

*2 hours cooking time*

*Ingredients for 5-6 servings*

2 oxtails
4 carrots
1½ tablespoons claret
2 tablespoons plain flour
1 cup diced celery
4 whole cloves
1 parsnip

2 tablespoons butter
1 teaspoon salt
1 cup tomatoes
½ teaspoon white pepper
2 cups water
3 small onions

1   Roll oxtail pieces in flour and brown.
2   Add water, tomatoes, salt and pepper and cloves.
3   Cover and simmer for 2 hours.
4   Add onions, carrots and parsnip and celery.
5   Cook until tender.
6   Add claret and blend well.
7   Serve in heated baking dish.

# OXTAIL RAGOUT

*3-4 hours cooking time*

*Ingredients for 5-6 servings*

1 kg (2 lb) oxtails
¾ cup butter
1 teaspoon salt
1 bay leaf
6-8 carrots, sliced

2 cups water
1 cup claret
¼ teaspoon white pepper
8 onions
½ cup celery, sliced

1   Brown oxtails on all sides and sprinkle with salt and pepper.
2   Add bay leaf, water and wine.
3   Simmer for 3-4 hours, adding more water if necessary.
4   Add vegetables and simmer for 20 minutes longer.
5   Thicken gravy with flour and water.
6   Serve immediately.

# CLARET POT ROAST

*2 hours cooking time*

*Ingredients for 8-10 servings*

1.5-2 kg (3-4 lb) meat in one piece
    (topside, round or chuck steak)
3 slices lemon
1 teaspoon ginger
1 rasher bacon, diced
1 bay leaf
4 cloves
1 cup claret

1 onion, sliced
4 tablespoons brown sugar
12 peppercorns
2 teaspoons salt
2 tablespoons dripping
2 tablespoons plain flour, blended with
    stock or water

1   Tie pot roast with string and place in a large bowl.
2   Mix next 10 ingredients together and pour over meat. Allow meat to marinate.
3   Remove meat from marinade next morning.
4   Heat dripping in a large saucepan, add meat and brown well on all sides.
5   Add marinade, cover, and cook gently for 2 hours.
6   Remove from heat.
7   Thicken gravy with blended flour.
8   Serve hot over sliced meat.
9   Garnish with parsley and serve with vegetables in season.

# BEEF STROGANOFF — A LA RUSSE

*25 minutes cooking time*

*Ingredients for 3-4 servings*

500 g (1 lb) rump or other good
  grilling steak
2 tablespoons butter or oil
2 onions, finely chopped
2 tomatoes, peeled and sliced
2 tablespoons flour

1¼ cups beef stock
¼ teaspoon salt
⅛ teaspoon white pepper
¼ teaspoon nutmeg
60 g (2 oz) mushrooms
1 cup sour cream

1   Freeze meat so that it is easy to cut finely, cut into thin strips 4-5 centimetres (1½-2 in) long.
2   Heat butter or oil, add meat, fry quickly until brown.
3   Remove from pan and keep hot.
4   Fry tomato, remove from pan and keep hot.
5   Fry onions until crisp and brown, keep hot.
6   Add flour to remaining butter in pan to make a paste, sometimes it may be necessary to add a little more butter here. Cook 1 minute.
7   Add stock, salt and pepper and nutmeg and stir until sauce boils.
8   Add mushrooms, and simmer for 2 minutes. Remove from heat, stir in half the sour cream.
9   Arrange all cooked ingredients on a heated platter, pour sauce over these, then trickle remaining sour cream over.
10   Serve with rice or small fried potato chips.

# QUICK BEEF AND VEGETABLE PIE

*35 minutes cooking time*

*Ingredients for 4-6 servings*

375 g (12 oz) packet pastry mix
½ cup water

450 g (1 lb) can beef and vegetable
  casserole

1   Combine pastry mix and water.
2   Knead together lightly.
3   Allow to rest for 15 minutes.
4   Roll out half the pastry and line a 23 centimetre (9 in) pie plate.
5   Pour in contents of can.
6   Cover with remaining pastry and bake in moderate oven 200°C (400°F) for 30-35 minutes.
7   Garnish with parsley.

# BURGUNDIAN CASSEROLE

*3 hours cooking time*

*Ingredients for 4-6 servings*

1.5 kg (3 lb) bladebone steak
2 tablespoons flour
3 tablespoons butter
2 onions
500 g (1 lb) tomatoes
1 small veal knuckle

2½ cups burgundy
3 carrots
3 cloves
1½ teaspoons salt
⅛ teaspoon white pepper

1   Cut steak in 5-8 centimetre (2-3 in) squares and dip in flour.
2   Melt butter and fry meat until browned.
3   Place in casserole dish when ready.
4   Brown sliced onions and add tomatoes.
5   Cook until tender.
6   Add burgundy, bring nearly to the boil, then pour into casserole dish.
7   Cook for 2 hours.
8   Add carrots, salt, pepper and cloves to casserole.
9   Add veal knuckle.
10   Cook for 1 hour before serving.

# BEEF CASSEROLE A LA CHABLIS

*2½ hours cooking time*

*Ingredients for 4-5 servings*

1 kg (2 lb) round steak
3 onions
⅛ teaspoon white pepper
1 clove garlic
2 cups stock
3 parsnips
1 tablespoon plain flour

125 g (4 oz) bacon
1 teaspoon salt
marjoram
1 cup Chablis
500 g (1 lb) potatoes
3 carrots

1   Cut steak into 5 centimetre (2 in) cubes.
2   Cut bacon and fry until brown.
3   Chop the onions and add to bacon.
4   Add meat, salt, pepper, crushed garlic, marjoram and wine, bring to boil.
5   Cover and simmer for 45 minutes, lower heat.
6   Prepare vegetables and add to casserole with flour, blended well.
7   Serve when completely cooked, about 1½ hours.

# RAGOUT OF BEEF WITH CELERY AND WALNUTS

*2 hours cooking time*

*Ingredients for 4-6 servings*

**750 g (1½ lb) chuck or skirt steak**
**2 tablespoons dripping**
**1 bouquet garni**
**2½ cups stock**
**¼ teaspoon salt**
**1 head celery**
**30 g (1 oz) walnuts, shelled**
**¾ cup red wine**

**12 button onions**
**3 teaspoons flour**
**1 clove garlic, crushed with salt**
**⅛ teaspoon white pepper**
**2 teaspoons butter**
**2 teaspoons orange rind, shredded and and blanched**

1  Cut beef into 5 centimetre (2 in) squares.
2  Peel onions.
3  Heat thick casserole and put in fat.
4  When smoking lay in pieces of meat until brown, turning once.
5  Take out meat, add onions and fry slowly.
6  Draw off heat, drain so that only 1 tablespoon of fat is left in the casserole.
7  Stir in flour, add red wine, meat, bouquet garni and garlic.
8  Barely cover with stock, season, bring slowly to the boil, cover and simmer gently until tender.
9  Cut the trimmed head of celery into slices.
10  Heat the butter in a frying pan, put in walnuts.
11  Toss over a medium heat with a pinch of salt.
12  Then shred and cook orange rind in boiling water until tender, drain and rinse.
13  Dish up ragout, or leave in casserole for serving, and scatter mixture of celery, orange rind and walnuts on the top.

# STEAK AND MUSHROOM PIE

*35 minutes cooking time*

*Ingredients for 6-8 servings*

**375 g (12 oz) packet pastry mix**
**½ cup water**
**1 tablespoon butter**
**1 onion**
**milk for glazing**

**500 g (1 lb) minced steak**
**1 packet mushroom soup**
**1 cup extra water**
**1 teaspoon salt**
**250 g (8 oz) mushrooms**

1  Combine pastry mix with half cup water.
2  Knead lightly, refrigerate 15 minutes.
3  Roll out half the pastry on lightly floured board.
4  Line a 23 centimetre (9 in) pie plate.
5  Chop onion, sauté in melted butter.
6  Add meat and brown well.
7  Add mushrooms, soup mix and extra water.
8  Season if necessary with a little salt.
9  Cool and spoon into pie shell.
10  Roll out remaining pastry, cover top of pie and trim. Glaze with milk. Bake in a moderate oven 180°C (350°F) for 35 minutes.

# RUMP STEAK AND KIDNEY PIE

*1½ hours cooking time*

*Ingredients for 5-6 servings*

**750 g (1½ lb) rump steak**
**500 g (1 lb) beef kidney**
**1 tablespoon plain flour**
**¼ teaspoon white pepper**

**¼ teaspoon salt**
**⅛ teaspoon nutmeg**
**plain pie pastry**
**stock or water**

1  Split kidneys and remove core, skin and hard matter.
2  Cut into 5 centimetre (2 in) pieces, and cover with salt water for 1 hour.
3  Drain, and wipe beef with cold cloth.
4  Cut into 5 centimetre (2 in) pieces.
5  Sprinkle kidney and beef with flour, salt, pepper, nutmeg and a little stock.
6  Line the sides of a baking dish with pastry.
7  Place beef and kidneys in dish and allow to cook for 1½ hours.

# STIFADO

*2 hours cooking time*

*Ingredients for 4-6 servings*

1 kg (2 lb) round steak
2 teaspoons salt
freshly ground black pepper
2 tablespoons butter
12 small white onions
⅓ cup claret
1 tablespoon malt vinegar
½ cup tomato paste

1 tablespoon brown sugar
1 tablespoon beef extract
1 clove garlic
1 bay leaf
1 small stick cinnamon
4 cloves
1 tablespoon raisins
chopped parsley

1   Cut meat into 2.5 centimetre (1 in) slices, discarding any fat.
2   Season meat with the salt and black pepper.
3   Melt the butter in a frying pan, add meat, and cook long enough to coat meat with butter.
4   Transfer meat to a 7½ cup casserole.
5   Measure liquid in pan, make up to half cup with water.
6   Pour over the meat.
7   Peel the onions and place on top of the meat.
8   Mix together claret, malt vinegar, tomato paste, sugar, beef extract and crushed garlic clove.
9   Pour sauce over meat and onions, add bay leaf, cinnamon stick and cloves.
10  Sprinkle raisins and parsley over the top.
11  Bake in a moderate oven 180°C (350°F) for 2 hours.

# SCALLOPED BEEF AND ONIONS

*15-20 minutes cooking time*

*Ingredients for 6-8 servings*

3 cups roast beef, cold
1 tablespoon chopped parsley
2 teaspoons onion juice

2 cups medium white sauce
2 cups breadcrumbs

1   Combine all ingredients but breadcrumbs.
2   Place a layer of breadcrumbs in a greased dish.
3   Alternate layers of meat mixture and crumbs.
4   Bake in oven at 220°C (425°F) with breadcrumbs on top.

# CARBONADE DE BOEUF

*2 hours cooking time*

*Ingredients for 4-5 servings*

| | |
|---|---|
| 1 kg (2 lb) topside, round or chuck steak | ¼ teaspoon salt |
| 2 tablespoons oil | ⅛ teaspoon white pepper |
| 2 tablespoons butter | 1 small bottle stout |
| 2-3 large onions | 2 teaspoons prepared mustard |
| | 1 small French loaf |

1 Cut the meat into small thin squares and slice the onions.
2 Heat the oil in a frying pan, brown the meat on all sides, remove and drain.
3 Add the onions and sauté until brown.
4 Add the butter to pan and melt, then stir in the flour and seasoning.
5 Arrange the meat and sliced onions in layers in the casserole.
6 Pour the stout into frying pan and heat.
7 When it comes to the boil, pour into casserole and cook in moderate oven 180°C (350°F) for 2 hours.
8 Slice the bread, spread with mustard, then take off casserole lid, and place the bread slices on top of the meat.
9 Increase oven heat to hot and bake, uncovered, for 15 minutes.

# GOULASH WITH RED WINE

*1½ hours cooking time*

*Ingredients for 4-6 servings*

| | |
|---|---|
| 750 g (1½ lb) round steak | 2 teaspoons oil |
| ½ cup beef stock | ½ teaspoon salt |
| ⅛ teaspoon white pepper | ½ cup red wine |
| 1 teaspoon paprika | 1 large onion |

1 Cut meat into 2.5 centimetre (1 in) slices, and combine stock and wine and warm in small pot.
2 Heat oil in saucepan, and add meat and brown all over.
3 Then add the sliced onion, brown a little.
4 Add salt, pepper and paprika, and blend well, then pour warmed stock and wine over.
5 Boil, reduce heat, cover and simmer for 1½ hours.
6 Serve with rice, mashed potatoes or noodles.

# SAVOURY BEEF WITH PEPPERS

*1½ hours cooking time*

*Ingredients for 4-6 servings*

**750 g (1½ lb) round steak**
flour
**1 tablespoon oil**
**1 green pepper**
**1 onion**
**2 teaspoons Worcestershire sauce**
**½ teaspoon salt**

**1 tablespoon chutney**
**2 tomatoes**
pinch thyme
**½ cup beef stock**
**1 cup claret**
**¾ teaspoon white pepper**

1 Seed and chop green pepper, chop onion and peel and chop tomatoes.
2 Trim any fat from steak, cut into 10 centimetre (4 in) squares.
3 Dredge lightly with flour.
4 Heat oil in electric frypan and brown meat on all sides.
5 Drain away any excess fat.
6 Add remaining ingredients and bring to the boil.
7 Reduce heat and cover, simmer gently for 1½ hours.
8 Taste and adjust seasoning.

# MEAT AND PASTRY ROLL UPS

*55 minutes cooking time*

*Ingredients for 6-8 servings*

**2 chopped onions**
**2 tablespoons butter**
**1 kg (2 lb) ground beef**
**1 teaspoon salt**

**⅛ teaspoon white pepper**
**pastry made with ¾ teaspoon baking**
**powder**

1 Melt butter, add onions and brown.
2 Add meat and brown.
3 Season with salt and pepper.
4 Roll dough thinly into a small square.
5 Spread with meat mixture and roll and slice.
6 Place in a greased baking dish and bake for 55 minutes in moderate oven 190°C (375°F).

# STUFFED ROLL OF SIRLOIN

*2 hours cooking time*

*Ingredients for 5-6 servings*

**500 g (1 lb) sirloin**
**2 cups boiled spaghetti**
**1 onion, chopped**
**1 stick celery, chopped**
**1 teaspoon salt**
**¼ teaspoon white pepper**

**1 tablespoon chopped parsley**
**2 tablespoons plain flour**
**2 tablespoons butter**
**2 cups water**
**1 teaspoon mixed herbs**

1  Wipe meat with damp cloth, and mix spaghetti, onion, celery, salt and spices together.
2  Spread on meat with white pepper and parsley.
3  Roll and skewer securely.
4  Dot with a tablespoon of flour.
5  Melt butter and brown all over.
6  Transfer to greased dish, and add liquid.
7  Bake in a moderate oven 180°C (350°F) for 2 hours.
8  Place roll on hot serving dish and thicken remaining liquid with flour and water.
9  Pour over meat.
10  Serve immediately.

# LEFT OVER BEEF

*50 minutes cooking time*

*Ingredients for 6-8 servings*

**2 cups cooked roast beef**
**3 cups boiled potatoes**
**½ cup milk**
**¼ teaspoon salt**

**½ teaspoon white pepper**
**1 teaspoon Worcestershire sauce**
**½ cup chopped onion**
**1 tablespoon butter**

1  Blend thoroughly all ingredients but fat.
2  Spread evenly in a greased pan and fry slowly over a moderate heat.
3  Turn and fold as an omelette, and place on a hot platter.
4  Garnish with parsley.
5  Serve immediately.

# FILLET AND KIDNEY PIE WITH SPAGHETTI

*1¼ hours cooking time*

*Ingredients for 6-8 servings*

| | |
|---|---|
| 500 g (1 lb) fillet steak | 1 tablespoon butter |
| 5 lamb kidneys | 1 cup boiled spaghetti |
| 1 large onion, chopped | plain pie pastry |
| 1 teaspoon salt | ¼ teaspoon white pepper |
| 2 tablespoons plain flour | |

1  Wash and split kidneys in half, remove cores and tubes. Soak 45 minutes in cold water.
2  Drain and dry.
3  Cut into small pieces.
4  Wipe fillet with cold damp cloth and cut into small pieces.
5  Place fillet and kidneys in saucepan with cold water, make sure to cover meat.
6  Bring to boiling point and add onion, salt and pepper.
7  Reduce heat and simmer until tender, about 35 minutes.
8  Mix flour and butter, and blend into ingredients.
9  Add hot spaghetti, mix well.
10  Line baking dish, and pour in cooked ingredients.
11  Bake in a hot oven 220°C (425°F) for 30 minutes.

# STEAK WITH TOMATO SAUCE

*2 hours cooking time*

*Ingredients for 5-6 servings*

| | |
|---|---|
| 750 g (1½ lb) flank steak | 1 cup thick tomato soup |
| 1 onion, chopped | ½ teaspoon white pepper |
| 2 tablespoons butter | 2 tablespoons plain flour |
| 1 teaspoon salt | |

1  Wipe meat with cold cloth and melt butter.
2  Add onion and brown.
3  Add meat and brown.
4  Sprinkle with salt and pepper and cover with water.
5  Add half the soup and bake in a moderate oven for 1½ hours.
6  Add remaining soup for last 15 minutes.
7  Serve immediately with this gravy.

# SWISS MEAT BALLS AND DUMPLINGS

*1½ hours cooking time*

*Ingredients for 6-8 servings*

**750 g (1½ lb) chuck steak**
**1 teaspoon salt**
**¼ teaspoon white pepper**
**2 tablespoons butter**

**1 medium sliced onion**
**6 dumplings**
**2 tablespoons plain flour**

1. Season meat with salt and pepper.
2. Round meat into small patties.
3. Melt butter and fry onion and meat cakes until brown.
4. Cover with boiling water and let simmer for 45 minutes.
5. Remove meat and add dumplings; make sure to cover tightly.
6. Cook for 10-15 minutes.
7. Take out dumplings and place on a hot platter.
8. Mix flour with cold water and stir in liquid for gravy.
9. Serve immediately.

# ASIAN BEEF

*1½ hours cooking time*

*Ingredients for 6 servings*

**1 kg (2 lb) chuck steak**
**2 onions**
**2 carrots**
**3 sticks celery**

**2 tablespoons soy sauce**
**1 beef stock cube**
**1 cup water**
**3 tablespoons butter**

1. Cube meat and chop onion.
2. Melt butter and brown meat and chopped onions.
3. Add water and stock cube.
4. Cover.
5. Simmer for 1¼ hours.
6. Add carrots, cut into slices, and celery, sliced.
7. Cook 10 minutes.
8. Thicken; season to taste.
9. Serve with rice.

# AMERICAN BEEFSTEAK PIE

*1¾ hours cooking time*

*Ingredients for 4-6 servings*

**1 kg (2 lb) chuck steak**
**1 teaspoon salt**
**⅛ teaspoon white pepper**
**2 tablespoons flour**
**3 tablespoons water**
**½ cup celery, chopped**

**1 cup boiled carrots**
**2 cups boiled potatoes**
**1 medium onion, sliced**
**2 tablespoons butter**
**pie pastry**

1  Wipe meat with wet cloth.
2  Cut in 2.5 centimetre (1 in) cubes and sprinkle with salt and pepper.
3  Put meat and onion in pan, cover with hot water and let simmer for 1 hour.
4  Line sides of buttered dish with pastry.
5  Place a layer of meat and onion in dish.
6  Thicken liquor in pan with paste of flour and cold water, pour over meat and onion in dish.
7  Place carrots and potatoes, dotted with butter, in dish.
8  Add another layer of meat and onion together with celery. Cover with pastry.
9  Bake in hot oven 220°C (425°F) for 30 minutes.

# CIVET OF BEEF

*1 hour cooking time*

*Ingredients for 6-8 servings*

**1 kg (2 lb) beef**
**½ cup flour**
**1½ teaspoons salt**
**¾ teaspoon white pepper**
**2 tablespoons butter**

**1 tablespoon plain flour**
**diced carrot**
**diced onion**
**2 tablespoons Worcestershire sauce**

1  Wipe meat with damp cloth and cut into small squares.
2  Add half the salt, pepper and Worcestershire sauce.
3  Melt butter in saucepan and add meat.
4  Brown well.
5  Mix in 1 tablespoon flour and add 1 cup boiling water.
6  Bring to boil.
7  Add balance of salt and pepper, carrot, onion and Worcestershire sauce.
8  Cover and simmer for 1 hour.

# BRAISED BEEF WITH VEGETABLES

*3 hours cooking time*

*Ingredients for 8-10 servings*

**1.25 kg (2½ lb) chuck steak**
**fat for browning**
**1 teaspoon salt**
**⅛ teaspoon white pepper**
**3 tablespoons plain flour**

**½ cup diced carrots**
**½ cup diced onion**
**½ cup diced celery**
**½ cup diced turnip**
**2½ cups boiling water**

1  Wipe meat with cold cloth and cut into small cubes.
2  Dot with salt, pepper and flour.
3  Brown in frying pan with fat.
4  Bake in oven at 150°C (300°F) for 3 hours.
5  Add vegetables after 30 minutes.

# BEEF AND TOMATOES SPECIAL

*1 hour cooking time*

*Ingredients for 4-6 servings*

**1 kg (2 lb) skirt steak**
**3 cups stewed tomatoes**
**⅛ teaspoon white pepper**

**3 large onions**
**1 teaspoon salt**

1  Wipe meat with damp cloth.
2  Cut into 6-7 pieces.
3  Melt fat and put meat in pan.
4  Place onion on top and add tomatoes.
5  Add salt and pepper.
6  Simmer at low heat for about 1 hour.

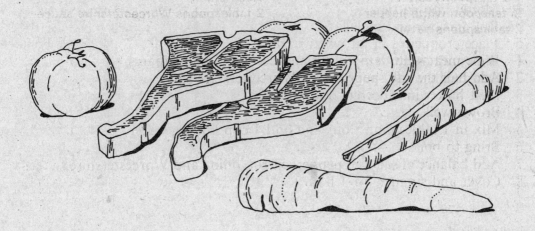

# CHILLI CON CARNE

*1½ hours cooking time*

*Ingredients for 4-6 servings*

| | |
|---|---|
| 1 kg (2 lb) beef | 2 cups canned red kidney beans |
| 5 tablespoons butter | 4 celery stalks, chopped |
| 4 onions, chopped | 1 teaspoon salt |
| 2 cups stewed tomatoes | 1 teaspoon red pepper |
| 1 teaspoon chilli powder | |

1  Wipe beef with cold damp cloth.
2  Cut beef into small cubes.
3  Melt butter and sauté meat and onions.
4  Place in saucepan.
5  Add tomatoes and beans.
6  Add celery, salt and pepper, chilli powder and red pepper and simmer for 1½ hours.

# CROQUETTES

*30 minutes cooking time*

*Ingredients for 6-8 servings*

| | |
|---|---|
| 500 g (1 lb) pork | ¼ teaspoon white pepper |
| 500 g (1 lb) beef | 1 tablespoon chopped parsley |
| 1 tablespoon chopped celery | 1 cup plain flour |
| 1 tablespoon chopped onion | ¼ cup butter |
| 1 teaspoon sage | 1 teaspoon salt |

1  Wipe meat with damp cloth, grind both pork and beef together.
2  Combine thoroughly celery, onion, sage, salt, pepper and parsley with meat.
3  Mould into patties.
4  Roll in flour and melt fat.
5  Place croquettes in fat when sizzling.
6  Brown all over.
7  Serve with white sauce.

# MEXICAN BEEF CASSEROLE

*2¼ hours cooking time*

*Ingredients for 8 servings*

1 kg (2 lb) round or chuck steak
2 tablespoons Mexican chilli powder
1 clove garlic, minced or mashed
¼ teaspoon pepper
2 tablespoons prepared mustard
1 chopped onion
¾ cup boiling water

2 tablespoons oil
2 tablespoons butter
½ cup uncooked long-grain rice
1 large can tomatoes
1 can red kidney beans
1 beef stock cube
1 teaspoon paprika

1  Spread meat with a mixture of half the chilli powder, garlic, pepper and prepared mustard, and cut it into 2.5 centimetre (1 in) squares.
2  Fry the onion in oil and butter until golden.
3  Put half the meat in bottom of a large casserole and cover with half the onions.
4  Sprinkle with half the rice and add half the tomatoes.
5  Repeat layers.
6  Top with the beans mixed with remaining tablespoon of chilli powder.
7  Dissolve stock cube in boiling water and pour over to almost cover.
8  Sprinkle with paprika.
9  Bake uncovered in a moderate oven 180°C (350°F) for about 2 hours, adding more stock if needed.

# FILLET OF BEEF

*30 minutes cooking time*

*Ingredients for 3-4 servings*

1 kg (2 lb) fillet of beef
butter or fat

¼ teaspoon white pepper
3 tablespoons flour

1  Wipe meat with damp cloth and place in saucepan.
2  Brush meat with fat and sprinkle with salt.
3  Add pepper and 2-3 tablespoons plain flour.
4  Brown, then place in ovenproof dish.
5  Bake in moderate oven for 30 minutes.
6  For gravy, thicken liquid, stirring constantly.

# BEEF CAKE

*1 hour cooking time*

*Ingredients for 4-6 servings*

500 g (1 lb) round steak
1 cup plain flour, sifted
2 cups milk

1 egg, beaten
1 teaspoon salt
⅛ teaspoon white pepper

1 Wipe meat with damp cloth and dice.
2 Make a batter with flour, milk, egg and half of the salt and pepper.
3 Grease a baking dish and place meat in.
4 Sprinkle with balance of salt and pepper.
5 Pour over the batter and bake for 1 hour.

# WESTERN GOULASH

*30 minutes cooking time*

*Ingredients for 4-5 servings*

3 tablespoons fat
500 g (1 lb) beef
finely chopped onion
1 cup beef stock

2 cups spaghetti
1 teaspoon salt
¼ teaspoon white pepper
2 teaspoons Worcestershire sauce

1 Melt fat and add steak and onions.
2 When brown, transfer to oven proof dish with other ingredients.
3 Cover and cook in moderate oven.

# CORNED BEEF

*Ingredients for 4-6 servings*

2.5 kg (5 lb) brisket
30 g (1 oz) whole black pepper
30 g (1 oz) whole allspice

6 cloves garlic
¼ teaspoon saltpetre
4 bay leaves

1 Let meat stand in brine for 24 hours.
2 Throw brine away and add fresh water.
3 Add saltpetre and spices.
4 Let stand for 2 weeks.
5 Add salt.

# BAKED RAGOUT OF RUMP

*3 hours cooking time*

*Ingredients for 6-8 servings*

**500 g (1 lb) rump steak**
**¼ cup plain flour**
**1 teaspoon salt**
**¼ teaspoon white pepper**
**2 sliced onions**

**2 cups lima beans**
**1 cup canned stewed tomatoes**
**1 tablespoon Worcestershire sauce**
**2 tablespoons butter**
**1 sliced carrot**

1 Combine flour, salt and pepper.
2 Roll meat in this mixture and melt butter in pan.
3 Sauté meat and onions.
4 Place alternate layers of meat and beans and carrot in greased dish.
5 Add tomatoes and Worcestershire sauce.
6 Cover and bake in moderate oven.

# POT ROAST

*4 hours cooking time*

*Ingredients for 8 servings*

**2 kg (4 lb) beef**
**4 tablespoons flour**
**1 teaspoon salt**
**¼ teaspoon pepper**
**3 tablespoons oil**
**½ cup diced celery**

**½ cup diced carrot**
**½ cup diced turnip**
**½ cup diced onion**
**1 tablespoon chopped parsley**
**1 bay leaf**
**boiling water**

1 Buy an inexpensive cut of meat, solid or rolled.
2 Sprinkle with flour, salt and pepper, and brown on all sides in oil.
3 Transfer meat to a large pan, surround with vegetables.
4 Add water to half cover meat.
5 Cover and simmer below the boiling point for about 4 hours.
6 Place meat on hot platter and surround with drained vegetables.
7 Thicken liquid with flour for gravy.

# BEEF GOULASH

*2¼ hours cooking time*

*Ingredients for 4-6 servings*

**750 g (1½ lb) blade steak**
**1 tablespoon butter**
**2 medium onions, chopped**
**1 clove garlic, chopped**
**pinch marjoram**
**pinch caraway seed**

**1 teaspoon paprika**
**1 teaspoon salt**
**1 green pepper, sliced**
**2 tomatoes, peeled and quartered**
**4 medium potatoes, diced**

1  Cut the steak into 2.5 centimetre (1 in) cubes.
2  Lightly fry the onions in melted butter.
3  Add the steak, garlic, caraway seed, marjoram, paprika and salt.
4  Cover with water and simmer.
5  Stir occasionally and add extra water if necessary.
6  After 1 hour add the green pepper, tomatoes and potatoes.
7  Cover and simmer until tender (about 1 hour).
8  Serve with rice, dumplings or noodles.

# GERMAN BEEF STEW

*3 hours cooking time*

*Ingredients for 8 servings*

**2.5 kg (5 lb) gravy beef, with bone**
**1½ teaspoons salt**
**½ teaspoon pepper**
**4 tablespoons flour**
**3 cups cubed potatoes**
**1 onion, diced**

**1 cup turnip, diced**
**1 cup carrot, diced**
**1 cup vinegar**
**10 whole cloves**
**boiling water**

1  Cut meat in 2.5 centimetre (1 in) cubes; sprinkle with salt, pepper and flour.
2  Melt some meat fat in frying pan and brown beef.
3  Put meat in large pan; add bones, drippings from frying pan, vinegar, and cover with boiling water.
4  Boil for 5 minutes; reduce heat and simmer for 2 hours.
5  Add carrot, turnip, cloves and onion, simmer 30 minutes longer.
6  Add potatoes and cook 30 minutes longer.
7  Remove bones and skim fat from surface of stew.

# EASY BEEF CASSEROLE

*2-3 hours cooking time*

*Ingredients for 6 servings*

| | |
|---|---|
| 1 kg (2 lb) boneless stewing steak | 1½ teaspoons salt |
| 20 small white onions | ½ teaspoon gravy sauce browning |
| 6 whole cloves | 1 tablespoon vinegar |
| 2 tablespoons sugar | ¼ teaspoon thyme |
| 1 cup water | 1 bay leaf |
| 2 tablespoons flour | |

1  Cut meat into 2.5 centimetre (1 in) pieces and put in casserole.
2  Add onions, stuck with cloves.
3  Heat the sugar in a frying pan, stirring until melted and caramelised to a dark golden brown.
4  Remove from heat, add the water, then stir again over heat until the sugar has redissolved.
5  Stir in the salt, gravy browning, vinegar, thyme and bay leaf.
6  Pour over meat in casserole.
7  Cover and bake in a moderate oven 160°C (325°F) for 2 to 3 hours until the meat is tender.
8  Blend the flour with 2 tablespoons water and stir into the meat gravy.
9  Continue cooking until thickened.

# CREAMED BEEF

*15-20 minutes cooking time*

*Ingredients for 5-6 servings*

| | |
|---|---|
| 500 g (1 lb) dried beef | ½ cup milk |
| 2 tablespoons butter | 1 tablespoon plain flour |
| 1 cup cream | parsley |

1  Soak beef in cold water for 15-20 minutes.
2  Drain and pick into thin pieces.
3  Melt butter and brown beef.
4  Add milk and cream and bring to the boil.
5  Thicken with flour and serve hot.

# BURGUNDY BEEF

*2 hours cooking time*

*Ingredients for 4-5 servings*

250 g (8 oz) small white onions, peeled
3 rashers lean bacon, diced
1 tablespoon butter
1 kg (2 lb) chuck beef
1½ tablespoons brandy (optional)
1 teaspoon salt

½ teaspoon pepper
1 cup red wine
2 whole cloves garlic, peeled
1 cup small sliced fresh mushrooms
1 cup water
bouquet garni
3 tablespoons flour

1  Brown onions and bacon in butter in heavy flameproof casserole; remove onions and bacon and set aside.
2  Brown meat on all sides.
3  Pour brandy over beef and set alight, tilting pan to keep flame going as long as possible.
4  Sprinkle meat with salt and pepper.
5  Add wine, garlic, mushrooms, water, onions and bacon.
6  Make a bouquet garni by tying together in a piece of cheesecloth the parsley, celery, carrot, bay leaf and thyme, and add to pan.
7  Cover and simmer for about 1½ hours until the meat is tender.
8  Lift beef, mushrooms and onions out of the pan with a slotted spoon; arrange in a covered baking dish.
9  Strain the liquid through a sieve, discarding bouquet garni, garlic and bacon.
10  Mix flour to a smooth paste with the cold water; stir into meat stock and cook, stirring, until gravy is thick and smooth.
11  Pour gravy over meat and serve immediately, or refrigerate and reheat, covered, in a moderate oven 180°C (350°F) for about 35 minutes, or until hot and bubbly.

# PARMESAN BEEF

*2 hours cooking time*

*Ingredients for 4 servings*

500 g (1 lb) gravy beef
½ cup sherry
60 g (2 oz) Parmesan cheese
1 teaspoon dried tarragon
1 tablespoon chopped parsley

½ teaspoon salt
¼ teaspoon pepper
1 slice ham
1 cup beef stock

1  Cut meat into 2.5 centimetre (1 in) pieces.
2  Combine the sherry, cheese, tarragon, parsley, salt and pepper.
3  Soak meat in this mixture overnight.
4  Cut the ham into 2.5 centimetre (1 in) cubes and alternate layers of meat and ham in a casserole dish.
5  Cover with remaining marinade and the stock.
6  Cover and cook in a moderate oven 160°C (325°F) for 1½ hours.
7  Remove the lid and continue cooking until meat is tender.
8  Serve with rice.

# SWISS STEAK

*2¼ hours cooking time*

*Ingredients for 4 servings*

750 g (1½ lb) blade steak, 1 cm (½ in) thick
6 tablespoons flour
1 teaspoon salt
¼ teaspoon pepper

1 onion, chopped
2 tablespoons oil
¼ cup chopped green pepper
1 cup tinned tomatoes
1 cup boiling water

1  Mix flour, salt and pepper, and pound into steak.
2  Brown steak and onions in fat in heavy pan.
3  Add green pepper, tomatoes and water.
4  Cover and simmer until meat is tender, about 2 hours.
5  Add more water if needed during cooking.
6  The liquor can be thickened with flour paste for gravy.

# BEEF AND KIDNEY CIVET

*30 minutes cooking time*

*Ingredients for 4-5 servings*

| | |
|---|---|
| **6 lamb kidneys** | **500 g (1 lb) round steak** |
| **½ cup onion, sliced** | **1½ cups boiling water** |
| **1 teaspoon mustard** | **2 teaspoons salt** |
| **¼ teaspoon white pepper** | **1 tablespoon plain flour** |
| **2 teaspoons butter** | **½ cup dry red wine** |
| **buttered toast** | |

1  After preparing the kidneys by soaking in water and removing tubes, drain thoroughly and dry.
2  Cut both steak and kidney into small squares, and place kidneys and beef in casserole dish.
3  Add onion and water, bake for 20 minutes in moderate oven about 180°C (350°F).
4  Combine mustard, salt, pepper, flour and butter, cream well.
5  Stir in the cooked meat, until blended thoroughly.
6  Add the wine and bake for further 15-20 minutes.
7  Serve with rice or buttered toast.

# CASSEROLE OF SPARERIBS

*2½ hours cooking time*

*Ingredients for 6 servings*

| | |
|---|---|
| **1 kg (2 lb) beef spareribs** | **2 cups beef stock** |
| **3 tablespoons French dressing** | **6 small potatoes, peeled** |
| **2 sliced onions** | |

1  Brush meat with French dressing and let stand for 1 hour.
2  Put in greased baking dish and put onion on top of meat.
3  Add stock.
4  Cover and bake in moderate oven 180°C (350°F) for 1 hour.
5  Add potatoes to dish.
6  Re-cover and bake for 1 hour, then uncover and bake for 30 minutes more.

# ALL IN TOGETHER

*1 hour cooking time*

*Ingredients for 5-6 servings*

**1 kg (2 lb) minced steak**
**1 small can cream of mushroom soup**
**½ teaspoon salt**
**3 cups mashed potatoes**
**2 sliced carrots**
**60 g (2 oz) shredded cheese**

**1 cup onion, chopped**
**1 small can tomato soup**
**¼ teaspoon white pepper**
**½ cup water**
**green beans**

1  Brown mince and onion, pour off surplus fat.
2  Add soups, water, salt and pepper.
3  Add vegetables and place in casserole.
4  Cover with mashed potatoes and put in oven for 50 minutes.
5  Cover with cheese and serve.

# BEEF AND LIMA BEAN STEW

*4 hours cooking time*

*Ingredients for 5-6 servings*

**500 g (1 lb) lima beans**
**60 g (2 oz) finely grated suet**
**¼ teaspoon white pepper**
**3 tablespoons butter**
**2 finely chopped onions**

**1 kg (2 lb) chuck steak**
**½ teaspoon salt**
**500 g (1 lb) peeled tomatoes**
**5 cm (2 in) stick cinnamon**
**chopped parsley**

1  Soak lima beans overnight, drain and place in saucepan, add salt and cover with cold water.
2  Boil gently for 2 hours, drain again.
3  Heat butter in saucepan, add onions and suet.
4  Cook for 10 minutes and remove from saucepan.
5  Add cubed meat and brown on all sides, then replace onions and add tomatoes and cinnamon.
6  Simmer for 1½ hours or until tender.
7  Stir in lima beans, simmer for 15-20 minutes and sprinkle with parsley.

# SWISS STEAK CASSEROLE

*3 hours cooking time*

*Ingredients for 4-5 servings*

2 tablespoons butter
500 g (1 lb) topside steak
1 onion, sliced
2 tablespoons plain flour
1¼ cups water
¼ teaspoon white pepper

3 gherkins, cut into strips
1 tablespoon vinegar
1 tablespoon Worcestershire sauce
1 tablespoon tomato sauce
½ teaspoon salt
2 teaspoons brown sugar

1  Melt butter and add meat, brown on all sides.
2  Remove.
3  Add onions and sauté until golden brown and then add flour.
4  Add water and flavourings, gherkins, and return to heat.
5  Bring gently to the boil, then simmer for 2-3 hours.

# SWEET POTATO MINCE PIE

*20-30 minutes cooking time*

*Ingredients for 5-6 servings*

500 g-1 kg (1-2 lb) minced steak
¼ teaspoon white pepper
3 apples, peeled, cored and sliced
¼ cup brown sugar
sprinkle nutmeg

1 tablespoon butter
½ teaspoon salt
1 kg (2 lb) sweet potatoes, cooked,
   salted and thoroughly mashed

1  Sauté mince and add salt.
2  Add pepper.
3  Drain off fat and cover bottom of greased dish, top with sweet potato.
4  Add sliced apple, brown sugar and nutmeg.
5  Dot with butter and bake for 20-30 minutes.

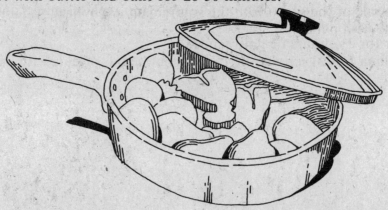

# HAMBURGER CASSEROLE

*45 minutes cooking time*

*Ingredients for 4 servings*

2 tablespoons butter
2 onions, sliced
500 g (1 lb) minced beef
1 tin tomato soup

1 large tin corn
1 cup mashed potatoes
1 beaten egg yolk

1  Melt butter in pan and fry onions and meat until brown.
2  Add soup and corn and mix.
3  Put into a greased baking dish and cover with potatoes.
4  Brush top with beaten egg yolk.
5  Bake in hot oven 230°C (450°F) until brown.

# HUNGARIAN BEEF STEW

*2 hours cooking time*

*Ingredients for 4-5 servings*

1 kg (2 lb) chuck steak
seasoned flour
2 tablespoons butter
chopped onions
½ teaspoon salt
2 teaspoons paprika

2 cups beef stock
375 g (12 oz) sliced mushrooms
½ cup cream
½ teaspoon lemon juice
¼ teaspoon white pepper
chopped parsley

1  Stir lemon juice into cream and let stand.
2  Cube meat and toss in seasoned flour.
3  Heat butter and add onions, brown lightly.
4  Remove onions and place meat in saucepan.
5  Brown meat and return onions to saucepan with mushrooms, stock, salt, pepper, paprika and simmer for 2 hours.
6  Blend some of the sauce with the sour cream and reheat.
7  Sprinkle with parsley.

# HAMBURGER AND RICE CASSEROLE

*30 minutes cooking time*

*Ingredients for 6 servings*

**750 g (1½ lb) coarse minced beef**
**1 onion, chopped finely**
**1 teaspoon salt**

**¼ teaspoon pepper**
**½ teaspoon powdered sage**
**3 cups cooked, drained rice**

1　Combine meat, onion, salt, pepper and sage.
2　Put in saucepan with 1 cup water and cook over low heat for 15 minutes.
3　Line a greased casserole dish with half the rice.
4　Add meat and cover with remaining rice.
5　Bake in moderate oven 180°C (350°F) for 15-20 minutes.

# WINTER HOT POT

*2½ hours cooking time*

*Ingredients for 5-6 servings*

**2 tablespoons butter**
**1 kg (2 lb) topside steak**
**2 teaspoons sugar**
**2 teaspoons plain flour**
**2 cups stock or water**
**¼ teaspoon white pepper**
**peas**

**2 tomatoes, skinned**
**2 green peppers**
**1 bay leaf**
**pinch of thyme**
**½ teaspoon salt**
**noodles**

1　Melt butter and add cubed meat, brown on all sides.
2　Sprinkle with sugar and continue browning.
3　Sprinkle over flour and brown.
4　Remove from heat and add beef stock, tomatoes, peppers, bay leaf, thyme, salt and pepper.
5　Bring to the boil and simmer gently for 2-2½ hours.
6　Serve with buttered noodles and buttered peas.

# CURRIED STEAK AND RICE

*20 minutes cooking time*

*Ingredients for 4-5 servings*

1 banana
1 cooking apple
2 medium onions
1 carrot
¼ teaspoon white pepper
500 g (1 lb) minced steak

2 teaspoons chopped parsley
3 teaspoons curry powder
1 cup cooked rice
½ teaspoon salt
1 potato
1 cup beef stock

1  Peel and chop fruit and vegetables.
2  Put steak and curry powder into large saucepan.
3  Cook over low heat.
4  Add vegetables, parsley and stock.
5  Simmer for 15 minutes.
6  Remove from heat, stir in rice, season to taste.
7  Serve with slices of toast.

# CRISPY CASSEROLE

*40 minutes cooking time*

*Ingredients for 2-4 servings*

1 kg (2 lb) blade steak

1 packet mixed vegetables

## CHEESE PASTRY

185 g (6 oz) self-raising flour
¼ teaspoon white pepper
90 g (3 oz) finely grated cheese
½ cup milk

½ teaspoon salt
90 g (3 oz) shredded suet
1 beaten egg

1  Cube meat then brown, drain and place in casserole dish.
2  Cook vegetables, strain then add to the meat.
3  To prepare pastry, sift flour with salt and pepper.
4  Stir in cheese and suet.
5  Mix together and bind with milk.
6  Roll out prepared pastry and brush with beaten egg that is left.
7  Cover meat with pastry and bake in moderate oven 190°C (375° F).

# BOILED BEEF WITH CARROTS

*3-4 hours cooking time*

*Ingredients for 6-8 servings*

2-2.5 kg (4-5 lb) round of beef
2-4 large carrots
2 stalks celery
1 teaspoon salt
1 bouquet garni

10 cups water
2 onions
8 peppercorns
2 cloves

1  Wash and prepare vegetables, tie beef securely in shape.
2  Cover meat and vegetables with water and bring to boil, simmer for 20-30 minutes.
3  Skim.
4  Add peppercorns, salt, cloves, bouquet garni and simmer for 3-4 hours.
5  Remove meat and place in heated dish.
6  Accompany with onion sauce.

# FRUITED BEEF AND WINE CASSEROLE

*3 hours cooking time*

*Ingredients for 5-6 servings*

2 tablespoons butter
1 kg (2 lb) topside steak
2 rashers bacon
2 onions, chopped
2 carrots, sliced
grated cheese

250 g (8 oz) prunes
½ teaspoon salt
¼ teaspoon white pepper
1½ cups dry red wine
250 g (8 oz) noodles

1  Melt butter and brown cubed meat.
2  Remove.
3  Add bacon, onions, carrots and sauté for 5 minutes.
4  Add prunes, salt, pepper and wine and the meat.
5  Bring to the boil and simmer for 2-3 hours.
6  Cook noodles and arrange on dish.
7  Sprinkle with grated cheese.

# GREEK STEW

*1½ hours cooking time*

*Ingredients for 5-6 servings*

1.25 kg (2½ lb) stewing beef
flour
oil
10 small onions
1 cup tomato paste
¼ teaspoon white pepper

1 cup water
2 cups red wine
3 sliced carrots
3 potatoes, cubed
½ teaspoon salt
2 teaspoons cinnamon

1　Cube meat, dip into flour.
2　Brown in oil and place in casserole dish.
3　Brown onions and add to casserole.
4　Add tomato paste, water and red wine.
5　Cover and bake in moderate oven 180°C (350°F) for 1 hour.
6　Add carrots, potatoes, salt, pepper and cinnamon.
7　Cover and cook for a further 30 minutes.

# STEAK AND PINEAPPLE CASSEROLE

*1½ hours cooking time*

*Ingredients for 4-6 servings*

1 kg (2 lb) topside steak
2 onions
1 small tin pineapple pieces
1 cup stock

½ teaspoon salt
¾ teaspoon white pepper
1½ tablespoons butter
1 tablespoon plain flour

1　Chop onions and brown in butter, remove to one side of pan.
2　Add salt and pepper and cubed meat which has been dipped into flour.
3　Brown on all sides.
4　Add wine and stock, drained pineapple pieces.
5　Place lid on saucepan and simmer gently for 1¼ hours.
6　Add chopped parsley when cooked.
7　Serve immediately.

# FOUNDATION BROWN STEW

*2 hours cooking time*

*Ingredients for 4 servings*

| | |
|---|---|
| 500 g (1 lb) chuck steak | 2 tablespoons plain flour |
| 1 tablespoon butter | 2½ cups water or stock |
| 1 onion, chopped | ½ teaspoon salt |
| ¼ teaspoon white pepper | chopped parsley |

1 Trim meat and cube, brown in butter.
2 Remove meat.
3 Add onion and sauté for 2 minutes.
4 Add liquid and bring to the boil.
5 Season with salt and pepper and return to heat. Simmer for 2 hours, thickening slowly with flour paste.

# CABBAGE ROLLS

*1 hour cooking time*

*Ingredients for 8 servings*

| | |
|---|---|
| 750 g (1½ lb) ground beef | 1½ teaspoons salt |
| 375 g (12 oz) ground pork | ½ teaspoon pepper |
| 2 chopped onions | 1 cabbage |
| 2 teaspoons sugar | 2 tablespoons butter |
| 2 cups cooked rice | 1 cup cream |

1 Combine meat, onion, sugar, seasoning.
2 Add rice.
3 Blanche cabbage leaves in boiling water.
4 Roll each cabbage leaf around 3 tablespoons of meat-rice mixture and secure with toothpicks.
5 Place rolls in greased baking pan and dot with butter; add 1½ cups water.
6 Bake in moderate oven 180°C (350°F) 30 minutes on each side.
7 Heat cream and pour over rolls to serve.

# STUFFED CUCUMBERS

*45 minutes cooking time*

*Ingredients for 4 servings*

4 medium-sized cucumbers
500 g (1 lb) ground beef
2 chopped onions
125 g (4 oz) chopped mushrooms

2 tablespoons butter
1 teaspoon salt
½ teaspoon pepper
½ cup tomato juice

1   Peel cucumbers, slice lengthwise and remove seeds. Boil in salted water for 3-4 minutes only, then remove from pan.
2   Fry meat, onions, salt and pepper in butter for 5 minutes, add chopped mushrooms and fry gently for 5 minutes more.
3   Fill centre of cucumbers with meat mixture and place in baking pan.
4   Add tomato juice to pan and cook in moderate oven 180°C (350°F) for 30 minutes.

# LENINGRAD BEEF

*2 hours 20 minutes cooking time*

*Ingredients for 4 servings*

750 g (1½ lb) steak
1 tablespoon plain flour
1½ teaspoons salt
3 raw potatoes
6 peppercorns
3 tomatoes

1 tablespoon vinegar
½ teaspoon pepper
2 tablespoons butter
2 carrots
6 cabbage leaves
1 onion

1   Beat the steak well. Cut into 10 centimetre (4 in) squares and coat with seasoned flour.
2   Fry in butter until brown and place in a deep casserole dish.
3   Add sliced potato, whole cabbage leaves and sliced carrot.
4   Add vinegar, peppercorns and sliced tomato.
5   Add 1 tablespoon water and cook in covered dish for 2 hours at 180°C (350°F).

# BEEF AND OLIVES

*1½ hours cooking time*

*Ingredients for 4 servings*

**750 g (1½ lb) beef, cubed**
**1 teaspoon salt**
pinch marjoram
**375 g (12 oz) small white onions,**
**peeled**
**½ cup stuffed green olives**

**½ teaspoon pepper**
**4 tablespoons butter**
**8 small carrots, scraped**
**2 cups beef bouillon**
**¼ cup flour**

1　Dust meat with flour, salt, pepper and marjoram.
2　Brown meat in butter and place in casserole dish.
3　Add onions and carrots. Pour over bouillon and cover.
4　Bake in moderate oven for 1 hour and add olives 20 minutes before serving.
5　Pour off juices, thicken with butter and flour and serve.

# BEEF AND SPINACH CASSEROLE

*45 minutes cooking time*

*Ingredients for 4-6 servings*

**1.25 kg (2½ lb) ground beef**
**2 large bunches spinach**
**¾ cup chopped onion**
**2 teaspoons salt**
**1 teaspoon pepper**

**3 cloves garlic, minced**
**1½ tablespoons olive oil**
**juice of ½ lemon**
**6 cups water**

1　Fry ground beef, garlic and onion in olive oil for 5 minutes, then add salt and pepper and simmer for 10 minutes.
2　Cut base stalks off spinach and tear leaves into pieces before adding to meat.
3　Cook for 15-25 minutes, or until water is absorbed.
4　Sprinkle with lemon juice before serving.

# STEAK AND VEGETABLES

*1 hour 15 minutes cooking time*

*Ingredients for 4 servings*

750 g (1½ lb) round steak, cubed
½ cup shredded Cheddar cheese
1 onion, sliced
1 teaspoon salt
½ green pepper, sliced
1 tomato, peeled and sliced

1 tablespoon olive oil
1 teaspoon basil
¼ cup uncooked rice
6 fresh mushrooms, sliced
125 g (4 oz) fresh beans, sliced
1 cup sliced carrot

1  Brown meat in oil and arrange one third of vegetables in casserole.
2  Place half of the meat pieces over vegetables and sprinkle with a little rice and seasonings.
3  Add another third of vegetables, remaining meat and a little more seasonings. Add remaining rice.
4  Top with remaining vegetables and cover. Bake in casserole for 45 minutes. Sprinkle with cheese and bake for further 15-20 minutes.

# BROAD BEAN-MEATBALL CASSEROLE

*45 minutes cooking time*

*Ingredients for 6 servings*

500 g (1 lb) ground beef
2 eggs
½ cup breadcrumbs
4 tablespoons butter
1 packet frozen broad beans

1 clove garlic
1 teaspoon salt
½ teaspoon pepper
⅓ cup milk
1 cup sour cream

1  Cook broad beans according to directions, drain (save liquid) and top with half the butter.
2  Mix milk, meat, breadcrumbs, minced garlic, salt and pepper and shape into meat balls.
3  Brown meat balls in remaining butter and transfer to greased casserole dish.
4  Pour ½ cup liquid from cooked beans into pan and heat to boiling, pour over meatballs.
5  Mix broad beans with sour cream and put over meat balls; cover and bake in low oven 150°C (300°F) for 30 minutes.

# CURRY CABBAGE COMBINATION

*40 minutes cooking time*

*Ingredients for 6-8 servings*

750 g (1½ lb) ground beef
¾ cup chopped onion
¾ cup fresh peas
10 cups chicken stock
3 tablespoons butter
1 cup chopped cabbage

250 g (8 oz) uncooked rice
1½ tablespoons curry powder
1 teaspoon salt
½ teaspoon pepper
2 cloves minced garlic

1   Fry meat, onion, garlic and curry powder in butter for 10 minutes.
2   Add seasoning, stock and rice and simmer for 20 minutes.
3   Add peas and cabbage and cook for further 10 minutes.

# SILVERSIDE

*2 hours cooking time*

*Ingredients for 6 servings*

750 g (1½ lb) silverside
45 g (1½ oz) Parmesan cheese
½ teaspoon pepper
45 g (1½ oz) plain flour
185 g (6 oz) tomato purée
250 g (8 oz) onions
3 green peppers

bouquet garni
1 teaspoon salt
45 g (1½ oz) dripping
4 cups stock
375 g (12 oz) tomatoes
500 g (1 lb) potatoes
500 g (1 lb) carrots

1   Chop onions and cook gently in dripping for 3 minutes.
2   Skin and remove seeds from tomatoes.
3   Cube silverside and coat in seasoned flour.
4   Brown in fat and add flour, tomatoes, and purée; mix in stock gradually and boil.
5   Place these ingredients in casserole and add chopped peppers, carrots, seasonings and bouquet garni.
6   Add potatoes and cover.
7   Cook for 2 hours in moderate oven and when ready to serve, sprinkle with Parmesan cheese.

# MACARONI BEEF SUPPER

*50 minutes cooking time*

*Ingredients for 4-5 servings*

500 g (1 lb) ground beef
½ cup butter
1 chopped onion
250 g (8 oz) cooked, drained macaroni
⅛ cup beef stock
⅛ cup tomato sauce
½ cup grated Cheddar cheese
5 tablespoons chopped parsley

1 teaspoon salt
3 tablespoons flour
1¼ cups milk
½ teaspoon pepper
½ teaspoon dry mustard
½ teaspoon oregano
1 teaspoon Worcestershire sauce
2 beaten eggs

1　Melt half the butter and fry meat and onion until meat is thoroughly brown.
2　Mix meat and onions with beef stock, cooked macaroni, tomato sauce, half the cheese, parsley, salt, pepper, oregano and Worcestershire sauce and place in casserole.
3　Melt the rest of the butter, stir in flour, then add milk and stir over heat until thickened.
4　Pour white sauce slowly into beaten eggs, stirring.
5　Then pour white sauce into casserole, top with rest of cheese and bake in moderate oven 180°C (350°F) for 30-40 minutes.
6　Stand for 10 minutes before serving.

# TRIPE NANCY

*6 hours cooking time*

*Ingredients for 4 servings*

1 kg (2 lb) tripe
1 teaspoon salt
4 cloves
2 carrots
½ cup brandy
3 tablespoons chopped parsley

½ teaspoon pepper
5 leeks
2½ cups white wine
4 onions
2 sprigs thyme
2 bay leaves

1　Wash tripe and blanch it. Cut into small pieces.
2　Season and add herbs and onions and place in casserole.
3　Add sliced leeks and carrots, wine and brandy. Cover and cook gently for 6 hours in slow oven 150°C (300°F).
4　Remove herbs and skim the surface before serving.

# MOUSSAKA

*1 hour 45 minutes cooking time*

*Ingredients for 4-6 servings*

500 g (1 lb) ground beef
500 g (1 lb) potatoes
2 large eggplants
4 sliced onions
4 sliced tomatoes
125 g (4 oz) butter

1 teaspoon salt
½ teaspoon pepper
1¼ cups milk
60 g (2 oz) flour
1 egg
125 g (4 oz) grated cheese

1  Fry sliced onions in half the butter for 5 minutes; remove and fry sliced potatoes and eggplant and remove.
2  Add remaining butter to pan, then flour and stir well.
3  Pour milk into pan and cook gently until thickened, then add salt and pepper.
4  Remove from heat, add beaten eggs and cheese.
5  Layer potatoes, meat, onion, eggplant and tomato in casserole, topping each layer with sauce.
6  Bake in moderate oven 180°C (350°) for 1½ hours.

# SPAGHETTI CASSEROLE

*40 minutes cooking time*

*Ingredients for 6-8 servings*

750 g (1½ lb) ground beef
250 g (8 oz) thin spaghetti
250 g (8 oz) grated tasty cheese
½ cup chopped onion
3 tablespoons olive oil
1 large tin tomato soup

1 teaspoon salt
½ teaspoon pepper
1 large tin whole corn
125 g (4 oz) fresh mushrooms, chopped
2 cups water

1  Fry meat and onion in olive oil.
2  Mix meat with soup and drained corn in casserole.
3  Add water and stir in broken spaghetti and seasonings.
4  Top with cheese and bake in moderate oven 180°C (350°F) for 30-35 minutes.

# SPARERIBS IN BLACK BEAN SAUCE

*1 hour 20 minutes cooking time*

*Ingredients for 6 servings*

**1.5 kg (3 lb) spareribs, cut
    into 2.5 cm (1 in) pieces**
**4 tablespoons black beans**
**½ teaspoon ground ginger**
**2 teaspoons soy sauce**
**3 tablespoons vinegar**
**2 teaspoons sugar**

**2 spring onions, chopped**
**3 cloves garlic**
**2 teaspoons cornflour**
**4 tablespoons chicken stock**
**2 tablespoons peanut oil**
**4 tablespoons sherry**

1  Put spareribs in boiling water for 5 minutes, drain and rinse in cold water.
2  Crush black beans with garlic and ginger.
3  Mix sugar, cornflour, soy sauce, vinegar, chicken stock and sherry.
4  Heat oil and brown spareribs. Add black bean mixture and stir.
5  Pour soy sauce mixture over spareribs and add spring onions. Transfer to ovenproof dish and bake for 1 hour in moderate oven.

# CLAREMONT MEAT PIE

*1 hour cooking time*

*Ingredients for 6 servings*

**500 g (1 lb) ground beef**
**1 chopped onion**
**2 raw eggs**
**2 hardboiled eggs**
**12 pitted black olives**

**½ teaspoon cayenne pepper**
**½ teaspoon oregano**
**¼ cup canned consommé**
**1 large can creamed corn**
**1 teaspoon salt**

1  Mix meat with onion, chopped olives and chopped hardboiled eggs.
2  Add oregano, consommé, salt and cayenne pepper to meat.
3  Mix beaten eggs with corn.
4  Line greased pie plate with meat mixture, fill with corn and egg mixture and bake for 40 minutes at 180°C (350°F) then 20 minutes at 200°C (400°F).
5  Cool for ten minutes before cutting to serve in wedges.

# PADUAN BEEF

*2 hours cooking time*

*Ingredients for 4-5 servings*

1 kg (2 lb) chuck steak
1 teaspoon salt
2 tablespoons olive oil
1 tin whole tomatoes
1 tablespoon chopped parsley

1 tablespoon minced onion
½ teaspoon pepper
4 slices Mozzarella cheese
½ teaspoon dried oregano
1 garlic clove, minced

1  Preheat oven to 180°C (350°F).
2  Arrange steak, cut into pieces, in a baking dish.
3  Mash the tomatoes with a spoon and spread over steak.
4  Sprinkle with oregano, parsley, garlic and onion. Season with salt and pepper. Dot with oil and bake uncovered for 1½ hours.
5  Top with cheese and bake for a further 15-20 minutes.

# JOANNE'S BEEF CASSEROLE

*40 minutes cooking time*

*Ingredients for 4-5 servings*

500 g (1 lb) ground beef
1 chopped onion
½ cup grated Cheddar cheese
¼ cup butter
125 g (4 oz) macaroni
5 tablespoons tomato sauce
5 tablespoons white wine

1½ teaspoons salt
½ teaspoon pepper
2 tablespoons chopped parsley
4 tablespoons plain flour
1¼ cups milk
1 teaspoon dry mustard
1 egg

1  Fry ground beef and onion in half the butter, and add to cooked macaroni, wine, tomato sauce, half the cheese, salt, pepper and parsley.
2  Pour into greased casserole.
3  Heat remaining butter, stir in flour and cook for 2-3 minutes before adding milk and mustard; pour gradually into beaten egg and then pour into casserole.
4  Top with grated cheese and bake for 40 minutes in moderate oven 180°C (350°F).

# TAMALE PIE

*Ingredients for 8-10 servings*

*1 hour 30 minutes cooking time*

1 kg (2 lb) ground beef
3 chopped onions
1 teaspoon salt
½ teaspoon oregano
½ teaspoon basil
3 tablespoons Mexican chilli powder
2 teaspoons sugar

1 large can tomatoes
1 small can tomato paste
1 cup yellow maize meal
1 cup pitted ripe olives
½ cup chopped Pepperoni sausage
⅓ cup grated Cheddar cheese
2 tablespoons olive oil

1  Cook onions in oil until brown, then add meat and cook 10 minutes.
2  Add salt, oregano, basil, chilli powder, and sugar, then tomatoes and tomato paste and simmer for 1 hour.
3  Mix maize meal with ½ cup cold water and add ½ teaspoon salt. Stir into 3 cups boiling water and cook, stirring for about 10 minutes.
4  Put layer of corn meal in large greased casserole, add meat and olives, then put remaining corn meal on top.
5  Top with sausage and cheese and brown in hot oven for 10-15 minutes.

# BATTER-TOPPED BEEF

*Ingredients for 4-6 servings*

*15 minutes cooking time*

500 g (1 lb) ground beef
1 small tin cream of mushroom soup
125 g (4 oz) sliced mushrooms
1 chopped onion
1 tablespoon butter
1 teaspoon salt

½ teaspoon pepper
1 tablespoon Worcestershire sauce
125 g (4 oz) plain flour
2 eggs
4 tablespoons cream
4 tablespoons water

1  Mix meat, Worcestershire sauce, salt and pepper, stir in soup and place in casserole.
2  Cook onions in butter for 5 minutes, add to casserole and cook in oven for 10 minutes at 200°C (400°F), then add mushrooms.
3  Make batter of remaining ingredients and spoon on top of casserole. Return to oven for 30 minutes.

# DIANE'S BEEF WITH CAULIFLOWER

*40 minutes cooking time*

*Ingredients for 6-8 servings*

1 kg (2 lb) ground beef
2 chopped onions
2 tablespoons butter
2 tablespoons Worcestershire sauce
½ cup chopped green pepper

1½ cups white sauce
½ cup grated cheese
1 cauliflower, cut into flowerets
1 teaspoon salt
½ teaspoon pepper

1   Parboil cauliflower for 10 minutes.
2   Fry onion and pepper in butter for 5 minutes, then add meat, Worcestershire sauce and salt and pepper and cook until brown.
3   Add all but 4 tablespoons grated cheese to white sauce, mix with meat and cauliflower and spoon into casserole.
4   Bake in oven at 200°C (400°F) for 10 minutes, top with remaining cheese and cook 5 minutes longer.

# BEEF STEW

*2 hours cooking time*

*Ingredients for 4 servings*

375 g (12 oz) beef, cubed
⅓ cup plain flour
1 tablespoon Worcestershire sauce
1 onion, sliced
½ teaspoon pepper

1 cup broad beans, boiled
½ cup tinned tomatoes
1 sliced carrot
1 tablespoon butter
½ teaspoon salt

1   Combine flour, salt, pepper and coat meat.
2   Melt butter and sauté meat gently.
3   Place alternate layers of meat and vegetables in casserole dish.
4   Pour in tomatoes and Worcestershire sauce and cover.
5   Bake in moderate oven for 2 hours.

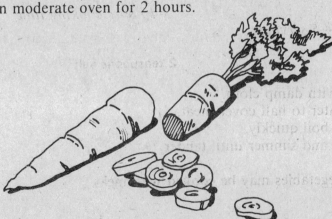

# ORIENTAL STEAK

*2 hours cooking time*

*Ingredients for 2-3 servings*

2 tablespoons olive oil
3 tablespoons sherry
500 g-1 kg (1-2 lb) grilling steak

1 tablespoon soy sauce
2 cloves garlic

1 Mix oil, soy sauce, sherry with chopped garlic.
2 Cut steak into serving pieces and leave to soak for 2 hours.
3 Drain.
4 Cook under hot grill for 8-10 minutes.
5 Serve with mixed vegetables.

# HONG KONG HASH

*1 hour cooking time*

*Ingredients for 4 servings*

250 g (8 oz) ground beef
1 chopped onion
1 can mushroom soup
½ cup raw rice
⅛ cup soy sauce

¼ teaspoon pepper
1 tablespoon oil
½ cup sliced celery
½ cup bean sprouts

1 Brown meat in oil, add celery, onions, soup and ¾ cup warm water.
2 Stir in pepper, rice and soy sauce and turn into greased casserole.
3 Cook in moderate oven 180°C (350°F) for 30 minutes covered, then uncover and cook 30 minutes longer.

# SIMMERED BEEF

*3-4 hours cooking time*

*Ingredients for 4-5 servings*

2 kg (4 lb) beef

2 teaspoons salt

1 Wipe meat with damp cloth.
2 Add cold water to half cover meat.
3 Bring to the boil quickly.
4 Reduce heat and simmer until tender.
5 Add salt.
6 If desired, vegetables may be cooked with meat.

# Lamb

## SPICY LAMB CASSEROLE

*Ingredients for 4 servings*

*1¼ hours cooking time*

| | |
|---|---|
| 750 g (1½ lb) boned shoulder of lamb | 1 onion, sliced |
| 1 teaspoon salt | 1 carrot, sliced |
| ½ teaspoon pepper | ¼ cup vinegar |
| ¼ teaspoon mixed herbs | 1 cup cooked rice |
| 1 sprig parsley or chopped parsley | 3 tablespoons raisins |

1 Remove fat from meat and cut into 2.5 centimetre (1 in) cubes.
2 Place in casserole with salt, pepper, herbs, onion, carrot and vinegar and marinate for 2 hours.
3 Add just enough water to cover.
4 Place casserole in a moderate oven 180°C (350°F) and cook covered for 1 hour.
5 Cook the rice and add to the casserole with the raisins.
6 Cook for further 5-10 minutes then serve sprinkled with chopped parsley.

# ROAST LAMB CASSEROLE

*1¼ hours cooking time*

*Ingredients for 4 servings*

12 slices cooked lamb
3 sliced onions
125 g (4 oz) sliced fresh mushrooms
½ red pepper, chopped
1 tablespoon butter
1½ cups stock

1 tablespoon tomato purée
1 teaspoon salt
¼ teaspoon pepper
1 cooking apple, peeled and sliced
2 tablespoons chopped parsley

1   Place meat in a casserole dish.
2   Lightly sauté the onions in the melted butter until golden.
3   Add the mushrooms and cook for 3 minutes.
4   Combine chopped pepper, stock and tomato purée and pour the mixture over the lamb.
5   Cover and bake in a moderate oven 180°C (350°F) for 30 minutes.
6   Add the slices of apple to the casserole, then cover again and cook for a further 30 minutes.
7   To serve, sprinkle with parsley.

# NAVARIN LAMB

*1 hour cooking time*

*Ingredients for 5-6 servings*

1.5 kg (3 lb) middle neck chops
1 small piece turnip
1 tablespoon butter
1 tablespoon plain flour
1¼ cups stock
1 bouquet garni

3 carrots
3 onions, quartered
sugar
1 teaspoon salt
½ teaspoon white pepper

1    Cut and trim meat, cut carrots and turnip.
2    Heat a shallow casserole, and add butter.
3    When smoking lay in the meat.
4    Brown the meat on all sides, then take out.
5    Put the vegetables in and fry slowly.
6    Add a pinch of sugar.
7    Now stir in flour and add stock.
8    Bring to the boil and replace meat in casserole.
9    Season with bouquet garni and cover.
10   Simmer for 1 hour.
11   Serve with creamed potatoes.

# POTTED LAMB WITH ONIONS

*3 hours cooking time*

*Ingredients for 5-6 servings*

**1.5-2 kg (3-4 lb) lamb**
**7 potatoes, sliced**
**5 sliced onions**

**1 tablespoon plain flour**
**2½ teaspoons salt**
**1 teaspoon white pepper**

1 Wipe meat with damp cloth.
2 Salt, pepper and flour should be combined thoroughly.
3 Cut meat into squares and roll in mixture.
4 Place layer of meat, onions and potatoes in a pot having layer of potatoes on top.
5 Cover, and bake for 3 hours in moderate oven 180°C (350°F).

# LAMB CHOPS CASSEROLE

*45 minutes cooking time*

*Ingredients for 4-5 servings*

**8 thin lamb chops**
**2 tablespoons butter**
**1 teaspoon salt**
**¼ teaspoon white pepper**
**4 cored and peeled apples**

**4 small onions**
**4 potatoes**
**1 can tomatoes**
**4 sliced tomatoes**

1 Wipe meat with damp cloth.
2 Melt butter in frying pan.
3 Lightly brown meat on both sides.
4 Sprinkle with salt and pepper.
5 Place sliced tomatoes, apples, onions and potatoes in dish, lay chops on top, pour in canned tomatoes and cover.
6 Bake in moderate oven 180°C (350°F).

# IRISH STEW

*Ingredients for 6 servings*

*2 hours cooking time*

12 best end of neck chops
3 medium onions
6 large potatoes
1 teaspoon salt

½ teaspoon pepper
3 cups vegetable or meat stock
1 tablespoon chopped parsley

1  Layer chops, sliced onions and sliced potatoes in a large pan, sprinkling each layer with salt and pepper.
2  Add stock.
3  Boil and spoon off fat.
4  Reduce heat, cover and simmer for about 1½ hours.
5  Sprinkle with chopped parsley to serve.

# LAMB STEW

*Ingredients for 5-6 servings*

*1½ hours cooking time*

1 kg (2 lb) lamb leg chops
1 tablespoon butter
1 teaspoon salt
4 small onions
1 teaspoon sugar
2 cups water
1 cup cooked peas

2 large tomatoes
4 carrots
¼ teaspoon white pepper
1 clove garlic
1 tablespoon plain flour
4 potatoes
3 tablespoons sherry or marsala

1  Sprinkle the chops with pepper and salt and brown.
2  Drain the fat and lower heat.
3  Sprinkle in garlic and flour, cook until absorbed.
4  Stir in water and chopped tomato.
5  Place in casserole and add 1 onion and 1 carrot.
6  Bake for 30 minutes in moderate oven 180°C (350°F).
7  Heat fat once more and add vegetables, except peas, and cook until tender.
8  Before serving, add peas and sherry or marsala.

# LAMB CIVET

*1½ hours cooking time*

*Ingredients for 5-6 servings*

1 kg (2 lb) lamb
2 tablespoons butter
½ cup sliced onion
3 cups diced turnips

1 chopped green pepper
1 chopped red pepper
1 teaspoon salt
¼ teaspoon white pepper

1 Wipe meat with damp cloth.
2 Cut lamb into pieces and roll in flour.
3 Melt butter and add onion.
4 Add meat and sauté.
5 When cooked remove meat and onions and place in baking dish.
6 Pour 5 cups water into dish, cover and simmer.
7 After 1 hour, add turnip and green and red peppers.
8 Serve immediately.

# LAMB STROGANOFF

*1¼ hours cooking time*

*Ingredients for 5-6 servings*

2 tablespoons butter
2 onions, sliced
750 g (1½ lb) neck chops
1 teaspoon salt
1½ cups stock
3 tablespoons sherry

500 g (1 lb) mushrooms
2 cloves garlic
½ cup plain flour
½ teaspoon white pepper
3 tomatoes, peeled
4 tablespoons sour cream

1 Melt butter, saute mushrooms, onions and garlic.
2 Coat meat in flour and seasoning, sauté in pan.
3 Add stock, tomatoes, mushrooms, onions and meat; cover and simmer for 1 hour.
4 Blend flour with a little water and add to the saucepan.
5 Add sherry and sour cream, do not allow mixture to boil.
6 Serve with boiled rice or noodles and green peas.

# LAMB CASSEROLE

*30 minutes cooking time*

*Ingredients for 4-5 servings*

3 cups roast lamb
1 tablespoon butter
1 cup carrots, diced
1 cup potato, diced
2 cups brown sauce
1 teaspoon Worcestershire sauce

8 small onions, boiled
1 cup French beans
½ cup boiled peas
1 teaspoon salt
⅛ teaspoon white pepper

1  Sauté lamb in hot butter and place in baking dish.
2  Add vegetables and brown sauce together with salt and pepper and Worcestershire sauce.
3  Cover and bake in very hot oven 230°C (450°F) for 20-30 minutes.
4  Serve with boiled rice or noodles.

# LAMB CUTLETS IN PORT

*2 hours cooking time*

*Ingredients for 5-6 servings*

1.5 kg (3 lb) lamb cutlets
1 tablespoon butter
3 onions
4 tomatoes
1 tablespoon plain flour
1 glass port wine

celery salt
¼ teaspoon white pepper
1 small lemon
chopped parsley
2 teaspoons red currant jelly
2½ cups stock

1  Trim and brown cutlets on both sides in butter.
2  Brown onions separately.
3  Put cutlets and onions in a baking dish and add tomatoes.
4  Brown plain flour in fat and add stock, celery, salt and pepper.
5  Squeeze lemon, and pour into this sauce.
6  Add to dish and cover, bake in slow oven 150°C (300°F) for 2 hours.
7  Just before serving, add jelly, port and parsley.

# LAMB CURRY

*40 minutes cooking time*

*Ingredients for 5-6 servings*

1 shoulder of lamb
2 tablespoons butter
2 tablespoons chopped onion
8 tablespoons cream

2 teaspoons curry powder
1 tablespoon plain flour
1¼ cups stock

1 Cube meat and season with salt and pepper.
2 Melt butter and sauté meat.
3 Fry onion and add curry powder.
4 Stir in flour, then add stock and stir.
5 Boil for 10-15 minutes and add cream.
6 Serve with rice.

# PILAU D'AGNEAU

*1 hour cooking time*

*Ingredients for 6-8 servings*

1 shoulder of lamb
2 tablespoons finely chopped onion
butter

250 g (8 oz) long-grain rice
2 cups stock

1 Cube meat and cook slowly in butter.
2 Brown onion separately and add rice.
3 Drain.
4 Add stock and cover.
5 Cook for 20 minutes.
6 Mix with meat and serve with sauce.

## SAUCE

1.25 kg (2½ lb) ripe tomatoes
½ teaspoon salt
1 clove garlic

2 teaspoons chopped parsley
¼ teaspoon white pepper
8 tablespoons olive oil

1 Peel tomatoes and remove seeds.
2 Chop and place in pan with other ingredients.
3 Cover and simmer for 30 minutes.

# LAMB AND TOMATO CASSEROLE

*2 hours cooking time*

*Ingredients for 5-6 servings*

**1-1.25 kg (2-2½ lb) lamb**
**¼ teaspoon white pepper**
**2 onions**
**2-4 tablespoons sour cream**

**½ teaspoon salt**
**1 tablespoon butter**
**2 cups tomato purée**
**1 tablespoon chopped parsley**

1    Divide meat into pieces and rub with seasoning.
2    Melt butter and brown meat and sliced onions.
3    Take out meat and onions and place tomatoes in dish.
4    Simmer for 10 minutes.
5    Return meat and onions to dish with tomatoes and cook slowly for 1-2 hours.
6    Serve with boiled potatoes.

# LAMB AND POTATO CASSEROLE

*2½ hours cooking time*

*Ingredients for 5-6 servings*

**1 kg (2 lb) lamb neck chops**
**8 potatoes**
**4 large onions**
**2 cups water**

**3 teaspoons salt**
**1 teaspoon white pepper**
**1 teaspoon thyme**

1    Trim chops and peel potatoes and cut into large, even slices.
2    Put sliced potatoes in base of large casserole.
3    Add thickly sliced onions and arrange meat evenly.
4    Sprinkle with salt, pepper, thyme and add remaining sliced onions.
5    Top with potatoes.
6    Sprinkle with more salt and pepper.
7    Add liquid, cover with foil and place lid on top.
8    Cook in moderate oven 180°C (350°F) for 2½ hours.
9    Serve with boiled carrots and rice.

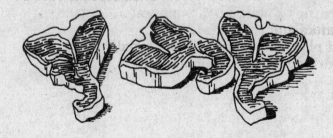

# HARICOT STEW

*2½ hours cooking time*

*Ingredients for 4-5 servings*

1 kg (2 lb) leg chops
1 onion
2 carrots
1 small parsnip
½ cup vinegar

2 stalks celery
2 tablespoons butter
2 teaspoons sugar
2 tablespoons plain flour

1   Trim chops and cut into 3-4 pieces.
2   Chop onion, carrot, parsnip and celery.
3   Melt butter and brown meat.
4   Remove meat and add vegetables, sprinkled with sugar.
5   Sauté until brown, add flour and bring to boil.
6   Return meat, flavour with salt and pepper and vinegar.
7   Simmer for 2½ hours.

# DEVILLED LAMB CHOPS

*1¼ hours cooking time*

*Ingredients for 4-5 servings*

4 lamb chump chops
prepared mustard
seasoned flour
1 green pepper
¾ teaspoon white pepper
grated lemon rind

2 large onions
1 can tomato soup
½ soup can water
1 teaspoon salt
chopped parsley

1   Trim chops and spread on one side with mustard.
2   Dust with seasoned flour.
3   Heat fat and brown on all sides.
4   Drain.
5   Place in a greased casserole dish.
6   Arrange green peppers and onions over chops.
7   Sprinkle lightly with lemon rind.
8   Pour over the combined soup and water.
9   Cover and bake for 1-1¼ hours.
10  Serve with sprinkled parsley.

# MINTY CASSEROLE

*1½ hours cooking time*

*Ingredients for 4-5 servings*

| | |
|---|---|
| 5 lamb chops | 3 tablespoons seasoned plain flour |
| 1 tablespoon butter | 1 chicken stock cube |
| 1 tablespoon chopped mint | 1 teaspoon sugar |
| ½ teaspoon salt | ⅛ teaspoon white pepper |
| 1 cup water | lemon juice |

1  Trim chops and season with flour.
2  Melt butter and add mint and chops and brown.
3  Transfer to casserole dish.
4  Add remaining flour to butter in pan and cook for 3 minutes.
5  Remove from heat and gradually add water in which stock cube has been dissolved.
6  Add lemon juice and sugar, pour over meat.
7  Cover and bake in a moderate oven 180°C (350°F) for 1-1½ hours.
8  Season to taste.
9  Serve immediately.

# BAKED STUFFED CHOPS

*30 minutes cooking time*

*Ingredients for 4-5 servings*

| | |
|---|---|
| 6 mutton chops | ½ teaspoon white pepper |
| 2 teaspoons onion juice | 2 sheep's kidneys, minced |
| ½ teaspoon salt | seasoned flour |

1  Preheat oven to 190°C (375°F) and trim meat.
2  Make an incision from the outside edge of each chop.
3  Add onion and seasoning to the kidney and fill the cavities in the chops.
4  Skewer to hold edges together.
5  Dip in seasoned flour and place in baking dish.
6  Bake for 30 minutes.

# HUNTER CASSEROLE

*2 hours cooking time*

*Ingredients for 4 servings*

6 potatoes, peeled and sliced
1 kg (2 lb) lamb shoulder
¼ teaspoon white pepper
250 g (8 oz) mushrooms, sliced
2 tablespoons butter

1 onion, peeled and sliced
½ teaspoon salt
2 lamb kidneys, sliced
1 cup red wine

1 Brown onions.
2 Place half the potato slices in casserole dish.
3 Cube meat and roll in flour.
4 Sauté in butter.
5 Add meat to casserole dish and cover with onion and mushrooms.
6 Add salt and pepper.
7 Add wine and place remaining potatoes on top.
8 Brush with melted butter and cook in moderate oven 190°C (375°F) for 2 hours.

# LAMB MUSHROOM CASSEROLE

*1-2 hours cooking time*

*Ingredients for 4-5 servings*

1 kg (2 lb) lamb neck chops
2 tablespoons butter
1 tablespoon chopped onion
2 tablespoons plain flour
1 teaspoon cayenne pepper

1 cup stock
1 can sliced mushrooms
1 cup sliced tomatoes
1 teaspoon salt

1 Preheat oven to moderate.
2 Cube meat and brown in butter.
3 Remove meat and fry onion.
4 Add flour and make gravy with stock and mushrooms.
5 Add meat and tomatoes and flavourings.
6 Place in casserole and cover.
7 Bake for 2 hours.

# SPICY LAMB

*1-2 hours cooking time*

*Ingredients for 7-8 servings*

1 kg (2 lb) boned lamb
½ cup white wine
½ cup white vinegar
1 onion, sliced
1 teaspoon salt

pinch thyme
pinch marjoram
water to cover
1 cup cooked rice
3 tablespoons raisins

1  Cube meat and remove fat.
2  Marinate one hour in wine and vinegar.
3  Add sliced onion, salt, thyme and marjoram.
4  Put all these ingredients into greased casserole dish.
5  Add water and cover. Cook gently for 1-2 hours.
6  Add rice and raisins and serve.

# LAMB STEAKS WITH GINGER

*35 minutes cooking time*

*Ingredients for 4-5 servings*

4-5 lamb steaks
450 g (15 oz) can pineapple

1 teaspoon ground ginger
1 teaspoon curry powder

## GINGER RICE

reserved marinade
water

1 teaspoon salt
250 g (8 oz) rice

1  Place steaks in single layer in shallow dish.
2  Combine pineapple, ginger and curry powder and sprinkle over meat.
3  Leave for 12 hours, turning occasionally.
4  Drain steaks and reserve marinade.
5  To prepare ginger rice, measure marinade and make 3 cups up with water.
6  Boil in saucepan, stir in salt and add rice.
7  Cover and simmer for 20-30 minutes.
8  Grill or pan fry steaks and spoon hot ginger rice on top of chops.

# LAMB KEBABS

*2 hours cooking time*

*Ingredients for 4 servings*

1 kg (2 lb) lamb from leg
250 g (8 oz) mushrooms
1 red pepper
1 green pepper
rice

1 large tomato
¼ cup claret
8 small onions
2 tablespoons butter

1 Cube meat and peel mushrooms.
2 Cut peppers and tomatoes into thick slices.
3 Soak lamb in claret for 2 hours, then thread alternate layers of lamb, mushrooms, onions, peppers and tomato on skewer.
4 Brush with melted butter and place under grill.
5 Serve on a bed of rice.

# LAMB FRUITS CURRY

*2½ hours cooking time*

*Ingredients for 4-5 servings*

8 dried apricots
8 prunes
12 lima beans
¼ teaspoon white pepper
2 cups water
500 g (1 lb) lamb chops

2 teaspoons curry powder
8 dates
½ teaspoon salt
juice of ½ lemon
2 tablespoons butter

1 Soak apricots, prunes and lima beans in water.
2 Trim chops and sauté in butter until brown.
3 Add curry powder, cook approximately 20 minutes.
4 Add dates and the soaked fruits.
5 Add water and boil, add salt, pepper and lemon juice.
6 Simmer for 2 hours.

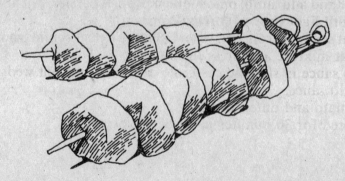

# LAMB RISOTTO

*30 minutes cooking time*

*Ingredients for 4-6 servings*

1 tablespoon butter
250 g (8 oz) carrots
1 can tomatoes
1 bay leaf
¼ teaspoon white pepper
chopped parsley

1 onion
250 g (8 oz) long-grain rice
1¼ cups water
½ teaspoon salt
250 g (8 oz) cooked lamb

1   Melt butter and fry onions, add peeled and thinly sliced carrots and rice and cook for a few minutes.
2   Stir in the peeled tomatoes, the water, bay leaf, salt and pepper, bring to boil.
3   Cover and simmer for 20 minutes.
4   When cooked add chopped meat and serve.
5   Sprinkle with chopped parsley.

# LAMB-FILLED EGGPLANT

*45 minutes cooking time*

*Ingredients for 6 servings*

1 large eggplant, cut into six pieces
4 tomatoes, quartered
4 tablespoons butter
2 onions, chopped
3 tablespoons chopped parsley
½ teaspoon garlic salt

1 teaspoon salt
4 onions, quartered
500 g (1 lb) minced lamb
8 tablespoons chopped green pepper
1 cup tomato sauce

1   Sprinkle eggplant with salt and stand for 1 hour on kitchen towelling.
2   Melt butter and fry eggplant wedges.
3   Place eggplant skin down on baking sheet in hot oven 200°C (400°F) for 10 minutes.
4   Reheat butter and add lamb, onion, green pepper, parsley, salt and garlic salt. Cook until light brown, stirring constantly.
5   Split eggplant sections from end to end making a pocket and press open.
6   Fill with meat mixture and press firmly.
7   Pour tomato sauce in shallow casserole dish. Set eggplant wedges skin side down into sauce.
8   Top with tomato and onion wedges.
9   Bake uncovered for 30 minutes in moderate oven.

# LAMB AND WHITE SAUCE

*30 minutes cooking time*

*Ingredients for 4-5 servings*

**1 kg (2 lb) cold roast lamb**
**2 cups medium white sauce,**
**more if desired**

**2 cups breadcrumbs**
**1 tablespoon chopped parsley**

1  Mix lamb and sauce together and put layer of mixture in greased dish.
2  Cover with layer of breadcrumbs.
3  Dot with parsley and repeat.
4  Bake in a hot oven 200°C (400°F) for 20-30 minutes.
5  Serve with parsley sprinkled on top.

# BOILED LAMB

*20 minutes cooking time*

*Ingredients for 4-5 servings*

**1 kg (2 lb) cooked lamb**
**2 teaspoons salt**

**½ teaspoon white pepper**
**15 slices bacon**

1  Season diced lamb with salt and pepper.
2  Shape into 12 flat cakes and place a strip of bacon around each.
3  Arrange on greased dish and grill for 10 minutes, turn and repeat.
4  Serve immediately.

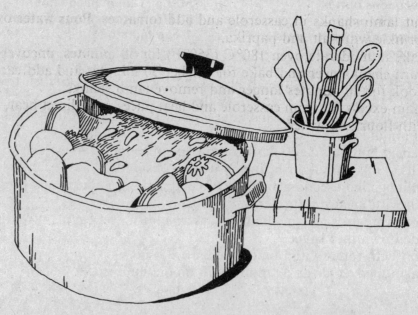

# LIVER WITH ONIONS

*1 hour cooking time*

*Ingredients for 6 servings*

750 g (1½ lb) liver
4 cups water
2 tablespoons cornflour
½ teaspoon pepper

250 g (8 oz) thawed frozen peas
3 tablespoons corn oil
½ teaspoon salt
1 packet onion soup

1  Trim liver and cut into slices. Coat with seasoned cornflour and heat corn oil.
2  Add liver to oil and fry gently. Remove to casserole dish and add onion soup to pan.
3  Stir in water and bring to boil. Pour over liver and bake in moderate oven for 45 minutes, covered.
4  Add peas 15-20 minutes before serving.

# LAMB SHANKS

*1½ hours cooking time*

*Ingredients for 6 servings*

6 lamb shanks, cracked
¼ cup flour
2 teaspoons paprika
3 tomatoes, peeled and quartered

10 carrots, peeled and cut in half
2 teaspoons salt
3 cups water

1  Put lamb shanks in casserole and add tomatoes. Pour water over and sprinkle with salt and paprika.
2  Bake in moderate oven 180°C (350°F) for 30 minutes, uncovered.
3  Turn shanks over and bake for further 30 minutes and add carrots.
4  Cook for 30 minutes longer and remove lamb shanks.
5  Skim excess fat from casserole and heat juices over direct heat, thicken with flour and water.

# Pork

## CUTLETS

*Ingredients for 5-6 servings*

*20 minutes cooking time*

1.5 kg (3 lb) lean pork chops
2 cups breadcrumbs
1 egg
1 cup water

½ teaspoon white pepper
2 tablespoons butter
2 teaspoons salt

1  Trim chops and cube.
2  Mince pork and place in a bowl.
3  Add 1 cup breadcrumbs, beaten egg, water, salt, pepper and mix thoroughly.
4  Form into oblong shapes and roll in remaining breadcrumbs, then flatten with knife.
5  Melt butter and fry for 15-20 minutes.
6  Serve immediately.

# PORK FILLETS WITH SOUR CREAM SAUCE

*30 minutes cooking time*

*Ingredients for 6-8 servings*

**1.5 kg (3 lb) pork fillet**
**125 g (4 oz) butter**
**3 onions**
**1 tablespoon plain flour**
**2 cups sour cream**
**1 chicken stock cube**

**1 cup water**
**2 tablespoons tomato purée**
**2 tablespoons capers**
**2 tablespoons chopped parsley**
**½ teaspoon salt**
**¼ teaspoon white pepper**

1　Cut pork fillets into 1 centimetre (½ in) slices and flatten.
2　Melt butter and fry until brown.
3　Add chopped onion, tomato purée and stir in flour.
4　Cook for 2 minutes.
5　Add sour cream, water, stock cube and stir.
6　Return to medium heat and continue to stir.
7　Add capers, chopped parsley, salt and pepper.
8　Pour sauce on fillets.

# LULU'S PORK CHOPS

*1 hour 10 minutes cooking time*

*Ingredients for 6 servings*

**6 loin pork chops**
**1 teaspoon salt**
**1½ tablespoons flour**
**¼ cup sultanas**
**3 apples, peeled and quartered**

**3 sweet potatoes**
**½ teaspoon pepper**
**1 cup water**
**1½ tablespoons lemon juice**

1　Trim fat off chops and place a little of it in frying pan. Coat pan lightly.
2　Discard excess fat and rub meat with salt and pepper.
3　Sauté meat in pan and remove.
4　In same pan add flour, and gradually stir in water and raisins. Stir and add lemon juice.
5　Simmer for 5 minutes and layer half of the apples and potatoes in casserole dish.
6　Place chops on top and cover with remaining apples and potatoes.
7　Pour sauce over and cover. Bake for 1 hour in moderate oven 180°C (350°F).

# PORK CHOPS IN PAPRIKA

*1 hour cooking time*

*Ingredients for 5-6 servings*

6 pork chops
¾ cup flour
½ teaspoon salt
1 tablespoon oil
1 onion
1 clove garlic
1 cup water

1 teaspoon dried dill
1 chicken stock cube
½ teaspoon white pepper
6 tablespoons sour cream
1 tablespoon plain flour
2 tablespoons plain paprika

1   Coat chops in flour and season with salt and pepper.
2   Heat oil in large deep frying pan and add chops.
3   Remove chops and add chopped onion and crushed garlic.
4   Sauté.
5   Stir in paprika, dill, water and crumbled stock cube.
6   Add chops and reduce heat, simmer for 45 minutes.
7   Lift chops onto serving dish and keep hot.
8   Combine sour cream and flour in bowl, add to sauce.
9   Cook gently, season to taste with salt and pepper.

# PORK CHOPS WITH APPLE

*30 minutes cooking time*

*Ingredients for 4-5 servings*

4-5 thick pork chops
1 teaspoon chopped parsley
1 teaspoon salt
fresh breadcrumbs
sautéed sliced apples

1 teaspoon onion
1 egg
freshly ground black pepper
olive oil
sautéed potato slices

1   Combine onion, parsley and egg.
2   Beat well.
3   Season with salt and pepper.
4   Trim meat and dip into seasoning mixture.
5   Drain well and dip in breadcrumbs.
6   Allow to stand for 30 minutes.
7   Fry chops and serve with sautéed apples and potatoes.

# PORK CAPRICE

*Ingredients for 5-6 servings*

*45 minutes cooking time*

**7** pork chops
**2** tablespoons butter
**1** clove garlic
**½** teaspoon salt
**1** tablespoon tomato paste

**2** cups water
**2** green peppers, chopped
**250 g (8 oz)** mushrooms, sliced
**¼** teaspoon white pepper

1  Melt butter and add chops.
2  Brown.
3  Season with salt and pepper.
4  Remove.
5  Dilute tomato paste with water.
6  Add peppers, mushrooms and garlic and bring to the boil.
7  Simmer for 15 minutes.
8  Place chops back in saucepan and simmer for further 30 minutes.

# PICKLED PORK

*Ingredients for 3-4 servings*

*1½ hours cooking time*

**1 kg (2 lb)** pickled pork
**1** peeled onion
**5** cloves
**6** peppercorns
chopped parsley

**1** bay leaf
**2** carrots
**2** turnips
**2** parsnips

1  Soak pork in cold water for 1 hour.
2  Remove and place in saucepan and cover with fresh water.
3  Bring to boil and remove scum.
4  Add peeled onion with cloves, peppercorns and bay leaf.
5  Cover and simmer for 1½ hours.
6  Add carrot, parsnip and turnip 1 hour before serving.
7  When ready, place on serving dish with vegetables.

# PORK CURRY

*Ingredients for 2-3 servings*

*1 hour cooking time*

2 tablespoons butter
500 g (1 lb) pork
1 onion, chopped
2 carrots
¼ teaspoon white pepper
2 teaspoons curry powder
12 dried prunes

1 cup water
1 tablespoon tomato paste
2 teaspoons chutney
½ teaspoon salt
1 tomato
12 dried apricots

1  Melt butter and fry meat until brown.
2  Remove and add onion, carrots, and tomato to pan.
3  Sauté for 2 minutes then add curry powder and cook for further 2 minutes.
4  Add water and bring to boil.
5  Add all remaining ingredients and simmer for 1 hour.


# TIVOLI PORK

*Ingredients for 6-8 servings*

*1¼ hours cooking time*

2 fillets of pork
6 sage leaves
2 onions
250 g (8 oz) shelled peas
4 tablespoons tomato purée
2 tablespoons flour
2½ tablespoons butter

1½ teaspoons salt
½ teaspoon pepper
250 g (8 oz) mushrooms
24 asparagus tips
2 bay leaves
2 cups stock

1  Cut meat into slices and melt butter in pan.
2  Fry meat until brown on both sides and place in casserole dish.
3  Fry onions in butter then add to meat.
4  Add flour to pan and heat gently.
5  Add stock and bring to boil, add tomato purée, bay leaves and sage. Season with salt and pepper.
6  Bake in moderate oven 180°C (350°F) for 1 hour.
7  Peel mushrooms and add to casserole.
8  Cook peas and asparagus tips separately and add to casserole.
9  Heat through before serving.

# BRAISED PORK CHOPS

*1 hour cooking time*

*Ingredients for 5-6 servings*

5-6 lean pork chops
seasoned plain flour
2 tablespoons butter
½ teaspoon salt

500 g (1 lb) tomatoes
1 cup tomato paste
2 medium onions
¼ teaspoon white pepper

1 Trim chops and toss in seasoned flour.
2 Melt butter and sauté chops.
3 Transfer to casserole.
4 Add tomatoes.
5 Add onion, tomato paste and salt and pepper to taste.
6 Cook for 1 hour in moderate oven 180°C (350°F).
7 Serve with grated cheese and hot noodles.

# PEPPERED PORK

*1½ hours cooking time*

*Ingredients for 3-4 servings*

6 medium green peppers
125-155 g (4-5 oz) rice
250 g (8 oz) cooked pork
½ teaspoon mixed herbs

½ teaspoon salt
cayenne pepper
tomato soup

1 Preheat oven to moderate and cut tops off peppers.
2 Scoop out seeds.
3 Boil rice in salted water for 15 minutes.
4 Drain.
5 Mince pork with the rice, herbs and seasoning.
6 Fill the peppers with this and place in a buttered casserole dish. Pour the tomato soup over and bake for 1 hour.

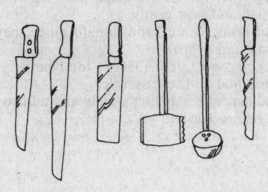

# CHINESE PORK

*20 minutes cooking time*

*Ingredients for 3-4 servings*

500 g (1 lb) lean pork
1 tablespoon butter
3 onions, sliced
750 g (1½ lb) green beans, cooked

1 tablespoon soy sauce
¼ teaspoon white pepper
boiled rice

1   Cut pork into strips and fry together with onion in butter.
2   Add cooked beans and cook for further 10 minutes.
3   Stir in soy sauce, season with white pepper.
4   Serve with rice.

# PORK AND VEGETABLE MEDLEY

*25 minutes cooking time*

*Ingredients for 4-5 servings*

4-5 pork chops
½ teaspoon salt
1 green pepper
250 g (8 oz) tomatoes
freshly ground pepper

1 tablespoon butter
¼ teaspoon white pepper
1 small marrow
250 g (8 oz) cooked potatoes

1   Wipe chops with damp cloth and brush with melted butter.
2   Sprinkle with salt and pepper and cook under medium grill.
3   Arrange prepared vegetables on serving dish and top with pork chops.

# FRUITED PORK CHOPS

*20 minutes cooking time*

*Ingredients for 4-5 servings*

6 pork chops
450 g (16 oz) can apricots
¼ teaspoon white pepper

1 quantity veal forcemeat
½ teaspoon salt

1   Drain apricots and fill with veal forcemeat.
2   Place chops under griller and grill for 15 minutes.
3   Arrange apricot halves on top of chops and grill for 5 minutes.

# SWISS PORK CHOPS

*1½ hours cooking time*

*Ingredients for 4 servings*

750 g (1½ lb) pork chops
1 onion
1½ cups tomato juice
1 green pepper, sliced into rings

1 lemon, sliced
1 tablespoon butter
1 teaspoon salt
½ teaspoon pepper

1   Slice onion into rings.
2   Put chops in greased casserole and cover with lemon juice, onion rings and green pepper rings.
3   Season with salt and pepper and pour over tomato juice.
4   Dot with butter and bake for 1½ hours in moderate oven 180°C (350°F).

# FRANKFURTER CASSEROLE

*30 minutes cooking time*

*Ingredients for 6 servings*

12 frankfurters
⅓ cup butter
1½ teaspoons salt
4 cups tinned tomatoes
2 chopped onions

2½ cups diced carrots
½ teaspoon pepper
2 tablespoons tomato sauce
⅓ cup flour

1   Melt butter and brown onions.
2   Stir in flour and blend well.
3   Add tomatoes, cook until mixture thickens and season with salt, pepper and tomato sauce.
4   Add carrots and split frankfurters and pour into casserole.
5   Bake for 30 minutes in moderate oven 180°C (350°F).

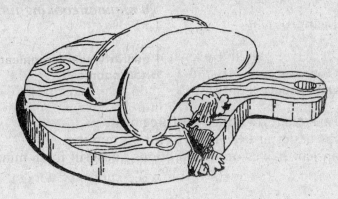

# Veal

## ITALIAN VEAL

*Ingredients for 4 servings*

*2 hours cooking time*

8 veal chops
2 onions, chopped
1 rasher bacon, diced
2 tablespoons butter

2 tablespoons flour
1 tin mushrooms in butter sauce
1 large tin tomatoes
1 bay leaf

1   Melt the butter in pan and brown the veal chops.
2   Remove from pan and place in a casserole.
3   Fry onions and bacon until brown, add the flour and stir well.
4   Stir until boiling and cook for 1 minute.
5   Add the bay leaf, tomatoes and mushrooms and pour the mixture over the chops.
6   Cover and place the casserole in an oven at 180°C (350°F) and continue cooking for about 1½ hours or until the chops are tender.

# VEAL FRICASSÉE

*1½ hours cooking time*

*Ingredients for 6 servings*

| | |
|---|---|
| **1 kg (2 lb) boned shin of veal** | **½ turnip, chopped** |
| **2 cups water** | **1 beef stock cube** |
| **1 teaspoon salt** | **½ cup milk** |
| **6 peppercorns** | **1 tablespoon butter** |
| **½ cup celery, chopped** | **2 tablespoons flour** |
| **1 onion, chopped** | |

1  Cut meat into 2.5 centimetre (1 in) pieces and place with water, salt and peppercorns in a saucepan and bring to the boil.
2  Add the vegetables and cover.
3  Simmer gently until cooked, about 1 hour.
4  Remove the fat and lift out the meat and vegetables.
5  Discard peppercorns.
6  Make a white sauce using 1¼ cups of stock from the meat, half cup of milk, butter and flour.
7  Bring to the boil, stirring, and cook for 2 minutes.
8  Add the meat and vegetables to the sauce.

# VEAL CHOPS WITH SPAGHETTI

*2½ hours cooking time*

*Ingredients for 4-6 servings*

| | |
|---|---|
| **750 g (1½ lb) veal chops** | **250 g (8 oz) lean bacon** |
| **1 cup diced mixed vegetables** | **½ cup sliced onion** |
| **1 tablespoon plain flour** | **1 sliced tomato** |
| **1¼ cups water** | **1¼ cups white wine** |
| **½ teaspoon salt** | **¼ teaspoon white pepper** |
| **125 g (4 oz) spaghetti** | **chopped parsley** |

1  Roll chops in flour and chop bacon.
2  Heat pan and fry bacon.
3  Add veal and brown.
4  Fry vegetables and onion.
5  Add tomato, white wine, flour, salt, pepper and water.
6  Cover.
7  Cook veal until tender, 2 hours.
8  Wash spaghetti and lay around edge of dish about 30 minutes before serving.
9  Sprinkle with parsley and serve.

# FRENCH VEAL LOAF

*3 hours cooking time*

*Ingredients for 4-5 servings*

1.5-2 kg (3-4 lb) lean veal
1 cup breadcrumbs
1 egg
1 tablespoon chopped onion
1 tablespoon chopped parsley
2 tablespoons melted butter

4 tablespoons cream
1 tablespoon salt
1 teaspoon white pepper
⅛ teaspoon nutmeg
3 tablespoons fat

1  Mix all ingredients and press as a loaf into the pan.
2  Cook in a slow oven for 2¾-3 hours.
3  Prick top every 30 minutes.
4  Serve immediately.


# FRENCH VEAL STEW

*2 hours cooking time*

*Ingredients for 4-6 servings*

1 kg (2 lb) veal
water
2 carrots
garlic
bouquet garni
3 tablespoons flour
½ teaspoon salt

mushrooms
small onions, whole
1 onion, chopped
3 egg yolks
lemon juice
3 tablespoons butter

1  Cut the meat into about 12 squares and place in a saucepan with cold water to cover, add salt.
2  Bring to boil.
3  Add carrots, onion and bouquet garni.
4  Cover saucepan and cook for 1½ hours.
5  Melt 3 tablespoons butter and add flour.
6  Cook for few minutes.
7  Gradually add the liquid from the veal.
8  Add mushrooms and small onions and simmer for 15 minutes.
9  Just before serving, add beaten egg yolks and lemon juice to sauce.
10  Place veal in serving dish and garnish with mushrooms and onions.

# SAUTÉ DE VEAU A LA MÉNAGÈRE

*1½ hours cooking time*

*Ingredients for 5-6 servings*

| | |
|---|---|
| **1 kg (2 lb) veal** | **4 onions** |
| **½ teaspoon salt** | **¾ teaspoon white pepper** |
| **plain flour** | **1 kg (2 lb) tomatoes** |
| **3 tablespoons oil** | **1 clove garlic** |
| **2 tablespoons butter** | **1 cup white wine** |

1  Cube veal and coat in seasoned flour.
2  Heat oil and butter, add meat and chopped onions.
3  Sauté.
4  Add wine and tomatoes and simmer for 1½ hours.
5  Add chopped garlic.
6  Serve with potatoes and red peppers.

# VEAL SPECIALTY

*45 minutes cooking time*

*Ingredients for 5-6 servings*

| | |
|---|---|
| **500 g (1 lb) veal steak** | **½ cup plain flour** |
| **250 g (8 oz) pork, sliced thinly** | **1 teaspoon salt** |
| **¼ teaspoon white pepper** | **2 tablespoons butter** |

1  Wipe meat with damp cloth.
2  Cut veal in squares.
3  Cut pork in squares.
4  Roll pork and veal in mixture of salt and pepper.
5  Roll in flour.
6  Put alternate slices of meat on small skewers.
7  Sauté until well browned and cover.
8  Cook slowly.
9  Serve with brown sauce.

# VEAL SCALOPPINE

*45 minutes cooking time*

*Ingredients for 8 servings*

3 tablespoons plain flour
2 teaspoons salt
¾ teaspoon white pepper
1 kg (2 lb) veal fillets
4 tablespoons butter
2 cloves garlic
1 bay leaf

2 medium onions, sliced
tomato purée
brown sugar
1 cup stock
500 g (1 lb) mushrooms
Parmesan cheese
½ teaspoon oregano

1  Combine the flour, salt and pepper and coat the veal.
2  Heat the butter and brown veal.
3  Add garlic and onions and fry gently.
4  Remove, and fry mushrooms.
5  Pour tomato purée into the pan and add sugar.
6  Add stock and herbs and simmer for 5 minutes.
7  Return the veal and onions to sauce and cook for 30-40 minutes.
8  Serve with cheese.

# VEAL CHOPS WITH MUSHROOMS

*30 minutes cooking time*

*Ingredients for 4 servings*

4-5 veal chops
310 g (10 oz) can creamed mushroom
  soup
1 small can button mushrooms
¾ teaspoon white pepper

2 tablespoons butter
8 small onions
1 teaspoon salt
milk
chopped parsley

1  Trim chops.
2  Melt butter and add chops.
3  Brown well.
4  Set chops aside and brown onions.
5  Arrange chops, onions and drained mushrooms in greased casserole dish.
6  Season with salt and pepper.
7  Add prepared soup, pouring slowly over chops.
8  Cover and bake in moderate oven for 30 minutes.
9  Sprinkle with chopped parsley.

# STUFFED VEAL

*30 minutes cooking time*

*Ingredients for 4-6 servings*

**shoulder of veal, boned**
**½ teaspoon salt**
**¼ teaspoon white pepper**

**2 tablespoons plain flour**
**2 cups stuffing**

1  Wipe meat with damp cloth and dot with salt, pepper and flour.
2  Stuff.
3  Place in pan with a little fat.
4  Sear for 15 minutes.
5  Place in hot oven 230°C (450°F).
6  Reduce heat to 160°C (325°F) and cook for 25 minutes.
7  Baste every 15 minutes.

# VEAL LOUISA

*1½ hours cooking time*

*Ingredients for 4-5 servings*

**1 kg (2 lb) lean stewing veal**
**1 teaspoon paprika**
**1 teaspoon salt**
**3 tablespoons plain flour**
**5 tablespoons oil**
**1 onion**

**2 teaspoons Worcestershire sauce**
**1 cup chicken stock**
**1 cup dry white wine**
**2 cups sour cream**
**1 clove garlic**

1  Crush garlic.
2  Chop onion and cut meat into 5 centimetre (2 in) pieces.
3  Toss in combination of paprika, salt and pepper.
4  Heat oil and brown meat well.
5  Add garlic, onion, Worcestershire sauce, stock and wine.
6  Simmer for 1 hour or until tender.
7  Just before serving add sour cream and season with salt and pepper.
8  Serve with hot noodles or rice, sprinkled with parsley.

# COATED VEAL

*35 minutes cooking time*

*Ingredients for 4-5 servings*

| | |
|---|---|
| **500 g (1 lb) veal steak** | **⅛ teaspoon white pepper** |
| **¼ cup flour** | **2 tablespoons butter** |
| **½ teaspoon salt** | **⅓ cup redcurrant jelly** |

1 Roll meat in mixture of flour, salt and pepper.
2 Melt fat in pan.
3 Add veal and brown.
4 Cook slowly, turning all the time.
5 Heat jelly and add water.
6 Pour liquid over meat and cook for 30 minutes.

# VEAL PIE

*1½ hours cooking time*

*Ingredients for 4-5 servings*

| | |
|---|---|
| **1 kg (2 lb) veal rump** | **125 g (4 oz) chopped cooked ham** |
| **2 tablespoons plain flour** | **2 hardboiled eggs** |
| **2 tablespoons butter** | **chopped parsley** |
| **1 onion** | **250 g (8 oz) puff pastry** |
| **1¼ cups stock** | **milk** |
| **½ teaspoon salt** | **cayenne pepper** |

1 Preheat oven to hot.
2 Cube veal and toss in flour.
3 Melt the butter and fry onions.
4 Add veal and continue cooking for 5 minutes.
5 Pour the stock over the top and add salt.
6 Add cayenne pepper to taste.
7 Bring to boil, then simmer with the lid on for 1 hour.
8 Allow the veal to cool, then add chopped ham.
9 Place in a pie dish and place sliced hardboiled eggs on top.
10 Sprinkle with parsley.
11 Cover with pastry and brush lightly with milk.
12 Bake for 20 minutes, then reduce heat and continue baking for 10 minutes.

# VEAL HAWAIIAN

*1½ hours cooking time*

*Ingredients for 3-4 servings*

2 tablespoons butter
4 veal chops
½ teaspoon salt
½ cup hot water

4 dried prunes
2 carrots
¼ teaspoon white pepper
4 pineapple rings

1  Melt butter and brown the chops in it.
2  Season with salt and pepper.
3  Place a pineapple ring on top of each chop with 1 prune in centre.
4  Add carrots and water, cover and simmer for 1½ hours.

# VEAL STEAK

*1½ hours cooking time*

*Ingredients for 4 servings*

500 g (1 lb) veal steak
1 teaspoon salt
¼ teaspoon pepper

2 cups milk
1 tablespoon flour

1  Dice meat.
2  Place in casserole with milk, pepper and salt.
3  Cook for 1 hour 15 minutes and thicken with flour mixed with cold water.

# ITALIAN VEAL LOAF

*2 hours cooking time*

*Ingredients for 5-6 servings*

1 kg (2 lb) yearling veal steak
1 rasher bacon
½ teaspoon salt

3 hardboiled eggs
1 tablespoon butter
¼ teaspoon white pepper

1  Trim meat and season the top side.
2  Lay the bacon rasher on top then add the hardboiled eggs.
3  Roll up the meat and tie securely with string.
4  Heat the butter and brown the meat.
5  Transfer to casserole and season well with salt.
6  Cover and cook for 2 hours.

# MARSALA VEAL

*30 minutes cooking time*

*Ingredients for 5-6 servings*

1 kg (2 lb) veal cutlets
½ teaspoon salt
1 tablespoon plain flour
2 tablespoons butter

1 cup marsala
¼ teaspoon white pepper
2 tablespoons stock
buttered rice

1　Pound veal and cut into pieces.
2　Sprinkle with seasoned flour.
3　Melt butter and brown.
4　Add marsala, let meat cook 1 minute longer.
5　Place meat on top of buttered rice and serve.

# VEAL SUPREME

*1 hour cooking time*

*Ingredients for 4-5 servings*

1.5 kg (3 lb) stewing veal
5 onions
250 g (8 oz) mushrooms
1 red pepper
1 green pepper
125 g (4 oz) butter
¼ teaspoon white pepper

1 packet tomato soup
1 tablespoon paprika
2 cups water
2 beef cubes
lemon juice
½ teaspoon salt

1　Cut veal into cubes and slice onions and mushrooms.
2　Slice peppers.
3　Melt butter and add onions and peppers, sauté until brown.
4　Add veal, brown and remove from heat.
5　Stir in tomato soup and paprika.
6　Add water in which stock cubes have been dissolved.
7　Return to heat.
8　Reduce heat and simmer for 1 hour.
9　Add mushrooms in the last 15 minutes of cooking.
10　Season with lemon juice, salt and pepper.

# VEAL PINEAPPLE

*30 minutes cooking time*

*Ingredients for 3-4 servings*

**8 thin slices veal**
**½ teaspoon salt**
**1 tablespoon butter**
**½-¾ cup cream**

**4 slices pineapple**
**¼ teaspoon white pepper**
**125 g (4 oz) mushrooms, sliced**

1   Beat veal and sprinkle with salt and pepper.
2   Fry gently in butter and remove from pan.
3   Place in oven.
4   Cook the pineapple in butter and set aside with veal.
5   Cook the mushrooms in butter and arrange veal on serving dish with pineapple and mushrooms. Stir in the cream and pour over the dish.

# VEAL AND ASPARAGUS

*30 minutes cooking time*

*Ingredients for 3-4 servings*

**750 g (1½ lb) veal fillet**
**plain flour**
**½ teaspoon salt**
**3 tablespoons butter**
**½ cup water or stock**

**1 can asparagus tips**
**2 tablespoons butter**
**¼ teaspoon white pepper**
**½ teaspoon sugar**

1   Slice veal and coat in seasoned flour with salt and pepper.
2   Fry in melted butter until brown.
3   Pour off excess butter and add water or stock.
4   Cover and simmer until tender.
5   Drain asparagus and heat in butter.
6   Add sugar and salt slowly.
7   When serving lay asparagus on top.

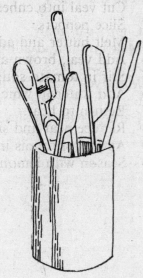

# PEACHY VEAL CASSEROLE

*1½ hours cooking time*

*Ingredients for 3-4 servings*

| | |
|---|---|
| 1 kg (2 lb) veal fillet | 250 g (8 oz) tomatoes |
| 3 tablespoons seasoned flour | 450 g (15 oz) can peaches |
| 3 tablespoons butter | 1¼ cups stock |
| 2 onions | parsley and lemon juice |

1 Preheat oven to 190°C (375°F) and cut veal into cubes.
2 Toss in seasoned flour.
3 Melt butter and brown the meat.
4 Remove and add chopped onions.
5 Fry lightly.
6 Place layers of meat, onion, tomato and peaches in a casserole.
7 Cover with stock.
8 Place lid on casserole and bake for 1½ hours.
9 To serve, sprinkle with lemon juice and parsley.

# SCRAMBLED VEAL

*10 minutes cooking time*

*Ingredients for 2-3 servings*

| | |
|---|---|
| 250 g (8 oz) cooked veal | 2 eggs, beaten |
| 1 tablespoon butter | ½ teaspoon salt |
| 1 cup tomato purée | ⅛ teaspoon white pepper |
| buttered toast | parsley |

1 Chop veal finely.
2 Melt butter and add tomato purée.
3 Add veal, eggs, salt and pepper.
4 Mix over heat until hot and thickened.
5 Serve on pieces of buttered toast.
6 Garnish with parsley.

# VEAL COOKED WITH SHALLOTS

*Ingredients for 3-4 servings*

*1½ hours cooking time*

1 kg (2 lb) veal fillet
1 small onion
cayenne pepper
2 sticks celery
1¼ cups stock
2 tablespoons butter
6 shallots or small pickling onions

yolks of 4 eggs
½ teaspoon salt
½ turnip
1 teaspoon chopped parsley
juice of 1 lemon
5 tablespoons cream
mashed potatoes and green beans

1 Slice veal and place in saucepan with stock.
2 Simmer for 1 hour.
3 Add vegetables, pre-cooked.
4 Lift out meat, drain.
5 Heat butter, fry shallots, but do not brown.
6 Add stock and yolks and stir gently.
7 Add salt, pepper, parsley, lemon juice and cream.
8 Return fillets to saucepan and reheat.
9 Serve on hot dish with mashed potatoes and green beans.

# BRANDY BAKE

*Ingredients for 5-6 servings*

*45 minutes cooking time*

2 tablespoons butter
6 thin slices veal
8 shallots
1 tablespoon brandy
2 teaspoons chopped parsley
4 tablespoons cream

1 cup stock
1 tablespoon finely chopped ginger
1 can pears
½ teaspoon salt
¼ teaspoon white pepper

1 Melt butter and brown veal on all sides.
2 Add shallots, brandy and chopped parsley.
3 Add half the cream, stock, sliced pears, ginger, salt and pepper.
4 Place lid on saucepan and simmer for 15 minutes, then add more cream, simmer for 30 minutes.

# FARMER'S VEAL

*1 hour 20 minutes cooking time*

*Ingredients for 6 servings*

1 medium onion
2 tablespoons chopped parsley
30 g (1 oz) breadcrumbs
½ teaspoon salt
2 tablespoons flour
450 g (15 oz) cream of mushroom
  soup
6 veal chops

1½ cups mashed potato
90 g (3 oz) mushrooms
1 teaspoon mixed herbs
½ teaspoon pepper
½ cup water
2 tablespoons butter
1 beaten egg
1½ tablespoons suet, chopped

1 Slice onion thinly and fry for 5 minutes in butter.
2 Remove from pan and prepare stuffing from breadcrumbs, parsley, herbs, seasonings, suet and egg.
3 Trim chops and top with stuffing. Fry for 2 minutes on both sides. Place in casserole dish and cover with onions.
4 Add flour to pan and blend with remaining liquid. Add water and soup, bring to boil and season. Pour into casserole and cook for 1 hour in moderate oven.
5 Garnish with mushrooms and parsley.

# VEAL A LA BACON

*30 minutes cooking time*

*Ingredients for 4-6 servings*

1 kg (2 lb) veal for roasting
½ cup plain flour
1 egg
1½ cups breadcrumbs

1 teaspoon salt
¼ teaspoon white pepper
2 tablespoons butter
4 rashers bacon, halved

1 Wipe meat with damp cloth.
2 Cut into pieces.
3 Dip in beaten egg, diluted with water.
4 Cover with breadcrumbs.
5 Sprinkle with salt and pepper.
6 Put in a baking dish and dot with butter and bacon slices.
7 Serve with white sauce.

# VEAL AND RICE PIE

*50 minutes cooking time*

*Ingredients for 8 servings*

750 g (1½ lb) chopped cooked veal
2 cups white sauce
½ teaspoon pepper
2½ cups boiled rice

½ cup mild cheese, shredded
short pastry
1 teaspoon salt

1  Combine veal, white sauce, cheese and rice.
2  Mix well and season with salt and pepper.
3  Place mixture in greased dish on half the pie pastry and cover with remaining pastry. Make 3-4 holes in top of pastry.
4  Bake for 45-50 minutes in moderate oven.

# VEAL AND MUSHROOMS

*1 hour cooking time*

*Ingredients for 6 servings*

1 kg (2 lb) veal steak
1 green pepper, seeded and cut into strips
1½ cups chicken stock
½ cup salad oil
1 teaspoon salt
1 clove garlic, minced
4 tablespoons butter

250 g (8 oz) fresh mushrooms, sliced
½ cup lemon juice
1 teaspoon paprika
1 teaspoon prepared mustard
¼ teaspoon nutmeg
½ cup flour
2 onions, sliced

1  Marinate meat in oil, paprika, lemon juice, salt, garlic, nutmeg and mustard for 30 minutes.
2  Remove meat and dredge in flour.
3  Brown meat in butter, remove to casserole.
4  Mix the remaining marinade, stock, green pepper and mushrooms, and pour over veal.
5  Cover and bake for 30 minutes in moderate oven 180°C (350°F).
6  Remove cover and top with sliced onion. Bake for 15 minutes and serve.

# VEAL IN CREAM

*1 hour cooking time*

*Ingredients for 4 servings*

500 g (1 lb) minced steak
½ teaspoon pepper
2 tablespoons chopped parsley
2 tablespoons dried breadcrumbs
4 pieces veal

1 teaspoon salt
¼ teaspoon nutmeg
1 egg, beaten
1 tablespoon melted butter
4 tablespoons sour cream

1 Mix steak with salt, pepper, nutmeg, parsley, egg and breadcrumbs. Refrigerate for 2 hours.
2 Brown veal in butter, coat with steak mixture, arrange in a baking dish, sprinkle with salt and pepper.
3 Place veal steaks on top of each other and bake for 40 minutes.
4 Dot each steak with sour cream and let it melt. Serve.

# VEAL PARMESAN

*20 minutes cooking time*

*Ingredients for 4 servings*

4 veal cutlets
2 tablespoons seasoned flour
2 eggs, beaten with milk

60 g (2 oz) Parmesan cheese
90 g (3 oz) butter
125 g (4 oz) dry breadcrumbs

1 Pound veal cutlets until they are thin.
2 Toss in seasoned flour, then dip into egg.
3 Mix parmesan cheese with breadcrumbs and coat meat.
4 Melt butter and fry cutlets for 20 minutes.
5 Serve immediately.

# Vegetables

# EGGPLANT LOUISIANA

*Ingredients for 4 servings*

*1 hour cooking time*

1 eggplant, peeled and diced
1 teaspoon salt
¼ cup fine breadcrumbs
pinch ground cloves
1½ cups strained tinned tomatoes

1 onion, minced
1 tablespoon grated cheese
3 teaspoons brown sugar
2 tablespoons plain flour
1 green pepper, chopped

1 Preheat oven to 180°C (350°F).
2 Rub casserole with butter and drop diced eggplant into 1 cup boiling water with a little salt. Cover and cook for 10 minutes.
3 Drain and place cooked eggplant in casserole.
4 Fry onion and pepper in melted butter for 5 minutes.
5 Add flour and blend, add tomatoes, salt and brown sugar. Mix well and add ground cloves.
6 Stir and simmer for 6 minutes, pour over eggplant.
7 Mix cheese and breadcrumbs and sprinkle over eggplant, bake for 30 minutes.

# SAUERKRAUT AND TOMATOES

*25 minutes cooking time*

*Ingredients for 4 servings*

¼ teaspoon salt
2 cups tinned tomatoes
2 tablespoons butter

2 cups sauerkraut
¼ teaspoon pepper
1½ cups breadcrumbs

1  Drain tomatoes and reserve juice.
2  Layer tomatoes, sauerkraut and breadcrumbs in casserole, dotting with butter and finishing with a layer of breadcrumbs.
3  Pour over reserved tomato juice from tin.
4  Sprinkle with salt and pepper and bake for 25 minutes in hot oven 200°C (400°F).

# ZUCCHINI BAKE

*35 minutes cooking time*

*Ingredients for 6 servings*

750 g (1½ lb) zucchini
½ teaspoon salt
1½ tablespoons olive oil

½ cup grated tasty cheese
1½ cups drained tinned tomatoes
2 onions, chopped

1  Preheat oven to 180°C (350°F) and prepare casserole dish by rubbing with butter.
2  Wash and cut zucchini in thin slices.
3  Fry onion in oil for 2 minutes.
4  Add zucchini and cook for 5 minutes.
5  Add tomatoes and season with salt and pepper.
6  Cover and simmer for 5 minutes.
7  Place in casserole dish and top with cheese.
8  Bake for 15-20 minutes.
9  Serve immediately.

# RATATOUILLE

*1½ hours cooking time*

*Ingredients for 6 servings*

| | |
|---|---|
| 1 onion, sliced | 2 tablespoons olive oil |
| 2 tablespoons chopped parsley | 1 teaspoon salt |
| ½ teaspoon basil | 1 green pepper, cut into chunks |
| 4 tomatoes | 3 zucchini, sliced thickly |
| 1 clove garlic, crushed | 1 small eggplant, cut into cubes |

1  In casserole dish, place onion, garlic, eggplant, zucchini and 2 tomatoes, diced. Add pepper and season with salt and basil.
2  Spread olive oil over and cover. Bake for 1½ hours in moderate oven.
3  Uncover for last 30 minutes. Remove from oven and garnish with tomato slices and parsley.

# ASPARAGUS AND SOUR CREAM

*15 minutes cooking time*

*Ingredients for 4 servings*

| | |
|---|---|
| 1½ cups boiled asparagus | ¾ cup buttered breadcrumbs |
| ¼ cup sour cream | |

1  Cut asparagus into pieces and drain.
2  Lay in single layer in baking dish greased with butter.
3  Cover with breadcrumbs and sour cream and bake for 15 minutes.

# SCALLOPED CABBAGE

*25 minutes cooking time*

*Ingredients for 4 servings*

| | |
|---|---|
| 2 cups shredded cooked cabbage | ⅓ cup grated Cheddar cheese |
| 1½ cups white sauce | ¾ cup soft breadcrumbs |
| 1 teaspoon salt | |

1  Mix cabbage and white sauce together. Season with salt.
2  Layer cabbage and breadcrumbs in greased casserole dish.
3  Sprinkle with cheese and bake for 25 minutes in moderate oven 180°C (350°F).

# CELERY IN CHEESE SAUCE

*40 minutes cooking time*

*Ingredients for 6 servings*

3 tablespoons butter
3 tablespoons flour
4 cups chopped cooked celery
⅔ cup grated tasty cheese

½ cup buttered dry breadcrumbs
⅔ cup evaporated milk
⅔ cup chicken stock

1  Preheat oven to 180°C (350°F).
2  Rub casserole dish with butter.
3  Melt butter and add flour. Add milk slowly and season with salt and pepper.
4  Add chicken stock and stir for 5 minutes.
5  Add grated cheese and stir until it melts.
6  Arrange celery in baking or casserole dish and pour sauce over.
7  Sprinkle with breadcrumbs and bake for 25-30 minutes.

# MUSHROOM TARTS

*30 minutes cooking time*

*Ingredients for 4 servings*

## PASTRY

220 g (7 oz) flour
125 g (4 oz) butter

1 egg
1 tablespoon warm salted water

## FILLING

500 g (1 lb) mushrooms
3 tablespoons chopped onions
½ cup cream
½ teaspoon pepper

2 tablespoons butter
2 teaspoons flour
1 teaspoon salt
juice of 1 lemon

1  Make pastry and allow to rest, roll out thinly and cut into tarts with a buttered pastry cutter. Bake blind.
2  Chop and cook mushrooms in butter.
3  Add chopped onions and sprinkle in flour.
4  Stir and add cream, season and add lemon juice.
5  Simmer gently for 4-5 minutes and fill hot tart cases with mixture.

# CORN AND PEPPER

*25 minutes cooking time*

*Ingredients for 4 servings*

| | |
|---|---|
| **1 green pepper, chopped** | **1½ tablespoons butter** |
| **⅛ teaspoon pepper** | **½ teaspoon salt** |
| **¼ cup evaporated milk** | **1 egg, well beaten** |
| **1½ cups tinned sweet corn** | **⅔ cup breadcrumbs** |

1   Preheat oven to 180°C (350°F).
2   Rub casserole dish with butter.
3   Fry pepper in butter and add corn slowly. Mix well and cook for 4 minutes.
4   Soak breadcrumbs in egg mixed with milk and season with salt and pepper.
5   Combine with corn mixture and bake for 20 minutes.

# BEETROOT AND TOMATO

*25 minutes cooking time*

*Ingredients for 4 servings*

| | |
|---|---|
| **2 cups boiled beetroot** | **1 teaspoon salt** |
| **¼ teaspoon pepper** | **1½ tablespoons butter** |
| **1½ cups breadcrumbs** | **⅓ cup grated cheese** |
| **2 cups tinned tomatoes** | |

1   Dice beets and place half in baking dish greased with butter; pour in half the tomatoes.
2   Add half the cheese and season with salt and pepper, top with half the breadcrumbs.
3   Repeat layers, dot with butter.
4   Bake in moderate oven 180°C (350°F) for 25 minutes.

# TASTY CABBAGE

*2 hours cooking time*

*Ingredients for 8 servings*

1 small cabbage
3 apples
125 g (4 oz) lard
1 teaspoon caraway seed
250 g (8 oz) garlic sausage

250 g (8 oz) pork
½ teaspoon salt
2 tablespoons vinegar
½ cup tomato sauce

1  Shred cabbage and peel and shred apples.
2  Cut meat into pieces and fry in lard in a deep pan.
3  Transfer to casserole, add cabbage and apples and season with salt, vinegar and caraway seed. Cover and cook slowly for 2 hours. Add a little cold water from time to time.
4  Peel and dice sausage, place in pot for last 15 minutes.

# BROCCOLI CASSEROLE

*45 minutes cooking time*

*Ingredients for 4 servings*

250 g (8 oz) frozen broccoli
2 eggs, well beaten
½ tablespoon minced onion
1½ tablespoons melted butter
2 cups milk

½ cup mayonnaise
¼ teaspoon pepper
1½ tablespoons plain flour
½ teaspoon salt

1  Cook broccoli in boiling water and drain.
2  Chop broccoli and add melted butter and flour to pan with broccoli.
3  Cook for 2 minutes and add milk, cook gently, stirring constantly.
4  Remove from heat and stir in onion, pepper, salt, mayonnaise and eggs, mix gently.
5  Place in casserole dish and bake for 30 minutes.

# ASPARAGUS IN WINE

*Ingredients for 4 servings*

*30 minutes cooking time*

**2 eggs, well beaten**
**1 tin drained, cut asparagus**
**½ teaspoon salt**
**¼ teaspoon pepper**
**¾ cup breadcrumbs**

**1 cup cubed cheese**
**2 tablespoons melted butter**
**1 cup milk**
**1 pimento, cut into small pieces**

1   To beaten eggs add salt, pepper, breadcrumbs, cheese and milk.
2   Stir and add asparagus. Stir once more and pour into greased casserole
    dish.
3   Top with melted butter and cook in moderate oven for 30 minutes.

# Index

# FAMILY FAVOURITES

# FAMILY FAVOURITES

# Contents

# Introduction

## FAMILY FAVOURITES

In this cookery book you will find recipes to please all members of the family, from the good old standards, like pumpkin soup, chicken pie and carpet bag steaks, to the more exotic curries, grilled dishes and desserts.

Many of the recipes can be prepared and served in less than half an hour, making this an excellent aid to the busy cook.

The art of dressing up simple ingredients skilfully, to make them look and taste appetizing is explored in detail, so that a better cooking is attained.

Family favourites should be eating artistically pleasing.

An imaginative use of herbs and spices together with garnishes and sauces is encouraged, so that a beautiful attractive meal can be presented in the best possible time.

At the end of the book is a place for you to put your own family favourites which might be recipes cut from magazines, or they might be the traditional recipes handed down from one family generation to the next.

# Introduction

## FAMILY FAVOURITES

In this cookery book you will find recipes to please all members of the family, from the good old standards, like pumpkin soup, chicken pie and carpet bag steaks, to the more exotic curries, seafood dishes and desserts.

Many of the recipes can be prepared and served in less than half an hour, making this an excellent aid to the busy cook.

The art of dressing up simple ingredients skillfully, to make them look and taste appetizing is exploited to the full, so that whether cooking for guests or family, the results should be enthusiastically received.

An imaginative use of herbs and spices, together with garnishes and sauces is encouraged, so that a balanced, attractive meal can be presented in the least possible time.

At the end of the book is a space in which to put your own family favourites, which might be recipes cut from magazines or they might be the traditional recipes handed down from one generation to the next.

# Soups

## CHICKEN BISQUE

*30 minutes cooking time*

*Ingredients for 4 servings*

**2 tablespoons butter or margarine**
**1½ tablespoons flour**
**3 cups chicken stock**
**¼ cup thick cream**

**1 cup minced cooked chicken**
**¾ cup thin cream**
**½ teaspoon salt**
**chopped watercress**

1  Melt butter, blend in flour, add chicken stock and chicken.
2  Stir and simmer until smooth and thick.
3  Heat the thin cream, add, stirring to mix well. Add salt.
4  Pour into serving bowls.
5  Whip the heavy cream.
6  Add 2 tablespoonfuls to each serving and sprinkle washed and drained watercress over each.

# BUTTERMILK SOUP

*Ingredients for 6 servings*

4 cups buttermilk
½ medium cucumber, peeled and
  diced
1 cup cooked chicken meat, finely
  chopped

1 teaspoon mustard
1 teaspoon salt
⅛ teaspoon pepper (optional)
fresh herbs
1 tablespoon minced celery leaves

1  Mix all ingredients thoroughly. Chill.
2  Beat well and serve in chilled cups. Fresh herbs such as dill, chervil or summer savory may be chopped and a few bits sprinkled on each serving.

# COCK-A- LEEKIE

*4 hours cooking time*

*Ingredients for 6 servings*

1 boiling chicken, about 1.25 kg
  (2½ lb)
5 cups stock or water

4 leeks
salt and pepper

1  Cover the chicken with stock or water and add the sliced leeks and seasoning.
2  Bring to the boil and simmer gently for 3½ hours.
3  Remove the chicken from the stock, carve off the meat and cut into fairly large pieces.
4  Serve the soup with the chicken pieces in it, or serve the soup on its own, with the chicken as a main course.

# CHICKEN-PRAWN SOUP

*1¼ hours cooking time*

*Ingredients for 4-6 servings*

1 1.5-kg (3½-lb) chicken, cut in pieces
1½ teaspoons salt
1 teaspoon pepper
¼ cup butter or margarine
3 small onions, finely chopped
1 clove garlic, minced or mashed

3 tablespoons minced parsley
1 cup port wine or apple juice
2 cups tomato sauce
1½ teaspoons crumbled basil
500 g (1 lb) uncooked, shelled and
  de-veined prawns

1  Sprinkle chicken with salt and pepper.
2  Melt butter in a large frying pan and lightly brown chicken on all sides.
3  Remove chicken from pan; add onions and garlic and cook until soft, about 3 minutes.
4  Stir in parsley, wine or apple juice, tomato sauce, and basil; simmer about 5 minutes.
5  Return chicken to pan, cover, and simmer about 35 minutes or until tender.
6  Remove cover and bring mixture to a slow boil; add prawns and cook just until they turn pink, 3 or 4 minutes.
7  In large bowls, serve chicken and sauté topped with prawns.

# CREAMED LETTUCE SOUP

*1½ hours cooking time*

*Ingredients for 4 servings*

| | |
|---|---|
| **1 small head lettuce** | **1 cup milk** |
| **90 g (3 oz) butter** | **1 small onion** |
| **5 cups chicken stock** | **2 egg yolks** |
| **1½ tablespoons flour** | **1 tablespoon thick cream** |

1  Melt butter in a heavy saucepan and add shredded lettuce.
2  Cover, simmer until lettuce is soft, add chicken stock and simmer gently for 45 minutes.
3  Blend flour with cold water, add 6 tablespoons hot stock, then add to soup.
4  Scald milk and onion together.
5  Add to saucepan, stir and simmer for 1 minute, then remove from heat.
6  When cool, strain through a sieve and place in refrigerator until you are ready to serve the soup.
7  Remove from refrigerator and place soup in the top of a double boiler over medium heat.
8  When soup is hot, lightly beat egg yolks in a cup.
9  Add a little of the hot soup to the cup gradually.
10  Stir into soup.
11  Serve topped with a tablespoon of cream and a sprinkling of chopped parsley or chives and a dash of paprika.

# CREAM OF PUMPKIN SOUP

*25 minutes cooking time*

*Ingredients for 4-6 servings*

| | |
|---|---|
| **1 kg (2 lb) pumpkin** | **2 teaspoons chopped dried savory** |
| **2 tablespoons sugar** | **thick cream** |
| **salt and pepper** | **cinnamon** |
| **2½ cups chicken stock** | |

1  Chop and peel the pumpkin.
2  Boil with sugar and some salt in barely enough water to cover.
3  When soft, sieve thoroughly or purée in a blender.
4  Add the chicken stock to the pumpkin purée, stirring well, then add chopped savory, and salt and pepper to taste.
5  Heat and serve with a spoonful of cream and a dusting of cinnamon.

# CHICKEN BROTH

*4 hours cooking time*

*Ingredients for 6 servings*

1 small boiling chicken (or 1 chicken carcase)
10 cups cold water
2 teaspoons salt
1 onion

2 medium carrots
1 25-cm (10-in) stalk celery with leaves
60 g (2 oz) long-grain rice
4 peppercorns
chopped parsley

1　Chop celery, onion and carrot finely.
2　Put chicken and vegetables into a large pan, cover with water and add salt and pepper.
3　Bring to the boil; simmer for 3 to 3½ hours, adding more water if necessary.
4　Strain, remove any grease with a metal spoon.
5　Return the broth to the pan, add the rice, bring to the boil and simmer for 15-20 minutes, until the rice is soft.
6　Sprinkle with chopped parsley just before serving. (Some of the meat can be finely chopped and added to the broth.) If a chicken carcase is used, it will only need to be simmered for 1 to 1½ hours.

# VICHYSSOISE

*30 minutes cooking time*

*Ingredients for 6-8 servings*

3 leeks
⅓ cup butter
3 cups chicken stock
1 stalk celery, chopped
1 raw potato, sliced
dash ground mace

dash Worcestershire sauce
1 cup thin cream
1 cup thick cream
½ teaspoon salt
¼ teaspoon white pepper

1　Wash leeks, cut off green top and any root whiskers, chop and sauté in half the butter, cooking slowly and stirring until tender but not browned.
2　Add stock, chopped celery, sliced potato and Worcestershire sauce.
3　Cover and simmer until potato slices are very tender.
4　Force through a sieve.
5　Place soup over very low heat and add thin cream and rest of the butter.
6　Heat and stir but do not let liquid reach simmering point.
7　Add thick cream, salt, pepper and mace.
8　Serve hot or well chilled.

# CHICKEN SOUP WITH BAMBOO SHOOTS

*30 minutes cooking time*

*Ingredients for 4 servings*

125 g (4 oz) chicken breasts
¼ teaspoon pepper
1 tablespoon chopped ham
125 g (4 oz) tinned bamboo shoots
5 cups chicken stock

½ teaspoon salt
1 egg
2 tablespoons chopped spring onions
1 tablespoon vegetable oil
1 piece fresh green ginger

1   Cut chicken and bamboo shoots into thin strips.
2   Heat oil and sauté chicken. Remove to a large saucepan and pour in chicken stock, bamboo shoots and ginger.
3   Cover and boil. Simmer for 5 minutes and season.
4   Beat egg and pour into soup. Simmer for 3 minutes and serve with chopped ham and spring onions.

# CHICKEN MULLIGATAWNEY

*1¾ hours cooking time*

*Ingredients for 4 servings*

4 chicken breasts
4 peppercorns
1 teaspoon ground turmeric
2 teaspoons ground coriander
1 onion

10 cups water
2 teaspoons vinegar
2.5 cm (1 in) fresh ginger, grated
30 g (1 oz) ghee
2 chillies

1   Place chicken in water and add peppercorns. Bring to boil and simmer until chicken is cooked.
2   Mix turmeric, ginger, coriander and vinegar into a paste.
3   Heat ghee in a frying pan and fry chopped, deseeded chillies and sliced onion. Cook for 3 minutes and add paste.
4   Cook for 4-5 minutes and turn chicken and stock into pan. Boil for 5 minutes and serve.

# CREAM OF CHICKEN SOUP

*1½ hours cooking time*

*Ingredients for 4 servings*

½ green pepper
1 onion
2 tablespoons butter
2 tablespoons plain flour
2½ cups chicken stock
1¼ cups milk

½ cup chicken pieces
60 g (2 oz) mushrooms
125 g (4 oz) peas
1 bay leaf
salt and pepper
toast croutons

1  Sauté the pepper and chopped onion in the butter for 5 minutes.
2  Add the flour and stir, then mix in the stock and milk gradually.
3  Add the chicken, mushrooms, peas, bay leaf and seasoning and bring to the boil, stirring constantly.
4  Simmer for 1 hour.
5  Serve with croutons of toast.

# CHICKEN AND ALMOND SOUP

*30 minutes cooking time*

*Ingredients for 6 servings*

2 tablespoons olive oil
125 g (4 oz) finely chopped almonds
1 tablespoon chopped onion
2 cloves chopped garlic
2 teaspoons chopped parsley

30 g (1 oz) breadcrumbs
6 cups chicken stock
1 teaspoon salt
½ teaspoon pepper

1  Heat the olive oil and slowly cook in it the chopped almonds, onion, garlic and half the parsley, stirring all the time until onions are transparent.
2  Add the breadcrumbs and cook very slowly for 3 minutes.
3  Add the stock, season, and simmer for 15 minutes.
4  Serve with chopped parsley.

# CURRIED CREAM OF CHICKEN SOUP

*30 minutes cooking time*

*Ingredients for 6 servings*

¼ cup minced onion
2 tablespoons butter
1 tablespoon curry powder
2 cups chicken stock
2½ cups thick cream

3 egg yolks
salt and pepper
1 large apple, finely diced
1½ tablespoons lemon juice

1  Cook minced onion in butter until transparent; stir in curry powder and then chicken stock.
2  Simmer for 5 minutes, add cream, and bring to a boil.
3  Beat the egg yolks slightly and beat half a cup of stock into them slowly.
4  Combine mixtures and cook gently until thickened, but do not boil.
5  Season with salt and pepper and chill.
6  Serve garnished with the diced apple that has been soaked in lemon juice.

# CHICKEN GUMBO

*3 hours cooking time*

*Ingredients for 6 servings*

1.5 kg (3 lb) stewing chicken
375 g (12 oz) lean veal, cubed
¼ cup drippings or chicken fat
1 onion, sliced
7 cups boiling water

1 cup fresh or canned sweet corn
1 cup sliced fresh or canned okra
1 tablespoon salt
2½ cups fresh oysters and liquor
1 crushed bay leaf

1   Have chicken cut in serving pieces.
2   Wipe the veal with clean, damp cloth and cut the meat in small pieces.
3   Heat the fat in a large heavy saucepan.
4   Brown the chicken and meat lightly on all sides.
5   Add the onion and cook 5 minutes more.
6   Add water, corn, okra and salt.
7   Cover and simmer 2 hours.
8   Remove the chicken, cut meat from bones, discard the bones and return the meat to the gumbo.
9   Add the oysters and simmer 2 or 3 minutes.
10  Add bay leaf, mix well and serve at once.

# EGG FLOWER SOUP

*Ingredients for 6 servings*

*20 minutes cooking time*

5 cups chicken stock
6 eggs
2 tablespoons soy sauce

1 teaspoon vinegar
½ teaspoon salt
2 spring onions

1  Heat the stock in a saucepan.
2  Beat the eggs well, pour in a thin stream into the soup, stirring.
3  Add the soy sauce, vinegar and salt and simmer for 1 minute.
4  Garnish with finely chopped spring onions.

# SWEET CORN SOUP

*Ingredients for 6 servings*

*1 hour cooking time*

1 cup canned sweet corn
250 g (8 oz) chopped cooked chicken
5 cups chicken stock
2 tablespoons sweet sherry

½ teaspoon salt
1 egg
30 g (1 oz) chopped ham
2 tablespoons chopped spring onion

1  Place the sweet corn and the chopped meat into the stock and simmer.
2  Add sherry and correct seasoning.
3  Beat egg lightly and stir briskly into hot soup.
4  Serve sprinkled with chopped ham and shallots.

# ASPARAGUS SOUP

*Ingredients for 4 servings*

*25 minutes cooking time*

5 cups chicken stock
1 cup shredded cooked chicken
1 tin asparagus pieces

1 spring onion
monosodium glutamate (optional)
1 teaspoon salt

1  Bring chicken stock to the boil.
2  Add shredded chicken and asparagus pieces with juice.
3  Chop spring onion, add to soup and season with pinch monosodium glutamate (if desired) and salt.
4  Simmer for 5 minutes.

# CHICKEN AND LETTUCE SOUP

*30 minutes cooking time*

*Ingredients for 8 servings*

2 chicken breasts
½ teaspoon sugar
1 teaspoon soy sauce
1 teaspoon cornflour
1 tablespoon vegetable oil

½ teaspoon pepper
2 slices fresh ginger
5 cups boiling water
salt
1 small head lettuce

1   Slice the chicken breasts into small pieces.
2   Mix the sugar, soy sauce, cornflour, oil and pepper to a smooth paste and soak the chicken pieces in this mixture for 30 minutes.
3   Pour a teaspoon of oil into a heavy saucepan and fry the ginger gently for 1 minute.
4   Add the boiling water and salt, and when boiling plunge in the shredded lettuce leaves.
5   Simmer 4 minutes in a covered saucepan.
6   Add the chicken pieces and simmer until the chicken is tender.

# CHICKEN AND MUSHROOM SOUP

*20 minutes cooking time*

*Ingredients for 6 servings*

250 g (8 oz) fresh mushrooms
4 tablespoons butter
2 cups chicken stock
dash pepper

3 egg yolks
1 cup light cream
¼ teaspoon salt
3 tablespoons sherry

1 Sauté chopped mushrooms in butter for 5 minutes.
2 Set aside 6 slices for garnish.
3 Mix stock with mushrooms, then add egg yolks, beat for 3 minutes.
4 Turn into a saucepan, add cream and heat slowly, stirring constantly, until slightly thickened.
5 Season with salt, pepper and sherry.
6 Garnish with sliced mushrooms or slivered almonds.

# EGG AND LEMON SOUP

*45 minutes cooking time*

*Ingredients for 6 servings*

7½ cups chicken stock
¾ cup rice
½ teaspoon salt

juice of 1 lemon
3 egg yolks

1 Boil chicken stock, add juice and simmer 15 minutes.
2 Beat the lemon juice with the egg yolks.
3 Add 2 cups of the hot broth to the egg yolk mixture gradually, stirring constantly.
4 When the rice is tender, pour the egg mixture into the soup.
5 Heat until just about to boil, remove from heat and leave tightly covered for about 5 minutes.
6 Serve very hot with some chopped parsley sprinkled on top.

# CREAMED FISH SOUP

*Ingredients for 6-8 servings*

*40 minutes cooking time*

1 chopped onion
¼ cup chopped celery
4 tablespoons butter
6 cups fish stock
1¼ cups milk
⅓ cup cream

500 g (1 lb) fillet of sole
1 tablespoon lemon juice
125 g (4 oz) ground rice
1 teaspoon salt
½ teaspoon paprika

1  Melt 1 tablespoon of butter and fry onion and celery gently for 5 minutes.
2  In another pan, melt remaining butter, add lemon juice, and fry all but one of the fillets of sole, then purée in food mill or blender.
3  Pour fish stock over vegetables, bring to boil.
4  Combine milk with ground rice, add to soup and stir well, then add fish purée, salt and paprika.
5  Immerse remaining fillet of sole in boiling water for 2 minutes, remove, drain and cut into strips.
6  Add strips to soup, stir in cream and serve immediately.

# TUNA COMBO SOUP

*Ingredients for 6 servings*

*20 minutes cooking time*

2 cans pea soup
5 cups water
½ teaspoon pepper
6 tablespoons cooked rice

2 small onions, grated
½ teaspoon salt
1 tablespoon chopped chives
250 g (8 oz) tuna

1  Drain tuna, reserve juice.
2  Mix together pea soup, onion and water.
3  Pour into saucepan and heat for 15 minutes.
4  Add flaked fish and rice.
5  Season with salt and pepper.
6  Add tuna liquid and heat through.
7  Garnish with chopped chives.

# CRAB AND CORN SOUP

*5 minutes cooking time*

*Ingredients for 6 servings*

185 g (6 oz) tinned crab meat
5 cups chicken stock
½ teaspoon salt
½ teaspoon sesame oil
1½ teaspoons cornflour
2 egg whites

125 g (4 oz) sweet corn
¼ teaspoon monosodium glutamate
  (optional)
1½ teaspoons sherry
2 tablespoons water

1  Shred crab meat and beat egg white lightly.
2  Add crab meat to egg and mix through.
3  Set aside.
4  Bring stock to boil and add corn.
5  Season with salt and add monosodium glutamate (if desired), sesame oil,
   sherry and a little pepper.
6  Blend cornflour and water, stir into stock and boil for 1 minute.
7  Add crab meat and egg mixture and bring to boil. Serve.

# MUSHROOM CRAB SOUP

*10 minutes cooking time*

*Ingredients for 4 servings*

155 g (5 oz) crab meat
¼ cup chopped cashews
¼ teaspoon pepper
½ onion, minced
¾ cup milk
¾ cup cream

450 g (16 oz) can condensed cream of
  mushroom soup
½ teaspoon salt
⅓ cup cream, whipped
2 tablespoons sherry

1  Combine crab meat, onion, sherry, milk and soup. Season with salt and
   pepper.
2  Heat to boiling point and pour into dishes.
3  Serve topped with whipped cream and sprinkle with chopped cashews.

# TOMATO CRAB SOUP

*7 minutes cooking time*

*Ingredients for 4 servings*

185 g (6 oz) crab meat, drained
½ teaspoon salt
450 g (16 oz) condensed cream of
  tomato soup
1½ cups milk

⅛ teaspoon paprika
¼ teaspoon pepper
¾ cup cream
2 tablespoons sherry
½ cup whipped cream

1  Combine crab meat, onion, sherry, milk and cream; season with salt and
   pepper.
2  Bring to boil and stir.
3  Chill.
4  Pour into serving dishes and serve topped with whipped cream and dotted
   with paprika.

# PRAWN SOUP

*30 minutes cooking time*

*Ingredients for 5-6 servings*

750 g (1½ lb) shelled prawns
60g (2 oz) long-grain rice
5 cups stock
1 tablespoon butter
1 carrot, chopped

½ cup cream
¼ teaspoon salt
¼ teaspoon cayenne pepper
1 onion, chopped

1  Save about 20 prawns for garnish.
2  Boil the rice until tender in salted water.
3  Add rice to the rest of the prawns which have been pounded into the
   butter.
4  Put rice, prawns and butter in a saucepan; stir over the heat for 2 minutes.
5  Add stock made from prawn shells and tails, carrot and onion, and
   simmer for 20 minutes.
6  Pass the soup through a sieve, return to pan and add the cream.
7  Serve with whole prawns.

# FRESH TOMATO SOUP

*15 minutes cooking time*

*Ingredients for 6 servings*

**2 tablespoons butter**
**¼ teaspoon pepper**
**2 tablespoons lemon juice**
**6 tomatoes**

**½ teaspoon salt**
**2 teaspoons sugar**
**3 cups chicken stock**
**6 chopped spring onions**

1  Peel and dice tomatoes.
2  Melt butter in frying pan and add tomatoes.
3  Cover and simmer for 5-6 minutes.
4  Pour in chicken stock, lemon juice, sugar, onions, salt and pepper.
5  Bring to boil and simmer for further 10 minutes.

# ELSA'S TOMATO BOUILLON

*10 minutes cooking time*

*Ingredients for 6-8 servings*

**6 cups tomato juice**
**2 chopped onions**
**2 tablespoons butter**
**½ cup chopped celery**

**4 cloves**
**2 tablespoons chopped parsley**
**1 tablespoon chopped basil**
**1 bay leaf**

1  Fry onions gently in butter for 5 minutes.
2  Add remaining ingredients and bring to the boil.
3  Strain and serve topped with whipped or sour cream.

# CITRUS-TOMATO SOUP

*10 minutes cooking time*

*Ingredients for 4 servings*

**4 cups tomato juice**
**2 teaspoons sugar**
**½ teaspoon pepper**
**1 onion, minced**

**½ cup concentrated orange juice**
**½ teaspoon salt**
**4 orange slices**

1  Heat tomato juice till boiling and add orange juice, sugar, onion and season with salt and pepper.
2  Heat through and pour into serving cups.
3  Top each serving with orange slice and serve.

# CREAMED TOMATO SOUP

*30 minutes cooking time*

*Ingredients for 5-6 servings*

| | |
|---|---|
| 1 cup tinned tomatoes | 4 tablespoons butter |
| 1 small onion, chopped | 4 tablespoons flour |
| 1 teaspoon sugar | 2 teaspoons salt |
| ¼ cup chopped celery | ½ teaspoon pepper |
| 2 cups milk | 4 tablespoons chopped parsley |

1 Combine tomatoes, celery, onion and sugar and simmer for 15 minutes.
2 Melt butter, stir in flour and add milk. Simmer slowly, stirring until thickened.
3 Add to tomato mixture, add salt and pepper and stir in parsley.

# JELLIED TOMATO BOUILLON

*15 minutes cooking time*

*Ingredients for 3-4 servings*

| | |
|---|---|
| 1½ cups tomato juice | 1 teaspoon salt |
| 1½ cups light stock | 1 teaspoon celery salt |
| 1 tablespoon gelatine | ½ teaspoon pepper |
| 3 tablespoons lemon juice | 2 tablespoons chopped parsley |

1 Soak gelatine in ¼ cup cold water for 5 minutes.
2 Heat tomato juice, stock, salt, pepper and celery salt to boiling and dissolve gelatine in hot mixture.
3 Cool, add lemon juice, pour into wet mould and chill.
4 Sprinkle with chopped parsley to serve.

# VEGETABLE HERB SOUP

*15 minutes cooking time*

*Ingredients for 6 servings*

| | |
|---|---|
| 1 small head of lettuce | 1 cup fresh or frozen peas |
| 6 spring onions | 5 cups chicken stock |
| 5 cm (2 in) fresh mint | ½ teaspoon salt |
| 6 leaves of tarragon | ¼ teaspoon pepper |
| 1 tablespoon chopped parsley or | |
|   1 teaspoon dried herbs | |

1   Shred lettuce finely and place in a saucepan with chopped spring onions, finely chopped herbs and peas.
2   Add chicken stock; season with salt and pepper.
3   Cover and simmer gently for 15 minutes.

# CURRIED CAULIFLOWER SOUP

*40 minutes cooking time*

*Ingredients for 4 servings*

| | |
|---|---|
| ½ small cauliflower | 1 capsicum |
| 2 onions, chopped | 2 tablespoons ghee |
| 1½ teaspoons turmeric | ½ teaspoon chilli powder |
| 4 chicken stock cubes | 1½ cups water |
| 1½ tablespoons lentil flour | ¾ cup milk |
| ½ cup yoghurt | 1 teaspoon garam masala |
| ½ teaspoon salt | 3 tablespoons chopped parsley |

1   Cut cauliflower into small flowers and slice capsicum thinly.
2   Heat ghee and fry vegetables for 5-10 minutes.
3   Stir in turmeric and chilli powder.
4   Add chicken stock cubes and water.
5   Cover and simmer for 20 minutes.
6   In separate bowl, mix lentil flour with 2 tablespoons milk, gradually add remaining milk and add to soup.
7   Bring to the boil and simmer.
8   Stir in yoghurt and add garam masala.
9   Season with salt and dot with chopped parsley.

# ONION SOUP

*25 minutes cooking time*

*Ingredients for 6 servings*

| | |
|---|---|
| 3 large onions | 6 tablespoons Parmesan cheese |
| ½ teaspoon pepper | ½ teaspoon salt |
| 1½ teaspoons sugar | 3 tablespoons butter |
| 6 cups stock | |

1   Sauté onions in butter and stir in sugar.
2   Cook for 10 minutes.
3   Pour heated stock over onions and season with salt and pepper.
4   Heat for further 15 minutes and serve with Parmesan cheese.

# CAULIFLOWER SOUP

*30 minutes cooking time*

*Ingredients for 4-5 servings*

| | |
|---|---|
| 1 small cauliflower | 2 leeks |
| 125 g (4 oz) diced ham | 6 cups stock |
| 1 tablespoon whole meal flour | 2 tablespoons butter |
| 1¼ cups milk | 3 egg yolks |
| ½ cup cream | ½ teaspoon salt |
| ¾ teaspoon white pepper | 2 grated carrots |

1  Melt the butter and combine with flour.
2  Mix thoroughly and cook for 3 minutes.
3  Add stock and bring to the boil, stirring constantly.
4  Add the chopped cauliflower and carrots. Stir.
5  Add chopped leeks and ham and simmer for 10 minutes.
6  Season with salt and pepper.
7  Add milk, eggs and cream.
8  Simmer for 5 minutes and serve.

# CREAMED CELERY SOUP

*30 minutes cooking time*

*Ingredients for 6 servings*

| | |
|---|---|
| 1 cup celery | ½ teaspoon chervil |
| ¼ cup butter | ¼ teaspoon white pepper |
| ¼ cup flour | 2 teaspoons grated onion |
| 5 cups cold chicken stock | 1 teaspoon salt |
| 1½ cups milk | parsley |
| dash of nutmeg | |

1  Cook chopped celery in butter until crisp but tender.
2  Add flour and gradually add half of the stock.
3  Cook, stirring constantly, until sauce boils for 1 minute.
4  Blend sauce in blender for 1 minute and return to saucepan.
5  Stir milk into remaining stock; add to celery mixture, along with nutmeg, chervil, pepper, salt and onion.
6  Heat slowly.
7  Garnish with parsley.

# CUCUMBER SOUP

*50 minutes cooking time*

*Ingredients for 6 servings*

½ cup dried prawns
2 slices fresh ginger
3 tablespoons sherry
6 cups chicken stock
2 cucumbers
⅔ cup chopped ham

1 teaspoon salt
½ teaspoon monosodium glutamate
   (optional)
1 tablespoon soy sauce
8 dried mushrooms

1  Soak prawns overnight and prepare mushrooms by soaking in hot water for 30 minutes, then cut into strips.
2  Score cucumbers with a fork and peel.
3  Cut lengthwise, scoop out seeds and slice.
4  Put soy sauce, salt, stock and ginger in a saucepan. Bring to boil and add mushrooms.
5  Add prawns and liquid they soaked in. Simmer for 35 minutes, add cucumber and cook for 5 minutes.
6  Season with monosodium glutamate and sprinkle with chopped ham.

# PORK AND LEEK SOUP

*20 minutes cooking time*

*Ingredients for 6 servings*

8 tablespoons thinly-sliced raw pork
½ teaspoon monosodium glutamate
   (optional)
2 small leeks

½ teaspoon salt
½ teaspoon sugar
2 teaspoons cornflour
6 cups chicken stock

1  Cut meat diagonally into thin slices.
2  Place in a small bowl, add seasonings and sherry and mix well.
3  Add 1 teaspoon cornflour and work through; set aside.
4  Cut the white part of the leek into very thin slices.
5  Boil stock, add leek and cook for 5 minutes.
6  Add pork and cook for 8 minutes.
7  Blend remaining cornflour with 1 tablespoon water and stir into soup. Cook for 1-2 minutes and serve.

# CREAMY ONION SOUP

*30 minutes cooking time*

*Ingredients for 8 servings*

3 tablespoons butter
3 tablespoons flour
½ teaspoon pepper
250 g (8 oz) grated cheddar cheese

6 onions, sliced
1 teaspoon salt
8 slices toasted french bread
7½ cups milk

1   Sauté onions in butter; cover and cook over low heat for 20 minutes.
2   Stir in flour and season with salt and pepper.
3   Add milk and stir constantly. Bring to boil and add cheese.
4   Float toast rounds on top and serve.

# PUMPKIN SOUP

*20 minutes cooking time*

*Ingredients for 4-5 servings*

500 g (1 lb) butternut pumpkin
7½ cups chicken stock
¼ teaspoon white pepper
60 g (2 oz) butter

3 onions, chopped
½ teaspoon salt
2 teaspoons orange rind

1   Brown the onions in butter and add chopped pumpkin.
2   Stir constantly and add stock.
3   Cook for 5 minutes.
4   Season with salt and pepper.
5   Add orange rind and heat for further 10-15 minutes.

# FRESH PEA SOUP

*45 minutes cooking time*

*Ingredients for 3-4 servings*

2 cups shelled green peas
1 onion, finely chopped
2 sprigs parsley
2½ cups chicken stock

½ head lettuce, shredded
2 stalks celery
1 tablespoon butter
½ bay leaf

1 Melt butter and gently fry onion, celery, lettuce and parsley.
2 Add half the chicken stock, half the peas and bay leaf and simmer for 30 minutes, then put soup through food grinder and strain.
3 Heat remaining stock and add remaining peas, cook for 10 minutes, then add to strained soup.

# WATERCRESS SOUP

*10 minutes cooking time*

*Ingredients for 6-8 servings*

**1 cup chopped watercress**
**1 teaspoon salt**

**4 cups chicken stock**
**½ teaspoon pepper**

1 Heat stock with salt and pepper to boiling.
2 Add watercress and simmer for 5 minutes only.
3 Serve immediately, before cress turns dark green.

# IRISH POTATO SOUP

*50 minutes cooking time*

*Ingredients for 6 servings*

**2 onions**
**4 peeled potatoes**
**60 g (2 oz) butter**
**1 teaspoon salt**
**½ teaspoon pepper**
**1 clove garlic**

**5 cups milk**
**½ cup cream**
**2 tablespoons chopped parsley**
**2 tablespoons chopped chives**
**bouquet garni**

1 Slice onions and potatoes thinly and toss in melted butter in pan; cover with foil and cook over low heat for 10 minutes.
2 Remove foil, add salt, pepper, crushed garlic clove, bouquet garni and milk and simmer for 30 minutes.
3 Remove bouquet garni and purée soup in blender or through a sieve, then reheat.
4 Put 2 tablespoons cream and some chive-parsley mixture in the bottom of bowls, top with soup and stir once before serving.

# BAVARIAN CHERRY SOUP

*15 minutes cooking time*

*Ingredients for 3-4 servings*

| | |
|---|---|
| **250 g pitted cherries** | **1 cup water** |
| **½ cup red wine** | **½ teaspoon arrowroot** |
| **⅛ cup sugar** | **½ teaspoon grated orange rind** |

1  Combine fruit, sugar, wine, orange rind and water in enamel pan.
2  Cook for 10 minutes, then sieve or put through blender.
3  Blend with arrowroot, return to heat for 2-3 minutes, until reheated.
4  Serve hot as dessert, or chilled as an appetiser.

# BORSCH

*No cooking time*

*Ingredients for 4 servings*

| | |
|---|---|
| **375 g (12 oz) sliced beetroot and juice** | **1 cup beef stock** |
| **1½ cups sour cream** | **½ teaspoon salt** |
| **¼ teaspoon pepper** | **1 tablespoon chopped dill** |
| | **1½ tablespoons sugar** |

1  Combine beetroot, juice, stock, 1 cup sour cream and sugar, and transfer to blender.
2  Blend at high speed until smooth.
3  Place in serving dishes and season with salt and pepper.
4  Combine remaining sour cream, a little salt and chopped dill.
5  Top beetroot mixture with sour cream and serve.

# SCANDINAVIAN SEAFOOD SOUP

*30 minutes cooking time*

*Ingredients for 6 servings*

| | |
|---|---|
| **500 g (1 lb) fish fillets** | **2 tablespoons chopped parsley** |
| **3 chicken stock cubes** | **185 g (6 oz) bacon** |
| **2 chopped onions** | **2 tablespoons butter** |
| **4 cups chopped cabbage** | **4 potatoes** |
| **2 apples** | **1 teaspoon salt** |
| **½ teaspoon pepper** | |

1 Melt butter, fry bacon and chopped onion.
2 Add cabbage and 10 cups boiling water, reduce heat and simmer.
3 Cook 10 minutes, covered, then add fish pieces.
4 Add diced peeled potatoes and grated apple, season with salt and pepper.
5 Add stock cubes and simmer for 20-25 minutes.
6 Serve garnished with chopped parsley.

# GRUYÈRE SOUP

*20 minutes cooking time*

*Ingredients for 4-5 servings*

**5 cups stock**
**1 tablespoon butter**
**2 cups grated gruyère cheese**
**¼ teaspoon white pepper**

**1 tablespoon wholemeal flour**
**3 chopped onions**
**½ teaspoon salt**

1 Brown the onions in butter or margarine and add flour.
2 Add the stock and cook for 5 minutes.
3 Simmer for 10 minutes, then add cheese.
4 Season with salt and pepper.
5 Serve.

# JAPANESE PRAWN AND WATERCRESS SOUP

*15 minutes cooking time*

*Ingredients for 4-6 servings*

**18 small green prawns**
**5 cups chicken stock**
**1 bunch watercress**

**1 teaspoon salt**
**2 tablespoons cornflour**
**2 teaspoons soy sauce**

1 Shell prawns, leaving tails on, and wash carefully before coating with cornflour.
2 Cook in boiling water for 2-3 minutes.
3 Boil stock with salt and soy sauce.
4 Place prawns in soup bowls, cover with chopped watercress and pour over boiling soup to serve.

# JAPANESE EGG DROP SOUP

*20 minutes cooking time*

*Ingredients for 4-6 servings*

5 cups clear chicken broth
½ cup fresh green peas
3 eggs
2 teaspoons light soy sauce

1 teaspoon salt
½ teaspoon monosodium glutamate (optional)

1  Parboil peas for 10 minutes.
2  Boil stock with salt, soy sauce and monosodium glutamate (if desired).
3  Pour well-beaten eggs in thin stream into swirling stock.
4  Continue to stir stock in one direction until egg threads are cooked.
5  Pour soup over green peas in bowls to serve.

# SPEEDY MINESTRONE

*12 minutes cooking time*

*Ingredients for 8 servings*

2 cans beef consommé
½ teaspoon dried basil
½ teaspoon salt
½ cup grated Parmesan cheese

450 g (1 lb) tinned tomatoes
1½ cups thin noodles
¼ teaspoon pepper

1  Combine all ingredients (except cheese) and break up tomatoes in a saucepan.
2  Cook for 12 minutes, uncovered, over medium heat and dot with grated Parmesan cheese.

# GAZPACHO

*No cooking time*

*Ingredients for 3-4 servings*

1 green pepper
3 large ripe tomatoes
½ cup olive oil
2 cups chilled chicken stock
1 clove garlic
2 tablespoons lemon juice

1 teaspoon salt
½ teaspoon ground black pepper
1 diced onion
1 seeded, peeled, diced cucumber
1 cup croutons
¼ cup chopped parsley, chives and basil

1   Combine tomatoes, stock, olive oil, herbs, salt and pepper, garlic and lemon juice in blender and mix until smooth.
2   Stir in chopped onion and cucumber.
3   Pour into bowl over ice cubes and top with croutons.

# COLD CUCUMBER SOUP

*No cooking time*

*Ingredients for 5-6 servings*

3 large cucumbers
½ cup chopped walnuts
1 clove garlic, minced
2 tablespoons chopped fresh dill
2 tablespoons olive oil

1½ cups plain yoghurt
1 teaspoon salt
½ teaspoon paprika
2 tablespoons chopped parsley

1   Peel and chop cucumber and mix with all ingredients except yoghurt.
2   Refrigerate for 2-3 hours.
3   To serve, stir cucumber mixture into yoghurt and pour into bowls over ice cubes.

# COLD CURRIED SOUP

*5 minutes cooking time*

*Ingredients for 4 servings*

2 small tins condensed cream of chicken soup
¾ cup thickened cream
4 tablespoons chopped parsley

½ cup whipped cream
1½ cups milk
2 tablespoons curry powder

1   Mix soup, milk and ¾ cup thickened cream.
2   Place ½ cup of this mixture into saucepan and bring to boil.
3   Add curry powder and mix well. Stir this mixture into remaining soup mixture and chill.
4   Serve topped with whipped cream and chopped parsley.

# CHILLED PEA SOUP

*No cooking time*

*Ingredients for 4 servings*

450 g (16 oz) can condensed cream of
  pea soup
¾ cup cream
2 tablespoons sherry
½ cup sour cream
1 tomato, sliced

1½ cups milk
green food colouring
½ onion, minced
1 tablespoon chopped mint
¼ teaspoon salt

1   Combine pea soup, onion, mint, sherry, cream, milk and 2 or 3 drops
    food colouring.
2   Mix well and chill.
3   Combine sour cream and salt.
4   Garnish with tomato slices, topped with sour cream.

# CHILLED VEGETABLE SOUP

*25 minutes cooking time*

*Ingredients for 4-5 servings*

3 potatoes, peeled and sliced
2 tablespoons butter
2 leeks
3 cups chicken broth
1 onion, chopped

1 teaspoon salt
1½ cups cream
3 tablespoons chopped chives
½ teaspoon pepper

1   Chop leeks and fry gently with onion in butter for 5 minutes.
2   Add sliced potatoes and stock and simmer for 20 minutes.
3   Force through sieve or put through blender, add cream, salt and pepper.
4   Top with chopped chives to serve, or chill for 2 hours and serve.

# Seafood

## CRAB CANTONESE

*Ingredients for 8 servings*

*8 minutes cooking time*

8 tablespoons peanut oil
1 teaspoon salt
500 g (16 oz) crab meat, flaked
2½ cups chicken stock
2 tablespoons water
2 tablespoons chopped parsley
5 tablespoons milk

500 g (8 oz) bamboo shoots, cut into strips
½ teaspoon monosodium glutamate (optional)
5 teaspoons sherry
3 teaspoons cornflour

1  Heat half of the oil and fry bamboo shoots. Season with salt, sugar and monosodium glutamate, if desired. Cook for 4 minutes and turn into heated dish.
2  Wipe out pan and add remaining oil. Add crab meat and sherry, stock and salt.
3  Toss and add cornflour blended with water, stir and boil.
4  Add milk and bring to boil.
5  Return bamboo shoots and heat for 30 seconds. Turn into heated dish and garnish with chopped parsley.

# ORIENTAL CRAB OMELETTE

*15 minutes cooking time*

*Ingredients for 6 servings*

6 eggs
2½ tablespoons peanut oil
½ teaspoon pepper
315 g (10 oz) bean sprouts

1½ cups crab meat
½ teaspoon salt
⅛ teaspoon garlic powder
8 chopped spring onions

1  Flake crab meat.
2  Beat eggs.
3  Wash and drain bean sprouts.
4  Combine eggs, sprouts, onions, crab meat, salt, pepper and garlic. Mix lightly.
5  Heat oil in frying pan.
6  Use ¼ cup of mixture for each omelette, cook as pancakes and remove to serving dish.
7  Pour over Foo Yung Sauce and serve.

## FOO YUNG SAUCE

1 teaspoon cornflour
2 teaspoons soy sauce
¾ cup chicken stock

1 teaspoon sugar
1 teaspoon vinegar

1  Combine all ingredients and heat over gentle flame.
2  Pour over crab omelette.

# CRAB COCKTAIL

*No cooking time*

*Ingredients for 4 servings*

375 g (12 oz) crab meat
½ cup mayonnaise
2 chopped gherkins
¼ teaspoon pepper

1 diced avocado
1 teaspoon chilli sauce
½ teaspoon salt
½ tablespoon minced onion

1  Drain crab meat and place in serving dishes.
2  Add diced avocado and mix mayonnaise, gherkins, minced onion and chilli sauce.
3  Mix well and season with salt and pepper.
4  Serve chilled, with mayonnaise mixture spooned over top.

# CRAB CASSEROLE

*30 minutes cooking time*

*Ingredients for 6 servings*

250 g (8 oz) tinned crab
3 tablespoons butter
½ teaspoon pepper
2 onions, chopped
⅓ cup milk
1½ cups chopped celery

250 g (8 oz) tinned lobster
1 teaspoon salt
1 cup mayonnaise
1 teaspoon Worchestershire sauce
1½ cups soft breadcrumbs

1   Drain crab and lobster.
2   Cut into pieces and combine with celery, mayonnaise, milk, onion, Worcestershire sauce and 1 cup breadcrumbs.
3   Spoon into casserole dish and combine remaining breadcrumbs with butter, sprinkle around edges of dish and bake for 30 minutes.

# CRAB MORNAY

*15 minutes cooking time*

*Ingredients for 4 servings*

500 g (16 oz) tinned crab
90 g (3 oz) cheese, grated
½ teaspoon pepper
8 potatoes, mashed

90 g (3 oz) butter
1 teaspoon salt
1¼ cups milk
2 tablespoons flour

1   Place milk and 1¼ cups hot water in saucepan and boil.
2   Melt butter in second pan. Add flour and stir in milk. Season with salt and pepper.
3   Bring to boil and add cheese. Add crab and mix well.
4   Place mashed potato in piping bag and pipe around edge of serving dish. Pour in crab mixture and sprinkle with extra grated cheese.
5   Place dish under grill and cook until brown.

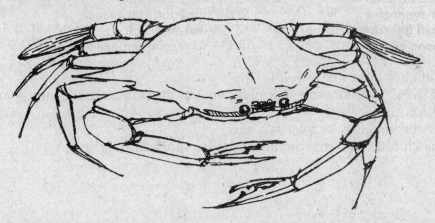

# CRAB-STUFFED MUSHROOMS

*10 minutes cooking time*

*Ingredients for 4 servings*

| | |
|---|---|
| **375 g (12 oz) mushrooms** | **2 tablespoons butter** |
| **2 spring onions, chopped** | **½ teaspoon salt** |
| **½ teaspoon pepper** | **½ teaspoon dry mustard** |
| **185 g tinned crab** | **2 tablespoons mayonnaise** |
| **3 tablespoons cream** | |

1   Remove stems from mushrooms and save.
2   Flake drained crab and combine with chopped onions.
3   Add mayonnaise, cream, salt, pepper and mustard and mix well.
4   Place spoonfuls of crab mixture into mushroom centres.
5   Pour melted butter into casserole dish and add mushrooms.
6   Bake for 8-10 minutes and serve.

# PRAWN-FILLED PEPPERS

*30 minutes cooking time*

*Ingredients for 4 servings*

| | |
|---|---|
| **4 green peppers** | **45 g (1½ oz) grated cheddar cheese** |
| **60 g (2 oz) macaroni, cooked** | **2 tablespoons butter** |
| **2 tablespoons flour** | **½ teaspoon salt** |
| **pinch basil** | **1½ cups milk** |
| **¼ teaspoon Worcestershire sauce** | **⅓ cup chopped celery** |
| **375 g (12 oz) shelled prawns** | |

1   Cut tops off green peppers and remove seeds.
2   Scallop edges and precook in boiling water. Drain.
3   Melt butter in frying pan, blend in flour and salt, mix and add basil and milk.
4   Stir well and add Worcestershire sauce. Mix once more and add celery.
5   Dice prawns and add to sauce with macaroni.
6   Salt inside of peppers and fill with prawn mixture. Place upright in dish and cook uncovered for 25 minutes.
7   Sprinkle with cheese and serve.

# CURRIED EGGS AND PRAWNS

*30 minutes cooking time*

*Ingredients for 8 servings*

375 g (12 oz) shelled prawns
250 g (8 oz) breadcrumbs
2½ cups white sauce
3 teaspoons curry powder
8 hardboiled eggs
½ teaspoon pepper

60 g (2 oz) butter
2 tablespoons chopped parsley
½ teaspoon dry mustard
1 teaspoon salt
4 tablespoons mayonnaise

1 Halve hardboiled eggs and remove yolks.
2 Mash and mix with seasonings and mayonnaise; refill whites.
3 Put in baking dish.
4 Make white sauce.
5 Add prawns and reheat gently. Pour this mixture over eggs and bake for 15-20 minutes in moderate oven.
6 Garnish with chopped parsley and serve with rice.

# PRAWNS A L'AUBERGINE

*25 minutes cooking time*

*Ingredients for 6 servings*

375 g (12 oz) shelled prawns
3 tablespoons butter
1½ teaspoons salt
½ teaspoon thyme
1 large eggplant
2 green peppers, chopped
2 onions, chopped

2 cups soft breadcrumbs
2 cups cooked rice
½ teaspoon pepper
375 g (12 oz) tinned tomatoes, chopped
⅓ cup butter
2 garlic cloves, crushed

1 Split prawns lengthwise and place aside.
2 Sauté onion, green pepper and garlic in butter.
3 Peel eggplant, cut into cubes and add to frying pan.
4 Add tomatoes and season with salt and pepper.
5 Add thyme and cover. Simmer for 8 minutes and stir in prawns. Mix well.
6 Add rice and spoon into individual ovenproof dishes.
7 Bake in moderate oven for 15 minutes with buttered breadcrumbs on top.

# PRAWNS IN BLACK BEAN SAUCE

*5 minutes cooking time*

*Ingredients for 8 servings*

15 large prawns
½ teaspoon salt
½ teaspoon monosodium glutamate
 (optional)
5 slices fresh ginger
5 tablespoons black soy beans
2 teaspoons soy sauce

4 teaspoons water
¼ teaspoon pepper
½ teaspoon sugar
4 tablespoons peanut oil
2 garlic cloves, crushed
1¼ cups hot chicken stock
2 teaspoons cornflour

1   Halve the shelled prawns and remove veins.
2   Cut prawns diagonally into small pieces, sprinkle with monosodium glutamate (if desired), pepper, sugar, salt and mix well.
3   Heat oil and add ginger and garlic, cook for 90 seconds and discard. Add beans and cook for 20 seconds, tossing.
4   Add prawns and cook for 2 minutes.
5   Add stock, soy sauce and cornflour blended with water. Boil for 1 minute and turn into serving dish.

# PRAWN VINDALOO

*25 minutes cooking time*

*Ingredients for 4 servings*

1 kg (2 lb) prawns
2 teaspoons cumin
1 tablespoon onion juice
2 teaspoons tamarind purée
125 g (4 oz) coconut cream
½ cup ghee

1 tablespoon grated fresh ginger
4 teaspoons coriander
1 teaspoon crushed garlic
½ cup water
1 teaspoon salt

1   Shell and de-vein prawns.
2   Heat ghee and fry grated ginger, cumin and coriander gently for 3 minutes.
3   Add onion juice and garlic, mix well and add tamarind purée and water.
4   Simmer for 10 minutes and add coconut cream and dissolve.
5   Add salt and stir in prawns.
6   Simmer for 10 minutes and serve.

# FIESTA PRAWNS

*25 minutes cooking time*

*Ingredients for 6 servings*

500 g (1 lb) cooked prawns
1 teaspoon salt
2 egg yolks
2 onions
4 tablespoons brandy
185 g (6 oz) mushrooms
375 g (12 oz) long-grain rice

½ teaspoon pepper
5 tablespoons butter
1 green pepper
juice of 1 lemon
1¼ cups cream
8 tablespoons white wine

1   Melt half butter and add prawns. Cook gently for 2 minutes.
2   Add rice to pan of boiling water and cook until tender.
3   Slice mushrooms, green pepper, onions and fry in remaining butter for 5 minutes.
4   Add lemon juice and wine to prawns and cook 1 minute more.
5   Pour brandy onto heated spoon and ignite it. Pour over prawns and repeat. Leave prawns until flame dies out.
6   Stir in cream and season with salt and pepper.
7   Drain rice and mix with vegetables; arrange on serving dish.
8   Add yolks to prawn mixture and stir well until sauce thickens.
9   Pile in centre of rice and garnish with lemon slices.

# PINEAPPLE PRAWNS

*20 minutes cooking time*

*Ingredients for 6 servings*

750 g (1½ lb) raw prawns
1½ teaspoons salt
10 cups milk
2.5 cm (1 in) piece fresh ginger
2 tablespoons milk

3 eggs
185 g (6 oz) plain flour
1⅓ cups peanut oil
1 small tin pineapple pieces

1   Beat eggs with salt, add sifted flour and a little milk.
2   Clean and shell prawns and dip in batter.
3   Heat oil in pan with grated ginger, then deep fry prawns, remove and drain.
4   Surround with pineapple pieces to serve.

# PRAWN CURRY

*Ingredients for 5-6 servings*

*20-25 minutes cooking time*

750 g (1½ lb) prawns, halved
1 tablespoon curry powder
2 small tins condensed cream of
  celery soup
¼ teaspoon salt
¼ cup butter

2 tablespoons chopped parsley
¾ cup onion, chopped
¼ teaspoon pepper
90 g (3 oz) mushrooms
¾ cup chopped celery
1 cup apple sauce

1　Melt butter and toss in onion and celery. Cook for 4-5 minutes and lower heat.
2　Add remaining ingredients and season with salt and pepper. Simmer uncovered for 15-20 minutes and serve garnished with chopped parsley.

# BUBBLING SEAFOOD

*20 minutes cooking time*

*Ingredients for 6 servings*

315 g (10 oz) crab meat
315 g (10 oz) prawns
3 cups milk
½ cup (125 g) butter
½ cup plain flour
250 g (8 oz) sliced mushrooms
½ teaspoon paprika

2 teaspoons marjoram
½ teaspoon salt
¼ teaspoon pepper
3 teaspoons Worcestershire sauce
4 tablespoons green olives, sliced
6 crumpets or muffins, toasted

1　Melt butter in frying pan and add flour, salt and pepper. Blend and add milk slowly.
2　Season with Worcestershire sauce and marjoram. Cook until sauce begins to thicken and add crab meat, prawns, olives and mushrooms.
3　Heat once again and serve on top of crumpets, sprinkled with paprika.

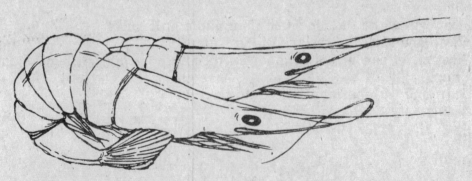

# SOUTH OF THE BORDER SEAFOOD

*20-25 minutes cooking time*

*Ingredients for 4 servings*

450 g (1 lb) can tomatoes
1 onion, sliced
½ teaspoon salt
12 black olives
250 g (8 oz) bottled oysters, drained
250 g (8 oz) crab meat
2 teaspoons chilli powder
2 tablespoons butter

4 tablespoons tomato sauce
1 clove garlic
½ teaspoon pepper
3 cups hot cooked rice
250 g (8 oz) prawns
2 tablespoons plain flour
¼ teaspoon Tabasco sauce
1½ teaspoons sugar

1  Combine tomatoes, tomato sauce, onion, garlic, sugar and Tabasco sauce, cook gently for 12 minutes and strain.
2  Melt butter in frying pan and add flour. Mix and add chilli powder and tomato sauce.
3  Boil and add crab meat, prawns, oysters and season with salt and pepper.
4  Heat for 10 minutes and arrange rice on serving dish.
5  Arrange tomato/prawn mixture in centre and garnish with olives.

# PRAWN COCKTAIL

*No cooking time*

*Ingredients for 4 servings*

750 g (1½ lb) shelled prawns
½ cup mayonnaise
½ teaspoon salt
1 tablespoon minced onion

250 g (8 oz) grapefruit sections
2 tablespoons grapefruit juice
¼ teaspoon pepper
1 teaspoon chilli sauce

1  Place prawns and grapefruit sections in serving dishes.
2  Combine mayonnaise, grapefruit juice, chilli sauce and minced onion.
3  Mix well and season with salt and pepper.
4  Pour over prawn/grapefruit mixture and serve.

# ELEGANT SCALLOPS

*15 minutes cooking time*

*Ingredients for 6 servings*

1 kg (2 lb) scallops
4 tablespoons sliced almonds
2 teaspoons butter

3 tablespoons sherry
3 tablespoons chicken broth
¼ teaspoon salt

1  Cut scallops in halves.
2  Brown almonds in butter in a frying pan and set aside.
3  Place chicken broth, seasoned with salt, in pan and bring to boil.
4  Add scallops and cover.
5  Simmer for 10 minutes and return almonds to pan.
6  Pour in sherry and simmer for 4 minutes.

# CREAMED SCALLOPS

*15 minutes cooking time*

*Ingredients for 6 servings*

1 kg (2 lb) scallops
1 teaspoon salt
3 tablespoons chopped parsley
4 spring onions

¾ cup white wine
½ teaspoon pepper
1½ cups cream

1  Place chopped spring onions, wine, salt, pepper and scallops in saucepan.
2  Bring to boil and simmer for 3 minutes.
3  Strain.
4  Boil the liquid again and add cream.
5  Boil until thickened and return other ingredients.
6  Heat through and garnish with chopped parsley.

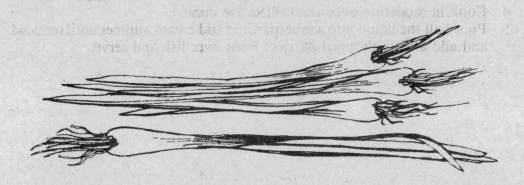

# BANANA FISH

*30 minutes cooking time*

*Ingredients for 4 servings*

1.5 kg (3 lb) white fish
2 teaspoons sugar
3 bananas
1 teaspoon salt
4 tablespoons olive oil

3 tablespoons tomato purée
2 tablespoons water
½ teaspoon dried mixed herbs
½ teaspoon pepper

1   Split fish and place in a greased baking dish.
2   Brush with oil and sprinkle with seasonings and herbs.
3   Mix tomato purée with 2 tablespoons oil and a little sugar. Mix and add remaining sugar.
4   Add water and pour around fish. Let a little go into the centre of the fish.
5   Peel and split bananas and place round fish.
6   Bake slowly for 30 minutes, basting occasionally.

# BERNESE FISH

*35 minutes cooking time*

*Ingredients for 6 servings*

1 kg (2 lb) flounder fillets
315 g (10 oz) mushrooms
2 tablespoons chopped parsley
4 tablespoons cream
1 teaspoon salt
125 g (4 oz) spring onions

1 tablespoon butter
5 tomatoes
1¼ cups white wine
juice of 1 lemon
⅛ teaspoon white pepper

1   Butter casserole and dot with chopped spring onions.
2   Place a layer of fillets seasoned with salt, pepper and lemon juice. Cover with chopped mushrooms and tomatoes. Dot with chopped parsley.
3   Put on another layer of fillets and moisten with white wine.
4   Cook in moderate oven until fillets are done.
5   Pour half the liquid into a saucepan and add cream, simmer until reduced and add a little chopped parsley. Pour over fish and serve.

# VALENCIA FISH

*1 hour cooking time*

*Ingredients for 6 servings*

| | |
|---|---|
| **750 g (1½ lb) fish fillets** | **1 teaspoon salt** |
| **½ teaspoon pepper** | **2 cloves garlic, chopped** |
| **1 red pepper, chopped** | **3 cups long-grain rice** |
| **1 teaspoon turmeric** | **4 tablespoons olive oil** |
| **1 tablespoon lemon juice** | **2 onions, chopped** |

1  Sprinkle fish with salt, pepper and lemon juice.
2  Sauté fish in oil and remove from pan.
3  Add onion, garlic and pepper to pan and cook until softened.
4  Stir in rice and fry. Add turmeric and 5 cups water, stir gently.
5  Bring to boil and cover.
6  Cook gently for 20 minutes and add fish.
7  Cook for 15 minutes.

# STEAMED FISH

*20-25 minutes cooking time*

*Ingredients for 5-6 servings*

| | |
|---|---|
| **1 2-kg (4½-lb) fish** | **3 tablespoons soy sauce** |
| **2 tablespoons crisp bacon pieces** | **3 cm (1 in) piece fresh ginger, shredded** |
| **½ teaspoon salt** | **¼ cup chopped spring onions** |
| **2 teaspoons sugar** | **¼ teaspoon pepper** |
| **3 tablespoons oil** | **8 dried mushrooms** |

1  Prepare mushrooms by soaking in warm water for 30 minutes, then discard stems and slice.
2  Clean fish, make two incisions across side and season with salt.
3  Sprinkle sugar on fish and pour on oil, soy sauce and ginger. Stand for 20 minutes.
4  Place mushrooms on top of fish and sprinkle with bacon.
5  Steam for 20 minutes and garnish with chopped spring onions.

# TUNA DELIGHT

*8 minutes cooking time*

*Ingredients for 6 servings*

½ cup evaporated milk
French dressing
375 g (12 oz) tinned tuna

2 slices white bread
3 hamburger buns

1   Drain tuna.
2   Split hamburger buns.
3   Remove crusts from bread.
4   Pour milk over bread and add salad dressing.
5   Stir with fork and stir in tuna.
6   Spoon mixture onto hamburger buns and place under griller.
7   Grill for 5-7 minutes and garnish with olives.

# SWEET AND SOUR TUNA

*15-20 minutes cooking time*

*Ingredients for 4 servings*

2 cups pineapple chunks
1½ tablespoons cornflour
1½ tablespoons butter
½ teaspoon salt
1½ tablespoons vinegar

4 tablespoons sugar
250 g (8 oz) tinned tuna, drained
½ cup chicken stock
1½ teaspoons soy sauce
1 green pepper, cut into slices

1   Break tuna into chunks and preheat skillet.
2   Drain pineapple and reserve liquid.
3   Mix together sugar, cornflour, salt and chicken stock, pineapple liquid and vinegar.
4   Mix well and add soy sauce.
5   Pour into skillet and cook for 2 minutes.
6   Add pineapple and green pepper, mix and add tuna and butter.
7   Cover and simmer for 10-15 minutes. Serve with fried noodles.

# FROSTED TUNA

*20 minutes cooking time*

*Ingredients for 6 servings*

750 g (24 oz) tinned tuna
1 teaspoon salt
¾ cup sour cream
6 potatoes, cooked
2 tablespoons chopped parsley

½ teaspoon pepper
1 green pepper, chopped
750 g (24 oz) condensed mushroom
  soup

1  Drain tuna and mix with mushroom soup.
2  Add green pepper and pour into greased casserole.
3  Mash potato and combine with sour cream and salt and pepper.
4  Mix well and spread over tuna. Bake for 20 minutes in hot oven.
5  Garnish with chopped parsley.

# TUNA PIE

*30 minutes cooking time*

*Ingredients for 8 servings*

3 cups cooked rice
1 egg, beaten
90 g (3 oz) butter, melted
1 teaspoon mixed herbs
125 g (4 oz) chopped pimento
2 tablespoons chopped parsley

375 g (12 oz) tinned tuna
2 small onions, grated
300 g (10 oz) tin condensed chicken
  soup
1 teaspoon salt

1  Combine cooked rice, butter, onion, herbs and egg. Mix and season with
   salt and pepper.
2  Press into greased casserole dish.
3  Combine soup, flaked tuna, parsley, salt, pepper and pimento and mix
   well.
4  Pour into casserole and bake for 30 minutes in moderate oven.

# TUNA PILAF

*Ingredients for 6 servings*

*10 minutes cooking time*

185 g (6 oz) tinned sliced mushrooms
4 tablespoons chopped green pepper
1 onion, chopped
3 cups cooked rice
½ teaspoon pepper
375 g (12 oz) tuna

3 tablespoons butter
½ cup chopped celery
1 teaspoon salt
½ teaspoon thyme
1½ teaspoons Worcestershire sauce

1  Sauté mushrooms, onion and celery in frying pan and add green pepper. Add rice, tuna, Worcestershire sauce and season with salt and pepper.
2  Stir and add thyme. Reduce heat and cook until heated through.

# LEATHERJACKET WITH FRUIT

*Ingredients for 6 servings*

*10 minutes cooking time*

12 leatherjacket fillets
½ teaspoon pepper
1½ tablespoons butter
1½ tablespoons flour
4 small tomatoes
3 spring onions, chopped

1 teaspoon salt
1 cup white wine
½ cup cream
2 cups grapes
3 cloves garlic
2 onions, chopped

1  Skin and slice tomatoes, season with salt and pepper.
2  Melt butter in ovenproof dish and add onion, spring onions, garlic cloves and place fish on top.
3  Spread tomato slices over and around fish. Pour wine over and cook for 10 minutes.
4  When cooked remove fish and place on serving dish. Remove garlic and pour over cream.
5  Combine butter and flour together and add to sauce, pour over fish.
6  Garnish with grapes.

# SOLE ROLL-UPS

*1 hour cooking time*

*Ingredients for 6 servings*

| | |
|---|---|
| **250 g (8 oz) small mushrooms** | **30 g (1 oz) butter** |
| **2 tablespoons chopped parsley** | **125 g (4 oz) peeled prawns** |
| **60 g (2 oz) butter** | **2 tablespoons lemon juice** |
| **1 teaspoon salt** | **½ teaspoon pepper** |
| **12 125 g (4 oz) sole fillets** | **⅛ cup milk** |
| **60 g (2 oz) fresh breadcrumbs** | |

1 Chop mushrooms and sauté in butter for 5 minutes. Remove from heat and stir in breadcrumbs. Add parsley, seasonings and milk to bind.
2 Skin fish and divide stuffing between the fillets. Roll up each fillet and place in casserole dish.
3 Melt butter and stir in lemon juice, pour over fish and add mushroom caps to casserole.
4 Cover and bake for 40 minutes in 190°C (375°F) oven.
5 5-10 minutes before serving add prawns and garnish with chopped parsley.

# SOLE A L'ORANGE

*15 minutes cooking time*

*Ingredients for 4 servings*

| | |
|---|---|
| **500 g (1 lb) sole fillets** | **2 oranges** |
| **8 walnut halves** | **2 tablespoons chopped parsley** |
| **1 teaspoon salt** | **½ teaspoon pepper** |
| **250 g (8 oz) fat** | **60 g (2 oz) butter** |

1 Grate orange rind and cut oranges into halves. Squeeze out juice.
2 Add 2 teaspoons grated rind and 3 tablespoons orange juice to melted butter. Keep warm.
3 Place fish skin down in grill pan and season.
4 Pour half orange butter over and grill for 3 minutes.
5 Turn fish and pour remaining orange butter over fish.
6 Top each fillet with walnut halves and continue to cook for 6-8 minutes.

# SURPRISE SOLE

*10 minutes cooking time*

*Ingredients for 6 servings*

| | |
|---|---|
| 12 fillets of sole | 1 teaspoon salt |
| ½ teaspoon pepper | 2 tablespoons chopped parsley |
| 250 g (8 oz) breadcrumbs | 1 egg, beaten |
| 2 tomatoes, peeled | 60 g (2 oz) raisins |
| 4 tablespoons lemon juice | 4 tablespoons chutney |

1   Season fish with salt and pepper.
2   Sprinkle with lemon juice.
3   Combine chopped tomatoes, chutney and raisins together.
4   Place a little of this mixture on each fillet.
5   Roll up and dip in egg, then breadcrumbs.
6   Fry in deep fat and drain.
7   Serve garnished with chopped parsley.

# SOLE AND MUSHROOMS

*30 minutes cooking time*

*Ingredients for 4 servings*

| | |
|---|---|
| 500 g (1 lb) sole fillets | 500 g (1 lb) mushrooms |
| 2 tablespoons chopped parsley | 3 tablespoons cream |
| 2 tablespoons flour | 1 chopped onion |
| 1 tablespoon butter | 1 teaspoon salt |
| ½ teaspoon pepper | ½ cup white wine |
| ⅓ cup chicken stock | |

1   Wash mushrooms and remove stems.
2   Arrange sole in greased casserole and pour over stock.
3   Season with salt and pepper and add mushrooms.
4   Bake for 30 minutes, covered.
5   Fry chopped onion in butter and stir in flour.
6   Cook and stir, remove and add chicken stock.
7   Return to heat and stir until sauce thickens.
8   Pour over fish and garnish with chopped parsley.

# LEMON SOLE FILLETS

*20 minutes cooking time*

*Ingredients for 6 servings*

1 kg (2 lb) sole fillets
1 teaspoon salt
4 tablespoons melted butter

2 tablespoons chopped parsley
½ teaspoon pepper
lemon slices

1   Season fillets with salt and pepper.
2   Place lemon slices on base of casserole.
3   Place fish on top of slices and sprinkle with salt.
4   Pour over melted butter and cover with foil.
5   Bake in moderate oven for 20 minutes.

# ROLLED SOLE

*20 minutes cooking time*

*Ingredients for 4 servings*

8 sole fillets
500 g (1 lb) packet frozen peas
4 spring onions
2 tablespoons chopped parsley
6 tablespoons mayonnaise
1 teaspoon salt
1 teaspoon mint, chopped

4 potatoes
1 can crab meat
3 tablespoons capers
3 gherkins, chopped
1½ teaspoons castor sugar
½ teaspoon pepper
lemon

1   In two separate saucepans, pour 5 centimetres (2 in) of hot water.
2   Peel and dice potato, place on foil square and season with salt and pepper.
3   Fold foil and twist top, place in saucepan and cover. Cook over moderate heat.
4   Spread each sole fillet with crab meat. Roll up and season with salt and pepper. Pour over a little lemon juice and place on foil square.
5   Fold and secure foil, and place in second saucepan.
6   Empty peas onto another piece of foil and season with mint. Add sugar and salt.
7   Secure and place with fillets. Cover pan and cook over moderate heat.
8   Chop gherkins, parsley, capers and shallots, add to mayonnaise and season.
9   Unwrap potatoes and dot with parsley; unwrap fish and peas; serve with sauce.

# KEDGEREE

*30 minutes cooking time*

*Ingredients for 4 servings*

| | |
|---|---|
| **125 g (4 oz) long-grain rice** | **4 hardboiled eggs** |
| **500 g (1 lb) smoked cod** | **60 g (2 oz) flour** |
| **2 tablespoons butter** | **2½ cups milk** |
| **2 tablespoons chopped parsley** | **1 teaspoon salt** |
| **½ teaspoon pepper** | |

1  Cook rice in boiling salted water.
2  Cut up cod and cover with cold water, heat to boiling and simmer.
3  Drain cooked cod and flake.
4  Add flour to melted butter and mix well, add milk and season with salt and pepper.
5  Add fish, drained rice and quartered eggs.
6  Mix well and top with parsley.

# EDINBURGH FISH

*20 minutes cooking time*

*Ingredients for 6 servings*

| | |
|---|---|
| **6 fillets smoked cod** | **2 cups milk** |
| **½ cup water** | **315 g (10 oz) mushrooms, sliced** |
| **2 tablespoons chopped parsley** | **2 tablespoons butter** |
| **¼ teaspoon pepper** | |

1  Wash fish and dry. Place in saucepan with milk and water and season with pepper.
2  Bring to boil and reduce heat.
3  Add mushrooms and simmer for 8 minutes.
4  Place fish on serving dish and keep warm.
5  Add butter and parsley to mushroom mixture and cook uncovered. Pour over fish and serve with mashed potatoes.

# COD'S ROE PROVENCAL

*15 minutes cooking time*

*Ingredients for 4 servings*

500 g (1 lb) boiled cod's roe
2 cloves garlic
4 tablespoons olive oil
1 teaspoon salt
¼ cup plain flour

4 onions
6 tomatoes, peeled and sliced
2 teaspoons capers
8 black olives
½ teaspoon pepper

1   Cut roe into 1 centimetre (½ in) slices and heat oil. Dip sliced roe in flour and season with salt and pepper.
2   Cook roe in very hot oil until well browned, remove from pan.
3   Crush garlic and add to pan with tomatoes and sliced onions.
4   Cook until soft and add fried roe.
5   Cover and cook for 5 minutes.
6   Stone olives and add to pan with capers. Heat through and serve with French bread.

# CREAMED SALMON

*15 minutes cooking time*

*Ingredients for 6 servings*

750 g (1½ lb) tinned red salmon
1 teaspoon salt
185 g (6 oz) butter
⅔ cup cream

3 tablespoons chopped parsley
½ teaspoon pepper
1 cup white wine
4 egg yolks

1   Flake and drain salmon.
2   Reserve liquid.
3   Fry salmon in melted butter for 4 minutes.
4   Add wine and simmer.
5   When reduced by half, remove from heat, add reserved salmon liquid and cream, stir and add egg yolks.
6   Return to heat and season with salt and pepper.
7   Garnish with chopped parsley.

# SALMON MILANESE

*30 minutes cooking time*

*Ingredients for 4 servings*

1 cooked pie crust
1 cup heavy cream
1 tablespoon flour
¼ teaspoon paprika
1 small onion, minced

375 g (12 oz) salmon
2 eggs
½ teaspoon salt
6 tablespoons chopped green pepper
1 small packet frozen mixed vegetables

1  Combine drained, flaked salmon and drained, cooked vegetables.
2  Add minced onion and chopped green pepper and spread over crust.
3  Combine cream, eggs, flour, paprika and salt.
4  Pour over salmon and vegetables and bake for 30 minutes in moderate oven, 180°C (350°F).

# SALMON AND MUSHROOMS

*No cooking time*

*Ingredients for 4 servings*

250 g (8 oz) sliced smoked salmon,
  cut into 2 cm (1 in) pieces
4 tablespoons minced green pepper
½ teaspoon salt
4 thick slices fresh tomato

¼ teaspoon pepper
155 g (5 oz) button mushrooms, sliced
½ cup peeled and shredded radish
4 teaspoons minced chives
½ cup mayonnaise

1  Chill all main ingredients.
2  Combine salmon, mushrooms, radish, green pepper, chives and mayonnaise.
3  Season with salt and pepper.
4  Serve well chilled, spooned on top of tomato slices.

# SALMON RICE CASSEROLE

*65 minutes cooking time*

*Ingredients for 6 servings*

2 cups flaked salmon
3 stalks celery, sliced
1 medium onion, chopped
2 cups long-grain rice

1 green pepper, cut into strips
3 tomatoes, chopped
1 tin mushrooms
1 tablespoon soy sauce

1  Combine flaked salmon and green pepper.
2  Add celery, onion, tomatoes, rice, mushrooms and soy sauce.
3  Mix well, then turn into casserole dish.
4  Bake in moderate oven 180°C, (350°F) for 1 hour and serve.

# STUFFED BREAM

*35 minutes cooking time*

*Ingredients for 4 servings*

1 kg (2 lb) bream
90 g (3 oz) prunes
1 teaspoon salt
½ teaspoon grated nutmeg

2 eggs, hardboiled
⅓ cup cooked rice
½ teaspoon pepper
2 teaspoons oil

1  Scale and clean bream, leaving head on.
2  Cook and stone prunes.
3  Chop eggs and prunes and combine with rice. Season with salt, pepper and nutmeg.
4  Stuff fish with this mixture and brush with oil.
5  Place in baking dish and bake for 35 minutes in moderate oven 180°C (350°F) and serve.

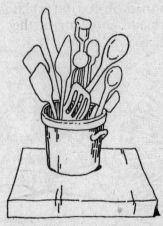

# BREAM WITH PORT

*30 minutes cooking time*

*Ingredients for 4-5 servings*

1 kg (2 lb) bream
1 teaspoon salt
1 tablespoon cream
½ cup port wine

1 tablespoon butter
½ teaspoon paprika
2 egg yolks

1 Season fish with salt and paprika.
2 Bake in butter in a covered ovenproof dish for 5 minutes and add port wine.
3 Cook until fish is tender and strain off liquid. Cook liquid in saucepan quickly to reduce it.
4 Cool and beat in the egg yolks, add cream and reheat gently. Pour the sauce over fish and serve with rice.

# DRESSY FISH FINGERS

*20 minutes cooking time*

*Ingredients for 8 servings*

500 g (1 lb) frozen fish fingers
1½ cups condensed cream of
  mushroom soup
2 lemons
1 teaspoon salt

375 g (12 oz) frozen chopped spinach
4 tablespoons milk
½ teaspoon nutmeg
½ teaspoon pepper

1 Place fish fingers in baking dish and bake for 12 minutes in hot oven.
2 Cook spinach according to directions and drain. Mix with soup, milk and nutmeg.
3 Heat and stir.
4 Spoon over fish fingers and cook for further 5-10 minutes.
5 Garnish with lemon slices and serve.

# ITALIAN SCHNAPPER

*30 minutes cooking time*

*Ingredients for 4 servings*

750 g (1½ lb) schnapper fillets
½ teaspoon pepper
2 tablespoons butter
1 cup tomato purée
2 onions, chopped

1 teaspoon salt
½ green pepper
1 cup cream
2 apples

1   Place fillets in greased casserole and bake for 10 minutes.
2   Mix cream, tomato purée, salt, pepper, chopped apple, chopped onion and sliced green pepper. Pour over fish.
3   Cook for 20 minutes in moderate oven.

# CURRIED FISH FINGERS

*25 minutes cooking time*

*Ingredients for 6 servings*

560 g (18 oz) fish fingers
2 tablespoons chopped parsley
½ teaspoon pepper
6 spring onions

1 teaspoon salt
2 teaspoons curry powder
1½ cups cream

1   Grease baking dish and place fish fillets in and bake in moderate oven for 10 minutes.
2   Combine 1 cup water, cream, chopped spring onions, salt, pepper and curry powder.
3   Pour over fish and bake for further 15 minutes.
4   Garnish with chopped parsley.

# Poultry

## CHICKEN LIVERS ROSEMARY

*15 minutes cooking time*

*Ingredients for 6 servings*

750 g (1½ lb) chicken livers
¾ cup white wine
pinch thyme
pinch paprika
¼ teaspoon pepper
2 tablespoons butter
2 tablespoons chopped parsley
1 clove garlic, crushed

5 tablespoons plain flour
2 teaspoons chicken stock
500 g (1 lb) mushrooms, quartered
1 teaspoon salt
2 tablespoons oil
1 onion, chopped
¼ teaspoon rosemary

1  Toss chicken livers in flour mixed with paprika, salt, pepper, and heat salad oil and butter.
2  Add chicken livers to pan and cook. Add garlic and stir occasionally.
3  Add onion, parsley, thyme and mushrooms.
4  Sauté until brown. Blend in chicken stock and cook for further 2 minutes.
5  Add rosemary and white wine. Cover and simmer for 4 minutes and serve.

# HONG KONG CHICKEN

*25 minutes cooking time*

*Ingredients for 4 servings*

2 chicken breasts
1½ tablespoons cornflour
2 teaspoons salt
½ teaspoon monosodium glutamate
   (optional)
6 tablespoons peanut oil
1 green pepper, sliced
250 g (8 oz) snow peas
1¼ cups chicken broth

½ teaspoon pepper
¾ teaspoon sugar
1½ tablespoons soy sauce
1½ cups celery, diced
4 onions, sliced
¾ cup bamboo shoots, sliced
125 g (4 oz) water chestnuts
125 g (4 oz) sliced fresh mushrooms

1  Drain and slice water chestnuts.
2  Bone chicken breasts and slice meat.
3  Brown chicken meat in oil and add celery.
4  Stir and add green pepper and onions.
5  Mix together and add snow peas, bamboo shoots, mushrooms and water chestnuts.
6  Stir, and when vegetables are tender add soy sauce, mixed with monosodium glutamate (if desired), sugar, salt, pepper and chicken broth.
7  Cover and simmer for 10 minutes and pour in cornflour which has been dissolved in a little water. When mixture thickens, serve with hot rice.

# CHICKEN LIVERS NAPOLI

*30 minutes cooking time*

*Ingredients for 6 servings*

90 g (3 oz) butter
2 cups long-grain rice
2 onions, chopped
6 rashers bacon
½ teaspoon salt

4 cups stock
2 tablespoons tomato purée
750 g (1½ lb) chicken livers
¼ cup chopped green pepper
½ teaspoon pepper

1  Sauté onion in butter and add chicken livers.
2  Add bacon and fry for 1 minute.
3  Add chopped pepper and tomato purée.
4  Add rice and stir for 5 minutes. Stir in hot stock and cover. Cook for 20 minutes.

# CHICKEN POT PIE

*20 minutes cooking time*

*Ingredients for 4 servings*

1 egg, beaten
½ teaspoon pepper
¼ cup milk
2 cups chicken stock
315 g (10 oz) cooked chicken, chopped
1 stick celery, chopped
2 tablespoons sherry

1 teaspoon salt
250 g (8 oz) puff pastry
60 g (2 oz) flour
¾ cup milk
185 g (6 oz) mushrooms, sliced
30 g (1 oz) blanched almonds
¼ teaspoon nutmeg

1  Roll out pastry to fit 1.5 litre (2 pint) casserole.
2  Place on baking tray and cut into 4 triangles. Brush with beaten egg and leave pastry in a cool place.
3  Melt butter and add flour. Stir over low heat and gradually add chicken stock and milk. Cook until sauce boils and thickens.
4  Add chicken, almonds, mushrooms, celery, sherry, salt, pepper and nutmeg.
5  Cover and cook in pan for 5 minutes. Turn into casserole dish and arrange pastry triangles on top. Cook for 10 minutes in hot oven, 230°C (450°F).

# APPLE CHICKEN

*1 hour cooking time*

*Ingredients for 4 servings*

1 kg (2 lb) chicken pieces
1½ tablespoons butter
1 onion, chopped
1 green pepper, deseeded and chopped
2 apples, peeled and chopped
¼ teaspoon pepper
¼ teaspoon paprika

125 g (4 oz) seasoned flour
¾ can condensed cream of chicken soup
2 tablespoons chopped parsley
125 g (4 oz) long-grain rice
1 teaspoon salt
pinch of thyme
1¼ cups water

1  Coat chicken in seasoned flour and fry in butter for 15 minutes.
2  In saucepan, combine chicken soup, parsley, onion, salt, thyme, pepper, paprika, apples and a little saffron.
3  Cook for 2 minutes and add water and rice to mixture, transfer to casserole.
4  Cook 40 minutes in moderate oven, 180°C (350°F).

# CHICKEN WITH WATER CHESTNUTS

*2 hours 40 minutes cooking time*

*Ingredients for 4 servings*

1.5 kg (3 lb) chicken
500 g (1 lb) dried chestnuts
2 spring onions
2 tablespoons soy sauce

2 cups water
6 slices fresh ginger
2 teaspoons salt
2 tablespoons sherry

1 Cook peeled chestnuts in 6 cups water for 2 hours.
2 Wash and cut chicken into pieces with a cleaver.
3 Cut onions into sections.
4 Place chicken in pan with water and boil.
5 Add soy sauce, sherry, ginger and onions.
6 Cook over low heat for 35 minutes.
7 Add chestnuts to chicken and cook for 15 minutes.

# CHICKEN CHOW MEIN

*20 minutes cooking time*

*Ingredients for 4 servings*

250 g (8 oz) egg noodles
¼ teaspoon pepper
1½ cups chicken stock
1½ tablespoons sherry
½ cup peanut oil
2 cups chopped chicken meat
1 cup green beans
½ teaspoon salt

1 tablespoon cornflour
1½ tablespoons soy sauce
½ teaspoon monosodium glutamate
  (optional)
6 dried mushrooms
1 egg
⅔ cup cooked ham
1 teaspoon sugar

1 Deep fry noodles in oil until crisp, drain and arrange on a plate.
2 Make a thin omelette with egg.
3 Combine mushrooms, ham and parboiled beans.
4 Place in pan with 2 tablespoons peanut oil, sauté for a few minutes, add chicken, salt and sugar and mix well.
5 Place on noodles and top with shredded egg, and keep warm.
6 Combine cornflour, a little water, and stock. Bring to boil and pour in soy sauce, sherry and monosodium glutamate if desired.
7 Simmer for 3 minutes and pour over chicken and noodles to serve.

# SPANISH CHICKEN AND RICE

*1 hour cooking time*

*Ingredients for 6 servings*

2.5 kg (5 lb) chicken
3 large onions
4 garlic cloves
560 g (18 oz) tinned tomatoes
4 bay leaves
1 tablespoon vinegar
2 cups cooked peas
2 tablespoons chopped parsley

1 cup olive oil
2 green peppers
125 g (4 oz) tomato paste
1 cup water
½ teaspoon salt
500 g (1 lb) mushrooms
½ cup stuffed black olives

1  Cut chicken into quarters and heat oil in pot.
2  Chop onions, peppers, garlic and place in oil.
3  Cook until onions are tender.
4  Add tomato paste, tomatoes, water, bay leaves and seasonings.
5  Add chicken, cover and cook gently for 45 minutes.
6  Add rice, lower heat and cook until tender.
7  When almost ready, add mushrooms, vinegar and peas.
8  To serve, remove chicken and pour sauce over and sprinkle with parsley.

# FRUITY CHICKEN

*1 hour cooking time*

*Ingredients for 6 servings*

1 chicken, cut into pieces
1 slice lemon rind
1¼ cups white wine
½ teaspoon pepper
1 red pepper
3 tablespoons flour

3 tablespoons oil
1¼ cups chicken stock
1 teaspoon salt
1 tin prunes
4 pears, peeled, cored and sliced

1  Strain prunes and reserve syrup.
2  Brown chicken in oil and place in ovenproof dish.
3  Sauté red peppers and add to ovenproof dish.
4  Add pear slices and prunes. Thicken juices with flour and add stock, wine and water, some of the prune syrup and lemon rind.
5  Season and pour into casserole; cover and cook for 1 hour in moderate oven, 190°C (375°F).

# CHICKEN CURRY WITH SLICED COCONUT

*1 hour cooking time*

*Ingredients for 4 servings*

1 chicken
1 onion, chopped
2 cardamom pods
5 cm (2 in) stick of cinnamon
1½ tablespoons curry powder
2 tablespoons tomato paste
½ cup sliced fresh coconut

2 cloves garlic, chopped
3 whole cloves
1 tablespoon curry paste
4 tablespoons ghee
1 teaspoon salt
2 tablespoons lemon juice

1  Fry onion, garlic and spices in ghee for 5 minutes.
2  Add curry powder and curry paste. Mix and fry for 5 minutes.
3  Add tomato paste and chicken, coconut and 1¼ cups of water. Mix through and cover pan.
4  Simmer until tender and season with salt and lemon juice.

# SPANISH PAELLA

*45 minutes cooking time*

*Ingredients for 6 servings*

1.5 kg (3 lb) chicken
2 garlic cloves, chopped
6 cups chicken stock
250 g (8 oz) long-grain rice
1 cooked lobster
1 packet frozen peas, cooked

2 onions, chopped
3 tablespoons olive oil
4 tomatoes
½ teaspoon saffron
12 mussels
125 g (4 oz) chopped pimentos

1  Cut chicken into pieces.
2  Fry onions and garlic in oil, brown chicken, then add half chicken stock.
3  Simmer for 20 minutes and add tomatoes, rice and remaining stock.
4  Stir in saffron.
5  Arrange lobster pieces, prawns, mussels and peas attractively with red pepper.
6  Continue cooking until rice is tender.
7  Serve.

# CHICKEN TAHITI

*Ingredients for 6 servings*

*2½ hours cooking time*

375 g (12 oz) long-grain rice
2 tablespoons oil
juice of 2 oranges
155 g (5 oz) sultanas
185 g (6 oz) glacé apricots, chopped
1.75 kg (3½ lb) chicken

½ teaspoon salt
juice of 1 lemon
2 beaten eggs
185 g (6 oz) glacé pineapple, chopped
90 g (3 oz) almond slivers

## SAUCE

3 tablespoons butter
3 tablespoons pineapple jam
3 pears, peeled, cored and sliced
2½ cups chicken stock

1½ tablespoons cornflour
rind of 1 orange, grated
watercress

1   Cook rice in salted water until tender, then drain.
2   Return rice to saucepan, add oil, beaten eggs, and one tablespoon of fruit juices.
3   Cook for 2 minutes over medium heat, then add half the sultanas, half the glacé fruits and half the almonds.
4   Allow to cool, fill six moulds with rice mixture, press down, refrigerate until needed.
5   Stuff chicken with remaining rice mixture and season with salt.
6   Place in roasting dish and cover with butter.
7   Roast in hot oven 220°C (425°F) for 20 minutes then reduce heat to moderate temperature 180°C (350°F).
8   Cook for 1½ hours, basting from time to time.
9   Dissolve pineapple jam in chicken stock and add grated fruit rind and remaining sultanas and glacé fruits.
10  Stir and add almonds. Bring to the boil and thicken slightly with cornflour.
11  Add the sliced pears and place chicken in serving dish and pour over sauce. Arrange rice moulds around the chicken and garnish with watercress.

# HERBED CHICKEN CASSEROLE

*1 hour 15 minutes cooking time*

*Ingredients for 6 servings*

3 tablespoons olive oil
1 teaspoon salt
2 teaspoons dried mixed herbs
1 tablespoon flour
3 tablespoons tomato sauce

6 chicken breasts
½ teaspoon pepper
250 g (8 oz) long-grain rice
2 cups stock
2 onions, chopped

1  Heat oil and fry chicken joints until brown.
2  Place in casserole and fry chopped onions for 5 minutes, stir in flour and cook for 1 minute.
3  Gradually add stock, tomato sauce and herbs and bring to boil, stirring continuously.
4  Season and pour over chicken.
5  Cover and cook for 50 minutes in moderate oven.

# LEMON CHICKEN

*35 minutes cooking time*

*Ingredients for 6 servings*

1 kg (2 lb) chicken breasts
2½ teaspoons sugar
½ teaspoon salt
2 tablespoons soy sauce
⅓ cup black beans

2½ teaspoons sesame oil
6 tablespoons cornflour
2 tablespoons sherry
2 cloves garlic
2 lemons

1  Chop chicken into 5 cm (2 in) pieces.
2  Blend sugar, salt, sesame oil, cornflour, soy sauce and sherry.
3  Mash beans with garlic and add to cornflour mixture.
4  Add chicken pieces and mix thoroughly, put in casserole.
5  Squeeze lemon juice over chicken, chop skin and put on top of chicken.
6  Cover casserole with waxed paper and put 5 cm (2 in) above boiling water.
7  Cover pan and simmer for 35 minutes.

# CHICKEN CURRY WITH LETTUCE

*45 minutes cooking time*

*Ingredients for 6 servings*

| | |
|---|---|
| 1 large chicken | 60 g (2 oz) ghee |
| 1 clove garlic, crushed | 2 cardamom pods |
| 2 tablespoons curry paste | 2 whole cloves |
| 2 tablespoons ground almonds | 2 tablespoons creamed coconut |
| 1 lettuce, shredded | 1½ teaspoons salt |
| 1 onion, chopped | 1 tablespoon lemon juice |

1 Fry onions, garlic and spices in ghee.
2 Add curry powder and almonds.
3 Mix thoroughly and cook for 5 minutes.
4 Add chicken pieces and creamed coconut and mix again.
5 Cover pan and cook for 35 minutes.
6 Add lettuce and cook for 3 minutes, and season with salt and lemon juice.

# Meat

## MILD LAMB CURRY

*Ingredients for 6 servings*

*1 hour 20 minutes cooking time*

| | |
|---|---|
| 12 large leg chops | 1½ cups yoghurt |
| 3 teaspoons curry powder | 1 teaspoon garam masala |
| ½ teaspoon black pepper | ½ cup sultanas |
| 10 dried apricots | 1½ teaspoons grated fresh ginger |
| 4 cloves garlic | 1½ teaspoons salt |
| 4 tablespoons ghee | 2 onions |

1  Cut chops from bone and cut into cubes.
2  Mix yoghurt and curry powder, pepper and garam masala.
3  Marinate meat in yoghurt mixture for 3 hours.
4  Slice apricots and place with sultanas in ½ cup water.
5  Slice onion, crush garlic and grate ginger.
6  Fry onion, garlic and ginger in ghee.
7  Add meat and drained fruit.
8  Fry for 5 minutes, stirring, and lower heat.
9  Season with salt and simmer for 1 hour.

# LAMB-FILLED EGGPLANT

*45 minutes cooking time*

*Ingredients for 6 servings*

1 large eggplant, cut into six wedges
4 tomatoes, quartered
4 tablespoons butter
2 onions, chopped
3 tablespoons chopped parsley
1 teaspoon salt

4 onions, quartered
500 g (1 lb) ground lamb
8 tablespoons chopped green pepper
½ teaspoon garlic salt
1 cup tomato sauce

1   Sprinkle eggplant with salt and stand for 1 hour on kitchen towelling.
2   Melt butter and fry eggplant wedges.
3   Place eggplant skin down on baking sheet in hot oven 200°C (400°F) for 10 minutes.
4   Reheat butter and add lamb, chopped onion, green pepper, parsley, salt and garlic salt. Cook until light brown, stirring constantly.
5   Split eggplant sections from end to end making a pocket and press open.
6   Fill with meat mixture and press sides of flesh firmly together.
7   Pour tomato sauce into shallow casserole dish. Set eggplant wedges skin side down into sauce.
8   Top with tomato and onion wedges.
9   Bake uncovered for 30 minutes in moderate oven.

# LAMB RISOTTO

*30 minutes cooking time*

*Ingredients for 6 servings*

4 large onions
185 g (6 oz) long-grain rice
4 cups stock
500 g (1 lb) diced cooked lamb
3 tablespoons chopped parsley

½ cup grated mild cheese
4 large tomatoes
125 g (4 oz) butter
½ teaspoon salt
90 g (3 oz) sultanas

1   Peel and slice onions and tomatoes.
2   Heat butter and toss vegetables and rice in. Allow onions to brown.
3   Add stock and bring to the boil.
4   Season with salt and pepper.
5   Cook for 10 minutes.
6   Add lamb and stir.
7   Cook for 20 minutes and stir in sultanas.
8   Pile onto serving dish and sprinkle with chopped parsley and grated cheese.

# LAMB WITH PEACHES

*1¼ hours cooking time*

*Ingredients for 4 servings*

| | |
|---|---|
| 1 lamb shoulder, boned | 1 teaspoon salt |
| ½ teaspoon pepper | 1 bay leaf |
| 60 g (2 oz) sugar | 1 green pepper |
| 1 cauliflower | 375 g (12 oz) peach halves |
| 1½ tablespoons vinegar | |

1  Cut cauliflower into flowerets.
2  Deseed and slice pepper.
3  Roll up shoulder, tie securely and place in ovenproof dish.
4  Add pepper, cauliflower and peach halves with a quarter of their juice, vinegar, sugar, bay leaves, salt and pepper.
5  Bake in moderate oven for 1 hour and 15 minutes.

# KIDNEY RISOTTO

*25 minutes cooking time*

*Ingredients for 6 servings*

| | |
|---|---|
| 90 g (3 oz) butter | 185 g (6 oz) mushrooms, sliced |
| 2 tablespoons tomato purée | ½ teaspoon salt |
| ½ teaspoon pepper | 12 lambs' kidneys |
| 2 stock cubes | 3 tablespoons red wine |
| 2 onions, chopped | 3 tablespoons cornflour |

1  Heat half butter and sauté onion. Fry kidneys which have been washed, skinned and cored, for 6 minutes.
2  Combine cornflour and onion and blend in wine and stock cubes dissolved in 2½ cups boiling water.
3  Boil for 2 minutes and add kidneys.
4  Season with salt and pepper, add tomato purée and mushrooms.
5  Simmer for 15 minutes and serve immediately on rice.

# GRILLED CHEESE CHOPS

*15 minutes cooking time*

*Ingredients for 4 servings*

**4 lamb chops**
**½ teaspoon salt**
**¼ cup grated Parmesan cheese**

**¼ teaspoon pepper**
**30 g (1 oz) butter**

1  Grill chops and blend remaining ingredients together.
2  Spread on chops and grill until cheese is brown. Serve immediately.

# LAMB SHANKS

*1½ hours cooking time*

*Ingredients for 6 servings*

**6 lamb shanks, cracked**
**¼ cup flour**
**2 teaspoons paprika**
**3 cups water**

**10 carrots, peeled and cut in half**
**2 teaspoons salt**
**3 tomatoes, peeled and quartered**

1  Put lamb shanks in casserole and add tomatoes. Pour water over and sprinkle with salt and paprika.
2  Bake in moderate oven 180°C (350°F) for 30 minutes, uncovered.
3  Turn shanks over and bake for further 30 minutes and add carrots.
4  Cook for 30 mintues longer and remove lamb shanks.
5  Skim excess fat from casserole and heat juices over direct heat, thicken with flour and water.

# SLICED BEEF WITH CUCUMBER

*10 minutes cooking time*

*Ingredients for 5-6 servings*

2 large cucumbers
1 tablespoon sherry
1 teaspoon salt
2 tablespoons water
3 tablespoons peanut oil

2 tablespoons soy sauce
1 teaspoon sugar
1 tablespoon cornflour
750 g (1½ lb) beef

1   Cut meat into thin slices and mix with soy sauce, cornflour, sherry, sugar and water.
2   Peel cucumbers and scrape out seeds.
3   Slice thinly.
4   Heat oil and fry cucumbers for 90 seconds, then remove.
5   Cook meat in oil for 3 minutes and return cucumbers. Cook together for 1 minute and season with salt.

# BEEF VINDALOO

*1 hour 10 minutes cooking time*

*Ingredients for 6 servings*

2 onions
2 tablespoons coriander
1 teaspoon cumin seed
1 teaspoon red chillies
6 tablespoons ghee
6 tablespoons vinegar

4 cloves garlic
5 teaspoons turmeric
1 teaspoon ground ginger
1½ teaspoons mustard seed
750 g (1½ lb) cubed beef

1   Mince onion and garlic cloves.
2   Combine onion, coriander, garlic, turmeric, cumin seed, ginger, mustard seed and chillies with vinegar to make a paste.
3   Mix meat in this mixture and stand for 6 hours.
4   In saucepan, heat ghee and add meat and remaining liquid, it may be necessary to add a little water.
5   Cover and simmer until cooked. Season with salt.

# BEEF WITH CELERY

*10 minutes cooking time*

*Ingredients for 4 servings*

| | |
|---|---|
| 185 g (6 oz) steak | 3 slices fresh ginger |
| 4 sticks celery | ¼ cup peanut oil |
| ½ teaspoon salt | ½ teaspoon sugar |
| ¼ teaspoon monosodium glutamate (optional) | 1 cup hot chicken stock |
| | 1 tablespoon water |
| 1 teaspoon cornflour | 1 teaspoon soy sauce |
| 2 garlic cloves, crushed | |

1   Cut meat into thin slices; halve celery lengthwise, then chop into 2 cm (1 in) pieces.
2   Place meat and ginger in a bowl, add 1 teaspoon of oil, salt, sugar and monosodium glutamate, if desired, 2 tablespoons stock and cornflour blended with water.
3   Heat half of the oil and fry celery for 1 minute, remove and wipe pan.
4   Heat remaining oil and fry garlic for 1 minute then discard. Add drained meat and ginger, fry for 4 minutes and remove.
5   Add liquid in which meat soaked and soy sauce. Bring to boil and stir in remaining cornflour blended with water.
6   Cook for 2 minutes, return beef and celery to pan, heat through and serve.


# BRANDIED STEAK

*15 minutes cooking time*

*Ingredients for 4 servings*

| | |
|---|---|
| 4 small fillet steaks | 2 tablespoons olive oil |
| 1 teaspoon salt | ½ teaspoon pepper |
| 1 packet frozen potato gems | 6 tomatoes |
| 250 g (8 oz) frozen peas | 6 tablespoons brandy |
| 4 tablespoons butter | |

1   Brush steaks with oil and season with salt and pepper. Cook peas in salted water.
2   Heat half the butter and fry potato gems, gently, covered.
3   Halve the tomatoes and season with salt and pepper. In another frying pan, melt butter and fry steaks for 2 minutes on each side.
4   Lower heat and pour in warmed brandy, light and add tomatoes.
5   Cook gently for 3 minutes, add peas and serve.

# STEAK AND VEGETABLES

*1¼ hours cooking time*

*Ingredients for 4 servings*

750 g (1½ lb) round steak, cubed
½ cup shredded cheddar cheese
1 onion, sliced
1 teaspoon salt
1 cup sliced carrot
½ green pepper, sliced

1 tablespoon olive oil
1 teaspoon basil
¼ cup uncooked rice
6 fresh mushrooms, sliced
125 g (4 oz) fresh beans, sliced
1 tomato, peeled and sliced

1  Brown meat in oil and arrange one third of vegetables in casserole.
2  Place half the meat pieces over vegetables and sprinkle with a little rice and seasonings.
3  Add another third of vegetables, remaining meat and a little more seasonings. Add remaining rice.
4  Top with remaining vegetables and cover. Bake in casserole for 45 minutes. Sprinkle with cheese and bake for further 15-20 minutes.

# BEEF AND OLIVES

*1½ hours cooking time*

*Ingredients for 4 servings*

750 g (1½ lb) beef, cubed
1 teaspoon salt
pinch marjoram
375 g (12 oz) small white onions,
  peeled
8 small carrots, scraped

2 cups beef bouillon
½ cup stuffed green olives
¼ cup flour
2 tablespoons butter
½ teaspoon pepper

1  Dust meat with flour, salt, pepper and marjoram.
2  Brown meat in butter and place in casserole dish.
3  Add onions and carrots. Pour over bouillon and cover.
4  Bake in moderate oven for 1 hour and add olives 20 minutes before serving.
5  Pour off juices, thicken with butter and flour and serve.

# STEAK AND BEER

*Ingredients for 4 servings*

*4½ hours cooking time*

4 pieces chuck steak
1 teaspoon salt
3 onions, sliced
250 g (8 oz) button mushrooms
1 bottle beer
1 clove garlic

3 tablespoons oil
½ teaspoon pepper
2 tablespoons butter
¼ cup flour
30 g (1 oz) sugar

1   Marinate the meat in mixture of oil, salt and pepper overnight.
2   Sauté onions in butter and place in a casserole with washed mushrooms.
3   Dip steaks in flour and fry in butter. Add any remaining marinade.
4   Place steaks on top of vegetables in casserole dish.
5   Mix together beer, sugar and crushed garlic.
6   Pour over meat and cover. Cook in slow oven 140°C (275°F) for 4 hours.

# CAPER BURGERS

*Ingredients for 4 servings*

*1¼ hours cooking time*

1 kg (2 lb) steak
1 onion, chopped
2 tablespoons capers
1 tablespoon lard
1½ teaspoons salt

60 g (2 oz) bacon
2 ½ tablespoons French mustard
¾ cup sour cream
⅛ cup flour
½ teaspoon pepper

1   Cut steak into four pieces.
2   Remove all fat and snip the edges to prevent curling.
3   Season with salt and pepper. Sprinkle with flour.
4   Heat lard and fry bacon and onion. Add meat and fry quickly; add mustard, capers and 1 cup water.
5   Transfer to casserole and bake in moderate oven for 45 minutes.
6   Remove steaks, add cream to gravy with 1 tablespoon flour and bring to boil. Cook until thickened and return steaks to sauce.

# CALCUTTA BEEF CURRY

*1 hour 45 minutes cooking time*

*Ingredients for 3-4 servings*

juice of ½ lemon
1 teaspoon salt
500 g (1 lb) beef, cubed
1 tablespoon ground coriander
1 teaspoon ground cumin seed
1 teaspoon ground black pepper
60 g (2 oz) ghee

2 cloves garlic, minced
90 g (3 oz) coconut cream
½ teaspoon turmeric
1 teaspoon ground chilli
1 teaspoon ground ginger
2 chopped onions

1  Mix spices to a paste with a little vinegar and fry onion, garlic and paste in ghee.
2  Fry for 5 minutes and add meat which has been partially cooked in water.
3  Add a little of this water and bring to the boil.
4  Add 1¼ cups hot water in which coconut cream has been disssolved, season with salt and lemon juice; simmer gently for 1½ hours.

# CARPET BAG STEAKS

*10 minutes cooking time*

*Ingredients for 4 servings*

4 fillet steaks, 4 cm (1½ in) thick
½ teaspoon salt
2 tablespoons butter

½ cup small oysters
¼ teaspoon pepper

1  Make a pocket in each fillet and mix oysters with butter. Season with salt and pepper.
2  Stuff each fillet with oysters and close pocket with skewers.
3  Brush steak with butter and grill for 5-8 minutes.
4  Season with salt and pepper.
5  Serve immediately.

# BEEF WITH BEAN SPROUTS

*10 minutes cooking time*

*Ingredients for 8 servings*

250 g (8 oz) bean sprouts
½ teaspoon salt
½ teaspoon sugar
½ cup peanut oil
2 teaspoons cornflour
1 teaspoon sherry
250 g (8 oz) topside steak

2 chopped garlic cloves
½ teaspoon monosodium glutamate
 (optional)
½ teaspoon pepper
1 teaspoon soy sauce
1¼ cups hot chicken stock
parsley sprigs

1  Add chopped garlic to sprouts and cut steak into thin strips.
2  Place the meat in bowl with salt, sugar, pepper and monosodium glutamate, if desired.
3  Add 2 teaspoons peanut oil, 1 teaspoon cornflour mixed in 2 teaspoons water, and soy sauce.
4  Heat half the remaining oil and fry sprouts for 1 minute. Transfer the sprouts to a heated dish and keep hot.
5  Empty oil from pan, wipe with paper towel and heat remaining oil. Add prepared steak and garlic to pan and cook for 2 minutes over high heat, remove steak to dish with bean sprouts.
6  Add stock and sherry, bring to boil and add remaining cornflour mixed with 2 tablespoons water.
7  Boil for 2 minutes and add bean sprouts and steak.
8  Turn into heated dish and serve.

# MUSHROOM FILLET

*15 minutes cooking time*

*Ingredients for 4 servings*

1.5 kg (3 lb) fillet steak, thickly cut
½ teaspoon pepper
250 g (8 oz) sliced mushrooms

4 tablespoons butter
½ teaspoon salt

1  Place steaks in frying pan and sauté in butter.
2  Cook for 5 minutes on each side and remove to serving dish.
3  Add mushrooms to frying pan and cook for 5-6 minutes, stirring occasionally.
4  Spoon cooked mushrooms over steaks.

# MILWAUKEE BEEF

*2 hours cooking time*

*Ingredients for 4 servings*

| | |
|---|---|
| 750 g (1½ lb) ground beef | ¼ cup beef stock |
| 1½ cups beer | 1½ tablespoons brown sugar |
| 250 g (8 oz) sliced onions | 1 tablespoon chopped parsley |
| 1 teaspoon salt | 1 tablespoon vinegar |
| 1 teaspoon pepper | 1 tablespoon cornflour |
| 1 clove garlic, minced | 1 tablespoon olive oil |

1   Heat oil and fry meat for 5 minutes, reduce heat and gently cook onions and garlic for 5 minutes more.
2   Add salt, pepper, mix well and spoon into casserole.
3   Mix beef stock with parsley and brown sugar and pour over casserole.
4   Add beer and cook in moderate oven 180°C (350°F) for 1 hour and 40 minutes.
5   Mix cornflour and vinegar and add to casserole, return to oven for another 20 minutes.

# SOUR CREAM TOPPED MEATLOAF

*1 hour cooking time*

*Ingredients for 6-8 servings*

| | |
|---|---|
| 500 g (1 lb) ground beef | 2 egg yolks |
| 500 g (1 lb) ground pork | 1 cup sour cream |
| 1 large eggplant | 6 tablespoons chopped parsley |
| 1 minced onion | ½ teaspoon ground cloves |
| 2 cloves garlic, minced | ½ teaspoon oregano |
| 1 teaspoon salt | |

1   Peel eggplant and chop very finely, then mix with meats and minced onion.
2   Put mixture into frying pan, add garlic, cloves, oregano, and salt.
3   Cook gently, stirring, for 15 minutes, or until mixture is dry.
4   Put mixture through food grinder with finest blade, then pack into greased loaf tin.
5   Combine sour cream with beaten egg yolks and spread over top of meat.
6   Bake in slow oven 160°C (325°F) for 40-45 minutes.

# SWEET AND SOUR MEATBALLS

*40 minutes cooking time*

*Ingredients for 4 servings*

**500 g (1 lb) ground steak**
**1 egg**
**1 cup breadcrumbs**
**2 chopped onions**
**1 teaspoon salt**
**⅓ cup vinegar**
**1 tin pineapple pieces**
**1½ teaspoons cornflour**
**2 teaspoons butter**

**½ teaspoon pepper**
**1 large tomato**
**½ cucumber**
**½ cup chopped celery**
**1 sliced green pepper**
**1 teaspoon sugar**
**2 teaspoons soy sauce**
**½ teaspoon ground ginger**
**1 sliced carrot**

1  Mix steak, egg, breadcrumbs, half the onion, salt and pepper and form into meatballs, and brown in butter, remove and keep warm.
2  In same pan, fry chopped cucumber, tomato, green pepper, carrot and celery for 2-3 minutes, remove and keep warm with meatballs.
3  Combine remaining ingredients in pan and heat to boiling. Add meatballs and cook for 15 minutes, thicken with cornflour, then add vegetables and cook for further 5 minutes.

# TARRAGON PATTIES

*20 minutes cooking time*

*Ingredients for 4 servings*

**500 g (1 lb) ground beef**
**3 tablespoons chopped onion,
  browned in butter**
**2 tablespoons tarragon vinegar**
**1 teaspoon salt**

**½ teaspoon pepper**
**4 hamburger buns**
**4 slices tasty cheese**
**1 ripe avocado**

1  Combine meat, salt and pepper and form into patties.
2  Place patties in baking pan and sprinkle with vinegar and onions.
3  Bake in moderately hot oven 190°C (375°F) for 20 minutes (for medium hamburgers, five minutes less for rare, five minutes more for well done).
4  Cut buns in half, butter and toast.
5  Place cheese on half of buns and melt under griller.
6  Place hamburger pattie on other half of buns and top with avocado slices.
7  Serve separately, with salad.

# BAVARIAN CABBAGE ROLLS

*1 hour 20 minutes cooking time*

*Ingredients for 8 servings*

| | |
|---|---|
| 1 kg (2 lb) ground beef | 2½ cups stock |
| 250 g (8 oz) chopped mushrooms | 2 tablespoons flour |
| 3 cups cooked rice | ½ cup tomato paste |
| 4 tablespoons butter | 2½ cups sour cream |
| 2 teaspoons salt | 4 teaspoons sugar |
| 1 teaspoon pepper | juice of one lemon |
| 16 large cabbage leaves | 4 chopped onions |

1  Fry onions in half the butter, then add meat, salt, pepper and mushrooms and fry gently for 5-10 minutes.
2  Remove from stove and add eggs, rice and ¼ cup stock.
3  Dip cabbage leaves in boiling water to soften, then put some meat mixture on each cabbage leaf and roll up, securing with toothpicks.
4  Melt remaining butter and stir in flour, add remaining stock and stir until thick, then add tomato paste, lemon juice and stock.
5  Pour over cabbage rolls in casserole and cook in oven at 200 °C (400°F) for 1 hour.

# MEATBALLS WITH RICE

*55 minutes cooking time*

*Ingredients for 4 servings*

| | |
|---|---|
| ½ cup long-grain rice | 450 g (1 lb) tin tomatoes |
| 4 teaspoons dried rosemary | 1 teaspoon salt |
| 250 g (8 oz) ground beef | ½ teaspoon dried sage |
| ½ teaspoon pepper | ⅓ cup breadcrumbs |
| 1 egg, lightly beaten | 1 cup shredded cheese |
| 3 tablespoons butter | |

1  Combine rice, tomatoes, 1 tablespoon butter, salt, rosemary and sage in top of double boiler.
2  Heat, stirring, cover and cook over boiling water until rice is cooked, about 20 minutes.
3  Mix ground beef, pepper, egg, breadcrumbs and milk.
4  Form into balls and fry in remaining butter.
5  Turn rice into greased casserole and place meat on top. Sprinkle with cheese and bake in moderate oven 180°C (350°F) for 25 minutes.

# TORTILLA TAMALE PIE

*45 minutes cooking time*

*Ingredients for 6-8 servings*

1 kg (2 lb) ground beef
1 chopped onion
3 cloves garlic, minced
1 teaspoon olive oil
24 pitted ripe olives

1 teaspoon salt
½ teaspoon marjoram
1 tablespoon flour
1 cup chilli sauce
12 corn tortillas

1  Fry meat in olive oil, add onion, salt, marjoram and garlic and fry for 5 minutes.
2  Sift flour over pan, stir in and add chilli sauce and 2 cups water, simmer 10 minutes.
3  Heat oil in frying pan and fry tortillas until crisp.
4  Cover base of baking dish with tortillas, saving 3 or 4 for top.
5  Fill with chilli mixture and top with left over tortillas.
6  Bake in moderate oven 180°C (350°F) for 30 minutes.

# MEAT-FILLED TOMATOES

*1½ hours cooking time*

*Ingredients for 5 servings*

10 large tomatoes
2 tablespoons chopped parsley
1 teaspoon castor sugar
½ teaspoon pepper
60 g (2 oz) long-grain rice
1 onion

500 g (1 lb) minced beef
1 teaspoon chopped dill
½ teaspoon salt
1 teaspoon brandy
⅛ cup breadcrumbs
185 g (6 oz) butter

1  Scoop out the tomatoes and leave a hinged lid.
2  Strain all seeds and chop up the cores.
3  Place a little salt in each tomato and turn upside down to drain.
4  Add a dash of pepper and sugar to each.
5  Fry minced onion in butter and add meat. Add chopped parsley and dill, rice and brandy.
6  Stuff tomatoes with meat and place in baking dish. Sprinkle with breadcrumbs and a little melted butter.
7  Add juice from tomatoes and remaining butter.
8  Cook in slow oven for 1½ hours.

# FRUIT SURPRISE MEATLOAF

*Ingredients for 4 servings*

*1¹/₄ hours cooking time*

375 g (12 oz) ground beef
1 small onion, chopped
2 tablespoons butter
1 small tin ham spread
1 egg
¼ cup milk
¼ cup breadcrumbs
1 teaspoon sugar
1 teaspoon salt
½ teaspoon pepper
½ cup cooked, pitted prunes

pinch allspice
2 rashers bacon
½ cup prune juice
2 teaspoons grated lemon peel
¼ cup firmly packed brown sugar
½ teaspoon cinnamon
1 tablespoon lemon juice
½ tablespoon tarragon vinegar
2 teaspoons prepared mustard
1 tablespoon flour
pinch cloves

1  Melt one tablespoon butter and fry onion for 5 minutes.
2  Mix onion and butter with ground beef, ham spread, breadcrumbs, salt, pepper, sugar and egg, and put half the mixture into greased loaf pan.
3  Arrange prunes on top of the meat and cover with remaining meat mixture, cover with bacon rashers.
4  Bake in moderate oven 180°C (350°F) for 1 hour.
5  Mix prune juice, lemon juice, lemon peel, brown sugar, vinegar, mustard, spices, bring to the boil in a small pan and simmer for 10 minutes.
6  Melt remaining tablespoon of butter in another pan, stir in flour, then blend in 6 tablespoons of fruit sauce, mix well and add to remaining fruit sauce.
7  Pour sauce over thick slices of meatloaf to serve.

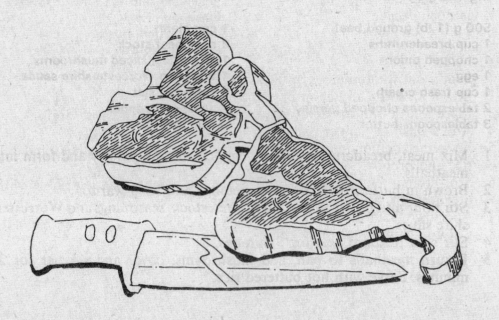

# COMO CASSEROLE

*2 hours cooking time*

*Ingredients for 5-6 servings*

500 g (1 lb) ground beef
1 chopped onion
1 clove garlic, minced
125 g (4 oz ) mushrooms, sliced
½ teaspoon oregano
½ teaspoon basil
1 teaspoon salt
1 teaspoon pepper
250 g (8 oz) macaroni

1 small tin tomato paste
1 package frozen chopped spinach, thawed
¼ cup chopped parsley
¼ cup grated cheese
½ teaspoon sage
1 cup breadcrumbs
¼ cup olive oil

1  Fry meat, onion and garlic until brown.
2  Add seasonings, herbs, tomato paste and simmer for 1 hour. Add sliced mushrooms.
3  Combine remaining ingredients except macaroni in large bowl, mix well.
4  Cook macaroni in boiling salted water.
5  Layer greased casserole with macaroni, spinach mixture and meat mixture, ending with meat mixture.
6  Bake uncovered in moderate oven 180°C (350°F) for 45 minutes.

# MEATBALLS IN WINE SAUCE

*45 minutes cooking time*

*Ingredients for 4 servings*

500 g (1 lb) ground beef
1 cup breadcrumbs
1 chopped onion
1 egg
1 cup fresh cream
2 tablespoons chopped parsley
3 tablespoons butter

1 cup claret
2 cups beef stock
125 g (4 oz) sliced mushrooms
1 teaspoon Worcestershire sauce
1 teaspoon salt
½ teaspoon pepper
⅛ cup plain flour

1  Mix meat, breadcrumbs, onion, egg, cream and parsley and form into meatballs.
2  Brown in butter for 20 minutes, remove and keep warm.
3  Stir flour into butter in pan, add claret, stock, seasonings and Worcestershire sauce.
4  Stir over medium heat for 5 minutes.
5  Return meatballs to pan, add mushrooms, cover and simmer for 20 minutes. Serve with hot buttered rice.

# MACARONI BEEF SUPPER

*50 minutes cooking time*

*Ingredients for 4-5 servings*

500 g (1 lb) ground beef
½ cup butter
1 chopped onion
250 g (8 oz) cooked, drained
   macaroni
⅛ cup beef stock
⅛ cup tomato sauce
½ cup grated cheddar cheese
5 tablespoons chopped parsley

1 teaspoon salt
3 tablespoons flour
1¼ cups milk
½ teaspoon pepper
½ teaspoon dry mustard
½ teaspoon oregano
1 teaspoon Worcestershire sauce
2 beaten eggs

1  Melt half the butter and fry meat and onion until meat is thoroughly brown.
2  Mix meat and onions with beef stock, cooked macaroni, tomato sauce, half the cheese, parsley, salt, pepper, oregano and Worcestershire sauce.
3  Melt the rest of the butter, stir in flour, then add milk and stir over heat until thickened.
4  Pour white sauce slowly into beaten eggs, stirring.
5  Then pour white sauce into casserole, top with rest of cheese and bake in moderate oven 180°C (350°F) for 30-40 minutes.
6  Stand for 10 minutes before serving.

# BUDGET STROGANOFF

*20 minutes cooking time*

*Ingredients for 6-8 servings*

1 kg (2 lb) ground beef
4 chopped onions
½ cup breadcrumbs
1 egg
1 teaspoon salt

1 carton sour cream
¼ cup sherry
1 tin whole mushrooms
2 tablespoons chopped parsley
½ teaspoon pepper

1  Shape mixed meat, onions, breadcrumbs, egg and seasoning into balls.
2  Fry gently until evenly browned.
3  In separate pan combine remaining ingredients and heat.
4  Pour cream sauce over meatballs and serve sprinkled with parsley over rice.

# MEATBALLS NAPOLI

*30 minutes cooking time*

*Ingredients for 4-6 servings*

500 g (1 lb) ground beef
2 chopped onions
½ cup breadcrumbs
2 eggs
125 g (4 oz) finely chopped bacon
2½ cups beef stock
60 g (2 oz) grated Parmesan cheese

2 tablespoons flour
1 teaspoon salt
½ teaspoon oregano
½ teaspoon pepper
¼ teaspoon nutmeg
3 tablespoons butter

1  Mix meat, onions, breadcrumbs, bacon, eggs, oregano and nutmeg.
2  Roll into meatballs and dust with flour.
3  Fry in butter until brown, drain and poach in stock for 20 minutes.

# CLARET CHEESE BURGERS

*10-12 minutes cooking time*

*Ingredients for 4 servings*

750 g (1½ lb) minced beef
1½ teaspoons salt
½ cup claret
4 slices Roquefort cheese

4 tablespoons chopped parsley
½ teaspoon pepper
2 chopped spring onions

1  Mix meat with parsley and spring onion.
2  Season with salt and pepper.
3  Shape into burgers and make a depression in centre.
4  Put into shallow pan and pour over wine.
5  Chill for 4 hours and remove from marinade.
6  Grill and place slice of cheese on top. Let cheese melt a little and serve garnished with chopped parsley.

# SOUTH SEAS BEEF AND BACON BURGERS

*10 minutes cooking time*

*Ingredients for 6-8 servings*

1 kg (2 lb) ground beef
1 tin pineapple rings
250 g (8 oz) bacon rashers
2 chopped onions
2 teaspoons salt

1 teaspoon Worcestershire sauce
½ cup breadcrumbs
2 eggs
2 sliced tomatoes
1 teaspoon pepper

1  Combine meat, chopped bacon, onion, seasoning, breadcrumbs, Worcestershire sauce and eggs, mix well and form into patties.
2  Grill on one side for 4-5 minutes, turn carefully.
3  Top with 1 slice tomato and 1 pineapple ring and grill 5 minutes more.

# MEATBALLS IN BUTTERMILK

*1 hour cooking time*

*Ingredients for 4 servings*

500 g (1 lb) ground beef
2 tablespoons chopped green pepper
1 small chopped onion
¾ cup long-grain rice
1 egg
1¼ cups buttermilk

1 teaspoon salt
½ teaspoon pepper
1 small tin cream of mushroom soup
1 small tin mushroom pieces
¼ cup chopped celery

1  Mix meat, onion, green pepper, egg, rice, salt, pepper and celery and form into small balls.
2  Place in greased casserole.
3  Combine soup, buttermilk and mushrooms and mix well, then pour over meatballs.
4  Bake in moderate oven 180°C (350°F) for one hour.

# BUDGET PEPPER STEAK

*10-15 minutes cooking time*

*Ingredients for 6-8 servings*

| | |
|---|---|
| **1 kg (2½ lb) ground beef** | **2 tablespoons Worcestershire sauce** |
| **2 tablespoons lemon juice** | **½ teaspoon Tabasco sauce** |
| **2 teaspoons salt** | **3 tablespoons warmed brandy** |
| **freshly ground black peppercorns** | **2 tablespoons chopped parsley** |

1   Combine meat, lemon juice, salt, Worcestershire sauce, Tabasco sauce and chopped parsley and form into square patties.
2   Press fresh ground black peppercorns into each side of the patties and grill 4-5 minutes on each side.
3   Melt butter, add brandy, and pour over each patty before serving.

# SKILLET DINNER

*25 minutes cooking time*

*Ingredients for 6 servings*

| | |
|---|---|
| **750 g (1½ lb) minced beef** | **1 onion, chopped** |
| **375 g (12 oz) condensed beef stock** | **1 teaspoon salt** |
| **½ teaspoon pepper** | **500 g (1 lb) creamed corn** |
| **3 potatoes, diced** | |

1   Brown beef in frying pan and add chopped onion.
2   Add stock and potatoes. Season with salt and pepper.
3   Mix and cook covered for 20 minutes over low heat and stir in corn.
4   Heat through and serve.

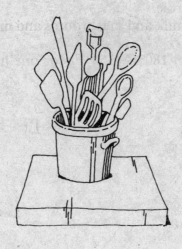

# CAPER STEAKS

*15 minutes cooking time*

*Ingredients for 6 servings*

750 g (1½ lb) minced steak
3 tablespoons capers
½ cup breadcrumbs
½ teaspoon salt
2 eggs

2 small onions
90 g (3 oz) butter
⅔ cup milk
½ teaspoon pepper

1  Mix chopped onion, capers, eggs, salt, pepper and meat together.
2  Add milk slowly and beat well.
3  Roll into balls and coat with breadcrumbs.
4  Flatten into cakes and fry in butter.

# TROPICAL BURGERS

*20 minutes cooking time*

*Ingredients for 4-6 servings*

1 tin pineapple rings
2 bananas, mashed
750 g (1½ lb) ground steak
1 teaspoon salt

1 teaspoon pepper
1 tablespoon Worcestershire sauce
4 tablespoons tomato sauce
4 tablespoons minced onion

1  Mix meat, seasonings, onion and Worcestershire and tomato sauces.
2  Form into patties, grill for 10 minutes on one side under moderate heat.
3  Turn patties, top each with layer of banana and 1 slice pineapple; return to heat for 10 minutes.

# SPEEDY LASAGNE

*Ingredients for 8 servings*

*30 minutes cooking time*

**375 g (12 oz) wide noodles**
**2 cups cottage cheese**
**½ teaspoon oregano**
**½ teaspoon pepper**

**1 teaspoon salt**
**375 g (12 oz) Mozzarella cheese, sliced**
**2 large tins spaghetti sauce with meat**

1 Cook noodles in boiling salted water.
2 Drain.
3 Mix spaghetti sauce with oregano and pepper.
4 In baking dish, place alternate layers of noodles, cottage cheese, Mozzarella and sauce, ending with a layer of sauce.
5 Bake for 20 minutes in moderate oven and serve immediately.

# KIDNEY CASSEROLE

*1 hour cooking time*

*Ingredients for 6 servings*

**2½ cups beef kidneys**
**1½ teaspoons salt**
**1½ cups diced carrots**
**½ teaspoon pepper**
**1 cup tinned tomatoes**

**½ teaspoon Worcestershire sauce**
**2 potatoes, peeled and sliced**
**¼ teaspoon paprika**
**1 onion, sliced**

1 Soak kidneys in cold water for 3 hours, changing water from time to time. Drain.
2 Pour boiling water over them and remove skin and tubes.
3 Cut into very small pieces and season with salt and pepper.
4 Combine onion, carrots and kidney pieces.
5 Cover with water and simmer for 30 minutes.
6 Pour mixture into casserole dish and add potatoes, tomatoes, salt, paprika, Worcestershire sauce and pepper.
7 Cook for 30 minutes in hot oven 200°C (400°F).

# VEAL AND MUSHROOMS

*1 hour cooking time*

*Ingredients for 6 servings*

2 onions, sliced
1 green pepper, seeded and cut
  into strips
1½ cups chicken stock
½ cup salad oil
1 teaspoon salt
1 clove garlic, minced
4 tablespoons butter

250 g (8 oz) fresh mushrooms, sliced
1 kg (2 lb) veal steak
½ cup lemon juice
1 teaspoon paprika
1 teaspoon prepared mustard
½ cup flour
¼ teaspoon nutmeg

1  Marinate meat in oil, paprika, lemon juice, salt, garlic, nutmeg and
   mustard for 30 minutes.
2  Remove meat and dredge in flour.
3  Brown meat in butter, remove to casserole.
4  Mix the remaining marinade, stock, green pepper and mushrooms and
   pour over veal.
5  Cover and bake for 30 minutes in moderate oven 180°C (350°F).
6  Remove cover and top with sliced onion. Bake for 15 minutes and serve.

# VEAL DELUXE

*15 minutes cooking time*

*Ingredients for 6 servings*

12 slices veal
¾ teaspoon sage
1 teaspoon garlic salt
4 tablespoons white wine

12 slices cooked ham
3 tablespoons butter
2 tablespoons chopped parsley
½ lemon, sliced

1  Pound veal and place ham and a little sage on each piece.
2  Fold in half and seal.
3  Sauté meat in butter and sprinkle with garlic salt.
4  Place lemon slice on each and add wine.
5  Simmer for 10 minutes and garnish with chopped parsley.

# APPLE VEAL

*20 minutes cooking time*

*Ingredients for 6 servings*

**6 veal cutlets**
**60 g (2 oz) butter**
**½ teaspoon salt**
**1 tablespoon chopped parsley**
**½ cup cider**
**1½ apples, grated**

**1 tablespoon oil**
**2 tablespoons lemon juice**
**½ teaspoon pepper**
**1 cup stock**
**3 onions, chopped**
**2½ tablespoons flour**

1  Season cutlets with salt and pepper and sprinkle with lemon juice.
2  Heat butter and oil together, fry cutlets on both sides and remove from heat to warm oven.
3  Fry onions and stir in apple, cook for 3 minutes and stir in flour, cider and stock.
4  Bring to boil and cook for 4 minutes. Season with salt and pepper.
5  Place cutlets in sauce and heat through.
6  Serve garnished with chopped parsley.

# VEAL PARMESAN

*20 minutes cooking time*

*Ingredients for 6 servings*

**1 kg (2 lb) veal cutlets**
**½ teaspoon pepper**
**2 eggs, beaten**
**½ cup breadcrumbs**
**1 teaspoon basil**

**1 teaspoon salt**
**lemon slices**
**½ cup olive oil**
**5 tablespoons Parmesan cheese**

1  Season meat with salt, pepper and basil.
2  Dip meat into mixture of Parmesan and breadcrumbs.
3  Dip into beaten eggs and again into crumbs.
4  Chill for 1 hour and heat oil.
5  Brown cutlets and cook uncovered for 20 minutes.
6  Serve with lemon slices.

# SCHNITZEL

*20 minutes cooking time*

*Ingredients for 4 servings*

| | |
|---|---|
| **4 pieces veal steak** | **1 teaspoon salt** |
| **½ teaspoon pepper** | **8 stuffed olives** |
| **¼ cup plain flour** | **¼ cup breadcrumbs** |
| **2 eggs** | **1 lemon** |
| **4 tablespoons butter** | **8 anchovy fillets** |

1  Hard boil one egg, and beat the other.
2  Pound veal steaks and dip into seasoned flour.
3  Brush meat with beaten egg and toss in breadcrumbs.
4  Melt butter, brown fillets and cook gently for 10 minutes on each side.
5  Place cooked steaks on serving dish and garnish with anchovies and olives, lemon wedges and hardboiled egg.

# SWISS LIVER ROLLS

*15 minutes cooking time*

*Ingredients for 4 servings*

| | |
|---|---|
| **250 g (8 oz) calves liver** | **1 teaspoon salt** |
| **2 teaspoons mustard** | **12 rashers bacon** |
| **250 g (8 oz) noodles** | **2 tablespoons butter** |

1  Cut liver into 5 centimetre (2 in) pieces.
2  Spread bacon rashers with mustard.
3  Cook noodles in boiling salted water for 15 minutes.
4  Roll liver and bacon together and secure.
5  Melt butter in pan and place meat rolls in; cook for 7-10 minutes.
6  Toss drained noodles in butter and serve with liver/bacon rolls.

# CONTINENTAL LIVER

*30 minutes cooking time*

*Ingredients for 4 servings*

**750 g (1½ lb) liver**
**1 teaspoon salt**
**750 g (1½ lb) potatoes**
**250 g (8 oz) mushrooms**
**6 tablespoons butter**

**½ cup plain flour**
**½ teaspoon pepper**
**¾ cup dry white wine**
**4 onions**

1   Peel, slice, boil and mash potatoes.
2   Slice liver and dust with seasoned flour. Melt butter and when very hot fry liver until brown.
3   Peel and slice onions, halve the mushrooms and add to pan.
4   Cook gently for 2-5 minutes and add wine; cook one minute longer.

# PORK VINDALOO

*1½ hours cooking time*

*Ingredients for 8 servings*

**3 onions**
**3 tablespoons coriander**
**2 teaspoons cumin**
**1½ teaspoons ground ginger**
**1 teaspoon pepper**
**2 tablespoons tamarind pulp**
**2 teaspoons salt**

**8 cloves garlic**
**1½ tablespoons turmeric**
**1½ teaspoons chilli**
**2 teaspoons mustard seeds**
**3 tablespoons vinegar**
**1 kg (2 lb) pork**
**½ cup ghee**

1   Combine minced onion and garlic, coriander, cumin, turmeric, chilli, ginger, mustard seeds and pepper. Toss lightly.
2   Add vinegar and tamarind pulp to pork meat, which has been cut into small pieces, and stand overnight.
3   Heat ghee and add meat mixture; stir in salt, cover and cook slowly for 1½ hours.

# PORK AND CASHEWS

*15 minutes cooking time*

*Ingredients for 6 servings*

½ cup thinly-sliced raw pork
3 teaspoons cornflour
1 teaspoon salt
½ teaspoon white pepper
¼ cup tinned bamboo shoots
½ cup peanut oil
4 teaspoons sesame oil
3 teaspoons cornflour
8 tablespoons roasted cashew nuts

3 teaspoons sherry
½ teaspoon monosodium glutamate
   (optional)
¼ cup raw carrot
¼ cup tinned water chestnuts
1 large onion
⅓ cup hot chicken stock
1 teaspoon soy sauce

1   In a bowl place meat, cornflour mixed with water, sherry, salt, monosodium glutamate (if desired) and pepper, work well into meat. Stand for a few minutes.
2   Cut carrot into match sticks, slice bamboo shoots and water chestnuts and chop onion.
3   Place three-quarters of oil in pan.
4   Heat 1 tablespoon of oil in another pan and fry onion. Add carrot, chestnuts and bamboo shoots, and cook for 1 minute.
5   Add liquid drained from meat, stock, sesame oil, and soy sauce, bring to boil and cook for 2 minutes.
6   Deep fry pork in oil, add to vegetables and cook for 2 minutes.
7   Turn this mixture into heated serving dish and wipe out pan. Add 1 teaspoon of peanut oil and cashew nuts.
8   When nuts are brown, add to meat mixture and serve at once.

# SWISS PORK CHOPS

*1½ hours cooking time*

*Ingredients for 4 servings*

750 g (1½ lb) pork chops
1 onion
1½ cups tomato juice
1 green pepper, sliced into rings

1 lemon, sliced
1 tablespoon butter
1 teaspoon salt
½ teaspoon pepper

1   Slice onion into rings.
2   Put chops in greased casserole and cover with lemon juice, onion rings and green pepper rings.
3   Season with salt and pepper and pour over tomato juice.
4   Dot with butter and bake for 1½ hours in moderate oven 180°C (350°F).

# PORK SAMBAL

*30 minutes cooking time*

*Ingredients for 6-8 servings*

1 kg (2 lb) pork meat, cubed
6 garlic cloves
1½ tablespoons fennel seed
juice of 1 lemon
90 g (3 oz) ghee
2 teaspoons salt

3 brown onions
3 dried chillies
8 cm (3 in) stick cinnamon
1½ teaspoons salt
60 g (2 oz) copha

1  Mince onion and garlic.
2  Grind fennel seeds and deseeded chillies.
3  Heat ghee and copha in pan and fry onion and spices until brown.
4  Add meat and cinnamon stick, salt and a little water. Simmer for 25 minutes and remove from heat.
5  Add lemon juice and serve.

# MACARONI HAM

*1 hour cooking time*

*Ingredients for 4 servings*

1½ cups macaroni
125 g (4 oz) mushrooms, sliced
1 tablespoon lemon juice
185 g (6 oz) tomato sauce
1 cup cooked chopped ham

¼ cup butter
4 teaspoons chopped chives
2 tablespoons grated Parmesan cheese
2 eggs, separated

1  Cook macaroni in boiling water for 15 minutes. Drain and cool.
2  Cream butter and egg yolks with ham. Mix through and add to macaroni.
3  Beat egg whites until they form stiff peaks.
4  Mix quickly into macaroni mixture and turn into buttered casserole dish. Sprinkle with cheese and bake uncovered for 45 minutes in moderate oven.
4  Combine tomato sauce, ¼ cup water, lemon juice, chives and mushrooms in small pan. Heat through and spoon over casserole.

# LUAU HAM

*15 minutes cooking time*

*Ingredients for 8 servings*

| | |
|---|---|
| 4 cups cubed cooked ham | 2½ cups cooked rice |
| 1½ cups pineapple chunks | 1 teaspoon ground ginger |
| 3 teaspoons dry mustard | 2 tablespoons brown sugar |
| 1 cup pineapple juice | ½ cup chopped green pepper |
| 2 tablespoons cornflour | 4 tablespoons butter |

1. Brown ham and green pepper in butter.
2. Combine cornflour with ⅔ cup water, add sugar, mustard, ginger and pineapple juice.
3. Pour over ham, cook, stirring until sauce clears and thickens.
4. Add pineapple and heat for 3 minutes.
5. Serve over rice.

# HAM PANCAKES

*15 minutes cooking time*

*Ingredients for 4 servings*

| | |
|---|---|
| 125 g (4 oz) plain flour | 8 slices ham |
| 185 g (6 oz) butter | 1¼ cups water |
| 2 cups milk | 155 g (5 oz) cheese |
| 2 eggs | |

1. Place 2 tablespoons flour in a bowl and add salt and eggs. Stir and mix to a smooth batter.
2. Melt a little fat in frying pan and pour in enough batter to form a thin layer over base.
3. Cook pancake on both sides and keep hot. Repeat until batter is used.
4. Grate half the cheese and place a slice of ham and grated cheese onto each pancake and roll.

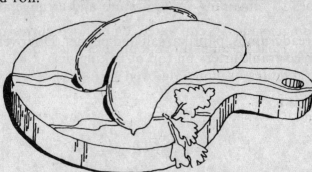

# MIAMI CASSEROLE

*25 minutes cooking time*

*Ingredients for 4 servings*

**750 g (1½ lb) tinned ham**
**⅓ cup breadcrumbs**
**½ teaspoon salt**
**2 tablespoons chopped parsley**

**2 tins creamed corn**
**60 g (2 oz) butter**
**¼ teaspoon pepper**

1   Preheat oven to 180°C (350°F) and dice ham.
2   Grease casserole dish and add diced ham and corn. Season with salt and pepper.
3   Dot with breadcrumbs and butter.
4   Heat for 25 minutes and serve garnished with chopped parsley.

# FRANKFURTERS A LA BERLIN

*30 minutes cooking time*

*Ingredients for 4 servings*

**8 frankfurters**
**½ cup mayonnaise**
**½ teaspoon pepper**
**½ cup breadcrumbs**
**1½ cups sauerkraut, drained**
**1 teaspoon caraway seeds**

**1 small tin condensed cream of
   mushroom soup**
**1 teaspoon salt**
**½ teaspoon paprika**
**3 cups diced cooked potatoes**

1   Halve 4 frankfurters and slice remaining ones into 5 millimetre (¼ in) thick slices.
2   Mix soup and mayonnaise, combine sliced frankfurters and half soup mixture and add caraway seeds.
3   Mix and add sauerkraut.
4   Spread into baking dish.
5   Add potatoes to remaining soup mixture and arrange around edge of dish.
6   Combine breadcrumbs, paprika, salt and pepper. Dot over potatoes and arrange halved frankfurters on top of baking dish.
7   Bake for 25 minutes in moderate oven.

# MISSISSIPPI RICE

*1 hour 10 minutes cooking time*

*Ingredients for 6 servings*

1 cup long-grain rice
½ cup tomato paste
4 spring onions, sliced
¼ teaspoon pepper

500 g (1 lb) thin sausages
3 onions, chopped
2 green peppers, chopped
1 cup cooked ham, cubed

1   Cook rice.
2   Cut sausages into 3 centimetre (1 in) lengths, brown lightly and remove from pan.
3   Pour off excess fat, retaining 2 tablespoons, sauté chopped onions.
4   Stir in tomato paste, peppers, onions and ham cubes. Toss and add sausage lengths.
5   Cook over low heat, stirring for 10 minutes.
6   Combine with cooked rice and place all ingredients in casserole dish.
7   Season with salt and pepper.
8   Bake in moderate oven 180°C (350°F) for 45 minutes.

# FRANKFURTER CASSEROLE

*30 minutes cooking time*

*Ingredients for 6 servings*

⅓ cup butter
12 frankfurters
1½ teaspoons salt
4 cups tinned tomatoes
2 chopped onions

2½ cups diced carrots
½ teaspoon pepper
2 tablespoons tomato sauce
⅓ cup flour

1   Melt butter and brown onion.
2   Stir in flour and blend well.
3   Add tomatoes, cook until mixture thickens and season with salt, pepper and tomato sauce.
4   Add carrots and split frankfurters, pour into casserole.
5   Bake for 30 minutes in moderate oven 180°C (350°F).

# SINGAPORE BEANS AND BACON

*20 minutes cooking time*

*Ingredients for 4 servings*

3 rashers bacon
1 garlic clove
750 g (1½ lb) green beans

1 chopped onion
1½ tablespoons soy sauce

1  Crush garlic clove.
2  Chop beans, cook 10 minutes in boiling salted water and drain.
3  Cook bacon until crisp and reserve a little fat.
4  Crumble bacon and cook onion and garlic in reserved fat.
5  Stir in soy sauce and add beans.

# Salads

## ANN'S POTATO SALAD

*Ingredients for 6 servings*

*20 minutes cooking time*

1 kg (2 lb) small new potatoes
2 tablespoons grated onion
1 teaspoon prepared mustard
2 tablespoons white vinegar
freshly ground black pepper

½ cup sour cream
1 tablespoon chopped parsley
1 tablespoon sugar
1 teaspoon salt

1 Cook potatoes in salted water until tender, and peel.
2 Blend sugar and vinegar, sprinkle over potatoes.
3 Mix remaining ingredients well and pour over potatoes, toss gently.
4 Chill before serving.

# MOULDED APPLE DELIGHT

*15 minutes cooking time*

*Ingredients for 4 servings*

2 cups water
4 large cooking apples
125 g (4 oz) crushed pineapple
60 g (2 oz) gelatine
2 tablespoons mayonnaise

red food colouring
½ cup sugar
¼ cup chopped walnuts
1 head lettuce

1  Peel and core apples.
2  Drain pineapple.
3  Tint water with red food colouring.
4  Place apples in water and sprinkle with sugar.
5  Cover and simmer for 15 minutes. Cool in liquid. Remove apples and reserve liquid.
6  Place each apple in deep cup. Mix pineapple and nuts, and stuff the apple cavities with this mixture.
7  Heat 2 cups of the liquid and dissolve gelatine in it. Cool and pour over apples.
8  Chill until firm, unmould apples and serve on lettuce leaves, dotted with mayonnaise.

# EGG-FILLED TOMATOES

*No cooking time*

*Ingredients for 6 servings*

6 small tomatoes
3 teaspoons prepared mustard
1 lettuce
10 hardboiled eggs
3 tablespoons minced onion
1½ teaspoons salt

⅓ cup lemon juice
⅓ cup mayonnaise
½ teaspoon cayenne pepper
1 cup minced celery
3 tablespoons French dressing

1  Remove stem end of the tomatoes.
2  Wash and cut each tomato into quarters, making sure not to cut all the way through.
3  Press petals back and sprinkle with pepper.
4  Add salt and some of the dressing.
5  Chill.
6  Add chopped eggs to remaining ingredients and mix thoroughly.
7  Top the tomatoes with egg mixture and pour over remaining dressing.
8  Serve on a bed of lettuce leaves.

# RIVIERA SALAD

*No cooking time*

*Ingredients for 6-8 appetiser servings or 4 main servings*

| | |
|---|---|
| 1 cup olive oil | ½ cup wine vinegar |
| 1 teaspoon salt | ½ teaspoon black pepper |
| 3 tablespoons chopped chives | 3 tablespoons chopped parsley |
| 4 large boiled potatoes | 500 g (1 lb) green beans |
| 3 tomatoes | 4 hardboiled eggs |
| 20 anchovy fillets | 2 tablespoons capers |
| 1 head lettuce | 2 large tins tuna |

1 Combine olive oil, vinegar, chives, parsley, salt and pepper. Shake vigorously and chill.
2 When potatoes are cool, peel and slice.
3 Dot with dressing and place in refrigerator for 30 minutes, covered.
4 Cut beans into 2.5 centimetre (1 in) lengths; cook in boiling salted water. Cool, drain and dot with dressing. Cover and chill for 30 minutes.
5 On a serving dish, pile the potato salad in centre on lettuce leaves and arrange beans around edge of tuna with capers.
6 Peel tomatoes and cut in quarters. Halve the boiled eggs and alternate eggs and tomato quarters around beans.

# CUCUMBER CHEESE SALAD

*No cooking time*

*Ingredients for 4 servings*

| | |
|---|---|
| 2 medium cucumbers | ½ teaspoon salt |
| ½ teaspoon pepper | 2 tablespoons chopped parsley |
| 1 lettuce | 1 cup cottage cheese |
| 2 tablespoons vinegar | 1 spring onion, chopped |

1 Peel cucumbers and slice after they have been cut lengthwise.
2 Season with salt and set aside.
3 Mix cottage cheese, vinegar, onion, pepper and parsley.
4 Beat with electric mixer until blended and combine with drained cucumbers.
5 Chill and serve on lettuce leaves.

# MOULDED CHICKEN SALAD

*15 minutes cooking time*

*Ingredients for 3-4 servings*

2 tablespoons gelatine
½ cup chicken stock
1 cup diced cooked chicken
⅔ cup thickened cream
½ teaspoon paprika
90 g (3 oz) stuffed olives

⅛ cup cold water
1 egg yolk
⅓ cup chopped pecans
1 teaspoon salt
4 tablespoons mayonnaise
2 tomatoes, sliced

1　Whip cream.
2　Beat egg yolk well.
3　Soak gelatine in cold water for 5 minutes.
4　Boil stock and pour a little into egg mixture.
5　Stir well, then pour egg mixture into stock and simmer for 5 minutes, stirring constantly.
6　Stir gelatine mixture into stock.
7　Chill until thickened then fold in chicken.
8　Add nuts, whipped cream and turn into mould.
9　Chill then unmould and garnish with mayonnaise, tomato slices and olives.

# RANGOON CUCUMBER SALAD

*15 minutes cooking time*

*Ingredients for 6 servings*

2 cucumbers
3 onions
¼ cup olive oil
1 tablespoon roasted sesame seeds
½ teaspoon sugar

6 tablespoons vinegar
6 cloves garlic
1 teaspoon turmeric
½ teaspoon salt

1　Peel cucumbers, cut lengthwise and remove seeds.
2　Chop into 5 centimetre (2 in) by 7.5 centimetre (3 in) slices and boil in 1 cup water, to which half the vinegar has been added, for 2 minutes.
3　Drain and sprinkle with salt.
4　Heat olive oil and fry chopped onions and garlic for 8 minutes, drain.
5　Put sugar, salt and turmeric into pan and fry for 1 minute, then remove from heat and add remaining vinegar.
6　Combine all ingredients and chill.

# PRAWN MACARONI SALAD

*No cooking time*

*Ingredients for 6 servings*

**375 g (12 oz) shelled prawns**
**½ teaspoon paprika**
**1 clove garlic, crushed**
**3 dessertspoons red wine vinegar**
**½ cup chopped celery**
**¼ cup chopped parsley**

**1 cup cooked shell macaroni**
**½ teaspoon dry mustard**
**1 tablespoon lemon juice**
**⅔ cup mayonnaise**
**2 teaspoons chopped pimento**

1  Cut prawns in half and mix with macaroni; add celery, pimento and chopped parsley.
2  Mix mayonnaise, vinegar, lemon juice, crushed garlic clove, salt, mustard and paprika.
3  Add prawn mixture to dressing and toss gently.
4  Serve chilled.

# GREEN BEAN-TUNA SALAD

*No cooking time*

*Ingredients for 4 servings*

**440 g (14 oz) tinned tuna fish**
**1 tablespoon capers**
**½ cup French dressing**
**750 g (1½ lb) green beans**
**¼ teaspoon pepper**

**⅓ cup bottled Italian dressing**
**1 onion, chopped**
**1 head lettuce**
**½ teaspoon salt**

1  Drain tuna and break into chunks, mix with chopped beans.
2  Marinate in mixture of Italian dressing and seasonings.
3  Arrange lettuce leaves in salad bowl and add onion, French dressing and seasonings.
4  Add tuna fish and capers.

# VEAL SALAD

*No cooking time*

*Ingredients for 6-8 servings*

½ teaspoon salt
1½ cups boiled green beans
6 hardboiled eggs
4 tomatoes
1 head lettuce

½ cup diced celery
2½ cups cooked cold veal
5 tablespoons dressing
2 tablespoons chopped parsley
6 tablespoons mayonnaise

1 Coarsely chop the eggs and combine with veal.
2 Blend thoroughly.
3 Add string beans and celery, oil, salt and pepper.
4 Marinate for 1 hour.
5 Add mayonnaise.
6 Form into a mould and spread on lettuce leaves.
7 Place sliced tomato around the edge and garnish with chopped parsley.

# LOBSTER ORANGE SALAD

*No cooking time*

*Ingredients for 4 servings*

375 g (12 oz) tinned lobster
1 head lettuce
2 tablespoons lemon juice
1 teaspoon salt
⅔ cup chopped celery

3 spring onions, chopped
4 mandarins, peeled
½ cup mayonnaise
½ teaspoon pepper

1 Chill mixture of lobster and celery.
2 Mix lemon juice, salt and mayonnaise together.
3 Arrange mandarin slices in circles on lettuce leaves and toss lobster in dressing.
4 Place this mixture on top of mandarins and garnish with chopped spring onion.

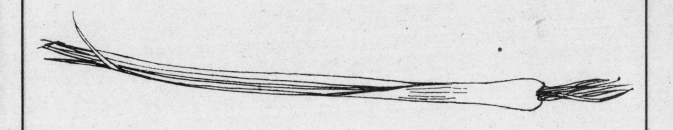

# COTTAGE CHEESE COMBINATION SALAD

*No cooking time*

*Ingredients for 6 servings*

1 cup sour cream
1 teaspoon salt
½ cup sliced onion
2 cups cottage cheese
½ cup sliced green pepper

10 green olives
½ teaspoon pepper
3 tablespoons chopped pimento
1 head lettuce

1  Combine sour cream and cottage cheese, mix well and stir in cold vegetables.
2  Serve with lettuce and olives.

# COLD MEAT SALAD

*No cooking time*

*Ingredients for 6 servings*

1 large head lettuce
2 onions, sliced in rings
315 g (10 oz) small tomatoes

1 tin anchovy fillets, drained
500 g (1 lb) roast beef, cut into strips

## DRESSING

½ teaspoon salt
1 teaspoon dry mustard
3 tablespoons vinegar
1 teaspoon sugar

¼ teaspoon pepper
6 tablespoons oil
1 tablespoon horseradish

1  Toss lettuce, anchovies, and onion rings.
2  Place tomatoes and beef on top of salad.
3  Place all ingredients for dressing in jar and shake. Pour over salad and serve.

# DUSSELDORF SALAD

*No cooking time*

*Ingredients for 4 servings*

lettuce leaves
½ teaspoon sugar
pinch aniseed
1 tablespoon chopped parsley
1 small apple

1½ tablespoons sour cream
½ teaspoon caraway seed
375 g (12 oz) drained chopped
   sauerkraut

1  Mix sauerkraut with parsley and add caraway seed.
2  Add aniseed, sugar and sour cream.
3  Blend well and cover.
4  Chill for 4 hours and add diced apple when ready to serve.
5  Serve in lettuce leaves.

# HAM-STUFFED PEPPERS

*No cooking time*

*Ingredients for 6-8 servings*

1½ cups cooked ham
½ teaspoon pepper
1 cup diced celery
2 tablespoons chopped parsley

½ teaspoon salt
6-8 small green peppers
250 g (8 oz) cream cheese

1  Combine ham and celery with cream cheese.
2  Mix well and add parsley.
3  Season with salt and pepper.
4  Scoop out centres of peppers and place mixture inside.
5  Chill.
6  Top with French dressing and serve.

# ASPARAGUS SALAD

*No cooking time*

*Ingredients for 5-6 servings*

1 cup diced celery
½ cup French dressing
500 g (1 lb) cooked asparagus
3 tablespoons chopped chives

1 head lettuce
½ cup mayonnaise
3 tablespoons chopped pimento
1 teaspoon salt

1 Combine celery and pimento.
2 Season with salt.
3 Add chives and mix thoroughly.
4 Arrange asparagus on lettuce.
5 Pour over dressing.
6 Add mayonnaise.
7 Add celery mixture and chill before serving.

# BACON SPINACH SALAD

*No cooking time*

*Ingredients for 4 servings*

2 bunches spinach
2 tablespoons Parmesan cheese,
  grated
½ teaspoon salt

4 crisp cooked rashers bacon
French dressing
¼ teaspoon pepper

1 Pick out tender leaves from spinach and wash.
2 Drain and slice into shreds. Place in bowl.
3 Crumble bacon slices and mix with Parmesan cheese.
4 Add to spinach and, when ready to serve, pour over French dressing.

# CREAMY CARROT SALAD

*No cooking time*

*Ingredients for 6-8 servings*

2½ cups chopped carrot
½ cup chopped walnuts
2 tablespoons chopped parsley

1½ cups chopped celery
3 tablespoons chopped onion
¾ cup mayonnaise

1   Blend all ingredients thoroughly.
2   Chill for 30 minutes before serving.

# SALMON ORANGE SALAD

*No cooking time*

*Ingredients for 4 servings*

2 medium oranges
1 small tin fruit salad
1 cucumber

90 g (3 oz) smoked salmon
4 tablespoons vermouth
1 head lettuce

1   Halve the orange and remove pulp.
2   Mix orange pulp and drained fruit salad.
3   Add vermouth and salmon. Combine well.
4   Serve on lettuce leaves and garnish with cucumber.

# APPLE SLAW

*10 minutes cooking time*

*Ingredients for 6-8 servings*

1 small cabbage
2 cups diced apple
1 teaspoon salt

¾ cup French dressing
½ teaspoon pepper

1   Shred cabbage.
2   Boil in salted water.
3   Drain and dry until crisp.
4   Combine with apples and mix in salad dressing.
5   Season with pepper and salt.

# GOURMET CRAB SALAD

*No cooking time*

*Ingredients for 4 servings*

4 hardboiled eggs, halved
185 g (6 oz) crab meat
1 head lettuce
1½ teaspoons lemon juice
¾ cup mayonnaise

250 g (8 oz) artichoke hearts
315 g (10 oz) crab legs
½ teaspoon salt
⅓ cup tomato sauce
½ cup cream

1  Whip cream and add mayonnaise, tomato sauce, salt and lemon juice.
2  Top lettuce with crab meat and crab legs, artichoke hearts and halved eggs.
3  Add cream mixture, toss gently and serve.

# PEACH SURPRISE SALAD

*No cooking time*

*Ingredients for 4 servings*

1 head lettuce
1 cup chopped olives
90 g (3 oz) chopped almonds
75 g (2½ oz) cream cheese

2 peaches
½ teaspoon paprika
1 tablespoon mayonnaise

1  Cut peaches into halves.
2  Blend olives, cream cheese and mayonnaise.
3  Arrange peach halves on a bed of lettuce leaves.
4  Fill peach centres with cheese and olive mixture.
5  Sprinkle with chopped almonds and paprika.

# SESAME CUCUMBER SALAD

*No cooking time*

*Ingredients for 4 servings*

1 carton sour cream
3 tablespoons sesame seeds
1 teaspoon salt

2 cucumbers
½ teaspoon pepper
2 tablespoons lemon juice

1 Wash cucumber, split lengthwise and scoop out seeds.
2 Chop into 1 centimetre (½ in) pieces and mix with sour cream, salt and pepper.
3 Brown sesame seeds in dry frying pan and add to cucumber.
4 Mix in lemon juice and serve.

# EASY COTTAGE CHEESE SALAD

*No cooking time*

*Ingredients for 8 servings*

1½ cups cottage cheese
5 tablespoons cream
2 green peppers

2½ tablespoons chopped mixed nuts
½ teaspoon paprika
½ teaspoon salt

1 Remove seeds then slice green peppers into rings.
2 Blend cheese and cream thoroughly.
3 Place mounds of cheese in centre of pepper rings.
4 Season with salt.
5 Garnish with nuts and paprika.

# *Vegetables*

## SWEET AND SOUR CABBAGE

*15 minutes cooking time*

*Ingredients for 4 servings*

500 g (1 lb) cabbage
2 tablespoons sugar
1 tablespoon cornflour
1 teaspoon salt

1 cup water
2 tablespoons vinegar
2 tablespoons peanut oil

1 Wash cabbage and cut into 2.5 centimetre (1 in) pieces.
2 Mix vinegar, sugar, cornflour and ¼ cup water.
3 Heat oil, stir cabbage in it for 1 minute, then add water and salt.
4 Add remaining ingredients and stir.
5 When juice clears, serve.

# CAULIFLOWER AU GRATIN

*25 minutes cooking time*

*Ingredients for 6 servings*

1 cauliflower
6 rashers bacon
¼ teaspoon pepper
2½ cups milk
2 tablespoons lemon juice

125 g (4 oz) white breadcrumbs
½ teaspoon salt
3 tablespoons butter
250 g (8 oz) grated cheese

1  Remove rind from bacon.
2  Trim cauliflower and cut into flowerets.
3  Boil in salted water with lemon juice until tender.
4  Pour off ½ cup of liquid and drain cauliflower.
5  Arrange in baking dish. Fry bacon until crisp, drain and chop.
6  Melt butter and stir in flour. Cook for 2 minutes and remove from heat, add ½ cup of liquid and the milk.
7  Bring to boil and stir. Remove from heat and add diced bacon, cheese and season with salt and pepper.
8  Pour over cauliflower.
9  Dot with remaining cheese and mixed breadcrumbs.
10  Brown under griller or in oven.

# EGGPLANT LOUISIANA

*1 hour cooking time*

*Ingredients for 4 servings*

1 eggplant, peeled and diced
1 teaspoon salt
¼ cup fine breadcrumbs
pinch ground cloves
1½ cups strained tinned tomatoes

1 onion, minced
1 tablespoon grated cheese
3 teaspoons brown sugar
2 tablespoons plain flour

1  Preheat oven to 180°C (350°F).
2  Rub casserole with butter and drop diced eggplant into 1 cup boiling water with a little salt. Cover and cook for 10 minutes.
3  Drain and place cooked eggplant in casserole.
4  Fry onion and pepper in melted butter for 5 minutes.
5  Add flour and blend, add tomatoes, salt and brown sugar. Mix well and add ground cloves.
6  Stir and simmer for 6 minutes, pour over eggplant, mix cheese and breadcrumbs and sprinkle over eggplant; bake for 30 minutes.

# SCANDINAVIAN TOMATOES

*10 minutes cooking time*

*Ingredients for 4 servings*

| | |
|---|---|
| ⅓ cup sour cream | ¼ cup mayonnaise |
| 1½ tablespoons chopped onion | 1 teaspoon fresh dill, chopped |
| ¼ teaspoon salt | 2 large tomatoes |
| 1 tablespoon butter | ⅛ teaspoon pepper |

1  Mix sour cream, mayonnaise, onion, dill and salt together.
2  Cut chilled tomatoes in half crosswise and season with salt and pepper.
3  Dot with butter.
4  Grill for 5-10 minutes and spoon over sauce.

# PARMESAN TOMATOES

*8-10 minutes cooking time*

*Ingredients for 4 servings*

| | |
|---|---|
| 4 tomatoes | 1 tablespoon chopped parsley |
| ½ teaspoon pepper | 1 teaspoon salt |
| 1 tablespoon butter | 1 tablespoon Parmesan cheese, grated |

1  Cut tomatoes in half and season with salt and pepper.
2  Dot with Parmesan cheese and a little butter.
3  Grill for 8-10 minutes about 20 centimetres (8 in) from griller and serve dotted with chopped parsley.

# CHEESE ZUCCHINI

*8-10 minutes cooking time*

*Ingredients for 6 servings*

| | |
|---|---|
| 8 small zucchini, thinly sliced | 3 tablespoons grated Parmesan cheese |
| 1 teaspoon salt | 4 tablespoons butter |
| ½ teaspoon pepper | |

1  Place zucchini in butter and cook gently, covered, for 5 minutes.
2  Season with salt and pepper.
3  Turn zucchini from time to time and sprinkle with grated cheese.
4  Cook for further 3-5 minutes and serve.

# CRUNCHY POTATOES

*25-30 minutes cooking time*

*Ingredients for 6 servings*

**6 tablespoons butter**
**½ teaspoon pepper**
**1½ cups shredded cheese**
**6 potatoes, peeled, cut into 5 mm
(¼ in) slices**

**1 teaspoon salt**
**1½ teaspoons paprika**
**1 cup crushed corn flakes**

1   Melt butter in pan and add single layer of potatoes. Turn and add cheese
    and corn flakes.
2   Sprinkle with salt, pepper and paprika.
3   Bake for 25-30 minutes in moderate oven.

# FRIED EGGPLANT

*6-10 minutes cooking time*

*Ingredients for 6 servings*

**2 large eggplants**
**½ cup butter**

**½ cup seasoned plain flour**

1   Wash and peel eggplant.
2   Slice thickly and coat with seasoned flour.
3   Fry in hot butter for 3 minutes on each side.

# YUKON POTATOES

*15 minutes cooking time*

*Ingredients for 4 servings*

**6 mashed potatoes**
**2 eggs, separated**
**1 teaspoon lemon juice**
**½ teaspoon pepper**

**3 tablespoons butter**
**2 chopped spring onions**
**3 tablespoons mayonnaise**
**1 teaspoon salt**

1   Add butter, salt, onion, pepper and egg yolks to cooked potatoes.
2   Place 4 mounds onto baking dish and beat egg whites.
3   When whites are stiff fold in mayonnaise and lemon juice. Top each
    mound of potatoes with this mixture and bake for 15 minutes.

# QUICK TASTY POTATOES

*15 minutes cooking time*

*Ingredients for 6 servings*

4 large potatoes, mashed
3 teaspoons prepared mustard
1 chopped spring onion

¾ cup sour cream
1 teaspoon sugar

1  Heat sour cream and stir in mustard, salt and sugar.
2  Mix into mashed potatoes and add onions.
3  Place all ingredients in casserole dish and bake for 10 minutes in hot oven.

# CHEESEY ONIONS

*10 minutes cooking time*

*Ingredients for 8 servings*

8 onions
1 teaspoon sugar
½ teaspoon pepper
4 tablespoons grated Parmesan
  cheese

1 teaspoon monosodium glutatmate
  (optional)
1 teaspoon salt
½ cup butter
⅔ cup sherry

1  Slice onions and season with salt, pepper, sugar and monosodium glutamate (if desired).
2  Cook in butter for 10 minutes and add sherry.
3  Sprinkle with grated Parmesan cheese and serve.

# DILLED PEAS

*10 minutes cooking time*

*Ingredients for 6 servings*

1 kg (2 lb) fresh peas
6 tablespoons chopped dill pickle
1 teaspoon salt

½ cup melted butter
½ teaspoon pepper

1  Shell peas and drop into boiling salted water.
2  Cook until tender and combine dill pickle with butter. Season with salt and pepper.
3  Pour over drained peas and serve.

# INDIAN PEACHES

*20 minutes cooking time*

*Ingredients for 6 servings*

**12 peach halves**
**4 tablespoons chutney**

**2 tablespoons melted butter**

1 Place peach halves in baking dish and brush with melted butter.
2 Spoon a little chutney into each and bake for 20 minutes in moderate oven.
3 Serve hot.

# SPECIAL MASHED POTATOES

*25 minutes cooking time*

*Ingredients for 6 servings*

**6 large potatoes, cooked and mashed**
**¼ cup chopped onion**

**1½ cups cottage cheese**
**1 teaspoon salt**

1 Combine mashed potato and onions. Mix well.
2 Fold in cheese and place in casserole dish.
3 Bake for 25 minutes in moderate oven and serve.

# NUTTY ASPARAGUS

*20 minutes cooking time*

*Ingredients for 6 servings*

**1 kg (2 lb) fresh asparagus**
**1 tablespoon lemon juice**
**½ cup salted cashews**

**½ cup butter**
**½ teaspoon marjoram**

1 Break cashews lengthwise and cut into halves.
2 Cook asparagus in salted water until tender, and drain.
3 Arrange on serving platter and melt butter in small frying pan.
4 Add lemon juice, marjoram and cashews.
5 Cook over low heat and pour over cooked asparagus.

# SPINACH AND SOUR CREAM COMBINATION

*40 minutes cooking time*

*Ingredients for 4 servings*

½ teaspoon grated nutmeg
1 packet onion soup
½ teaspoon salt

¾ cup sour cream
625 g (20 oz) frozen chopped spinach

1  Cook spinach in boiling salted water and drain.
2  Place sour cream, soup mix and salt in blender. Mix thoroughly.
3  Combine sour cream mixture with cooked spinach and pour into casserole dish.
4  Sprinkle with nutmeg and bake uncovered in moderate oven for 25 minutes.

# APPLE-POTATO PANCAKES

*15 minutes cooking time*

*Ingredients for 6 servings*

4 eggs, beaten
1 teaspoon salt
6 tablespoons flour

1 jar apple sauce
½ teaspoon pepper
6 potatoes

1  Peel and shred potatoes.
2  Place potatoes in water for 5-7 minutes and drain.
3  Pour potatoes into bowl and mix with flour, salt and pepper.
4  Add beaten eggs and blend well.
5  Drop spoonfuls of batter into oiled frying pan and bake until brown.
6  Serve rolled around apple sauce.

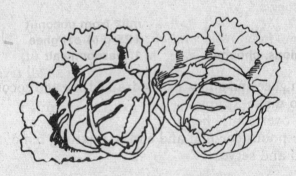

# SCALLOPED CABBAGE

*25 minutes cooking time*

*Ingredients for 4 servings*

2 cups shredded cooked cabbage
1½ cups white sauce
1 teaspoon salt

⅓ cup grated cheddar cheese
¾ cup soft breadcrumbs

1   Mix cabbage and white sauce together. Season with salt.
2   Layer cabbage and breadcrumbs in greased casserole dish.
3   Sprinkle with cheese and bake for 25 minutes in moderate oven 180°C (350°F).

# CHEESE RICE

*30 minutes cooking time*

*Ingredients for 6 servings*

1¼ cups long-grain rice
1½ tablespoons butter
1½ cups grated cheese

3 cups chicken stock
pinch powdered saffron

1   Combine rice with chicken stock and pour into pan.
2   Add butter and cook, covered, over very low heat for 20 minutes.
3   Mix saffron with ⅓ cup hot water and add to rice.
4   Cook for 10 minutes and when cooked fold in grated cheese.

# COCONUT RICE

*20 minutes cooking time*

*Ingredients for 4 servings*

1 small coconut
500 g (1 lb) rice
2 tablespoons onions, chopped

milk from coconut
125 g (4 oz) ghee
1 teaspoon salt

1   Fry onions in ghee and add washed, drained rice and coconut milk mixed with water to make 5 cups.
2   Cook slowly over gentle heat.
3   Grate 3 tablespoons coconut and add to mixture, remove from heat, let liquid absorb and serve.

# FRIED CELERY

*8 minutes cooking time*

*Ingredients for 6 servings*

6 celery stalks
2 slices fresh ginger, crushed
½ teaspoon salt
½ teaspoon monosodium glutamate
  (optional)
1 teaspoon sherry

2 cloves garlic, crushed
2 tablespoons peanut oil
½ teaspoon sugar
½ teaspoon pepper
1¼ cups hot chicken stock

1  Cut celery stalks diagonally into 2.5 centimetre (1 in) strips.
2  Heat oil and cook garlic and ginger, discard them.
3  Add celery, seasonings, sherry and stock to pan.
4  Cook for 6 minutes.
5  Turn into heated dish and serve.

# CALCUTTA PILAU

*1½ hours cooking time*

*Ingredients for 3-4 servings*

250 g (8 oz) long-grain rice
1 teaspoon caraway seeds
2 cups hot water
2 tablespoons butter
2 pieces cinnamon

1 teaspoon salt
½ teaspoon turmeric
250 g (8 oz) shelled peas
8 cloves

1  Wash and soak rice for 40 minutes in water.
2  Heat butter and place cloves and cinnamon, turmeric and caraway seeds
   in it.
3  Fry for one minute over low heat.
4  Add rice, salt and peas.
5  Fry for 5 minutes and stir continually.
6  Add hot water and mix well, bring to boil.
7  Lower heat and cook for 30 minutes.
8  Serve.

# CORN AND PEPPER

*Ingredients for 4 servings*

*25 minutes cooking time*

1 green pepper, chopped
⅛ teaspoon pepper
¼ cup evaporated milk
1½ cups tinned sweet corn, drained

1½ tablespoons butter
½ teaspoon salt
1 egg, well beaten
⅔ cup breadcrumbs

1   Preheat oven to 180°C (350°F).
2   Rub casserole dish with butter.
3   Fry pepper in butter and add corn slowly. Mix well and cook for 4 minutes.
4   Soak breadcrumbs in egg mixed with milk and season with salt and pepper.
5   Combine with corn mixture and bake for 20 minutes.

# ASPARAGUS IN WINE

*Ingredients for 4 servings*

*30 minutes cooking time*

2 eggs, well beaten
1 tin drained, cut asparagus
½ teaspoon salt
¾ cup breadcrumbs
1 cup cubed cheese

2 tablespoons melted butter
1 cup milk
¼ teaspoon pepper
1 pimento, cut into small pieces

1   To beaten eggs add salt, pepper, breadcrumbs, cheese and milk.
2   Stir and add asparagus. Stir once more and pour into greased casserole dish.
3   Top with melted butter and cook in moderate oven for 30 minutes.

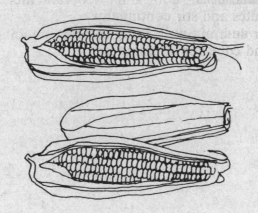

# FRIED ZUCCHINI

*8 minutes cooking time*

*Ingredients for 4 servings*

3 small zucchini
3 thin slices fresh ginger, crushed
1 teaspoon salt
1 teaspoon sugar
1 teaspoon sherry
2 garlic cloves, crushed

2 tablespoons peanut oil
1 teaspoon monosodium glutamate
 (optional)
½ teaspoon pepper
1¼ cups hot chicken stock

1  Cut zucchini into thin slices diagonally.
2  Fry garlic and ginger in oil and then discard.
3  Add slices of zucchini and toss for 1 minute.
4  Sprinkle with seasonings and sherry.
5  Toss for 1 minute.
6  Add the hot stock and cook for 5 minutes.

# CARROT CUSTARD

*10 minutes cooking time*

*Ingredients for 4 servings*

⅛ teaspoon ground mace
2 tablespoons butter
1 tablespoon flour
1½ cups mashed cooked carrots

½ teaspoon salt
⅔ cup evaporated milk
2 eggs, beaten
¼ onion, chopped finely

1  Preheat oven to 180°C (350°F).
2  Rub casserole dish with butter and fill shallow baking pan with hot water.
3  Melt butter and sauté onions.
4  Add flour to onions and blend, add milk and stir.
5  Simmer for 5 minutes and cool; add carrots and mix, pour in beaten eggs and mace.
6  Place in casserole and bake for 25 minutes standing in baking pan of water in oven.

# SCALLOPED POTATOES

*45 minutes cooking time*

*Ingredients for 6 servings*

625 g (1¼ lb) raw potatoes,
  peeled and thinly sliced
2½ cups milk
1 teaspoon salt

3 tablespoons flour
¼ teaspoon pepper
3 tablespoons butter

1  Preheat oven to 180°C (350°F) and rub casserole dish with butter.
2  Arrange half potato slices in soufflé dish and sprinkle with flour. Dot with half of the butter and season with salt and pepper.
3  Add remaining potatoes and pour over milk.
4  Add remaining seasonings and butter.
5  Cover dish.
6  Bake for 30 minutes and uncover, bake for 15 minutes longer.
7  Serve immediately.

# RATATOUILLE

*1½ hours cooking time*

*Ingredients for 6 servings*

1 onion, sliced
2 tablespoons parsley, chopped
½ teaspoon basil
2 tomatoes, cut into chunks
1 clove garlic, crushed
3 zucchini, sliced thickly

2 sliced tomatoes
2 tablespoons olive oil
1 teaspoon salt
1 green pepper, cut into chunks
1 small egg plant, cut into cubes

1  In casserole dish place onion, garlic, eggplant, zucchini and tomatoes. Add pepper and season with salt and basil.
2  Spread olive oil over and cover. Bake for 1½ hours in moderate oven.
3  Uncover during last 30 minutes then remove from oven. Garnish with tomato slices and parsley.

# ORANGE RICE

*45 minutes cooking time*

*Ingredients for 6 servings*

125 g (4 oz) butter
¼ teaspoon dried thyme
2 onions, chopped
½ teaspoon powdered saffron

5 cups orange juice
2 teaspoons salt
2½ cups long-grain rice

1 Melt butter in saucepan and fry onion until soft.
2 Add rice and fry for 4 minutes.
3 Add saffron and heated orange juice.
4 Add thyme and salt and stir.
5 Bring to the boil and reduce heat.
6 Cover and simmer for 30 minutes on low heat.

# SPINACH SOUFFLÉ

*30 minutes cooking time*

*Ingredients for 4 servings*

2 cups boiled spinach
½ teaspoon pepper
1 beaten egg
1 tablespoon butter

½ teaspoon salt
⅓ cup milk
1 tablespoon flour
½ teaspoon nutmeg

1 Chop spinach finely and rub through coarse sieve.
2 Reheat and add butter mixed with flour and seasonings.
3 Add milk, egg and beat for 3 minutes.
4 Place in individual baking dishes and bake for 15-20 minutes in moderate oven 180°C (350°F).

# CHEESE-FILLED TOMATOES

*20 minutes cooking time*

*Ingredients for 4 servings*

8 large tomatoes
2 onions, chopped
½ teaspoon pepper
½ cup sour cream

250 g (8 oz) grated cheese
½ teaspoon salt
fresh herbs, chopped

1  Cut tomatoes in half and remove seeds and cores.
2  Mix cheese, onion, salt, pepper and herbs. Fill tomatoes with this mixture and pour sour cream on top.
3  Bake in hot oven 200°C (400°F).

# RICE AND CARROTS

*45 minutes cooking time*

*Ingredients for 6 servings*

¾ cup long-grain rice
½ teaspoon powdered ginger
2 tablespoons chopped parsley
2 cups chicken stock

1½ cups chopped carrots
½ teaspoon grated orange rind
6 tablespoons chopped onion
3 tablespoons butter

1  Put rice in shallow pan and brown in hot oven 200°C (400°F) for 8 minutes.
2  Place rice and butter in casserole and mix with carrots, ginger, orange rind, parsley and onion.
3  Pour stock over rice mixture.
4  Cover and bake in hot oven for 30 minutes.

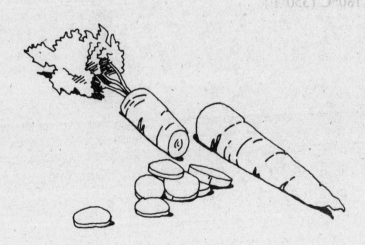

# RICH MACARONI AND CHEESE BAKE

*25 minutes cooking time*

*Ingredients for 6 servings*

250 g (8 oz) cooked macaroni
2 tablespoons chopped parsley
185 g (6 oz) fresh cream
½ teaspoon salt
185 g (6 oz) cheddar cheese, grated

185 g (6 oz) cottage cheese
¼ teaspoon paprika
2 eggs, beaten
½ teaspoon pepper

1  Combine cream, egg, salt, pepper and cottage cheese. Mix well and add grated cheddar cheese.
2  Stir cheese mixture into cooked macaroni and pour into casserole.
3  Season with paprika and bake for 25 minutes in hot oven. Garnish with chopped parsley.

# Desserts

## BAKED ALASKA

*5 minutes cooking time*

*Ingredients for 4 servings*

**4 tablespoons castor sugar**
**1 small pineapple**
**¼ cup sweet sherry**

**3 egg whites**
**½ Swiss roll**
**small block vanilla ice cream**

1 Slice Swiss roll into four pieces.
2 Peel pineapple, core and slice.
3 Place Swiss roll rounds onto ovenproof dish.
4 Moisten sponge with sherry and add a ring of pineapple to top.
5 Beat egg whites until stiff.
6 When egg whites are stiffly beaten, add castor sugar and beat once more.
7 Place firm ice cream on top of pineapple rings and cover with egg white mixture — make sure that no part of ice cream or sponge is uncovered.
8 Dot with sugar and bake in very hot oven for 5 minutes, until brown.

# ORANGE BANANAS

*20 minutes cooking time*

*Ingredients for 4 servings*

6 bananas
¼ cup rum
⅓ cup brown sugar

¾ cup orange juice
3 tablespoons orange rind, grated
2 tablespoons butter

1  Peel and cut bananas lengthwise and arrange in buttered baking dish.
2  Pour over mixture of juice and rum.
3  Add orange rind and sugar, and dot with butter.
4  Bake for 20 minutes in moderate oven.

# APRICOT WHIP

*10 minutes cooking time*

*Ingredients for 4 servings*

750 g (1½ lb) tinned apricot halves
15 marshmallows

¾ cup cream

1  Drain apricots and reserve syrup.
2  Mash apricots and combine with marshmallows and ¼ cup syrup.
3  Cook and stir for 10 minutes.
4  Chill and fold in whipped cream.

# NO BAKE PIE

*No cooking time*

*Ingredients for 8 servings*

2 cups biscuit crumbs
1½ teaspoons grated lemon rind
2½ cups sweetened condensed milk
1 cup lemon juice

2 eggs
1 cup melted butter
½ cup sugar

1  Combine crumbs, sugar and melted butter. Press into greased pie plate and chill.
2  Combine eggs, lemon rind, lemon juice and condensed milk. Beat until mixture thickens and pour into chilled pie crusts.
3  Serve well chilled.

# BANANA SUPREME

*No cooking time*

*Ingredients for 6 servings*

6 ripe bananas
4 tablespoons lemon juice
1¼ cups whipped cream

90 g (3 oz) chocolate, grated
¼ teaspoon vanilla essence
3 tablespoons castor sugar

1  Peel bananas.
2  Mash and beat in sugar.
3  When sugar dissolves, fold in cream and vanilla essence.
4  Add lemon juice and place in individual serving dishes.
5  Decorate with grated chocolate and serve chilled.

# APPLE CRUNCH

*30 minutes cooking time*

*Ingredients for 6 servings*

½ cup plain flour
1 teaspoon baking powder
½ teaspoon vanilla essence
¼ teaspoon salt

¾ cup sugar
1 egg, beaten
1 cup chopped apples
½ cup chopped walnuts

1  Mix sugar and vanilla essence with egg.
2  Sift salt, flour and baking powder, add to egg mixture and stir well.
3  Mix in nuts and apples and bake in moderate oven for 30 minutes.

# RED GLAZED PEARS

*10 minutes cooking time*

*Ingredients for 4 servings*

4 pears
4 teaspoons redcurrant jelly

⅛ cup melted butter

1  Prepare pears by peeling, cutting in halves and removing cores.
2  Brush halves with melted butter and grill for 5 minutes.
3  Turn pears over and brush with butter. Grill for further 5 minutes and fill hollow of each pear with currant jelly.
4  Serve warm.

# RICH STRAWBERRIES

*No cooking time*

*Ingredients for 4 servings*

**315 g (10 oz) cream cheese**
⅓ cup sour cream
¾ cup icing sugar

⅓ cup cream
**2 punnets strawberries**

1   Crush cheese with fork until completely smooth and stir in cream, sour cream and icing sugar.
2   Hull strawberries and serve with cream mixture.

# SUNSHINE PIE

*25 minutes cooking time*

*Ingredients for 4 servings*

**185 g (6 oz) cream cheese**
**375 g (12 oz) tinned fruit**
¾ cup sour cream
¼ teaspoon vanilla essence

**4 tablespoons orange marmalade**
**20 cm (8 in) biscuit-crumb pie crust**
¼ cup sugar

1   Mix cream cheese with sour cream, sugar and vanilla.
2   Blend thoroughly and pour into pie crust.
3   Bake for 25 minutes in moderate oven and chill.
4   Drain fruit and arrange on pie.
5   Stir marmalade and spoon over fruits.

# GRILLED BANANAS

*8-10 minutes cooking time*

*Ingredients for 4 servings*

**4 bananas**
**1 lemon, quartered**

**2 tablespoons butter**

1   Place unpeeled bananas on top of barbecue.
2   Cook, turning once in a while, until skin turns black.
3   Serve with butter and lemon wedges.

# PINEAPPLE HONEY

*No cooking time*

*Ingredients for 8 servings*

**1 large pineapple**　　　　　**3 teaspoons honey**
**1½ cups yoghurt**　　　　　　**8 mint leaves**

1　Peel pineapple and cut into chunks and chill.
2　Mix honey and yoghurt. Blend well and stir in pineapple chunks.
3　Garnish with mint leaves and serve.

# TROPICAL CREAM

*10 minutes cooking time*

*Ingredients for 6 servings*

**185 g (6 oz) dried apricots**　　　**3 passionfruit**
**⅓ cup sugar**　　　　　　　　　**2½ cups cream**

1　Quarter apricots and place in saucepan with 2 cups water and ¼ cup sugar.
2　Simmer for 10 minutes and strain.
3　Chill and reserve liquid.
4　Beat cream with remaining sugar until stiff and fold in apricots.
5　Add passionfruit pulp and reserved liquid.
6　Serve chilled.

# STRAWBERRY CHARGERS

*No cooking time*

*Ingredients for 4 servings*

**1½ punnets strawberries**　　　**⅓ cup brown sugar**
**¾ cup sour cream**　　　　　　**2 tablespoons chopped mint**

1　Wash and hull strawberries and place in a bowl.
2　Dot with half the brown sugar and stir in sour cream and mint.
3　Use half the remaining sugar to sprinkle again and chill for 1½ hours.
4　Spoon into serving dishes and sprinkle with remaining sugar.

# PORT PRUNES

*No cooking time*

*Ingredients for 4 servings*

750 g (1½ lb) stewed prunes
1 tablespoon lemon rind, grated
¾ cup port wine

⅓ cup sugar
⅛ teaspoon salt
½ cup whipped cream

1  Marinate prunes in port wine for 25-30 minutes in refrigerator.
2  Add sugar, lemon rind and salt.
3  Serve with whipped cream.

# QUICK COCONUT CAKE

*30 minutes cooking time*

*Ingredients for 8 servings*

2 eggs
¼ teaspoon vanilla essence
½ cup milk
1 teaspoon baking powder

3 tablespoons butter
½ teaspoon salt
1 cup plain flour
1 cup sugar

## COCONUT TOPPING

⅓ cup butter
1½ tablespoons cream

¾ cup brown sugar
2 cups shredded coconut

1  Beat eggs and gradually add sugar; continue beating until mixture is thick and light.
2  Sift flour and add baking powder.
3  Add salt and blend flour mixture with eggs.
4  Scald milk and add butter, mix and add a little vanilla essence.
5  Blend milk mixture into flour and pour into greased tin.
6  Bake for 25 minutes in moderate oven and spread with topping.
7  Place under griller for 2 minutes and cut into squares and serve.

## TOPPING

1  Melt butter in frying pan and remove from heat.
2  Mix in brown sugar, cream and coconut. Blend thoroughly and spread onto cake.

# SWEET SPICED PEACHES

*7-10 minutes cooking time*

*Ingredients for 4 servings*

**750 g (1½ lb) canned peach halves**
**1½ tablespoons sugar**
**juice of ½ orange**

**⅓ cup sauterne wine**
**10 cm (4 in) cinnamon stick**

1 Break cinnamon stick in half and drain peaches.
2 Combine half the peach syrup with sugar and cinnamon.
3 Place in saucepan and bring to boil. Remove from heat and blend in orange juice.
4 Add wine to taste and pour over peaches.
5 Chill overnight.

# *Index*

# Y

Yukon potatoes 115

# Z

Zucchini
   cheese 14
   fried 122

# LOW CALORIE HEALTH

# Contents

# Contents

# Introduction

One of the most important changes in our eating habits has come about in the last few years with an increased interest in "health foods" or "natural foods". Health food stores are growing steadily in number and their stock is improving constantly.

For a long time, health food has conjured up images of ascetic meals of nuts and dried fruits, but this need not be the case. It is possible to get all nutritional requirements from vegetables, but it is most important to pay close attention to the level of protein in the vegetarian diet — foods such as lentils and soy beans must be emphasized.

However, it is not necessary to delete meat from the diet entirely. What is important is that food should be properly grown and processed. Modern science has discovered many ways to increase the output of many products, but the quality of foods grown with chemical fertilizers, protected with chemical insecticides and sprayed with chemical additives must be considered in addition to the increased quantity.

Modern processing methods remove great deal of the natural nutrients and vitamins which are present in natural foods, and though some firms advertise special nutrients, these cannot compensate for the value of the food when this has been lost through processing.

Many foods are now available which are grown organically, without the usual chemicals of any place. These must be better for you and if you are serious about it, you can also buy bread, fish, chicken and eggs which have been raised on natural feed. You are only getting the wholesale benefits of, not the disadvantages, something along the way.

Designed as a daily reference guide for the user of health food and the owner of a small health food store, this book was especially intended to explain the workings of the book. Care have been designed to give simple variations on basic appealing dishes which will appeal to your family and friends.

# Introduction

One of the most important changes in our eating habits has come about in the last few years with an increasing interest in 'health foods' or 'natural foods'. Health food stores are growing rapidly in number and their stocks improve constantly.

For a long time, health food has conjured up images of ascetic meals of nuts and dried fruits, but this need not be the case. It is possible to get all nutritional requirements from vegetables, but it is most important to pay close attention to the level of protein in the vegetarian diet — foods such as lentils and soy beans must be emphasized.

However, it is not necessary to delete meat from the diet entirely. What is important is that food should be naturally grown and processed. Modern science has discovered many ways to increase the output of many products, but the **quality** of foods grown with chemical fertilizers, protected with chemical insecticides and preserved with chemical additives must be considered in addition to the increased quantity.

Modern processing methods remove a great deal of the natural nutrients and vitamins which are present in natural foods, and though some brands advertise special 'additions', these are no substitute for the value of the food which has been lost through processing.

Many foods are now available which are grown 'organically' without the use of chemicals at any stage. These must be better for you and if you are serious about it, you can also find meat, fish, chicken and eggs which have been raised on natural foods — so you are only getting the wholesome food value, not the chemicals encountered along the way.

One important thing to remember is that a meal of health food need not consist of a small pile of beans next to a few raw vegetables, followed by plain dried fruit. The recipes in this book have been designed to give simple variations of basic, appetizing dishes which will appeal to your family and friends.

# Drinks

## WATERMELON

*Ingredients for 2 servings*

**6 cups watermelon**                    **honey to taste**

1   Combine ingredients and blend.
2   Serve chilled.


## ASPARAGUS

*Ingredients for 2 servings*

**juice of 3 lemons**                    **1 cup pineapple juice**
**2 cups asparagus, mashed**             **1 teaspoon onion juice**

1   Combine all ingredients and blend.
2   Serve chilled.

# CARROT

*Ingredients for 2 servings*

**2 cups pineapple juice**
**½ teaspoon salt**

**2 cups grated carrots**

1 Combine all ingredients and blend.
2 Serve chilled.

# RADISH

*Ingredients for 2 servings*

**2 cups pineapple juice**
**1 teaspoon chopped chives**

**2 cups radishes, chopped**

1 Combine all ingredients and blend.
2 Serve chilled.

# CELERY

*Ingredients for 2 servings*

**2 cups pineapple juice**
**1 teaspoon onion juice**

**4 cups celery, diced**

1 Blend all ingredients.
2 Serve chilled.

# RHUBARB

*Ingredients for 2 servings*

**2 cups pineapple juice**
**creamed honey to taste**

**2 cups rhubarb, cooked**

1 Combine all ingredients and blend.
2 Serve chilled.

# PARSNIP

*Ingredients for 2 servings*

**2 cups grated parsnips**　　　　**2 cups pineapple juice**
**1 teaspoon chopped chives**

1　Combine all ingredients and blend.
2　Chill.

# CABBAGE

*Ingredients for 2 servings*

**2 cups pineapple juice**　　　　**chopped cabbage**
**½ teaspoon salt**

1　Combine all ingredients and blend.
2　Serve chilled.

# CHERRY COCKTAIL

*Ingredients for 2 servings*

**1 cup pineapple juice**　　　　**2 cups pitted cherries**
**¼ teaspoon salt**

1　Combine all ingredients and blend.
2　Strain and serve chilled.

# MIXED

*Ingredients*

**1 cup tomato juice**　　　　**1 tablespoon chopped parsley**
**1 cup diced carrots**

1　Combine all ingredients and blend.
2　Serve chilled.

# SPINACH COCKTAIL

*Ingredients for 2 servings*

2 cups pineapple juice
juice of 2 lemons

2 cups spinach, cooked
honey to taste

1 Combine all ingredients and blend.
2 Serve chilled.


# TOMATO

*Ingredients for 2 servings*

2 cups diced tomatoes
½ teaspoon vinegar

½ teaspoon salt
1 teaspoon lemon juice

1 Combine all ingredients and blend.
2 Chill.


# CARROT MILK

*Ingredients for 2 servings*

1 cup nut milk
½ teaspoon nutmeg

2 cups diced, cooked carrots
½ teaspoon white pepper

1 Blend nut milk, carrots and pepper.
2 Sprinkle with nutmeg.
3 Serve chilled.


# RHUBARB AND CARROT COCKTAIL

*Ingredients for 2 servings*

2 cups water
½ cup carrot, grated

3 cups diced rhubarb
½ teaspoon salt

1 Combine all ingredients and blend thoroughly.
2 Serve chilled.

# BLACKBERRY

*Ingredients for 2 servings*

**1 cup pineapple juice**
**2 egg yolks**

**1 cup blackberry juice**
**½ teaspoon salt**

1  Combine all ingredients and blend.
2  Strain and serve chilled.

# LIQUID AVOCADO

*Ingredients for 2 servings*

**2 cups water**
**2 tablespoons honey**

**2 avocados, mashed**
**1 teaspoon nutmeg**

1  Combine all ingredients and blend.
2  Use blender if possible, if not, mix thoroughly.
3  Serve chilled.

# ROCK MELON

*Ingredients for 2 servings*

**1 whole rock melon**
**½ teaspoon salt**

**1 cup pineapple juice**

1  Peel and seed rock melon and combine inside with other ingredients.
2  Blend thoroughly.
3  Serve chilled.

# GRAPE

*Ingredients for 2 servings*

**250 g (8 oz) white grapes**

water

1  Combine grapes and water and blend.
2  Strain seeds and serve chilled.

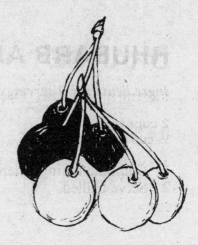

# GRAPEFRUIT

*Ingredients for 2 servings*

**2 whole grapefruit**
**¼ teaspoon honey**

**2 cups water**

1   Peel and seed grapefruit and combine with other ingredients.
2   Blend.
3   Serve chilled.

# PEACH

*Ingredients for 2 servings*

**1 cup milk**
**1 teaspoon honey**

**2 cups peeled fresh peaches**
**¼ teaspoon cinnamon**

1   Combine all ingredients and blend.
2   Serve chilled.

# PEAR

*Ingredients for 2 servings*

**1 cup pineapple juice**
**2 cups peeled fresh pears**

**¼ teaspoon cinnamon**

1   Combine all ingredients and blend.
2   Serve chilled.

# ORANGE

*Ingredients for 2 servings*

**4 oranges, peeled**

**1 teaspoon honey**

1   Combine ingredients and blend.
2   Serve chilled.

# PINEAPPLE

*Ingredients for 2 servings*

1 cup milk
chopped mint

2 cups fresh pineapple
¼ teaspoon nutmeg

1   Combine all ingredients and blend.
2   Serve chilled.

# STRAWBERRY

*Ingredients for 2 servings*

2 cups water
cinnamon to taste

3 cups strawberries

1   Combine ingredients and blend.
2   Serve chilled.

# *Soups*

# CAULIFLOWER SOUP

*30 minutes cooking time*

*Ingredients for 4-5 servings*

| | |
|---|---|
| 1 cauliflower | 2 leeks, chopped |
| 125 g (4 oz) diced ham | 6 cups stock |
| 30 g (1 oz) wholemeal flour | 60 g (2 oz) butter |
| 1¼ cups milk | 3 egg yolks |
| ½ cup cream | ½ teaspoon salt |
| ¾ teaspoon white pepper | 2 grated carrots |

1  Melt the butter and combine with flour.
2  Mix thoroughly and cook for 3 minutes.
3  Add stock and bring to the boil, stirring constantly.
4  Add the chopped cauliflower and carrots.
5  Stir.
6  Add chopped leeks and ham and simmer for 10 minutes.
7  Season with salt and pepper.
8  Add milk, egg yolks and cream.
9  Simmer for 5 minutes and serve.

# PLEASANT SOUP

*Ingredients for 4-5 servings*

*20 minutes cooking time*

**5 cups stock**
**2 grated carrots**
**2 grated parsnips**
**½ teaspoon salt**
**¼ teaspoon white pepper**

**1 cup barley**
**2 grated onions**
**1 tablespoon chopped parsley**
**2 chopped green peppers**

1   Wash the barley and add to stock.
2   Cook for 10 minutes.
3   Season with salt and pepper.
4   Add carrots, onions, parsnips and peppers.
5   Cook for further 10 minutes.
6   Dot with chopped parsley.

# VEGETABLE SOUP

*Ingredients for 4-5 servings*

*10 minutes cooking time*

**5 cups stock**
**2 grated onions**
**2 finely chopped green peppers**
**½ teaspoon salt**

**¼ teaspoon white pepper**
**2 grated carrots**
**2 sticks celery, chopped**
**1 tablespoon chopped parsley**

1   Place prepared vegetables in boiling stock and cook for 5 minutes.
2   Season with salt and pepper.
3   Cook for further 5 minutes.

# BEAN SPROUT SOUP

*Ingredients for 4-5 servings*

*20 minutes cooking time*

**5 cups stock**
**3 cups bean sprouts**

**4 tablespoons chopped parsley**
**4 eggs, beaten**

1   Heat stock and add bean sprouts.
2   Simmer for 10 minutes and remove from heat.
3   Stir in eggs and garnish with chopped parsley.

# TRIPE SOUP

*30 minutes cooking time*

*Ingredients for 4-5 servings*

2 onions, chopped
2 potatoes, diced
5 cups beef stock
1 tablespoon chopped parsley

3 tablespoons yeast
500 g (1 lb) tripe, cooked and diced
1 teaspoon salt

1  Combine vegetables, season with salt and add stock and yeast.
2  Heat gently and simmer.
3  Add tripe when vegetables are cooked and re-heat.
4  Garnish with chopped parsley.

# CREAMED SOY BEAN SOUP

*20 minutes cooking time*

*Ingredients for 4-5 servings*

4 cups soy beans, puréed
2 cups stock
1 cup cream

½ cup milk
3 tablespoons brewer's yeast

1  Blend beans and milk together.
2  Heat for 5 minutes and remove from heat.
3  Add stock, brewer's yeast and cream and stir thoroughly.
4  Reheat and serve.

# MIXED HERB SOUP

*30 minutes cooking time*

*Ingredients for 4-5 servings*

5 cups stock
3 tablespoons brewer's yeast
1 cup chopped parsley
2 egg yolks

½ teaspoon chervil
1 bunch sorrel
1 cup chopped chives
1 small carton plain yoghurt

1  Blend all ingredients until smooth, reserving a little yoghurt.
2  Chill.
3  Add a teaspoon of yoghurt to each bowl before serving.

# GRUYÈRE SOUP

*20 minutes cooking time*

*Ingredients for 4-5 servings*

5 cups stock
1 tablespoon butter
2 cups grated gruyère cheese
¼ teaspoon white pepper

1 tablespoon wholemeal flour
3 chopped onions
½ teaspoon salt

1 Brown the onions in butter and add flour.
2 Add the stock and cook for 5 minutes.
3 Simmer for 10 minutes, then add cheese.
4 Season with salt and pepper and simmer 5 minutes longer.
5 Serve hot.

# TURKISH SOUP

*30 minutes cooking time*

*Ingredients for 4-5 servings*

1.5 kg (3 lb) tripe, cooked and diced
5 cups stock
1 clove garlic
¼ teaspoon white pepper
juice of 1 orange

3 tablespoons brewer's yeast
2 eggs
1 teaspoon salt
juice of 1 lemon

1 Blend tripe and stock together.
2 Add garlic, salt, brewer's yeast and pepper.
3 Heat gently.
4 Remove from heat and beat eggs with lemon and orange juice.
5 Add egg mixture to soup and reheat.

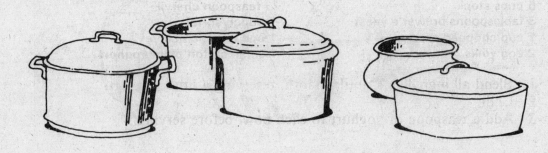

# LENTIL AND CELERY SOUP

*45 minutes cooking time*

*Ingredients for 4-5 servings*

2 cups lentils, washed
5 cups stock
3 cups chopped celery
1 teaspoon salt
3 tablespoons brewer's yeast

1 tablespoon celery seeds
3 onions, chopped
2 tablespoons oil
½ teaspoon pepper

1 Place lentils, stock, brewer's yeast and pepper in a large pot.
2 Simmer for 40 minutes, and add onions and celery.
3 Add oil and simmer for 5 minutes.
4 Heat through and serve.

# PUMPKIN SOUP

*20 minutes cooking time*

*Ingredients for 4-5 servings*

1.5 kg (3 lb) butternut pumpkin
7½ cups chicken stock
¼ teaspoon white pepper
2 tablespoons butter

3 onions, chopped
½ teaspoon salt
2 teaspoons grated orange rind

1 Brown the onions in butter and add cooked pumpkin.
2 Stir constantly and add stock.
3 Cook for 5 minutes.
4 Season with salt and pepper.
5 Add orange rind and heat for further 10-15 minutes.

# KIDNEY SOUP

*Ingredients for 4-5 servings*

*30 minutes cooking time*

3 tablespoons oil
3 calves' kidneys
3 egg yolks
3 tablespoons milk

1 bay leaf
3 tablespoons whole wheat flour
3 tablespoons brewer's yeast
2 tablespoons chopped parsley

1  Heat oil and sauté kidneys.
2  Add bay leaf, stock, flour and brewer's yeast.
3  Bring to the boil and simmer.
4  Add beaten egg yolks and milk to mixture.
5  Reheat and serve garnished with chopped parsley.

# BAVARIAN CHERRY SOUP

*Ingredients for 4 servings*

*1 hour cooking time*

500 g (1 lb) cherries
¼ teaspoon white pepper
red food colouring
½ cup port
1 bay leaf
10 cm (4 in) piece of celery
1 onion, sliced

½ teaspoon salt
1 tablespoon arrowroot
30 g (1 oz) sugar
2½ cups stock
4 cloves
1 tomato

1  Remove stones from cherries and crack a few stones and tie in a muslin bag.
2  Slice vegetables and put in pan with cherries.
3  Mix gently.
4  Add bay leaf, sugar, crushed stones and stock.
5  Stir and bring to boil. Cook for 50 minutes and strain.
6  Combine arrowroot and port.
7  Mix into cherry mixture.
8  Stir and bring to boil once more, add food colouring and garnish with a few cherries.

# LAURIE'S ONION SOUP

*35 minutes cooking time*

*Ingredients for 6 servings*

**8 cups water**
**630 g (20 oz) sliced onion**
**1 teaspoon garlic powder**

**6 beef stock cubes**
**6 slices bread**
**½ teaspoon salt**

1 Combine water, stock cubes and onions.
2 Over gentle heat, cook for 20 minutes, stirring.
3 Put bread in baking dish and add ¼ cup stock.
4 Season bread with salt and garlic powder.
5 Turn and repeat.
6 Bake for 10 minutes in hot oven and cut each bread slice into four and serve with soup.

# WATERCRESS SOUP

*20 minutes cooking time*

*Ingredients for 8 servings*

**1 teaspoon salt**
**3 bunches watercress**
**1½ tablespoons flour**
**5 cups chicken stock**
**bouquet garni**

**½ teaspoon pepper**
**2 egg yolks**
**60 g (2 oz) butter**
**1¼ cups milk**

1 Wash watercress and reserve a few leaves for garnishing.
2 Dip those for garnish into boiling water and drain. Set aside.
3 Chop remaining leaves and cook for 5 minutes in butter.
4 Pour in stock and season with salt and pepper. Mix and add bouquet garni.
5 Cook for 5 minutes and sieve.
6 Blend flour and a little milk, stir into soup and simmer for 5 minutes.
7 Cool and add beaten egg yolk, reheat gently but do not boil. Garnish with watercress leaves.

# VEGETABLE SOUP

*30 minutes cooking time*

*Ingredients for 8 servings*

8 carrots, diced
7 tablespoons chopped parsley
1 teaspoon salt
5 litres (8 pints) boiling water

250 g (8 oz) spinach, chopped
¼ teaspoon pepper
2 tablespoons minced onion
1 cup celery, diced

1 Combine celery and onion, and add to boiling water.
2 Add carrots and cook for 10 minutes, covered.
3 Add remaining vegetables and season with salt and pepper.
4 Cook for 20 minutes and serve.

# BUTTERMILK SOUP

*Ingredients for 8 servings*

15 cups chilled buttermilk
2 tablespoons chopped chives
1 cucumber, diced

3 tablespoons chopped parsley
¼ teaspoon paprika
¼ teaspoon chopped fresh dill

1 Mix cucumber and chives together.
2 Combine parsley, dill and buttermilk and mix with cucumber mixture.
3 Chill and dot with paprika.

# CELERY SOUP

*35 minutes cooking time*

*Ingredients for 6 servings*

750 g (1½ lb) tomatoes
5 cups chicken stock
1 teaspoon salt
1 teaspoon brown sugar

90 g (3 oz) butter
30 g (1 oz) cornflour
½ teaspoon pepper
1 head of celery

1 Dice tomatoes and celery, and simmer in stock for 20 minutes.
2 Sieve and return to pan with butter and cornflour which has been blended in water.
3 Bring to boil, add sugar, and cook. Stir until thickened.

# TOMATO SOUP

*25 minutes cooking time*

*Ingredients for 4 servings*

2½ cups stock
1 onion
1 teaspoon tomato purée
1 tablespoon cream
¼ teaspoon pepper

250 g (8 oz) tomatoes
1 garlic clove
1 bay leaf
2 tablespoons chives, chopped

1  Chop tomatoes and dice onion.
2  Cut garlic thinly and bring stock to boil.
3  Add vegetables and bay leaf.
4  Simmer, covered.
5  When onion is tender, sieve and return to pan.
6  Simmer for 1 minute and season with salt, pepper and tomato purée.
7  Stir in cream gently and garnish with chopped chives.

# SOUP À ROUEN

*30 minutes cooking time*

*Ingredients for 4 servings*

4 cups water
3 beef stock cubes
2 tomatoes, peeled, deseeded and
  chopped
pinch saffron
2 garlic cloves
1½ cups tomato juice

2 chicken stock cubes
90 g (3 oz) diced carrots
1 tablespoon chopped celery leaves
1 cup frozen green beans
1 cup diced zucchini
1½ tablespoons cooking oil
2 tablespoons basil leaves

1  Boil tomato juice in pan until reduced by half.
2  Combine water, seasonings, onions and carrots in saucepan and cook for 10 minutes.
3  Add tomatoes, celery, beans, zucchini and a pinch of saffron.
4  Simmer for 15 minutes and stir occasionally.
5  Combine garlic, basil and tomato juice in blender and add oil.
6  Blend at medium speed for 1-2 minutes and just before serving pour tomato mixture into soup.

# BORTSCH

*Ingredients for 4 servings*

*5 minutes cooking time*

2½ cups beef stock
½ cup yoghurt
½ teaspoon pepper
500 g (1 lb) cooked beetroot

1½ teaspoons vinegar
½ teaspoon salt
½ teaspoon sugar
1 raw beetroot

1  Peel raw beetroot, grate it and mix with vinegar.
2  Chop cooked beetroot.
3  Bring stock to boil, season with salt, pepper and a pinch of sugar.
4  Drop in cooked beetroot strips and boil for 2 minutes.
5  Squeeze raw beetroot and vinegar in muslin and add juice to soup.
6  Serve topped with yoghurt.

# CUCUMBER SOUP

*Ingredients for 6 servings*

*40 minutes cooking time*

1 cucumber
¼ teaspoon pepper
1 teaspoon chopped mint
1 tablespoon butter
4 cups vegetable stock

½ teaspoon salt
green food colouring
1 tablespoon flour
2 teaspoons chopped onion
1 egg yolk

1  Peel cucumber and cut into very thin slices.
2  Reserve a few slices and place the rest in stock.
3  Combine chopped onion and seasonings.
4  Mix into stock and bring to boil.
5  Simmer for 25 minutes and strain.
6  Melt butter and stir in flour. Work in cucumber stock and stir until boiling.
7  Cook, stirring, for 5 minutes and add food colouring.
8  Stir in cucumber and mint.
9  After soup has cooled slightly, add beaten egg yolk and stir gently.
10  Serve garnished with reserved cucumber slices.

# COLD TOMATO SOUP

*20 minutes cooking time*

*Ingredients for 2 servings*

375 g (12 oz) tomatoes
1¼ cups chicken stock
½ teaspoon pepper
¼ teaspoon Worcestershire sauce
1 bay leaf

1 onion, chopped
½ teaspoon salt
½ teaspoon vinegar
¼ cup chopped celery
2 slices fresh beetroot

1 Place all ingredients together in saucepan and cook for 20 minutes.
2 Remove bay leaf and beetroot.
3 Rub ingredients through a sieve and pour into freezing tray.
4 Chill until slightly iced.
5 Garnish with lemon wedges to serve.

# MUSHROOM SOUP

*45 minutes cooking time*

*Ingredients for 8 servings*

375 g (12 oz) mushrooms
4 egg yolks
½ teaspoon grated nutmeg
2 tablespoons chopped parsley

1½ teaspoons salt
6 tablespoons cream
¼ teaspoon pepper
5 cups chicken stock

1 Prepare mushrooms and place in frying pan with melted butter.
2 Cover and cook for 10 minutes. Add stock.
3 Season with salt, pepper and nutmeg.
4 Bring to boil and then simmer for 30 minutes.
5 Sieve and blend, until smooth, with remaining ingredients.
6 Return to pan and heat. Remove pan from stove and cool.
7 Add beaten egg yolks and cream, stirring gently. Do not boil.
8 Garnish with chopped parsley and serve.

# VICHYSSOISE

*30 minutes cooking time*

*Ingredients for 4 servings*

| | |
|---|---|
| 1½ cups sliced leeks | 1 bay leaf |
| 1½ cups yoghurt | 1½ cups skimmed milk |
| ½ teaspoon celery seed | 1 teaspoon salt |
| 3 chicken stock cubes | 2½ cups water |
| ¼ teaspoon cayenne pepper | 2 tablespoons chopped chives |

1  Combine water, chicken cubes, leeks, celery seed, bay leaf and salt and pepper in saucepan.
2  Cover and simmer for 25 minutes.
3  Strain, add milk to the purée and blend.
4  Bring to boil.
5  Chill thoroughly.
6  Beat in yoghurt and sprinkle with chopped chives to serve.

# MINESTRONE

*40 minutes cooking time*

*Ingredients for 3-4 servings*

| | |
|---|---|
| ½ carrot | 4 cups stock |
| 1 teaspoon salt | ½ teaspoon pepper |
| 1 tomato, peeled | ½ onion |
| 1 stick celery | ½ small turnip |
| 1 white leek | 30 g (1 oz) peas |
| 30 g (1 oz) broad beans | 30 g (1 oz) cabbage |
| 30 g (1 oz) bacon | 1 clove garlic |
| 60 g (2 oz) grated Parmesan cheese | 2 tablespoons chopped parsley |
| 1 teaspoon chopped basil | 30 g (1 oz) green beans |

1  Trim bacon and dice, fry slowly.
2  Chop carrot, turnip and leek into small pieces and fry with bacon.
3  Add onion and crushed garlic, fry until brown and add stock and basil.
4  Cook for 20 minutes.
5  Season with salt and pepper.
6  Add remaining vegetables and cook for 15 minutes.
7  Add grated Parmesan cheese and mix through.
8  Serve garnished with chopped parsley.

# EGG AND LEMON SOUP

*15 minutes cooking time*

*Ingredients for 6 servings*

4 cups chicken stock
½ teaspoon salt
2 eggs

4 tablespoons lemon juice
¼ teaspoon pepper

1　Heat stock.
2　Beat lemon juice and egg together.
3　Fold into stock and season with salt and pepper.
4　Simmer and serve.

# SPINACH SOUP

*30 minutes cooking time*

*Ingredients for 4 servings*

250 g (8 oz) spinach
1¼ cups stock
¼ teaspoon pepper
¼ teaspoon nutmeg

2 small onions
1¼ cups milk
½ teaspoon salt

1　Wash spinach and pull off largest stalks.
2　Bring the stock to boil and add spinach and chopped onions.
3　When soft put through a sieve and return to pan.
4　Season with salt and pepper.
5　Add milk and nutmeg.

# Salads

## BEAN SPROUT SALAD

*Ingredients for 4-5 servings*

| | |
|---|---|
| 1 lettuce | ½ cup chopped green pepper |
| ½ cabbage | 4 tomatoes |
| 2 cups bean sprouts | ½ cup chopped onions |
| ½ cup chopped chives | ½ cup French dressing |

1  Shred lettuce and cabbage.
2  Add chopped pepper, onions, chives and bean sprouts.
3  Toss with dressing.
4  Top with tomato slices.

# AVOCADO AND CELERY SALAD

*Ingredients for 5-6 servings*

3 avocados                                oil and vinegar
1 cup chopped celery

1   Halve avocados, scoop out and mash insides.
2   Combine with celery and put back in shells.
3   Pour over oil and vinegar to taste.
4   Serve immediately.

# AVOCADO AND MAYONNAISE SALAD

*Ingredients for 4-5 servings*

4 mashed avocados                         1 lettuce
2 cups chopped onions                     mayonnaise
7 tomatoes, halved

1   Mash avocados and combine with chopped onions.
2   Place on a bed of lettuce leaves with tomato halves.
3   Add mayonnaise.

# MUSHROOM AND WATERCRESS SALAD

*Ingredients for 4-5 servings*

1 lettuce                                 1 cup grated cheddar cheese
½ cabbage                                 1 bunch watercress
20 small mushrooms

1   Shred lettuce and cabbage.
2   Sauté mushrooms in butter and slice.
3   Combine mushrooms with cheese and torn watercress and serve on a bed
    of lettuce and cabbage.

# AVOCADO AND CUCUMBER SALAD

*Ingredients for 5-6 servings*

**3 avocados** **oil and vinegar**
**½ cucumber, seeded and chopped**

1 Halve avocados, scoop out and mash insides.
2 Combine with cucumber and put back in shells.
3 Pour over oil and vinegar.
4 Serve immediately.

# AVOCADO AND CHIVES SALAD

*Ingredients for 5-6 servings*

**3 avocados** **oil and vinegar**
**1 cup chopped chives**

1 Halve avocados, scoop out and mash insides.
2 Combine with chopped chives and replace in shells.
3 Pour over oil and vinegar.
4 Serve immediately.

# AVOCADO AND TOMATO SALAD

*Ingredients for 5-6 servings*

**3 avocados** **oil and vinegar**
**2 peeled and diced tomatoes**

1 Halve avocados, scoop out and mash insides.
2 Combine with tomato and put back in shells.
3 Pour over oil and vinegar.
4 Serve immediately.

# AVOCADO AND YOGHURT SALAD

*Ingredients for 5-6 servings*

3 avocados
oil and vinegar

1 cup chopped chives
½ cup yoghurt

1  Halve avocados, scoop out and mash insides.
2  Combine with chopped chives and yoghurt.
3  Replace in shells and pour over a little oil and vinegar.
4  Serve immediately.

# DATE SALAD

*Ingredients for 4-5 servings*

1 cup chopped dates
1 banana, sliced
1 tablespoon honey

½ cup walnuts, chopped
1 orange, diced
lettuce leaves

1  Combine walnuts, dates and orange.
2  Pour over honey and add bananas.
3  Mix thoroughly.
4  Serve on a bed of lettuce leaves.

# AVOCADO AND ONION SALAD

*Ingredients for 5-6 servings*

3 avocados
1 cup chopped onions

oil and vinegar

1  Halve avocados, scoop out and mash insides.
2  Combine with chopped onions and replace in shells.
3  Pour over oil and vinegar.
4  Serve immediately.

# WALNUT SALAD

*Ingredients for 4-5 servings*

| | |
|---|---|
| **2 tablespoons gelatine** | **1 cup cold water** |
| **1 cup honey** | **1 cup hot water** |
| **1 cup lemon juice** | **¾ cup chopped walnuts** |

1  Dissolve gelatine in 1 cup cold water.
2  Add honey and hot water.
3  Blend thoroughly.
4  Stir until dissolved and add lemon juice.
5  Chill until partly set, stir in walnuts and continue to chill until firm.

# FIG AND GRAPE SALAD

*Ingredients for 4-5 servings*

| | |
|---|---|
| **10 fresh figs** | **3 cups grapes** |
| **3 cups chopped walnuts** | **2 tablespoons mayonnaise** |
| **lettuce leaves** | **chopped parsley** |

1  Mix figs, grapes, walnuts and mayonnaise.
2  Blend thoroughly.
3  Dot with chopped parsley.
4  Serve on a bed of lettuce leaves.

# BANANA SALAD

*Ingredients for 4-5 servings*

| | |
|---|---|
| **2 bananas, peeled and sliced** | **lettuce leaves** |
| **1 cup chopped walnuts** | **mayonnaise** |

1  Combine bananas, mayonnaise and walnuts.
2  Mix thoroughly.
3  Serve on a bed of lettuce leaves and garnish with chopped parsley.

# CREAM CHEESE SALAD

*Ingredients for 4-5 servings*

½ cup heavy cream
155 g (5 oz) grated cheddar cheese
lettuce leaves

155 g (5 oz) cream cheese
½ teaspoon salt
chopped parsley

1  Combine cream, cream cheese and cheddar cheese.
2  Add salt and chopped parsley.
3  Combine and mix thoroughly.
4  Serve on a bed of lettuce leaves.

# TOMATO AND CELERY SALAD

*Ingredients for 4-5 servings*

4 tomatoes
1 tablespoon coconut

2 cups chopped celery
1 cup mayonnaise

1  Cut tomatoes into wedges and combine with chopped celery.
2  Dot with coconut and toss.
3  Top with mayonnaise and serve immediately.

# TOMATO CAYENNE SALAD

*Ingredients for 4-5 servings*

5 tomatoes
1 teaspoon cayenne pepper

2 cups chopped onions
oil and vinegar

1  Combine onions and tomatoes, cut into wedges.
2  Toss.
3  Pour over oil and vinegar.
4  Sprinkle with cayenne pepper.
5  Serve immediately.

# TOMATO SUPREME SALAD

*Ingredients for 4-5 servings*

**4 tomatoes, halved**
**½ cup mayonnaise**
**½ cup sliced cucumber**

**½ cup yoghurt**
**½ cup chopped onions**

1  Combine tomatoes and cucumber.
2  Add onions and pour over mayonnaise.
3  Toss.
4  Just before serving top with yoghurt.

# CARROTS AND CABBAGE SALAD

*Ingredients for 4-5 servings*

**3 carrots, chopped**
**oil and vinegar**

**3 cups chopped and shredded cabbage**
**pinch of rosemary**

1  Combine carrots and shredded cabbage.
2  Add pinch of rosemary and pour over oil and vinegar.
3  Serve immediately.

# TOMATO AND LIMA BEAN SALAD

*Ingredients for 5-6 servings*

**4 tomatoes, halved**
**½ cup yoghurt**
**½ teaspoon salt**

**1 cup prepared lima beans**
**½ cup mayonnaise**
**¼ teaspoon white pepper**

1  Combine tomatoes and lima beans.
2  Combine yoghurt and mayonnaise.
3  Season with salt and pepper.
4  Add to tomatoes and lima beans and toss.
5  Serve immediately.

# CARROT AND CELERY SALAD

*Ingredients for 4-5 servings*

3 carrots, chopped
oil and vinegar

2 cups chopped celery
pinch of thyme

1   Combine carrots and celery.
2   Add pinch of thyme and pour over oil and vinegar.
3   Serve immediately.

# TOMATO AND RADISH SALAD

*Ingredients for 5-6 servings*

4 tomatoes, halved
oil and vinegar

4 radishes, chopped

1   Combine tomatoes with radishes.
2   Toss.
3   Pour over oil and vinegar and serve chilled.

# CABBAGE AND CELERY SALAD

*Ingredients for 4-5 servings*

½ cup onions, chopped
oil and vinegar

½ cabbage, shredded
1 cup chopped celery

1   Combine cabbage, onions and celery.
2   Pour over oil and vinegar.
3   Toss.
4   Serve immediately.

# CARROTS AND PARSNIP SALAD

*Ingredients for 4-5 servings*

**3 carrots, chopped**
**oil and vinegar**

**3 parsnips, chopped**
**pinch of basil**

1  Combine carrots and parsnips and add basil.
2  Pour over oil and vinegar.
3  Toss.
4  Serve immediately.

# CARROT AND LETTUCE SALAD

*Ingredients for 4-5 servings*

**1 whole lettuce, shredded**
**oil and vinegar**

**4 carrots, chopped**
**ginger to taste**

1  Combine lettuce and carrots.
2  Toss.
3  Pour over oil and vinegar and toss once more.
4  Add ginger to taste and serve immediately.

# CARROTS AND POTATO SALAD

*Ingredients for 4-5 servings*

**3 carrots, chopped**
**oil and vinegar**

**2 large cooked potatoes, cubed**

1  Combine carrots and potatoes.
2  Pour over oil and vinegar.
3  Toss.
4  Serve immediately.

# CABBAGE AND TOMATO SALAD

*Ingredients for 4-5 servings*

½ cabbage, shredded
oil and vinegar
½ teaspoon salt

4 tomatoes, quartered
½ teaspoon cinnamon

1 Combine cabbage and tomatoes.
2 Toss and dot with cinnamon.
3 Season with salt.
4 Pour over oil and vinegar and serve immediately.

# CABBAGE AND ONION SALAD

*Ingredients for 4-5 servings*

½ cabbage, shredded
½ cup yoghurt
1 cup chopped parsley

2 cups chopped onions
½ cup mayonnaise

1 Combine cabbage, onions and parsley.
2 Toss.
3 Combine yoghurt and mayonnaise.
4 Pour over ingredients and serve chilled.

# CABBAGE AND MUSHROOMS SALAD

*Ingredients for 4-5 servings*

250 g (8 oz) chopped mushrooms
½ cabbage, shredded
½ cup yoghurt

2 cups chopped onions
½ cup mayonnaise

1 Combine mushrooms, onions and cabbage.
2 Toss.
3 Mix yoghurt and mayonnaise.
4 Pour over ingredients and serve immediately.

# CARROT-RAISINS SALAD

*Ingredients for 3-4 servings*

3 carrots, shredded
1 cup diced celery
lettuce leaves

1 cup raisins
3 tablespoons mayonnaise
chopped parsley

1  Mix carrots, raisins and celery.
2  Blend thoroughly.
3  Spoon over mayonnaise and dot with chopped parsley.
4  Serve on a bed of lettuce leaves.

# AVOCADO CHEESE SALAD

*Ingredients for 3-4 servings*

2 cups diced avocado
2 cups diced cheddar cheese
lettuce leaves
¼ cup pineapple juice

1 cup diced pineapple
1 tablespoon honey
chopped mint leaves
¼ teaspoon salt

1  Mix diced avocado, pineapple, cheese, honey and a little salt.
2  Mix through and pour over a little pineapple juice.
3  Serve on a bed of lettuce leaves.
4  Garnish with mint leaves.

# RAISIN-NUT SALAD

*Ingredients for 3-4 servings*

1 cup raisins
½ cup chopped nuts
lettuce leaves

1 cup chopped walnuts
2 tablespoons mayonnaise
watercress

1  Mix raisins, walnuts and nuts.
2  Blend thoroughly.
3  Spoon over mayonnaise and dot with watercress.
4  Serve on a bed of lettuce leaves.

# ONION-NUT SALAD

*Ingredients for 3-4 servings*

3 cups chopped nuts
5 tablespoons mayonnaise
lettuce leaves

3 tablespoons chopped onion
½ cup lemon juice
pimentos

1 Mix chopped nuts, chopped onion and lemon juice.
2 Blend thoroughly.
3 Top with mayonnaise and garnish with pimentos.
4 Serve on a bed of lettuce leaves.

# BEAN SALAD

*Ingredients for 4-5 servings*

3 cups assorted beans
½ cup mayonnaise
lettuce leaves

1 cup diced celery
1 teaspoon chopped onion

1 Combine assorted beans and celery.
2 Add mayonnaise and chopped onion.
3 Blend thoroughly.
4 Serve on a bed of lettuce leaves.

# POTATO SALAD

*Ingredients for 4-5 servings*

4 cups potatoes, cooked and diced
2 hardboiled eggs
1 cup mayonnaise
2 teaspoons celery seed

¼ cup vinegar
1 green pepper, chopped
chopped chives or parsley
lettuce leaves

1 Combine potatoes, pepper and a little salt.
2 Mix thoroughly.
3 Add mayonnaise, vinegar, celery seed and chopped chives or parsley.
4 Mix thoroughly.
5 Serve on a bed of lettuce leaves.

# COLESLAW

*Ingredients for 4-5 servings*

| | |
|---|---|
| **3 cups shredded cabbage** | **2 cups grated carrot** |
| **½ cup lemon juice** | **½ cup mayonnaise** |
| **½ teaspoon salt** | **lettuce leaves** |
| **chopped chives** | |

1  Combine shredded cabbage and grated carrot.
2  Mix thoroughly.
3  Pour over lemon juice and mayonnaise.
4  Add salt and mix thoroughly.
5  Serve on a bed of lettuce leaves.
6  Dot with chives.

# CELERY SALAD

*Ingredients for 4-5 servings*

| | |
|---|---|
| **3 cups chopped celery** | **3 cups grated cheddar cheese** |
| **1 cup mayonnaise** | **1 cup chopped parsley** |
| **½ teaspoon salt** | **¼ teaspoon paprika** |
| **lettuce leaves** | |

1  Combine celery and cheese.
2  Mix thoroughly.
3  Add salt and paprika.
4  Add mayonnaise and blend.
5  Mix in parsley and serve with lettuce.

# WALNUT SALAD

*Ingredients for 4-5 servings*

2 cups chopped celery
5 tablespoons lemon juice
lettuce leaves

2 cups chopped walnuts
½ teaspoon salt
6 tablespoons mayonnaise

1  Combine celery and walnuts.
2  Add lemon juice and mix thoroughly.
3  Add salt and mayonnaise.
4  Mix thoroughly.
5  Serve on a bed of lettuce leaves.

# CAULIFLOWER SALAD

*Ingredients for 4-5 servings*

3 cups uncooked cauliflower
½ teaspoon salt
1 teaspoon lemon juice

1 cup sour cream
1 cup grated cheese
lettuce leaves

1  Combine the cauliflower and sour cream.
2  Add grated cheese and lemon juice.
3  Add salt, thoroughly blend and serve on a bed of lettuce leaves.

# SOUTHERN SALAD

*Ingredients for 4-5 servings*

4 green peppers, chopped
½ cup lemon juice
½ teaspoon paprika

4 tomatoes diced
½ teaspoon salt

1  Mix green peppers and tomatoes.
2  Pour over lemon juice and season with salt.
3  Mix thoroughly and add paprika.
4  Serve on a bed of lettuce leaves.

# CARROT AND PEA SALAD

*Ingredients for 4-5 servings*

2 cups peas
mayonnaise
¼ cup lemon juice

2 cups chopped carrots
lettuce leaves

1  Combine peas, carrots and lemon juice.
2  Pour over mayonnaise.
3  Serve on lettuce leaves.

# CARROT AND PARSLEY SALAD

*Ingredients for 4-5 servings*

2 cups chopped carrots
mayonnaise
½ teaspoon salt

2 cups chopped parsley
lettuce leaves
½ cup chopped chives

1  Combine carrots, parsley and chives.
2  Sprinkle with salt and pour mayonnaise over.
3  Serve on a bed of lettuce leaves.

# CELERY AND RADISH SALAD

*Ingredients for 4-5 servings*

1 cup radishes
mayonnaise
¼ teaspoon white pepper

3 cups chopped celery
lettuce leaves

1  Combine radishes, celery and pepper.
2  Toss.
3  Pour over mayonnaise.
4  Serve on a bed of lettuce leaves.

# ONION AND TOMATO SALAD

*Ingredients for 4-5 servings*

4 onions, sliced
lettuce leaves
1 tablespoon vinegar

4 tomatoes, sliced
mayonnaise

1   Combine tomatoes and onions.
2   Mix mayonnaise and vinegar.
3   Combine all ingredients and blend thoroughly.
4   Serve on a bed of lettuce leaves.

# RADISH SALAD

*Ingredients for 4-5 servings*

2 cups shredded radishes
½ cup shredded cabbage

salad oil

1   Combine all ingredients and mix thoroughly.

# ASPARAGUS AND CUCUMBER SALAD

*Ingredients for 4-5 servings*

3 cups asparagus
1 cup yoghurt

3 cups cucumber, sliced
1 cup mayonnaise

1   Combine cucumber and asparagus.
2   Mix yoghurt and mayonnaise.
3   Pour mayonnaise over and serve on a bed of lettuce leaves.

# BEETROOT AND CELERY SALAD

*Ingredients for 4-5 servings*

**2 cups sliced beetroot**
**1 cup chopped onion**
**¼ teaspoon white pepper**
**lettuce leaves**

**2 cups chopped celery**
**½ teaspoon salt**
**mayonnaise**

1  Combine onion, beetroot, celery and salt.
2  Pour over mayonnaise and sprinkle with pepper.
3  Serve on a bed of lettuce leaves.

# CABBAGE AND ONION SALAD

*Ingredients for 2 servings*

**2 cups shredded cabbage**
**mayonnaise**

**2 cups chopped onions**
**lettuce leaves**

1  Combine cabbage and onions.
2  Pour over mayonnaise and serve on a bed of lettuce leaves.

# ARTICHOKE AND PEA SALAD

*Ingredients for 4-5 servings*

**4 artichoke hearts, minced**
**mayonnaise**

**2 cups peas**
**lettuce leaves**

1  Combine peas and artichokes.
2  Pour over mayonnaise and serve on a bed of lettuce leaves.

# ARTICHOKE AND CHEESE SALAD

*Ingredients for 4-5 servings*

**4 artichoke hearts, minced**　　　　**1 cup grated cheese**
**mayonnaise**　　　　　　　　　　　　**lettuce leaves**
**½ cup chives, chopped**

1　Combine artichokes, cheese, chives and pour mayonnaise over.
2　Dot with chives and serve on a bed of lettuce leaves.

# ARTICHOKE SALAD

*Ingredients for 4-5 servings*

**lettuce leaves**　　　　　　　　　　**12 minced artichoke hearts**
**mayonnaise**

1　Pour mayonnaise over artichoke hearts and serve on a bed of lettuce leaves.

# ASPARAGUS AND CAULIFLOWER SALAD

*Ingredients for 4-5 servings*

**3 cups cauliflower**　　　　　　　　**2 cups asparagus**
**mayonnaise**　　　　　　　　　　　　**lettuce leaves**
**½ teaspoon salt**

1　Combine cauliflower (broken into small pieces), salt and asparagus.
2　Top with mayonnaise and serve on a bed of lettuce leaves.

# APPLE AND ORANGE SALAD

*Ingredients for 4-5 servings*

2 diced apples
salad oil
chopped mint

2 diced oranges
lettuce leaves

1  Combine all ingredients and dot with mint.
2  Serve on a bed of lettuce leaves.

# NUT SALAD

*Ingredients for 2-3 servings*

2 cups cream
1 tablespoon honey
1 cup chopped green pepper
lettuce leaves

2 beaten eggs
1 cup carrots, diced
½ teaspoon salt
½ cup celery, chopped

1  Scald cream and pour over beaten eggs.
2  Simmer for 3 minutes and blend with carrots, salt and honey.
3  Simmer for further 3 minutes and add celery and green pepper.
4  Chill.
5  Serve with lettuce leaves.

# PINEAPPLE AND BANANA SALAD

*Ingredients for 4-5 servings*

1 pineapple, diced
¼ cup salad oil
chopped parsley

3 bananas, sliced
lettuce leaves

1  Combine pineapple and banana.
2  Toss lightly.
3  Add oil and serve on a bed of lettuce leaves.
4  Dot with chopped parsley.

# ASPARAGUS AND ONION SALAD

*Ingredients for 4-5 servings*

2 cups chopped onion
½ teaspoon salt
lettuce leaves

2 cups asparagus
¼ teaspoon white pepper
mayonnaise

1   Combine all ingredients and top with mayonnaise.
2   Serve on a bed of lettuce leaves.

# PEAR CHEESE SALAD

*Ingredients for 4-5 servings*

2 fresh pears, diced
1 cup mayonnaise
lettuce leaves

2 cups cheddar cheese, diced
chopped mint

1   Combine pears and cheese.
2   Top with mayonnaise and dot with chopped mint.
3   Serve on a bed of lettuce leaves.

# APPLE WALNUT SALAD

*Ingredients for 4-5 servings*

1 cup chopped walnuts
mayonnaise
1 teaspoon lemon juice

2 large apples, grated
lettuce leaves
chopped parsley

1   Combine walnuts, grated apples and mayonnaise.
2   Mix thoroughly.
3   Dot with lemon juice.
4   Serve on a bed of lettuce leaves.
5   Sprinkle with chopped parsley.

# AVOCADO SALAD

*Ingredients for 4-5 servings*

**2 diced avocados**
**1 cup ripe olives**
**½ teaspoon salt**

**1 cup chopped walnuts**
**lemon juice**
**½ teaspoon paprika**

1  Mix avocado, chopped walnuts and olives.
2  Pour over lemon juice and season with salt and paprika.
3  Serve on lettuce leaves.

# GRAPE SALAD

*Ingredients for 4-5 servings*

**2 cups green grapes**
**lettuce leaves**
**chopped parsley**

**1 cup pineapple**
**1 tablespoon honey**
**½ cup chopped walnuts**

1  Combine grapes, pineapple, nuts and honey.
2  Mix thoroughly.
3  Dot with chopped parsley and serve on bed of lettuce leaves,

# CUCUMBER AND BROAD BEAN SALAD

*Ingredients for 4 servings*

**185 g (6 oz) broad beans**
**1 tablespoon chopped parsley**
**½ teaspoon salt**
**1 tablespoon oil**

**1 cucumber**
**2 tablespoons lemon juice**
**¼ teaspoon pepper**
**1 garlic clove, crushed**

1  Shell beans and slice cucumber into rounds.
2  Combine remaining ingredients and pour over cucumber and beans.
3  Toss gently and serve.

# QUEENSLAND SALAD

*Ingredients for 6 servings*

3 bananas
1 head lettuce
250 g (8 oz) cottage cheese

1 bunch watercress
5 tomatoes, sliced
1 tablespoon lemon juice

1 Slice bananas and dot with lemon juice.
2 Place lettuce in dish and pile watercress on top.
3 Add mounds of cottage cheese.
4 Circle lettuce with bananas and tomatoes.
5 Serve chilled.

# MILDURA SALAD

*Ingredients for 4 servings*

500 g (1 lb) cooked prawns, shelled
3 tablespoons lemon juice
¼ teaspoon pepper
1 garlic clove, crushed
1 tablespoon chopped parsley

250 g (8 oz) broad beans
½ teaspoon salt
1 tablespoon oil
1 teaspoon fresh dill, chopped

1 Shell beans and mix lightly with prepared prawns.
2 Combine remaining ingredients and mix gently.
3 Pour over prawn/broad bean mixture and toss gently.

# MIAMI SALAD

*Ingredients for 4 servings*

250 g (8 oz) tinned grapefruit
2 tablespoons mayonnaise
¼ teaspoon pepper
¾ cup diced celery

1½ tablespoons lemon juice
½ teaspoon salt
1 head lettuce
1½ cups cooked chicken, diced

1   Drain grapefruit.
2   Combine chicken and celery in a separate bowl and mix in lemon juice, mayonnaise and seasonings.
3   Add to grapefruit and serve on lettuce.

# SALMON SALAD

*Ingredients for 8 servings*

3½ cups tinned salmon
¼ cup mayonnaise
1½ cups chopped celery

1½ lemons
8 olives
1 head lettuce

1   Mix drained, flaked salmon with celery and mayonnaise.
2   Arrange on a bed of lettuce leaves.
3   Garnish with sliced olives and serve with sliced lemon.

# PADUAN FISH SALAD

*Ingredients for 4 servings*

500 g (1 lb) cooked fish
4 hardboiled eggs
½ teaspoon pepper
½ lettuce, shredded

2 tablespoons mayonnaise
½ teaspoon salt
4 tablespoons fennel, shredded

1   Flake fish, and place in large salad bowl.
2   Add lettuce and shredded fennel.
3   Season with salt and pepper.
4   Mix in mayonnaise and garnish with chopped hardboiled eggs.

# COLESLAW WITH SULTANAS

*Ingredients for 3 servings*

| | |
|---|---|
| 1 carrot, grated | ⅓ white cabbage |
| 1 onion | 2 tablespoons lemon juice |
| ½ teaspoon prepared mustard | ¼ teaspoon pepper |
| ½ teaspoon salt | 4 tablespoons sultanas |
| 4 tablespoons oil | 2 tablespoons chopped parsley |

1 Cut cabbage into thin shreds and slice onion.
2 Place carrot, cabbage and onion in bowl and dot with sultanas.
3 Add chopped parsley and mix lemon juice, mustard and seasonings with oil.
4 Add dressing to ingredients and toss gently.

# GRAPEFRUIT CHEESE SALAD

*Ingredients for 4 servings*

| | |
|---|---|
| 2 grapefruit | 1 head lettuce |
| 125 g (4 oz) cheese, grated | 4 tomatoes |
| 2 apples | |

1 Remove pips from grapefruit and separate sections.
2 Arrange grapefruit on lettuce and add sliced tomato and diced apple.
3 Top with grated cheese.

# WALDORF SALAD

*Ingredients for 6 servings*

| | |
|---|---|
| 4 large carrots | 2 apples, peeled and diced |
| 1 head lettuce | 3 ounces raisins |
| 2 tablespoons lemon juice | 2 tablespoons chopped parsley |

1 Mix grated carrot with raisins and apples.
2 Add lemon juice and parsley and mix well.
3 Serve heaped on lettuce leaves.

# ORANGE CAULIFLOWER SALAD

*Ingredients for 4 servings*

½ teaspoon celery salt
3 sticks celery, chopped
1 teaspoon salt
1 small cauliflower

3 tablespoons salad dressing
2 oranges, peeled and chopped
¼ teaspoon pepper
2 apples, peeled and chopped

1  Divide cauliflower into flowerets.
2  Mix with sections of orange and toss with chopped apple.
3  Add celery and celery salt.
4  Season with salt and pepper.
5  Add dressing and serve.

# CAPSICUM SALAD

*Ingredients for 4 servings*

4 green capsicums
6 chopped gherkins
1 head lettuce
½ teaspoon pepper
2 red capsicums

¼ cup salad dressing
4 tomatoes
1½ teaspoons salt
250 g (8 oz) grated cheese

1  Cut piece off one end of each green pepper.
2  Scoop out seeds and mix grated cheese with salad dressing.
3  Add chopped red pepper, gherkins and chopped tomatoes and season with salt and pepper.
4  Place in centre of each green pepper and serve.

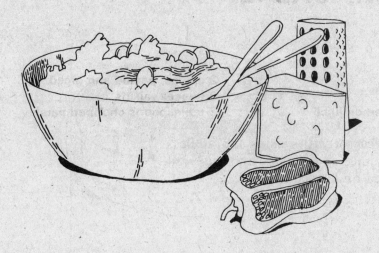

# BEETROOT SALAD

*5 minutes cooking time*

*Ingredients for 4 servings*

1 tin beetroot
1½ teaspoons minced onion
½ cup chopped celery
½ cup orange juice

2 teaspoons vinegar
½ teaspoon salt
1 teaspoon horseradish
30 g (1 oz) gelatine

1   Drain juice from beetroot and measure ½ cup into saucepan. Bring to boil and dissolve gelatine.
2   Add remaining ingredients except celery and when mixture has thickened add celery and beetroot.
3   Turn into mould and chill.

# CIDER SALAD

*3 minutes cooking time*

*Ingredients for 4 servings*

2 cups cider
¼ cup chopped nuts
¾ cup chopped apple
1½ tablespoons gelatine

¼ teaspoon salt
1½ tablespoons chopped parsley
⅓ cup chopped celery

1   Soak gelatine in ½ cup of cider. Bring remaining cider to boil.
2   Pour in gelatine and stir.
3   Cool.
4   When mixture starts to thicken pour in remaining ingredients.
5   Pour into moulds and chill.
6   Serve with mayonnaise.

# APPLE FISH SALAD

*Ingredients for 6 servings*

| | |
|---|---|
| 375 g (12 oz) cooked fish | 2 apples, peeled and diced |
| 1 lemon | 1 head lettuce |
| ¼ teaspoon pepper | ½ teaspoon salt |

1　Mix flaked fish with apple and season with salt and pepper.
2　Serve with lemon wedges on crisp lettuce.

# MUSHROOM SALAD

*Ingredients for 4 servings*

| | |
|---|---|
| 250 g (8 oz) raw mushrooms | 1 garlic clove, crushed |
| 2 tablespoons lemon juice | ½ teaspoon salt |
| ¼ teaspoon pepper | 1 tablespoon oil |
| 1 tablespoon chopped parsley | 1 tablespoon chopped chives |

1　Cut stalks off mushrooms and slice thinly.
2　Combine remaining ingredients and mix well.
3　Pour over mushrooms and toss gently.
4　Stand for 2-3 hours before serving.

# FRUIT SLAW

*Ingredients for 4 servings*

| | |
|---|---|
| 2 oranges | 3 cups shredded cabbage |
| 2 tablespoons mayonnaise | 1 tablespoon pineapple juice |
| ½ teaspoon salt | ¼ cup crushed pineapple |
| ½ chopped green pepper | |

1　Peel orange sections and add cabbage, pineapple and green pepper; toss.
2　Combine mayonnaise and pineapple juice and season with salt.
3　Pour dressing over salad and mix well.

# TOMATO EGG SALAD

*10 minutes cooking time*

*Ingredients for 6 servings*

6 hardboiled eggs
4 tablespoons salad dressing
8 tomatoes
1 teaspoon salt

½ cup chopped watercress
2 tablespoons chopped parsley
½ teaspoon pepper

1　Cut eggs in half and remove yolks. Mix yolks with finely chopped watercress and add a little salad dressing.
2　Fill egg whites with this mixture and season with salt and pepper.
3　Cut tomatoes in halves and place on serving dish.
4　Lay eggs, filling downwards, on slices of tomato and coat with salad dressing.
5　Add a little chopped parsley to garnish.

# CURRIED FISH SALAD

*Ingredients for 4 servings*

¾ cup cooked fish
½ cup diced celery
1 head lettuce
½ teaspoon salt
1½ tablespoons lemon juice

pinch dry mustard
½ cup diced apple
½ teaspoon curry powder
⅓ cup dressing

1　Flake fish and sprinkle with lemon juice.
2　Add remaining ingredients and mix.
3　Place in lettuce cups and chill.

# MOULDED FISH SALAD

*Ingredients for 6 servings*

**750 g (1½ lb) lobster meat**
**½ cucumber**
**185 g (6 oz) broad beans, cooked**
**1 lettuce**
**2½ cups aspic jelly**

**3 tomatoes**
**250 g (8 oz) peas, cooked**
**2 cooked carrots, diced**
**2 hardboiled eggs**

1  Flake lobster meat.
2  Peel tomato, remove seeds and dice flesh.
3  Peel cucumber and slice it.
4  Pour a little aspic jelly into mould and set.
5  Pour a little aspic jelly over sliced cucumber and hardboiled eggs for the garnish.
6  To mould previously set aside, add beans, peas and carrots. Mix in tomatoes and fish.
7  When cold and set, dip mould into hot water and turn out onto serving dish. Garnish with tomato, lettuce leaves and cucumber slices.

# MOULDED CHICKEN SUNSHINE

*5 minutes cooking time*

*Ingredients for 8 servings*

**60 g (2 oz) gelatine**
**¾ cup diced tinned pineapple**
**3 tablespoons lemon juice**
**3 chicken stock cubes**

**1½ saccharine tablets**
**2 cups diced cooked chicken**
**½ teaspoon salt**
**2 cups water**

1  Sprinkle gelatine into a little water and dissolve.
2  Combine remaining water with stock cubes and salt, bring to boil and remove from heat.
3  Stir in softened gelatine and add lemon juice and saccharine.
4  Chill until thickened.
5  Fold in pineapple and chicken. Place in mould and chill.

# TOMATO ASPIC

*5 minutes cooking time*

*Ingredients for 6 servings*

45 g (1½ oz) gelatine
1½ tablespoons lemon juice
¼ teaspoon pepper

3 cups tomato juice
½ teaspoon salt

1　Dot gelatine on a little cold tomato juice and soften.
2　Heat remaining tomato juice.
3　Add softened gelatine and seasonings.
4　Stir and add lemon juice.
5　Pour into mould and chill.

# ORANGE ASPIC

*3 minutes cooking time*

*Ingredients for 4 servings*

¾ tablespoon gelatine
¾ cup orange juice
¼ teaspoon cayenne pepper

½ cup condensed tomato soup
¼ teaspoon salt
½ cup chopped celery

1　Soak gelatine in a little orange juice.
2　Dissolve over hot water.
3　Mix in remaining juice and add soup.
4　Season with salt and pepper. Chill.
5　When mixture begins to thicken add celery and pour into moulds. Chill and serve.

# Dressings

## COOKED DRESSING

*Ingredients for 2 cups*

*10 minutes cooking time*

½ cup cold water
2 tablespoons butter
3 saccharine tablets
1½ cups boiling water
2 teaspoons salt

1 tablespoon gelatine
2 eggs, beaten
½ cup vinegar
½ teaspoon paprika
2 teaspoons dry mustard

1 Sprinkle gelatine on cold water in top of double boiler.
2 Mix mustard, salt and paprika together.
3 Add boiling water and mustard mixture to softened gelatine.
4 Remove mixture from heat, stir and add beaten eggs.
5 Return to double boiler and cook, stirring.
6 When mixture begins to thicken remove and add saccharine.
7 Stir in vinegar slowly and chill for 10 minutes.
8 Beat thoroughly and store in refrigerator.

# EGG MAYONNAISE

*Ingredients for 2 servings*

1 cup evaporated milk
½ teaspoon salt
1 cup olive oil

3 tablespoons lemon juice
¼ teaspoon white pepper
2 hardboiled eggs

1  Combine evaporated milk, lemon juice, hardboiled eggs and salt.
2  Blend thoroughly.
3  Add salt and pepper.
4  Add olive oil and mix in blender.

# CELERY MAYONNAISE

*Ingredients for 2 servings*

2 egg yolks
1 teaspoon paprika
2 tablespoons lemon juice

2 teaspoons mashed celery
2½ cups salad oil

1  Mix all ingredients and blend thoroughly.
2  Serve chilled.

# AVOCADO AND LEMON MAYONNAISE

*Ingredients for 2 servings*

2 egg yolks, beaten
¼ teaspoon white pepper
2 teaspoons chopped celery

½ teaspoon salt
2 cups avocado pulp

1  Combine all ingredients and mix thoroughly.
2  Serve chilled.

# BANANA DRESSING

*Ingredients for 4-5 servings*

**5 ripe mashed bananas**          **3 tablespoons thickened cream**

1  Combine ingredients and mix thoroughly.
2  Serve chilled.

# FRUIT DRESSING

*Ingredients for 4-5 servings*

**1 cup orange juice**          **1 cup whole wheat flour**
**1 cup warmed honey**          **2 eggs, beaten**
**2 cups whipped cream**

1  Blend honey, orange juice and whole wheat flour.
2  Mix thoroughly.
3  Add beaten eggs and whipped cream.

# LEMON DRESSING

*Ingredients for 2-3 servings*

**2 tablespoons honey**          **2 tablespoons lemon juice**
**1 teaspoon cinnamon**          **2 cups whipped cream**

1  Combine all ingredients.
2  Mix thoroughly.
3  Serve chilled.

# CREAMED HONEY DRESSING

*10 minutes cooking time*

*Ingredients for 2-3 servings*

1 cup honey
1 tablespoon sugar
1 cup whipped cream

1 cup whole wheat flour
juice of 2 oranges

1   Combine honey, wheat flour and sugar and heat, stirring.
2   When this mixture has thickened, add orange juice and cream.
3   Chill and serve.

# CHEESE DRESSING

*Ingredients for 1 cup*

½ cup cottage cheese
1½ tablespoons lemon juice
½ teaspoon salt

⅓ cup grapefruit juice
½ teaspoon grated lemon rind
¼ teaspoon pepper

1   Combine all ingredients.
2   Place in blender and mix for 1 minute.
3   Chill and serve.

# RICH DRESSING

*Ingredients for 2 cups*

2 teaspoons gelatine
2 teaspoons salt
½ teaspoon pepper
½ cup cold skim milk

8 tablespoons lemon juice
¼ teaspoon dry mustard
1 cup hot skim milk

1   Soften gelatine in cold milk and add hot milk.
2   Stir until gelatine dissolves and mix in remaining ingredients and beat
    thoroughly.
3   Chill and serve.

# SLIMMERS' MAYONNAISE

*10 minutes cooking time*

*Ingredients for 1 cup*

**1 teaspoon salt**
**½ teaspoon paprika**
**½ cup milk**
**½ teaspoon mustard**

**¼ teaspoon cayenne pepper**
**4 tablespoons vinegar**
**2 eggs**

1   Combine all ingredients and place bowl in frying pan with water. Bring to boil and beat mixture.
2   When mixture thickens remove from heat and continue to beat until smooth.
3   Pour into jar and chill.

# Vegetable Dishes

## VEGETABLE LOAF

55 minutes cooking time

*Ingredients for 4-5 servings*

3 eggs
1 cup whole wheat breadcrumbs
1 cup chopped carrots
1 cup chopped onions
¼ teaspoon white pepper

2 cups milk
1 cup chopped celery
1 cup chopped parsnip
1 cup ground nuts
½ teaspoon salt

1 Beat eggs and milk.
2 Stand for 5 minutes.
3 Combine breadcrumbs, celery, carrots, parsnip, onions and nuts.
4 Season with salt and pepper.
5 Form into a loaf and bake at 190°C (375°F) for 55 minutes.

# CARROT LOAF

*45 minutes cooking time*

*Ingredients for 4-5 servings*

| | |
|---|---|
| 3 tablespoons whole wheat flour | 3 tablespoons butter |
| 2 cups roasted nuts | 3 cups chopped carrots |
| 1 cup chopped parsley | 1 teaspoon salt |
| ¼ teaspoon white pepper | 1 cup tomato juice |

1　Blend flour, butter and tomato juice.
2　Stir until thick and then cook for 2 minutes.
3　Combine roasted nuts, carrots and parsley.
4　Add to sauce and season with salt and pepper.
5　Form into a loaf and bake for 35 minutes.

# VEGETABLE CASSEROLE

*45 minutes cooking time*

*Ingredients for 4-5 servings*

| | |
|---|---|
| 4 cups diced carrots | 2 cups chopped celery |
| 2 tablespoons corn | 2 cups cream |
| ½ teaspoon salt | ¾ teaspoon white pepper |
| 1 cup diced parsnip | |

1　In buttered casserole dish, layer carrots, celery, parsnip, corn and cream.
2　Season with salt and pepper.
3　Bake in moderate oven for 45-50 minutes.

# CARROT CASSEROLE

*40 minutes cooking time*

*Ingredients for 4-5 servings*

| | |
|---|---|
| 5 eggs, beaten | 2 tablespoons grated onions |
| 4 cups grated carrots | 1 cup whole wheat breadcrumbs |
| 1 cup grated mushrooms | 1 cup chopped parsley |

1　Mix all ingredients and blend thoroughly.
2　Place in greased casserole dish.
3　Bake in moderate oven for 40 minutes and garnish with chopped parsley.

# POTATOES AND APPLES

*10 minutes cooking time*

*Ingredients for 4-5 servings*

4 cups mashed potatoes
½ cup sugar
chopped parsley

3 cups apple sauce
½ teaspoon salt

1   Combine potatoes, apple sauce, sugar and salt.
2   Dot with chopped parsley and serve.

# POTATO PUFF

*40 minutes cooking time*

*Ingredients for 4-5 servings*

3 cups mashed potatoes
5 beaten eggs
1 teaspoon salt

½ cup butter
½ cup sugar
½ teaspoon white pepper

1   Combine all ingredients and place in well-oiled dish.
2   Place in oven and bake for 40 minutes or until brown on top.

# TOMATOES STUFFED WITH CHEDDAR CHEESE

*20 minutes cooking time*

*Ingredients for 4 servings*

6 tomatoes
250 g (8 oz) cheddar cheese
4 teaspoons lemon juice

2 tablespoons butter
½ teaspoon salt

1   Scoop out top of 4 tomatoes and place a little salt in each tomato.
2   Dice two tomatoes and mix with melted cheese and butter.
3   Combine with lemon juice and replace in scooped out tomatoes.
4   Bake in oven for 20 minutes and dot with parsley.

# CARROTS AND MINT

*20 minutes cooking time*

*Ingredients for 4-5 servings*

4 medium carrots, sliced    ½ cup chopped mint
3 tablespoons butter

1  Boil carrots in water until cooked.
2  Drain and add butter and mint.
3  Toss and serve immediately.

# PEAS AND MINT

*15 minutes cooking time*

*Ingredients for 4-5 servings*

3 cups shelled peas    ½ cup chopped mint
1 teaspoon sugar    3 tablespoons butter

1  Boil peas in sugared water and drain when cooked.
2  Add butter and mint.
3  Toss and serve.

# CARROT RING

*30 minutes cooking time*

*Ingredients for 4-5 servings*

4 cups raw carrots, grated    ½ cup milk
3 eggs, beaten    ½ cup milk powder
1 tablespoon chopped mint    3 tablespoons brewer's yeast
3 tablespoons oil

1  Combine all ingredients and turn into oiled mould.
2  Bake for 30 minutes and serve.

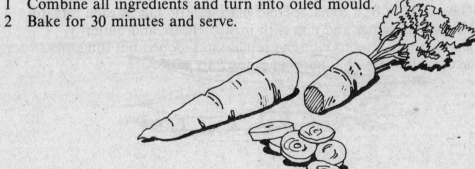

# MUSHROOM-FILLED TOMATOES

*25 minutes cooking time*

*Ingredients for 4 servings*

4 tomatoes
½ teaspoon salt
2 tablespoons butter
2 tablespoons chopped parsley

2 eggs
¼ teaspoon pepper
4 mushrooms

1 Chop mushrooms and cook in hot butter.
2 Remove tops from tomatoes and scoop out centre.
3 Add tomato pulp to mushrooms with beaten eggs.
4 Season and cook until mixture begins to stiffen.
5 Place mixture into tomato cases and bake for 10-15 minutes. Garnish with chopped parsley.

# PEAS WITH LETTUCE

*1 hour cooking time*

*Ingredients for 4 servings*

4 cups shelled peas
½ teaspoon salt
1 teaspoon sugar
1 lettuce
1 tablespoon butter

90 g (3 oz) spring onions, chopped
⅛ teaspoon white pepper
1 teaspoon plain flour
60 g (2 oz) bacon

1 Cut bacon into strips.
2 Place peas in saucepan with sugar, bacon and spring onions.
3 Add chopped lettuce and season with salt and pepper.
4 Pour enough water in to just cover ingredients.
5 Add 2 teaspoons butter and cover.
6 Cook until tender and combine remaining butter with flour and gradually add to pan.
7 Cook until mixture thickens and stir constantly.
8 Serve.

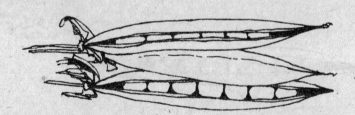

# ASPARAGUS MOULD

*Ingredients for 6 servings*

*10 minutes cooking time*

| | |
|---|---|
| 1½ tablespoons gelatine | 2 cups tomato juice |
| 4 tablespoons cider vinegar | ½ cup diced pimento |
| 4 tablespoons diced celery | 2½ cups cut-up asparagus |
| dash Tabasco sauce | 4 saccharine tablets |
| 1 teaspoon salt | |

1  Sprinkle gelatine over half cup tomato juice and soften.
2  Cook over low heat and when gelatine dissolves, stir in remaining tomato juice.
3  Add vinegar, salt, saccharine and Tabasco sauce.
4  Chill.
5  Fold in asparagus, pimento and celery.
6  Spoon into moulds and serve chilled.

# TIFFANY'S BRAISED CELERY

*Ingredients for 4 servings*

*1 hour 45 minutes cooking time*

| | |
|---|---|
| 1 large head of celery | 45 g (1½ oz) lean ham |
| 155 g (5 oz) carrot | 155 g (5 oz) onion |
| 30 g (1 oz) dripping | ½ teaspoon salt |
| ⅛ teaspoon white pepper | 1 tablespoon chopped parsley |
| bouquet garni | 90 g (3 oz) turnip |
| 2 teaspoons cornflour | |

1  Wash celery and cut into short lengths.
2  Tie together in little bundles and peel remaining vegetables.
3  Cut into large pieces and melt dripping.
4  Fry ham, carrot, onion and turnip.
5  Pour off excess fat and add cornflour and seasonings.
6  Place celery on top of ingredients and cover.
7  Cook over slow heat for 1½ hours.

# CARROT AND ONION LOAF

*40 minutes cooking time*

*Ingredients for 4-5 servings*

6 cups cooked mashed carrots
5 eggs, beaten
4 onions, chopped
¼ teaspoon white pepper

1 cup whole wheat breadcrumbs
2 tablespoons chopped parsley
½ teaspoon salt
¼ teaspoon cayenne pepper

1　Combine carrots and breadcrumbs.
2　Mix well and add eggs.
3　Add chopped parsley, onion, salt, white pepper and cayenne pepper.
4　Form into a loaf and bake in moderate oven for 40 minutes.
5　Serve immediately.

# TOMATO CASSEROLE

*1 hour cooking time*

*Ingredients for 4-5 servings*

3 tablespoons butter
3 onions, chopped
¼ teaspoon white pepper
2 cups tomato juice

1¼ cups beef stock
1 teaspoon salt
¼ teaspoon paprika
1 cup cooked brown rice

1　Melt butter and sauté chopped onions.
2　Add rice and tomato juice.
3　Cook for 2 minutes, then add stock and season with salt, pepper and paprika.
4　Cook for 1 hour and serve immediately.

# MUSHROOMS AND MINT

*5 minutes cooking time*

*Ingredients for 4-5 servings*

500 g (1 lb) medium mushrooms
½ cup chopped mint

3 tablespoons butter

1　Cook mushrooms in butter.
2　Just before serving add mint.

# PEA AND PARSLEY LOAF

*40 minutes cooking time*

*Ingredients for 4-5 servings*

**4 cups mashed peas**
**4 tablespoons chopped parsley**
**¼ teaspoon white pepper**

**4 tablespoons oil**
**½ teaspoon salt**
**2 tablespoons butter**

1 Blend peas and parsley.
2 Mix thoroughly.
3 Season with salt and pepper.
4 Bind with oil and butter.
5 Mix thoroughly.
6 Form into a loaf and bake for 40 minutes in a moderate oven.

# CARROTS AND ONIONS

*20 minutes cooking time*

*Ingredients for 4-5 servings*

**5 carrots, chopped**
**4 onions, chopped**

**3 tablespoons oil**
**stock to cover**

1 Sauté onions and carrots in oil.
2 Place in casserole dish and add stock.
3 Simmer for 20 minutes and serve.

# BEANS WITH MINT

*10 minutes cooking time*

*Ingredients for 4-5 servings*

**3 cups cooked beans**
**3 tablespoons butter**
**½ teaspoon pepper**

**½ cup chopped mint**
**¾ teaspoon salt**

1 Combine ingredients and season with salt and pepper.
2 Heat and serve.

# SPINACH SOUFFLÉ

*30 minutes cooking time*

*Ingredients for 4 servings*

2 cups boiled spinach
½ teaspoon pepper
1 beaten egg
1 tablespoon butter

½ teaspoon salt
⅓ cup skim milk
1 tablespoon flour
½ teaspoon nutmeg

1  Chop spinach finely and rub through coarse sieve.
2  Reheat and add butter mixed with flour and seasonings.
3  Add milk, egg and beat for 3 minutes.
4  Place in individual baking dishes and bake for 15-20 minutes in moderate oven 180°C (350°F).

# SPINACH AND SOUR CREAM COMBINATION

*40 minutes cooking time*

*Ingredients for 4 servings*

½ teaspoon grated nutmeg
1 packet onion soup
630 g (20 oz) frozen chopped spinach

½ teaspoon salt
½ cup reduced sour cream

1  Cook spinach in boiling salted water and drain.
2  Place sour cream, soup mix and salt in blender. Mix thoroughly.
3  Combine sour cream mixture with cooked spinach and pour into casserole dish.
4  Sprinkle with nutmeg and bake uncovered in moderate oven for 25 minutes.

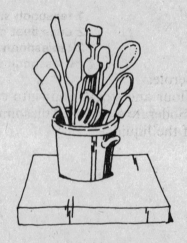

# BRAISED CABBAGE

*10 minutes cooking time*

*Ingredients for 4 servings*

3 cups shredded cabbage
1 garlic clove
¼ teaspoon pepper

1½ tablespoons vinegar
½ teaspoon salt

1   Place cabbage and remaining ingredients in frying pan.
2   Cover and cook over low heat, stirring occasionally, for 10 minutes or
    until cabbage is cooked.

# ASPARAGUS VINAIGRETTE

*Ingredients for 4 servings*

½ cup herb vinegar
⅛ teaspoon cayenne pepper
½ teaspoon paprika

½ teaspoon garlic salt
500 g (1 lb) cooked cold asparagus
½ cup water

1   Combine water, paprika, salt, cayenne and vinegar.
2   Pour over asparagus and stand overnight.
3   Serve chilled.

# ONION CASSEROLE

*1 hour cooking time*

*Ingredients for 6 servings*

12 onions
½ teaspoon pepper
3 tablespoons butter

1 teaspoon salt
2 cups beef stock
2 tablespoons flour

1   Place onions in casserole.
2   Melt butter, stir in flour and stock; pour into casserole.
3   Bake for 2 hours in moderate oven, after seasoning with salt and pepper.
4   Serve with a little of the liquid.

# WINSBORO CELERY

*15 minutes cooking time*

*Ingredients for 2 servings*

1 cup sliced celery
1 bay leaf
pinch thyme
3 drops Tabasco sauce
½ onion, chopped

½ tomato, chopped
pinch basil
⅛ teaspoon chilli powder
1 chicken stock cube
½ green pepper, chopped

1   Combine ingredients in saucepan.
2   Cover and simmer for 15 minutes.

# TASTY GREEN BEANS

*5 minutes cooking time*

*Ingredients for 3 servings*

2 cups green beans
2 teaspoons prepared mustard
½ teaspoon salt

pinch cayenne pepper
½ teaspoon Worcestershire sauce
¼ teaspoon pepper

1   Cook beans in boiling salted water for 5 minutes, drain.
2   Combine all remaining ingredients and toss in beans.

# ITALIAN ZUCCHINI

*10 minutes cooking time*

*Ingredients for 6 servings*

750 g (1½ lb) zucchini
½ cup minced onion
½ teaspoon salt
1 tablespoon chopped parsley
pinch thyme

2 tomatoes, chopped
1 garlic clove, crushed
¼ teaspoon pepper
pinch basil
1 bay leaf

1   Slice zucchini into 1 centimetre (½ in) rounds and place in pan with remaining ingredients.
2   Cover.
3   Simmer for 10 minutes and serve.

# STUFFED EGGPLANT

*Ingredients for 4 servings*

*30 minutes cooking time*

2 small eggplants
⅛ teaspoon white pepper
1 tablespoon chopped parsley
1 tablespoon butter

½ teaspoon salt
6 tablespoons tomato sauce
¼ cup breadcrumbs
4 hardboiled eggs

1   Steam eggplants until tender.
2   Remove stalk.
3   Cut in halves lengthwise and scoop out pulp.
4   Chop well and add chopped eggs to mixture. Season with salt and pepper.
5   Fill the half skins with mixture and dot with breadcrumbs.
6   Bake on greased baking dish in hot oven.
7   Serve sprinkled with parsley and pour over tomato sauce.

# BROCCOLI CASSEROLE

*Ingredients for 4 servings*

*45 minutes cooking time*

250 g (8 oz) frozen broccoli
2 eggs, well beaten
½ tablespoon minced onion
½ teaspoon salt
2 cups milk

½ cup mayonnaise
¼ teaspoon pepper
1½ tablespoons plain flour
1½ tablespoons melted butter

1   Cook broccoli in boiling water and drain.
2   Chop broccoli and add melted butter and flour to pan with broccoli.
3   Cook for 2 minutes and add milk, cook gently, stirring constantly.
4   Remove from heat and stir in onion, pepper, salt, mayonnaise and eggs, mix gently.
5   Place in casserole dish and bake for 30 minutes.

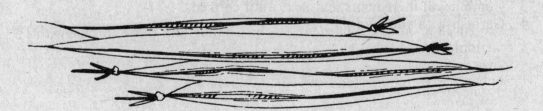

# MIXED VEGETABLES

*25 minutes cooking time*

*Ingredients for 4 servings*

2 heads lettuce
185 g (6 oz) green peas
2 tablespoons chopped parsley

½ cup chicken stock
125 g (4 oz) onion wedges
1 tablespoon margarine

1  Cut lettuce into four wedges.
2  Tie each wedge with string and in a saucepan cook combined stock, lettuce, peas, onions and parsley.
3  Mix gently.
4  Cook covered for 25 minutes and turn into heated serving dish.
5  Add margarine and serve.

# BASIC RICE

4 cups boiling stock          2 cups brown rice

1  Pour stock over washed rice and stir.
2  Cover and stand overnight.
3  Reheat when serving.

# RICE AND CELERY

*20 minutes cooking time*

*Ingredients for 4-5 servings*

3 tablespoons oil
2 cups chopped celery
2 cups brown rice

2 tablespoons brewer's yeast
2 cups boiling stock
½ cup yoghurt

1  Brown celery in oil.
2  Drain.
3  Combine all ingredients and heat until cooked.
4  Garnish with chopped parsley.

# RICE LOAF

*45 minutes cooking time*

*Ingredients for 3-4 servings*

2 cups cooked brown rice
1 cup whole wheat breadcrumbs
3 tablespoons butter
1½ cups milk

1 chopped green pepper
½ teaspoon salt
3 tablespoons whole wheat flour
2 beaten eggs

1 Combine brown rice and breadcrumbs.
2 Blend thoroughly.
3 In a separate bowl blend the butter, salt, whole wheat flour, milk and chopped pepper.
4 Combine both mixtures.
5 Add beaten eggs and bind.
6 Form into a loaf and place in oven 190°C (375°F) for 45 minutes.

# RICE PATTIES

*20 minutes cooking time*

*Ingredients for 4-5 servings*

1 cup brown rice, cooked
1 tablespoon oil
½ cup chopped mushrooms

2 teaspoons brewer's yeast
4 teaspoons milk powder

1 Combine all ingredients and mix thoroughly.
2 Shape into patties and place on oiled baking dish.
3 Heat and serve immediately.

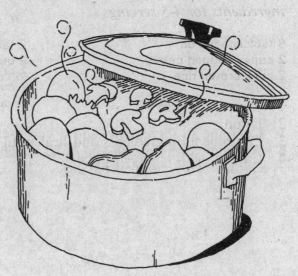

# BEAN SOUFFLÉ

*30 minutes cooking time*

*Ingredients for 4-5 servings*

4 egg yolks
1 cup chopped onions
2 tablespoons chopped parsley

3 cups soy beans
½ teaspoon salt
1 cup wholemeal breadcrumbs

1   Beat the egg yolks and combine with soy beans, salt, breadcrumbs, onions and parsley.
2   Beat the egg whites and fold into this mixture.
3   Bake in a moderate oven for 30 minutes.

# STEWED BEANS

*10 minutes cooking time*

*Ingredients for 4-5 servings*

3 cups soy beans
3 tablespoons brewer's yeast
1 bay leaf

2 onions, chopped
½ teaspoon salt
2 tablespoons chopped parsley

1   Mix all ingredients except parsley and simmer for 10 minutes.
2   Garnish with chopped parsley.

# CORN AND BEAN CASSEROLE

*40 minutes cooking time*

*Ingredients for 4-5 servings*

3 cups soy beans
3 cups corn
3 cups stewed tomatoes

1 crushed bay leaf
1 cup chopped parsley
½ cup wheat germ

1   Combine all ingredients and if you prefer add a little stock.
2   Place in casserole dish and bake for 40 minutes.
3   Garnish with chopped parsley.

# BEAN CASSEROLE

*30 minutes cooking time*

*Ingredients for 4-5 servings*

2 cups soy beans
1 cup chopped onion
1 cup grated cheddar cheese
½ teaspoon salt

2 cups carrots, diced
4 tomatoes, sliced
1 cup wholemeal breadcrumbs
¼ teaspoon white pepper

1 Combine cooked beans and carrots and blend thoroughly.
2 Season with salt and pepper.
3 Add breadcrumbs and onion.
4 Mix thoroughly.
5 Add tomatoes and cheese.
6 Bake in moderate oven for 30 minutes.

# Egg and Cheese Dishes

## EGGS BAKED IN TOMATOES

*15 minutes cooking time*

*Ingredients for 2 servings*

2 tomatoes
1 tablespoon chopped chives
¼ teaspoon pepper

2 eggs
½ teaspoon salt

1 Cut tops off the tomatoes.
2 Scoop out pulp and stand upside down for 6 minutes.
3 Season with salt and pepper.
4 Break one egg into each tomato cup and sprinkle with chives.
5 Bake for 15 minutes in moderate oven 180°C (350°F) and serve.

# CHEESE LOAF

*30 minutes cooking time*

*Ingredients for 4-5 servings*

2 beaten eggs
1 cup whole wheat breadcrumbs
1 cup milk

2 cups chopped walnuts
3 cups grated cheddar cheese

1 Combine eggs and milk.
2 Mix thoroughly.
3 Mix chopped walnuts, cheese and breadcrumbs.
4 Combine with eggs and milk.
5 Form into a loaf and bake for 30 minutes in oven 190°C (375°F).

# CHEESE SQUARES

*10 minutes cooking time*

*Ingredients for 4-5 servings*

3 eggs, beaten
4 tablespoons oil
1 cup chopped parsley

2 cups cheddar cheese, grated
6 slices wholewheat toast

1 Combine eggs and oil.
2 Dip bread cubes into this mixture and sprinkle with cheese.
3 Place on oiled sheet and bake for 7-10 minutes.
4 Serve with salad.

# ASPARAGUS AND EGGS

*8-10 minutes cooking time*

*Ingredients for 6 servings*

8 eggs
1 teaspoon salt
375 g (12 oz) asparagus tips

½ cup tomato sauce
½ teaspoon pepper
250 g (8 oz) mushrooms

1 Hardboil eggs and slice half of them.
2 Chop the white part of the other eggs and add to sauce, seasoning with salt and pepper.
3 Place in dish and add sliced eggs; sieve remaining yolks over top.
4 Serve with asparagus tips and grilled mushrooms.

# EGGS AND KIPPERS

*15 minutes cooking time*

*Ingredients for 4 servings*

4 eggs
½ teaspoon salt
8 slices buttered toast
60 g (2 oz) butter

3 kippers
¼ teaspoon pepper
4 tablespoons skim milk

1  Cook kippers in boiling water and when cool remove the bones, and mash. Sieve flesh.
2  Place flesh in small pan with milk and butter.
3  Beat eggs slightly and add to kippers.
4  Season with pepper and a little salt.
5  Cook and stir until eggs thicken.
6  Serve with buttered toast.

# CHEESE SOUFFLÉ

*25 minutes cooking time*

*Ingredients for 4 servings*

3 eggs
1 tablespoon butter
2 tablespoons skim milk
¼ teaspoon pepper

½ teaspoon dry mustard
1 carton cottage cheese
½ teaspoon salt

1  Melt butter and add milk.
2  Add cheese and beat until smooth.
3  Separate egg yolks from whites and season yolks with salt, pepper and mustard.
4  Beat egg yolks lightly with beater and add to cheese mixture.
5  Beat egg whites until stiff and fold into mixture.
6  Pour into prepared soufflé dish and bake for 25 minutes in hot oven 200°C (400°F).

# BAKED EGGS

*5 minutes cooking time*

*Ingredients for 4 servings*

| | |
|---|---|
| **4 eggs** | **2 tablespoons chopped ham** |
| **1½ teaspoons chopped onion** | **¼ cup breadcrumbs** |
| **½ teaspoon salt** | **⅛ teaspoon white pepper** |
| **1 tablespoon chopped parsley** | **3 teaspoons butter** |
| **4 tablespoons grated cheese** | **2 tablespoons skim milk** |

1. Melt butter and fry onion and ham.
2. Remove this mixture and place on the bottom of 4 greased ovenproof dishes.
3. Break an egg into each mould, add seasonings, milk and grated cheese.
4. Dot with breadcrumbs and a little butter.
5. Bake in hot oven until eggs set.
6. Garnish with chopped parsley and serve.

# TOMATO CHEESE SOUFFLÉ

*35 minutes cooking time*

*Ingredients for 6 servings*

| | |
|---|---|
| **2 tablespoons butter** | **1¼ cups tomato juice** |
| **½ teaspoon salt** | **¼ teaspoon pepper** |
| **125 g (4 oz) grated cheese** | **4 eggs** |
| **½ teaspoon dry mustard** | **30 g (1 oz) cornflour** |

1. Heat butter, remove from heat and stir in cornflour.
2. Return to flame and heat gently for 4 minutes.
3. Add tomato juice away from flame and stir constantly.
4. Cook until sauce thickens and season with salt and pepper.
5. Stir in beaten egg yolks, mustard and cheese.
6. Beat egg whites until stiff.
7. Fold into mixture and pour into soufflé dish.
8. Bake for 25 minutes in moderate oven.
9. Serve immediately.

# TOMATOES AND CHEESE

*30 minutes cooking time*

*Ingredients for 6 servings*

750 g (1½ lb) tomatoes
½ teaspoon salt
125 g (4 oz) grated cheese

2 onions, sliced
¼ teaspoon pepper
1 cucumber, peeled and sliced

1    Place half sliced tomatoes in casserole and add half of the cucumber.
2    Add onion and season with salt and pepper.
3    Repeat layers and top with tomatoes.
4    Dot with cheese and bake for 30 minutes in moderate oven 180°C (350°F).

# BAKED HAM AND EGGS

*10 minutes cooking time*

*Ingredients for 4 servings*

8 eggs
¼ cup grated cheese
½ teaspoon salt

4 ham slices
¼ teaspoon pepper
2 tablespoons butter

1    Melt butter in frying pan and add slices of ham.
2    Break eggs on top and season with pepper and salt.
3    Dot with cheese and bake until cheese melts and eggs have set.

# EGGS WITH TOMATOES

*25 minutes cooking time*

*Ingredients for 2 servings*

2 eggs, poached
2 tomatoes
cheese sauce
¼ teaspoon pepper

2 onions
¼ cup grated cheese
½ teaspoon salt

1    Boil chopped onion and drain. Season.
2    Heat chopped tomatoes and half-fill fireproof dishes with mixture of tomatoes and onions.
3    Add poached egg and cover with cheese sauce.
4    Add grated cheese and brown under griller.

# COTTAGE CHEESE LOAF

*1 hour cooking time*

*Ingredients for 4-5 servings*

**2 cups cottage cheese**
**½ teaspoon salt**
**3 tablespoons tomato pulp**

**2 cups brown rice**
**¼ teaspoon white pepper**
**3 tablespoons chopped onion**

1. Mix brown rice and cottage cheese.
2. Blend thoroughly.
3. Add chopped onion and tomato pulp.
4. Mix well.
5. Season with salt and pepper.
6. Form into a loaf and bake for 1 hour.

# Seafood

## FISHERMAN'S SCOTCH EGGS

*15 minutes cooking time*

*Ingredients for 4 servings*

4 hardboiled eggs
⅛ teaspoon white pepper
155 g (5 oz) smoked haddock
1 tablespoon butter
1 tablespoon flour

½ teaspoon salt
½ cup skim milk
1 egg
¼ cup breadcrumbs

1  Flake haddock and melt butter, add flour and fry until it forms a sandy mixture.
2  Add most of the milk and stir until boiling.
3  Season and smooth mixture.
4  Beat in haddock and leave to cool.
5  Shell eggs and roll in flour, divide fish mixture into four and flatten.
6  Wrap one circle around each egg and smooth over.
7  Dip in beaten egg and then in breadcrumbs.
8  Fry in oil and serve with chopped parsley.

# FISHERMAN'S STEW

*30 minutes cooking time*

*Ingredients for 3-4 servings*

1 whiting
½ cup crab meat
1½ onions, chopped
½ cup white wine
pinch saffron
½ teaspoon salt
1 garlic clove
2 tablespoons chopped parsley
1 clove

1 red mullet
1 John Dory cutlet
1 large tomato, peeled and deseeded
1 bay leaf
½ lemon
1½ tablespoons olive oil
¼ teaspoon white pepper
1 leek

1   Cut the fish into pieces and heat oil in pan.
2   Chop onions and cook until brown. Add fish and cover with water. Add muslin bag with bay leaf and crushed garlic clove.
3   Add tomato pulp, juice from lemon and chopped leek. Mix and add wine and parsley and season with salt and pepper.
4   Bring to boil and simmer over low heat for 15 minutes. Remove bag and stir in saffron.
5   Serve with French bread.

# PRAWNS AND CAULIFLOWER

*30 minutes cooking time*

*Ingredients for 6 servings*

1 cauliflower
2 teaspoons lemon juice
¼ teaspoon pepper
2½ cups tomato juice
125 g (4 oz) grated Cheddar cheese

45 g (1½ oz) cornflour
½ teaspoon salt
60 g (2 oz) butter
250 g (8 oz) peeled prawns
1½ teaspoons Worcestershire sauce

1   Cook cauliflower in boiling water.
2   Drain and place on serving dish. Keep hot.
3   Combine butter, cornflour and tomato juice. Mix well and add lemon juice, Worcestershire sauce and season with salt and pepper.
4   Stir in the prawns and half the cheese.
5   When sauce has thickened, pour over cauliflower and dot with remaining cheese.
6   Brown under griller and serve.

# FISH MADRID

*15-20 minutes cooking time*

*Ingredients for 2-3 servings*

500 g (1 lb) fish fillets
1 tablespoon chopped parsley
2 teaspoons vinegar
4 tablespoons chopped pimento

2 teaspoons Worcestershire sauce
½ cup tomato juice
2 teaspoons brown sugar
1 onion, sliced

1   Place fish fillets in baking dish and cover with mixture of remaining ingredients.
2   Season and bake for 15-20 minutes.

# BAKED SCHNAPPER WITH ELEGANT SAUCE

*20 minutes cooking time*

*Ingredients for 6 servings*

2 chicken stock cubes
1 crumbled bay leaf
6 schnapper fillets

1½ cups boiling water
pinch saffron
1½ green peppers, cut into rings

## SAUCE

¼ cup onion bouillon
1 clove garlic, crushed
1¼ cups tomato juice

3 green peppers, seeded and sliced
2 pimentos, sliced
dash Tabasco sauce

1   Combine stock, water, bay leaf, pinch of saffron and stand for 15 minutes.
2   Pour over fish and bake for 10 minutes in moderate oven.
3   Garnish with green pepper rings.
4   Combine bouillon, peppers and garlic in pan.
5   Cook for 10 minutes over low heat and transfer to blender.
6   Add tomato juice, reduced to half by boiling, pimentos and Tabasco sauce.
7   Blend for 1 minute and spoon over fish.

# FISH SPECIALTY

*25 minutes cooking time*

*Ingredients for 4 servings*

1 kg (2 lb) flounder fillets
½ teaspoon dill
2 tomatoes, chopped
2 tablespoons lemon juice
½ teaspoon pepper

2 teaspoons salt
1 cucumber, sliced
1 cup beef stock
2 teaspoons margarine

1 Season fillets with salt, pepper and lemon juice.
2 Stand for 20 minutes and combine stock and margarine in saucepan.
3 Pour over fish in baking pan.
4 Mix tomatoes, cucumber and dill.
5 Spoon over half of this mixture and bake for 15 minutes.
6 Just before serving add remaining ingredients and brown lightly.

# TUNA MOULD

*3 minutes cooking time*

*Ingredients for 8 servings*

3 cups tuna, flaked
1½ tablespoons lemon juice
1½ tablespoons gelatine
3 tablespoons chopped parsley
1 cup salad dressing

½ cup watercress
½ teaspoon salt
dash pepper
1½ cups chopped celery

1 Combine parsley, celery, salt, pepper and drained tuna.
2 Soak gelatine in water and dissolve over hot water.
3 Add gelatine to 1 cup salad dressing and mix in with other ingredients.
4 Pour into moulds and chill.
5 Unmould and garnish with watercress.

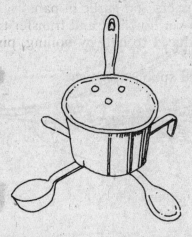

# STUFFED SOLE

*30 minutes cooking time*

*Ingredients for 6 servings*

| | |
|---|---|
| 6 large fillets of sole | 2 tablespoons lemon juice |
| 125 g (4 oz) mushrooms | 125 g (4 oz) diced celery |
| 1 teaspoon salt | ½ teaspoon pepper |
| 2 teaspoons grated lemon rind | 2 tablespoons chopped parsley |
| 1 tablespoon butter | |

1  Chop mushrooms and mix with celery, sliced mushrooms, parsley, lemon rind and juice.
2  Spread on fillets and season with salt and pepper.
3  Roll up firmly and place in ovenproof dish with melted butter. Cover.
4  Bake for 30 minutes in moderate oven 180°C (350°F).

# SLIM SCALLOPS

*10 minutes cooking time*

*Ingredients for 4 servings*

| | |
|---|---|
| 1 kg (2 lb) scallops | 1½ teaspoons salt |
| ½ teaspoon pepper | 1 cup clam juice |
| 2 garlic cloves, crushed | 1 tablespoon chopped parsley |
| 4 tablespoons lemon juice | 3 tablespoons margarine |

1  Season scallops with salt and pepper.
2  Place in baking dish and mix garlic, clam juice, parsley and lemon juice in pan.
3  Cook for a few minutes over low heat and pour mixture over scallops.
4  Grill for 5 minutes and add margarine to scallops.

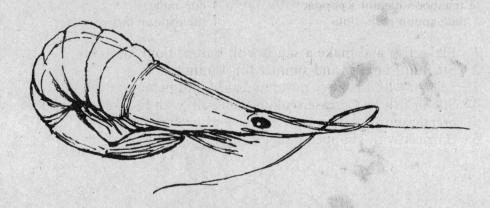

# CAPRICORN PRAWN CURRY

*45 minutes cooking time*

*Ingredients for 8 servings*

1 kg (2 lb) raw shelled prawns
2 cloves garlic
2 tablespoons butter
90 g (3 oz) tomatoes
½ teaspoon pepper
2 tablespoons chopped parsley
½ lemon, sliced
1¼ cups fish stock

125 g (4 oz) onions
1 teaspoon treacle
2 tablespoons lemon juice
½ teaspoon salt
15 g (½ oz) rice flour
90 g (3 oz) apple
1 tablespoon curry powder
½ tablespoon desiccated coconut

1  Peel garlic and crush. Peel onion and chop.
2  Peel apple and dice.
3  Fry in butter and stir in curry powder.
4  Add coconut, treacle and stock.
5  Season with salt and pepper and add tomato flesh.
6  Bring to boil and simmer for 30 minutes.
7  Blend rice flour with ¼ cup cold stock and stir into sauce.
8  Bring to boil, stirring constantly and simmer for 4 minutes.
9  Place shelled prawns in sauce and heat for a few minutes.
10  Garnish with lemon slices.

# SCALLOPED FISH

*15 minutes cooking time*

*Ingredients for 6 servings*

750 g (1½ lb) cooked fish
½ teaspoon prepared mustard
2 tablespoons chopped parsley
¼ teaspoon cayenne pepper
1 tablespoon plain flour

1 teaspoon anchovy paste
¼ cup breadcrumbs
1 lemon
1 cup milk
1 tablespoon butter

1  Flake fish and make a sauce with butter, flour and milk.
2  Stir until boiling and simmer for 4 minutes.
3  Season with anchovy paste, mustard and pepper.
4  Stir in fish and grease scallop shells, fill with fish mixture and dot with breadcrumbs. Add a little butter and brown.
5  Garnish with chopped parsley and lemon.

# PRAWNS AND EGGPLANT

*50 minutes cooking time*

*Ingredients for 4 servings*

⅓ cup chopped onion
½ cup prepared prawns
½ teaspoon salt
⅛ teaspoon oregano
½ green pepper, chopped
¼ cup celery, sliced

¾ cup tinned tomatoes
375 g (12 oz) eggplant
¼ teaspoon pepper
1 clove garlic, crushed
2 tablespoons consommé

1   Mix consommé, onion, celery and seasonings in saucepan.
2   Cover and simmer for 15 minutes, add green pepper, garlic, tomatoes, oregano and blend well.
3   Peel eggplant and cube. Arrange layer of eggplant in casserole and top with remaining ingredients. Repeat layers.
4   Top with prawns and bake for 35 minutes in moderate oven 180°C (350°F).

# TOMATO PRAWN MOULD

*5 minutes cooking time*

*Ingredients for 6 servings*

2½ cups tomato juice
4 minced gherkins
500 g (1 lb) shelled prawns
½ teaspoon salt
30 g (1 oz) gelatine

3 teaspoons lemon juice
½ cucumber, sliced
¼ teaspoon pepper
1 teaspoon Worcestershire sauce
1 head lettuce

1   Soften gelatine in water and dissolve over heat.
2   Stir in half the tomato juice and mix.
3   Cool with remaining tomato juice and add flavourings.
4   Season with salt and pepper.
5   Stir in prawns and small cucumber cubes.
6   When mixture has thickened spoon into mould and when ready to serve turn out on to lettuce.

# ACAPULCO FISH

*10 minutes cooking time*

*Ingredients for 6 servings*

| | |
|---|---|
| 1½ packets frozen fish fillets | 3 tablespoons lemon juice |
| ½ cup pineapple chunks | 1 teaspoon salt |
| ½ cup chilli sauce | |

1  Thaw fillets.
2  Cube fish fillets and arrange under griller.
3  Sprinkle with lemon juice, salt and chilli sauce.
4  Add pineapple chunks and grill for 10 minutes.

# CREAMED ROES

*15 minutes cooking time*

*Ingredients for 4 servings*

| | |
|---|---|
| 375 g (12 oz) soft roes | ½ teaspoon salt |
| ¼ teaspoon pepper | 1 tablespoon chopped parsley |
| lemon wedges | 2 teaspoons flour |
| 2 teaspoons butter | 1 cup milk |

1  Wash and season roes.
2  Simmer in milk for 5-6 minutes and mash through a sieve.
3  Melt butter in pan and add flour. Work in milk and add mashed roes.
4  Bring to boil and season with salt and pepper.
5  Serve on toast with chopped parsley and lemon wedges.

# SCALLOP KEBAB

*10 minutes cooking time*

*Ingredients for 6 servings*

| | |
|---|---|
| 750 g (1½ lb) scallops | 250 g (8 oz) bacon rashers |
| 6 pineapple slices | ½ teaspoon pepper |
| 1 teaspoon salt | |

1  Cut scallops in halves and cut rashers into 10 centimetre (4 in) lengths.
2  Roll each scallop in bacon and place 4 on each skewer.
3  Season and cook under grill.
4  Serve on pineapple slices.

# BAKED SOLE

*15 minutes cooking time*

*Ingredients for 4 servings*

750 g (1½ lb) sole fillets
½ teaspoon pepper
2 slices bread, rolled into crumbs
4 tablespoons water

1 teaspoon salt
3 cups chopped spinach
6 tablespoons dry nonfat milk
½ cup chopped onion

1  Season fish with salt and pepper. Lay fillets in baking dish.
2  Combine spinach, breadcrumbs, milk, water, and onion.
3  Mix and spoon mixture into baking dish over fish.
4  Bake for 15 minutes and serve.

# SOLE WITH MUSHROOMS

*10 minutes cooking time*

*Ingredients for 6 servings*

3 cups fresh mushrooms, sliced
1.5 kg (3 lb) sole fillets
4 tablespoons chopped parsley

¾ cup lemon juice
½ cup chopped onion

1  Combine mushrooms, parsley and onion.
2  Place in baking dish and place fillets on top of mixture.
3  Pour over lemon juice and bake for 10 minutes in moderate oven 190°C (375°F).

# SMOKED COD CASSEROLE

*30 minutes cooking time*

*Ingredients for 4 servings*

750 g (1½ lb) smoked cod
½ teaspoon salt
1¼ cups tomato juice

1 onion, chopped
¼ teaspoon pepper
1 teaspoon Worcestershire sauce

1  Place cod in casserole.
2  Season with salt and pepper.
3  Add chopped onion and pour over tomato juice and Worcestershire sauce.
4  Cook in moderate oven for 25-30 minutes.

# BAKED COD'S ROE

*20 minutes cooking time*

*Ingredients for 2 servings*

3 tomatoes
375 g (12 oz) soft roes
¼ teaspoon pepper
2 teaspoons lemon juice
1 teaspoon onion juice

¼ cup breadcrumbs
½ teaspoon salt
4 tablespoons white wine
1 tablespoon chopped parsley

1  Skin tomatoes.
2  Remove seeds and chop.
3  Grease baking dish and lay seasoned roes in.
4  Mix tomato, onion juice and parsley together with lemon juice and spread over roes.
5  Pour over white wine and cover with foil or greased paper.
6  Bake for 15-20 minutes in moderate to slow oven.

# ROLLED SOLE

*20 minutes cooking time*

*Ingredients for 4 servings*

4 sole fillets
½ teaspoon pepper
2 tablespoons chopped parsley
juice of 1 lemon

1 teaspoon salt
2 bay leaves
1 tablespoon butter

1  Combine parsley, butter and lemon juice together.
2  Season with salt and pepper.
3  Spread on fillets and roll up.
4  Place fillets in deep dish and just cover with water.
5  Add bay leaf.
6  Cover and cook for 20 minutes in moderate oven.

# TOMATO STUFFED SOLE

*30 minutes cooking time*

*Ingredients for 2 servings*

4 small fillets of sole
2 tomatoes
½ teaspoon salt
1 tablespoon lemon juice

1 tablespoon butter
1 teaspoon capers
¼ teaspoon pepper
¼ teaspoon chopped thyme

1   Skin and chop tomatoes. Combine with chopped capers, thyme, salt, pepper and lemon juice.
2   Spread fillets with above mixture and roll up firmly.
3   Place in buttered dish and bake for 30 minutes in moderate oven 180°C (350°F).

# FISH COOKED IN VINEGAR

*20 minutes cooking time*

*Ingredients for 4-5 servings*

3 pieces sole
½ teaspoon salt
1 tablespoon butter

4 tablespoons vinegar
½ teaspoon white pepper
2 cups cold water

1   Place water in frying pan and add fish.
2   Season with salt and pepper.
3   Pour in vinegar and dot with butter.
4   Simmer for 20 minutes and serve immediately.

# Poultry

## CHICKEN WITH JUICE

*1 hour cooking time*

*Ingredients for 4-5 servings*

1.5 kg (3 lb) chicken
½ cup pineapple juice
1 teaspoon salt
5 tablespoons butter

4 tablespoons lemon juice
¼ cup flour
¼ teaspoon white pepper

1   Cut chicken into serving pieces.
2   Wash chicken, drain and dry.
3   Combine flour, salt and pepper.
4   Dip chicken pieces into seasoned flour.
5   Sauté chicken pieces in butter, cover and cook for 5 minutes.
6   Add lemon juice and pineapple juice.
7   Cover and cook slowly for 45 minutes.

# BOILED CHICKEN

*1¼ hours cooking time*

*Ingredients for 3-4 servings*

| | |
|---|---|
| **1 chicken** | **2 tablespoons lemon juice** |
| **5 cups stock** | **6 peppercorns** |
| **bouquet garni** | **1 carrot** |
| **1 turnip** | **1 onion** |
| **1½ tablespoons plain flour** | **1½ tablespoons butter** |
| **1 tablespoon chopped parsley** | **2 hardboiled eggs, chopped** |

1   Clean and truss chicken. Rub with lemon juice.
2   Place chicken in boiling stock.
3   Add bouquet garni, peppercorns, carrot and turnip. Stir and add onion.
4   Cook for approximately 1 hour.
5   Melt butter and stir in flour.
6   Add ¾ cup stock slowly and mix gently.
7   Cook for 2 minutes and add chopped hardboiled eggs and parsley.
8   Pour over chicken and serve.

# CHICKEN WITH ONIONS

*1 hour 10 minutes cooking time*

*Ingredients for 6 servings*

| | |
|---|---|
| **750 g (1½ lb) chicken pieces** | **1 tablespoon lemon juice** |
| **2 teaspoons Worcestershire sauce** | **1 teaspoon salt** |
| **¼ teaspoon pepper** | **2 onions, sliced** |

1   Place chicken pieces in buttered casserole.
2   Cover with onion.
3   Add lemon juice.
4   Season with salt, pepper and Worcestershire sauce.
5   Bake for 1 hour 10 minutes in moderate oven 180°C (350°F).

# CHICKEN AND LEEKS

*3 hours cooking time*

*Ingredients for 4-5 servings*

½ boiling chicken
1 tablespoon rice
2 cloves
250 g (8 oz) leeks
½ carrot
½ teaspoon pepper

½ onion
1 tablespoon chopped parsley
5 cups water
½ turnip
½ teaspoon salt

1  Trim and cut leeks into short lengths.
2  Place chicken into pan and cover with water.
3  Season with salt and bring to boil.
4  Season with pepper and add sliced carrot and turnip.
5  After you have peeled the onion, stick cloves in it and place in pot. Cook for 3 hours.
6  Strain broth and add rice and leeks to pan with broth.
7  Boil for 20 minutes and dice a little chicken flesh. Place chicken meat in broth and garnish with chopped parsley.

# TASTY GRILLED CHICKEN

*25 minutes cooking time*

*Ingredients for 6 servings*

3 small chickens
1 teaspoon pepper
3 tablespoons mustard

2 teaspoons salt
60 g (2 oz) butter
2 tablespoons lemon juice

1  Cut chickens in halves and season with salt and pepper.
2  Place under griller for 4 minutes on each side.
3  Remove from griller.
4  Spread with mixture of mustard, lemon juice and butter.
5  Grill under moderate heat, turning occasionally, for 15 minutes.
6  Baste with drippings from pan and serve.

# PEKING BARBECUED CHICKEN

*1½ hours cooking time*

*Ingredients for 4 servings*

1 1.5-kg (3-lb) chicken
¼ teaspoon pepper
3 teaspoons fresh ginger, grated
1 tablespoon peanut oil

1 garlic clove, minced
1 teaspoon dry mustard
⅓ cup soy sauce

1 Combine all ingredients except chicken, and mix well.
2 Place chicken in pan, brush with marinade and stand for 1 hour.
3 Spit and rotate over medium coals for 1½ hours. Baste occasionally.

# Meat

# BEEF STEW

*2¹/₄ hours cooking time*

*Ingredients for 4 servings*

**500 g (1 lb) chuck steak**
**¼ teaspoon pepper**
**bouquet garni**
**2 carrots**
**2 onions**

**½ teaspoon salt**
**1 turnip**
**2 cups stock**
**2 teaspoons butter**

1  Wipe meat and cut into cubes.
2  Cut vegetables into cubes and melt butter in frying pan.
3  Fry vegetables until golden brown and remove.
4  Brown meat in same pan and remove.
5  Add flour to pan and mix. Add stock and bring to boil.
6  Add bouquet garni, and season with salt and pepper.
7  Place meat and vegetables back into pan and cover.
8  Cook for 2 hours and serve with chopped parsley.

# MUSTARD STEAK

*15 minutes cooking time*

*Ingredients for 6 servings*

| | |
|---|---|
| **750 g (1½ lb) chuck steak** | **3 teaspoons lemon juice** |
| **½ teaspoon pepper** | **1½ teaspoons salt** |

1  Season steaks with salt and pepper.
2  Spoon over lemon juice and grill for 6 minutes on each side.

## MUSTARD SAUCE

| | |
|---|---|
| **1 tablespoon brown mustard** | **2 tablespoons margarine** |
| **2 tablespoons chopped parsley** | **3 teaspoons lemon juice** |
| **½ teaspoon pepper** | |

1  Combine ingredients in mixing bowl and stir with spatula until ingredients are smooth.
2  Spoon over steaks and serve.

# CIDER BEEF

*1½ hours cooking time*

*Ingredients for 6 servings*

| | |
|---|---|
| **1 kg (2 lb) stewing steak** | **1¼ cups cider** |
| **2 stock cubes** | **2 cloves garlic, crushed** |
| **3 carrots, cut into strips** | **3 onions, sliced** |
| **3 oranges** | **1 teaspoon salt** |
| **2½ tablespoons corn oil** | **60 g (2 oz) cornflour** |
| **½ teaspoon pepper** | |

1  Trim meat and cube. Coat with seasoned cornflour and heat corn oil.
2  Add meat, onion and garlic. Fry gently.
3  Remove and place in casserole dish.
4  Peel oranges thinly and blanch peel and cut into strips.
5  Squeeze oranges and add juice to cider.
6  Make up to 5 cups with water and add stock cubes and any remaining cornflour to frying pan. Stir in liquid and bring to boil. Simmer for 1-2 minutes and pour into casserole.
7  Cover and cook for 1½ hours in moderate oven.
8  Garnish with remaining orange strips.

# STEAK WITH MUSHROOMS

*8 minutes cooking time*

*Ingredients for 6 servings*

| | |
|---|---|
| **1.5 kg (3 lb) steak** | **½ teaspoon salt** |
| **½ teaspoon pepper** | **250 g (8 oz) mushroom caps** |

1 Preheat griller.
2 Put meat on rack under griller.
3 Cook until meat is browned and season with salt and pepper.
4 Turn meat and top with mushrooms. Brown and serve.

# STEAK TARTARE

*No cooking time*

*Ingredients for 4 servings*

| | |
|---|---|
| **500 g (1 lb) rump steak** | **4 egg yolks** |
| **1 finely chopped onion** | **8 tablespoons capers** |
| **1 teaspoon salt** | **½ teaspoon pepper** |

1 Scrape steak with a knife along the grain.
2 When steak breaks down to a fibreless mush, season with salt and pepper.
3 Stir in chopped onion and capers.
4 Break egg yolks into a little dent in the centre of each portion.
5 Serve with green salad.

# MEAT LOAF

*2 hours cooking time*

*Ingredients for 4-5 servings*

| | |
|---|---|
| **1 kg (2 lb) round steak** | **2 cups milk** |
| **1 cup chopped onion** | **2 teaspoons raw sugar** |
| **1 cup grated lemon rind** | **½ teaspoon salt** |
| **¼ teaspoon white pepper** | |

1 Cut meat into cubes, then mash or mince.
2 Mix with milk, sugar, onion and lemon rind.
3 Season with salt and pepper.
4 Form into a loaf and bake for 2 hours.
5 Serve immediately.

# GOULASH

*Ingredients for 6 servings*

*1 hour 10 minutes cooking time*

750 g (1½ lb) beef
2 cloves garlic
white pepper
bouquet garni
75 g (2½ oz) bacon

250 g (8 oz) onions
½ teaspoon salt
½ teaspoon crushed aniseed
1½ tablespoons flour
15 g (½ oz) paprika

1  Chop bacon into small pieces and fry with onion and garlic.
2  Add meat and fry. Season with salt and pepper.
3  Sprinkle with flour and paprika.
4  Pour stock over meat and bring to boil.
5  Add bouquet garni and aniseed.
6  Simmer for 1 hour and remove garlic and bouquet garni before serving.

# SUKIYAKI

*Ingredients for 6 servings*

*15 minutes cooking time*

750 g (1½ lb) round steak
3 saccharine tablets
2 chicken stock cubes
4 cups raw spinach
4 sticks celery, diced
375 g (12 oz) mushrooms, sliced

315 g (10 oz) bamboo shoots, sliced
½ cup soy sauce
⅔ cup hot water
2 onions, sliced
12 spring onions, in 5 cm (2 in) pieces

1  Cut meat diagonally into very thin strips.
2  Rub pan with fat and brown meat. Add all ingredients except spinach.
3  Simmer for 8 minutes and add spinach.
4  Cook for 5 minutes and serve with rice.

# RICH MEAT LOAF

*45 minutes cooking time*

*Ingredients for 4-5 servings*

| | |
|---|---|
| 1 kg (2 lb) ground beef | 1 cup milk powder |
| 2 onions, grated | 1 teaspoon salt |
| 2 cups tomatoes | 3 tablespoons brewer's yeast |
| 2 eggs, beaten | 1 cup stock |

1  Combine beef, milk powder, onions and salt.
2  Mix thoroughly.
3  Add tomatoes, brewer's yeast, eggs and stock.
4  Blend thoroughly.
5  Place in oiled loaf pan and bake for 40 minutes.

# MIXED GRILL

*15 minutes cooking time*

*Ingredients for 4-5 servings*

| | |
|---|---|
| 6 small fillet steaks | 5 tomatoes, sliced |
| 6 lamb chops | 2 peeled bananas, halved |
| 1 green pepper, chopped | |

1  Place ingredients alternately on oiled rack.
2  Cook under the grill for 6 minutes and turn.
3  Cook for further 6 minutes and serve immediately.

# BRAISED LAMB CHOPS

*30 minutes cooking time*

*Ingredients for 4-5 servings*

| | |
|---|---|
| 6 chump chops | ½ teaspoon salt |
| ¼ teaspoon white pepper | 1 cup chopped celery |
| 1 cup chopped parsnips | |

1  Braise chops in usual manner.
2  Season with salt and pepper.
3  Add parsnips and celery.
4  Simmer for 20 minutes and serve.

# LAMB STEW

*2 hours cooking time*

*Ingredients for 4-5 servings*

1.5 kg (3 lb) lamb, cut into cubes
water
2 cups chopped onions
1 cup chopped parsley
2 tablespoons wholemeal flour

½ teaspoon salt
2 cups chopped carrots
2 cups diced potatoes
1 cup fresh peas

1 Season lamb with salt.
2 Cover with water and simmer for 1 hour.
3 Add carrots, onions, parsley and potatoes.
4 Simmer for further 20 minutes.
5 Thicken with flour.
6 Add peas and simmer for further 20 minutes.
7 Serve immediately.

# LAMB WITH BEANS

*20 minutes cooking time*

*Ingredients for 4-5 servings*

1.25 kg (2½ lb) lamb
2 teaspoons lemon juice
½ teaspoon salt
¼ teaspoon white pepper

2 tablespoons wholemeal flour
1 kg (2 lb) string beans
2 cups tomato purée

1 Slice lamb and boil for 10 minutes.
2 Season with salt and pepper.
3 Add string beans and tomato purée.
4 Simmer for 5 minutes.
5 Add lemon juice.
6 Simmer for 5 minutes, then thicken with flour.
7 Serve immediately.

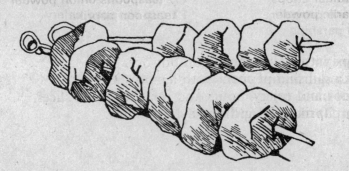

# KEBAB

*20 minutes cooking time*

*Ingredients for 4-5 servings*

1 kg (2 lb) lamb, cut into cubes
½ teaspoon salt
pineapple slices

2 tablespoons olive oil
2 tablespoons lemon juice
3 tomatoes, cut in half

1 Marinate meat in mixture of oil and lemon juice for 6 hours.
2 Season with salt.
3 Place meat on skewers alternately with pineapple and tomato.
4 Grill, turning once.
5 Serve immediately.

# PEPPERED LAMB

*30 minutes cooking time*

*Ingredients for 4-5 servings*

500 g (1 lb) ground lamb
3 green peppers, chopped
3 tablespoons chopped onions

3 tablespoons chopped parsley
2 tablespoons butter
½ teaspoon salt

1 Cook peppers for 10 minutes in butter.
2 Brown onion and meat in butter and season with salt.
3 Add chopped parsley and serve when cooked through.
4 Serve with rice or salad.

# TASTY LAMB CHOPS

*8-10 minutes cooking time*

*Ingredients for 6 servings*

6 large lamb shoulder chops
1½ teaspoons garlic powder
½ lemon, sliced

1½ teaspoons onion powder
1 teaspoon paprika

1 Season chops with garlic and onion powder.
2 Place in baking dish and cover with lemon slices.
3 Stand in cool place for 24 hours and remove lemon slices.
4 Season with paprika and grill for 8-10 minutes.

# LAMB STUFFED CABBAGE

*55 minutes cooking time*

*Ingredients for 2 servings*

| | |
|---|---|
| 1 cup ground lamb | 1 egg, beaten |
| ½ small cabbage | ½ teaspoon salt |
| pinch nutmeg | ¼ teaspoon pepper |
| ½ cup stock | ½ onion, grated |

1  Cut core from cabbage and peel off 6 leaves. Drop into boiling salted water, and cook for 3 minutes.
2  Remove and drain.
3  Shred finely 1 cup remaining cabbage and mix with onion, egg, nutmeg, lamb, salt and pepper.
4  Mix thoroughly and place mixture into centre of each whole cabbage leaf.
5  Wrap leaf around filling and pour stock over.
6  Bake for 50 minutes in moderate oven 180°C (350°F), basting occasionally.

# POTTED LAMB

*2¾ hours cooking time*

*Ingredients for 4 servings*

| | |
|---|---|
| 1 kg (2 lb) lamb | 3 tablespoons flour |
| 2 teaspoons salt | ½ teaspoon pepper |
| 4 potatoes, sliced | 3 onions, sliced |

1  Wipe meat with damp cloth.
2  Cut into 2.5 centimetre (1 in) cubes and roll in seasoned flour.
3  Place alternate layers of meat, onions and potatoes in pan; finish with potatoes.
4  Fill with warm water and cover.
5  Bake for 2¾ hours in moderate oven.

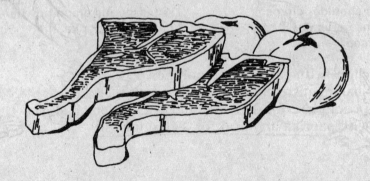

# PORK

*3 hours cooking time*

*Ingredients for 5-6 servings*

2 kg (4 lb) pork
3 cloves garlic
3 brown onions
2 tablespoons wholemeal flour
¼ teaspoon white pepper
chopped parsley

3 oranges
2 teaspoons honey
thyme
½ teaspoon salt
2 tablespoons oil

1 Combine onion, garlic, thyme, salt, oil, parsley and pepper.
2 Mix thoroughly.
3 Rub over meat and bake for 2½-3 hours.
4 While meat is baking, squeeze oranges and reserve juice.
5 Make sauce with orange juice and honey thickened with flour.

# PORK LOAF

*1½ hours cooking time*

*Ingredients for 4-5 servings*

1 kg (2 lb) ground pork
1 cup milk
1 cup wholewheat breadcrumbs

2 eggs
1 small can tomato purée

1 Combine 1 tablespoon tomato purée with pork and breadcrumbs.
2 Mix well.
3 Add eggs and milk.
4 Form into a loaf and pour over remaining purée.
5 Cover and bake for 1½ hours.

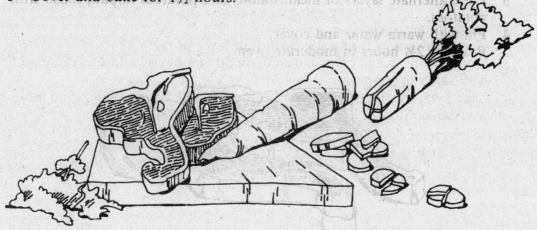

# VEAL DELUXE

*1 hour 10 minutes cooking time*

*Ingredients for 4 servings*

500 g (1 lb) veal fillet
½ teaspoon salt
1 teaspoon lemon juice
2 cups stock
125 g (4 oz) button onions
60 g (2 oz) butter
¼ teaspoon pepper
4 tablespoons white wine

bouquet garni
1¼ cups skim milk
1 egg yolk
125 g (4 oz) button mushrooms
1 tablespoon plain flour
½ teaspoon salt
1 tablespoon chopped parsley

1  Wipe meat and cube. Slice mushrooms and place stock, wine, veal, mushrooms and onions in saucepan.
2  Add bouquet garni and simmer for 1 hour.
3  Melt butter in another pan and add flour. Fry for a few seconds and add milk, 1¼ cups of the stock and wine.
4  Add cooked veal and vegetables. Season with salt, pepper and lemon juice. Remove from heat.
5  Stir in egg yolk and reheat. Do not boil.
6  Garnish with chopped parsley.

# CALVES' LIVER AND ONIONS

*40 minutes cooking time*

*Ingredients for 4 servings*

375 g (12 oz) calves' liver
½ teaspoon salt
3 tablespoons olive oil

500 g (1 lb) onions
¼ teaspoon pepper
2 cups cooked rice

1  Slice onions finely.
2  Cover bottom of frying pan with thin layer of oil.
3  Place onions in and cook, covered, for 30 minutes over low heat. Season with salt and pepper.
4  Slice liver very thinly and add to onions. Cook for 5 minutes and serve with boiled rice.

# LIVER KEBABS

*10 minutes cooking time*

*Ingredients for 4 servings*

| | |
|---|---|
| **500 g (1 lb) sheep's liver** | **250 g (8 oz) bacon** |
| **2 onions** | **250 g (8 oz) mushrooms** |
| **1 lemon** | **¼ teaspoon thyme** |
| **½ teaspoon salt** | **¼ teaspoon pepper** |
| **4 tablespoons olive oil** | |

1  Slice liver thickly and divide slices into four pieces.
2  Season with salt, pepper and thyme and squeeze lemon juice over.
3  Remove rind from bacon, chop into pieces; slice onion thickly.
4  Remove stalks from mushrooms and thread liver, bacon, onion and mushrooms alternately on skewers.
5  Brush with olive oil and heat grill pan.
6  Grill for 4-5 minutes, turn and grill another 4-5 minutes.

# LIVER COOKED IN ORANGE
# AND LEMON

*20 minutes cooking time*

*Ingredients for 4-5 servings*

| | |
|---|---|
| **2 lambs' fries** | **juice of 3 oranges** |
| **juice of 3 lemons** | **2 onions, chopped** |
| **2 tablespoons butter** | **2 cloves garlic** |
| **½ cup red wine** | **2 tablespoons wholemeal flour** |

1  Sauté lamb's fry and onion in butter.
2  Crush garlic and add to pan.
3  Pour juice of oranges and lemons into lamb's fry and onion.
4  Cook for 10 minutes and then add red wine.
5  Thicken with wholemeal flour and serve.

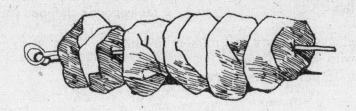

# LIVER WITH APPLES

*1½ hours cooking time*

*Ingredients for 4 servings*

4 rashers bacon
375 g (12 oz) liver, sliced
¼ teaspoon pepper

1½ apples, diced
1 teaspoon salt
1 onion, chopped

1  Cut bacon slices into two and combine with liver, onion, apples and seasonings in greased ovenproof dish.
2  Bake for 1½ hours in moderate oven and serve.

# WASHINGTON LIVER

*10 minutes cooking time*

*Ingredients for 6 servings*

750 g (1½ lb) sheep's liver
3 garlic cloves
3 tablespoons oil
½ teaspoon pepper

1 cup skim milk
2 tablespoons chopped parsley
½ teaspoon salt
2 teaspoons lemon juice

1  Slice liver into strips and soak in milk.
2  Leave for 3 hours.
3  Dry and season with salt and pepper.
4  Heat oil in pan and add liver.
5  Add crushed garlic and cook for 5 minutes.
6  Add squeeze of lemon juice and serve.

# KIDNEYS IN BUTTER

*20 minutes cooking time*

*Ingredients for 4-5 servings*

5 kidneys, cut in half
155 g (5 oz) butter
½ teaspoon salt

4 tablespoons chopped shallots
¾ teaspoon white pepper
2 tablespoons chopped parsley

1  Sauté kidneys, shallots and parsley in butter.
2  Season with salt and pepper.
3  Cook for 15 minutes and serve.

# KIDNEY CASSEROLE

*1 hour cooking time*

*Ingredients for 6 servings*

| | |
|---|---|
| **2½ cups beef kidneys** | **½ teaspoon Worcestershire sauce** |
| **1½ cups diced carrots** | **2 potatoes, peeled and sliced** |
| **1½ teaspoons salt** | **¼ teaspoon paprika** |
| **½ teaspoon pepper** | **1 cup tinned tomatoes** |
| **1 onion, sliced** | |

1  Soak kidneys in cold water for 3 hours, changing water from time to time. Drain.
2  Pour boiling water over them and remove skin and tubes.
3  Cut into very small pieces and season with salt and pepper.
4  Combine onion, carrots and kidney pieces.
5  Cover with water and simmer for 30 minutes.
6  Pour mixture into casserole dish and add potatoes, tomatoes, salt, paprika, Worcestershire sauce and pepper.
7  Cook for 30 minutes in hot oven 200°C (400°F).

# KIDNEY-STUFFED ONIONS

*1½ hours cooking time*

*Ingredients for 3 servings*

| | |
|---|---|
| **6 large onions** | **6 lambs' kidneys** |
| **1 teaspoon salt** | **¼ teaspoon pepper** |
| **2 cups beef stock** | |

1  Cut slice from top of each onion and remove centres.
2  Chop centres and add to stock.
3  Season with salt and pepper.
4  Pour into casserole.
5  Stuff a seasoned kidney into each onion, place in casserole.
6  Place slices back on top of onions and cover.
7  Cook for 1½ hours in moderate oven 190°C (375°F).

# STEWED KIDNEYS

*30 minutes cooking time*

*Ingredients for 6 servings*

750 g (1½ lb) lambs' kidneys
3 tablespoons dry sherry
1 clove garlic, halved
1 teaspoon salt
3 tablespoons chopped parsley

⅔ cup sliced mushrooms
1½ cups bouillon
1 bay leaf
½ teaspoon pepper

1   Wash kidneys and place in boiling water.
2   Remove after 1 minute and drain.
3   Remove skin, split, remove tubes and fat.
4   Soak in salted water for 30 minutes and drain.
5   Slice and combine with mushrooms, bouillon, bay leaf, salt, pepper, garlic and sherry.
6   Cover and simmer for 20 minutes.
7   Remove garlic and bay leaf.
8   Add parsley and serve.

# TRIPE AND ONIONS

*55 minutes cooking time*

*Ingredients for 4 servings*

500 g (1 lb) tripe
½ teaspoon salt
1 tablespoon chopped parsley
155 g (5 oz) onions

1 teaspoon plain flour
¼ teaspoon pepper
2 teaspoons butter
1¼ cups milk

1   Cut tripe into pieces.
2   Slice onions and place them with the tripe in milk and bring to boil.
3   Lower heat and simmer until cooked.
4   Combine butter and flour together, mix and add slowly to pan.
5   Stir and season.
6   Pour into serving dish and garnish with chopped parsley.

# BOILED BEEF TONGUE

*3 hours cooking time*

*Ingredients for 4 servings*

| | |
|---|---|
| **1 small beef tongue** | **1 bay leaf** |
| **8 peppercorns** | **2 cloves** |
| **1½ teaspoons salt** | **¼ teaspoon pepper** |
| **2 tablespoons chopped parsley** | **½ cup diced celery** |
| **1 sliced onion** | **1 sliced carrot** |

1   Wash tongue.
2   Cover tongue with water and add remaining ingredients.
3   Bring to boil and simmer over low heat for 3 hours.
4   Remove tongue and remove skin and throat part from tongue.
5   Serve sliced with horseradish.


# SCRAMBLED BRAINS

*15 minutes cooking time*

*Ingredients for 2 servings*

| | |
|---|---|
| **1 set sheep brains** | **1 tablespoon lemon juice** |
| **1 onion, sliced** | **6 peppercorns** |
| **4 eggs** | **½ teaspoon salt** |
| **1 teaspoon vinegar** | **1 tablespoon melted butter** |
| **⅛ teaspoon pepper** | |

1   Soak brains in salted water, clean and parboil in salted water, containing lemon juice, sliced onion and peppercorns.
2   Drain brains and chop into small pieces.
3   Beat 4 eggs and vinegar, salt, pepper and melted butter.
4   Stir in chopped brains and heat mixture, stirring constantly, until set.

# Sauces

## GREEN AVOCADO SAUCE

*Ingredients for 4-5 servings*

| | |
|---|---|
| 2 large avocados | 2 tablespoons dressing |
| 1½ tablespoons sour cream | ½ teaspoon salt |
| ¼ teaspoon white pepper | 1 teaspoon chopped chives |

1  Mash the avocados and beat in dressing.
2  Dot with chives.
3  Season with salt and pepper.
4  Top with sour cream and serve immediately.

# ONION-TOMATO SAUCE

*5 minutes cooking time*

*Ingredients for 4-5 servings*

3 cups tomato juice
2 cups chopped onions
¼ teaspoon white pepper

2 tablespoons butter
½ teaspoon salt

1   Sauté onions in butter and stir.
2   Add tomato juice and stir constantly.
3   Season with salt and pepper.
4   Serve.

# MUSHROOM AND PARSLEY SAUCE

*5 minutes cooking time*

*Ingredients for 2-3 servings*

1 cup chopped mushrooms
2 tablespoons wholemeal flour
½ cup cream
1 cup chopped parsley

4 tablespoons melted butter
½ cup chicken or celery soup
¼ teaspoon salt

1   Brown the mushrooms in butter.
2   Add flour and blend with soup; then add cream.
3   Stir constantly until mixture thickens.
4   Season with salt.
5   Add chopped parsley and stir.

# CHOPPED NUT SAUCE

*Ingredients for 4-5 servings*

125 g (4 oz) butter
5 tablespoons chopped nuts
¼ teaspoon white pepper

2 tablespoons lemon juice
½ teaspoon salt

1   Beat butter until fluffy and add lemon juice.
2   Combine with chopped nuts and season with salt and pepper.

# TOMATO SAUCE

*5 minutes cooking time*

*Ingredients for 4-5 servings*

1 can tomatoes
½ teaspoon salt

1 cup grated gruyère cheese
¼ teaspoon white pepper

1 Combine cheese and tomatoes and stir constantly.
2 Heat over very low heat until cheese melts.
3 Season with salt and pepper.
4 Simmer.

# ONION SAUCE

*10 minutes cooking time*

*Ingredients for 4-5 servings*

6 brown onions, chopped
½ teaspoon salt

2 tablespoons butter
¼ teaspoon white pepper

1 Brown the onions in butter and add salt and pepper.
2 Bring to the boil and serve.

# CHEESE SAUCE

*5 minutes cooking time*

*Ingredients for 2 servings*

3 tablespoons butter
¼ teaspoon salt
1 cup grated gruyère cheese

2 tablespoons wholemeal flour
1 cup milk

1 Melt butter and blend in flour.
2 Add milk and stir over heat.
3 When mixture starts to thicken add salt and cheese.
4 Simmer but do not boil for 2 minutes.

# LEMON SAUCE

*10 minutes cooking time*

*Ingredients for 4-5 servings*

1 cup sugar
grated rind of 2 lemons
1 cup water

2 tablespoons wholemeal flour
3 tablespoons butter

1   Melt the butter.
2   Mix sugar, flour and lemon rind together.
3   Combine with butter.
4   Add boiling water and stir constantly until mixture thickens.

# SOUR CREAM SAUCE

*10 minutes cooking time*

*Ingredients for 4-5 servings*

2 tablespoons butter
2 cups sour cream
¼ teaspoon white pepper

2 tablespoons wholemeal flour
½ teaspoon salt

1   Blend all ingredients and stir constantly.
2   Heat over very low heat and stir.
3   Do not boil.

# ORANGE SAUCE

*10 minutes cooking time*

*Ingredients for 4-5 servings*

1 cup sugar
grated rind of 2 oranges
1 cup water

2 tablespoons wholemeal flour
3 tablespoons butter

1   Melt the butter.
2   Mix sugar, flour and orange rind.
3   Combine with butter.
4   Add boiling water and stir constantly until mixture thickens.

# SAUCE FOR FISH

*5 minutes cooking time*

*Ingredients for 4-5 servings*

| | |
|---|---|
| 4 minced onions | 2 cloves garlic, minced |
| 2 cups tomato purée | ½ cup water |
| 6 cloves | ½ teaspoon salt |
| 2 tablespoons olive oil | |

1 Sauté the onions in olive oil.
2 Then combine all ingredients and simmer for 5 minutes.
3 If you prefer, add a little rosemary and simmer for further 5 minutes.

# GRAVY

*5 minutes cooking time*

*Ingredients for 4-5 servings*

| | |
|---|---|
| 2 tablespoons wholemeal flour | 2 tablespoons fat or dripping |
| 2 cups hot water | ½ teaspoon salt |

1 Blend the flour and dripping or fat together. Mix thoroughly, removing all lumps.
2 Over very low heat add the water and stir constantly.
3 Season with salt and thicken slowly.

# Desserts

## FRUIT SALAD

*Ingredients for 6 servings*

**2 pears**
**7 tablespoons lemon juice**
**2 peaches**
**1 cup water**
**12 cherries, pitted**
**6 apricots**

**1 orange**
**1 apple**
**1 tin drained figs**
**4 saccharine tablets**
**2 bananas**

1 Prepare pears and remove centres.
2 Peel and core apples and cut into sections; peel orange and cut into segments.
3 Cut apricots in halves and slice into pieces.
4 Mix all fruits in chilled bowl and add sliced banana and cherries.
5 Add figs.
6 Pour over lemon juice mixed with water and saccharine tablets.

# CRÈME ANDALUSE

*15 minutes cooking time*

*Ingredients for 4 servings*

| | |
|---|---|
| 1 tablespoon gelatine | 1½ teaspoons liquid non-calorie |
| 1½ cups skim milk | sweetener |
| 2 eggs | 1 teaspoon vanilla |
| ⅛ teaspoon nutmeg | ¼ teaspoon salt |

1 Soften gelatine in milk and place in top of double boiler.
2 Heat over boiling water until gelatine is dissolved.
3 Gradually pour mixture over beaten egg yolks and stir.
4 Add nutmeg, salt and sweetener.
5 Return mixture to boiler and stir constantly for 10 minutes over boiling water.
6 Add vanilla and chill.
7 Fold in beaten egg whites and pour into mould.
8 Serve chilled.

# MOCK EGGNOGG PUDDING

*10 minutes cooking time*

*Ingredients for 6 servings*

| | |
|---|---|
| 1½ tablespoons gelatine | 5 saccharine tablets |
| 2 teaspoons rum | 1 teaspoon grated nutmeg |
| 2 cups hot water | ½ teaspoon salt |
| 6 eggs, separated | ½ cup cold water |

1 Sprinkle gelatine on cold water and soften. Beat egg yolks and add salt.
2 When light and fluffy add hot water to yolks and cook over simmering water. Stir until mixture coats spoon and remove from heat.
3 Add softened gelatine and saccharine, rum and nutmeg. When gelatine has dissolved, chill and beat in egg whites. Blend. Pour into mould and chill.

# LEMON JELLY

*5 minutes cooking time*

*Ingredients for 8 servings*

**3 tablespoons gelatine**
**grated rind of 1 lemon**

**1 cup lemon juice**
**⅓ cup sugar**

1 Soak gelatine in 1 cup cold water and add sugar.
2 Pour into 1½ cups boiling water and when dissolved add lemon juice and rind.
3 Mix and strain. Pour into mould and chill.

# ORANGE SHERBET

*5 minutes cooking time*

*Ingredients for 8 servings*

**2 tablespoons gelatine**
**⅔ cup lemon juice**
**3 cups orange juice**

**4 cups skim milk**
**4 tablespoons liquid sweetener**

1 Sprinkle gelatine over half cup orange juice and soften.
2 Place over hot water and blend in milk, lemon juice and remaining orange juice.
3 Add dissolved gelatine and sweetener.
4 Pour into freezing tray and chill.
5 Beat thoroughly and freeze.

# PLUM FOOL

*15 minutes cooking time*

*Ingredients for 6 servings*

**750 g (1½ lb) plums**
**6 glacé cherries**
**4 tablespoons water**

**1 cup yoghurt**
**4 saccharine tablets**

1 Place plums in water and simmer with saccharine.
2 Remove stones and rub through sieve.
3 Beat plum mixture with yoghurt and place in individual serving dishes.
4 Cool.
5 Garnish with glacé cherries.

# LEMON FLUFF

*Ingredients for 4 servings*

*15 minutes cooking time*

| | |
|---|---|
| **1 tablespoon gelatine** | **1 lemon** |
| **⅓ cup cold water** | **1 teaspoon lemon rind, grated** |
| **2 cups boiling water** | **¼ cup lemon juice** |
| **1 egg white** | **12 saccharine tablets** |

1  Dot gelatine on cold water and soften.
2  Add lemon rind and juice to boiling water.
3  Bring to boil once more and add gelatine and saccharine.
4  Remove from heat and stir to dissolve gelatine.
5  Chill and add white of egg. Beat until fluffy and place in container of ice.
6  Beat until mixture holds its shape and turn into mould.
7  Chill and serve with lemon wedges.

# YOGHURT WHIP

*Ingredients for 4-5 servings*

| | |
|---|---|
| **1 tablespoon gelatine** | **2 tablespoons honey** |
| **½ cup chilled grapefruit juice** | **1 tablespoon orange juice** |
| **1½ cups apple, oranges and lemons, mashed and puréed** | **¾ teaspoon salt** |
| | **2 cups yoghurt** |

1  Soften gelatine in orange juice.
2  Add puréed fruit, honey, grapefruit juice and salt.
3  Chill.
4  Beat until thick.
5  Add yoghurt and pour into mould.
6  Chill and serve with fresh fruit.

# STRAWBERRY MOUSSE

*Ingredients for 4-5 servings*

2½ cups thick cream
4 cups strawberries, hulled and washed

½ cup honey
3 teaspoons sugar

1 Whip cream.
2 Blend strawberries, honey and sugar.
3 Fold into whipped cream and chill.
4 Garnish with a strawberry on top of each serving.

# ORANGE CREAM

*Ingredients for 4-5 servings*

3 cups sour cream
½ cup sugar

2 cups orange juice

1 Combine all ingredients and mix thoroughly.
2 Stand and chill.
3 Serve with whipped cream.

# GRAPEFRUIT SHERBET

*Ingredients for 4-5 servings*

3 egg whites, beaten
½ cup cold water
4 tablespoons gelatine
½ cup sugar

3 egg yolks, beaten
2 cups honey
2 cups grapefruit juice
1 teaspoon nutmeg

1 Dissolve gelatine in cold water.
2 Add honey.
3 Add grapefruit juice, nutmeg and cinnamon.
4 Add beaten egg whites and salt.
5 Freeze.

# WHIPPED COFFEE MOULD

*5 minutes cooking time*

*Ingredients for 6-8 servings*

4 egg whites
30 g (1 oz) gelatine
2 tablespoons single cream
1¼ cups strong coffee

4 tablespoons chopped almonds
2½ cups skim milk
4 saccharine tablets

1  Dissolve gelatine in black coffee.
2  Heat milk and sweeten with saccharine and add gelatine.
3  Allow to cool and when mixture begins to set whisk in stiffly beaten egg whites and cream.
4  Chill and serve topped with chopped almonds.

# COFFEE JELLY

*Ingredients for 8 servings*

3 tablespoons gelatine
½ cup sugar

1¼ cups strong coffee

1  Soak gelatine in 1 cup cold water and add 2 cups boiling water.
2  Stir and add coffee and sugar when dissolved.
3  Pour into individual moulds and chill.

# BAKED FRUIT COMBINATION

*25 minutes cooking time*

*Ingredients for 4 servings*

1½ cups water
1 pear, cored and cut into wedges
2 plums, halved and pitted
1 peach, halved and pitted

1 teaspoon vanilla essence
4 apricots
6 saccharine tablets

1  Place water and vanilla essence in saucepan.
2  Bring to boil and add fruit.
3  Simmer for 20 minutes and add sweetener.
4  Serve chilled.

# STRAWBERRY CREAM

*Ingredients for 4-5 servings*

3 egg yolks
2½ cups thick cream
3 egg whites, beaten

2 cups honey
5 cups mashed strawberries
1 teaspoon cinnamon

1  Mix egg yolks and honey.
2  Stand for 10 minutes.
3  Whip cream and add strawberries.
4  Add to yolks.
5  Fold in egg whites and dot with cinnamon.
6  Freeze.

# APRICOT DELIGHT

*Ingredients for 6 servings*

½ cup water
½ cup instant nonfat dry milk
1 tablespoon lemon juice

1 jar strained apricot-apple sauce
  (baby food)

1  Place water in deep bowl.
2  Add milk and lemon juice.
3  Beat until stiff and beat in apricot-apple sauce.
4  Pour into mould and chill.

# SPICED FRUITS

*10 minutes cooking time*

*Ingredients for 4-5 servings*

500 g (1 lb) prunes
½ cup honey
3 cloves

500 g (1 lb) grapes
2 teaspoons cinnamon
¼ teaspoon salt

1  Stew prunes and grapes.
2  Add honey, cinnamon and salt.
3  Simmer for 5 minutes.
4  Add cloves and cook for 2 minutes.
5  Chill and serve.

# RAISIN MOUSSE

*Ingredients for 4-5 servings*

2 cups thick cream
3 tablespoons honey
2 cups raisins

1 cup apple cider
3 egg yolks
¼ teaspoon salt

1 Combine cream and honey in blender.
2 Turn into a bowl.
3 Add raisins, cider, salt and egg yolks.
4 Cook over hot water, stirring until thick.
5 Freeze in ice tray and serve.

# LEMON MERINGUE

*10 minutes cooking time*

*Ingredients for 4-5 servings*

1½ cups sugar
5 tablespoons cornflour
½ teaspoon salt
2 cups boiling water
6 tablespoons sugar

3 eggs, separated
½ cup lemon juice
2 tablespoons grated lemon rind
3 tablespoons butter

1 Combine 1½ cups sugar, cornflour and salt in a saucepan.
2 Add boiling water and stir.
3 Cook over low heat and stir.
4 Beat egg yolks and pour over mixture in saucepan.
5 Remove from heat and stir in lemon juice, lemon rind and butter.
6 Chill.
7 Pour into baked pie crusts.
8 Beat egg whites and 6 tablespoons sugar until stiff.
9 Bake in moderate oven 180°C (350°F) until brown.

# COFFEE CUSTARD

*1½ hours cooking time*

*Ingredients for 6 servings*

¾ cup strong coffee
3 saccharine tablets
4 eggs

½ teaspoon nutmeg
1¾ cups skim milk

1 Beat egg yolks with milk and coffee.
2 Add saccharine tablets and mix well.
3 Fold in beaten egg whites.
4 Place bowl in dish of cold water.
4 Cook for 1½ hours in slow oven 150°C (300°F).

# CIDER PEARS

*5 hours cooking time*

*Ingredients for 6 servings*

1 kg (2 lb) cooking pears
3 saccharine tablets

2½ cups cider
2½ cups water

1 Peel pears and leave whole.
2 Put into casserole dish, packed closely, and cover with equal amounts of water and cider.
3 Cover and cook for 5 hours in slow oven 150°C (300°F).
4 Remove pears to serving dish. Boil syrup until it has reduced by half.
5 Add saccharine to syrup and pour over pears.

# RICE RING

*40 minutes cooking time*

*Ingredients for 4-5 servings*

3 cups cooked rice
2 cups milk
3 eggs, separated
¼ teaspoon salt

½ cup honey
3 eggs, beaten
grated rind of 2 lemons

1 Blend all ingredients except egg whites.
2 Beat egg whites until stiff and fold into mixture.
3 Turn into ring mould and bake for 30-40 minutes.

# WALNUT PIE

*1 hour cooking time*

*Ingredients for 4-5 servings*

4 tablespoons butter
6 tablespoons brown sugar
3 tablespoons flour
1 teaspoon salt

½ cup water
4 beaten egg yolks
2 cups chopped walnuts
4 beaten egg whites

1　Cream butter with sugar and flour.
2　Add salt, water and egg yolks.
3　Stir in walnuts and fold in egg whites.
4　Bake in a moderate oven for 50-60 minutes.

# RAISIN PIE

*30 minutes cooking time*

*Ingredients for 4-5 servings*

juice of 2 lemons
3 tablespoons cream
2 eggs
3 tablespoons butter

rind of 1 lemon
2 cups chopped raisins
½ cup honey

1　Beat eggs and combine with honey.
2　Fold in raisins and other ingredients and pour into pie dish.
3　Bake in moderate oven for 30 minutes.

# CUSTARD PIE

*20 minutes cooking time*

*Ingredients for 4-5 servings*

4 eggs
½ cup honey
½ teaspoon vanilla

2 cups milk
½ teaspoon salt
½ teaspoon cinnamon

1　Combine eggs, honey, salt, vanilla and cinnamon.
2　Beat well.
3　Heat milk and add to other ingredients.
4　Pour into pie crust and bake for 20 minutes.
5　Dot with cinnamon and serve with cream.

# BAKED ORANGES

*2 hours cooking time*

*Ingredients for 4 servings*

**4 oranges**
**2 teaspoons cornflour**
**1 tablespoon curacao**
**2 saccharine tablets**

**4 cups water**
**2 cups orange juice**
**4 teaspoons butter**

1  Cover oranges with water in saucepan and place lid on.
2  Boil for 30 minutes and cool.
3  Cut a slice off the top and remove core and pips. Place a half of a saccharine tablet in a teaspoon of butter and add to each orange.
4  Pack into casserole and add water to half way up.
5  Cover and cook for 1½ hours in moderate oven.
6  Transfer oranges to serving dish and blend cornflour and orange juice together.
7  Add cooking liquid and boil. Add curacao and pour over oranges.

# STEWED RHUBARB

*40 minutes cooking time*

*Ingredients for 6 servings*

**750 g (1½ lb) rhubarb**
**2 tablespoons water**
**3 eggs**

**3 saccharine tablets**
**1½ tablespoons butter**
**60 g (2 oz) sugar**

1  Place rhubarb in saucepan with water and cook until soft.
2  Beat mixture until quite smooth and add butter, dissolved saccharine tablets and beaten egg yolks.
3  Pour into dish and bake for 25 minutes in hot oven. Remove and lower heat to 180°C (350°F).
4  Beat egg whites until stiff and fold in sugar.
5  Top rhubarb with the meringue and bake at 180°C (350°F) for 15 minutes.

# STUFFED DATES

*Ingredients for 3 servings*

**12 dates**                    **2 cups cream cheese**

Pit dates and stuff with cream cheese.

# DATE NUTS

*Ingredients for 3 servings*

**12 dates**                    **1 cup chopped walnuts**

1   Pit dates.
2   Stuff with chopped walnuts.

# NUT BALLS

*10 minutes cooking time*

*Ingredients for 4-5 servings*

**3 cups honey**                **1 teaspoon cinnamon**
**2 cups cocoa**                **3 cups chopped almonds**
**1 cup chopped walnuts**

1   Combine all ingredients and stir over very low heat.
2   When mixture thickens remove from stove.
3   Cool.
4   Roll into balls and serve.

# Cakes and Bread

## LO-CAL SPONGE CAKE

*25 minutes cooking time*

*Ingredients for 8 servings*

6 eggs, separated
½ teaspoon vanilla essence
60 g (2 oz) sugar

6 saccharine tablets
250 g (8 oz) self-raising flour

1 Beat egg whites until stiff.
2 Add sugar, egg yolks and vanilla essence and beat well.
3 Fold in sifted flour and saccharine dissolved in 2 tablespoons hot water.
4 Turn into greased sandwich tins.
5 Bake for 25 minutes in moderate oven 180°C (350°F).

# CORN CAKES

*20 minutes cooking time*

*Ingredients for 3 servings*

3 cups corn meal
3 cups hot water
3 tablespoons butter
1 teaspoon cinnamon

1 teaspoon salt
3 egg yolks
2 egg whites

1 Combine corn meal, salt, hot water and cinnamon.
2 Mix well.
3 Add egg yolks and butter.
4 Beat the egg whites and fold in.
5 Form into small cakes and bake in moderate oven for 20 minutes.

# WHOLE WHEAT CAKES

*50 minutes cooking time*

*Ingredients for 4 servings*

4 cups whole wheat flour
2 cups sour milk
2 teaspoons butter

1 teaspoon salt
3 egg yolks, well beaten
2 egg whites, well beaten

1 Combine whole wheat flour and salt.
2 Mix well.
3 Add milk, egg yolks and butter; fold in beaten egg whites.
4 Form into small cakes and bake in moderate oven for 50 minutes.

# SOY CAKES

*40 minutes cooking time*

*Ingredients for 3-4 servings*

2 cups soy flour
2 teaspoons baking powder
4 tablespoons dates

1 teaspoon salt
2 eggs, beaten
2 cups milk

1 Combine flour, salt and baking powder.
2 Mix well.
3 Add beaten eggs, chopped dates and milk.
4 Bake in oiled muffin tins and serve after 40 minutes.

# FRUIT CAKES

*Ingredients for 4-5 servings*

*30 minutes cooking time*

2 cups soy flour
1 teaspoon baking powder
1 cup dried figs
2 tablespoons butter

1 cup whole wheat flour
½ teaspoon salt
1 teaspoon lemon juice
5 eggs

1  Combine all ingredients, adding one at a time, and mix thoroughly.
2  Bake in oiled muffin tins for 30 minutes and serve.

# EGG BREAD

*Ingredients for 3-4 servings*

*30 minutes cooking time*

750 g (1½ lb) whole wheat flour
2 cups milk
4 beaten eggs
3 teaspoons baking powder

2 teaspoons salt
2 teaspoons butter or margarine
2 teaspoons honey

1  Sift flour, baking powder and salt together.
2  Add milk, melted butter and honey.
3  Combine and add eggs.
4  Bake in well-oiled tin for 30 minutes and serve.

# CORN BREAD

*Ingredients for 3-4 servings*

*40 minutes cooking time*

3 cups milk
2 tablespoons butter
2 eggs, beaten

1 cup corn meal
4 tablespoons melted cheese

1  Scald milk and add corn meal.
2  Add melted butter and cheese.
3  Add eggs and blend thoroughly.
4  Spread on a board and cube.
5  Bake in moderate oven for 40 minutes and serve with cheese.

# RAISIN BREAD

*40 minutes cooking time*

*Ingredients for 4-5 servings*

5 cups whole wheat flour
4 teaspoons baking powder
2 cups chopped walnuts
5 eggs, beaten
3 cups milk

½ cup wheat germ
1 teaspoon salt
2 cups raisins
4 tablespoons butter

1   Sift flour and wheat germ, baking powder and salt.
2   Add walnuts, raisins and a little salt.
3   Beat together eggs, milk, butter and fold into dry ingredients.
4   Bake in moderate oven for 40 minutes.

# OATMEAL BREAD

*50 minutes cooking time*

*Ingredients for 4-5 servings*

3 cups oatmeal
1 cup soy flour
1 teaspoon baking powder
3 tablespoons sugar

2 teaspoons salt
2 cups whole wheat flour
3 tablespoons butter
3 beaten eggs

1   Combine oatmeal, salt, soy flour and whole wheat flour.
2   Add baking powder and blend.
3   Add oil or butter, sugar and beaten egg.
4   Mix thoroughly.
5   Bake in oven for 50 minutes and serve.

# Index

# CHINESE & ASIAN

# Contents

# Introduction

## CHINESE AND ASIAN COOKERY

Chinese cooking can be simple or elegant, bland or spicy, but it is sure to be a favourite with your family and friends. It utilizes many ingredients which are readily available in Australia; even the exotic additions can be obtained in the Australian cities and towns which have a Chinese population and shops which import the unusual ingredients.

One very important rule in all Oriental cooking is to use fresh ingredients. Most dishes are cooked only long enough to combine the flavours of the ingredients — not to stew them into oblivion — so tender meat and fresh vegetables are essential.

Chopping and slicing are important for two reasons: it is almost impossible to pick up and bite off a piece of a slippery hunk of food with chopsticks (try it with a large piece of abalone in sauce some time!), so small, bite-size pieces are necessary. Secondly, Oriental dishes require uniform pieces of food which will cook at the same rate so all ingredients will be done at the same time.

Oriental cooking can be done with the Western cooking utensils you already own. The most useful addition to your kitchen would be a wok. This is a round, curved pan which sits on a ring directly over the heat. It is used mainly for the 'stir-frying' method of cooking which is used in many recipes. Because of its shape, the wok is ideal for frying as the oil collects in the bottom of the pan.

It is important to use the wok over very high heat. Gas is by far the best as it can be controlled easily and quickly. If you have an electric stove, the best idea is to use two burners — one on full and one at medium heat — so the temperature can be controlled by moving the wok from one element to the other.

The essence of stir-frying is keeping the food moving constantly — it should be tossed from the bottom to the sides of the pan all the time. The protein foods (meat and fish) should be cooked until just tender and juicy and the vegetables should be barely tender and retain their crisp texture and bright colours. Because of the brief cooking times and high temperatures used, it is important to have all the ingredients prepared and easily available. You can't leave a wok to 'simmer' while you race to the refrigerator for a forgotten ingredient. This means, of course, that all the preparation can be done well in advance, so you don't have to be in the kitchen until you are ready to serve the meal.

A wok can be used as a steamer by placing a round cake rack in it and covering it with a lid. An electric fry-pan can also be adapted in the same way. The food should be about 5 centimetres (2 in) above the water level so the water does not bubble up into the food. A cloth over the top of the pan under the lid will keep condensed steam from dripping on the food.

Presentation of food is almost as important to the Oriental cook as the preparation. Contrasting colours and textures are a basic element of Oriental cooking, and imaginative garnishes add to the pleasure of the dishes.

# Appetizers and Soups

## DIM SIMS

*30 minutes cooking time*

*Ingredients for 5-6 servings*

| | |
|---|---|
| 500 g (1 lb) pork mince | 1½ teaspoons sugar |
| 2 teaspoons soy sauce | 2 tablespoons water |
| ¼ teaspoon pepper | ½ teaspoon salt |
| 125 g (4 oz) mushrooms, cooked in butter | 90 g (3 oz) fat |
| | 7.5 cm (3 in) square noodles |

1  Combine first 8 ingredients.
2  Spoon this mixture onto the noodles and secure.
3  Fill in the top with last of the mixture and steam for 30-40 minutes.

# PRAWN SLICES

*10 minutes cooking time*

*Ingredients for 5-6 servings*

500 g (1 lb) shelled prawns
2 onions
2 eggs
2 tablespoons soy sauce

½ teaspoon salt
1 tablespoon sherry
slices of bread
oil

1  Mince prawns and combine with chopped onions.
2  Add egg white, soy sauce, salt and sherry.
3  Cut bread into shape desired and place dessertspoon of mixture on top.
4  Dip in beaten egg yolk and deep fry.
5  Drain and serve immediately.

# DUMPLINGS

*20 minutes cooking time*

*Ingredients for 4-5 servings*

10 prawns
½ teaspoon salt
1 teaspoon oil
185-250 g (6-8 oz) wheat starch
hot water

2 tablespoons chopped pork
2 teaspoons sherry
½ teaspoon monosodium glutamate
   (optional)

1  Clean and prepare the prawns.
2  Cut pork and prawns into small pieces and pound.
3  Add sherry, salt, oil and monosodium glutamate (if desired).
4  Combine well.
5  Place the wheat starch on a board and make an impression in the centre, add hot water drop by drop.
6  Place paste in basin and steam for 5 minutes.
7  Remove the paste and form into a roll.
8  Cut into 12 pieces and press each round into 6 centimetre (2½ in) circles.
9  Spread with prawn paste and fold in half.
10  Make sure that edges have been secured.
11  Steam for 15 minutes and serve immediately.

# DEEP FRIED CHICKEN LIVERS

*10 minutes cooking time*

*Ingredients for 5-6 servings*

**750 g (1½ lb) chicken livers**
**3 tablespoons soy sauce**
**2 tablespoons sherry**
**½ cup plain flour**
**¼ teaspoon pepper**

**1 teaspoon baking powder**
**3 tablespoons vinegar**
**oil**
**½ teaspoon salt**

1  Cut livers into shape desired and marinate in soy sauce, sherry, vinegar and salt and pepper for 20 minutes.
2  Mix flour and baking powder and add water to make a thick batter.
3  Combine well.
4  Dip chicken livers into this mixture and deep fry.
5  Drain and serve immediately.

# PRAWN PUFFS APPETIZER

*10 minutes cooking time*

*Ingredients for 5-6 servings*

**750 g (1½ lb) raw prawns**
**2 egg whites**
**½ teaspoon salt**

**2 teaspoons soy sauce**
**oil**

1  Clean and prepare prawns.
2  Combine with soy sauce and salt.
3  Fold prawn mixture into beaten egg whites.
4  Drop teaspoonfuls of this mixture into hot oil and deep fry.
5  Drain.

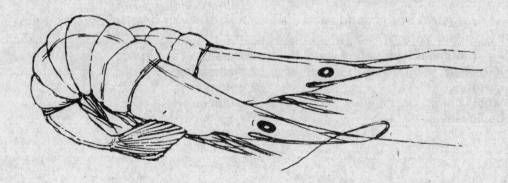

## EGG SOUP

*20 minutes cooking time*

*Ingredients for 5-6 servings*

chicken stock
½ teaspoon white pepper
3 eggs
chopped Chinese parsley

½ teaspoon salt
½ teaspoon monosodium glutamate
(optional)

1  Boil chicken stock and monosodium glutamate (if desired) and season with salt and pepper; add chopped parsley.
2  Beat eggs together and pour into stock.
3  Cook for 5 minutes then add a little more chopped parsley.

## SCALLOPS AND EGG SOUP

*30 minutes cooking time*

*Ingredients for 5-6 servings*

500 g (1 lb) fresh scallops
chicken stock
½ teaspoon salt

4 eggs, beaten
2 chopped shallots
¼ teaspoon white pepper

1  Shred scallops and place in chicken stock.
2  Season with salt and pepper.
3.  Bring to the boil and simmer for 20-30 minutes.
4  Beat in eggs, shallots and more salt and pepper to taste.
5  Serve immediately.

## BASIC MEAT STOCK

*2 hours cooking time*

*Ingredients for 5-6 servings*

1 kg (2 lb) meat bones
250 g (8 oz) soup meat
2 carrots
1 whole onion
2 garlic cloves

water
2 stalks celery
2 onions
6 peppercorns

1 Brown the bones, soup meat and onion under griller.
2 Placc in stock pot with enough water to just cover.
3 Add vegetables and bring to the boil.
4 Add garlic cloves and peppercorns.
5 Simmer for 2 hours, then strain fat off.
6 Store in refrigerator.

# BASIC FISH STOCK

*• 1½ hours cooking time*

*Ingredients for 5-6 servings*

**crab and lobster shells**
**⅛ cup chopped celery**
**2 carrots**
**1 teaspoon vinegar**

**7½ cups water**
**2 white onions**
**6 peppercorns**
**sliced ginger**

1 Wash shells thoroughly.
2 Cover with water and add chopped vegetables, peppercorns, ginger and vinegar.
3 Bring to the boil and simmer for 1½ hours.
4 Strain and allow to cool.
5 Use in soup or stock recipes.

# SHORT SOUP

*30 minutes cooking time*

*Ingredients for 5-6 servings*

**noodle paste, cut into 5 cm (2 in)**
**  squares**
**½ cup pork mince, lean**
**500 g (1 lb) raw prawns**
**1 teaspoon salt**

**3 cups chicken stock**
**90 g (3 oz) dried mushrooms**
**1 teaspoon soy sauce**
**2 egg whites**

1 Soak mushrooms in hot water for 1 hour.
2 Combine pork and prawns and season with salt and soy sauce.
3 Bind together with egg white.
4 Place a teaspoon of mixture on each square and wrap tightly.
5 Serve in soup, or fry with vegetables.

# BEEF AND SWEET CORN SOUP

*20 minutes cooking time*

*Ingredients for 5-6 servings*

1 tin corn kernels
500 g (1 lb) beef
1 teaspoon soy sauce
½ teaspoon monosodium glutamate
(optional)

1 cm (½ in) green ginger, crushed
beef stock
2 eggs
oil
½ teaspoon salt

1  Cube meat and season with salt and soy sauce.
2  Add crushed ginger to oil in pan and sauté meat for 5 minutes.
3  Pour in stock and simmer, add corn and simmer for further 5 minutes.
4  Add beaten eggs and monosodium glutamate (if desired).
5  Serve immediately.

# SWEET CORN AND CRAB SOUP

*5 minutes cooking time*

*Ingredients for 4-5 servings*

185 g (6 oz) cooked crab meat
2½ cups chicken stock
½ teaspoon monosodium glutamate
(optional)
1 teaspoon cornflour
½ teaspoon pepper

375 g (12 oz) sweet corn
2 tablespoons sherry
½ teaspoon salt
2 eggs
1 tablespoon water

1  Shred the crab meat.
2  Place sweet corn into a pan with stock and bring to the boil.
3  Add crab meat, sherry, and monosodium glutamate (if desired).
4  Separate yolks and stir them into the soup.
5  Add mixed cornflour and water.
6  Stir constantly until boiling.
7  Fold in beaten egg whites and cook for 2 minutes.
8  Season with salt and pepper and serve immediately.

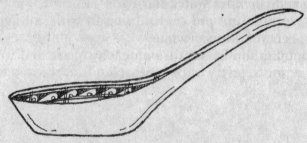

# SOUR SOUP

*10 minutes cooking time*

*Ingredients for 4-5 servings*

125 g (4 oz) dried mushrooms
185 g (6 oz) chopped ham
2 tablespoons soy sauce
1 tablespoon cornflour
2 eggs
½ teaspoon monosodium glutamate
  (optional)

90 g (3 oz) canned bamboo shoots
5 cups chicken stock
1 tablespoon vinegar
3 tablespoons water
½ teaspoon white pepper
1 teaspoon salt

1   Soak the mushrooms for 30 minutes.
2   Shred mushrooms and bamboo shoots.
3   Shred ham.
4   Bring chicken stock to boil and add mushrooms, bamboo shoots, ham and cook for 5 minutes.
5   Add soy sauce, vinegar, cornflour, water, and cook for 2 minutes.
6   Drop the beaten eggs into this mixture and stir.
7   Season with salt, pepper and monosodium glutamate (if desired).
8   Serve immediately.

# NOODLES IN BEEF SOUP

*30 minutes cooking time*

*Ingredients for 5-6 servings*

315 g (10 oz) dried egg noodles
1 tablespoon oil
½ teaspoon white pepper
soy sauce
chopped Chinese parsley
½ carrot, shredded

4 cups beef stock
½ teaspoon salt
sesame oil
sliced green ginger
2 chopped shallots

1   Cook egg noodles in water for 5-6 minutes.
2   Loosen bundles as they cook.
3   Drain and run cold water through.
4   Place green ginger and oil in frying pan.
5   Place vegetables in saucepan with stock and heat through.
6   Add noodles and a few drops of sesame oil.
7   Serve immediately with soy sauce and more chopped parsley.

# PORK AND ABALONE SOUP

*15 minutes cooking time*

*Ingredients for 4-5 servings*

30 g (1 oz) lean pork
60 g (2 oz) dried mushrooms
1 teaspoon sherry
4 cups chicken stock
2 shallots, chopped
½ teaspoon monosodium glutamate
  (optional)

60 g (2 oz) bamboo shoots
½ teaspoon cornflour
8 snow peas or ⅛ cup peas
1 cm (½ in) fresh green ginger, chopped
60 g (2 oz) canned abalone, sliced
½ teaspoon salt

1  Slice the pork, bamboo shoots and soaked mushrooms thinly.
2  Add cornflour and sherry.
3  Cut off ends of snow peas and blanch for 2 minutes, or boil peas for 4 minutes.
4  Bring stock to boiling point and add snow peas, ginger, shallots and pork ingredients.
5  Cook for 5 minutes, add abalone and monosodium glutamate (if desired).
6  Boil for 2 minutes and add salt.
7  Remove ginger and onion and pour soup into serving bowl.
8  Serve immediately.

# PORK SOUP

*30 minutes cooking time*

*Ingredients for 5-6 servings*

750 g (1½ lb) minced pork
½ teaspoon salt
2 tablespoons soy sauce
2 egg yolks
1 beaten egg

6 peppercorns
stock
Chinese spinach
1 teaspoon monosodium glutamate
  (optional)

1  Combine soy sauce, beaten egg yolks and minced pork.
2  Roll into small balls and bring to boil in stock.
3  Simmer for 15 minutes and add spinach cut into pieces.
4  Cook for 5 minutes and season with salt and peppercorns.
5  Add beaten egg and monosodium glutamate (if desired).
6  Serve immediately.

# ASPARAGUS SOUP WITH GINGER

*15 minutes cooking time*

*Ingredients for 4-5 servings*

**5 cups chicken stock**
**1 cup shredded chicken**
**1 tin asparagus spears**
**½ teaspoon green ginger, grated**

**shallots, chopped**
**½ teaspoon monosodium glutamate**
  **(optional)**
**salt**

1  Bring chicken stock to boil and add shredded chicken pieces and green ginger.
2  Add asparagus spears and simmer for 5 minutes.
3  Before serving add shallots, monosodium glutamate (if desired) and salt.
4  Serve immediately.

# BAMBOO SHOOT SOUP

*30 minutes cooking time*

*Ingredients for 5-6 servings*

**500 g (1 lb) canned bamboo shoots**
**½ teaspoon white pepper**
**2 teaspoons vegetable oil**
**chicken stock**

**1 teaspoon salt**
**3 eggs, beaten**
**chopped ham**
**chopped shallots**

1  Cut bamboo into strips. Toss in hot oil for 3 minutes.
2  Pour in chicken stock.
3  Cover and allow to boil. Simmer for 10 minutes.
4  Add seasonings and beaten eggs. Add ham and simmer for 5 minutes.
5  Add chopped shallots and serve immediately.

# CHICKEN AND SWEET CORN SOUP

*40 minutes cooking time*

*Ingredients for 5-6 servings*

1 1-kg (2-lb) chicken
1½ tablespoons salt
1 can sweet corn kernels
2 onions, chopped
3 stalks celery, chopped

6 peppercorns
7½ cups water
chopped Chinese parsley
2 carrots, chopped
3 cloves garlic, crushed

1  Place cleaned chicken, chopped vegetables and peppercorns in salted water.
2  Bring to the boil and simmer for 30 minutes.
3  Remove chicken and vegetables, strain.
4  Bring soup to boil and add corn.
5  Return chicken and vegetables and add crushed garlic.
6  Season with a little salt and dot with chopped parsley.
7  Serve immediately.

# SCALLOP-MEAT SOUP

*10 minutes cooking time*

*Ingredients for 8 servings*

375 g (12 oz) pork meat
1 tablespoon cornflour
250 g (8 oz) scallops

1 teaspoon salt
1 tablespoon soy sauce
7 cups water

1  Cut meat into thin strips and mix with cornflour.
2  Clean scallops and cut into 4 round slices.
3  Place scallops in water and heat to boiling, lower heat and simmer for 3 minutes with soy sauce.
4  Add salt and meat, cook for 3 minutes and serve.

# HAM AND CABBAGE SOUP

*10 minutes cooking time*

*Ingredients for 4 servings*

250 g (8 oz) cured ham
1 teaspoon salt

500 g (1 lb) Chinese cabbage
4 cups water

1  Cut meat thinly.
2  Heat water to boiling point, add ham and simmer 15 minutes.
3  Cut Chinese cabbage into shreds.
4  Add shredded cabbage and salt to water and cook for 5-6 minutes.

# CRAB AND CORN SOUP

*5 minutes cooking time*

*Ingredients for 6 servings*

185 g (6 oz) tinned crab meat
5 cups chicken stock
½ teaspoon salt
½ teaspoon sesame oil
1½ teaspoons cornflour
1½ teaspoons sherry

2 egg whites
125 g (4 oz) sweet corn
¼ teaspoon monosodium glutamate
  (optional)
2 tablespoons water

1  Shred crab meat and beat egg white lightly.
2  Add crab meat to egg and mix through.
3  Set aside.
4  Bring stock to boil and add corn.
5  Season with salt and add monosodium glutamate (if desired), sesame oil,
   sherry and a little pepper.
6  Blend cornflour and water, stir into stock and boil for 1 minute.
7  Add crab meat and egg mixture and bring to boil. Serve.

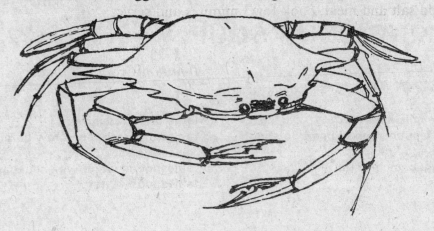

# PRAWN SOUP WITH EGG

*20 minutes cooking time*

*Ingredients for 4 servings*

3 spring onions
1 tablespoon sherry
½ teaspoon sugar
1 cup peeled prawns
½ teaspoon salt

2½ cups chicken stock
¼ teaspoon monosodium glutamate
   (optional)
1 teaspoon soy sauce
1 egg

1   Chop onions and put into boiling stock and simmer for 15 minutes.
2   Add sherry, sugar, soy sauce, monosodium glutamate (if desired) and prawns. Cook gently for 2 minutes.
3   Pour in beaten egg and stir briskly. Season with salt and serve.

# MEAT AND BEAN CURD SOUP

*10 minutes cooking time*

*Ingredients for 8 servings*

375 g (12 oz) pork meat
½ teaspoon monosodium glutamate
   (optional)
1 teaspoon salt
½ tablespoon cornflour

1 tablespoon sherry
2½ cups bean curd
2 tablespoons soy sauce
7 cups water

1   Cut meat into thin slices and mix with cornflour.
2   Cut bean curd into small cubes.
3   Boil water and add bean curd.
4   Boil for 3 minutes and add seasonings.
5   Add meat and boil for 5 minutes.

# PEKING SOUR SOUP

*40 minutes cooking time*

*Ingredients for 6-8 servings*

5 cups chicken stock
4 tablespoons tinned bamboo shoots
½ teaspoon pepper
2 teaspoons cornflour
2 eggs

1 large dried mushroom
8 tablespoons chopped raw ham
½ teaspoon salt
2 tablespoons white wine vinegar
1 tablespoon water

1   Soak mushroom in cold water for 1 hour and slice. Discard stem.
2   Bring stock to boil and add ham, simmer for 2 minutes and add bamboo shoots.
3   Season with salt and pepper.
4   Add vinegar and cover, simmer for 30-35 minutes.
5   Blend cornflour and water, add to soup, stir and simmer for 2 minutes. Remove from heat.
6   Pour beaten eggs into soup slowly, stirring constantly.

## DRIED PRAWN AND CABBAGE SOUP

*35 minutes cooking time*

*Ingredients for 6 servings*

90 g (3 oz) dried prawns
500 g (1 lb) Chinese cabbage

7 cups water
1 teaspoon salt

1   Chop cabbage.
2   Place dried prawns in pot with cold water and heat until boiling, simmer for 25 minutes.
3   Add cabbage and salt.
4   Cook for 10 minutes over low heat.

## CHICKEN SOUP WITH BAMBOO SHOOTS

*30 minutes cooking time*

*Ingredients for 4 servings*

125 g (4 oz) chicken breasts
¼ teaspoon pepper
1 tablespoon chopped ham
125 g (4 oz) tinned bamboo shoots
5 cups chicken stock

½ teaspoon salt
1 egg
2 tablespoons chopped spring onions
1 tablespoon vegetable oil
1 piece fresh green ginger

1   Cut chicken and bamboo shoots into thin strips.
2   Heat oil and sauté chicken. Remove to a large saucepan and pour in chicken stock, bamboo shoots and ginger.
3   Cover and boil. Simmer for 5 minutes and season.
4   Beat egg and pour into soup. Simmer for 3 minutes and serve with chopped ham and spring onions.

# RADISH SCALLOP SOUP

*45 minutes cooking time*

*Ingredients for 4 servings*

20 radishes
1½ teaspoons salt

5 cups water
375 g (12 oz) fresh scallops

1  Peel radishes and wash scallops.
2  Place scallops in heavy pot with radishes and water.
3  Cook for 10 minutes over low heat and add salt.
4  Cook for 30-35 minutes and serve.

# VEGETABLE BEEF SOUP

*12 minutes cooking time*

*Ingredients for 8 servings*

185 g (6 oz) beef
4 spring onions
250 g (8 oz) bamboo shoots
5 cups beef stock
½ teaspoon salt
½ teaspoon white pepper

2 tomatoes
10 water chestnuts
8 dried mushrooms
½ teaspoon monosodium glutamate
  (optional)

1  Cut beef into thin strips and skin and quarter tomato.
2  Slice onions, water chestnuts and bamboo shoot.
3  Soak mushrooms in warm water for 30 minutes, and cut into thin slices.
4  Boil stock, add beef and simmer for 4 minutes.
5  Add vegetables and cook for 4 minutes. Add monosodium glutamate (if desired) and salt and pepper.

# CHICKEN AND MUSHROOM SOUP

*10 minutes cooking time*

*Ingredients for 6 servings*

185 g (6 oz) raw chicken
155 g (5 oz) tinned bamboo shoots
¼ teaspoon monosodium glutamate
  (optional)

90 g (3 oz) fresh mushrooms
5 cups chicken stock
½ teaspoon salt

1 Chop chicken into small pieces.
2 Slice mushrooms and bamboo shoots.
3 Bring stock to boil and drop chicken into it, cook for 3-4 minutes.
4 Add mushrooms and cook for 45 seconds.
5 Add bamboo shoots, cook for 1 minute, add seasonings and serve.

# WON TON SOUP

*20 minutes cooking time*

*Ingredients for 4 servings*

2 cups chicken stock
8 won ton skins
2 chopped spring onions
¼ teaspoon pepper

1 egg white
½ teaspoon salt
90 g (3 oz) cooked chicken
90 g (3 oz) cooked prawns

1 Boil stock and add salt and pepper.
2 Mince chicken, prawns and spring onions together. Place some of this filling on each won ton skin.
3 Moisten edges with egg white, fold and press edges together.
4 Drop into boiling stock and cook for 15 minutes.

# FISH SOUP

*10 minutes cooking time*

*Ingredients for 6 servings*

500 g (1 lb) flounder fillet
1 teaspoon salt
1 tablespoon cornflour
½ onion

6 cups water
2 tablespoons sherry
2 tablespoons soy sauce

1 Slice fish into 2.5 centimetre (1 in) squares.
2 Mix with sherry, soy sauce and cornflour.
3 Chop onion and add to sherry mixture.
4 Add all ingredients except fish to water and boil.
5 Add fish and boil for 3 minutes and serve.

# BIRD'S NEST SOUP

*2 hours 10 minutes cooking time*

*Ingredients for 8 servings*

125 g (4 oz) processed bird's nest
10 cups chicken stock
½ cup sherry

1 1.5-kg (3-lb) chicken
1 teaspoon salt
90 g (3 oz) ham

1 Soak and wash bird's nest.
2 Place in the centre of clean chicken.
3 Put in saucepan and pour chicken stock over, add salt.
4 Simmer for 2 hours and correct seasoning.
5 Pour in sherry and simmer for 10 minutes.
6 Add more stock if necessary. Serve sprinkled with chopped ham.

# PORK AND LEEK SOUP

*20 minutes cooking time*

*Ingredients for 6 servings*

8 tablespoons thinly-sliced raw pork
½ teaspoon monosodium glutamate
  (optional)
2 small leeks
¼ cup sherry

½ teaspoon salt
½ teaspoon sugar
2 teaspoons cornflour
6 cups chicken stock

1 Cut meat diagonally into thin slices.
2 Place in a small bowl, add seasonings and sherry and mix well.
3 Add 1 teaspoon cornflour and work through; set aside.
4 Cut the white part of the leek into very thin slices.
5 Boil stock, add leek and cook for 5 minutes.
6 Add pork and cook for 8 minutes.
7 Blend remaining cornflour with 1 tablespoon water and stir into soup.
  Cook for 1-2 minutes and serve.

# FRESH TOMATO SOUP

*30 minutes cooking time*

*Ingredients for 6 servings*

6 tomatoes
2 tablespoons peanut oil
¼ teaspoon monosodium glutamate
  (optional)
¼ teaspoon pepper

2 onions
5 cups chicken stock
1 teaspoon salt
1 egg, beaten

1   Skin and chop tomatoes and onions.
2   Fry tomatoes and onions for 5 minutes in hot oil.
3   Drain excess oil and add salt, pepper, stock and monosodium glutamate
    (if desired).
4   Simmer for 20 minutes, stir briskly while adding egg.

# CHICKEN NOODLE SOUP

*15 minutes cooking time*

*Ingredients for 6 servings*

375 g (12 oz) transparent noodles
3 cups chicken broth
½ teaspoon sugar

2 teaspoons soy sauce
1 chicken breast, cooked and sliced
  into thin strips

1   Cook noodles in boiling water until tender, rinse and drain.
2   Place in serving dish and bring broth to boil.
3   Season with soy sauce and sugar, pour over noodles and top with chicken
    strips.

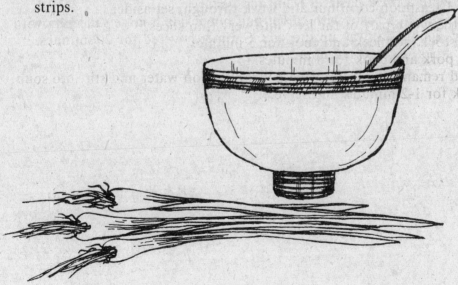

## DUMPLING SOUP

*2½ hours cooking time*

*Ingredients for 4 servings*

7½ cups chicken stock
½ teaspoon coriander seed, crushed
1 kg (2 lb) chicken backs

1 onion, sliced
2 slices fresh ginger
12 shrimp won ton

1   Combine chicken stock, coriander seed, ginger and chicken.
2   Simmer for 2 hours and strain.
3   Reheat stock, add won ton and simmer for 8 minutes.

## FILLED OMELETTE SOUP

*40 minutes cooking time*

*Ingredients for 4 servings*

1½ cups minced cooked pork
¼ teaspoon pepper
¼ teaspoon monosodium glutamate
   (optional)
4 cups beef stock
flour and water

½ teaspoon salt
2 teaspoons soy sauce
1 teaspoon cornflour
2 eggs
1 carrot, sliced
1 tablespoon peanut oil

1   Combine pork, soy sauce, salt, pepper, monosodium glutamate (if desired) and cornflour.
2   Beat eggs and make 2 small omelettes.
3   Spread a thin layer of the pork mixture on each omelette and roll, coat edges with a thick paste of flour and water.
4   Place rolls in a basin with carrot and put inside a large saucepan with water coming halfway up the side. Simmer covered for 20 minutes.
5   Heat stock in large saucepan.
6   Pour over quartered egg rolls in individual dishes.

# MUSHROOM SOUP

*Ingredients for 6 servings*

2 spring onions, chopped
185 g (6 oz) button mushrooms
2 tablespoons sherry

5 cm (2 in) piece fresh ginger, grated
5 cups chicken stock
1 teaspoon salt

1   Slice mushrooms.
2   Place stock in saucepan with spring onions and ginger. Cover and simmer for 30 minutes.
3   Add mushrooms and simmer for 10 minutes, and add sherry and salt.

# ASPARAGUS SOUP

*10 minutes cooking time*

*Ingredients for 8 servings*

10 cups chicken stock
2 tins asparagus pieces
½ teaspoon monosodium glutamate (optional)

1 cup cooked chicken
¼ cup chopped spring onions
1½ teaspoons salt

1   Bring stock to boil and add chopped chicken meat.
2   Add asparagus and salt and simmer for 5-6 minutes.
3   Add monosodium glutamate (if desired) and spring onions just before serving.

# HEAVENLY SOUP

*Ingredients for 4 servings*

5 cups boiling water
1½ shallots cut into 6 pieces
1½ teaspoons salt

2½ tablespoons soy sauce
1½ teaspoons sesame oil
3 slices fresh ginger

1   Place seasonings in a bowl.
2   Pour boiling water in and serve.

# MANDARIN OXTAIL SOUP

*Ingredients for 4 servings*

| | |
|---|---|
| 1 2-kg (4-lb) oxtail | 3 teaspoons soy sauce |
| 3 chopped spring onions | 3 tablespoons sherry |
| skin of ½ orange | 125 g (4 oz) raw shelled peanuts |
| 1 teaspoon salt | ½ teaspoon peppercorns |

1  Chop oxtail into sections. Brown under griller.
2  Cover with hot water and simmer until tender with orange skin, peanuts, salt, peppercorns, sherry and soy sauce.
3  Remove orange skin and peppercorns.
4  Garnish with spring onions to serve.

# SHARK'S FIN SOUP

*2 hours 40 minutes cooking time*

*Ingredients for 8 servings*

| | |
|---|---|
| 185 g (6 oz) dried shark's fin | 7½ cups chicken stock |
| 2 tablespoons peanut oil | 2 teaspoons fresh ginger, grated |
| 4 spring onions | 185 g (6 oz) crab meat |
| 185 g (6 oz) bamboo shoots | 2 tablespoons sherry |
| 1 tablespoon cornflour | 1½ teaspoons soy sauce |
| ½ teaspoon monosodium glutamate (optional) | ½ teaspoon salt |
| | ¼ teaspoon pepper |

1  Soak shark's fin for 8 hours.
2  Place in boiling water, cover and simmer for 2 hours, then drain.
3  Combine grated ginger and chopped onions, chop crab meat and slice bamboo shoot.
4  Fry ginger and spring onions for 5 minutes in hot oil and add stock, sherry and shark's fin.
5  Bring to boil and simmer for 30 minutes.
6  Mix cornflour with seasonings, soy sauce and monosodium glutamate (if desired).
7  Add to pan and simmer, stirring, for 4-5 minutes.
8  Add crab meat and bamboo shoots. Reheat and serve.

# SCALLOP SOUP

*35 minutes cooking time*

*Ingredients for 8 servings*

250 g (8 oz) dried scallops
7½ cups chicken stock
1 teaspoon salt

2 eggs, beaten
¼ cup chopped spring onions
¼ teaspoon pepper

1  Chop scallops and add to stock with salt and pepper.
2  Bring to boil and simmer for 30 minutes, stir briskly and pour in eggs. Top with chopped spring onion.

# TURNIP AND STEAK SOUP

*1 hour cooking time*

*Ingredients for 4 servings*

500 g (1 lb) steak
375 g (12 oz) turnips
4 tablespoons chopped spring onions
2 teaspoons peanut oil

½ dried mandarin skin
1 teaspoon salt
½ teaspoon peppercorns
2 onions

1  Cut steak into cubes; dice onion.
2  Brown meat and onions in oil.
3  Cover with water, add peppercorns and simmer for 40 minutes.
4  Soak mandarin skin in water and cut into fine strips.
5  Wash and peel turnips, and cut into small pieces. Place mandarin skin with turnips in soup and add more water, if necessary.
6  Simmer until turnip is cooked and season with salt.
7  Remove peppercorns and garnish with spring onions.

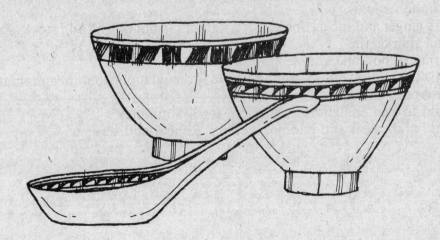

# MEATBALL SOUP

*Ingredients for 6 servings*

*30 minutes cooking time*

**500 g (1 lb) minced pork**
**1½ tablespoons soy sauce**
**½ teaspoon monosodium glutamate**
  **(optional)**

**½ teaspoon salt**
**1 egg yolk**
**7½ cups chicken stock**
**1 cup spinach**

1  Mix pork with salt, soy sauce and beaten egg yolk.
2  Shape into small balls and drop into boiling chicken stock. Cook for 15 minutes.
3  Chop spinach, add to soup and cook for 10 minutes, add salt.
4  Add monosodium glutamate (if desired) and serve with oyster sauce.

# WATERCRESS SOUP

*Ingredients for 4 servings*

*20 minutes cooking time*

**4 cups chicken stock**
**½ teaspoon sugar**
**4 slices fresh ginger**
**2 tablespoons chopped spring onions**

**¼ teaspoon salt**
**1½ teaspoons soy sauce**
**⅓ cup water**
**1 bunch watercress**

1  Remove stems from watercress and break into sprigs.
2  Combine chicken stock, soy sauce, salt, sugar, ginger and water.
3  Cook for 15 minutes over low heat.
4  Bring to boil and add watercress and spring onions.
5  Cover and simmer for 4 minutes.

# PORK AND CUCUMBER SOUP

*10 minutes cooking time*

*Ingredients for 4 servings*

**1 cucumber**
**½ tablespoon cornflour**
**1 tablespoon sherry**
**1 teaspoon salt**

**250 g (8 oz) pork**
**2½ tablespoons soy sauce**
**6 cups water**

1  Peel and slice cucumber thinly.
2  Cut pork into thin slices and mix with cornflour.
3  Add soy sauce and sherry to meat mixture.
4  Boil water and add salt, then add cucumber and boil for 1-2 minutes.
5  Add meat, boil for 2-3 minutes and serve.

# BEAN CURD SOUP

*30 minutes cooking time*

*Ingredients for 4 servings*

**5 cups chicken stock**
**½ teaspoon sugar**
**2 dried mushrooms**
**2½ cups bean curd**

**2 teaspoons soy sauce**
**250 g (8 oz) fresh pork**
**2 tablespoons chopped spring onions**

1  Soak mushrooms in warm water for 30 minutes.
2  Mix stock, soy sauce, and sugar in pan.
3  Cut pork into thin strips and slice mushrooms.
4  Boil broth, add pork, onion and mushrooms.
5  Simmer for 15 minutes and add bean curd, cook 15 minutes more; garnish with chopped spring onion to serve.

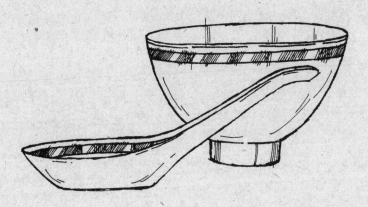

# CUCUMBER SOUP

*50 minutes cooking time*

*Ingredients for 6 servings*

½ cup dried prawns
2 slices fresh ginger
3 tablespoons sherry
6 cups chicken stock
2 cucumbers
1 tablespoon soy sauce

1 teaspoon salt
½ teaspoon monosodium glutamate
  (optional)
⅔ cup chopped ham
8 dried mushrooms

1   Soak prawns overnight and prepare mushrooms by soaking in hot water for 30 minutes, then cut into strips.
2   Score cucumbers with a fork and peel.
3   Cut lengthwise, scoop out seeds and slice.
4   Put soy sauce, salt, stock and ginger in a saucepan. Bring to boil and add mushrooms.
5   Add prawns with liquid they soaked in. Simmer for 35 minutes, add cucumber and cook for 5 minutes.
6   Season with monosodium glutamate and sprinkle with chopped ham.

# Rice
# and Noodles

## FRIED RICE

*Ingredients for 5-6 servings*

*20 minutes cooking time*

3 cups cooked rice
3 bacon rashers
4 eggs
½ teaspoon salt
¼ teaspoon pepper

chopped chives
1 teaspoon monosodium glutamate
  (optional)
1½ tablespoons soy sauce

1   Cook bacon until crisp, shred.
2   Heat oil in pan and add beaten eggs.
3   Just before the eggs set, add rice and season with salt and pepper.
4   Add bacon, chives, monosodium glutamate (if desired) and soy sauce.
5   Serve immediately.

# BOILED RICE

*25 minutes cooking time*

*Ingredients for 5-6 servings*

**750 g (1½ lb) long-grain rice**
**4 cups boiling water**

**4 small pairs Chinese salami**

1  Wash rice in water. Cover with cold fresh water and bring to the boil.
2  Boil until water has evaporated and reduce heat to the lowest level.
3  Chop salami and place on top of rice.
4  Steam for 20 minutes and serve immediately.

# RICE AND BEANS

*1½ hours cooking time*

*Ingredients for 5-6 servings*

**5 tablespoons red beans**
**250 g (8 oz) rice**

**6 cups water**
**6 tablespoons sugar**

1  Soak beans overnight in warm water.
2  Wash and rinse a few times.
3  Place beans and rice in saucepan with water.
4  Bring to the boil and simmer for 1½ hours.
5  Add sugar when serving.

# PEKING RICE

*30 minutes cooking time*

*Ingredients for 5-6 servings*

**5 cups cold cooked rice**
**1 cup toasted almonds**
**oil**
**6 eggs**

**½ teaspoon salt**
**125 g (4 oz) ham, cooked and diced**
**soy sauce to taste**

1  Combine eggs and salt.
2  Shred ham and heat oil.
3  Pour eggs into pan and add rice just before eggs start to set.
4  Add ham and dot with soy sauce.
5  Mix well and serve with toasted almonds on top.
6  Serve immediately.

# BUTTERED RICE

*Ingredients for 5-6 servings*

**1 cup hot steamed rice, seasoned
  with salt**
**3 teaspoons butter**

**2 teaspoons soy sauce
chopped Chinese parsley**

1   Melt butter into rice.
2   Mix with soy sauce.
3   Dot with chopped Chinese parsley and remove to serving dish.

# GREEN RICE

*20 minutes cooking time*

*Ingredients for 5-6 servings*

**375 g (12 oz) uncooked rice**
**2 tablespoons cooked cabbage**
**125 g (4 oz) butter**

**60 g (2 oz) grated Parmesan cheese**
**2 cloves garlic, chopped**
**½ teaspoon sage**

1   Cook the rice in boiling salted water.
2   Sauté garlic, sage and cabbage in butter.
3   Stir into cooked rice.
4   Mix well and sprinkle with cheese.

# RICE AND ALMONDS

*15 minutes cooking time*

*Ingredients for 5-6 servings*

**1½ cups uncooked rice**
**½ cup raisins**
**2 cups stock**
**½ teaspoon salt**

**½ cup toasted slivered almonds**
**3 tablespoons butter**
**grated green ginger**

1   Combine rice, stock, butter, raisins, salt and green ginger.
2   Bring to the boil and stir.
3   Cover and simmer for 15 minutes, add almonds and combine thoroughly.

# SAVOURY RICE AND CHEESE

*15 minutes cooking time*

*Ingredients for 5-6 servings*

1 cup uncooked rice
3 tomatoes, peeled and chopped
½ teaspoon salt

250 g (8 oz) grated cheese
½ cup green pepper, chopped
green ginger, grated

1   While cooking the rice in boiling salted water, chop the green peppers and add to rice.
2   Drain when cooked and add tomatoes, half of the cheese, salt and grated green ginger.
3   Combine and mix well.
4   Serve immediately, topped with remaining cheese.

# CRUSHED GINGER RICE

*20 minutes cooking time*

*Ingredients for 5-6 servings*

1 cup rice
butter
3 cups water
1 teaspoon white pepper

saffron
green ginger syrup
½ teaspoon salt

1   Place rice in saucepan with water and bring to the boil.
2   Season with salt and saffron and boil until tender.
3   Drain and add ginger syrup to rice.
4   Place butter on top and mix well.
5   Serve immediately.

# KOWLOON RICE

*20 minutes cooking time*

*Ingredients for 6-8 servings*

5 cups cooked rice
125 g (4 oz) diced ham
½ cup green pepper, chopped
60 g (2 oz) mushrooms, sliced
oil

125 g (4 oz) diced pork
125 g (4 oz) chopped prawns
1 small onion, chopped
2 teaspoons soy sauce
1 teaspoon mixed spices

1 Heat oil in pan and sauté ham, mushrooms, pork, onion, prawns, green pepper and spices. Cook for 2 minutes.
2 Remove from pan and sauté rice.
3 Return vegetable-meat mixture to pan and mix through rice.
4 Add soy sauce and season with salt and pepper.
5 Cook for 10 minutes and serve immediately.

# GINGER RICE AND BUTTER

*15 minutes cooking time*

*Ingredients for 4-5 servings*

**2 cups rice**
**3 cups water**
**1 teaspoon salt**

**saffron**
**½ cup ginger syrup**
**125 g (4 oz) butter**

1 Wash rice and cook in boiling salted water and saffron.
2 Drain ginger and add syrup to rice with a little butter.
3 Cook for 15 minutes and add remaining butter.
4 Serve immediately.

# SPICED RICE

*1 hour cooking time*

*Ingredients for 4-5 servings*

**2 cups rice**
**2 cloves garlic, chopped**
**3 cups water**
**½ teaspoon cinnamon**

**4 onions, sliced**
**6 cloves**
**250 g (8 oz) butter**
**½ teaspoon nutmeg**

1 Fry the onion, garlic and spices in oil.
2 Add water and bring to the boil.
3 Add washed rice and mix well.
4 Cook over low heat for 1 hour.
5 Serve when water has been absorbed.
6 Serve hot, garnished with chopped Chinese parsley.

# RICE WITH PEAS

*15 minutes cooking time*

*Ingredients for 4-5 servings*

125 g (4 oz) butter
½ cup chopped Chinese parsley
salted boiling water
grated lemon peel
½ teaspoon pepper

½ cup sliced onions
½ clove garlic
250 g packet frozen peas
3 cups cooked rice
2 teaspoons soy sauce

1   Heat butter in pan and sauté onions, parsley and garlic.
2   Cook peas in boiling water, remove from heat, drain.
3   Add the rice, lemon peel, soy sauce, and pepper to frying pan.
4   Add peas.
5   Stir gently and serve immediately.

# RICE AND BEAN SPROUTS

*5 minutes cooking time*

*Ingredients for 4-5 servings*

4 tablespoons toasted sesame seeds
2 cloves garlic, crushed
2 cups bean sprouts
2 teaspoons soy sauce

3 minced onions
sesame oil
3 cups hot cooked rice

1   Mix sesame seeds with onions and garlic.
2   Combine well and sauté in oil for 5 minutes.
3   Add bean sprouts and heat through.
4   Add hot rice and soy sauce. Mix gently.
5   Serve immediately.

# RICE WITH EGGS

*30 minutes cooking time*

*Ingredients for 4-5 servings*

4 cups cooked rice
4 eggs
oil
1 teaspoon salt

1 cup diced pork
5 shallots, chopped
2 tablespoons soy sauce
½ teaspoon pepper

1   Beat the eggs lightly.
2   Heat the oil and add rice and cook for 2 minutes.
3   Stir constantly to prevent going lumpy.
4   Stir in salt and pepper, add shallots and pork.
5   Mix thoroughly and form a hollow in the middle of the pan.
6   Scramble the eggs gently in hollow, then stir into surrounding rice mixture.
7   Sprinkle with soy sauce and serve immediately.

# STEAMED RICE WITH SAUSAGES

*40 minutes cooking time*

*Ingredients for 4-5 servings*

**250 g (8 oz) long-grain rice**
**1½ Chinese sausages**

**2½ cups water**

1   Wash rice and rub gently between the hands.
2   Drain.
3   Place into a bowl and add water; leave for 20 minutes.
4   Cover and place rice in a bowl and place in a steamer for 30-40 minutes.
5   Place sausage on top of rice half way through cooking.
6   Serve immediately.

# ORIENTAL COMBINATION

*20 minutes cooking time*

*Ingredients for 4-5 servings*

**3 cups cooked rice, cold**
**1 cup diced cooked pork**
**2 cups Chinese cabbage, shredded**
**2 tablespoons oil**
**½ teaspoon salt**

**½ cup breadcrumbs**
**185 g (6 oz) cooked prawns, minced**
**½ cup chopped shallots**
**2 tablespoons soy sauce**

1   Heat the oil and add the prawns and salt.
2   Toss and turn until heated.
3   Add the pork, shallots and breadcrumbs.
4   Add cabbage and rice.
5   Fry for 5 minutes.
6   Add soy sauce and pile into serving dish.

# SAVOURY NOODLES

*20 minutes cooking time*

*Ingredients for 4-5 servings*

250 g (8 oz) pork, diced
1 chopped onion
3 eggs
½ teaspoon salt
cooking oil
1½ tablespoons soy sauce

breadcrumbs
250 g (8 oz) chicken, diced
1½ tablespoons sesame oil
90 g (3 oz) dry noodles
¼ teaspoon pepper

1   Combine diced meats and onion together.
2   Mix in beaten eggs and season with salt and pepper.
3   Add soy sauce and sesame oil.
4   Add breadcrumbs and blend in with other ingredients.
5   Roll into balls and then roll in crushed noodles.
6   Deep fry and drain.
7   Serve immediately.

# NOODLE SALAD

*10 minutes cooking time*

*Ingredients for 4-5 servings*

250 g (8 oz) egg noodles
vegetable oil
90 g (3 oz) cooked chicken
2 tablespoons soy sauce

1 red chilli
2 tablespoons sesame oil
315 g (10 oz) cooked ham
chopped shallots

1   Cook noodles in boiling salted water. Rinse and drain.
2   Fry in vegetable oil and cool.
3   Shred chicken, ham and chilli.
4   Mix with sesame oil and soy sauce.
5   Add noodles and chill.
6   Sprinkle with chopped shallots.

# MIXED FRIED NOODLES

*Ingredients for 5-6 servings*

*10-15 minutes cooking time*

**500 g (1 lb) fine noodles**
**500 g (1 lb) pork, cubed**
**12 shelled prawns**

salt to taste
3 teaspoons soy sauce
oil

1   Combine prawns and pork, mix together thoroughly.
2   Season with salt and soy sauce and place these ingredients into prepared noodles.
3   Fold and deep fry.

# Seafood

## BUTTERFLIES

*10 minutes cooking time*

*Ingredients for 5-6 servings*

| | |
|---|---|
| **1.5 kg (3 lb) raw prawns** | **batter** |
| cornflour | oil |
| bacon | chopped Chinese parsley |

1  Prepare prawns by washing and cleaning. Leave tails on.
2  Split into half and wind bacon pieces around.
3  Secure with toothpicks.
4  Sprinkle with cornflour and dip into batter.
5  Deep fry prawns.
6  Remove to warmed plate and deep fry parsley.
7  Serve immediately.

# FISH ROE

*Ingredients for 5-6 servings*

*20 minutes cooking time*

**500 g (1 lb) fish roes**
**breadcrumbs**
**lemon slices**
**1 tablespoon soy sauce**

**cornflour**
**oil**
**1 teaspoon salt**
**2 eggs**

1  Beat eggs with soy sauce and salt.
2  Cover roes with cornflour and dip into egg mixture, then into breadcrumbs.
3  Deep fry and serve with lemon slices.

# STEAMED GINGER PRAWNS

*Ingredients for 4-5 servings*

*15 minutes cooking time*

**750 g (1½ lb) whole raw prawns**
**1 teaspoon salt**

**2 tablespoons oil**
**5 cm (2 in) green ginger, shredded**

1  Wash prawns and place them in a shallow bowl.
2  Sprinkle with salt and oil.
3  Place ginger on top.
4  Steam for 15-20 minutes.
5  Chill prawns and serve with salad.

# PRAWNS IN ASPIC

*Ingredients for 5-6 servings*

*2 hours cooking time*

**500 g (1 lb) raw prawns**
**green ginger, shredded**
**2 tablespoons soy sauce**
**1 teaspoon sesame oil**

**6 teaspoons gelatine**
**3 cups water**
**sliced cucumber**
**1 teaspoon salt**

1  Cook prawns in boiling water and add ginger.
2  Season with salt, soy sauce, and sesame oil.
3  Boil water and dissolve gelatine.
4  Cool when prawns have been poured in.
5  Chill for 2 hours and garnish with sliced cucumber.

# FRIED RICE AND PRAWNS

*15 minutes cooking time*

*Ingredients for 4-5 servings*

3 cups cooked rice
3 teaspoons chopped onions
2 tablespoons tomato paste
1 teaspoon curry powder
1 teaspoon salt

1 kg (2 lb) prawns, peeled
1 clove garlic, chopped
3 teaspoons butter
1 sliced cucumber
Chinese parsley

1  Fry the garlic in butter and add prawns.
2  Add curry powder, onion, tomato paste and salt.
3  Cover and simmer for 5 minutes.
4  Add cooked rice and stir thoroughly.
5  Cook for 5 minutes and garnish with sliced cucumber or chopped Chinese parsley.

# STUFFED CRABS

*20 minutes cooking time*

*Ingredients for 4-5 servings*

6 small crabs, uncooked
250 g (8 oz) pork mince
1½ teaspoons soy sauce
1½ teaspoons salt
2 teaspoons sugar
tomatoes

6 chestnuts
2 egg whites
cooking oil
green ginger (optional)
cucumbers
lettuce

1  Boil crabs, remove meat and leave shells intact.
2  Season meat with salt, sugar and soy sauce.
3  Peel chestnuts and mince them.
4  Add to pork mince and crab meat.
5  Mix in beaten egg whites and place in shells.
6  Steam for 10 minutes.
7  Season with a little ginger on top.
8  Drain and deep fry, drain once more and serve with lettuce, tomatoes and cucumber.

# PRAWNS AND ARTICHOKES

*Ingredients for 4-5 servings*

*10 minutes cooking time*

1 kg (2 lb) raw prawns
6 canned artichoke hearts
salt
2 tablespoons oil

5 cm (2 in) green ginger, sliced
1 teaspoon sugar
1 teaspoon cornflour
2 tablespoons soy sauce

1  Wash and clean prawns, slice in half.
2  Simmer prawns in water with sugar for 8 minutes. Remove.
3  Heat oil in pan and add salt, ginger and prawns.
4  Add artichokes and blend in cornflour and soy sauce.
5  Cook for 2 minutes and serve immediately.

# CRAB AND ASPARAGUS

*Ingredients for 2-3 servings*

*10 minutes cooking time*

1 large crab
8 pieces fresh asparagus
2 tablespoons cooking oil
soy sauce

5 cm (2 in) green ginger, grated
1 teaspoon sugar
1 teaspoon cornflour
1 teaspoon salt

1  Clean crab meat and season with salt and ginger.
2  Prepare asparagus by simmering for 2 minutes in sugar and water.
3  Fry crab meat in oil and spoon in asparagus.
4  Blend in cornflour and soy sauce.
5  Cook for 5 minutes and serve immediately.

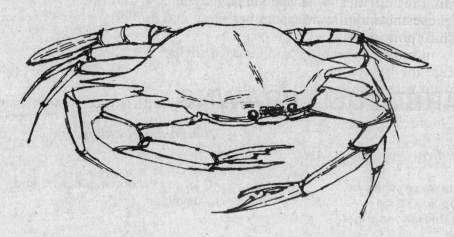

# CRAB BALLS

*10 minutes cooking time*

*Ingredients for 4-5 servings*

2 large crabs
salt
2 tablespoons soy sauce

oil
2 egg whites
black pepper

1  Clean and remove meat from crab shells.
2  Mince meat and season with salt.
3  Beat egg whites and thoroughly blend with meat mixture.
4  Drop teaspoons of this mixture in hot oil and brown evenly.
5  Drain.
6  Season with soy sauce and black pepper.
7  Serve immediately.

# CUCUMBER ROLL

*Ingredients for 4-5 servings*

3 large cucumbers
salt to taste
6 hardboiled eggs

500 g (1 lb) crab meat
4 tablespoons mayonnaise

1  Peel cucumbers and halve them crosswise.
2  Place in salted water and stand for 1 hour.
3  Cut cucumber into 2 millimetre (⅛ in) thick slices, full length.
4  Discard centre.
5  Dry well.
6  Mix the crab meat with egg yolks, mayonnaise and salt.
7  Spread this mixture on cucumber piece and lie flat.
8  Chill for 2 hours.

# BARBECUED PRAWNS

*20 minutes cooking time*

*Ingredients for 4-5 servings*

¾ cup sweet sherry
½ cup soy sauce
1½ tablespoons sugar

40 large raw prawns, peeled and
   deveined

1 In a saucepan, combine sherry, soy sauce and sugar.
2 Bring to the boil.
3 Dip skewered prawns in sauce and grill over hot coals.
4 Brush constantly with sauce until prawns are glazed.

# LOBSTER AND SWEET AND SOUR PICKLES

*Ingredients for 4-5 servings*

1 whole lobster, washed and prepared,
  broken up into serving pieces
lettuce

4 hardboiled eggs
chopped parsley
sweet and sour pickles

1 Prepare lettuce by washing and breaking up leaves.
2 Place in a salad bowl.
3 Pour in lobster pieces, pickles and quartered eggs.
4 Add chopped parsley and serve with salad dressing.

# JAPANESE FISH TERIYAKI

*15 minutes cooking time*

*Ingredients for 4-5 servings*

1 cup soy sauce
½ cup salad oil
2 cloves garlic, crushed
1 tablespoon sesame seed

½ cup sugar
green ginger
1.5 kg (3 lb) fish fillets
shredded lettuce

1 Combine soy sauce, sugar, oil, ginger, and garlic.
2 Marinate fillets in this mixture for 2 hours.
3 Line a baking pan with foil and lift fillets into pan.
4 Grill for 10 minutes and brush with marinade.
5 Sprinkle with sesame seed and grill for further 10 minutes.
6 Serve immediately.

# SALTED FISH

*30 minutes cooking time*

*Ingredients for 5-6 servings*

1 large piece salt fish
1 teaspoon green ginger, crushed
½ teaspoon salt

1½ teaspoons sugar
2 tablespoons vegetable oil
375 g (12 oz) beef mince

1   Season mince with salt and sugar.
2   Form into flat surface and place salt fish on mince in a shallow dish.
3   Season with ginger.
4   Pour vegetable oil over and steam for 30 minutes.
5   Dot with chopped shallots and serve immediately.

# FISH SQUARES

*10 minutes cooking time*

*Ingredients for 5-6 servings*

500 g (1 lb) fish fillets
½ teaspoon salt
cornflour
oil

crushed green ginger
fish stock
250 g (8 oz) crab meat
milk

1   Cut fish into squares and season with salt.
2   Heat oil and cover fish with cornflour.
3   Deep fry.
4   Season with ginger and drain.
5   Remove to serving plate.
6   Blend cornflour, stock and milk.
7   Bring to the boil and add crab meat.
8   Combine well.
9   Pour over squares and garnish with chopped shallots.

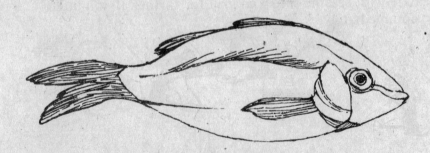

# PAPER-WRAPPED PRAWNS

*5 minutes cooking time*

*Ingredients for 4-5 servings*

| | |
|---|---|
| **4 prawns** | **chopped Chinese parsley** |
| **½ teaspoon salt** | **¼ teaspoon white pepper** |
| **⅛ teaspoon monosodium glutamate (optional)** | **1 teaspoon sherry** |
| | **peanut oil** |
| **slices green ginger** | **shallots** |
| **8 snow peas** | **greaseproof paper** |

1  Remove the shells from prawns and slice them in half lengthwise.
2  Season with salt and pepper, sherry and monosodium glutamate (if desired).
3  Cut paper into large squares and rub each piece with a little oil.
4  Place one slice each of prawn, ginger and shallot and one snow pea on the paper.
5  Fold opposite corners and fold the edge.
6  Heat oil and deep fry, flap side down.
7  Serve immediately.

# SQUID WITH CABBAGE

*20 minutes cooking time*

*Ingredients for 4-5 servings*

| | |
|---|---|
| **500 g (1 lb) fresh squid** | **1 teaspoon sugar** |
| **3 tablespoons oil** | **½ teaspoon salt** |
| **2 cloves garlic, crushed** | **6 tablespoons stock** |
| **1 tablespoon cornflour** | **2 tablespoons sherry** |
| **green ginger, crushed** | **2 tablespoons oyster sauce** |
| **250 g (8 oz) cabbage, shredded** | **4 tablespoons chopped parsley** |

1  Wash and clean squid.
2  Slash inside making a hatched pattern.
3  Heat oil in pan and add ginger, garlic and a little salt.
4  Fry squid for 5 minutes, while cabbage boils in salt water for 1 minute. Add cabbage to squid.
5  Make sauce of cornflour, sherry, sugar, oyster sauce, salt, stock and chopped parsley and pour over squid just before serving.

# BRAISED SHARK FINS

*40 minutes cooking time*

*Ingredients for 6-8 servings*

250 g (8 oz) prepared shark fins
2 tablespoons lotus flour
1½ tablespoons soy sauce
salt
1 teaspoon monosodium glutamate
(optional)

oil
1 tablespoon sherry
¾ cup cooked crab meat
4 eggs
¾ cup chicken stock

1 Soak the fins in hot water for 1 hour.
2 Drain.
3 Beat eggs lightly and shred crab meat.
4 Add crab meat, fins, salt and monosodium glutamate (if desired) to eggs.
5 Place tablespoons of this mixture on porcelain spoons and steam for 25 minutes.
6 Heat oil and fry shark fins.
7 For the sauce, combine lotus flour, chicken stock, sherry and soy sauce and simmer for 10 minutes then add fins and egg puffs.
8 Serve immediately.

# TUNA WITH GINGER RICE

*20 minutes cooking time*

*Ingredients for 4-5 servings*

1 large can tuna
1 cup green beans
2 teaspoons cornflour
1½ cups water
2 teaspoons soy sauce
4 cups cooked rice

1 cup sliced celery
2 onions, chopped
1 teaspoon sugar
90 g (3 oz) butter
½ teaspoon salt
2 teaspoons green ginger, grated

1 Blend the cornflour with a little water.
2 Melt the butter and fry onion.
3 Add the celery, beans, salt and more water.
4 Bring to the boil, cover and simmer for 5 minutes. Add the cornflour, sugar, soy sauce and cook for 5 minutes.
5 Add drained tuna and reheat.
6 Heat the cooked rice in a saucepan.
7 When hot, sprinkle ginger over the rice and mix all ingredients thoroughly.

# SEAFOOD CURRY SALAD

*Ingredients for 6-8 servings*

3 cups cooked rice
2 cups cooked scallops
lettuce leaves or cabbage
1 red pepper, chopped
1 cup dressing

750 g (1½ lb) prawns, cooked and
  peeled
500 g (1 lb) tomatoes, chopped
2 tablespoons curry paste

1   Chop half the prawns and scallops into small pieces.
2   Mix thoroughly with rice.
3   Add the tomatoes and red pepper.
4   Mix.
5   Add curry paste and dressing.
6   Line a bowl with lettuce or cabbage leaves and fill with this mixture.
7   Decorate the top of the bowl with remaining prawns and scallops.
8   Serve chilled.

# PRAWNS AND LEMON RICE

*30 minutes cooking time*

*Ingredients for 4-5 servings*

2½ cups lemon rice
½ cup diced celery
2 cloves garlic
oil

1.5 kg (3 lb) prawns, shelled
½ cup diced cucumber
1 cup yoghurt
2 lemons

1   Sauté celery, cucumber and garlic in oil.
2   Add prawns and cook.
3   Drain and chill, then mix with yoghurt.

## LEMON RICE

1   Combine hot rice with juice of 2 lemons.
2   Add oil, salt and pepper, toss.
3   Serve combined with prawn mixture.

# PRAWN CHOW MEIN

*30 minutes cooking time*

*Ingredients for 4-5 servings*

| | |
|---|---|
| 2½ cups cooking oil | 16 soaked dried mushrooms |
| 315 g (10 oz) egg noodles | ½ cup stock |
| 60 g (2 oz) green beans | 2 tablespoons cooking sherry |
| 6 tinned water chestnuts | 1 tablespoon soy sauce |
| 2 stalks celery | 1 thick slice cooked ham |
| 500 g (1 lb) cooked prawns | |

1  Fry noodles in oil until brown and drain on absorbent paper.
2  Peel prawns and slice beans, chestnuts and celery.
3  Cut mushrooms into lengths and place in a bowl with stock and sherry.
4  Pour remaining oil out of frying pan and sauté celery and green beans, mushrooms, chestnuts, stock, sherry, soy sauce and prawns.
5  Mix thoroughly and heat through. Serve with dried noodles in centre of prawn mixture. Sprinkle with chopped ham.

# FRIED LOBSTER BALLS

*10 minutes cooking time*

*Ingredients for 8 servings*

| | |
|---|---|
| 250 g (8 oz) self-raising flour | 2 eggs |
| 2 cups water | 500 g (1 lb) lobster meat |
| 1 teaspoon salt | 1 teaspoon sugar |
| 1 teaspoon monosodium glutamate (optional) | 1½ tablespoons cornflour |
| 1 cup peanut oil | 2 tablespoons chopped parsley |

1  Sift flour into a basin and work in egg. Gradually beat in water and leave to stand for 1-2 hours.
2  Cut lobster into suitable pieces and trim off ragged bits. Dust with seasonings and roll in cornflour. Coat with batter and drain.
3  Heat oil and drop balls into it. Cook for 8-10 minutes and drain. Serve with chopped parsley.

# STEAMED FISH

*20-25 minutes cooking time*

*Ingredients for 5-6 servings*

1 2-kg (4½-lb) fish
2 tablespoons crisp bacon pieces
½ teaspoon salt
2 teaspoons sugar
3 tablespoons oil
3 tablespoons soy sauce

2.5 cm (1 in) piece fresh ginger,
  shredded
¼ cup chopped spring onions
¼ teaspoon pepper
8 dried mushrooms

1   Prepare mushrooms by soaking in warm water for 30 minutes, then discard stems and slice.
2   Clean fish, make two incisions across side and season with salt.
3   Sprinkle sugar on fish and pour on oil, soy sauce and ginger. Stand for 20 minutes.
4   Place mushrooms on top of fish and sprinkle with bacon.
5   Steam for 20 minutes and garnish with chopped spring onions.

# FISH AND BEAN CURD

*40 minutes cooking time*

*Ingredients for 6 servings*

1 1.5-kg (3-lb) fish
½ teaspoon pepper
2.5 cm (1 in) piece fresh ginger, grated
10 squares fresh bean curd
3 tablespoons black bean sauce
60 g (2 oz) cubed pork fat
2 teaspoons sesame oil

½ teaspoon salt
1½ tablespoons sherry
10 squares fried bean curd
4 tablespoons chopped spring onions
1½ tablespoons peanut oil
2 tablespoons soy sauce
1 teaspoon sugar

1   Clean fish and leave head on. Score the skin.
2   Mix black bean sauce with peanut oil and add fried pork fat.
3   Mix in sesame oil, soy sauce, sugar, sherry, salt and pepper.
4   Place fish in steamer and sprinkle with shredded ginger.
5   Pour black bean sauce over the fish and place fresh and fried bean curd alongside it.
6   Steam for 25 minutes and serve topped with chopped spring onions.

# PRAWN CUTLETS

*5 minutes cooking time*

*Ingredients for 6 servings*

1.25 kg (2½ lb) raw king prawns
¼ cup cornflour
2 teaspoons soy sauce
1 teaspoon salt

½ cup breadcrumbs
1 cup peanut oil
2 eggs

1 Shell prawns (leaving tail on) and clean by slitting back gently, being careful not to cut right through. Remove black vein and any sand.
2 Beat eggs together with soy sauce and salt.
3 Cover prawns in cornflour and dip into egg mixture.
4 Sprinkle with breadcrumbs and press out cut side gently to flatten.
5 Deep fry in oil. Drain and serve immediately.


# PRAWN PUFFS

*2 minutes cooking time*

*Ingredients for 6 servings*

12 prawns
½ teaspoon salt
¼ teaspoon monosodium glutamate (optional)
6 tablespoons peanut oil

¼ teaspoon pepper
½ teaspoon sugar
1 egg, beaten
1 lettuce

1 Halve the shelled prawns lengthwise.
2 Remove black veins and trim off tails, chop finely and roll into balls.
3 Combine pepper, salt, sugar and monosodium glutamate (if desired), dust prawns with this mixture and add the egg, mix well.
4 Heat oil and fry prawns for 2 minutes.
5 Serve prawns on lettuce.

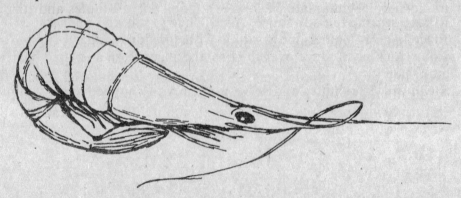

# CURRIED CRAB

*20 minutes cooking time*

*Ingredients for 4 servings*

4 tablespoons peanut oil
2 garlic cloves, crushed
½ teaspoon sugar
1 sliced onion
2 large crabs
4 tomatoes, quartered
1 egg, beaten

½ cup chopped pork
1 teaspoon salt
1 tablespoon curry powder
1 green pepper, chopped
1½ cups chicken stock
3 teaspoons cornflour

1  Heat oil in pan, add pork and cook until browned.
2  Add garlic, salt, sugar and curry, and stir.
3  Add onion and green pepper, stir for 2 minutes and add crab and stock. Cover and cook for 4 minutes.
4  Add tomatoes and cornflour mixed with 2 tablespoons of water.
5  Cook for 2 minutes and stir in egg. Serve immediately.

# CRAB CANTONESE

*8 minutes cooking time*

*Ingredients for 8 servings*

8 tablespoons peanut oil
1 teaspoon salt
500 g (1 lb) crab meat, flaked
2½ cups chicken stock
2 tablespoons water
2 tablespoons chopped parsley
5 tablespoons milk

250 g (8 oz) bamboo shoots, cut into strips
½ teaspoon monosodium glutamate (optional)
5 teaspoons sherry
3 teaspoons cornflour

1  Heat half of the oil and fry bamboo shoots. Season with salt, sugar and monosodium glutamate (if desired). Cook for 4 minutes and turn into heated dish.
2  Wipe out pan and add remaining oil. Add crab meat and sherry, stock and salt.
3  Toss and add cornflour blended with water, stir and boil.
4  Add milk and bring to boil.
5  Return bamboo shoots and heat for ½ minute. Turn into heated dish and garnish with chopped parsley.

# ABALONE AND BROCCOLI

*20 minutes cooking time*

*Ingredients for 3 servings*

**1 tin abalone**
**2 tablespoons oyster sauce**
**375 g (12 oz) broccoli**
**2 tablespoons rosé wine**

**½ teaspoon salt**
**1 teaspoon sesame oil**
**1 tablespoon cornflour**

1 Cut abalone into thin slices and retain liquid.
2 Slice broccoli stems and cut flowers into small bunches.
3 Combine abalone liquid with water and cook broccoli stems until tender.
4 Add flowers, cook 1 minute and remove to plate.
5 Blend cornflour with wine, salt and oyster sauce.
6 Add stock from broccoli and abalone and mix in sesame oil and cook until abalone is tender.
7 Serve abalone on top of broccoli and ladle sauce over it.

# PRAWNS IN BLACK BEAN SAUCE

*5 minutes cooking time*

*Ingredients for 8 servings*

**15 prawns**
**½ teaspoon salt**
**½ teaspoon monosodium glutamate**
**(optional)**
**5 tablespoons black soy beans**
**2 teaspoons soy sauce**
**1 tablespoon water**

**¼ teaspoon pepper**
**½ teaspoon sugar**
**4 tablespoons peanut oil**
**2 garlic cloves, crushed**
**1¼ cups hot chicken stock**
**2 teaspoons cornflour**
**5 slices fresh ginger**

1 Halve the shelled prawns and remove veins.
2 Cut prawns diagonally into small pieces, sprinkle with monosodium glutamate (if desired), pepper, sugar, salt and mix well.
3 Heat oil and add ginger and garlic, cook for 90 seconds and discard. Add beans and cook for 20 seconds, tossing.
4 Add prawns and cook for 2 minutes.
5 Add stock, cornflour blended with water and soy sauce. Boil for 1 minute and turn into serving dish.

# SCALLOPS AND BAMBOO SHOOTS

*20 minutes cooking time*

*Ingredients for 6 servings*

500 g (1 lb) fresh scallops
3 teaspoons soy sauce
185 g (6 oz) tinned bamboo shoots
2 rings pineapple
4 tablespoons peanut oil
1 cup fish stock

2 teaspoons cornflour
1½ teaspoons sugar
3 sticks celery
2 onions
1 teaspoon salt

1 Cut scallops in half and mix with cornflour.
2 Add sugar, soy sauce and 1 tablespoon water.
3 Cut bamboo shoots and celery into thin strips, and cut pineapple into wedges.
4 Heat oil and sauté scallops until cooked, drain and keep warm.
5 Add bamboo shoots, pineapple, celery and chopped onion to pan. Fry for 5 minutes and season with salt.
6 Pour in stock and bring to boil. Simmer for 3 minutes and stir in cornflour mixture.
7 To serve, pour sauce over scallops.

# CRAB SWEET AND SOUR

*30 minutes cooking time*

*Ingredients for 4 servings*

4 crabs
2 tablespoons white vinegar
2 tablespoons soy sauce
2 onions, chopped
1 hot chilli
8 tablespoons vegetable oil

1 cup water
2 tablespoons sugar
1 tablespoon cornflour
3 cloves garlic
2.5 cm (1 in) piece fresh ginger

1 Scrub and wash crab carefully. Remove outer shell and clean away fibres inside.
2 Cut each half into three sections, take off claws and cut claws at joint.
3 Pound onion together with crushed garlic and chilli.
4 Crush ginger and place in pan with oil.
5 Add onion-chilli-garlic mixture and sauté 3 minutes, then sauté crab for 8 minutes.
6 Pour in water and cover. Simmer for 15 minutes then add vinegar, sugar, soy sauce and cornflour.
7 Cook for 5-10 minutes and serve.

# BARBECUED FISH

*45 minutes cooking time*

*Ingredients for 4 servings*

1 1.5-kg (3-lb) fish
1 piece green ginger
1 teaspoon salt

1 tablespoon soy sauce
1 clove garlic
1 tablespoon peanut oil

1  Clean fish, leaving head intact.
2  Combine salt, vegetable oil, soy sauce, crushed ginger and garlic, and marinate for 20 minutes.
3  Put skewer through fish and cook on spit or under griller for 12 minutes on each side.

# SHANGHAI BREAM

*25 minutes cooking time*

*Ingredients for 4 servings*

1 1.5-kg (3-lb) bream
1½ cups white wine
2 rashers bacon
1 tablespoon soy sauce
90 g (3 oz) toasted slivered almonds
2.5 cm (1 in) piece fresh ginger
2 stock cubes
1 carrot

½ teaspoon peppercorns
¼ cup chopped spring onions
125 g (4 oz) peanut oil
1½ teaspoons sesame oil
2 stalks celery
2 onions
1 teaspoon salt

1  Clean fish, keeping head on, and sprinkle with salt.
2  Chop onions, carrot, celery, ginger and coriander.
3  Crumble stock cubes in 6 cups water in large pan, add sliced vegetables, wine and peppercorns. Bring to boil.
4  Immerse fish gently and poach for 12 minutes over low heat.
5  Cut bacon into strips and fry.
6  Heat peanut oil and add 2 tablespoons of stock.
7  Top fish with spring onions, spoon over oil and sprinkle with bacon and almonds.

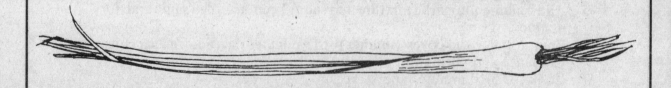

# FISH-FILLED MUSHROOMS

*25 minutes cooking time*

*Ingredients for 3 servings*

15 dried mushrooms
½ teaspoon salt
1 tablespoon soy sauce
6 teaspoons peanut oil
1½ teaspoons sesame oil

375 g (12 oz) fish fillets, chopped
8 tablespoons chopped spring onions
1 egg white
3 teaspoons sugar

1   Soak mushrooms in hot water for 30 minutes.
2   Squeeze dry and remove stems.
3   Combine fish fillets with salt, soy sauce and spring onions and egg white.
4   Sauté mushrooms in oil for 2 minutes and add sugar, sherry and stock. Remove and cool.
5   Pack fish filling on the underside of each mushroom and arrange on a shallow dish. Steam for 15-20 minutes and sprinkle with sesame oil before serving.

# SWEET AND SOUR PRAWNS

*10 minutes cooking time*

*Ingredients for 6 servings*

315 g (10 oz) prawns
1 onion
2 tomatoes, cut into wedges
1 hot chilli
3 teaspoons tomato purée
1 teaspoon salt
2 teaspoons cornflour

1½ tablespoons plain flour
6 tablespoons pineapple wedges
4 tablespoons peanut oil
4 tablespoons green pepper, diced
3 tablespoons sugar
1½ tablespoons water
6 tablespoons wine vinegar

1   Combine prawns and flour.
2   Chop onion, chilli, pineapple, tomato and green pepper.
3   Heat peanut oil and fry prawns, remove and fry onions.
4   Add tomato purée, sugar and salt.
5   Add chicken stock, vinegar and cornflour blended with water.
6   Cook for 2 minutes then add tomatoes, pepper and pineapple. Heat through and add prawns. Toss gently and serve.

# ABALONE AND LETTUCE

*15 minutes cooking time*

*Ingredients for 3 servings*

1 tin abalone
1 tablespoon cornflour
2 tablespoons warm water
1 lettuce

3 tablespoons peanut oil
185 g (6 oz) tinned button mushrooms
3 tablespoons oyster sauce
3 tablespoons chopped spring onions

1  Drain abalone and reserve liquid. Cut into thin slices and heat oil.
2  Fry abalone gently in oil and remove. Drain champignons and place in a deep saucepan.
3  Pour in half the abalone liquid and half the mushroom liquid and add oyster sauce.
4  Return abalone and braise until cooked. Blend cornflour with warm water and add to mixture slowly.
5  Serve over shredded lettuce and garnish with spring onions.

# CRAB IN BLACK BEAN SAUCE

*20 minutes cooking time*

*Ingredients for 4 servings*

2 large crabs
3 cloves garlic
3 tablespoons soy sauce
60 g (2 oz) chopped pork
2 teaspoons cornflour
2 tablespoons chopped green pepper

1 tablespoon black beans
1 teaspoon sugar
2 tablespoons peanut oil
6 tablespoons boiling water
1 tablespoon cold water
1 egg, beaten

1  Crack crab and clean, rinse well.
2  Wash and drain beans, crush with 1 clove of garlic and mix with soy sauce and sugar.
3  Heat oil in pan and add remaining garlic, cook for 1 minute and discard. Pour in boiling water and black bean mixture.
4  Cover and cook for 10 minutes.
5  Stir in cornflour blended with cold water and stir until thickened.
6  Add green pepper and beaten egg. Heat and serve immediately.

# PRAWN-STUFFED FISH

*20 minutes cooking time*

*Ingredients for 8 servings*

1 1-kg (2-lb) fish
2 spring onions, chopped
¼ teaspoon white pepper
5 prawns, cleaned and chopped
2 teaspoons sherry

2 slices fresh ginger
1 teaspoon salt
¼ teaspoon monosodium glutamate (optional)
1½ teaspoons cornflour

1  Scale, gut and wash fish.
2  Break spine at head and tail ends. Remove meat leaving head, tail and skin intact.
3  Remove any small bones and chop meat.
4  Add chopped ginger, onion, sherry and seasonings to meat. Mix well and add prawns.
5  Mix to a smooth paste and spread inside the fish which has been dotted with cornflour.
6  Shape the fish into its original form.
7  Place fish on oiled plate and steam for 20 minutes.

# PRAWNS AND NOODLES

*25 minutes cooking time*

*Ingredients for 6 servings*

185 g (6 oz) dried egg noodles
2 tablespoons peanut oil
1 lettuce
1 teaspoon soy sauce
1 slice fresh ginger, chopped

250 g (8 oz) peeled prawns
4 cups stock
1 teaspoon sesame oil
2 eggs
½ teaspoon salt

1  Cook noodles in boiling water for 5 minutes, drain and rinse with cold water.
2  Sauté prawns in oil with ginger and remove.
3  Beat eggs and cook into two thin omelettes.
4  When cool, cut into shreds. Pour stock into saucepan, season with salt and heat.
5  Shred lettuce and dip in hot soup.
6  Place lettuce in bottom of individual soup dishes.
7  Add prawns and egg noodles to soup. Spoon sesame oil on top of lettuce, pour soup over, sprinkle with shredded omelette.

# CANTONESE LOBSTER

*Ingredients for 4 servings*

*10 minutes cooking time*

1 lobster
3 tablespoons peanut oil
1 teaspoon sherry
½ teaspoon salt
¼ teaspoon monosodium glutamate
   (optional)
1½ teaspoons cornflour

90 g (3 oz) raw pork, chopped
2 cloves garlic, crushed
1 cup stock
½ teaspoon sugar
2 teaspoons tomato sauce
1 tablespoon water

1   Clean lobster and chop into 2.5 centimetre (1 in) slices.
2   Heat oil and fry garlic for 1 minute then discard. Fry pork for 1 minute and add lobster pieces.
3   Add sherry, chicken stock seasonings and tomato sauce. Blend in cornflour and water.
4   Bring to boil and cook for 2 minutes.

# PRAWN CURRY

*Ingredients for 4 servings*

*25 minutes cooking time*

1 kg (2 lb) raw prawns
1 potato
1½ cups coconut milk
2 tablespoons flour
3 cloves garlic, crushed
½ teaspoon pepper
2 tablespoons curry powder

3 onions, chopped
1 cup water
2 tablespoons butter
6 tablespoons peanut oil
1 teaspoon salt
5 cm (2 in) piece fresh ginger, grated

1   Peel and clean prawns.
2   Heat oil and fry garlic, ginger, salt and pepper for 2 minutes.
3   Sauté prawns until they turn pink, remove and keep warm.
4   Sauté onions, add curry powder, potato, and water. Cover and simmer until potato is cooked.
5   Blend butter with flour and pour into curry sauce gradually with coconut milk.
6   Add prawns and cook for 5 minutes.

# SESAME BATTER FISH

*8 minutes cooking time*

*Ingredients for 8 servings*

| | |
|---|---|
| 750 g (1½ lb) fish fillets | 2.5 cm (1 in) piece fresh ginger, grated |
| 2 onions | 2 tablespoons sherry |
| 1 teaspoon salt | ½ teaspoon pepper |
| 1½ tablespoons flour | 60 g (2 oz) cornflour |
| 30 g (1 oz) sesame seeds | 1 egg |
| 1 cup peanut oil | 2 teaspoons sugar |

1  Cut fish into 2.5 centimetre (1 in) squares.
2  Chop onions, mix with ginger, salt, sherry, pepper and sugar and marinate fish 30 minutes.
3  Sift cornflour and flour, add 5 tablespoons water and egg.
4  Dip drained fish in batter and roll in sesame seeds.
5  Fry in hot oil for 6 minutes and serve.

# STUFFED SNAPPER

*35 minutes cooking time*

*Ingredients for 4 servings*

| | |
|---|---|
| 1 whole snapper | 185 g (6 oz) minced pork |
| 10 mushrooms, sliced | 1 teaspoon salt |
| ¼ teaspoon pepper | 2 teaspoons cornflour |
| 2 teaspoons sesame oil | 6 tablespoons peanut oil |

1  Wash and clean fish, leaving head intact.
2  Slit open side of fish, remove backbone and all meat, without breaking skin.
3  Mix pork with mushrooms and combine with chopped meat.
4  Add salt, pepper and 1 tablespoon oil and stuff mixture back into fish.
5  Sew up side or fasten with poultry pins.
6  Sprinkle with cornflour and fry over low heat until brown on both sides.
7  Cover with lid and cook for 20 minutes.

# CRISP SKIN FISH

*Ingredients for 4 servings*

1.5 kg (3 lb) fish
½ cup breadcrumbs
½ teaspoon salt
2 teaspoons cornflour

1 egg
1 cup peanut oil
1 tablespoon soy sauce

1 Split fish in half and remove backbone.
2 Season with salt and soy sauce.
3 Sprinkle with cornflour and brush on beaten egg.
4 Cover with breadcrumbs and deep fry in oil.
5 Drain and remove to serving dish.

# PINEAPPLE PRAWNS

*20 minutes cooking time*

*Ingredients for 6 servings*

750 g (1½ lb) raw prawns
1½ teaspoons salt
1⅓ cups milk
8 cm (3 in) piece fresh ginger
1 small tin pineapple pieces

2 tablespoons milk
3 eggs
185 g (6 oz) plain flour
1½ cups peanut oil

1 Beat eggs with salt, add sifted flour and a little milk.
2 Clean and shell prawns and dip in batter.
3 Heat oil in pan and add grated ginger, then deep fry prawns, remove and drain.
4 Surround with pineapple pieces to serve.

# Poultry

## STEAMED CHICKEN

*40 minutes cooking time*

*Ingredients for 5-6 servings*

| | |
|---|---|
| 1 2-kg (4-lb) chicken | 2 chopped onions |
| ¼ cup chopped celery | 2 chopped carrots |
| 1 chopped red pepper | 1½ tablespoons salt |
| oil | 8 peppercorns |
| water | 2 teaspoons chopped green ginger |

1  Place chicken in boiling water; add salt, peppercorns and onions.
2  Simmer for 30 minutes and remove chicken.
3  Pour cold water over chicken.
4  When saucepan ingredients have cooled down, stir in chopped red pepper.
5  Drain chicken, brush with oil and serve.
6  Vegetables should be pre-cooked and served around chicken.

# STUFFED WINGS

*30 minutes cooking time*

*Ingredients for 5-6 servings*

12 chicken wings
12 bacon rashers, chopped
185 g (6 oz) bamboo shoots
125 g (4 oz) cooked pork
½ teaspoon salt

2 tablespoons cornflour
2 tablespoons sesame oil
6 tablespoons stock
chopped Chinese parsley
½ teaspoon pepper

1   Holding the middle joint of the chicken wing, cut through the joint. Loosen and remove bones.
2   Fill the cavity with chopped bacon, bamboo shoots and pork mixture.
3   Season with salt and pepper.
4   Sprinkle with cornflour and fry in sesame oil.
5   Add stock and cover, cook until tender.
6   Serve garnished with parsley.

# CHICKEN AND MUSHROOMS

*45 minutes cooking time*

*Ingredients for 5-6 servings*

1 2-kg (4-lb) chicken
4 tablespoons plain flour
1 teaspoon salt
2 teaspoons monosodium glutamate (optional)

20 dried mushrooms
3 tablespoons butter
¼ cup stock
4 tablespoons sherry
2 cups cream

1   Prepare chicken by washing and rubbing with salt.
2   Place in saucepan with mushrooms and soak for 1 hour.
3   Add monosodium glutamate (if desired) and water to cover.
4   Bring to the boil and simmer until cooked.
5   Drain.
6   Remove meat from chicken and dice mushrooms and chicken.
7   Slowly melt the butter and add flour. Cook for 1 minute.
8   Add chicken stock and cook, stirring, until thick. Combine all ingredients.
9   Dot with chopped Chinese parsley and serve immediately.

# SMOOTH CHICKEN

*Ingredients for 4-5 servings*

*20 minutes cooking time*

**4 chicken breasts**
**½ cup water**
**3 teaspoons cornflour**
**salt**
**6 egg whites**
**cooked shredded ham**

**250 g (8 oz) fat or oil**
**green ginger**
**1½ cups chicken stock**
**½ teaspoon monosodium glutamate**
  **(optional)**
**3 tablespoons sherry**

1 Slice chicken into thin pieces.
2 Mince meat and add a little water.
3 Season with cornflour, salt and monosodium glutamate (if desired) and pound.
4 Beat the egg whites and add to mixture.
5 Stir in remaining ingredients to chicken mixture.
6 Melt fat or oil and place chicken mixture in.
7 Drain the fat from this mixture and stir constantly.
8 Heat more oil in another pan and place tablespoons of chicken mixture into pan.
9 Brown on all sides and serve with sauce.

## SAUCE

Combine stock, salt, cooked ham and a little cornflour, heat and pour over chicken balls.

# FRIED CHICKEN

*20 minutes cooking time*

*Ingredients for 5-6 servings*

**2 cloves garlic, crushed**
**½ cup soy sauce**
**3 eggs**
**oil**
**1 tablespoon sugar**

**1 2-kg (4-lb) chicken**
**grated green ginger**
**breadcrumbs**
**1 teaspoon salt**
**1 cup sherry**

1 Cut chicken in serving pieces and place in bowl of sherry.
2 Season with soy sauce, sugar, salt, garlic and ginger and stand for 1 hour.
3 Beat eggs and dip chicken pieces into this mixture.
4 Dip into breadcrumbs and deep fry.
5 Drain before serving.

# CHICKEN AND ALMONDS

*45 minutes cooking time*

*Ingredients for 5-6 servings*

1 kg (2 lb) chicken meat
½ teaspoon bicarbonate soda
2 egg whites
2 tablespoons riesling
½ teaspoon monosodium glutamate
   (optional)
500 g (1 lb) prepared mushrooms
½ cup chopped celery

1 teaspoon salt
2 tablespoons cornflour
2 teaspoons sesame oil
oil
2 onions, chopped
½ cup chopped green beans
toasted almonds

1   Cut the chicken and dice.
2   Season with salt, soda, cornflour and add egg whites, sesame oil, wine and monosodium glutamate (if desired).
3   Deep fry chicken, remove and drain.
4   Chop all vegetables and add oil to pan.
5   Sauté vegetables and add a little water.
6   Season with salt.
7   Return chicken and combine all ingredients thoroughly.
8   Sprinkle with toasted almonds just before serving.

# CHICKEN WITH RED PEPPERS

*30 minutes cooking time*

*Ingredients for 4-5 servings*

1 1-kg (2-lb) chicken
1 teaspoon salt
cornflour
oil for cooking
4 onions

2 tablespoons butter
4 red peppers
1 cup chicken stock
1 teaspoon soy sauce

1   Sauté red peppers, already chopped and cleaned, in butter.
2   Cut the chicken into 5 centimetre (2 in) cubes and sprinkle with salt and cornflour.
3   Add soy sauce and deep fry in oil.
4   Remove and drain.
5   Add red peppers to chicken cubes and fry once more.
6   Sauté chopped onions and mix all ingredients.
7   Add one whole red chilli to this mixture and serve immediately.

# CREAMED MUSHROOM CHICKEN

*1 hour 20 minutes cooking time*

*Ingredients for 4-5 servings*

1 1.5-kg (3-lb) chicken
salt
chicken stock
1 cup cream
1 teaspoon monosodium glutamate
  (optional)

3 tablespoons butter
grated green ginger
sweet sherry to taste
315 g (10 oz) champignons, cooked in
  butter and garlic separately

1  Wash and clean the chicken, break into serving pieces and rub in salt.
2  Place in a bowl with ginger.
3  Add monosodium glutamate (if desired) and cover with water.
4  Simmer for 1 hour and remove from heat.
5  Drain and add fresh stock, heat slowly and thicken with cream.
6  Add sherry, a little butter and mushrooms.
7  This sauce should not be very thick.

# CHICKEN AND ARROWROOT

*20 minutes cooking time*

*Ingredients for 4-5 servings*

4 cups cooked rice
1 cup fresh beans
½ cup shredded parsnips
2 tablespoons arrowroot
2 cups chicken stock
2 teaspoons soy sauce

8 chicken pieces
½ cup shredded carrots
3 onions, chopped
2 tablespoons sherry
3 tablespoons oil

1  Place the chicken pieces in saucepan and add 1 cup of water and seasonings. Cover and simmer.
2  Remove chicken when tender.
3  Keep the liquid and make up to 2½ cups.
4  Heat the oil and sauté the onions until tender.
5  Reduce the heat and add the carrot and parsnip shreds. Stir in the chopped beans and simmer for 3 minutes.
6  Cover and simmer for 5 minutes.
7  Add soy sauce, sherry, stock and arrowroot.
8  Stir.
9  Place in serving dish and serve immediately with rice.

# SPICY CHICKEN LIVERS

*20 minutes cooking time*

*Ingredients for 5-6 servings*

**500 g (1 lb) chicken livers**
**½ cup chopped onions**
**1½ tablespoons sugar**
**2 teaspoons chopped ginger**

**1 cup soy sauce**
**½ cup sake**
**½ teaspoon aniseed**

1 Boil chicken livers in water and drain.
2 Add soy sauce, onions, sake, sugar, aniseed and ginger.
3 Bring to the boil and simmer for 15 minutes.
4 Chill.
5 Drain.
6 Slice into bite-size pieces and serve.

# EGG NOODLES AND CHICKEN PIECES

*10 minutes cooking time*

*Ingredients for 4-5 servings*

**125 g (4 oz) chicken pieces**
**4 snow peas**
**½ chopped carrot**
**½ teaspoon monosodium glutamate**
  **(optional)**
**½ teaspoon white pepper**
**1 tablespoon cornflour**

**2 dried mushrooms**
**egg noodles**
**½ teaspoon salt**
**1 teaspoon sherry**
**2½ cups chicken stock**
**1½ tablespoons water**
**4 tablespoons oil**

1 Cut chicken into small pieces and soak mushrooms.
2 Remove the rough part of the snow peas and cook egg noodles in boiling salted water.
3 Rinse in cold water and drain.
4 Heat oil and fry mushrooms, peas, carrot, chicken.
5 Add salt, sherry, monosodium glutamate (if desired) and pepper.
6 Add half of the chicken stock and thicken with cornflour.
7 Reheat the noodles and add to chicken mixture.
8 Serve immediately.

# LEMON AND PINEAPPLE CHICKEN

*30 minutes cooking time*

*Ingredients for 5-6 servings*

1 1.5-kg (3-lb) chicken
½ cup soy sauce
2 teaspoons sugar
1 teaspoon cornflour
oil

2 cloves garlic
1 can pineapple pieces
chopped Chinese parsley
grated rind of 2 lemons
2.5 cm (1 in) green ginger, grated

1  Wash chicken and mix together soy sauce, cornflour, salt, ginger, sugar and lemon rind.
2  Pour over chicken and stand for 30 minutes.
3  Heat oil in pan and add garlic, brown the chicken on all sides.
4  Add pineapple and 4 tablespoons juice and a little water.
5  Simmer, cut chicken into serving pieces and arrange on a warmed plate.
6  Pour over liquid and serve immediately.

# CURRIED CHICKEN

*20 minutes cooking time*

*Ingredients for 4-5 servings*

24 chicken wings
12 tablespoons water
6 tablespoons flour
2 teaspoons sugar
oil for frying

1 egg
cornflour
1 teaspoon salt
2 teaspoons curry powder
soy sauce

1  Cut wings at first joint.
2  Start at the small end of each large piece of wing.
3  Cut the meat from the bone.
4  Break egg into a bowl, beat with fork.
5  Add water, cornflour, flour, salt, sugar and curry powder.
6  Coat chicken pieces in this mixture and fry in hot oil.
7  Serve immediately with soy sauce.

# GRILLED CHICKEN LIVERS

*20 minutes cooking time*

*Ingredients for 4-5 servings*

500 g (1 lb) chicken livers, washed, drained and cut in half
bacon
2 small cloves garlic

whole water chestnuts
soy sauce
grated ginger

1 Fold liver around water chestnuts and wrap with a slice of bacon.
2 Secure with toothpicks.
3 Combine soy sauce, garlic and ginger.
4 Marinate the liver in this mixture for four hours.
5 Grill for 7-10 minutes or longer if preferred.

# CHICKEN WITH MIXED VEGETABLES

*1 hour cooking time*

*Ingredients for 6 servings*

1 1.5-kg (3-lb) chicken
2 tablespoons dry sherry
1 teaspoon salt
1 green pepper
2 stalks celery
2 tablespoons peanut oil
2 teaspoons chopped fresh ginger
3 spring onions, sliced
1 tablespoon brown sugar

3 tablespoons soy sauce
2 teaspoons sugar
3 rings pineapple
1 carrot
8 water chestnuts
2 garlic cloves, crushed
4 cups chicken stock
185 g (6 oz) spinach
2 tablespoons cornflour

1 Chop chicken into 12 pieces with cleaver.
2 Combine soy sauce, sugar, sherry and salt. Rub chicken with this mixture and stand for 30 minutes.
3 Cut pineapple into eighths and pepper and carrot into slices. Cook for 5 minutes in boiling water. Drain.
4 Slice celery and water chestnuts.
5 Fry garlic and ginger for 2 minutes in hot oil, add chicken pieces and cook 5 minutes. Pour off excess oil and add chicken stock.
6 Cover and simmer 40 minutes.
7 Add pineapple and vegetables to the pan and cook 5 minutes.
8 Arrange the chicken on a serving dish. Mix sugar and cornflour with a little water and add to cooking liquid.
9 Boil and stir for 3 minutes, season and serve with sauce poured over the chicken.

# FRUIT CHICKEN

*40 minutes cooking time*

*Ingredients for 8 servings*

| | |
|---|---|
| 4 whole chicken breasts | 2 egg whites |
| 3 teaspoons cornflour | ⅓ cup soy sauce |
| 1 tin lychees | 3 tablespoons vinegar |
| 3 tablespoons sugar | ⅓ cup peanut oil |
| 2 tablespoons candied ginger | 4 tablespoons chopped parsley |
| 1 tin sliced kumquats in syrup | |

1  Remove skin and bones from chicken and slice flesh thinly.
2  Combine egg whites and chicken and cornflour.
3  Mix soy sauce and 1 tablespoon of cornflour in separate bowl, with ¼ cup lychee syrup, vinegar and sugar.
4  Heat oil and add chicken mixture. When meat turns white add lychees and ginger and stir, then add cornflour and soy sauce mixture.
5  Cook until thickened and garnish with parsley and sliced cumquats.

# CHINESE CHICKEN

*30 minutes cooking time*

*Ingredients for 8 servings*

| | |
|---|---|
| 2 1.5-kg (3-lb) chickens | 1 teaspoon salt |
| ½ teaspoon pepper | 6 tablespoons soy sauce |
| 2 tablespoons sugar | 5 tablespoons sherry |
| 7.5 cm (3 in) fresh ginger, shredded | 7 teaspoons sesame oil |
| 20 dried mushrooms | ½ cup chopped spring onions |
| 3 tablespoons oil | 8 tablespoons chicken stock |

1  Chop chickens into pieces without removing bones.
2  Season with salt, soy sauce, pepper, sugar, ginger and sherry.
3  Marinate for 1 hour.
4  Soak mushrooms in hot water for 20 minutes.
5  In deep bowl, combine chicken and marinating liquid and mushrooms.
6  Pour over peanut oil, sesame oil and stock.
7  Steam for 30 minutes and sprinkle with spring onions.

# LEMON CHICKEN

*35 minutes cooking time*

*Ingredients for 6 servings*

2½ teaspoons sesame oil
2½ teaspoons sugar
½ teaspoon salt
2 tablespoons soy sauce
⅓ cup black beans

1 kg (2 lb) chicken breasts
6 tablespoons cornflour
2 tablespoons sherry
2 cloves garlic
2 lemons

1 Chop chicken into 5 centimetre (2 in) pieces.
2 Blend sugar, salt, sesame oil, cornflour, soy sauce and sherry.
3 Mash beans with garlic and add to cornflour mixture.
4 Add chicken pieces and mix thoroughly, put in casserole.
5 Squeeze lemon juice over chicken, chop peel and put on top of chicken.
6 Cover casserole with waxed paper and put 5 centimetres (2 in) above boiling water.
7 Cover pan and steam for 35 minutes.

# CHICKEN CHOW MEIN

*20 minutes cooking time*

*Ingredients for 4 servings*

250 g (8 oz) egg noodles
¼ teaspoon pepper
1½ cups chicken stock
1½ tablespoons sherry
½ cup peanut oil
2 cups chopped chicken meat
1 cup green beans
⅔ cup cooked ham

½ teaspoon salt
1 tablespoon cornflour
1½ tablespoons soy sauce
½ teaspoon monosodium glutamate (optional)
6 dried mushrooms
1 egg
1 teaspoon sugar

1 Deep fry noodles in oil until crisp, drain and arrange on a plate.
2 Make a thin omelette with egg.
3 Combine mushrooms, ham and parboiled beans.
4 Place in pan with 2 tablespoons peanut oil, sauté for a few minutes, add chicken, salt and sugar and mix well.
5 Place on noodles and top with shredded egg, and keep warm.
6 Combine cornflour, a little water, and stock. Bring to boil and pour in soy sauce, sherry, and monosodium glutamate (if desired).
7 Simmer for 3 minutes and pour over chicken and noodles to serve.

# ONION-STUFFED DUCK

*2 hours cooking time*

*Ingredients for 4 servings*

**1 2.5-kg (5-lb) duck**
**3 cups water**
**4 slices green ginger**
**20 spring onions, chopped**

**3 teaspoons sugar**
**3 tablespoons sherry**
**8 tablespoons soy sauce**

1  Wash duck and cut off tail.
2  Slice onions and mix with 2 tablespoons soy sauce, 1 teaspoon sugar and stuff duck with the mixture.
3  Place duck into heavy pot with 3 cups of water and remaining soy sauce, sherry and ginger.
4  Heat until boiling, simmer for 1 hour and add remaining sugar and simmer for another hour.

# CHICKEN AND CASHEWS

*10 minutes cooking time*

*Ingredients for 4 servings*

**2 chicken breasts**
**185 g (6 oz) mushrooms**
**315 g (10 oz) bamboo shoots**
**⅓ cup soy sauce**
**½ teaspoon salt**
**¼ cup peanut oil**

**155 g (5 oz) snow peas**
**4 spring onions**
**¾ cup chicken stock**
**2 tablespoons cornflour**
**½ teaspoon sugar**
**185 g (6 oz) cashew nuts**

1  Bone chicken, remove skin, and slice flesh thinly.
2  Remove tips and strings from snow peas.
3  Slice mushrooms and chop onions.
4  Combine soy sauce, sugar, cornflour and salt.
5  Heat 1 tablespoon of oil and add nuts. Cook for 1 minute, shaking pan from time to time, remove and drain.
6  Add chicken to pan and cook for 3 minutes then add peas and mushrooms.
7  Pour in stock and simmer for 3 minutes.
8  Add bamboo shoots and stir in soy sauce mixture.
9  Cook until thickened, stirring, add nuts and serve immediately.

# ROAST CHICKEN

*1 hour cooking time*

*Ingredients for 4 servings*

| | |
|---|---|
| 1 2-kg (4-lb) chicken | ½ cup sherry |
| 4 slices fresh ginger | 1 onion |
| 1 teaspoon salt | ½ cup soy sauce |
| 1 tablespoon sugar | 3 cups water |

1 Boil water with other ingredients and put in chicken, chopped into 12 pieces with cleaver.
2 Cook for 15 minutes and turn off. Let chicken stand in this mixture for 20 minutes.
3 Remove and roast for 25 minutes.

# STIR-FRIED CHICKEN

*20 minutes cooking time*

*Ingredients for 4 servings*

| | |
|---|---|
| 1 1.5-kg (3-lb) chicken | 4 tablespoons soy sauce |
| 2 tablespoons sherry | 4 slices fresh ginger |
| 1 onion | 3 tablespoons peanut oil |
| ½ cup water | 1 teaspoon salt |

1 Chop chicken into 5 centimetre (2 in) squares.
2 Mix in soy sauce, sherry, onion and ginger. Stand for 10 minutes.
3 Heat oil and put in chicken and marinade; stir for 5 minutes:
4 Add water and salt. Cover and cook for 5 minutes.

# CHICKEN WITH BEAN CURD

*20 minutes cooking time*

*Ingredients for 4 servings*

| | |
|---|---|
| 1¼ cups bean curd | 250 g (8 oz) chicken meat |
| 2 dried mushrooms | 2 teaspoons black bean sauce |
| 1 teaspoon soy sauce | 1 teaspoon sugar |
| ½ teaspoon cornflour | ¼ cup chicken stock |
| 2 teaspoons peanut oil | 4 spring onions, chopped |
| 125 g (4 oz) bamboo shoots, sliced | |

1  Cut bean curd into 2.5 centimetre (1 in) squares and drain.
2  Chop chicken, rinse mushrooms and slice.
3  Combine bean sauce, sugar, soy sauce, cornflour and broth.
4  Brown meat in oil and add mushrooms, bean curd and bamboo shoots. Pour sauce mixture into pan and cook for 10 minutes. Garnish with chopped onions.

# CHICKEN WITH WATER CHESTNUTS

*2 hours 40 minutes cooking time*

*Ingredients for 4 servings*

| | |
|---|---|
| **1.5 kg (3 lb) chicken** | **2 cups water** |
| **500 g (1 lb) dried water chestnuts** | **6 slices fresh ginger** |
| **2 spring onions** | **2 teaspoons salt** |
| **2 tablespoons soy sauce** | **2 tablespoons sherry** |

1  Cook peeled chestnuts in 6 cups water for 2 hours.
2  Wash chicken and cut into pieces with a cleaver.
3  Cut onions into sections.
4  Place chicken in pan with water and boil.
5  Add soy sauce, sherry, ginger and onion.
6  Cook over low heat for 35 minutes.
7  Add chestnuts to chicken and cook for 15 minutes.

# CHICKEN WITH CAULIFLOWER

*20 minutes cooking time*

*Ingredients for 6 servings*

| | |
|---|---|
| **750 g (1½ lb) cauliflower** | **3 egg whites** |
| **1 tablespoon cornflour** | **2 tablespoons oil** |
| **2 cups water** | **2 teaspoons salt** |
| **250 g (8 oz) chicken meat** | |

1  Break cauliflower into small flowers.
2  Place in pan with water and salt. Boil for 10 minutes and drain.
3  Mince chicken meat and add egg whites, cornflour, salt and 2 tablespoons water. Beat until ingredients puff up.
4  Heat oil and put beaten chicken mixture in. Stir for 3 minutes and add cauliflower, cook 2 minutes.

# MANDARIN CHICKEN

*50 minutes cooking time*

*Ingredients for 4 servings*

2 kg (4 lb) chicken
½ cup chopped onion
1 teaspoon chopped fresh ginger
¼ teaspoon allspice
⅛ teaspoon ground cloves

½ cup soy sauce
2 cloves garlic, crushed
½ teaspoon cinnamon
¼ teaspoon crushed aniseed
½ teaspoon pepper

1   Chop chicken into 16 pieces with cleaver.
2   Soak chicken in onion, soy sauce, garlic and ginger for 6 hours.
3   Drain chicken and put in shallow greased baking dish.
4   Mix spices and sprinkle over chicken.
5   Bake for 50 minutes in moderate oven 180°C (350°F).

# HOT CHICKEN CUBES

*5 minutes cooking time*

*Ingredients for 6 servings*

750 g (1½ lb) chicken meat
2 tablespoons water
3 spring onions
2 tablespoons soy sauce
4 tablespoons peanut oil
½ teaspoon hot chilli powder

1 teaspoon salt
1 tablespoon cornflour
2 tablespoons sherry
4 slices fresh ginger
1 tablespoon sugar

1   Cut chicken into cubes, mix with cornflour, sherry, water, chopped onion and chilli powder.
2   Heat oil and fry chicken for 2 minutes.
3   Mix soy sauce, salt and sugar and add to chicken, fry for 2 minutes more.

# STEAMED DUCK

*Ingredients for 4 servings*

*1 hour cooking time*

1 3-kg (6-lb) duck
2 pieces dried tangerine peel
6 stalks celery
185 g (6 oz) bamboo shoots
1 teaspoon sugar
4 chopped spring onions

½ cup soy sauce
6 dried mushrooms
½ cup white wine
3 tablespoons cornflour
3 tablespoons peanut oil
lettuce leaves

1    Marinate duck in soy sauce overnight.
2    Soak mushrooms and tangerine peel.
3    Drain duck and pour marinade into frying pan and boil, and place duck in.
4    Simmer for 10 minutes, add wine and baste.
5    Put 1 piece tangerine peel, 1 spring onion and 3 sprigs parsley inside duck.
6    Add rest of tangerine peel to pan, and add 2 cups hot water.
7    Cover and simmer for 2½ hours, then skim off fat.
8    Slice celery, add remaining spring onions and slice mushrooms.
9    Heat oil and fry bamboo shoots, celery, spring onions and mushrooms for 3 minutes.
10   Simmer for 5 minutes uncovered and combine cornflour, sugar and 3 tablespoons of the liquid drained from mushrooms.
11   Add to vegetables and cook until thickened and smooth.
12   Arrange lettuce leaves in a deep platter and put duck on top. Pour vegetables over and garnish with chopped parsley.

# DUCK BALLS

*Ingredients for 4-5 servings*

1 2-kg (4-lb) duck
1 tablespoon dry sherry

1 tablespoon soy sauce
1 tablespoon sake

1    Cut meat from bone and mince finely.
2    Mix the meat with soy sauce and wine.
3    Add sake.
4    Form into small balls and thread onto skewers.
5    Grill over hot coals until brown.
6    Serve immediately.

# TASTY DUCK

*2½ hours cooking time*

*Ingredients for 3-4 servings*

2 kg (4 lb) duck
⅔ cup pearl barley
6 dried mushrooms
3 bacon rashers
125 g (4 oz) water chestnuts
8 tablespoons soy sauce

3 cups chicken stock
1 onion
2 tablespoons peanut oil
3 tablespoons sherry
4 cups cooked cabbage

1  Marinate duck in soy sauce for 2 hours.
2  Cover barley with hot water and stand for 45 minutes, rinse and drain.
3  Soak mushrooms for 30 minutes, drain and slice.
4  Boil stock, add barley and duck's neck.
5  Simmer for 40 minutes, remove neck.
6  Cook bacon and add chopped onion and sliced giblets and cook 8-10 minutes.
7  Mix mushrooms with chopped onions, add sliced giblets and chestnuts, sherry and 2 tablespoons soy sauce. Cook for 2 minutes and add barley. Season with salt.
8  Stuff duck with barley mixture.
9  Heat oil in pan and add duck, brown all over and add 1 cup water, cover and simmer for 1½-2 hours.
10  Place duck on cabbage in serving dish and spoon some of the drippings over.

# POT-COOKED DUCK

*40 minutes cooking time*

*Ingredients for 6 servings*

1.5 kg (3 lb) duck breasts and legs
1½ tablespoons sherry
6 slices fresh ginger
4 tablespoons cornflour
3 tablespoons peanut oil

3 tablespoons soy sauce
2 spring onions
3 eggs
1½ teaspoons salt

1  Place duck meat in soy sauce, sherry, onion, and ginger. Stand for 1 hour.
2  Mix eggs, cornflour, salt and water together. Apply this coating to duck.
3  Heat oil and fry duck for 15 minutes on each side — about 30 minutes altogether.
4  Chop duck into 2.5 centimetre (1 in) pieces and serve.

# DICED PIGEON

*30 minutes cooking time*

*Ingredients for 5-6 servings*

2-3 pigeons
½ lettuce
1 teaspoon sugar
1 teaspoon cornflour

oil for frying
½ cup stock
2 tablespoons soy sauce

1  Prepare pigeons by washing and cleaning.
2  Remove meat and dice.
3  Chop lettuce.
4  Sauté the pigeon and lettuce in oil and cook until meat is tender.
5  Pour in sugar and soy sauce, thicken with cornflour and add stock.
6  Serve immediately with boiled rice.

# STEAMED PIGEONS

*2 hours cooking time*

*Ingredients for 5-6 servings*

3 pigeons
125-185 g (4-6 oz) mixed herbs
1 oup brandy

soy sauce to taste
1 teaspoon salt
chopped Chinese parsley

1  Clean and wash pigeons.
2  Place in a steamer with herbs, soy sauce, salt and cover bottom of pan with 8 centimetres (3 in) water.
3  Steam for 2 hours or until tender.
4  When serving, pour over brandy and garnish with chopped Chinese parsley.

# Meat

## BEEF CHOP SUEY

*30 minutes cooking time*

*Ingredients for 5-6 servings*

750 g (1½ lb) beef
4 tablespoons soy sauce
salt
2 cloves garlic, crushed
¾ cup stock

2 onions, chopped
½ cup celery
2 tablespoons sherry
2 tablespoons cornflour
¾ cup cabbage

1  Marinate sliced meat in mixture of soy sauce, salt, and sherry.
2  Slice vegetables and parboil.
3  Heat pan and add oil for frying and garlic.
4  Sauté vegetables in oil-garlic mixture.
5  Add more oil when vegetables are removed and sauté sliced meat.
6  Return vegetables and mix well together.
7  Add marinade and add blended cornflour and stock.
8  Cook for 5 minutes and serve with white fluffy rice.

# STEAK AND GHERKINS

*30 minutes cooking time*

*Ingredients for 5-6 servings*

500 g (1 lb) round steak
2.5 cm (1 in) green ginger, grated
¼ cup soy sauce
½ teaspoon salt
1 teaspoon cornflour

8 gherkins
2 tomatoes, skinned and chopped
2 teaspoons sesame oil
1 teaspoon sugar
shallots, chopped

1  In a bowl place green ginger, soy sauce and sliced meat.
2  Add salt and cornflour.
3  Marinate for 1 hour.
4  Slice gherkins and combine with drained meat, oil and tomatoes.
5  Sprinkle with sugar and steam for 30 minutes.
6  Add shallots just before serving.

# NOODLES WITH BEEF

*20 minutes cooking time*

*Ingredients for 5-6 servings*

egg noodles
500 g (1 lb) beef
soy sauce
½ teaspoon salt
oil
2 cloves garlic, crushed

green ginger
chopped Chinese parsley
1 cup stock
¼ teaspoon white pepper
1 tablespoon plain flour

1  Cooking noodles in hot water, drain.
2  Slice meat and season with salt and pepper, soy sauce and garlic.
3  Heat oil in pan and add green ginger, then sauté sliced meat.
4  Pour in stock and simmer for 5 minutes.
5  Mix flour with a little water and then with stock.
6  Stir in with noodles and mix all ingredients well.
7  Serve immediately with chopped Chinese parsley.

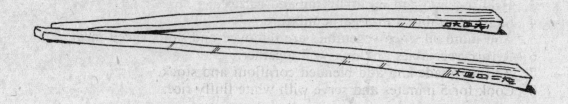

# CURRIED STEAK

*20 minutes cooking time*

*Ingredients for 4-5 servings*

750 g (1½ lb) steak
½ teaspoon salt
2 tablespoons soy sauce
oil
3 cups water
coconut milk

2 tablespoons curry powder
pepper to taste
2 onions, chopped
1 tablespoon curry paste
cornflour

1　Cube steak and sprinkle with salt and pepper.
2　Add soy sauce.
3　Heat oil in pan.
4　Sauté onions in oil then sauté steak.
5　Add curry powder and paste, cook for 1 minute.
6　Add water and simmer.
7　Thicken with coconut milk and cornflour.
8　Cook for a few minutes and serve immediately.

# OYSTER SLICES

*20 minutes cooking time*

*Ingredients for 5-6 servings*

750 g (1½ lb) beef steak
½ cup water
2 tablespoons white wine
2 tablespoons fat or oil
1 teaspoon sugar

3 onions, sliced
½ cup soy sauce
½ teaspoon salt
4 tablespoons oyster sauce

1　Slice steak into strips.
2　Add onions, soy sauce, wine, salt and a little water.
3　Mix well and pour over steaks.
4　Toss.
5　Heat oil or fat in frying pan and brown meat.
6　Over high heat add oyster sauce and sugar.
7　Cook and stir for 5 minutes.
8　Serve immediately.

# BEEF AND MUSHROOM SKEWERS

*30 minutes cooking time*

*Ingredients for 3-4 servings*

**375 g (12 oz) rump steak**
**2 teaspoons sesame oil**
**6 tablespoons salad oil**
**2 tablespoons sesame seeds, toasted**
**½ teaspoon sugar**
**2 onions**
**3-4 eggs, beaten**

**125 g (4 oz) sliced mushrooms, drained**
**4 tablespoons soy sauce**
**2 cloves garlic, crushed**
**white pepper**
**flour**
**oil for frying**

1  Cut meat in 6 millimetre (¼ in) strips.
2  Toss meat in a bowl with mushrooms, sesame oil, soy sauce, sesame seeds, garlic, sugar, white pepper and mix lightly.
3  Stand for 30 minutes.
4  Wash and cut onions.
5  On skewers, thread 2 pieces of meat, 2 pieces of onion, 2 mushroom slices, and then repeat.
6  Roll skewers in plain flour, then in beaten egg.
7  Stand for 20 minutes.
8  Cover bottom of pan with oil and brown skewers (approximately 10-15 minutes).
9  Serve immediately.

# RICE WITH BEEF CUBES

*10 minutes cooking time*

*Ingredients for 4-5 servings*

**500 g (1 lb) lean beef, cubed**
**2 tablespoons soy sauce**
**2 cloves garlic**
**green ginger, chopped**
**½ teaspoon salt**

**2 teaspoons cornflour**
**4 tablespoons oil**
**4 cups cooked rice**
**2 eggs**
**1 cup chicken stock**

1  Season cubed meat with soy sauce, garlic, ginger, salt and cornflour.
2  Heat oil in pan and fry meat.
3  Add rice and mix thoroughly.
4  Pour in beaten eggs and mix well.
5  Add chicken stock and simmer for 5 minutes.
6  Serve immediately, garnished with chopped Chinese parsley.

# PINE-MEAT BALLS

*30 minutes cooking time*

*Ingredients for 5-6 servings*

500 g (1 lb) steak
½ teaspoon salt
2 tablespoons sherry
¼ cup vinegar
4 chopped shallots
2 egg whites
¼ cup soy sauce

2 onions
1 cup pineapple juice
1 cup pineapple pieces
⅓ cup sugar
cornflour
oil

1  Mince steak and onion together.
2  Season with salt and sherry.
3  Pour in beaten egg whites and shape into balls.
4  Roll in cornflour.
5  Deep fry until cooked.
6  Add pineapple juice and pieces, cornflour, soy sauce, vinegar and sugar.
7  Cook for 1 minute then add chopped shallots.

# STEAK SUPREME

*15 minutes cooking time*

*Ingredients for 4-5 servings*

4 cups cooked rice
1 cup green peas
2 cloves garlic
cooking oil
3 tablespoons soy sauce
½ teaspoon white pepper

750 g (1½ lb) steak
2 onions, chopped
1 tablespoon sugar
2 teaspoons green ginger, grated
½ teaspoon salt

1  Chop the steak into thin strips.
2  Marinate meat in mixture of soy sauce, ginger, salt and 1 tablespoon oil.
3  Heat oil and fry garlic until browned, then remove.
4  Sauté the onion and meat and add cooked peas.
5  Mix well and simmer for 10 minutes.
6  Serve on a bed of rice.

## SEASONED BRAISED STEAK

*30 minutes cooking time*

*Ingredients for 5-6 servings*

| | |
|---|---|
| **750 g (1½ lb) steak** | **3 cloves garlic, crushed** |
| **oil** | **½ cup water** |
| **2.5 cm (1 in) green ginger, grated** | **½ teaspoon salt** |
| **1 teaspoon cornflour** | **½ teaspoon cinnamon** |

1  Cube steak and add to oil in pan.
2  Season with salt, garlic and ginger.
3  Sauté until cooked, add cinnamon and water.
4  Blend in cornflour and serve.

## MEAT BALLS

*30 minutes cooking time*

*Ingredients for 5-6 servings*

| | |
|---|---|
| **8 hardboiled eggs** | **4 onions** |
| **½ teaspoon salt** | **oil** |
| **3 tablespoons soy sauce** | **2 teaspoons cornflour** |
| **1 kg (2 lb) minced steak** | **1 cup water** |
| **1 cup tomato purée** | **2 tablespoons dry sherry** |
| **ginger (optional)** | |

1  Cut eggs in half and combine salt and soy sauce with beef.
2  Add half cup of tomato purée.
3  Mince the onions and add to beef mixture.
4  Chop eggs finely and brown in oil.
5  Blend in cornflour, water, sherry and remaining tomato purée.
6  Place meat balls in and simmer over low heat.

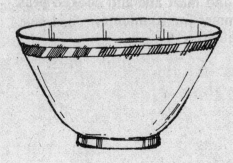

# BEEF AND GREEN BEANS

*30 minutes cooking time*

*Ingredients for 2 servings*

250 g (½ lb) green beans
250 g (½ lb) beef
1 tablespoon soy sauce
3 chopped spring onions

2 teaspoons sugar
4 tablespoons peanut oil
2 slices fresh ginger root
2 teaspoons cornflour

1   Slice beans into 2.5 centimetre (1 in) pieces.
2   Place in boiling water and cook for 2 minutes and drain, saving ½ cup of the liquid.
3   Cut beef into strips and mix with sugar, cornflour, and soy sauce; add 1 tablespoon oil and ginger.
4   Heat 3 tablespoons of oil in pan and add beans, stir for 5 minutes and remove from heat.
5   Add meat to oil and cook for 3 minutes.
6   Return beans to pan, add marinade and cook until sauce has thickened.
7   Serve garnished with chopped spring onions.

# SLICED BEEF WITH CUCUMBER

*10 minutes cooking time*

*Ingredients for 5-6 servings*

2 large cucumbers
1 tablespoon sherry
1 teaspoon salt
2 tablespoons water
3 tablespoons peanut oil

750 g (1½ lb) beef
2 tablespoons soy sauce
1 teaspoon sugar
1 tablespoon cornflour

1   Cut meat into thin slices and mix with soy sauce, cornflour, sherry, sugar and water.
2   Peel cucumbers and scrape out seeds.
3   Slice thinly.
4   Heat oil and fry cucumbers for 90 seconds, then remove.
5   Cook meat in oil for 3 minutes and return cucumbers. Cook together for 1 minute and season with salt.

# BEEF WITH CABBAGE

*10 minutes cooking time*

*Ingredients for 6 servings*

750 g (1½ lb) beef
3 tablespoons soy sauce
1 teaspoon sugar
1 teaspoon salt

500 g (1 lb) Chinese cabbage
1 tablespoon sherry
3 tablespoons peanut oil

1  Cut cabbage into thin strips.
2  Shred meat and mix with sherry, sugar, and soy sauce.
3  Heat oil and fry cabbage for 3 minutes, stirring constantly.
4  Remove cabbage and fry seasoned meat for 3 minutes.
5  Add cabbage and season with salt.
6  Cook for 1 minute and serve.

# BEEF WITH CELERY

*10 minutes cooking time*

*Ingredients for 4 servings*

185 g (6 oz) steak
4 sticks celery
½ teaspoon salt
¼ teaspoon monosodium glutamate
    (optional)
1 teaspoon cornflour
2 garlic cloves, crushed

3 slices fresh ginger
¼ cup peanut oil
½ teaspoon sugar
1 cup hot chicken stock
1 tablespoon water
1 teaspoon soy sauce

1  Cut meat into thin slices; halve celery lengthwise, then chop into 2.5 centimetre (1 in) pieces.
2  Place meat and ginger in a bowl, add 1 teaspoon of oil, salt, sugar and monosodium glutamate (if desired), 2 tablespoons stock and cornflour blended with water.
3  Heat half the oil and fry celery for 1 minute, remove and wipe pan.
4  Heat remaining oil and fry garlic for 1 minute then discard.
5  Add drained meat and ginger, fry for 4 minutes and remove.
6  Add liquid in which meat soaked and soy sauce. Bring to boil and stir in remaining cornflour blended with water.
7  Cook for 2 minutes, return beef and celery to pan, heat through and serve.

# SWEET AND SOUR BEEF

*4 minutes cooking time*

*Ingredients for 8 servings*

250 g (8 oz) steak
½ teaspoon sugar
¼ teaspoon pepper
1 teaspoon cornflour
2 tablespoons self-raising flour

½ teaspoon salt
¼ teaspoon monosodium glutamate (optional)
3 tablespoons beaten egg
1 cup peanut oil

## SAUCE

1 tablespoon sugar
¼ teaspoon white pepper
1 tablespoon malt vinegar
2 teaspoons soy sauce
1 teaspoon cornflour

½ teaspoon salt
½ teaspoon monosodium glutamate (optional)
2 teaspoons tomato sauce

1   Mix together ingredients of sauce except cornflour, add 8 tablespoons water and bring to the boil.
2   Stir in cornflour blended with 1 tablespoon water and boil for 2 more minutes, stirring.
3   Cut steak into thin 5 centimetre (2 in) strips and place in bowl with cornflour which has been mixed with 2 teaspoons water.
4   Mix well and stand for a few minutes.
5   Lift out and drop into self-raising flour.
6   Have the oil heated in deep pan and drop meat into pan, cook for 1 minute, then raise heat and cook until meat is very brown.
7   Pour sauce into heated dish, and place the steak on top.

# BEEF WITH BEAN SPROUTS

*10 minutes cooking time*

*Ingredients for 8 servings*

250 g (8 oz) bean sprouts
½ teaspoon salt
½ teaspoon sugar
½ cup peanut oil
2 teaspoons cornflour
1 teaspoon sherry
1¼ cups hot chicken stock

250 g (8 oz) topside steak
2 chopped garlic cloves
½ teaspoon monosodium glutamate (optional)
½ teaspoon pepper
1 teaspoon soy sauce
parsley sprigs

1  Add chopped garlic to sprouts and cut steak into thin strips.
2  Place the meat in bowl with salt, sugar, pepper and monosodium glutamate (if desired).
3  Add 2 teaspoons peanut oil, 1 teaspoon cornflour mixed in 2 teaspoons water, and soy sauce.
4  Heat half the remaining oil and fry sprouts for 1 minute. Transfer the sprouts to a heated dish and keep hot.
5  Empty oil from pan, wipe with kitchen towelling and heat remaining oil. Add prepared steak and garlic to pan and cook for 2 minutes over high heat, remove steak to dish with bean sprouts.
6  Add stock, sherry, salt, sugar and monosodium glutamate (if desired), bring to boil and add remaining cornflour mixed with 2 tablespoons water.
7  Boil for 2 minutes and add bean sprouts and steak.
8  Turn into heated dish to serve.

# BEEF AND MUSHROOMS

*15 minutes cooking time*

*Ingredients for 8 servings*

**750 g (1½ lb) beef**
**2 tablespoons peanut oil**
**4 tablespoons water**
**1½ tablespoons sherry**
**2 teaspoons salt**

**750 g (1½ lb) mushrooms**
**3 tablespoons soy sauce**
**2 tablespoons cornflour**
**2 teaspoons sugar**

1  Cut meat into thin slices and mix with sherry, water, cornflour, sugar and half the soy sauce.
2  Slice mushrooms.
3  Heat half oil and add mushrooms, stir for 2 minutes.
4  Remove mushrooms and brown meat in remaining oil.
5  When the meat is cooked, add salt and mushrooms and cook for 2 minutes.

# BEEF WITH BEAN CURD

*8 minutes cooking time*

*Ingredients for 4 servings*

185 g (6 oz) steak
½ teaspoon sugar
1½ tablespoons crushed yellow soy
  beans
2 garlic cloves, crushed
½ teaspoon soy sauce
1 tablespoon cold water

½ teaspoon salt
¼ teaspoon monosodium glutamate
  (optional)
2 tablespoons peanut oil
1 cup hot chicken stock
1 teaspoon cornflour

1  Cut steak into thin slices and place in basin with salt, sugar and monosodium glutamate (if desired). Add soy beans.
2  Heat half of the oil and fry garlic for 1 minute, then discard; add meat to
   frying pan.
3  Add remaining oil, soy sauce and chicken stock and boil.
   Blend cornflour with water, stir in and cook for 2 minutes.
4  Return meat to pan and heat for 1 minute, then serve immediately.

# BEEF IN OYSTER SAUCE

*12 minutes cooking time*

*Ingredients for 6 servings*

250 g (8 oz) steak, cut in thin slices
½ teaspoon sugar
1 teaspoon soy sauce
4 garlic cloves, crushed
1¼ cups hot chicken stock
1½ tablespoons tinned oyster sauce
2 teaspoons sherry

4 slices fresh ginger
½ teaspoon salt
¼ teaspoon monosodium glutamate
  (optional)
2 teaspoons cornflour
2 tablespoons peanut oil

1  Place steak and ginger in bowl and season with sugar, salt, monosodium
   glutamate (if desired), half the cornflour mixed with 1 teaspoon of water
   and mix well.
2  Heat oil, fry garlic for 1 minute and remove.
3  Fry meat in oil for 2 minutes then remove. Add sherry and stock to pan
   and bring to boil.
4  Add oyster sauce, remaining cornflour mixed with water.
5  Boil for 2 minutes, return meat to pan, and serve when heated.

# BEEF WITH GREEN VEGETABLES

*30 minutes cooking time*

*Ingredients for 6 servings*

250 g (8 oz) spinach
250 g (8 oz) Chinese cabbage
250 g (8 oz) beef
1 tablespoon cornflour
  blended with ½ cup water

4 tablespoons peanut oil
1 teaspoon sesame oil
2 teaspoons soy sauce
1 cup chicken stock
½ teaspoon salt

1  Chop greens coarsely.
2  Heat oil, add beef strips, mix and cook until meat is browned. Add sesame oil and sprinkle with half the salt and soy sauce; stir, remove meat.
3  Add 2 tablespoons oil; add greens, stir and cook for about 3 minutes, or until greens are crisp, season with salt and soy sauce and add broth.
4  Combine cornstarch and water, add to meat and cook until thickened.

# BROCCOLI AND BEEF SLICES

*15 minutes cooking time*

*Ingredients for 8 servings*

500 g (1 lb) steak
185 g (6 oz) egg noodles
2 tablespoons soy sauce
2 teaspoons sugar
½ teaspoon monosodium glutamate
  (optional)
3 tablespoons cornflour

3 onions
2 teaspoons chopped fresh ginger
2 tablespoons peanut oil
1 teaspoon salt
½ teaspoon pepper
1 cup beef stock
375 g (12 oz) cooked broccoli

1  Cut beef into strips and onions into wedges.
2  Cook noodles in boiling water and drain.
3  Place meat and ginger in soy sauce and marinate for 20 minutes.
4  Sauté beef in hot oil for 4 minutes.
5  Mix sugar, monosodium glutamate (if desired), salt, pepper, cornflour and beef stock well.
6  Add broccoli and stock mixture to pan and cook for 5-6 minutes.
7  Deep fry noodles in oil and drain.
8  Serve meat mixture on top of noodles.

# SLICED BEEF WITH GREEN PEPPER

*10 minutes cooking time*

*Ingredients for 6 servings*

3 tablespoons soy sauce
1½ teaspoons salt
4 tablespoons water
3 tablespoons peanut oil
4 green peppers

1 kg (2 lb) beef
1½ teaspoons sugar
2 tablespoons cornflour
1½ tablespoons sherry

1　Cut meat into thin slices and mix with soy sauce, sherry, cornflour, sugar and water.
2　Wash green peppers, remove seeds and cut into thin strips.
3　Heat for 2 minutes, then remove.
4　Cook meat in oil for 3 minutes and return peppers. Cook for 30 seconds and season with salt.

# FILET MARINADE

*5 minutes cooking time*

*Ingredients for 4 servings*

500 g (1 lb) fillet steak
4 tablespoons soy sauce
3 tablespoons peanut oil

2 teaspoons sugar
2 garlic cloves
2 tablespoons wine

1　Cut meat into thin slices and soak in sugar, soy sauce and wine for 90 minutes.
2　Heat oil, fry garlic for 1 minute and meat for 2 minutes.

# FUKIEN BEEF HEART

*8 minutes cooking time*

*Ingredients for 4 servings*

1 kg (2 lb) beef heart
1 teaspoon salt
4 tablespoons peanut oil
1 tablespoon cornflour
3 tablespoons sherry

5 slices fresh ginger
1 teaspoon sugar
2 tablespoons water
2 small onions
2 tablespoons soy sauce

1 Cut heart vertically in two. Cut into thin slices and remove blood vessels.
2 Wash meat and cut onions into 2.5 centimetre (1 in) sections.
3 Mix onion with soy sauce, cornstarch, sherry, water, salt, ginger, and sugar.
4 Heat oil and fry heart for 4 minutes, stirring; add soy mixture and cook 4 minutes longer.

# SPARERIBS IN BLACK BEAN SAUCE

*1 hour cooking time*

*Ingredients for 6 servings*

1.5 kg (3 lb) spareribs, cut into
   2.5 cm (1 in) pieces
4 tablespoons black beans
½ teaspoon ground ginger
2 teaspoons soy sauce
3 tablespoons vinegar
2 spring onions, chopped

3 cloves garlic
2 teaspoons sugar
2 teaspoons cornflour
4 tablespoons chicken stock
2 tablespoons peanut oil
4 tablespoons sherry

1 Put spareribs in boiling water for 5 minutes, drain and rinse in cold water.
2 Crush black beans with garlic and ginger.
3 Mix sugar, cornflour, soy sauce, vinegar, chicken stock and sherry.
4 Heat oil and brown spareribs. Add black bean mixture and stir.
5 Pour soy sauce mixture over spare ribs and add spring onions. Cover and simmer for 40 minutes.

# FRIED PORK

*40 minutes cooking time*

*Ingredients for 5-6 servings*

750 g (1½ lb) belly pork
4 tablespoons soy sauce
3 teaspoons sherry
aniseed
oil

2 eggs
2 tablespoons sugar
3 cups stock
cornflour

1 Combine soy sauce, sherry, aniseed and sugar.
2 Rub over pork.
3 Place in stock and simmer for 30 minutes. Drain.
4 Cut pork into pieces and dip in cornflour and egg mixture.
5 Deep fry and serve immediately.

# ROAST PORK AND BEAN SPROUTS

*20 minutes cooking time*

*Ingredients for 5-6 servings*

1 kg (2 lb) roast pork
sugar to taste
½ teaspoon salt
oil

500 g (1 lb) bean sprouts
2 tablespoons water
ginger (optional)

1   Heat oil in a pan and add ginger, salt and bean sprouts.
2   Dot with sugar and water.
3   Add cubed pork and cook for 10 minutes.
4   Serve immediately.

# ROAST PORK WITH PEAS

*10 minutes cooking time*

*Ingredients for 4-5 servings*

500 g (1 lb) fresh shelled peas
oil
2.5 cm (1 in) green ginger

500 g (1 lb) red roast pork
1 tablespoon sugar
1 tablespoon water

1   Heat pan and add oil. Shred ginger and add to oil.
2   Add cooked peas and sprinkle with sugar and water.
3   Add sliced pork and combine with other ingredients.
4   Cook for 5 minutes and serve immediately with boiled rice.

# BARBECUED PORK AND SHALLOTS

*30 minutes cooking time*

*Ingredients for 5-6 servings*

1 kg (2 lb) pork fillet
barbecue sauce
½ teaspoon salt
5 teaspoons soy sauce
ginger (optional)

chopped shallots
3 tablespoons oil
sugar to taste
honey to taste

1   Brush fillet with a mixture of sugar, honey, oil, barbecue sauce, salt and
    soy sauce. Add shallots.
2   Bake for 30 minutes at moderate heat.

# SWEET AND SOUR PORK

*30 minutes cooking time*

*Ingredients for 5-6 servings*

750 g (1½ lb) lean pork
1 tablespoon sugar
oil
2 tablespoons soy sauce
1 green pepper, chopped
2 tablespoons sherry

2 egg yolks
2 teaspoons cornflour
2 onions
2 carrots
1 cup pineapple pieces
1 teaspoon salt

1  Cube pork and place in a mixture of sugar, soy sauce, salt and sherry.
2  Stand for 30-60 minutes.
3  Add yolks and mix well.
4  Roll pork in cornflour and deep fry in oil.
5  Drain and place on warmed plate in slow oven.
6  Cut onions and carrots, fry with green pepper, then add to meat.
7  Pour over sweet and sour sauce, mix in pineapple pieces and serve immediately.

# SWEET AND SOUR SAUCE

½ cup vinegar
½ teaspoon salt
green ginger to taste
1-2 teaspoons cornflour

3 tablespoons sugar
2 teaspoons tomato sauce
1 cup pineapple juice
¼ cup cold water

1  Combine vinegar, sugar, salt, tomato sauce, ginger, pineapple juice and bring to the boil.
2  Blend cornflour and cold water and stir into pan.
3  Cook for further 2 minutes and serve.

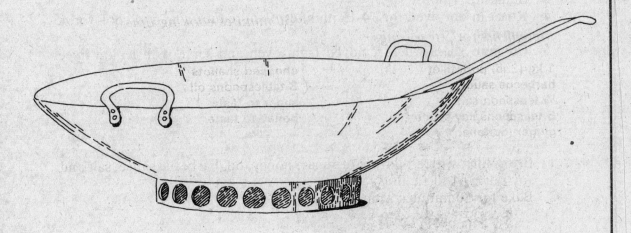

# RED ROAST PORK

*30 minutes cooking time*

*Ingredients for 6 servings*

750 g (1½ lb) lean leg of pork
½ teaspoon sugar
few drops cochineal
1½ tablespoons soy sauce
chopped parsley

½ teaspoon salt
½ teaspoon monosodium glutamate
  (optional)
2½ tablespoons red soy bean curd

1  Cut pork into strips, place in bowl and add salt, sugar, monosodium glutamate (if desired), cochineal, bean curd and soy sauce.
2  Work well together.
3  Skewer each piece of meat on wire hook and hang on a bar of the oven shelf. Place a drip tray underneath.
4  Bake for 30 minutes in hot oven.
5  Slice meat thinly across the grain and place on heated serving dish, pour over juice and serve garnished with chopped parsley.

# ROAST PORK

*1 hour cooking time*

*Ingredients for 5-6 servings*

1.5 kg (3 lb) pork fillet
5 tablespoons soy sauce
2 teaspoons thick red sauce
1 teaspoon mixed herbs

2 tablespoons sugar
salt to taste
green ginger
2 cloves garlic, crushed

1  Combine sauces, herbs, salt, sugar, ginger and garlic.
2  Brush over pork.
3  Stand for 1 hour.
4  Roast in hot oven for 14-15 minutes, then reduce heat and cook for 45 minutes.
5  Cut into slices when removed from oven and serve with lemon juice.

# PORK AND CUCUMBERS

*10 minutes cooking time*

*Ingredients for 4 servings*

155 g (5 oz) lean pork
½ teaspoon sugar
1½ teaspoons peanut oil
3 teaspoons water
1 cucumber
1 garlic clove, crushed
1 cup chicken stock
1 teaspoon soy sauce

½ teaspoon salt
½ teaspoon monosodium glutamate
  (optional)
1 onion
2 teaspoons cornflour
1½ tablespoons pork dripping
1 teaspoon sherry

1  Cut pork into thin slices and place in a bowl with salt, sugar and monosodium glutamate (if desired).
2  Add oil and 1 teaspoon of cornflour mixed with 1 teaspoon of water and mix well.
3  Cut onion and cucumber into quarters, then slice diagonally across cucumber.
4  Melt half of the dripping and fry garlic, discard it and fry pork for 4 minutes.
5  Sprinkle with sherry and remove the meat to a warm dish.
6  Wipe out pan, add remaining dripping and cook vegetables for 1 minute. Add soy sauce, cook for 3 minutes.
7  Stir in remaining cornflour mixed with water and blend with ingredients.
8  Boil for 2 minutes, add pork and cook 1 minute longer, then turn in heated serving dish.

# PORK ON SKEWERS

*20 minutes cooking time*

*Ingredients for 5-6 servings*

500 g (1 lb) lean pork
½ cup peanut butter
½ teaspoon salt

chilli powder to taste
2 teaspoons soy sauce
oil

1  Combine peanut butter, salt, chilli powder and cinnamon.
2  Add soy sauce.
3  Cube pork and rub over nut paste.
4  Stand for 15 minutes. Place on skewers.
5  Grill and baste with butter while cooking.

# PORK AND CAULIFLOWER

*15 minutes cooking time*

*Ingredients for 6 servings*

250 g (8 oz) pork
½ teaspoon salt
1 teaspoon soy sauce
2 teaspoons cornflour
3 garlic cloves, crushed
8 tablespoons chicken stock
½ teaspoon sugar

12 cauliflower flowers
¼ teaspoon pepper
¼ cup pork dripping
2 tablespoons water
¼ teaspoon monosodium glutamate
(optional)

1  Slice pork thinly.
2  Boil cauliflower for 5 minutes and drain.
3  Add salt, pepper, soy sauce and 2 teaspoons of melted pork dripping. Blend half the cornflour with the water and dip flowers in it.
4  Fry cauliflower in 1½ tablespoons of dripping and transfer to heated dish.
5  Wipe out pan and melt the remaining dripping.
6  Fry the pork and add salt, sugar, monosodium glutamate (if desired) and combine chicken stock and cornflour.
7  Blend all ingredients and return flowers to the pan. Heat through and serve.

# PORK WITH NOODLES

*10 minutes cooking time*

*Ingredients for 6 servings*

1½ cups chicken stock
1 teaspoon salt
375 g (12 oz) pork
2 onions, chopped
185 g (6 oz) sliced mushrooms

3 teaspoons soy sauce
3 tablespoons cornflour
6 celery stalks
500 g (1 lb) bamboo shoots
4 tablespoons peanut oil

1  Combine stock, soy sauce, salt and cornflour.
2  Slice pork, celery, onions and bamboo shoots.
3  Heat 2 tablespoons of oil, and cook pork for 2 minutes. Remove meat.
4  Add 2 tablespoons of oil and toss celery, onions; bamboo shoots and mushrooms for 3 minutes, add stock mixture.
5  Return meat and heat through; serve on cooked noodles.

# PORK WITH GREEN TEA

*10 minutes cooking time*

*Ingredients for 4 servings*

**500 g (1 lb) pork chops**
**1 teaspoon sugar**
**1 tablespoon cornflour**

**3 tablespoons soy sauce**
**3 tablespoons peanut oil**
**2 tablespoons green tea leaves**

1  Cut meat into slices, then into shreds.
2  Mix with cornflour, soy sauce and sugar.
3  Steep the tea leaves in boiling water for 10 minutes, strain and mix tea with meat.
4  Heat oil and stir in meat for 2-3 minutes. Add tea leaves, stir until well mixed, and serve immediately.

# PORK AND LEEKS

*10 minutes cooking time*

*Ingredients for 4 servings*

**1½ teaspoons sherry**
**½ teaspoon salt**
**¼ teaspoon sesame oil**
**1½ teaspoons water**
**2 tablespoons peanut oil**
**6 tablespoons leeks, sliced thinly**
**¼ teaspoon sugar**

**5 tablespoons raw pork**
**¼ teaspoon monosodium glutamate (optional)**
**1 teaspoon cornflour**
**1 slice fresh ginger**
**6 tablespoons hot chicken stock**

1  Cut pork into thin slices and put in bowl with salt, monosodium glutamate (if desired), pepper, ½ teaspoon sherry, sesame oil and cornflour mixed with water.
2  Heat oil in pan and fry chopped ginger.
3  Add drained pork and fry for 4 minutes, then add leeks and liquid from pork.
4  Add sugar and stock, cook for 3-4 minutes and serve sprinkled with remaining sherry.

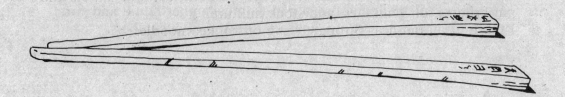

# BARBECUED SPARERIBS

*1 hour cooking time*

*Ingredients for 6 servings*

2 kg (4½ lb) pork spareribs
6 tablespoons vinegar
8 tablespoons soy sauce
5 cm (2 in) piece fresh ginger, chopped
2 tablespoons sherry

6 tablespoons honey
3 tablespoons sugar
6 cloves garlic, crushed
1½ cups stock

1   Mix honey, sugar, vinegar, soy sauce, ginger, garlic, stock and sherry. Chop spareribs and marinate overnight.
2   Roast in moderate oven 180°C (350°F) for 1 hour, basting at 10 minute intervals, and serve.

# MUSHROOM-STUFFED CUCUMBERS

*45 minutes cooking time*

*Ingredients for 4 servings*

4 thick cucumbers
1 tablespoon sherry
1 tablespoon cornflour
250 g (8 oz) ground lean pork

16 fresh mushrooms
2 tablespoons salt
1 egg

## GRAVY

2 tablespoons soy sauce
¼ cup cold water

1 tablespoon cornflour

1   Peel and cut cucumbers into 5 centimetre (2 in) pieces.
2   Use a teaspoon and dig out some of the seeds from one end only.
3   Mix ground meat with beaten egg, sherry, salt, and cornflour and stuff in each cucumber.
4   Cover cucumber section with mushroom and stand in pan with 1 cup water.
5   Cook slowly for 40 minutes and put cucumbers carefully in serving dish. Keep juice.
6   Mix all ingredients for gravy in pan with cucumber liquid and stir.
7   Boil for 30 seconds, stirring, and pour on top of cucumbers.

# PORK AND CASHEWS

*15 minutes cooking time*

*Ingredients for 6 servings*

½ cup thinly-sliced raw pork
3 teaspoons cornflour
1 teaspoon salt
½ teaspoon white pepper
¼ cup tinned bamboo shoots
½ cup peanut oil
4 teaspoons sesame oil
3 teaspoons cornflour
1 teaspoon soy sauce

3 teaspoons sherry
½ teaspoon monosodium glutamate
 (optional)
¼ cup raw carrot
¼ cup tinned water chestnuts
1 large onion
⅓ cup hot chicken stock
8 tablespoons roasted cashew nuts

1  In a bowl place meat, cornflour mixed with water, sherry, salt, mono-sodium glutamate (if desired) and pepper, work well into meat. Stand for a few minutes.
2  Cut carrot into match sticks, slice bamboo shoots and water chestnuts and chop onion.
3  Place three-quarters of oil in pan.
4  Heat 1 tablespoon of oil in another pan and fry onion. Add carrot, chestnuts, bamboo shoots and cook for 1 minute.
5  Add liquid drained from meat, stock, sesame oil, and soy sauce, bring to boil and cook for 2 minutes.
6  Deep fry pork in oil, add to vegetables and cook for 2 minutes.
7  Turn this mixture into heated serving dish and wipe out pan.
8  Heat 1 teaspoon of peanut oil and brown the cashew nuts.
9  Add nuts to meat mixture and serve at once.

# JAPANESE PORK TERIYAKI

*30 minutes cooking time*

*Ingredients for 4-5 servings*

1.25 kg (2½ lb) boneless pork, cubed
½ cup sweet sherry
1 teaspoon sugar

1 cup soy sauce
2 cloves garlic, crushed

1  Marinate meat in mixture of soy sauce, sherry, garlic and sugar.
2  Grill slowly.
3  Baste with marinade during cooking.
4  Serve immediately.

# PORK WITH GINGER

*Ingredients for 4 servings*

*1 hour 5 minutes cooking time*

1 kg (2 lb) pork chops, in one piece
3 cups water
2 tablespoons soy sauce
½ teaspoon salt
4 slices fresh ginger
½ teaspoon hot pepper sauce

1 spring onion
3 tablespoons peanut oil
2 cloves garlic
1 teaspoon sugar
½ teaspoon chilli oil

1   Boil meat gently for 1 hour and remove bones.
2   Slice cooled meat thinly.
3   Crush garlic and chop spring onion.
4   Heat oil, add garlic and meat and stir for 3 minutes. Add remaining
    ingredients and heat through.

# BARBECUED PORK

*Ingredients for 4 servings*

*40 minutes cooking time*

315 g (10 oz) raw pork
1 clove garlic, chopped
2 teaspoons red bean curd
½ teaspoon salt
½ teaspoon sugar
4 drops red food colouring

½ teaspoon powdered ginger
2 teaspoons soy beans
½ teaspoon sherry
½ teaspoon monosodium glutamate
(optional)

1   Cut pork into 15 centimetre (6 in) strips and sprinkle with ginger powder
    and garlic.
2   In a bowl, mash soy beans, bean curd and sherry, salt, sugar and mono-
    sodium glutamate if desired.
3   Lay pork pieces in greased baking dish.
4   Spread the bean mixture and then the colouring onto the meat and place
    dish in hottest part of hot oven 220°C (425°F).
5   Bake for 20 minutes, turn and bake for further 20 minutes. Cool and slice.

# BATTERED FRIED PORK

*30 minutes cooking time*

*Ingredients for 8 servings*

750 g (1½ lb) lean pork
1 tablespoon sugar
1 clove star anise
1 teaspoon salt
1 cup peanut oil
185 g (6 oz) self-raising flour

4 tablespoons soy sauce
2 tablespoons sherry
½ teaspoon monosodium glutamate
  (optional)
2 eggs

1  Cut pork into cubes and place in saucepan with sugar, 2 cups water, sherry, soy sauce, star anise, and monosodium glutamate (if desired). Simmer until tender and drain.
2  Mix flour and salt with eggs, add 1 cup water and beat well.
3  Coat pork with batter and fry in hot oil for 8 minutes. Drain and serve.

# PORK AND CABBAGE

*15 minutes cooking time*

*Ingredients for 6 servings*

½ small cabbage
1½ teaspoons sugar
4 tablespoons peanut oil
1½ teaspoons sherry
1 teaspoon soy sauce
2 cloves garlic, crushed
3 teaspoons cornflour

1 teaspoon salt
½ teaspoon monosodium glutamate
  (optional)
10 teaspoons water
250 g (8 oz) pork, cut into strips
1¼ cups hot chicken stock

1  Separate cabbage leaves and break them up.
2  Drop into boiling water and boil for 4 minutes, then drain.
3  Blend salt, monosodium glutamate (if desired), pepper, sugar and half the cornflour mixed with 2 teaspoons of water and mix well with meat.
4  Heat 2 tablespoons of oil in pan and cook cabbage pieces for 2 minutes and remove.
5  Wipe out pan and heat remaining oil, fry garlic and discard it.
6  Fry pork in oil for 4 minutes then add sherry, chicken stock and soy sauce. Bring to boil and stir in remaining cornflour mixed with water, and boil for 1½ minutes.
7  Return the cabbage to the pan and heat through.

# RED-COOKED MEAT

*3 hours cooking time*

*Ingredients for 5-6 servings*

2 kg (4 lb) shoulder of ham
1 tablespoon sugar
1 cup cold water

1 cup soy sauce
3 slices fresh ginger
1 cup sherry

1  Cut a few slashes on the sides of the ham.
2  Place in water, cover and boil.
3  Add sherry, soy sauce and ginger, and simmer over gentle heat for 1 hour.
4  Add sugar and cook for 1 hour more.

# LAMB AND BEAN SPROUTS

*10 minutes cooking time*

*Ingredients for 8 servings*

375 g (12 oz) lamb
½ teaspoon salt
1½ tablespoons cornflour
3 tablespoons brown sugar
2 tablespoons soy sauce
750 g (1½ lb) bean sprouts

1 carrot
3 teaspoons chopped fresh ginger
½ teaspoon pepper
3 tablespoons vinegar
2 spring onions
3 tablespoons peanut oil

1  Slice lamb thinly, chop spring onions into 2.5 centimetre (1 in) pieces and slice carrot.
2  Mix soy sauce, ginger, vinegar, brown sugar, salt, pepper and cornflour mixed with ⅓ cup water.
3  Heat oil and fry lamb for 3 minutes, then stir in cornflour mixture, carrot and spring onions.
4  Bring to boil and stir. Simmer for 2 minutes, add bean sprouts and cook for 3 minutes.

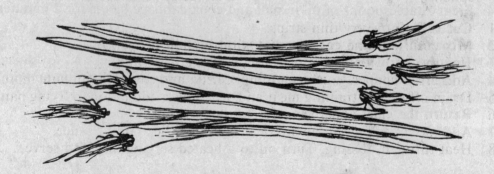

# LAMB WITH SPRING ONIONS

*20 minutes cooking time*

*Ingredients for 4 servings*

500 g (1 lb) lamb, cubed
1 egg white
4 slices fresh ginger root
5 teaspoons soy sauce
6 tablespoons sherry
10 spring onions

½ teaspoon five-spice powder
2 cloves garlic
2 tablespoons water
3 teaspoons cornflour
6 tablespoons soy sauce
2 tablespoons peanut oil

1  Mix lamb in a bowl with five-spice, egg white, garlic, ginger root, 1 teaspoon cornflour, 1 teaspoon soy sauce, and stand 10 minutes.
2  Meanwhile blend rest of cornflour, soy sauce, sherry and water.
3  Cut white part of each onion in half and chop tops.
4  Heat oil, add meat mixture and cook, stirring, until meat browns, return to bowl.
5  Add cornflour soy sauce mixture to pan with the white part of onion. Stir until mixture thickens.
6  Add meat and green tops. Reheat until simmering.

# LAMB AND VEGETABLES

*6 minutes cooking time*

*Ingredients for 6 servings*

250 g (8 oz) lamb
1 beaten egg
½ teaspoon pepper
1 green pepper, diced
2 tablespoons celery, diced
2 tablespoons spring onion, chopped
¼ teaspoon monosodium glutamate
   (optional)

1 teaspoon cornflour
½ teaspoon salt
4 tablespoons peanut oil
2 dried mushrooms, soaked for 1 hour,
   cut into thin strips
1½ tablespoons white wine
1 tablespoon soy sauce
2 cloves garlic, chopped

1  Cut lamb into very thin strips.
2  Mix cornflour and egg together with salt and pepper.
3  Heat peanut oil and fry meat for 1 minute.
4  Add green pepper, mushrooms and celery, and cook for 1 minute more.
5  Drain off oil by straining meat and vegetables; add onion to frying pan.
6  Return the meat and vegetables to pan and add white wine.
7  Add monosodium glutamate (if desired), garlic and soy sauce.
8  Heat through, tossing. Turn on to a heated serving dish and serve.

# VEAL AND MUSHROOMS

*20 minutes cooking time*

*Ingredients for 4 servings*

250 g (8 oz) fillet of veal
½ teaspoon salt
1 tablespoon peanut oil
1 teaspoon cornflour
6 tablespoons thinly-sliced
   mushrooms
1 tablespoon water

1 beaten egg
1 teaspoon soy sauce
¼ teaspoon pepper
2 tablespoons tinned bamboo shoots,
   diced
½ teaspoon monosodium glutamate
   (optional)

1  Cut veal into thin slices and mix with egg, soy sauce, pepper and salt.
2  Heat oil and add veal, fry for 5 minutes over high heat.
3  Transfer to serving dish and keep hot.
4  Fry bamboo shoots and mushrooms for 1 minute, add stock and monosodium glutamate (if desired), and cook for 1 minute more.
5  Blend cornflour with water, add to pan and stir for 30 seconds.
6  Pour vegetable mixture and sauce over the veal and serve.

# FRIED BRAINS

*30 minutes cooking time*

*Ingredients for 4 servings*

3 calves' brains
1 small onion
2 teaspoons salt

3½ tablespoons plain flour
4 tablespoons peanut oil
2 eggs

1  Wash brains and remove outer skin.
2  Remove small veins and place brains in pan with 2 cups water and 1 teaspoon salt.
3  Heat to boiling, lower heat and simmer for 25 minutes, cool and cut brains into 2.5 centimetre (1 in) pieces.
4  Mix cooking juice with beaten eggs, add flour, chopped onion and remaining salt.
5  Heat oil and dip each brain in batter.
6  Fry for 5 minutes and serve.

# Vegetables and Salads

## CUCUMBER SALAD

*Ingredients for 4-5 servings*

**2 large cucumbers**
**4 teaspoons sugar**
**2 teaspoons grated green ginger**

**white vinegar**
**1 teaspoon salt**

1 Cut cucumbers in half and remove any seeds.
2 Slice crosswise into thin slices.
3 Marinate in a mixture of vinegar, sugar, salt and ginger.
4 Chill in this marinade for 2 hours.

# SALAD BOWL

*Ingredients for 5-6 servings*

500 g (1 lb) bean sprouts
1 whole lettuce
chopped parsley
8 pickled onions

1 cup chopped cucumber
½ cup cooked celery
12 lychees

1 Steam the bean sprouts and chill.
2 Mix all ingredients into lettuce leaves and serve with salad dressing.

# SALAD DRESSING

*Ingredients for 5-6 servings*

4 tablespoons salad oil
1 teaspoon sugar
½ teaspoon mustard
¼ teaspoon salt

2 tablespoons vinegar
2 teaspoons soy sauce
2 cloves garlic, crushed

1 Combine all ingredients and mix thoroughly.
2 Shake.
3 Pour over green salad.

# ONION SALAD

*Ingredients for 5-6 servings*

5 large onions, peeled and cut into
  rings
250 g (8 oz) bean sprouts, steamed
  and chilled

1 leek, chopped
chopped Chinese parsley
sesame seeds, toasted

1 Combine bean sprouts, onions and leek.
2 Place in lettuce cups and dot with chopped parsley.
3 Sprinkle with sesame seeds and serve with salad dressing.

# OYSTER-MUSHROOM SALAD

*Ingredients for 5-6 servings*

24 oysters
500 g (1 lb) chopped mushrooms
sesame seeds, toasted

oyster sauce
green ginger

1  Combine all ingredients except for sesame seeds.
2  Pour over 3 tablespoons salad dressing and dot with sesame seeds.
3  This salad can be chilled for 1 hour before serving.

# MUSHROOMS IN WHITE SAUCE

*10 minutes cooking time*

*Ingredients for 4-5 servings*

20 mushrooms
6 tablespoons chicken stock
1 teaspoon cornflour
½ teaspoon salt
1 teaspoon chopped parsley
1 teaspoon chopped ham

peanut oil
6 tablespoons milk
1 tablespoon water
½ teaspoon monosodium glutamate
 (optional)

1  Remove stems from mushrooms.
2  Wash in water and drain.
3  Heat the oil and place mushrooms in. Cook on both sides.
4  Add chicken stock and bring to the boil.
5  Cook for 5 minutes and remove mushrooms.
6  Mix the milk, cornflour, salt and monosodium glutamate (if desired) together in pan and bring to the boil.
7  Pour over the mushrooms and dot with chopped ham and parsley.
8  Serve immediately.

# STUFFED CUCUMBER

*20 minutes cooking time*

*Ingredients for 4-5 servings*

1 cucumber
125 g (4 oz) minced pork
1 teaspoon shallot, chopped
1 tablespoon soy sauce
5 teaspoons sherry
2 teaspoons cornflour
½ cup chicken stock
peanut oil

1 teaspoon bamboo shoots, chopped
1 teaspoon chopped water chestnuts
1 teaspoon fresh green ginger, chopped
½ teaspoon salt
½ teaspoon monosodium glutamate (optional)
1 teaspoon sugar

1   Peel the cucumber and cut into 4-5 sections and remove seeds.
2   Combine pork with chestnuts, bamboo shoots, shallot and ginger.
3   Add soy sauce, sugar, sherry and monosodium glutamate (if desired).
4   Mix well.
5   Stuff cucumber.
6   Sprinkle the stuffing with cornflour and heat oil in pan.
7   Fry cucumber in oil for 2 minutes then add chicken stock, salt and soy sauce mixture.
8   Cover and cook for 15 minutes. Thicken with the cornflour mixed with 2 tablespoons water.
9   Serve immediately.

# CUCUMBER PICKLES

2 cucumbers
10 tablespoons sugar
10 tablespoons water

1 red chilli, chopped
10 tablespoons vinegar
3 teaspoons salt

1   Score cucumber with a fork and peel.
2   Cut in half and scoop out seeds.
3   Slice finely crosswise and place in a bowl.
4   Marinate in salt, sugar, vinegar, chilli and water and leave for 2 days.

# STUFFED GREEN PEPPERS

*15 minutes cooking time*

*Ingredients for 4-5 servings*

125-155 g (4-5 oz) sweet green
  peppers
90 g (3 oz) water chestnuts, chopped
fresh ginger, chopped
3 tablespoons sherry
½ teaspoon salt
½ teaspoon monosodium glutamate
  (optional)

185 g (6 oz) minced pork
90 g (3 oz) bamboo shoots, chopped
4 shallots, chopped
3 tablespoons soy sauce
1 teaspoon cornflour
1 teaspoon sugar
peanut oil

1  Cut the peppers in half and remove seeds.
2  Mix the pork, chestnuts, bamboo shoots, shallots and ginger together.
3  Add sherry, 1 tablespoon soy sauce and salt.
4  Stuff peppers with this mixture and sprinkle with cornflour.
5  Heat oil and fry peppers for 5 minutes.
6  Add sugar and remaining soy sauce, monosodium glutamate and half cup water.
7  Cook for 10 minutes and garnish with chopped parsley.
8  Serve immediately.

# CABBAGE PICKLES

*20 minutes cooking time*

*Ingredients for 1.75 litres*

2 small heads regular cabbage
5 shallots, chopped
2 red chillis, dried and crushed

salt to taste
2 cloves garlic, minced
2 teaspoons grated green ginger

1  Cut cabbage into pieces 3 centimetres by 3 centimetres (1 in by 1 in).
2  Sprinkle with salt, stand for 20 minutes.
3  Wash salted cabbage with cold water, add shallots, garlic, chilli, ginger and a little salt.
4  Cover with water.
5  Stand for 2 days.
6  Taste ingredients every few days, and by two weeks they should be acid enough to eat.

# STUFFED MUSHROOMS

*15 minutes cooking time*

*Ingredients for 4-5 servings*

10 dried black mushrooms
1 tablespoon bamboo shoots,
  chopped
4 shallots, chopped
½ teaspoon monosodium glutamate
  (optional)
chopped parsley

155 g (5 oz) minced pork
1½ tablespoons soy sauce
2 teaspoons sherry
½ teaspoon salt
2 tablespoons chicken stock
2 tablespoons peanut oil
1 teaspoon cornflour

1   Soak the mushrooms in warm water for 30 minutes.
2   Drain and remove stalks.
3   Mix the pork, bamboo shoots and shallots together.
4   Add soy sauce, sherry and monosodium glutamate (if desired).
5   Combine and mix to a paste.
6   Fill the mushroom caps and steam for 15 minutes.
7   Remove to serving dish and keep hot.
8   Heat the peanut oil and combine remaining ingredients.
9   Stir until boiling.
10  Pour over mushrooms and dot with chopped parsley.
11  Serve immediately.

# FRIED CELERY

*8 minutes cooking time*

*Ingredients for 6 servings*

6 celery stalks
2 slices fresh ginger, crushed
½ teaspoon salt
½ teaspoon monosodium glutamate
  (optional)
1 teaspoon sherry

2 cloves garlic, crushed
2 tablespoons peanut oil
½ teaspoon sugar
½ teaspoon pepper
1¼ cups hot chicken stock

1   Cut celery stalks diagonally into 2.5 centimetre (1 in) strips.
2   Heat oil and cook garlic and ginger, discard them.
3   Add celery, seasonings, sherry and stock to pan.
4   Cook for 6 minutes.
5   Turn into heated dish and serve.

# FRIED VEGETABLES

*5 minutes cooking time*

*Ingredients for 4-5 servings*

| | |
|---|---|
| 1 large dried mushroom | 90 g (3 oz) bamboo shoots |
| 1 cucumber, sliced | 30 g (1 oz) carrot |
| 1 onion | 60 g (2 oz) celery |
| 30 g (1 oz) water chestnuts | 90 g (3 oz) bean sprouts |
| oil for cooking | 1 teaspoon salt |
| ½ teaspoon sugar | 2 tablespoons soy sauce |
| 1 tablespoon sherry | ½ cup water |
| ¼ teaspoon monosodium glutamate (optional) | ½ tablespoon cornflour mixed with 2 tablespoons water |
| 1 teaspoon sesame oil | |

1  Soak the mushroom in hot water for 1 hour, cut into slices.
2  Slice bamboo shoots, cucumber, carrot, onion, celery, water chestnuts.
3  Clean sprouts.
4  Cook the onion, mushrooms, bamboo shoots for 1 minute then add celery, carrot and chestnuts. Cook for further 2 minutes.
5  Add salt, sugar, soy sauce, sherry, monosodium glutamate (if desired) and water.
6  Mix well.
7  Stir in cornflour and water, bring to the boil.
8  Sprinkle with oil and serve immediately.

# FRIED ZUCCHINI

*8 minutes cooking time*

*Ingredients for 4 servings*

| | |
|---|---|
| 3 small zucchini | 2 garlic cloves, crushed |
| 3 thin slices fresh ginger, crushed | 2 tablespoons peanut oil |
| 1 teaspoon salt | 1 teaspoon monosodium glutamate (optional) |
| 1 teaspoon sugar | ½ teaspoon pepper |
| 1 teaspoon sherry | |
| 1¼ cups hot chicken stock | |

1  Cut zucchini into thin slices, diagonally.
2  Fry garlic and ginger in oil and then discard.
3  Add slices of zucchini and toss for 1 minute.
4  Sprinkle with seasonings and sherry.
5  Toss for 1 minute.
6  Add the hot stock and cook for 5 minutes.

# FRIED BEAN SPROUTS

*10 minutes cooking time*

*Ingredients for 6 servings*

1 cup bean sprouts
2 thin slices fresh ginger
2 tablespoons peanut oil
1 teaspoon sugar
1 teaspoon sherry
6 tablespoons chicken stock

6 tablespoons thinly-sliced ham
1½ sliced onions
1 teaspoon salt
½ teaspoon monosodium glutamate
  (optional)
1½ teaspoons sesame oil

1  Rinse and dry the bean sprouts thoroughly.
2  Cut ham, ginger and onions into thin strips.
3  Heat half the oil and cook onion pieces for 2 minutes. Add ginger and cook for 1 minute.
4  Add bean sprouts, cook for 2 minutes then add seasonings and turn to combine.
5  Add sherry, sesame oil and stock. Heat through.
6  Heat remaining oil and toss in thin strips of ham until heated through.
7  Place ham on top of bean sprouts and serve.

# MUSHROOMS AND CABBAGE

*10 minutes cooking time*

*Ingredients for 3-4 servings*

250 g (8 oz) Chinese cabbage
¼ teaspoon monosodium glutamate
  (optional)
1 tablespoon soy sauce
3 tablespoons peanut oil

1 teaspoon sugar
185 g (6 oz) button mushrooms
¼ teaspoon pepper
½ green pepper

1  Clean and chop cabbage, fry for 3 minutes in oil.
2  Add pepper, cut in strips, to pan plus sugar, soy sauce and monosodium glutamate (if desired). Stir and add mushrooms.
3  Season with salt and pepper, add ¾ cup water. Cover and cook for 6 minutes and serve.

## FRIED BEAN CURD

*10 minutes cooking time*

*Ingredients for 4 servings*

**2 tablespoons oil**
**1 teaspoon salt**

**2½ cups bean curd**

1  Cut bean curd into 2.5 centimetre (1 in) cubes.
2  Heat oil and fry bean curd until browned and slightly crisp.
3  Season with salt and serve.

## BRAISED BEAN CURD

*5 minutes cooking time*

*Ingredients for 6 servings*

**2½ cups bean curd**
**2 tablespoons soy sauce**
**½ teaspoon salt**
**¼ cup water**

**1 tablespoon peanut oil**
**2 spring onions**
**1 tablespoon cornflour**

1  Cut bean curd into 6 pieces. Chop onion into small sections.
2  Heat oil and place bean curd in. After 4 minutes, add mixed seasonings and onion. Cook for 1 minute and serve.

## SNOW PEAS

*3 minutes cooking time*

*Ingredients for 6 servings*

**250 g (8 oz) snow peas**
**1 teaspoon salt**
**½ cup clear stock**

**2 teaspoons peanut oil**
**1 teaspoon sugar**

1  Prepare snow peas by washing and cutting off tips and strings.
2  Heat oil and add salt, sauté peas for 1 minute then add sugar and stock.
3  Cover and simmer for 2 minutes.

# STUFFED SNOW PEAS

*Ingredients for 4 servings*

**30 snow peas**
¼ teaspoon coriander
**185 g (6 oz) cream cheese**
**2 teaspoons mayonnaise**

¼ teaspoon mustard
½ teaspoon salt
**4 tablespoons tomato purée**

1   Pour boiling water over peas and soak for 1 minute. Drain and dry pods.
2   Cut through one side only with sharp knife.
3   Blend cheese, tomato purée, mayonnaise, mustard and coriander.
4   Pipe cheese mixture into peas and chill for 1-2 hours.

# STEAMED EGGPLANT

*25 minutes cooking time*

*Ingredients for 5-6 servings*

**1 eggplant**
**2 tablespoons peanut oil**
½ teaspoon salt
½ teaspoon sugar
**1¼ cups hot chicken stock**
½ teaspoon cornflour

**250 g (8 oz) pork**
**1 garlic clove, crushed**
½ teaspoon monosodium glutamate
    (optional)
½ teaspoon soy sauce

1   Wash the eggplant and steam for 20 minutes.
2   Chop pork finely and heat the oil.
3   Fry garlic and discard it. Add pork to oil and fry for 3 minutes; then add seasonings and soy sauce.
4   Add stock and bring to boil.
5   Add cornflour blended with 2 tablespoons water and boil for 2 minutes.
6   Place sliced eggplant in serving dish and pour over pork mixture.

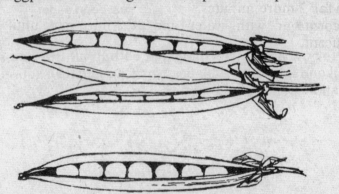

# ASPARAGUS AND CRAB SAUCE

*10 minutes cooking time*

*Ingredients for 4-5 servings*

**20 fresh asparagus spears**
**1¼ cups chicken stock**
**½ cup milk**
**1 tablespoon water**

**125 g (4 oz) crab meat**
**¼ teaspoon monosodium glutamate**
  **(optional)**
**½ tablespoon cornflour**

1  Prepare the asparagus spears by cutting off the ends.
2  Cook in boiling salted water until tender.
3  Remove soft bones from crab meat and bring chicken stock to boil.
4  Add meat, monosodium glutamate (if desired) and milk.
5  Cook for 5 minutes.
6  Mix cornflour and water, add to pan and stir until thickened.
7  Boil for 2 minutes.
8  Season with salt and pepper.
9  Place asparagus on serving dish and pour over sauce.
10  Serve immediately.

# BEAN CURD WITH MUSHROOMS

*8 minutes cooking time*

*Ingredients for 8 servings*

**375 g (12 oz) fresh mushrooms**
**2 tablespoons soy sauce**
**5 cups fresh bean curd**

**½ teaspoon salt**
**1 tablespoon cornflour**
**2 tablespoons peanut oil**

1  Wash mushrooms and slice thickly.
2  Cut bean curd the same way.
3  Heat oil and put mushrooms in first.
4  Stir and cook for 3 minutes, add bean curd, soy sauce and salt, cook gently for 2 more minutes.
5  Mix cornflour with water and stir into pan until juice becomes translucent.

# SWEET AND SOUR CABBAGE

*5 minutes cooking time*

*Ingredients for 4 servings*

| | |
|---|---|
| **500 g (1 lb) cabbage** | **1 cup water** |
| **2 tablespoons sugar** | **2 tablespoons vinegar** |
| **1 tablespoon cornflour** | **2 tablespoons peanut oil** |
| **1 teaspoon salt** | |

1  Wash cabbage and cut into 2.5 centimetre (1 in) pieces.
2  Mix vinegar, sugar, cornflour and ¼ cup water.
3  Heat oil, stir cabbage in it for 1 minute, then add water and salt.
4  Add remaining ingredients and stir.
5  When juice clears, serve.

# SWEET AND SOUR VEGETABLES

*10 minutes cooking time*

*Ingredients for 6 servings*

| | |
|---|---|
| **1 red pepper** | **1½ tablespoons soy sauce** |
| **1 green pepper** | **1 cup chicken stock** |
| **6 tablespoons brown sugar** | **½ teaspoon salt** |
| **4 sticks celery** | **1 tablespoon cornflour** |
| **1 carrot** | **2 onions** |
| **8 tablespoons vinegar** | |

1  Chop peppers into pieces 2.5 centimetre (1 in) square.
2  Cut onion into quarters and slice carrot.
3  Slice celery and put all vegetables into boiling water. Simmer for 5-6 minutes.
4  Mix cornflour with soy sauce and combine with stock, sugar and vinegar in a saucepan. Bring to boil and cook for 2 minutes.
5  Add vegetables, mix well and heat through.

# BRAISED LETTUCE

*3 minutes cooking time*

*Ingredients for 4-6 servings*

**1 large head lettuce**
**2 tablespoons peanut oil**
**½ teaspoon monosodium glutamate**
   **(optional)**

**5 cups chicken stock**
**1 teaspoon salt**
**1 teaspoon soy sauce**

1  Drop lettuce leaves into boiling stock and cook for 30 seconds.
2  Lift out and drain.
3  Combine oil and soy sauce and heat; add lettuce and stir gently for 1 minute.
4  Add seasonings, place lettuce into heated serving dish, and pour over sauce from pan.

# BEAN SPROUTS FUKIEN

*12 minutes cooking time*

*Ingredients for 4 servings*

**375 g (12 oz) bean sprouts**
**1 tablespoon peanut oil**
**½ cup chicken stock**
**½ teaspoon salt**
**¼ teaspoon pepper**

**3 spring onions**
**2 cloves garlic**
**¼ teaspoon monosodium glutamate**
   **(optional)**

1  Chop spring onions into 2.5 centimetre (1 in) lengths.
2  Heat oil and sauté garlic for 2 minutes, then discard it.
3  Add bean sprouts and spring onions, stir for 5 minutes, then add chicken stock and seasonings to pan.
4  Cook for 4 minutes and serve.

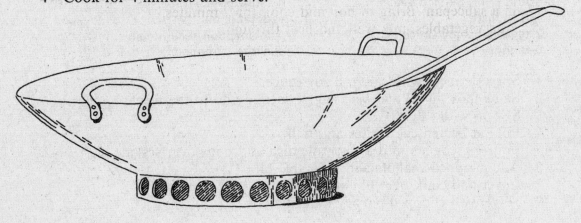

# Eggs

## STEAMED EGGS

*Ingredients for 5-6 servings*

*30 minutes cooking time*

500 g (1 lb) minced veal
salt to taste
2 teaspoons soy sauce
6-9 eggs

4 tablespoons milk
vegetable oil
1 tablespoon sesame oil
shallots, chopped

1  Sprinkle meat with salt and soy sauce.
2  Sauté meat in oil and beat egg yolks and add to the meat.
3  Season with salt.
4  Fold in beaten egg whites and milk.
5  Pour ingredients into a casserole dish and pour over sesame oil.
6  Add chopped shallots and vegetable oil.
7  Cover and cook over boiling water for 20-30 minutes.
8  Serve with chopped parsley immediately.

# SOY EGGS

*5 minutes cooking time*

*Ingredients for 4-5 servings*

| | |
|---|---|
| 6 eggs | sesame oil |
| 6 tablespoons soy sauce | ½ teaspoon salt |
| 7 tablespoons water | 2 teaspoons mayonnaise |
| chopped shallots | soy sauce |

1 Boil eggs for 5 minutes, chill and shell.
2 Place eggs into mixture of soy sauce, water, oil and salt. Simmer for 5 minutes.
3 Remove from heat and marinate for 10 minutes. Cut in half.
4 Mash yolks and combine with chopped shallots, mayonnaise and soy sauce. Place back into egg whites.

# STEAMED OMELETTE

*10 minutes cooking time*

*Ingredients for 4-5 servings*

| | |
|---|---|
| 5 eggs | 90 g (3 oz) minced pork |
| 1 teaspoon chopped water chestnuts | 1 teaspoon chopped onion |
| 1 teaspoon sherry | 1½ tablespoons soy sauce |
| ½ teaspoon salt | ¼ teaspoon monosodium glutamate |
| 1½ tablespoons water | (optional) |
| ½ teaspoon oil | |

1 Separate egg whites and yolks.
2 Beat the whites and mix with minced pork.
3 Add chopped chestnuts, onion, sherry and sauce.
4 Add salt, monosodium glutamate (if desired) and water.
5 Mix well.
6 Place this mixture into a deep bowl which has been rubbed with oil.
7 Add the yolks gently and place bowl in steamer for 10 minutes.

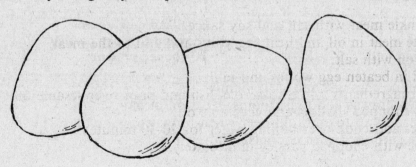

# HAM OMELETTE

*5-10 minutes cooking time*

*Ingredients for 5-6 servings*

6 eggs
½ teaspoon salt
2 pieces bamboo shoots
4 shallots, chopped

2 tablespoons cooked mushrooms
1 teaspoon soy sauce
2 tablespoons vegetable oil
500 g (1 lb) chopped cooked ham

1   Beat eggs lightly and add soy sauce and salt.
2   Sauté mushrooms and bamboo shoots in oil for a few seconds.
3   Pour in beaten eggs and mix thoroughly with other ingredients. Fold over.
4   Serve hot, garnished with chopped shallots.

# FRIED EGGS

*10 minutes cooking time*

*Ingredients for 4-5 servings*

5 eggs
vegetable oil
chopped parsley

2 tablespoons soy sauce
sesame oil

1   Heat oil in pan and break each egg in separately.
2   When starting to set dot with chopped parsley.
3   Remove and pour over soy sauce, vegetable oil and sesame oil.
4   Serve with rice.

# PRAWN OMELETTE

*10 minutes cooking time*

*Ingredients for 4-5 servings*

6 eggs
vegetable oil
1 teaspoon salt

8 cooked mushrooms
chopped Chinese parsley
20 cooked prawns

1   Combine eggs and salt. Mix lightly.
2   Mix in prawns and mushrooms. Heat oil in pan.
3   Pour in mixture and fold over when browned.
4   Serve garnished with chopped Chinese parsley.

# CRAB OMELETTE

*10 minutes cooking time*

*Ingredients for 5-6 servings*

**6-8 eggs**
**1½ teaspoons soy sauce**
**½ teaspoon salt**
**2 teaspoons dry sherry**

**oil**
**1 teaspoon cornflour**
**oyster sauce**
**250 g (8 oz) crab meat**

1  Mix beaten eggs, soy sauce and salt.
2  Combine crab meat with sherry and cornflour and mix into eggs.
3  Fry gently in hot oil until brown.
4  Fold, remove from pan and spoon over oyster sauce.

# Desserts

## SWEET BUNS

*50 minutes cooking time*

*Ingredients for 4-5 servings*

**1 package pie crust mix**
**2 egg yolks**

red bean paste
**2 tablespoons water**

1 Prepare pastry mix as directed on package.
2 Divide pastry into 4-5 rolled out rectangles.
3 Spread bean paste over pastry, almost to the edges.
4 Fold short ends of pastry over.
5 Place seam side down on baking sheet and flatten.
6 Beat egg yolks with water and brush over pastry.
7 Bake for 45-50 minutes and cool.

# ALMOND COOKIES

*40 minutes cooking time*

*Ingredients for 6-8 servings*

250 g (8 oz) lard
½ teaspoon almond extract
3 cups self-raising flour
1 egg yolk

1 cup sugar
yellow food colouring
blanched almonds
3 tablespoons water

1  Cream lard with sugar and blend in almond extract.
2  Add food colouring and thoroughly mix in 1 cup of flour at a time.
3  Measure 1 level tablespoon of the dough and press with your hands to form a flat round cake.
4  Place biscuits on baking sheet and gently press an almond into the centre of each biscuit.
5  Beat the egg yolk with water and brush over each biscuit.
6  Bake in moderate oven for 30 minutes then increase heat to hot and bake for 10 minutes.
7  Store in an air-tight tin.

# MOONSTONES

*Ingredients for 5-6 servings*

125 g (4 oz) agar-agar
4 cups orange juice
colouring

½ cup sugar
1½ teaspoons lemon juice

1  Rinse agar-agar in water.
2  Soak in fruit juice for 15 minutes.
3  Add sugar and bring to the boil.
4  Remove, add lemon juice and pour half, mixed with colouring, into a mould. Cool.
5  The remainder should be placed in another mould and cooled.
6  When set cut into squares or ball shapes and serve a mixture of both in tall glasses.

# SWEET RICE

*20 minutes cooking time*

*Ingredients for 5-6 servings*

250 g (8 oz) Chinese brown sugar
5 cups rice cereal
vinegar

1 tablespoon water
green ginger

1　Combine sugar and water, melt slowly.
2　When liquid is nearly setting pour in rice cereal.
3　Mix well.
4　Add ginger.
5　Add vinegar.
6　Pour onto greased tin and cut in strips.
7　Serve when set.

# PEANUT BRITTLE

*20 minutes cooking time*

*Ingredients for 5-6 servings*

3 cups brown sugar
500 g (1 lb) shelled peanuts

2 tablespoons water
5 tablespoons vinegar

1　Combine sugar, vinegar and water.
2　Bring to the boil and simmer until thick.
3　Grease a cake tin with oil and cover tin with cooked peanuts.
4　Pour over the syrup. Chill and cut into strips.

# ALMOND TEA

*10 minutes cooking time*

*Ingredients for 5-6 servings*

½ cup ground almond powder
4-5 cups water
lotus flour

1 cup unsweetened evaporated milk
toasted almonds
½ cup sugar

1　Combine almond powder, lotus flour and sugar.
2　Add milk and water.
3　Place all ingredients in a saucepan. Bring to the boil.
4　Stir constantly and simmer for 10 minutes.
5　Serve hot in bowls, sprinkled with almonds.

# *Index*

# W

# Z